NĀGARA AND COMMANDERY
Origins of the Southeast Asian Urban Traditions

by

Paul Wheatley
The University of Chicago

THE UNIVERSITY OF CHICAGO
DEPARTMENT OF GEOGRAPHY
RESEARCH PAPER NOS. 207-208
(Double Number)

1983

Copyright 1983 by Paul Wheatley
Published 1983 by the Department of Geography
The University of Chicago, Chicago, Illinois

Library of Congress Cataloging in Publication Data

Wheatley, Paul.
 Nāgara and commandery.
 (Research paper/University of Chicago, Department of Geography; nos. 207-208)
 Includes bibliographical references and index.
 1. Cities and towns, Ancient—Asia, Southeastern. 2. Urbanization—Asia, Southeastern—History. 3. Protohistory. I. Title. II. Series: Research paper (University of Chicago. Dept. of Geography); no. 207-208.
 H31.C514 no. 207-208 910s 83-18014
 [HT147.A785] [307.7'6'0959]
 ISBN 0-89065-113-2 (pbk.)

Research Papers are available from:
The University of Chicago
Department of Geography
5828 S. University Avenue
Chicago, Illinois 60637
Price: $8.00; $6.00 series subscription
Price of double number 207-208: $16.00

For

PUTERI PULAU LANGKAWI

> Sunt aliquot quoque res quarum unam dicere causam
> non satis est, verum pluris, unde una tamen sit;
> corpus ut exanimum siquod procul ipse iacere
> conspicias hominis, fit ut omnis dicere causas
> conveniat leti, dicatur ut illius una.
> nam neque eum ferro nec frigore vincere possis
> interiisse neque a morbo neque forte veneno,
> verum aliquid genere esse ex hoc quod contigit ei
> scimus. item in multis hoc rebus dicere habemus.
>
> Titus Lucretius Carus, *De Rerum Natura*,
> Book VI, lines 703-711.

Une ville ne croyait pas avoir le droit de rien oublier; car tout dans son histoire se liait à son culte.

L'histoire de la cité disait au citoyen tout ce qu'il devait croire et tout ce qu'il devait adorer.

> Numa Denys Fustel de Coulanges, *La Cité Antique* (Paris, 1864), pp. 198-199.

CONTENTS

LIST OF FIGURES ix

PREFACE xi

ABBREVIATIONS xv

Chapter

   1. THE CITY AND ITS ORIGINS 1

   2. OF CHIEFS AND CHIEFDOMS 43

   3. CITIES OF "THE HUNTER" 119

   4. CITIES OF THE PYŪ 165

   5. CITIES OF THE RMAÑ 199

   6. CITIES OF THE EARLY MALAYSIAN WORLD 231

   7. URBAN GENESIS IN THE INDIANIZED TERRITORIES 263

   8. BEYOND THE GATE OF GHOSTS 365

   9. ENVOI 419

APPENDIX: URBAN CENTERS IN THE PTOLEMAIC CORPUS 439

GENERAL INDEX 465

INDEX OF PRINCIPAL TEXTS AND INSCRIPTIONS 471

LIST OF FIGURES

1. Models of State Origins 22
2. Models for the Operation of Control Hierarchies 25
3. Locations of Southeast Asian Sites, Ethnonyms and Localities mentioned in Chapter 2 47
4. Competing Models of Ecotype Development 54
5. Spread of Geographic Races of *Oryza sativa* in Asia 84
6. Evolution of the Two Cultivated Species of Rice 86
7. Enceintes at Cô-lõa 92
8. Locations of Archeological Sites and Localities Mentioned in Chapter 3 122
9. Identifiable Ceremonial and Administrative Centers Mentioned in Pre-Aṅkor Epigraphy 126
10. Layout of the Ancient City at Oc-èo 129
11. Hydraulic System on the Oc-èo Plain 138
12. Locations of Archeological Sites, Ancient Toponyms and Ethnonyms Mentioned in Chapter 4 166
13. Remains of the City at Beikthano 168
14. Isometric Projection of a Brick Structure at Beikthano . . 171
15. Traces of the Ancient Enceinte at Hmawza 174
16. Locations of Archeological Sites, Ancient Toponyms and Ethnonyms Mentioned in Chapter 5 201
17. Urban Enceintes from the Dvāravatī Period 205
18. Moated Enclosures on the Khorat Plateau 217
19. Locations of Archeological Sites and Ancient Toponyms Mentioned in Chapter 6 235
20. The Protectorate-General of the Pacified South, c. A.D.800 375
21. Toponymy of Jih-nan Commandery in the 4th Century A.D. . . 386
22. Principal Urban Hierarchies in Southeast Asia in the Second Half of the 14th Century 426
23. Trans-Gangetic India in MS *Venet. Marc. 516 (R)* 456

PREFACE

This is the third in a series of studies seeking to elucidate the origins of the city, and by implication of the state, in East Asia. The preceding volumes were *The Pivot of the Four Quarters: a preliminary enquiry into the origins and character of the ancient Chinese city* (University of Edinburgh Press, Edinburgh and Aldine Publishing Company, Chicago, 1971) and (with Thomas See) *From Court to Capital: a tentative interpretation of the origins of the Japanese urban tradition* (University of Chicago Press, Chicago, 1978). The present volume traces the rise of urban hierarchies in that extensive tract of the earth's surface now known as Southeast Asia *sensu stricto*, specifically the region lying to the east of India and the south of China.

In many respects this was the most difficult of the three volumes to write. In the first place, it was necessary to elicit such information as was available — in studies of urban origins it is never anything but meager — from no less than five cultural traditions. And then a great deal of the evidence had first to be sifted from literary sources originating outside the cultures concerned before being interpreted in the context of a woefully inadequate archeological record. Third, this study involved both of the principal modes of urban genesis, namely generation and imposition, in contrast to the earlier volumes which had been concerned to explicate a single mode of origin. And fourth, the winds of a self-conscious revisionism are currently sweeping through Southeast Asian prehistory and protohistory so searchingly that it is no longer possible to set the study of urban and state origins within an assured and tested framework of political and social change. Instead the inquiry has to be accommodated to a flux of competing formulations, hardly any of which command universal assent.

Preface

It is not claimed that the present exposition is in any sense complete or definitive. The paucity of archeological evidence, which combines with the prevailing intractability of literary and epigraphic sources to induce a disconcerting fluidity of opinion about the early history of Southeast Asia, would effectively contradict such an assertion. But this study, like others of its type, further suffers from the lack of a comprehensive and sufficiently analytical theory of urban genesis. Some decades hence it may be possible to attain an enhanced understanding of social change in early Southeast Asia in terms of a more powerful and unified theory of urban and state origins; in the meanwhile, the present interpretation is offered as one tentative synthesis of diverse and sometimes seemingly contradictory facts into a coherent developmental sequence which seems to be consonant with currently developing thrusts in both the specific study of ancient Southeast Asian society and the comparative investigation of urban origins.

This book has been written for urbanists with a comparative cast of mind, relatively few of whom will be grounded in the intricacies of early Southeast Asian history. Yet an understanding of the urbanization process sufficiently informed to be of use in cross-cultural studies requires an appreciation of the nature and limitations of the sources on which the arguments and conclusions are based. Social, political, and economic processes assume their full significance only in the cultural contexts within which they occur: neither the nature of paramountcy nor the workings of the *nāgara* can be adequately comprehended, or indeed comprehended at all, without some understanding of sacred authority in ancient Southeast Asia; social and occupational deployment in Pre-Aṅkor Kampuchea are intelligible only in light of the prevailing *Tempelwirtschaft*; and so on. I have therefore included a good deal of background information which, although already available to historians of ancient Southeast Asia, may be less familiar to some professional urbanists. However, in order to render the somewhat involved narrative as readable as possible, such illustrative and elaborative material has usually been relegated to the "Notes and References" accompanying each chapter. It is not egregiously misleading to say that the text provides the argument while the notes furnish the context of that argument. As a very high proportion of the references consulted in the preparation of this volume are cited only once or twice and have no continuing relevance to the work as a whole, a formal bibliography has not been considered necessary. The reader who wishes to follow up a particular point can readily obtain the requisite guidance from the "Notes and References." Full bibliographic

Preface

citations are furnished on first mention in each chapter, but abbreviated titles for the rest of the chapter. Chinese characters are similarly provided only on the first occurrence of a term, name, or reference.

Few scholars command more than a fraction of the linguistic skills needed for worthwhile comparative investigation in ancient Southeast Asia, and my own competencies fall a good way short of the ideal. This means that I have frequently had to rely on translations of both historical texts and contemporary exegesis. My transcriptions have usually been modeled on those used in the major bodies of commentary. In Indochina, for instance, I have followed the practice of scholars of the Ecole Française d'Extrême-Orient, for the Pyū that of Otto Blagden and Gordon Luce. For modern Malay, I have employed the revised transcriptions set out in *Pedoman Umum Ejaan Bahasa Malaysia* (Kuala Lumpur, 1977), excepting only a few established names such as, for example, "Sumatra." For Sanskrit I have used the forms embodied in Sir Monier Monier-Williams's *Sanskrit-English Dictionary* (New edition, Oxford, 1970). The sounds of what is known technically as Ancient or Middle Chinese, that is the vocalization prevailing in north-central China in about A.D. 600, have been rendered according to Bernhard Karlgren's reconstructions in "Grammata Serica Recensa," *Bulletin of the Museum of Far Eastern Antiquities*, no. 29 (1957), pp. 1-323. For Modern Standard Chinese I have retained the Wade-Giles romanization. Although this system, even in its customary modified form, is not strictly logical in all its principles, it is employed consistently by its users, whereas the *pin-yin* system is so imprecisely and incompletely formulated that at one time or another, for example, it has to my knowledge permitted at least six versions of the Chinese for "our" (*wŏmend*, *wŏm de*, *wŏmde*, *wŏmd*, *wŏmen de*, and *wŏmende*). And thus far there are no comprehensive dictionaries, no complete gazetteers, and no reference works in *pin-yin*, which makes it almost impossible to use the system consistently and which probably accounts for the fact that only one major Sinological library in the English-speaking world is currently utilizing it. Moreover, the Wade-Giles romanization can be more readily vocalized by, say, a Sanskritist or an Indonesian historian with no Sinological expertise than can *pin-yin*.

It is sometimes said that those who seek to reconstruct events in the Indic past of Southeast Asia are attempting to know what cannot be known. Of course this is indisputably true if one is thinking of a sequence of specific happenings, a flow of temporally related events, or the interplay of particular personalities; but in the

Preface

study of urban and state origins, and only slightly less so in the study of urban imposition, we are concerned with *patterns* of development, with *types* of actions rather than with the motivations and achievements of this or that individual or group, with *forms* of social, political, and economic interaction, in short with generalized *institutional evolution*. Who reigned when is often, indeed for much of the period with which we are concerned almost always, debatable; who married whom is not infrequently irrecoverable; who begat whom a matter of speculation. But the nature of kingship, the valuation of women, alliances, descent groups, and kindreds, the political purpose of genealogies, both genuine and fictive, as well as the integrative power of redistributive institutions, the status-enhancing capacity of religious devotionalism and the role of sanctity as a functional equivalent of political power, all these and more can be discerned in outline in the grandiloquent *praśasti* and archetyped exploits that constitute the substance of early Southeast Asian epigraphy, and can occasionally be inferred even from archeological assemblages. It is in these patterns of ideal-typical relationships, laced with occasional (and always hazardous) dashes of comparative ethnography and historical retrojection, that I have sought tentatively to discriminate the core features of the processes involved in the transformation from tribe to state, from village to city. In this respect, I am, like so many concerned with this type of investigation, following inadequately in the footsteps of Max Weber. But the ideal type formulated in the following pages is only a beginning, as much a program for future inquiry as the results of accomplished research.

In conclusion, I would like to thank those colleagues who, through their counsel generously given over thirty years, have helped to shape my perception of ancient Southeast Asia, and at the same time to acknowledge my indebtedness to numerous other scholars of many nationalities, often known to me only through their writings, who have collectively established the framework for my exposition. I am also grateful to Mrs. T.H. Tsien for the elegant Chinese calligraphy that substantially enhances the appearance of the following pages, to Mr. Clifford Vaida and Miss Jane E. Benson for a great deal of assistance during the final stages in the preparation of this volume, and to Mr. Bernard Lalor for the care and skill with which he has supervised its production. But most of all am I beholden to that Langkawi Princess who through the years has made, and still makes, all things possible.

Langkasuka, Porter Beach, Indiana
July 1981

ABBREVIATIONS EMPLOYED IN CHAPTERS 3 - 8

AA	*Artibus Asiae* (Ascona)
AAAG	*Annals of the Association of American Geographers* (Washington, D.C.)
BCAI	*Bulletin de la Commission Archéologique de l'Indochine* (Paris)
BEFEO	*Bulletin de l'Ecole Française d'Extrême-Orient* (Hanoi, Paris)
BIIEH	*Bulletin de l'Institut Indochinois pour l'Etude de l'Homme* (Hanoi)
BKI	*Bijdragen tot de Taal-, Land- en Volkenkunde van Nederlandsch-Indië, uitgegeven door het Koninklijk Instituut voor Taal-, Land- en Volkenkunde van Nederlandsch-Indië* ('s Gravenhage)
BSEI	*Bulletin de la Société des Etudes Indochinoises* (Saigon)
BSOAS	*Bulletin of the School of Oriental and African Studies* (London)
HJAS	*Harvard Journal of Asiatic Studies* (Cambridge, Mass.)
IHQ	*The Indian Historical Quarterly* (Calcutta)
ISCC	Auguste Barth and Abel Bergaigne, *Inscriptions Sanscrites du Cambodge et de Campā*, Notices et Extraits des Manuscrits de la Bibliothèque Nationale XXVII (Paris, 1885, 1893).
JA	*Journal Asiatique* (Paris)
JAOS	*Journal of the American Oriental Society* (New Haven, Conn.)
JAS	*The Journal of Asian Studies* (Ann Arbor, Mich.)
JASB	*Journal of the Asiatic Society of Bengal* (Calcutta)
JBRS	*Journal of the Burma Research Society* (Rangoon)
JGIS	*Journal of the Greater India Society* (London)
JMBRAS	*Journal of the Malayan/Malaysian Branch of the Royal Asiatic Society* (Singapore, Petaling Jaya)
JRAS	*Journal of the Royal Asiatic Society* (London)
JSBRAS	*Journal of the Straits Branch of the Royal Asiatic Society* (Singapore)
JSEAH	*Journal of Southeast Asian History* (Singapore)
JSS	*Journal of the Siam Society* (Bangkok)
[M]JTG	*The [Malayan] Journal of Tropical Geography* (Singapore and Kuala Lumpur)
TBG	*Tijdschrift voor Indische Taal-, Land- en Volkenkunde uitgegeven door het Koninklijk Bataviaasch Genootschap van Kunsten en Wetenschappen* (Batavia, 's Gravenhage)
TP	*T'oung Pao* (Leiden)

CHAPTER 1

The City and Its Origins

The Concept of Urbanism

Urbanism is a term of manifold implications subsumed within a construct of equivocal import. In its grossest connotation it signifies no more than a particular level of sociocultural integration which becomes meaningful only when it is contrasted with a preceding, less complex level of segmental, egalitarian society, with a contemporaneous but equally poorly stratified state of non-urbanism, or with a rapidly approaching, and presumably more highly differentiated, post-urban society. This particular hierarchical patterning of societal relationships is invariably accorded material expression in a localized nexus of built forms that is recognized, in whatever cultural context it may occur, as a theater for the acting out of a distinctive manner of life characterized as urban. It is the forms and functions of these nexuses that constitute the subject matter of conventional urban studies, with inquiries focusing on the built form as (1) an arena for the interplay of both creative and destructive tensions in the disposition of volume and space; (2) a locale promoting a characteristic style of life, of production, and of thought,[1] and (3) a functional center of societal control, a creator of effective space as it has been called.[2] Each of these foci of inquiry is apt to present itself in starkly different terms to practitioners of different academic disciplines, each of which, by virtue of its distinctive repertoire of cognizances and skills, is capable of interpreting only a limited sector of the total urban reality.

At a generally more abstract level, the concept of urbanism has been explicated in terms of three supradisciplinary conceptions, namely the behavioral (involving a transformation of attitudes and values, an adjustment of personal conduct), the structural (focusing attention on the patterned activities of whole populations), and the processual (concerned primarily with a progressive concentration of population). From a somewhat different standpoint, both disciplinary and supradisciplinary investigations of urban phenomena can be subsumed into a series of paradigmatic models: an interactional model (emphasizing the growth and structure of specialized networks), a normative model (in which urbanism connotes a style of life), an economic model (designed to throw light on the character and location of production and service activities), and a demographic model (concerned with the statistical characteristics of population aggregates). Common to all these approaches is a view of the city proper — by which is meant pre-eminently the societal entity that develops within the environs of the built form — as the critical locality within which are located the institutions that establish and maintain order within the subsystems of society. To that extent, the structure of the city can be said to epitomize the pattern of society at large. Furthermore, within the confines of the city proper social process and spatial form are continuously interacting to fashion a cultural recorder, on which are chronicled both the best and the worst of human achievements.[3]

The first desideratum in any attempt to devise a definition of urbanism which can be rendered satisfactorily operational, and which is at the same time appropriate to our present theme, is to avoid restricting it to the point where it is unrecognizable to students of cities in the modern world. The sodality of professional urbanists, with understandably rare exceptions, is properly concerned with the large, dense, permanent aggregations of socially heterogeneous individuals that constitute the prevailing mode of urban expression at the present time, or at least with social entities either approaching or derived from that Wirthian category.[4] The sophisticated techniques of analysis employed by these scholars in their studies of the contemporary city, however, appear to be noticeably less incisive when applied to the ancient world. No doubt this is partly because in the latter case the scholars are denied the statistically ordered data for the manipulation of which their analytical apparati were devised, but it is also possible that their techniques are not entirely appropriate to the study of urban genesis, or possibly even to the study of the developed city in ancient times. In any case, the point to be made is that, in defining the category of urbanism in earlier ages, it is important not to depart so far from current conceptualizations that it becomes impracticable to sustain a profitable dialogue with students of contemporary urbanism.

The crux of the problem is essentially this. Urbanism is a concept which, enmeshed in a web of semantic ramifications, has persisted for some five millennia as a means of denoting sets of qualities possessed by certain of the larger, and usually more compact, clusters of settlement features that at any particular moment in time have represented centroids of continuous population movements. From the earliest recorded formulation of this concept, apparently in ancient Sumer, there have existed very clear perceptions of the role of these functionally more important nodes in the settlement pattern, often with moral valuations attached.[5] But no city, no urban tradition, indeed, has survived for more than a fraction of the time during which the concept has been in existence. Instead there has been a sequence of evolving and protean manifestations exhibiting a staggering variety of morphologies and functions. In other words, although urbanism, or something that translates into English under that term, has persisted as an enduring concept apparently immune to the passage of time, its substance has undergone numerous and profound transmutations. What this amounts to is an admission that "urbanism" is no more than a general term for a wide range of, perhaps any and all, ways of organizing complex societies. As societies have experienced progressive changes, so have the nodes of societal organization been transformed, together with the hierarchies into which they are grouped. The problem of definition in the present instance, then, is to devise a way of conceptualizing the phenomenon of urbanism so that it includes both ends of the developmental spectrum and all that falls between.

This conclusion raises a second major issue, which is sometimes grandly referred to as the problem of entitation: namely, that the permanent built forms which all cultures recognize as urban cannot be predicated as first-order objects of study, that is the most meaningful objects and the only ones, it is often claimed, which can be posited when functional performance is in question. A first-order object is, in fact, one which can be specified in terms of its morphology, taxonomy, composition, physiology, ecology, chorology, and chronology.[6] The city is not a unitary, self-contained system in this sense because its organizational efficacy does not, except in highly specific and easily explained instances, cease at the edge of the built form. Nor are the fields of operation of its institutions anything like congruent. Rather than constituting a unit at one scale level and a clearly defined component of a more inclusive unit at a higher level of scale, the city, on analysis, at least partially dissolves into an areal aggregate, a collection of elements closely juxtaposed but not necessarily structurally interdependent.[7] This makes for formidable difficulties of interpretation, for it is a fundamental premise of the Theory of Integrative Levels that a comprehensive evaluation of any organizational structure must be conducted at three levels: its own, where the mechanics of its operation are most directly accessible; the one below, which is the analytical level at which attention is transferred from the whole to the parts; and the level above, at which the organization under consideration becomes part of some more complex system.[8] Despite some attempts to treat the city as an organizational structure susceptible to this type of analysis,[9] a theoretical basis for the argument has been developed only with reference to the economic sectors of the urban entity, and then not wholly satisfactorily.

In attempting to devise an operational definition of the city which will be compatible with the purpose in hand, it is helpful to discriminate between two components of the urban concept, namely *urbanization* and the *urban process*.[10] Whereas the former can be interpreted as denoting the rate of change in the proportion of urban dwellers to total population (or, for Kingsley Davis and some others, the proportion itself[11]), which in practice means a change in the number and size of cities, the urban process is here to be understood as a complex nexus of functionally interrelated, parallel-trending changes by means of which increasing numbers of people in society at large become involved in some way in the affairs of the city.[12] Whether or not they live within its physical purlieus, they come under the influence, and more often than not, the control of its institutions. This means that an urbanized society subsumes both a spatially urban and a spatially rural component. On the one hand there is the city-dweller proper, the resident within the urban enclave; and on the other there is the urbanized countryman who lives in terms of the city but not in it, who is bound to the city (or perhaps more accurately to the institutions of state located within the city) in an asymmetrical structural relationship that requires him to produce in one form or another a fund of rent payable to power brokers based, if not always resident, within the urban enceinte.[13] It follows that only within the walls, either actual or metaphorical, of the city is there a significant measure of congruence between urbanization and the urban process as these concepts are defined here. It is for this reason that urbanized society is to be contrasted in the first instance not with that of the surrounding countryside (which it subsumes) but with pre- or non-urbanized society.

An important implication of this perspective on the city is that, from the point of view of the student of urban genesis, the urban process can be regarded as the systemic transformation of one qualitatively distinct level of sociocultural integration into another with a higher degree of complexity, which in turn enhances its potentialities for adaptation.[14] In broadly cultural terms the generalized integrative patterns involved in this transmutation of a folk into an urbanized society are those of relatively egalitarian, ascriptive, kin-based societies at the simpler level and stratified, politically structured, territorially defined societies as the more complex resultants of the process. In equally broad ecological terms they are levels, respectively, of reciprocally integrated Developed Village-Farming Efficiency and of redistributive integration about an administrative and ceremonial center that is distinguished from other settlements of the time by the presence of an assemblage of public ceremonial structures.[15]

The transformation between these particular levels of integration can be effected by means of two distinct and, for all analytical and most practical purposes, unrelated processes, namely *urban imposition* and *urban generation*. Whereas the first of these processes reflects an extension of symbolic and organizational patterns developed in one territory into another, the latter signifies a progressive differentiation of autonomous institutional spheres and the emergence of specialized collectivities and roles as a response to societal pressures generated internally within a specific region. The former results, initially at least, in suprastratification, the latter in true stratification.

Urban imposition constitutes a mode of urban diffusion that is virtually inseparable from the expansion of empire, and is usually accompanied by the establishment of an administrative organization designed to sustain the value system of the colonial power, the imposition of the legal definitions of property current in the colonists' homeland, and the introduction into the dependent territory of certain sectors of the metropolitan economy. To that extent it can be regarded as a mode of systems interaction, in particular of compound systems interaction.[16] By this is meant that three modes of interaction are involved simultaneously — or at least potentially involved. In the first mode each system, although itself comprising a complex compound set of relationships,[17] acts and responds as a unit. This type of interaction might represent reasonably accurately, for example, the operation of political linkages at government level between the colonizing power and its dependent territory, though Parsons and Shils, by referring to social collectivities as actors, would seem to extend its applicability to analysis of a very much wider range of social relationships.[18] In the second mode of interaction it is the components of the discrete systems (rather than the systems themselves) that act directly on each other in a manner that would seem to represent fairly accurately the most widely held conception of the social system. The third mode of interaction, which is probably less common in the colonial experience than the two preceding processes, operates when one system acts as a unit on one or more of the constituent components of another system. A representative example might be the founding by the central government of the metropolitan power (symbolizing one system in its entirety) of a fortified city (a component of the second system) for frontier defense in a colony.

Urban generation, the only alternative to urban imposition as a means of effecting a transformation of this sort, is a mode of processual change subsumed within the more inclusive field of social differentiation and stratification. If urban imposition is viewed as a case of systems interaction, then urban generation is to be regarded as a form of systemic evolution. At one extreme of the spectrum of systemic changes encompassed by this term are those situations in which cities have arisen when some particular conjunction of internal forces has induced spontaneous readjustments in institutional forms and relationships. In such circumstances the transition *ideally* may be conceived as the structural transformation of a closed system, though it needs no emphasis that in the real world social systems are seldom, if ever, of the closed type. Even ancient Sumer, the region with an undisputed claim to historical priority in the initiation of the process of urbanization, was by no means immune to external influences during and immediately preceding the emergence of its earliest urban forms. In fact, what entitles an evolving society at an appropriate level of complexity to be characterized as an instance of primary urban generation is not its degree of systemic closure so much as the fact that none of the external cultures able to influence its development is significantly more complex than the particular society under consideration. Although opinions may vary as to precisely which communities at one time or another have generated urban forms in this manner, there is a virtual consensus among scholars in the field that the Middle East was the first region to experience this quantum transformation of society. There might be a divergence of views, though, as to whether Mesopotamia and Egypt should be treated as separate manifestations of a single process or as discrete regions. Other realms of primary urban generation on which there would be very substantial scholarly agreement are the Indus valley, the North China plain, Middle America (where again there might be a division of opinion as to whether two realms or one have been involved), the central Andes, and — the realm on which there would probably be least agreement — the Yoruba territories of southwestern Nigeria.

On the peripheries of these core regions of primary urban generation, particularly in those sectors where political jurisdiction has lagged behind cultural imperialism, cities have often arisen as a result of a secondary diffusion of cultural traits that has stimulated the evolution of society towards an urban level of integration. In such circumstances the process has still been one of urban generation rather than of imposition, but it has been a generational process stimulated by the diffusion of cultural traits from already urbanized regions. It must be emphasized that it has been the diffusion of individual traits that has effected this transformation, not, as is true of urban imposition, the transference of the total set of functionally interrelated institutions that constitutes the city. In other words, it is not the artifact of the city itself that has been diffused but particular institutional components of an urbanized society.[19]

The operational view of urbanism as a level of sociocultural integration which we have advanced in the preceding paragraphs (as opposed to the more commonly essayed attempt to represent urban forms as something approaching first-order objects of study) implies that the city in the narrow material sense of the built form cannot profitably be isolated as a functioning unit from the totality of the society of which it is an epiphenomenal reflection. This is, of course, only another way of stating that the city is not merely an aggregation of population of critical size and density but also an organizing principle, an agent of regional integration, in John Friedmann's pithy phrase which we have previously appropriated, a creator of effective space.[20] There is, however, a significant exception to this generalization during the initial phase of urban imposition. When it is first established, the colonial city is essentially a subsystem of the metropolitan urban system that happens to have been transferred to a dependent territory. Its links with its environing territory are by definition rudimentary, so that the influence of its institutions not infrequently ceases more or less at the city wall. Only with the passage of time does a combined process of political absorption and cultural diffusion, often with assistance from the socially consolidatory mechanisms of economic exchange, induce the customary degree of interdependence between city and country. From that phase of development onwards, generated city and imposed city are structurally homologous, though significant ethnic and other distinctions within their populations may persist for many subsequent generations.

The emphasis that we have accorded the city as an organizing principle and the concomitant relational view of urbanism as a social process in which spatial and locational strategies are used to structure social accessibilities have important implications for the study of urban genesis, particularly in so far as the notions of primary and secondary urban generation are concerned. The creation of effective space, wherever and whenever it has occurred, has necessitated the restructuring of the functional subsystems of society, afforded opportunities for the concentration of power, wealth, and prestige, and initiated the evolution of an urban-orientated Great Tradition. At the same time the engrossing of power and authority by institutions located within the city ensured that relations between subsidiary settlements, which had hitherto been managed directly by the participants, were now mediated, notionally if not always physically, through the focally situated city. In other words, the generated city in its earlier phases was already furnished with a dependent territory, a circumstance clearly implying that city and state were coeval, and indeed, constituted differentially scaled spatial manifestations of the same societal processes.

It is at this juncture that the relationship between urban and state origins becomes apparent. From the point of view adopted in this volume, it is not possible to conceive of city-less statehood, though certain other definitions of urbanism, of course, might well permit the conceptualization of a conjunction of political, jurisdictional, and ekistical organizational structures which could be held to constitute a state lacking "urban" foci.[21] In any case, although the higher-level institutions of power and authority were almost invariably located within the built form of the city, their organizational capacities always extended beyond the physical limits of that form, so that it is debatable whether in the investigation of urban genesis it is at present more profitable to focus inquiry on the area of functional interaction in its totality or to concentrate on the restricted socio-political core within which the organizing institutions were aggregated: in short, whether the extended system (the state) or the limited system (the city) is the more manageable, and in the last analysis intellectually advantageous, category of investigation. A not negligible practical advantage in focusing on the city, however, is that its architectural form is often accessible to archeological scrutiny in a way that the state (even though it was the institutions of state which were aggregated in the city) is not.

At all events, from this point in time onwards, in order to minimize the friction of distance, virtually all the institutions providing leadership, reinforcement, and mediation in the state have been assembled within a restricted area which we have got into the habit of calling (or translating as) a city. Most important of all, the nodes in the communications networks are situated in cities, so that the messages they transmit originate predominantly with, and in any case inevitably carry the point of view of, those who, controlling the city, reside at the hub of the network. The messages which flow outwards to the rest of society are, therefore, impregnated with urban norms. In fact, what makes the city (in early or recent times) important from this point of view is less its role as a large, dense, heterogeneous collection of non-agricultural persons (when they are non-agricultural, that is) than its control of a communications hub in that society. This is essentially what we mean when we join John Friedmann in categorizing the city as a creator of effective space,[22] when we allegorize it as the summation of society,[23] or when we designate it as a living repository of culture.[24] The city, by virtue of being the site of the organizational foci of society, contrives, prescribes, modulates, and disseminates order throughout the subsystems of that society. Its most crucial export, as Scott Greer has reminded us, is control.[25] And because of its regulation of the communications (and more often than not the transportation) networks, the city is likely to become a focus of innovation, a locale whence new concepts and novel technologies are diffused through the larger society. What all this implies is that it is analytically profitable to discriminate two generalized types of central institutional transactions: those involved in the exchange and processing of information, and those involved in the exchange and processing of material goods. The former are obviously concerned with administration, ritual, and ceremony, and in a subsequent section of this work we shall discover that in ancient times the latter were engaged primarily in the redistribution and mobilization of resources.[26]

The Problem of Urban Genesis

The Construct of the Chiefdom

In the preceding paragraphs it has become evident that our approach by way of the city to the climacteric transformation of society variously categorized under ideal-type constructs such as from Status to Contract,[27] from *Societas* to *Civitas*,[28] from *Gemeinschaft* to *Gesellschaft*,[29] from mechanical to organic solidarity,[30] and so forth will develop closely parallel to the current approach to the same transformation by way of the state. Both approaches begin with the delineation of segmental, egalitarian, ascriptive, kin-structured groups living in villages, that is societies where the diffuseness of power is aptly epitomized by Father Le Jeune's phrase, "All the authority of their chief is in his tongue's end."[31] Thence both attempt to document, and each in its own way to provide an explanation of, the progressive institutionalization of centralized leadership; but at this point the urbanist tends to focus his research on the manner in which power and authority come to be concentrated in sets of institutions aggregated within a localized nexus of built forms, whereas the student of state origins tends to direct his attention more specifically to the changing nature and conceptions of government.[32] Both lines of inquiry, however, seek to elucidate the operation of a nexus of disjunctive processes by which a relatively undifferentiated system of societal integration is transformed into another possessing a higher degree of complexity. The scholars who pioneered this approach to urban genesis[33] dealt only with the two levels of integration defined on p. 5 above, though it is fair to say that they were patently aware that the transformation was not one of simple replacement. In no realm of primary or secondary urban generation so far investigated were kin-based institutions abruptly rejected in favor of patron-client relationships. Rather the old gentile groupings tended to persist

for varying, and often long, periods of time side by side with
incipient politicized structures, with which they articulated
through institutions such as the army, corporate craft
organizations, labor management on estate projects, and various
forms of clientage. In the process the kin groups were gradually
modified and absorbed as specialized dependent elements into the
more complex, emergent, socio-political fabric.

In attempting to refine our understanding of the mechanisms
of these processual changes, several recent investigators have
adopted the construct of the chiefdom, defined as a system of
chieftainships, as denoting a level of integration intermediate
between relatively undifferentiated folk or tribal society and
complex urban or state society.[34] The construct is a broad one,
constituting a continuum ranging at one end from non-ranked
chieftainships which, although exercising more than nominal
authority over local headships, are not always easily
distinguishable from segmentary tribes, through a variety of ranked
chieftainships in which the chief is usually assisted by a council,
court, or other functionally equivalent group of advisors, to
paramountcies which often approximate to true states.[35] It is
these last which, in Marshall Sahlins' words, illustrate the
economic and political limits of kinship (that is pre-state or
pre-urban) society.[36] But all three orders of chiefdom exhibit in
their respective degrees relatively permanent, centralized
leadership and hereditary hierarchical status arrangements informed
by an aristocratic ethos. What distinguishes them from true
states, in Service's view, is their lack of a formal legal
apparatus of forceful repression.[37] Even in advanced chiefdoms
of this type the segmentary principle characteristic of tribal
organization, at once structurally decentralized and functionally
generalized, is often still very much in evidence even though
constituent descent and community groups are hierarchically
arranged. In fact, in some of the more complex examples the
incipient class distinctions are still subsumed within a kinship
framework in the manner of so-called conical clans.[38]

Settlement Patterns. In her study of political and jurisdictional
organizations in East-Central Africa, Donna Taylor established that,
within the range of societies that she investigated, the more
highly centralized chiefdoms ("middle-range hierarchical societies"
in her terminology) were characterized by a three-level settlement
hierarchy manifesting a marked disparity in size between the center
of highest rank and those of the middle rank.[39] Less highly

centralized chiefdoms exhibited only two levels of development. This was essentially the conclusion of Gregory Johnson, whose application of central-place principles to archeological data from Khūzistān led him to infer the existence of a two-level decision-making and settlement hierarchy *above that of the general population* in the chiefdom phase of development on the Susiana plain,[40] and of Sanders and Price, who discerned social communities at two "levels of inclusiveness" in the chiefdoms of Prehispanic Mesoamerica.[41] The latter authors also proposed three possible settlement patterns (as distinct from hierarchical levels) compatible with chiefdom-type degrees of centralization, namely:

> (1) Ceremonial centers each with a civic precinct and a very small residential group made up of the chiefly lineage, together perhaps with a small cadre of service personnel. The rest of the population of the chiefdom in this case are dispersed through the surrounding countryside in nuclear-family, extended-family, or lineage settlements.
> (2) A single large compact center containing virtually all the inhabitants of the chiefdom.
> (3) A relatively large compact center with a substantial number of permanent inhabitants, and the balance of the population of the chiefdom residing in smaller settlements distributed through the dependent territory.[42]

Essentially these patterns are those previously observed to be associated with Mayan ceremonial centers by Gordon Willey[43] and S. W. Miles.[44] Type 1, which Sanders and Price regard as the typical arrangement of settlements within a chiefdom, represents a pattern termed "extended boundary town" by Miles,[45] "synchoritic settlement" by John Rowe,[46] and "dispersed ceremonial center" by Wheatley,[47] while Types 2 and 3, which are not at all uncommon in fully urbanized societies, are likely to be found only sporadically at the chiefdom phase of development, and then only under the stimulus of a powerful centripetalizing force such as the extreme localization of a critical resource or a state of chronic warfare.

Variability of Form. The model of chiefdom organization most commonly invoked in the literature on state origins seems to be that characteristic of the Polynesian high islands, particularly Hawaii, of pre-Islāmic Arabia, and of parts of Central Asia,[48] which exhibits

> hierarchical relations within and between local groups, a regional political frame maintained by a system of chiefs, major and minor, holding sway over segments of greater and lesser order and subordinate all to the one paramount.[49]

However, neither the range of variables nor the degree of
ethnographic variability appropriately subsumed under the construct
of chiefdom has yet been established definitively. Sahlins noted,
for example, that the "pyramidal political geometry" of Hawaii was
noticeably less strongly developed in Melanesian chiefdoms, and
also that there were significant differences in the manner and
purpose of economic centralization in the two culture realms.
Whereas in the former, commodities were appropriated from virtually
the entire population of the chiefdom mainly for the benefit of the
chiefly faction, in Melanesia they were exacted from a big-man's
faction for subsequent reallocation to the population of more or
less the whole chiefdom.[50] Among Donna Taylor's sample chiefdoms in
East-Central Africa, centralization not only tended to be less
strongly developed than in Polynesia but also operated unevenly on
the several subsystems of society.[51] Whether or not these and
numerous other ethnographic variations in incidence and intensity
of centralization are expressive of evolutionary progress along a
continuum remains to be determined.

Patrimonial domain. Whereas less developed chiefdoms would seem to
fall within the Weberian category of patriarchalism (under which
authority is exercised by a particular individual who is designated
by a definite rule of inheritance, but who lacks an administrative
staff under his personal control),[52] the paramountcies and probably
a substantial proportion of ranked chieftainships are evidently to
be comprehended within the ideal type of Weber's patrimonial
domain.[53] It is characteristic of this form of traditional rule,
which operates through a pervasive combination of traditionalism
and arbitrariness, that government and court administration
coincide. It is, in effect, an extension to political subjects of
a ruler's patriarchal control over his family. Political
transactions that do not directly involve the royal household are
nevertheless consolidated with the corresponding function of the
court. The ruler thereby treats all administration as his personal
affair, while his officials, appointed from among dependents on the
basis of the ruler's personal confidence in their abilities, and
maintained as members of the royal household, in turn regard their
administrative responsibilities as a personal service to their lord
in a context of duty and respect.

In these circumstances, the acquisition of large
extrapatrimonial territories which exceed the governmental capacity
of the ruler's resources and household management — and the
effectiveness of the chiefdom as an instrument of political

aggrandizement is a subject of frequent comment in ethnographic reporting[54]— inevitably induces an extension of the administrative staff to perform public duties beyond the scope of the royal household. In practice this means that the ruler is constrained to delegate authority by granting benefices in return for services rendered to the throne, and to assert his control over populations who do not necessarily recognize his legitimacy by raising and maintaining military forces.[55] As long as the benefice holders do not violate tradition or contravene the interests of their ruler, their control over their subjects is absolute, and as arbitrary as the ruler's is over them. Ultimately central bureaus are established, usually under the supervision of a high official of the vizier type, who is often a royal favorite. In order to counteract the decentralization and concomitant attenuation of duties of personal dependents which inevitably accompany the territorial extension of a patrimonial regime, the ruler not infrequently resorts to the chartering of associations which are held collectively responsible for the performance of public duties, especially for meeting the economic needs of the government. This liturgical method of public finance is,[56] in fact, a classic response to the central administrative problem of the chiefdom as soon as its coercive apparatus becomes incapable of enforcing the personal liability of political subjects inhabiting peripheral territories. This assignment of the power of enforcement to compulsory liturgical associations is typical of the mixture of traditionalism and arbitrariness that characterizes patrimonial regimes.[57]

Custom versus Law. In the matters of custom and law, a chiefdom, itself representing a functional and developmental stage between segmental, egalitarian society and the coercive state, is, not unexpectedly, ambivalent. It is usually capable of invoking certain attributes of both public law (resolving conflict between individuals and groups on the one hand and authority structures on the other) and private law (mediating legal contentions between "persons" in the form of individuals or groups), while yet relying to a very considerable extent on sanctioned custom as a mode of social control.[58] Each of the four attributes which Leopold Pospisil requires of a legal decision, namely authority, intention of universal application, true *obligatio*, and sanction,[59] can be found in varying degrees and combinations in chiefdoms, but never in the full and unambiguous development achieved in some state societies. A centralized permanent authority above the familistic level, for instance, is inherent in the structure of the chiefdom, but, lacking the means to impose coercive physical sanctions consistently, is often forced to rely on persuasion and conciliation in the settlement of disputes. When sanctions are involved in the sphere of private law, they are applied as often as not by peers, in the manner of egalitarian societies, rather than by an officially constituted authority acting as a third party in a dispute.[60] In the domain of public law, where transgressions are often viewed as offences against the person of the high chief, and therefore against the gods, sanctions typically take the form of supernatural punishments invoked by sacerdotal authority.[61] Moreover, the patrimonial ethic is always disposed to transform questions of law and adjudication into questions of administration, so that the decision of authority often incorporates an expediently variable political element. Where such a decision does carry an intention of universal application, and consequently conforms that much more closely to the modern concept of law, then it is prevailingly an interpretation of a formalized corpus of judgments on the pattern of the dooms of Teutonic, or the *themistes* of Homeric, chieftains. *Obligatio*, the third of Pospisil's attributes of law, defines "the rights of the entitled and the duties of the obligated parties."[62] As such it is a statement of the asymmetrical relationship of the litigants, who may include not only the living but also the dead and the incorporeal.[63] In theocratic chiefdoms it is invoked principally in connection with questions of conscience, morals, and tabus, penalties for the violation of which are often exacted supernaturally or experienced psychically. All in all, and allowing for the range of centralization subsumed under the term chiefdom, it is not practicable to generalize beyond the statement that law-like processes begin to manifest themselves during that phase of sociopolitical development, and that some attributes of law are almost invariably present in the more advanced chiefdoms, with the most law-like and comprehensive formulations probably to be found in paramountcies.

Economic Integration. In conformity with the centripetalizing organization of the chiefdom, which itself expresses the primacy accorded the integrative dimension by the central value system of societies at that stage of development, the dominant mode of economic exchange is redistribution, with mobilization developing concomitantly in the more advanced chiefdoms.[64] As redistribution is the mode of exchange associated specifically with the integrative subsystem of society, its operation contributes powerfully to the maintenance and reinforcement of the authority hierarchy. In fact, the main centers of allocation are typically also the main centers of decision-making, so that there is an almost perfect locational isomorphism between administrative and economic hierarchies. Furthermore, the structure of the chiefdom as a system of chieftainships under the rule of a high chief ensures that the range of highest-order functions in both these hierarchies is coincident with the extent of the society as a whole, with a resulting primate distribution in the settlement hierarchy (cp. p. 11 above).

The pre-eminence in the chiefdom of the redistributive system does not mean that other modes of economic integration are totally suppressed. We have already mentioned mobilization, which in any case in practice is not always easily distinguishable institutionally from redistribution, but which operates in support of broadly political, rather than integrative and allocative, goals. Reciprocity, in the sense of a network of instrumental exchanges grounded in family and neighborhood morality, is universal in chiefdoms, as indeed elsewhere. Nor is market exchange absent: on the contrary, it can assume impressive proportions. Indeed, as we have noted in a previous paragraph, the reallocative system itself is not everywhere equally strongly developed, nor is it structured on a uniform pattern in the major culture realms, or even within neighboring chiefdoms. But it is this superordinate redistributive system which, in greater or lesser degree and according to its organizational capacity, underpins and to no inconsiderable extent guarantees the integrity of the sociopolitical hierarchy. In this context the authority structure serves also as the redistributive structure, whose purpose it is to allocate to each class what is judged to be its just (in this case signifying what is necessary to maintain the social system) share of resources and facilities. And as the society comes to depend on, indeed is structured in terms of, the redistributive hierarchy, so it develops a vested interest in the continuity of the leadership at each of the constituent levels. Add to which the circumstance that at each level of the hierarchy, decision-makers controlling the redistributive process are able to impose devastating economic sanctions on those at lower levels who might contravene their interests. From this point of view, the redistributive mode of integration exerts a powerful stabilizing influence, and, generally speaking, operates in favor of the *status quo*.

Religion. Many descriptions of chiefdoms, particularly of those of the pre-modern world, have commented on the ritual and ceremonial ambience surrounding the seat of the high chief, which as often as not received concrete expression in variously elaborated complexes of public ceremonial structures. These were usually massive, often extensive, and included assemblages of such architectural features as pyramids, platform mounds, temples, palaces, terraces, staircases, courts, and stelae, all of which were apt to incorporate a highly developed plastic symbolism. In these systems of *religious symbolism* the paradigmatic figures of the old tribal religions with whom men formerly identified in ritual had been accorded specific, and often characteristic, attributes. They had been objectified, and were conceived as actively involved in the ordering of both the natural and human worlds, that is they had assumed the mantle of gods and, incidentally, showed a disposition to arrange themselves in a hierarchy closely paralleling that of the chiefly court. The prevailing world view was still monistic, but it was cast in terms of an increasingly more highly differentiated monism, in which a single all-embracing cosmology justified the existence and role of all things divine and human. In this schema the gods of the heavenly regions tended to hold supreme power.[65]

Religious action in the chiefdom took the primary form of cult. This was a response to a developing distinction, in contrast to tribal religion, between gods and men, a differentiation which necessitated the elaboration of a communication system effected through worship and sacrifice.[66] While permitting a higher degree of conscious volition on the part of the human participants, this mode of communication also entailed some uncertainty as to the divine response, which possibly helps to explain the indications of anxiety that some authors have claimed to discern in the representational art of certain ceremonial centers.

In the *religious organization* of the chiefdom, political and religious authority were but poorly discriminated, with higher status groups usually laying claim to superior religious status as well. In fact, the paramount ruler was often also the chief priest, and almost invariably the priesthood consecrated the high chief. Priestly offices were commonly the prerogative of noble families who asserted divine descent. Bellah sees the most significant limitation on religious organization at this stage to have been the failure to develop differentiated religious collectivities which included adherents other than priests.[67] The

18   *Nāgara and Commandery*

cult centers, he points out, afforded facilities for sacrifice and worship for what were essentially transient groups, mainly pilgrims and peasants at the seasonal festivals, who were not organized as coherent collectivites. Only the priesthood itself constituted such a closely knit group.

The *social implications* of this phase of religious development will become clear enough in the following chapters. Suffice it here to note that social structures and social practices were both subsumed within a divinely ordained cosmological scheme, so that there was relatively little tension between religious prescription and social conformity. All social action was, indeed, reinforced by religious authority, a situation which sometimes nurtured the seeds of its own dissolution, for as society became yet further differentiated, so the problem of legitimating the enhanced autonomy of discrete institutional spheres became increasingly difficult. Competing factions tended to espouse the causes of rival deities, thereby rending the fabric of the unitary world view, and leading sometimes to the inducement of messianic expectations. During the period of greatest vigor of the chiefdom, however, the ceremonial cycle at the paramount's seat was a powerfully integrative force which has been described so effectively by Elman Service that I have no hesitation in reproducing the relevant paragraph:

> Ceremonialism in and of itself has a great socially integrating effect, especially when rituals and ceremonies involve the attendance of large numbers of people and are for the purposes of the whole society. This latter aspect is in a sense a technological function of the authority system; the priest-chief is "getting something done" toward a good harvest, for example, by assuring a rainfall after the ceremony. That is good. But he needs the presence of his people and perhaps the actual participation of large numbers of them, dancing, chanting, clapping, or praying. All this is a common effort for the common good, but *led by authority*. This kind of ceremony is thus organismic in its nature, like the redistributional system. But it also has an important social-psychological dimension as the people collaborate in large groups with little likelihood of friction under such circumstances. And apparently the larger the group the greater the social intoxication of the melting of the individual into the collectivity.[68]

Like the student of state origins, the student of urban origins will take account of the characteristics of the chiefdom which have been specified in the preceding pages but he will focus his investigations primarily on the internal structures and external relations of the built forms within which the institutions of centralized control are aggregated. Especially will he be concerned with the ritual and ceremonial complex from which the chiefdom is governed. I have elsewhere characterized centers of this type as

> instruments for the generation of political, social, economic, sacred [and other] spaces, at the same time as they were symbols of cosmic, social, political, and moral order. Under the religious authority of divine monarchs and organized priesthoods, they elevated the redistributive and mobilizative modes of economic integration to positions of regional dominance, functioned as nodes in webs of administered trade,[69] and served as foci of craft specialization . . . . Above all they embodied the aspirations of brittle, pyramidal societies in which, typically, a sacerdotal elite, controlling a corps of officials and a palace guard, ruled over a peasantry whose business it was to produce a fund of rent which could be absorbed into the reservoir of resources controlled by the masters of the ceremonial center.[70]

This configuration of the ideal-type ceremonial center was elicited during investigations into specifically urban origins, but it accords closely with Service's ideal-type model of the classical chiefdom derived independently from his study of state origins.[71] Indeed, I regard Service's formulation of the construct of the chiefdom as an alternative statement of the proposition which I advanced in *The Pivot of the Four Quarters* that archaic urban developments in their classic forms were often ceremonial centers — proto-urban perhaps in the eyes of the purist — functioning as the foci of city-states.[72]

It is not overly difficult to justify the belief that the chiefdom mode of social organization, with its proto- or fully urban ceremonial center, represents in the long term a transient phase. The increasing heterogeneity of society, although at first most evident in the elaboration of ceremonial and cultic hierarchies, tends eventually to undermine the effectiveness of religious sanctions on the conduct of public affairs. Concomitantly the concentration of wealth in the hands of oligarchs in the ritual center offers strong inducements to the substitution of organized and sustained warfare for localized and sporadic raiding in the slack season of the farming year, a development which has led to the recognition of a militaristic phase as representative of the ensuing set of disjunctive processes in the evolution of urban society.[73] The predominant characteristic of this phase is the progressive differentiation of political and religious authority, with the legitimation of political power coming increasingly to depend on a balance of forces between secular (i.e. political) and sacral leadership. The simple social duality of the classical chiefdom stage, which was manifested in a dichotomy between rulers and ruled, is replaced by a quadripartite division in which cultural-religious and politico-military elites are opposed to lower-status rural (i.e. peasant) and urban (predominantly artisan and merchant) groups. Furthermore, whereas in the chiefdom phase the ruler's personal administrative staff had typically owned its own *means* of administration (whether in the form of money, construction or war material, vehicles, horses, and so forth), the bureaucrats of the ensuing militaristic phase had been deprived of those means and performed assigned duties as salaried servants of the central government.[74]

Finally, it is with this transition from chiefdom to state that the aims and intentions of the urbanist and political scientist begin to diverge more widely. As the incipient status distinction between the seat of the paramount ruler and those of subordinate chiefs develops into a fully fledged urban hierarchy of greater or lesser complexity, the hitherto mutually reinforcing concerns of the two disciplines become complementary rather than confirmatory. Whereas the political scientist focuses his attention on the nature of authority relationships, the urbanist is concerned less with the state as such than with a generalized level of sociocultural integration which manifests itself (as was stated at the beginning of this chapter) as:

(1) a built form disposed spatially in a combination of
  (a) legislated and unlegislated patterns of land use reflecting a division of labor;
  (b) residential neighborhoods reflecting an apportionment of rewards, both of which are coordinated through the agency of
  (c) organizational structures that produce and depend on a flow of messages, persons, and commodities along institutionalized channels.
(2) a way of life.[75]
(3) a hierarchy of centers of societal control, a system of cities, the development of which can be viewed as an increase in societal scale involving:
  (a) extension of the radii of societal interdependence;
  (b) an intensification of the degree of that interdependence;
  (c) enlargement of the range and content of the information flows that integrate societal action;
  (d) a consequent expansion of the sphere of compliance to, and control by, the metropolitan center.[76]

This sphere of compliance and control is, of course, normally the state, the national polity, but for the urbanist it has become an independent variable.

Approaches to the Study of Urban Genesis

Thus far we have delineated the morphology of the transformation by which a congeries of acephalous societies is converted into an integral, pyramidal polity in which the units of kinship organization higher than that of the separate local segments not infrequently exist as permanent institutions performing different and complementary functions for the reproduction of the entire society; and we have commented briefly on the further mutation of this chiefdom-style entity into the still more highly specialized regulative organization of the state, sustained by a bureaucracy operating basically on rational-legal principles, and staffed by officials whom Weber characterized as "propertyless strata having no social honor of their own."[77] But we have said nothing of the dynamics of this process, a topic which has provided a subject of speculation for sages since Antiquity and a field of research for social scientists at least since the middle of the 19th century.[78] Today the theme is still a central concern of all who are engaged in the great collaborative enterprise of devising a definition of man.

Until recently attempts to provide explanations of the emergence of the state or its epiphenomenal accompaniment, the city, have been cast, almost without exception, in terms of prime movers, those *fontes et origines* which are so accommodatable, indeed necessary, to the grand monistic interpretations of history. Among the causative agents invoked, either singly or in combination, within the framework of this paradigm have been trade, warfare, irrigation, fertility and/or productivity, population growth, cooperation and/or competition, the integrative power of religion, and, at least once, anxiety induced when a sustaining ecosystem turned maladaptive.[79] In almost all instances the prime movers have been seen as operating either to produce conflict of some sort or to induce some mode of managerial integration. During the past two decades, however, authors have tended to reject monistic explanations in favor of multivariate approaches. Henry T. Wright has documented this change in the style of argument, as well as provided a systematization of several of the more insightful models recently proposed.[80] The most sophisticated of these was certainly the comparative study of urban origins in Mesopotamia and Mesoamerica in which Robert Adams examined a complex nexus of interrelated variables involved in a processual

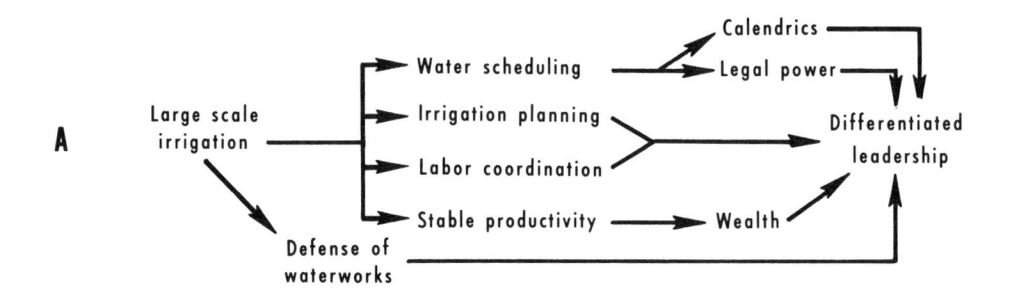

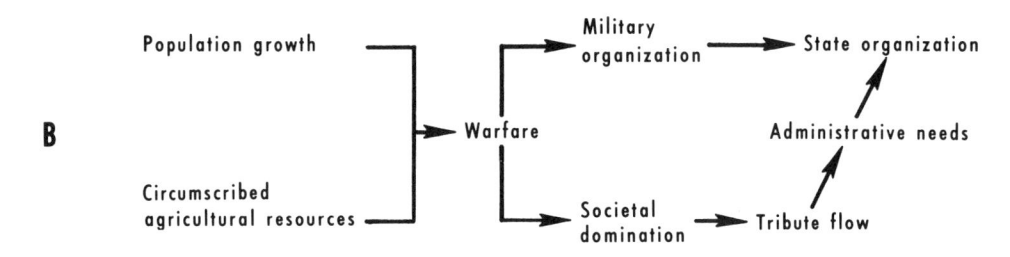

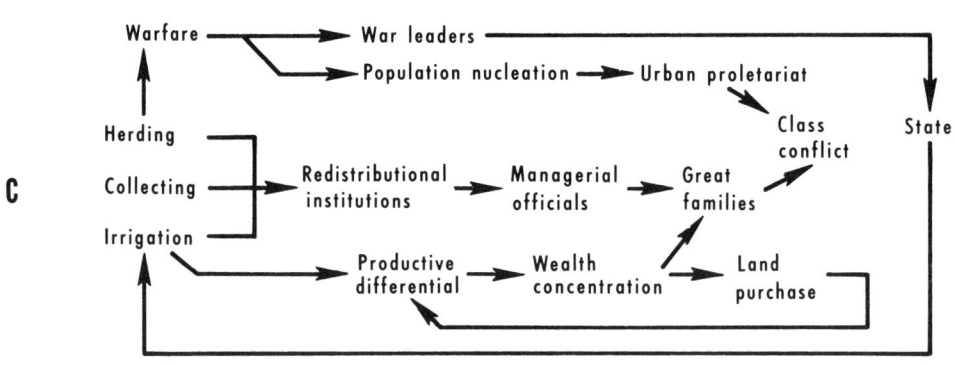

Fig. 1. Models of state origins proposed by [A] Karl Wittfogel; [B] Robert Carneiro; [C] Robert McC. Adams. After Henry T. Wright [*Toward an explanation of the origin of the state*. Paper prepared for a Symposium at the School of American Research on "Explanation of Prehistoric Organizational Change" (Santa Fe, 1970), mimeographed], modified by Kent V. Flannery, "The cultural evolution of civilizations," *Annual Review of Ecology and Systematics*, vol. 3 (1972), p. 408.

transformation between tribal (though he did not use that term) and urban levels of integration.[81] Shortly afterwards Wheatley interpreted the process of urban genesis on the North China plain[82] in terms of Duncan and Schnore's theory of the ecological complex, the functionally interrelated basic components of which are environment, population, technology, and social organization.[83] It goes without saying, of course, that the ecological approach incorporates a particular functionalist bias of a type better adapted to the analysis of distributional than of structural change. Of greater consequence, perhaps, was the failure of both Adams and Wheatley adequately to explain why the climacteric transformation from village to city occurred only in certain of the rather numerous regions which had seemingly attained the level of integration requisite for take-off into urbanism.[84] In fact, in some instances the arguments all but implied that the nexus of institutions of centralized control had arisen as random social mutations out of non-specific factors difficult, or even impossible, to generalize. It was Kent Flannery who carried the argument forward by suggesting how the transformational triggering mechanism may have worked.[85]

The essential components of Flannery's model can be specified as follows. If human society is postulated as a class of living system in the manner proposed by J. G. Miller,[86] then the state can be regarded as a system whose well-nigh incredible complexity can be comprehended in terms of the interaction of two processes: *segregation,* by which is denoted the degree of internal differentiation and specialization of its subsystems, and *centralization,* by which is meant the intensities and strengths of the linkages between the various subsystems and the highest order controls operating in a particular society. Flannery further discriminates between the *processes* themselves, the *mechanisms* by which they operate, and the *socio-environmental stresses* which select for those mechanisms. These are shrewdly conceived distinctions for, whereas both processes and mechanisms are viewed as universal in their application, the socio-environmental stresses are specific to particular regions and societies, thus providing a tool with which to probe the elusive problem of why state and/or urban generation should have occurred in so few of the regions technologically equipped to support it. The socio-environmental conditions envisaged by Flannery include both components of the ecological complex that formed the basis of analysis in the *Pivot* and an array of extra-cultural factors such as the managerial imperatives of various adaptive activities which in the earlier work were adduced as factors influencing the dependent variable.

The model of the ecotype adopted by Flannery as a framework for his analysis is specified as

> a series of subsystems arranged hierarchically, from lowest and most specific to highest and most general. Each subsystem is regulated by a control apparatus whose job is to keep all the variables in the subsystem within appropriate goal ranges — ranges which maintain homeostasis and do not threaten the survival of the system . . . . On all levels, the social control apparatus compares output values not merely with subsistence goals but with ideological values, the demands of deities and ancestral spirits, ethical and religious propositions — the human population's "cognized model" of the way the world is put together. The highest, most abstract, and most unchanging of these propositions lie in the highest-order (or "governmental") controls, which deal in policy more often than commands.[87]

Within the limits of this hierarchy of subsystems, the controls exercised by higher-order institutions extend to the output of lower-order institutions but not to the variables that they regulate, although in the event that a lower-order control fails to keep its subordinate variables within their appropriate ranges, the control apparatus at the next higher level may be activated. In terms of the Theory of Integrative Levels, the hierarchy of subsystems exemplifies the principle, to which we have already referred on p. 4, that, for an organization at any given level, its mechanism is to be investigated at the level below and its purpose at the level above.[88] This inclusion in the field of analysis of the highest of the three levels implies some concern with purpose, but not purpose in the teleological sense which assumes that the functions of a structure adequately account for its existence: rather purpose conceived as vectors built into organizations and manifesting themselves in the manner in which higher levels furnish direction to lower.

Adopting Slobodkin's formulation that the stress induced by variables transgressing their assigned goal ranges can bring about *either* the disruption of a system *or* its progressive evolution,[89] Flannery proposes that the processes of segregation and centralization are induced by the operation of two evolutionary mechanisms, which he terms respectively *promotion* and *linearization*. Promotion occurs when an institution rises from its original place in the control hierarchy to a position at a higher level. During this translation, either a new entity is born through the amplification and elaboration of a particular role within a pre-existing institution, or an already developed institution becomes less system-serving (special-purpose) and more self-serving

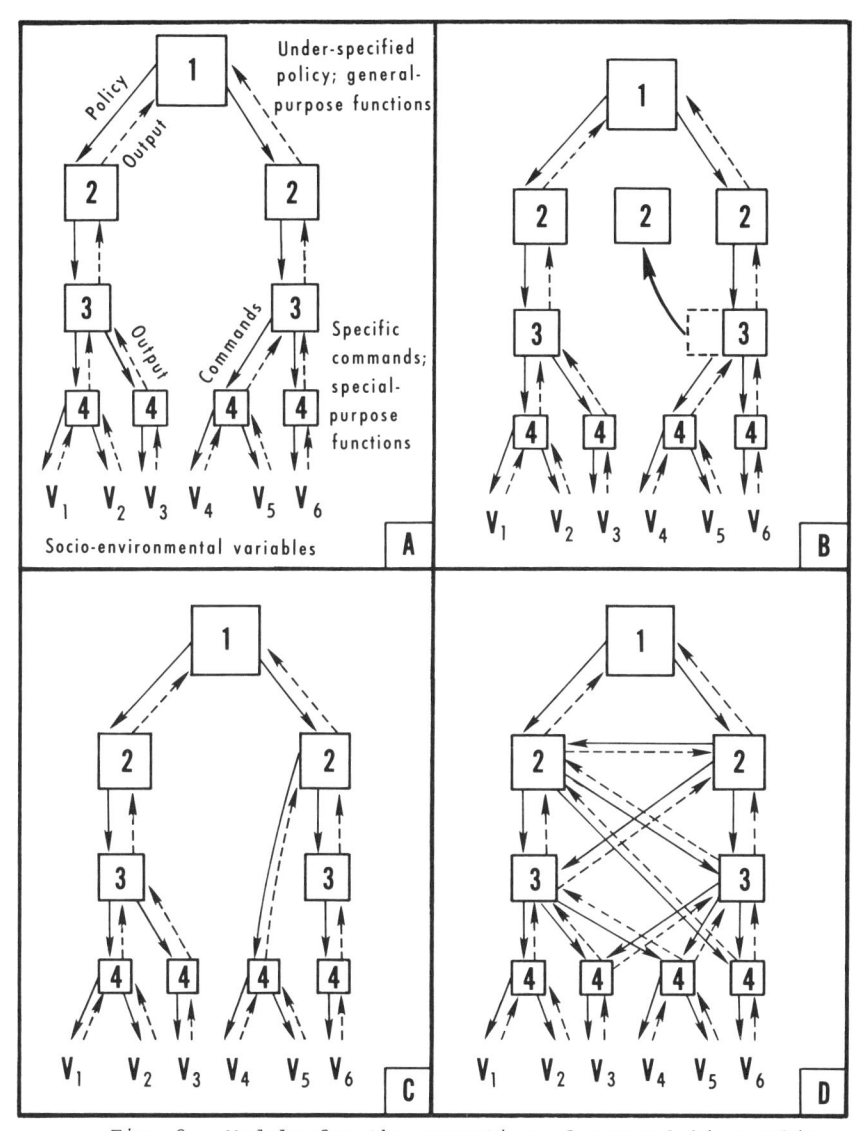

Fig. 2. Models for the operation of control hierarchies: [A] Stable functional hierarchy; [B] The mechanism of promotion; [C] The mechanism of linearization; [D] The pathology of hyper-coherence. Reproduced from Kent V. Flannery, "The cultural evolution of civilizations," *Annual Review of Ecology and Systematics*, vol. 3 (1972), p. 410.

(general purpose). Both occurrences are characteristic of evolutionary advance, primarily through their contributions to the process of segregation. Linearization, by contrast, makes its main contribution to the process of centralization. It is said to occur when lower-order controls are permanently (or at least repeatedly) bypassed by higher-order controls, a situation liable to arise when a lower-order institution fails for some critical period adequately to retain its variables within appropriate goal ranges.

In addition to these two functional mechanisms, the model also incorporates three dysfunctional mechanisms, or systemic pathologies as Rappaport calls them,[90] each of which can subject a system to additional stress and possibly, through the development of positive feedback loops, to increased segregation and centralization. The first of these pathologies is *usurpation,* defined as "the elevation of the purpose of one's own subsystem to a position of pre-eminence in a more inclusive system." It is induced by the proclivity of promoted institutions to serve their own interests rather than those of society at large. The second pathology is *meddling,* the direct subjection to a higher-order control of the variables properly regulated by lower-order controls. It occurs when linearization impairs the effectiveness of the controls that insulate one subsystem from perturbations in another. The third pathology is *hypercoherence,* which may be regarded as an excessive degree of centralization. It is a potentially unstable condition said to exist when institutions or subsystems are deprived of the autonomy proper to their status in the total system. As Flannery puts it, " . . . one by one, they are coupled more closely to each other and/or to the central hierarchical control until, like an old-fashioned string of Christmas tree lights set in linear sequence, change in one does in fact affect all the others too directly and rapidly."[91] Possibly the most common way in which hypercoherence occurs is through uncontrolled meddling. Needless to say, for any system to function effectively it must achieve a level of integration appropriate to its operational needs, so that the central problem inherent in an attempt to diagnose hypercoherence is that of recognizing the signs denoting an excessive deficiency in institutional autonomy.

The discrimination inherent in this model between mechanisms and processes, which are universal in their operation, and socio-environmental selection pressures, which are local, not only casts the problem of the so-called "prime movers" in a new light, but also focuses attention on systemic relationships between variables rather than on the variables themselves or on simple matter and energy exchanges.[92] In this type of interpretation, socio-environmental conditions and managerial imperatives are less direct mechanisms of cultural evolution than selectors for one of those mechanisms — or indeed for one of the pathologies. Population increases or organized warfare, for example, in any particular instance are to be regarded not so much as prime movers but rather as socio-environmental settings exerting potentially strong pressures for linearization and meddling, the end results of which are likely to be increased centralization. But linearization and meddling could both, in other circumstances, have been selected for by any one or more of a whole range of alternative socio-environmental factors. What the Flannery model does not specify is how the factors actually inducing centralization or segregation in any particular situation are to be discriminated within what is often a large array of potentially effective, mechanism-selecting, socio-environmental stresses. It is also true that the human ecosystem postulated by Flannery is one in which a hierarchically arranged series of subsystems, each furnished with its own specific control apparatus, already exists. It is not at all clear, however, how such a system comes into being in the first place. In other words, the model is better adapted to the study of differentiation and elaboration than of origins.

A major implication of the model is the importance for evolutionary advance of shifts in the hierarchical organization of decision-making procedures, from which it follows that information processing and ritual activities are likely to play a prominent part in any reasonably adequate interpretation of urban genesis. From this point of view, in fact, the city can be regarded as a multi-channelled instrument for the facilitation of human communication.[93] The secular aspects of the enormously complex flows of messages that constitute the communications network of even the smallest city have been studied by Richard Meier,[94] and the role of religious ritual as a regulatory mechanism will receive considerable attention in Chapter 7. Suffice it here to note that, as Rappaport puts it, human social organization is genetically underspecified.[95] The particular control mechanism operating in a specific situation is generally only one of a number that could maintain an appropriate degree of systemic coherence, and men, who are endowed with an adaptability that enables them to learn a whole range of social conventions, are quite capable of recognizing the essential arbitrariness of the set of conventions under which they do in fact at any time live. What sanctity can, and does, do is prescribe the options that the integrity of the particular social organization permits or demands. In Rappaport's apt phrase, sanctification transforms the arbitrary into the necessary. Indeed, it often goes farther, and castigates recalcitrance as sacrilege. In short, it reinforces the conventions that regulate society. As the output reference values of a regulatory mechanism derive not from the operation of that mechanism itself but from one at a level above, the reference value of a lower-order control has to be deduced from the cognized model of a higher-order control. It is, therefore, desirable that the goals of higher-order systems should be diffused through, and, as it were internalized by, lower-order systems so as to subvert possible attempts by social groups to "promote" (in the technical sense defined above) their own interests to positions of dominance in higher-level systems. In Rappaport's forthright language, "Sanctity helps to keep subsystems in their places."[96]

* * * * * * * * * *

Although, in succeeding chapters of this book, I shall attempt to elucidate the origin of the city in western (Indianized) Southeast Asia broadly within the conceptual framework just described, it is not my intention to impose any of the constituent models on the data. The deployment of sets of phenomena within the framework of an ideal type cannot itself generate explanation (although it may afford insights into principles of systemic organization). Instead, I shall allow my interpretation to develop out of the evidence as I understand it under the impulsion of its own intrinsic logic, and use the models, which embody the cumulative understandings of a century or more of inquiry into the problem of urban genesis, as flexible and accommodating principles of organization. It is improbable that the states and cities of Southeast Asia were all created by any single uniform and precisely repetitive process. Only after the origins of each of the urban traditions and, as far as is feasible, the subtraditions have been evaluated in their own right and the appropriate conclusions inferred will it perhaps be possible to discern recurrent trends in systemic change which, if they are at all comprehensive, may ultimately be recognized as constituting a paradigm (a model of models) of urban genesis in western Southeast Asia. However, this is a possible, not a necessary, conclusion, and one which I shall espouse only when confronted with compelling evidence. My purpose is not to subsume, disregard, or suppress the enormous diversity that characterizes urban forms within the region, but rather to render that diversity intelligible.

To this end, I shall first provide a summary statement of conditions in Southeast Asia late in the prehistoric period, thereby establishing a level of sociocultural integration as a datum plane from which to undertake the ensuing study of urban development in the so-called Indianized realms. Then I shall present the evidence for that transformation in the several major cultural divisions of the region, delineate the levels of integration that can be appropriately designated as urban, and offer an explication in broad systemic terms of the series of processual changes that gave rise to the states and cities of Indianized Southeast Asia. It will be evident from the following chapters that nowhere in Southeast Asia is the available evidence, either archeological or literary, for the formative phase of urban development sufficient in quantity or quality to permit the undertaking of statistically based locational analyses of the type recently pioneered by Gregory Johnson, Vincas Steponaitis, Ian Hodder, John Alden, Fred Plog, A. J. Chadwick, Jeffrey Eighmy, and others.[97] However, certain statistical techniques have been applied, with promising results, by Higham, Kijngam and Manly to a Khorat settlement pattern dating probably from the second half of the first millennium A.D.,[98] and similar approaches would surely prove profitable in Aṅkor Kampuchea, for which there is an abundance of settlement data. Finally I shall outline the contrasting process of urban imposition that obtained in the Việt and neighboring territories, and conclude with some comments on the urban hierarchies that evolved in the several cultural realms of Southeast Asia.

Notes and References

1. This aspect of urban studies is indissolubly associated with the name of Louis Wirth: "Urbanism as a way of life," *American Journal of Sociology,* vol. 44 (1938), pp. 3-24; reprinted on several occasions, perhaps most conveniently in Wirth's posthumous *Community life and social policy* (Chicago, 1956), pp. 110-132, and Albert J. Reiss, Jr., *On cities and social life* (Chicago, 1964), pp. 60-83. For a recent evaluation of Wirth's contribution to urban studies, together with a conspectus of alternative analyses of urbanism as a way of life, see Claude S. Fischer, "'Urbanism as a way of life': a review and an agenda," *Sociological Methods and Research,* vol. 1, no. 2 (1972), pp. 187-242.

2. John Friedmann, "Cities in social transformation," *Comparative Studies in Society and History,* vol. 4, no. 1 (1961), p. 92; Friedmann, "L'influence de l'intégration du système social sur le développement économique," *Diogène* vol. 33 (1961), pp. 80-104. The same author has applied the notion of the city as a creator of effective space to problems of development in several subsequent papers, which have been conveniently brought together in *Urbanization, planning, and national development* (Beverly Hills, Calif., and London, 1973).

3. The substance of this and the preceding paragraph is elaborated in Wheatley, "The concept of urbanism," in Peter J. Ucko, Ruth Tringham, and G. W. Dimbleby (eds.), *Man, settlement and urbanism* (London, 1972), pp. 601-637; reprinted in Tringham (ed.), *Urban settlements. The process of urbanization in archaeological settlements* (Andover, Mass., 1973), pp. Rl2: 1-37. Cf. also the "Foreword" to Robert R. Reed, *City of Pines: the origins of Baguio as a colonial hill station and regional capital.* Research Monograph No. 13 of the Center for South and Southeast Asia Studies, University of California (Berkeley, Calif., 1976).

4. Wirth's characterization of the city in roughly these terms occurs on p. 8 of the original printing of his paper on "Urbanism as a way of life": cp. note 1 above.

5. Awareness of the contrast between urban and rural life styles is clearly evident in, for example, Old Testament accounts of the urbanized Canaanites and certain nomadic Hebrew tribes [Cf. W. R. Jeremia, *Handbuch zum Alten Testament,* vol. 12 (Tübingen, 1958), pp. 207ff; M. Y. Ben-Gavriel, "Das nomadische Ideal in der Bibel," *Stimmen der Zeit,* vol. 88 (1962-63), pp. 253-263; J. O. Hertzler, *Social thought of the ancient civilizations* (New York, 1936), pp. 298ff.]. For Lucretius and the Epicureans much the same distinction was subsumed by the paired terms *concordia* and *justitia,* for Mencius [II, ii, 3, 6] by the opposition of court (*ch'ao t'ing*) and village (*hsiang tang*).

6. This is the definition provided by Brian T. Robson [*Urban growth: an approach* (London, 1973), p. 4], following earlier statements by G. P. Chapman [*The object of geographical analysis,* an unpublished paper presented to the Commission on Quantitative Methods of the International Geographical Union (Budapest, 1971)] and James K. Feibleman ["Theory of integrative levels," *British Journal for the Philosophy of Science,* vol. 5 (1954), pp. 59-66]. In less abstract language than that used in the text, a first-order object of study can be characterized as an object which has shape, which is composed of a set of identifiable elements determining its internal functioning, which can be related to other objects defined at a similar scale and having relationships with it at the next-higher scale level, and which varies over both space and time.

7. Robinson, *Urban growth,* p. 4.

8. Feibleman, "Theory of integrative levels," p. 61. Phrased differently the law becomes: the output of a higher-order control constitutes the reference

value for a lower-order control. Or, stated in yet a third way, a regulatory mechanism does not establish its own output reference values, but adopts those of a higher-order regulatory mechanism.

9. Notably by Brian J. L. Berry, "Cities as systems within systems of cities," *Papers and Proceedings of the Regional Science Association*, vol. 13 (1964), pp. 147-163.

10. This and the following eight paragraphs are reproduced substantially as they appeared in Wheatley and Thomas See, *From court to capital. A tentative interpretation of the origins of the Japanese urban tradition* (Chicago, 1978), pp. 3-8.

11. See, for example, Kingsley Davis and Hilda Hertz Golden, "Urbanization and the development of pre-industrial areas," *Economic Development and Cultural Change,* vol. 3 (1954), pp. 6-24.

12. At this point the reader must be cautioned that, although the vocabulary employed is shared by a number of other writers, several alternative terminologies are also in use. Kenneth Little, for instance, denotes by *urbanization* "the process whereby people acquire material and non-material elements of culture, behaviour patterns and ideas that originate in or are distinctive of the city" — which is substantially what we are designating as the *urban process* [Little, *Urbanization as a social process. An essay on movement and change in contemporary Africa* (London and Boston, 1974), *passim*]. More than a decade previously Scott Greer referred to this same process simply as "urbanism" ("the acculturation of subgroups to a society-wide normative structure") in *The emerging city: myth and reality* (New York, 1962), p. 49. Other authors prefer to speak of two senses of the term "urbanization": e.g., Manuel Castells, *The urban question: a Marxist approach* (Cambridge, Mass., 1977), p. 9.

13. Urbanized country dwellers of this type customarily figure in anthropological writings as peasants *sensu stricto*. See, for example, Robert Redfield, *The primitive world and its transformations* (Ithaca, N.Y., 1953), p. 53, and *Peasant society and culture* (Chicago, 1956), *passim*; Eric R. Wolf, *Peasants* (Englewood Cliffs, N.J., 1966), *passim*, but especially pp. 9-10.

14. The concept of levels of socio-cultural complexity comprising "a framework of functionally interconnected institutions forming the structural core of a distinctive set of social systems" was proposed by Julian H. Steward [*Theory of culture change* (Urbana, Ill., 1955)], and subsequently applied to the problem of urban genesis by Robert McC. Adams, *The evolution of urban society* (Chicago, 1966).

15. These levels of sociocultural integration are discussed in some detail in Wheatley, *The pivot of the four quarters. A preliminary enquiry into the origins and character of the ancient Chinese city* (Edinburgh and Chicago, 1971), pp. 316-330.

16. H. M. Blalock and A. B. Blalock, "Toward a classification of system analysis in the social sciences," *Philosophy of Science,* vol. 26 (1959), pp. 84-92.

17. J. Klir and M. Valach, *Cybernetic modelling* (London, 1967).

18. Talcott Parsons and Edward Shils (eds.), *Toward a general theory of action* (Cambridge, Mass., 1952), pp. 4, 39, 56, and 101.

19. Our categorization of realms of primary and secondary urban generation is, of course, analogous to Morton H. Fried's discrimination between what he terms pristine and secondary states [Briefly in "On the evolution of social stratification and the state," in Stanely Diamond (ed.), *Culture in history: essays in honor of Paul Radin* (New York, 1960), pp. 713 and 729-730; elaborated

in *The evolution of political society* (New York, 1967) *passim*].

There have been few attempts to generalize about the processes operating in either secondary urban generation or secondary state formation, but two such are Herbert S. Lewis, "The origins of African kingdoms," *Cahiers d'Etudes Africaines*, vol. 6 (1966), pp. 402-407 and Barbara J. Price, "Secondary state formation: an explanatory model," in Ronald Cohen and Elman R. Service (eds.), *Origins of the state: the anthropology of political evolution* (Philadelphia, 1978), pp. 161-186.

20. Note 2 above.

21. A notable example of an author who is prepared to accede to the notion of city-less statehood is Eric R. Wolf, who takes a somewhat narrower view of urbanism than that espoused in the present volume: *Peasants* (Englewood Cliffs, N.J., 1966), pp. 10-11. John A. Wilson seems to have been subscribing to the same notion when he contrived the formula "civilization without cities" in reference to the Nile valley before the rise of the New Kingdom: *The burden of Egypt* (Chicago, 1951), chap. 2 [Reprinted under the title *The culture of ancient Egypt* (1963)].

22. Note 2 above.

23. As was implicit in the works of, among others, Ferdinand Tönnies [*Gemeinschaft und Gesellschaft* (Eighth revised edition, Leipzig, 1935)], Emile Durkheim [*De la division du travail social: étude sur l'organisation des sociétés supérieures* (Paris, 1893)], Oswald Spengler [*Der Untergang des Abendlandes*, 2 vols. (München, 1922)], and José Ortega y Gasset [*The revolt of the masses* (New York, 1932)].

24. Richard L. Meier, "The organization of technological innovation in urban environments," in Oscar Handlin and John Burchard (eds.), *The historian and the city* (Cambridge, Mass., 1963), p. 75.

25. Scott Greer, *The emerging city: myth and reality* (New York, 1962), p. 34.

26. For further discussion of this distinction between central institutional transactions concerned with the transmission of information on the one hand and those dealing with the allocation of commodities on the other see Richard E. Blanton, "Anthropological Studies of Cities," *Annual Review of Anthropology*, vol. 5 (1976), pp. 249-264.

27. Sir Henry [Sumner] Maine, *Ancient law. Its connection with the early history of society and its relation to modern ideas* (London, 1961). Reprinted in 1916 with editorial notes by Frederick Pollock, and as Beacon Paperback No. 155 (Boston, 1963).

28. Lewis Henry Morgan, *Ancient society, or, researches in the lines of human progress from savagery through barbarism to civilization* (New York, 1877). Reprinted as Meridian Book No. 166, edited by Eleanor Burke Leacock (New York, 1963).

29. Ferdinand Tönnies, *Gemeinschaft und Gesellschaft* (Eighth revised edition, Leipzig, 1935).

30. Emile Durkheim, *De la division du travail social: étude sur l'organisation des sociétés supérieures* (Paris, 1893). Contrasts of this type had been incorporated in the works of numerous authors prior to the rise of the social sciences in the 19th century. Edmund Burke's *Reflections on the revolution in France* (1790), for instance, is structured about his distinction between "legitimate society" (compounded of kinship, class, religion, and locality, and cemented by tradition) and the new industrial society which he observed developing in Britain and Europe. Cf. also the same author's *A vindication of natural society* (1756). An analogous conception is also clearly evident in

Hegel's opposition of "family society" to "civic society." For a short
discussion of these and similar so-called "theories of contrast" see Wheatley,
"The concept of urbanism," pp. 602-605. The most comprehensive treatment of
these paired terms is still that by H. Becker, *Through values to social
interpretation* (Durham, N.C., 1950).

31. Quoted by Elman R. Service [*Origins of the state and civilization. The
process of cultural evolution* (New York, 1975), p. 51] from Ruben Gold Thwaites
(ed.), *The Jesuit relations and allied documents*, vol. 6 (Cleveland, 1897),
p. 243.

32. For varying views of what constitutes a state consult, *int. al.*, J. K.
Bluntschli, *The theory of the state* (London, 1892); Franz Oppenheimer, *The
state: its history and development viewed sociologically* (reprint edition: New
York, 1926); Richard Thurnwald, *Die menschliche Gesellschaft*, vol. 4
(Berlin-Leipzig, 1935); Otto Gierke, *Natural law and the theory of society*
(Boston, 1950); Wilhelm Koppers, "L'origine de l'état," *VIth International
Congress of Anthropological and Ethnological Sciences 1960*, vol. 2 (Paris, 1963),
pp. 159-168; Morton H. Fried, *The evolution of political society. An essay in
political anthropology* (New York, 1967), chap. 6; Lawrence Krader, *Formation of
the state* (Englewood Cliffs, N.J., 1968); and most recently Elman R. Service,
Origins of the state and civilization: the process of cultural evolution (New
York, 1975).

33. *Int. al.*, Robert McC. Adams, *The evolution of urban society: early
Mesopotamia and Prehispanic Mexico* (Chicago, 1966); Wheatley, *The pivot of the
four quarters* (Edinburgh and Chicago, 1971).

34. See particularly Service, *Origins of the state, passim;* Donna Taylor, *Some
locational aspects of middle-range hierarchical societies*. Unpublished Ph.D.
dissertation submitted to the Graduate Faculty in Anthropology, The City
University of New York, 1975; Blanton, "Anthropological studies of cities,"
passim.
The term "chiefdom" seems to have been first employed in a restricted technical
sense by Kalervo Oberg in 1955 ["Types of social structure among the lowland
tribes of South and Central America," *American Anthropologist*, vol. 57, no. 3,
pp. 472-487] as a designation for a certain type of circum-Caribbean society
exhibiting a degree of structural centralization somewhere between that of a
segmented tribe and that of a developed state. Subsequently Julian H. Steward
and Louis C. Faron gave wider currency to this usage by incorporating it in their
text entitled *Native peoples of South America* (New York, 1959), and a year or
two later Elman Service adopted the term to denote an evolutionary stage of
social development [*Primitive social organization: an evolutionary perspective*
(New York, 1962).] More recently the same author has used the concept as a
principal organizing theme in his study of the *Origins of the state*. Others who
have incorporated the concept in studies of early state development include:
Marshall D. Sahlins, *Tribesmen* (Englewood Cliffs, N.J., 1968), and *Stone age
economics* (Chicago, 1972); William T. Sanders and Barbara J. Price, *Mesoamerica:
the evolution of a civilization* (New York, 1968); Jeffrey R. Parsons,
Prehistoric settlement patterns in the Texcoco region, Mexico. Memoir No. 3 of
the Museum of Anthropology, University of Michigan (Ann Arbor, Mich., 1971);
Gregory A. Johnson, *Local exchange and early state development in southwest Iran.*
Anthropological Paper No. 51 of the Museum of Anthropology, University of
Michigan (Ann Arbor, 1973); Richard E. Blanton, *Prehispanic settlement patterns
of the Irtapalapa Peninsula region, Mexico*. Occasional Paper in Anthropology
No. 6, Department of Anthropology, The Pennsylvania State University (University
Park, Pennsylvania, 1972), and "Anthropological studies of cities" [See Note 26
above]; Taylor, *Some locational aspects of middle-range hierarchical societies*
(above). In this last work (p. 15) Dr. Taylor notes pertinently that, whereas
Steward's levels of sociocultural integration are based on a combination of
aspects of subsistence, technology and material culture, sociopolitical and
religious patterns, and a variety of other "culture elements," Service's
chiefdom is defined in terms of social-structural integration, particularly the

degree of centralization of economic, social, and religious activities. To that extent the chiefdom cannot justly be considered as an intermediate level of sociocultural integration between two of Steward's levels, but must be regarded as a sub-category separated out from the state level of integration on social-structural principles.

35. These are the groupings used by Donna Taylor in her study of African chiefdoms: *Some locational aspects, passim* but especially Chapter IV.

36. Sahlins, *Stone age economics,* p. 141.

37. Service, *Origins of the state,* p. 16, Cp. also Morton H. Fried, *The evolution of political society. An essay in political anthropology* (New York, 1967), p. 230.

38. "Conical clans" was the term proposed by Paul Kirchhof to denote extensive common descent groups, ranked and segmented on genealogical lines, which bound their members with familial ties while yet distributing wealth, social standing, and power according to consanguineal proximity to the main line of descent ["The principles of clanship in human society," *Davidson Journal of Anthropology,* vol. 1 (1955), pp. 1-10. Reprinted in Morton H. Fried (ed.), *Readings in anthropology,* vol. 2 (New York, 1959), pp. 260-270.] There is an admirable discussion of these social groups, felicitously characterized as "clanship made political," in Marshall D. Sahlins, *Tribesmen* (Englewood Cliffs, N.J., 1968), pp. 24-26. Raymond Firth categorized such conical groups as *ramages* (Old French = "branches"), a term which has usually been preferred by British social anthropologists and which has the advantage of drawing attention etymologically to the basic concept of the branching of genealogies. See *We, the Tikopia* (London, 1936).

39. Taylor, *Some locational aspects,* pp. 71-78 and 92.

40. Johnson, *Local exchange and early state development in southwestern Iran,* pp. 4-9, 87-90, and *passim.*

41. Sanders and Price, *Mesoamerica,* p. 229.

42. Sanders and Price, *Mesoamerica,* p. 116.

43. Gordon R. Willey, "Problems concerning prehistoric settlement patterns in the Maya lowlands," in Willey (ed.), *Prehistoric settlement patterns in the New World.* Viking Fund Publications in Anthropology No. 23 (New York, 1956), pp. 107-114.

44. S. W. Miles, "Maya settlement patterns: a problem for ethnology and archaeology," *Southwestern Journal of Anthropology,* vol. 13 (1957), pp. 239-248.

45. Miles, "Maya settlement patterns," p. 243, and "An urban type: extended boundary towns," *Southwestern Journal of Anthropology,* vol. 14, no. 4 (1958), pp. 339-351.

46. John Howland Rowe, "Urban settlements in ancient Peru," *Ñawpa Pacha,* vol. 1 (1963), p. 3.

47. Wheatley, *Pivot,* pp. 305-311 and 389. For a more general discussion of chiefdom settlement patterns see Vincas P. Stephanaitis, "Location theory and complex chiefdoms: a Mississippian example," in Bruce D. Smith (ed.), *Mississippian settlement patterns* (New York, 1978), pp. 417-453. There is also much of relevance to the present theme in Christopher S. Peebles and Susan M. Kus, "Some archaeological correlates of ranked societies," *American Antiquity,* vol. 42, no. 3 (1977), pp. 421-448.

48. For the ethnographic bases of these ascriptions, though not necessarily for

syntheses in terms of chiefdoms, see, *int. al.,* David Malo, *Hawaiian antiquities* (Honolulu, 1903); Douglas L. Oliver, *The Pacific islands* (Cambridge, Mass., 1951); Marshall D. Sahlins, *Social stratification in Polynesia* (Seattle, 1958); Timothy Earle, *Economic and social organization of a complex chiefdom: the Halelea district, Kaua'i, Hawaii*. Anthropological Paper, Museum of Anthropology, University of Michigan, No. 63 (Ann Arbor, Mich., 1978); Max Freiherr von Oppenheim, *Die Beduinen,* vols. 1 and 2 (Leipzig, 1939, 1943), vol. 3 (Wiesbaden, 1952); J. Otto Maenchen-Helfen, *The world of the Huns. Studies in their history and culture* (Berkeley and Los Angeles, 1973); W. Barthold, *Turkestan down to the Mongol invasion*. "E. J. W. Gibb Memorial" Series, New Series V (Third edition, London, 1968). Lawrence Krader, *Social organization of the Mongol-Turkic pastoral nomads* (New York and The Hague, 1963), and *Peoples of Central Asia* (Bloomington, Ind., 1963).

49. Sahlins, *Stone age economics,* p. 139. This also appears to be the model of the chiefdom against which Service measures his "modern primitive states," namely the Nguni (Zulu); Ankole (Uganda); Nupe, Ashanti, and Kongo (West Africa), the Cherokee, and Polynesian chiefdoms [*Origins of the state and civilization,* Part II].

50. Marshall Sahlins, "Poor man, rich man, big-man, chief: political types in Melanesia and Polynesia," *Comparative Studies in Society and History,* vol. 5 (1963), pp. 285-303. See also Douglas L. Oliver, *Studies in the anthropology of Bougainville, Solomon Islands*. Peabody Museum Papers, vol. 29 (Cambridge, Mass., 1949); Bronislaw Malinowski, *Argonauts of the western Pacific* (London, 1932); Marshall D. Sahlins, *Moala: culture and nature on a Fijian island* (Ann Arbor, Mich., 1962).

51. Taylor, *Some locational aspects of middle-range hierarchical societies, passim.*

52. Max Weber, *Wirtschaft und Gesellschaft. Grundriss der verstehenden Soziologie,* vol. 2 (Second edition, Tübingen, 1925), pp. 680-681, and the posthumously published essay "Die drei reinen Typen der legitimen Herrschaft," *Preussische Jahrbücher,* vol. 187 (1922), pp. 1-12; reprinted in *Staatssoziologie* (Berlin, 1956), pp. 99-110. A critical summary of Weber's types of traditional domination (*Herrschaft*) is incorporated in Reinhard Bendix, *Max Weber: an intellectual portrait* (New York, 1962), chap. 11. Note that Weber employed the term *Herrschaft* in a very restricted sense, excluding from its scope all situations in which power derived from constellations of interest: cf. Bendix, *op. cit.,* p. 291; Max Rheinstein (ed., Edward Shils and M. R., transl.), *Max Weber on law in economy and society*. Twentieth Century Legal Philosophy Series, vol. 6 (Cambridge, Mass., 1954), pp. 327-328.

53. Weber, *Wirtschaft und Gesellschaft,* vol. 2, pp. 679-752, and "Die drei reinen Typen der legitimen Herrschaft," *passim.*

54. See, *int. al.,* Paul Kirchhoff, "The principles of clanship in human society," in Morton H. Fried (ed.), *Readings in Anthropology,* vol. 2 (New York, 1959), pp. 260-270 [Originally written in 1935; first published in 1955 in *Davidson Journal of Anthropology,* vol. 1, pp. 1-10]; Jonathan Friedman, "Tribes, states, and transformations," in Maurice Bloch (ed.), *Marxist analyses and social anthropology*. Association of Social Anthropologists Studies No. 3 (London and New York, 1975), pp. 161-202.

55. When a ruler is in a position to use these military forces, in conjunction with an administrative corps loyal only to him, to extend his power "free of traditional restraint," then he has created a "sultanistic regime," Weber's term for the extreme form of personal despotism, and has transformed the chiefdom into a state. In his analysis of this particular transformation of traditional domination, Weber paid special attention to the social organization of military forces. His argument is conveniently summarized in Bendix, *Max Weber,* pp. 341-344.

The City and Its Origins 37

56. "Liturgical" was the term used by Max Weber to denote payments in kind made to a central authority [after the liturgies of the ancient Greek city-states, in which certain groups of the population were charged with the provision and maintenance of naval vessels or the furnishing of theatrical performances]. *Vide* Max Weber, *The theory of social and economic organization* (English transl., New York, 1947) pp. 310-315.

57. Bendix, *Max Weber,* p. 340.

58. "Sanctioned custom" is Service's term for the pressure of an immemorial tradition which, as is by no means always the case, is backed by either positive or negative reinforcements (that is sanctions): *Origins of the state and civilization,* p. 86. As far as I have been able to ascertain, pp. 83-90 of this volume comprise the only explicit discussion of chiefdom law, though the subject has, of course, received considerable attention in numerous ethnographic accounts of polities which were in fact chiefdoms, and Morton H. Fried includes perceptive sections on law in his discussions of simple egalitarian and rank societies [*The evolution of political society: an essay in political anthropology* (New York, 1967), pp. 90-94 and 144-153].

59. See, for example, Leopold Pospisil, *Anthropology of law. A comparative theory* (New York, 1971); *The ethnology of law.* McCaleb Modules in Anthropology No. 12 (Reading, Mass., 1972). Pospisil's original substantive work on primitive law, reported in *Kapauka Papuans and their law.* Yale University Publications in Anthropology No. 54 (New Haven, Conn., 1958), was carried out in a society which would meet our requirements for a low-level chiefdom. An earlier attempt by E. Adamson Hoebel to formulate a supracultural definition of "law" had proposed three necessary components: privileged force, official authority, and regularity. In effect, Hoebel was thinking along the same lines as Pospisil, but chose to ignore *obligatio,* the rights and duties of the litigants [*The law of primitive man* (Cambridge, Mass., 1954)].

60. This is the type of sanction that Bronislaw Malinowski had in mind when, nearly fifty years ago, he wrote:

> This positive aspect of compliance to primitive custom, the fact that obedience to rules is baited with premiums, that it is rewarded by counter-services, is as important, in my opinion, as the study of punitive sanctions; and these latter consist not in a punishment inflicted deliberately *ad hoc,* but rather in the natural retaliation of non-compliance in counter-services, of criticism and dissatisfaction within the relationship and within the institution.
>
> "Introduction" to H. Ian Hogbin, *Law and order in Polynesia* (London, 1934), p. xxxvi.

61. It should be noted that sanctions are not, as has sometimes been thought, necessarily indicative of law, the most obvious case to the contrary being the sanctions invoked against transgressors of *ad hoc* political fiats, which, though "legal" in the sense of not contravening custom or existing law, in no way themselves constitute law.

62. Pospisil, "The ethnology of law," pp. 22-23.

63. Service, *Origins of the state,* pp. 88-89.

64. In the Parsonian paradigm followed here, every society employs four primary modes of exchange, each corresponding to one of its functional subsystems, in a combination of emphases reflective of its value system, appropriate to the degree of differentiation of its social structure, and adapted to its external situation. The four modes of exchange are *reciprocity,* which obtains primarily among those social units such as families, neighborhood communities, and religious groups concerned with pattern maintenance and tension management;

redistribution, which involves the allocation of rewards and facilities in conformity with the integrative requirements of society; *mobilization,* which provides mechanisms for the acquisition, control, and disposal of resources in the pursuit of collective goals, that is broadly speaking in the political field; and *market exchange,* the main instrument for the production of such generalized facilities as enable the adaptive subsystem of society to achieve a variety of aims in a variety of situational contexts. At any one time the subsystems exhibit not only individual morphologies but also a particular collective configuration, but as the society evolves the sphere of operation of each of its subsystems changes in extent and intensity, thereby inducing parallel mutations in its associated modes of exchange. Cf. Talcott Parsons and Neil J. Smelser, *Economy and society. A study in the integration of economic and social theory* (London, 1956); Smelser, "A comparative view of exchange systems," *Economic Development and Cultural Change,* vol. 7 (1959), pp. 173-182, and *The sociology of economic life* (Englewood Cliffs, N.J., 1963).

65. I am, of course, here assimilating the religious system of the chiefdom to Robert N. Bellah's ideal-typical stage of Archaic Religion: "Religious evolution," *American Sociological Review,* vol. 29, no. 3 (1964), pp. 364-366. On the high god see Raffaele Pettazzoni, *The all-knowing god* (London, 1956).

66. On this point see the classic paper of Henri Hubert and Marcel Mauss, "Essai sur la nature et la fonction du sacrifice," *L'Année Sociologique,* vol. 2 (1897-98), pp. 29-138.

67. Bellah, "Religious evolution," p. 365.

68. Service, *Origins of the state and civilization,* p. 93.

69. I.e., any of several forms of wholesaling undertaken at government instigation and under government control. The term was first given this technical meaning in the works of Karl Polanyi: see, for instance, Polanyi, Conrad M. Arensberg, and Harry W. Pearson, *Trade and market in the early empires* (Glencoe, Ill., 1957), pp. 168ff. and 262ff., and "Traders and trade," in Jeremy A. Sabloff and C. C. Lamberg-Karlovsky, *Ancient civilization and trade* (Albuquerque, New Mexico, 1975), pp. 149-150; George Dalton (ed.), *Primitive, archaic and modern economies. Essays of Karl Polanyi* (New York, 1968), pp. 164ff. My use of Polanyi's term does not mean that I concur in all his conclusions, a fact which is evident enough from several sections of this work.

70. Paul Wheatley and Thomas See, *From court to capital. A tentative interpretation of the origins of the Japanese urban tradition* (Chicago, 1978) pp. 75-76. Cf. also Wheatley, *The pivot of the four quarters. A preliminary enquiry into the origins and character of the ancient Chinese city* (Edinburgh and Chicago, 1971), pp. 225-226.

71. Service, *Origins of the state and civilization,* pp. 15-16 and *passim.*

72. Wheatley, *The pivot of the four quarters,* chap. 3 and Conclusion.

73. In the Middle East this functional and developmental phase is usually known as the *Dynastic,* in the Central Andean Co-tradition by the equally expressive term *Expansionist* [E.g., Wendell C. Bennett and Junius B. Bird, *Andean culture history* (New York, 1949), pp. 135-148; J. Alden Mason, *The ancient civilizations of Peru* (Harmondsworth, England, 1957), pp. 88-95]. For an attempt to extend this style of terminology to all regions of nuclear urbanism, see Julian H. Steward *et al., Irrigation civilizations: a comparative study,* Pan American Union Social Science Monograph No. 1 (Washington, D.C., 1955), pp. 68-69.

74. Cf. Max Weber, "Politik als Beruf," in *Gesammelte Politische Schriften* (München, 1921), pp. 396-450.

75. See Note 1 above.

76. For a discussion of these aspects of increasing societal scale see Scott Greer, *The emerging city: myth and reality* (New York, 1962), pp. 41-54.

77. Weber, "Politik als Beruf," cited by H. H. Gerth and C. Wright Mills, *From Max Weber, Essays in sociology* (London and New York, 1958), p. 82.

78. This concern was central, for example, to the thought of Sir Henry Maine and Lewis Henry Morgan (Notes 27 and 28 above), Edward B. Tyler [*Primitive culture* (3rd edition, New York, 1889)], Karl Marx [*Zur Kritik der politischen Ökonomie* (Berlin, 1859) and *Das Kapital*, 3 vols. (Hamburg, 1867, 1885, 1894)], and Friedrich Engels [*The origin of the family, private property, and the state* (1st English edition, Chicago, 1904)].

79. Long-distance commerce has always been a favorite causative agent of urban historians, particularly those of the older school, while retail trade has been the preferred option of geographers, a notion encapsulated in the often cited dictum that permanent central-place systems develop out of periodic central-place systems. Warfare was accorded a pre-eminent role in the origin of the state by Herbert Spencer [*The evolution of society*. Edited, and with an introduction by Robert L. Carneiro (Chicago, 1967)], and has recently been invoked by Robert L. Carneiro as a prime mover (though not one which is alone adequate to the task) in state formation ["A theory of the origin of the state," *Science*, vol. 169 (1970), pp. 733-738, especially p. 734]. Irrigation is, of course, irrevocably associated with the name of Karl August Wittfogel: see his summary of many years' work in *Oriental despotism: a comparative study of total power* (New Haven, Conn., 1957), and a distillation of his thought in "The hydraulic civilizations," in William L. Thomas, Jr., (ed.), *Man's role in changing the face of the earth* (Chicago, 1956), pp. 152-164. A collaborative attempt to extend Wittfogel's formulation to realms outside the Orient was organized by Julian H. Steward *et al.*, *Irrigation civilizations*: cf. Note 73 above. Productivity and population growth as dependent variables were both implicit in V. Gordon Childe's classic exposition of urban genesis: "The urban revolution," *Town Planning Review*, vol. 21, no. 1 (1950), pp. 9-16. See also T. Cuyler Young, Jr., "Population densities and early Mesopotamian urbanism" in Peter J. Ucko, Ruth Tringham, and G. W. Dimbleby, *Man, settlement and urbanism* (London, 1972), pp. 827-842. Cooperation and competition have been proposed as processes which, though generalized, might yet exert a generative influence, by William T. Sanders and Barbara J. Price, *Mesoamerica. The evolution of a civilization* (New York, 1968), pp. 49 and 230. The integrative power of religion was the theme of Numa Denis Fustel de Coulanges, *La cité antique* (Paris, 1864), and more recently has been regarded somewhat sympathetically by Gordon R. Willey, "Mesoamerica," in Robert J. Braidwood and Willey (eds.), *Courses toward urban life. Archeological considerations of some cultural alternates* (Chicago, 1962), pp. 84-101, and "The early Great Styles and the rise of the Pre-Columbian civilizations," *American Anthropologist*, vol. 64 (1962), pp. 1-14. In spite of the circumstance that, for reasons of brevity, only one or two names have here been attached to the individual causative agents, each has in fact been proposed by several, and sometimes numerous, authors; but anxiety induced by deterioration of a habitat has, I think, been suggested (and then very tentatively) in only one instance: by Walter A. Fairservis, Jr., "The Harappan civilization — new evidence and more theory," *American Museum Novitates*, no. 2055 (1961), p. 18. It is true that Henri Frankfort was aware of the possible function of anxiety in the formation of Mesopotamian temple cities, but he derived it from an inability to cope with a particular environment rather than from general environmental deterioration: cf., for example, *The birth of civilization in the Near East* (Bloomington, Ind., 1951), chap. 3, especially p. 54.

80. Henry T. Wright, *Toward an explanation of the origin of the state*. Paper prepared for a Symposium at the School of American Research on "Explanation of Prehistoric Organizational Change" (Santa Fe, 1970). Mimeographed, but subsequently published in progressively expanded forms in James H. Hill (ed.), *Explanation of prehistoric change* (Albuquerque, N. Mex., 1977) and Ronald Cohen and Elman R. Service (eds.), *Origins of the state: the anthropology of political*

evolution (Philadelphia, 1978).

81. Robert McC. Adams, *The evolution of urban society: early Mesopotamia and Prehispanic Mexico* (Chicago, 1966).

82. Wheatley, *The pivot of the four quarters, passim*.

83. Otis Dudley Duncan and Leo F. Schnore, "Cultural, behavioral, and ecological perspectives in the study of social organization," *American Journal of Sociology*, vol. 65 (1959), pp. 132-146; Schnore, "Social morphology and human ecology," *American Journal of Sociology*, vol. 63 (1958), pp. 620-634; Duncan, "Human ecology and population studies," in Philip M. Hauser and Duncan (eds.), *The study of population* (Chicago, 1959), pp. 678-716. But for a contrary view see Sidney M. Wilhelm, "The concept of the 'ecological complex': a critique," *American Journal of Economics and Sociology*, vol. 23 (1964), pp. 241-248. The theory of the ecological complex owes a good deal to Emile Durkheim's work, particularly *De la division du travail social: étude sur l'organisation des sociétés supérieures* (Paris, 1893).

84. Possibly the most significant achievement of the attempt to elucidate the process of urban genesis in terms of the ecological complex was an enhanced awareness of the kinds and degrees of structural differentiation (or fusion) of the functional subsystems of society at succeeding levels of integration: the tendency to fuse pattern-maintenance and adaptive (so-called "economic") functions at the folk level of integration, integrative and adaptive functions at the level of the ceremonial-administrative center, and goal-attainment and adaptive functions during the expansionist phase of incipient empire.

85. Kent V. Flannery, "The cultural evolution of civilizations," *Annual Review of Ecology and Systematics*, vol. 3 (1972), pp. 399-426.

86. J. G. Miller, "Living systems: basic concepts," *Behavioral Scientist*, vol. 10, pt. 3 (1965), pp. 193-257.

87. Flannery, "The cultural evolution of civilizations," p. 409.

88. James K. Feibleman, "Theory of integrative levels," *British Journal for the Philosophy of Science*, vol. 5 (1954), p. 61. Or, phrased differently, the output of a higher-order control constitutes the reference value of a lower-order control. Or, stated in yet a third way, a regulatory mechanism does not establish its own output reference values, but adopts those of a higher-order regulatory mechanism.

89. L. B. Slobodkin, "Toward a predictive theory of evolution," in Richard O. Lewontin (ed.), *Population biology and evolution* (Syracuse, N.Y., 1968), pp. 187-205.

90. R. A. Rappaport, *Sanctity and adaptation*. Paper prepared for the Wenner-Gren Symposium on "The Moral and Esthetic structure of Human Adaptation" (1969). Cited by Flannery, "The cultural evolution of civilization," pp. 413-414.

91. Flannery, "The cultural evolution of civilizations," p. 420.

92. Flannery, *op. cit.*, p. 412.

93. Cp. p. 9 above.

94. Richard L. Meier, *A communications theory of urban growth* (Cambridge, Mass., 1962).

95. Roy A. Rappaport, "The sacred in human evolution," *Annual Review of Ecology and Systematics*, vol. 2 (1971), p. 32. On this topic generally see also the same

author's *Ecology, meaning, and religion* (Richmond, Calif., 1979), pp. 173-246.

96. Rappaport, "The sacred in human evolution," p. 36.

97. Gregory A. Johnson, "A test of the utility of Central Place Theory in archaeology," in Peter J. Ucko, Ruth Tringham, and G. W. Dimbleby (eds.), *Man, settlement and urbanism* (London, 1972), pp. 769-785; Johnson, "Aspects of regional analysis in archaeology," *Annual Review of Anthropology*, vol. 6 (1977), pp. 479-508; Johnson, "Information sources and the development of decision-making organizations," in C. L. Redman (ed.), *Social archeology: beyond subsistence and dating"* (New York, 1978), pp. 87-112; Vincas P. Stephanaitis, "Location theory and complex chiefdoms: a Mississippian example," in Bruce Smith (ed.), *Mississippian settlement patterns* (New York, 1978), pp. 417-453; Ian R. Hodder, "Locational models and the study of Romano-British settlement," in David L. Clarke (ed.), *Models in archaeology* (London, 1972), pp. 887-909; Hodder, "Simulating the growth of hierarchies," in Colin Renfrew and Kenneth L. Cooke (eds.), *Transformations: mathematical approaches to cultural change* (New York, 1979), pp. 117-144; John R. Alden, "A reconstruction of Toltec period political units in the Valley of Mexico," in Renfrew and Cooke, *Transformations*, pp. 169-200; Fred Plog, "Alternative models of prehistoric change," in Renfrew and Cooke, *Transformations*, pp. 221-236; A. J. Chadwick, "Settlement simulation," in Ian R. Hodder (ed.), *Simulation studies in archaeology* (Cambridge, England, 1978); Jeffrey L. Eighmy, "Logistic trends in Southwest population growth," in Renfrew and Cooke, *Transformations*, pp. 205-220.

98. Cf. note 88 to chapter 5.

CHAPTER 2

Of Chiefs and Chiefdoms

The Ethnological Basis of Southeast Asian Prehistory

At the beginning of the Christian era the territories today known as Southeast Asia *sensu stricto* were occupied by a mosaic of communities ranging in level of societal integration from band to chiefdom. Typically these communities exhibited relatively high degrees of self-sufficiency, possessed distinctive artifactual traditions, and exploited ecologically complementary natural environments. An earlier level of social integration within which archeologists are able to discriminate broad culture areas in terms of stone-ax types had already been partially obscured by new associations based on technological affinities in the working and use of metals, a development which served only to complicate an inherently intricate juxtaposition of degrees of technological achievement and, therefore by inference, of modes of ecological adaptation.

Attempts to discriminate the numerous integrative levels that were then coexisting side by side in Southeast Asia, to isolate individual components of the sociocultural pattern as it were, are rendered difficult enough in the first instance by appalling deficiencies in the archeological record. Vast tracts of the area are still archeologically unexplored and others have been subjected to only cursory survey, while an unduly large proportion of finds are only casually recorded or even wholly unprovenanced. Many, perhaps most, of the excavations undertaken prior to World War II exhibited what would now be regarded as inadequate stratigraphic controls, and the excavators necessarily relied predominantly on their own generalized skills rather than, as often happens today, on the combined competencies of a multi-disciplinary team of specialists.[1] The typological classification of artifacts, often on the basis of single elements of form or composition, appears to have been the primary concern of many authors. In fact, emphasis was more often than not on the refinement of the systematics of spatial and temporal distributions, to the virtual exclusion of any concern with developmental trends. Moreover, an inordinate proportion of the total archeological effort was expended on the study and preservation of statuary and monumental architecture from the historic period. Particularly in the French and Dutch colonies and protectorates, and to an only slightly lesser degree in Burma and Thailand, archeologists were preoccupied with epigraphic and esthetic matters relating to this period, while those who evinced an interest in earlier eras, generally speaking, tended to concentrate their attention on Pleistocene problems. The later stone ages received considerably less attention,[2] and, as far as excavation was concerned, the protohistoric period, which is our primary concern in the present instance, least of all. There was, though, a fairly extensive body of literature devoted to the development of typologies of the bronze artifacts characterized as Đông-sơn, particularly the famous drums that have come to light in most parts of Southeast Asia. Withal there was a pervasive tendency to interpret Southeast Asian archeological assemblages in terms of the European prehistoric experience, without regard to the possibility that development might have followed a rather different course in that corner of Asia.

Since World War II archeological investigation has progressed more slowly than might have been anticipated in, say, 1950. Political and economic problems inseparable from newly acquired nationhood have combined with a prevailing ethos understandably inclined to the fostering of modern developmental technologies rather than the recovery of past civilizations to ensure that funding for archeological work by the states of Southeast Asia has been minimal. In fact, as a cursory glance at the references to this chapter indicates, many of the excavations undertaken during the last two decades have been funded and staffed not by Southeast Asians but by archeologists from outside the region.

Probably even more important than economic constraints as inhibitors of archeological activities have been the insurrections and civil wars that have beset all the countries of the area, with

the exception of Thailand, at one time or another during the past
quarter of a century, and often for extended periods of time. Not
only have these disturbances occasionally resulted in the
disruption of excavations and the destruction of archeological
sites (Most massively at Oc-èo in the Democratic Republic of
Vietnam), but on a larger scale they have interdicted access to
potentially profitable locations. In the circumstances, it is
perhaps not surprising that a substantial number of excavations
remain completely unpublished, and full site reports are very few
indeed. The preliminary or interim archeological report is the
standard document with which the student of prehistoric Southeast
Asia must work. The chief exception to the conditions described in
this paragraph occurs in the Democratic Republic of Vietnam, mainly
in the northern half of the country where, since 1954,
archeological investigation has proceeded apace; yet even there
fully documented site reports are extremely rare, and the student
must rely on relatively brief notices in a variety of journals both
archeological and historical. Among the other countries of
Southeast Asia, only Thailand has attracted prehistoric researchers
in significant numbers.

    Difficult as it is by reason of these lacunae in the
archeological record to present a compendious account of Southeast
Asia in prehistoric times, the problem is further compounded by
radical changes in the conceptualization of the developmental
process that have been proposed during the past two decades. Prior
to World War II, virtually all prehistoric research in Southeast
Asia was undertaken within an evolutionary paradigm established by
the Vienna school of (diffusionistic) historical ethnology. In
this view, changes in the composition of archeological assemblages,
and presumably in the levels of societal integration that they
implied, were almost invariably interpreted as the results of
population movements (primary diffusion) or, if not of actual
migrations, at least in terms of the adoption of cultural traits
from outside the region (secondary diffusion). The implication was
that Southeast Asia had been populated by a succession of different
ethnic groups ("racial stocks" in the jargon of the paradigm), many
of whom have retained their genetic and cultural integrity down to
very recent times. This interpretation received its most elaborate
formulation in the work of Robert von Heine-Geldern during the
'thirties and 'forties of this century.[3] It subsequently underwent
numerous minor modifications at the hands of prehistorians
concerned with particular regions and periods, but persists in its

essentials even today as a framework for most textbook accounts of early Southeast Asia. What is often not made explicit, however, is that the reconstruction was based on very inadequate data. This was particularly true of the archeological component, which consisted solely of fortuitous surface finds and artifacts from a limited number of what have been characterized, with somewhat exaggerated deprecation, as "potholing expeditions."[4] Even more important was the failure of many writers who used Heine-Geldern's formulation to specify that it was a tool for, not a result of, research. The assemblages of traits by which that scholar defined periods in Southeast Asian prehistory were relatively high-level abstractions designed as heuristic aids to the discrimination of broad stages in a process of societal evolution. To that extent Heine-Geldern's developmental phases were ideal-type constructs rather than inductively derived generalizations.

The periodization that resulted from this schema can be summarized briefly as follows. The earliest material remains, other than their bones, left by inhabitants of Southeast Asia, biologically pre-Modern and exhibiting very little cultural differentiation, were caches of stone hand-axes which fell within a Palaeolithic industrial tradition extending across the whole of Eastern Asia, and which had been categorized by Hallam Movius as Chopper-Chopping Tools.[5] They were, and are, usually ascribed a Lower-Middle Pleistocene date, though it has been suggested that a Malaysian hoard of hand-axes from Kota Tampan in Perak may be of Early Pleistocene provenance.[6] The earliest representatives of a Sapient population were considered to have been ethnically diverse groups who, supposedly between ten and four thousand years ago, spread over most of Southeast Asia, carrying with them a variety of so-called Mesolithic industrial technologies. They were referred to collectively as Hoabinhians, after a type-site in the Democratic Republic of Vietnam which was formerly thought to have yielded a classical development of this culture.[7] They were dependent for their livelihood primarily on food gathering and hunting, with emphasis shifting from the former to the latter with the passing of the millennia. The Hoabinhians, in turn, were supposedly followed into Southeast Asia some four or five thousand years ago, allegedly from a culture-hearth in Southwest China, by an agricultural folk who ushered in the Neolithic period. Those farmers who colonized the archipelagic realms were identified as Proto-Malays, and were credited with the introduction of the Malay language, pottery, the outrigger canoe, domestication of draft animals, and wet-padi

Fig. 3. Locations of Southeast Asian sites, ethnonyms, and localities mentioned in this chapter. Names and transcriptions are those favored in the relevant literature.

cultivation, with all that this last implies as to permanence and concentration of settlement. Finally, rather more than two thousand years ago, a second migration of Malays — Deutero-Malays as they were often called — brought a knowledge of bronze and iron metallurgy to the island world. They, together with the metal-using peoples of the mainland, were usually rubricated as the Đông-sơn Culture. In Heine-Geldern's reconstruction, they represented the highest immediately pre-urban level of societal integration in Southeast Asia, although it was not supposed that they totally supplanted their predecessors. Rather they were held to have infiltrated the lowlands and intermontane valleys suitable for wet-padi farming, leaving the uplands to remnants of allegedly earlier, technologically less well-endowed groups.

George Coedès's characterization of the so-called Đông-sơn Culture will serve as well as any.[8]

Au point de vue matériel:	la culture de rizières irriguées; la domestication du boeuf et du buffle; l'usage rudimentaire des métaux; l'habilité à la navigation.
Au point de vue social:	l'importance du rôle attribué à la femme et à la filiation en ligne maternelle; l'organisation résultant des nécessités de la culture irriguée.
Au point de vue religieux:	l'animisme; le culte des ancêtres et du dieu du sol; l'installation des lieux de culte sur les hauteurs; l'inhumation des morts dans des jarres, ou des dolmens.
Au point de vue mythologique:	"un dualisme cosmologique où s'opposent la montagne et la mer, la gent ailée et la gent aquatique, les hommes des hauteurs et ceux des côtes."[9]
Au point de vue linguistique:	l'emploi de langues isolantes douées d'une riche faculté de dérivation par préfixes, suffixes et infixes.

In an earlier reconstruction of the culture of Java in what would subsequently come to be known as the Đông-sơn period, Nicholaas Krom had included the puppet theater (*wayang*), the orchestra (*gamelan*), and the *batik* process of dyeing cloth[10] (the weaving of textiles should in any case be included in the roster of technologies[11]), and other authors from time to time have proposed additional features, among them the domestication of the dog, pig, and fowl. Exception may be taken to some of the items in this schedule, notably the descent system that is envisaged and possibly the indigenous origin of the *wayang*, but generally speaking the reconstruction is not grossly contradictory of present-day views. What has been transformed rather radically is prevailing opinion as to (1) the periods when, and to a lesser extent the order in which, several of the items were added to the cultural inventory, and (2) the mechanisms which worked to induce societal and technological change. During the nineteen-fifties it had become increasingly clear that the old paradigm was no longer a medium for progressive and fruitful hypothesization. This failure alone could have been construed as a portent of impending change,[12] but during the 'sixties it became evident that the conventionalized framework of assumptions and preconceptions that had emerged some two decades previously was no longer capable of accommodating certain classes of data currently being elicited by archeological and linguistic researches. It was as a response to these apparent anomalies that a new framework for the investigation of Southeast Asian prehistory began to take shape.

Thus far a wholly satisfactory new synthesis able to account for all the genetic, cultural, and linguistic variations in Southeast Asian ethnology has not been forthcoming, though Wilhelm Solheim and Geoffrey Benjamin have proposed preliminary formulations. It is the latter who has rejected most decisively the notion of serial population influxes into the region,[13] though it is to be assumed that he does so in deference to ethnological theory rather than in response to the implications of new data. The available material evidence, which is still inadequate to sustain any but the most speculative hypothesis, in the abstract affords as much support for Viennese diffusionist theories as for current interpretations. But between the presentation of Heine-Geldern's construction and the present there have intervened four decades and more of ethnographic theorizing. In particular, doubts have been cast on the assumption, inherent in the old paradigm, of an indefinite persistence of close correspondences between cultures and phenotypically distinctive, bounded human populations.[14] Accordingly, Benjamin proposes that the ethnological pattern of present-day Southeast Asia be regarded as comprising not the perduring survivals of immigrant groups who found their way into the region in ancient times, but rather the outcome of a still continuing process of ethnic differentiation within a common cultural tradition. The key to the existing pattern, in his opinion, lies in an apparent tendency to introversive specialization, whereby culturally diverse but substantially self-sufficient groups have come to occupy distinct ecological niches. Several archeologists have, in fact, noted precisely such tendencies operating at different periods of Southeast Asian prehistory. Ian Glover, for instance, has commented on the strongly individual traditions of stone-working which, as early as the close of the late Pleistocene period, had developed within each of the Indonesian islands where remains have been found,[15] while Bennet Bronson encountered what he termed "sub-regional isolation and sociocultural stasis" in his investigation of the Late Metal Age in Central Thailand.[16] It is possible that Benjamin, in attempting to refute the older, wave theory of Southeast Asian ethnology, has unduly depreciated the part played by diffusion processes, but that is a matter for future archeological research to decide. In the meanwhile, he has performed a signal service in drawing attention to ecological specialization as a means by which culturally diverse groups in relatively close juxtaposition were enabled to preserve their cultural integrity through relatively long periods of time.

The emerging paradigm also differs from its predecessor in the matter of chronology. Whereas relative chronology has remained largely unchanged, the absolute dating of the more important technological innovations, and to a lesser degree of societal transformations, has been advanced by up to four millennia. This modification of the hitherto received chronology, although implicit in the improved stratigraphic control of recent excavators, has been confirmed by the use of Carbon-14 and, to a lesser extent, thermoluminescence dating techniques, both of which were unavailable to earlier researchers.[17] Tin-bronze metallurgy for instance, has been recorded conservatively by 2500 B.C., and possibly as early as 3500 B.C., in northeastern Thailand[18] and, it is claimed, at about 2000 B.C. at a site near Saigon,[19] while iron was apparently being forged early in the 1st millennium B.C.[20] The origins of agriculture, or at least of plant tending, are now discernible in northeastern Thailand perhaps as early as 10,000 B.C.[21] (which provides a certain amount of support for Carl Sauer's thesis, advanced more than a quarter of a century ago, that the earliest experiments in plant reproduction were undertaken in riparian situations in tropical forest environments[22]) and pottery by about 5,000 B.C. Concurrently animal domestication has been pushed back to a period prior to 3000 B.C. in mainland Southeast Asia, specifically a variety of cattle ancestral to those of present-day Khorat.[23] In fact, much of the technological complex that was formerly associated with the migration of so-called Proto-Malays some four or five millennia ago is now seen to have had its origins probably some four thousand years previously.[24]

The only attempt to integrate the disparate pieces of available evidence into a coherent periodization of Southeast Asian prehistory is owed to Wilhelm Solheim II.[25] In view of the relative paucity of reliable information, his essay may have been a little premature: certainly it depends excessively on unreplicated data from northern Thailand for the delineation of its earlier phases. On the positive side, though, it comprehends Carbon-14 and thermoluminescence datings that were not assimilable to the preceding paradigm, and appears to be capable of accommodating a growing body of linguistic inferences that are themselves currently being recast within a new conceptual framework.[26] Less satisfactory is Solheim's substitution for simple stages of technological development of stages defined arbitrarily in terms of a sequentially varying mix of technological, social (or perhaps better sociopolitical), and developmental features. However, for what they are worth, and as the only evolutionary framework currently being offered, these stages may be summarized as follows:[27]

1. *The Lithic Period,* which encompassed the Chopper-Chopping Tool Tradition mentioned above. It apparently lasted for some quarter of a million years until about forty millennia ago. The population was paleanthropic, exhibiting (as far as can be determined) little cultural differentiation.

This period corresponds to the Lower Paleolithic of the old classification.

2. *The Lignic Period* is inferred primarily from the character of certain stone-tool assemblages, found in association with Sapient skeletal remains and thought to be dated between 40,000 and 20,000 years ago. It was manifested in stone-flake industries which existed contemporaneously with Chopper-Chopping Tool cultures,[28] and in Hoabinhian tool industries (edge-wear on some specimens has been held to imply wood-working). Postulation of an emphasis on woods and fibers in the making of articles of material culture affords an opportune way in which to account for the retardation in the development of stone tools that is apparent at this time in the archeological record. For subsistence the several cultural

variants who inhabited Southeast Asia at this time depended primarily on river fishing and forest hunting and gathering: the typical Hoabinhian monofacial tool is admirably adapted to grubbing up roots from the soil or breaking bone. To ecotypes of this character and scale Gorman has applied the functionally descriptive phrase "broad-spectrum hunting, fishing and gathering."[29]

This period corresponds to the Upper Paleolithic and Lower Hoabinhian of the old classification.

3. *The Crystallitic Period*, from 20,000 to 10,000 years ago, was characterized by the differentiation of several distinctive cultures, each of which added to the old Lower Hoabinhian cultural inventory one or more (usually more) of the following: edge grinding of stone tools, manufacture of cord-marked pottery, and utilization of the vegetal resources of the home territory. Together these cultures seem to have constituted an area co-tradition of the type described by Wendell Bennett for the Central Andes in Precolumbian times.[30] Solheim emphasizes,[31] as did Sauer before him,[32] the high degree of interrelatedness and at least partial interdependence of several of the technological complexes developed during this period. The use of paddle and anvil in pottery manufacture, for instance, is paralleled by the use of beaters in the preparation of bark cloth. Moreover, the paddle used to create the distinctive Late-Hoabinhian markings on pots was wrapped or woven with cord or basketry, while the fibers employed for this purpose were also used in the plaiting of fish nets,[33] traps, and mats, and as cordage generally. These concerns with the maceration and retting of vegetable fibers would likely have facilitated the discovery not only of plant dyes for body, food, and clothing, but also of stupefying alkaloid substances used in the taking of fish (the quantities attested on archeological sites make it unlikely that all were caught individually). And a preoccupation with the uses of vegetable substances would have focused attention on individual plants, and perhaps led to their care, tending, and ultimately their domestication. In a zone of high ecological diversity in Northwest Thailand, Chester Gorman has excavated the remains of no less than twelve genera of humanly exploited plants which, in the aggregate, appear to have signalled a transition from broad-spectrum gathering to the repeated harvesting of certain favored plants.[34] Analogous conclusions can be drawn from a more limited range of functionally similar plant remains recovered by Ian Glover from cave sites in Timor.[35] It is noticeable that many of the plants involved in technological

complexes of this type were multipurpose, serving at one and the same time a combination of the following uses: as cordage, dye, oil, condiment, stimulant, poison, preservative, or sustenance, so that food production may well have afforded only one among several motives for devoting attention to plant reproduction. In any case, it was to be a long time before any Southeast Asian community became primarily dependent on horticulture, let alone agriculture in the normal sense of the term.

This period corresponds to the Middle and Upper Hoabinhian and early Neolithic of the old classification.

4. *The Extensionistic Period,* from 10,000 to 2,000 years ago, was a time of cultural consolidation and presumed population increase, both of which tended to promote a fuller development of the several co-traditions in Southeast Asia. The beginning of the period coincided with the post-Pleistocene rise in sea-level that would ultimately produce the disposition of land and sea that obtains today: a vast archipelago extending over a longitudinal distance of some 3,500 miles, embracing more than 4,000 islands (including both Indonesia and the Philippines), and linking the continents of Asia and Australia. The period is characterized by a general downward movement of foci of population concentration from intermontane valleys towards lowland plains, with a concomitant development of horticultural practices.[36] It was as an integral component in the series of adaptations necessitated by this movement that *padi* was adopted into certain Southeast Asian farming systems, probably by about 3500 B.C. David Harris is inclined to interpret the movement to lower elevations as reflecting a shift in emphasis from upland proto-cultivation in domestic gardens to a more specialized production of *padi,* probably in swidden clearings.[37] It is surely significant, moreover, that right down to recent times *padi* was treated in the same manner as a vegetable or tuber; that is, it was started in a seed bed, whence individual shoots were subsequently transplanted into the field. In other words, *padi* cultivation would appear to have been adopted into an already well integrated, vegetal farming regimen. Concurrently the spectrum of animal domestication was broadened to include *Bos indicus* by about 3000 B.C. at latest,[38] and the pig before 2000 B.C.[39]

During the second half of the Extensionistic Period metallurgy either developed in, or was introduced into, the continental territories of Southeast Asia, the ascribed dates of 3500 B.C. for a socketed tool of copper and of 2300 B.C. for bronze-casting from double molds at Non Nok Tha in northeastern Thailand being

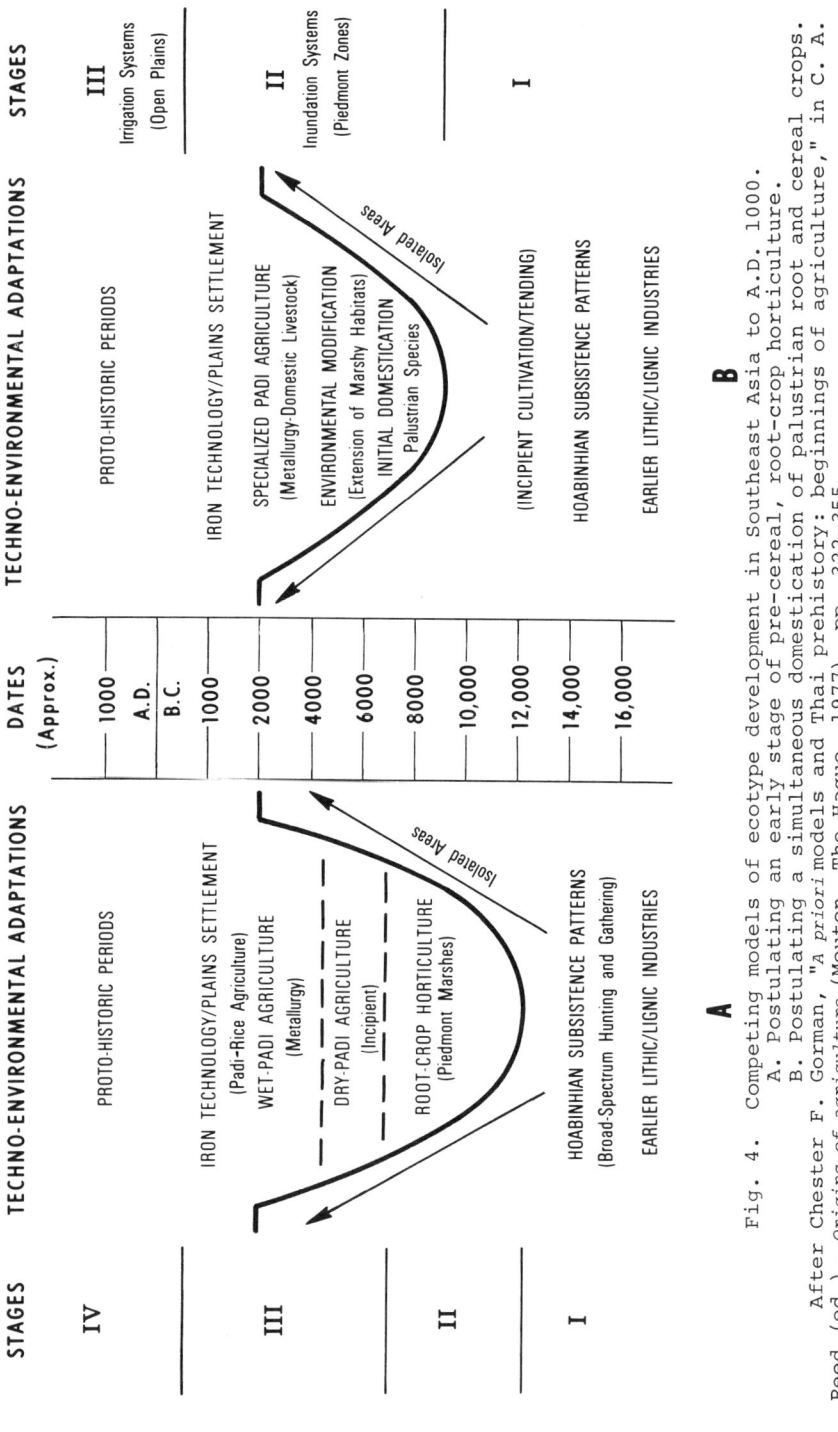

Fig. 4. Competing models of ecotype development in Southeast Asia to A.D. 1000.
A. Postulating an early stage of pre-cereal, root-crop horticulture.
B. Postulating a simultaneous domestication of palustrian root and cereal crops.
After Chester F. Gorman, "A priori models and Thai prehistory: beginnings of agriculture," in C. A. Reed (ed.), Origins of agriculture (Mouton, The Hague, 1977), pp. 322-355.

Of Chiefs and Chiefdoms 55

considerably prior to any recorded similar occurrences of metal-working in East Asia.⁴⁰ At a still earlier point in time, perhaps by the end of the 4th millennium B.C., the invention of the outrigger canoe permitted the dispersion of men and the diffusion of ideas outwards from mainland Southeast Asia into the archipelagic realms. As a result, the later phases of the Extensionistic Period witnessed an accelerated exchange of cultural elements between the different co-traditions that had formed in the region.

A third development which may have been initiated during the concluding phases of the Extensionistic Period was the incipient supplementation of indigenous systems of cultivation concerned primarily with vegetatively reproduced cultigens by seed-cultures based on wet *padi*. This can be inferred only from subsequent events, and in any case cannot have progressed very far, for over most of Southeast Asia wet-*padi* cultivation has been areally restricted until quite recent times. Harris suggests that *padi* was integrated into an ecologically unstable, seed-crop (primarily millet), swidden system as it diffused southwards into Southeast Asia from North and Central China.⁴¹

This period corresponds to the Middle and Late Neolithic and Early Đông-sơn of the old classification.

5. *The Period of Conflicting Empires* comprises the proto-historical and historical phases of Southeast Asian development, which witnessed a relatively rapid institutionalization of centralized leadership, the resultant formation of states, and the emergence of urban life. It represents the level of sociocultural integration whose origins it will be the purpose of this monograph to elucidate.

The preceding brief summary cannot do justice to the more detailed ramifications of Solheim's schema, which is pregnant with implications for the ethnological evolution not only of Southeast Asia but also of neighboring cultural realms. It must be emphasized, however, that, like Heine-Geldern's earlier model, Solheim's is an ideal-type construct, designed as a speculative framework for the structuring of future research. As such it invites testing against whatever new evidence becomes available, with consequent rejection, confirmation, or modification in whole or part as may prove necessary. That modifications will be required, possibly on a considerable scale, is rendered practically inevitable by the meager data base currently available to Professor Solheim. I suspect, for instance, that the emergence of a true

56   Nāgara and Commandery

agriculture, even in the specialized form of polycultural domestic
plots, has presently been assigned too early a date. What Solheim
seems to regard as developed horticulture will probably turn out, I
would conjecture, to be a more or less regular harvesting of
favorite plants, possibly some degree of plant tending perhaps, but
still only a form of proto-cultivation at most. On the other hand,
there is a considerable degree of congruence between the
ethnological inventory of Solheim's Extensionistic Period and that
proposed by Krom, Coedès, and others under the rubric of Đông-sơn
Culture. It should be emphasized, though, that in the immediately
pre-urban period the most advanced cultures occupied only limited
tracts of Southeast Asia, mainly the coastal and interior plains of
the mainland and of what would now be called western Indonesia.
The remaining territories comprised a mosaic of groups occupying a
range of ecological niches appropriate to their respective levels
of societal integration and technological advancement.

The Immediately Pre-Urban Period

The long eons during which this pattern of ethnic
differentiation developed need not concern us here. Our
investigation will focus on the transition from pre-urban to urban,
from Đông-sơn to Indianized or Sinicized state in the older
terminology, or from Extensionistic to Conflicting Empires in the
new. It is highly subversive of our purpose that this period of
climacteric social transformation is among the least well
documented of the phases of Southeast Asian history. Such evidence
as is available can be categorized as direct and indirect. Direct
evidence is provided by both archeological investigation and
textual analysis, as well as by epigraphs, which are often
archeological in the sense that they are acquired by excavation,
yet speak with the relative directness of a literary record. The
chief drawback of these latter is that they are only too frequently
instruments of self-validation, composed to glorify a historical
present, to establish a particular dynast as the ultimate source of
political, social, economic, moral, and religious order. Their
import is also almost invariably restricted to a narrow sector of
the spectrum of social and institutional development, chiefly that
concerned with ritual, ceremony, administration, government, and to
some extent education. Nor are the available literary texts by any
means free of this type of bias. It follows that, although texts
and epigraphs may rank as primary sources for the elicitation of
value systems, for the reconstruction of events they must usually

be considered as secondary.

Indirect (or circumstantial) evidence is also by its very nature of a secondary character, comprising retrospective inferences from the morphology, symbolism, and organization of the very cities whose mode of origin we are seeking to establish, as well as information derived from folklore and mythology. This last genre of material is especially difficult to handle. The collective memory of traditional society is by no means unresponsive to happenings in the past but, unable to retain individual persons and specific events, transforms them respectively into archetypes and categories, heroes and heroic situations. But this may not be the end of the matter. Such archetyped events, heroized personalities, and heroic contexts not infrequently have been manipulated and exploited in later times in the interests of the dynastic glorification mentioned above. When that has happened, it can be virtually impossible to peel back the layers of meaning imposed first by the archetyping process, and subsequently by the purposed idealization of exegetes of later ages, so as to recover an actual happening.

This is an appropriate point at which to draw attention to the study of historical linguistics, particularly the still controversial work of Paul Benedict, although its potential as a tool for prehistoric reconstruction will almost certainly be realized primarily in periods prior to the one with which we are here concerned. This author has reconstructed a language family, including Indonesian and the Austronesian languages in general, together with Thai, Kadai, two "para-Thai" languages (Kam-Sui and Ong-Be), and the Miao-Yao group, to which he has given the name Austro-Thai.[42] Apart from its general relevance to the elucidation of early Southeast Asian ecotypes, the main interest of Benedict's reconstruction for our present study is that he claims, not implausibly, to be able to document extensive cultural interaction between the Austro-Thai peoples and the early Chinese. The process, he writes "was essentially unidirectional, with the Chinese as the recipients rather than the donors."[43] The bulk of the loan-words involved were, in Benedict's view, from an obsolete Austro-Thai language, which he labels AT-x, not ancestral to any modern Austro-Thai speech. He further concludes that:

> The AT loan-words in Chinese, when viewed as an ensemble, constitute the outlines of a substantial material culture: the higher numerals (above 100); the fowl and egg (and perhaps the duck); horse, saddle, and riding; elephant and ivory; the pig and rabbit (but not the dog); cattle and goat/sheep; the bee (curiously prominent in this material)

and perhaps honey; garden and manure; plough; morter and hull grain
with pestle; seed, sow, and winnow; rice (various, including cooked
rice) and sugarcane (whence sugar); banana and coconut; ginger and
mustard; the dipper (made of coconut or gourd), ladle, and vessel
(container); salt; smoking (meat) and steaming (rice); bait (meat)
and net; metals (gold, copper, iron, tin/lead); the ax;
ladder/stairs; boat, rafts, and oars; washing (metals and rice);
hunting (but not the bow or arrow); crossbow (but precise origin
unknown); fireplace, kiln, and pottery; weaving and plaiting
(twisting rope); the needle and embroidery; basket and bag; indigo;
cowry (=money); market, price and sell.[44]

Benedict postulates a South-China origin for the Austro-Thai language family, and regards the speakers as those people who evolved wet-*padi* farming and metallurgy in Southeast Asia. He has not so far indicated a date for the full elaboration of Austro-Thai, but would seem to favor broadly the earlier half of the Extensionistic period. If he is able to substantiate this claim, his researches will obviously provide strong support for the sort of revised periodization proposed by Solheim. One of the main problems inhibiting a too-ready acceptance of Benedict's thesis at the present time is the incompatibility of his implied dating (understandably he is never too explicit on matters of chronology) for the devolution of the Austro-Thai Language family with what is currently known about the evolution and diversification of Proto-Austronesian.[45]

The Archeological Record

The sole material that can properly be regarded as primary in the investigation of protohistoric Southeast Asian social structures is scientifically acquired archeological evidence, but only a small proportion of excavations have yielded information pertaining to the immediately pre-urban period. The most thoroughly explored territory so far as this developmental phase is concerned is undoubtedly the northern tracts of the Democratic Republic of Việtnam, though even there the coverage is anything but adequate. In the whole of the rest of Southeast Asia, scarcely a handful of excavations have been directed to unravelling the complexities of this period. Such information of this type as does exist will be introduced at appropriate points in the following discussions, but one class of material remains merits separate discussion, namely the megalithic tradition which, despite a half-century of speculation, still remains essentially undated and functionally unexplained.

The Megalithic problem. One of the most persistent conundrums in the prehistory of Southeast Asia concerns the character, purpose, dating, and authorship of various types of stone constructions known collectively as megaliths. These comprise menhirs, singly, in clusters, and disposed so as to enclose (what was presumably ritual) space, dolmens, stone seats, terraces, platforms, pyramidal structures, stone pathways and plazas, stone urns, and possibly true stone tombs, though the existence of these last has sometimes been denied. Elements of this complex are found, in various forms of association, in an arcuate zone stretching from northern Indochina, through the Malay Peninsula, Sumatra, and Java to eastern Indonesia. Despite the availability of a sizeable descriptive literature accumulated over half a century, and despite the presence of a body of ethnographic data relating to contemporary or near-contemporary megalith builders in Assam, western Burma, and parts of Indonesia (specifically on the islands of Nias, Flores, Sumba, and central Sulawesi), none of the questions posed at the beginning of this paragraph has been answered satisfactorily. It is particularly unfortunate that no absolute chronology has so far been established, and only a suspect relative one.

The earliest attempt to deal systematically with the megalithic cultures of Southeast Asia was incorporated in a paper by Robert von Heine-Geldern in 1928.[46] Nearly two decades later, in the course of a summary statement,[47] this author found little reason to modify his original conclusions as to the purpose of the structures, but broke new ground in distinguishing between Older and Younger Megalithic traditions. The former, attributed on distributional grounds to the bearers of the Quadrangular Adze Culture which Heine-Geldern had already defined in a previous series of papers,[48] was exemplified in menhirs, dolmens, stone seats, terraces, pyramids, and suchlike. In accordance with the prevailing chronological ideas of the 'forties, the Quadrangular Adze Culture, and therefore the first appearance of the Older Megalithic, was dated to the second half of the 3rd millennium B.C. The Younger Megalithic was manifested in cist and dolmen graves, various types of sarcophagi, and stone statuary in the round and in relief. Within this last category are included the large figures, sculpted in a strongly dynamic idiom, which occur in some profusion in the Pasemah country, and which provide iconographic information about dress, ornaments, and weaponry of the time when they were carved. Some of the figures exhibit an apparent stylistic affinity with reliefs and sculptures of the Chinese Former Han dynasty, particularly with a statue erected in 117 B.C. on the tomb of

Huo Ch'iu-p'ing in Shenhsi Province. That two figures from Batu Gajah appear to represent warriors carrying a bronze kettledrum of a type known as Heger I has been taken to indicate an association with the Đông-sơn culture.[49] In fact, Heine-Geldern was explicit in assigning the Younger Megalithic to the metal age of Southeast Asia, by which he seems to have implied a period beginning during the second half of the 1st millennium B.C. Sculptures and other Younger Megalithic features occur in other localities in Indonesia from Java, through Bali, to the Lesser Sunda Islands.[50] Elsewhere in Southeast Asia the Younger Megalithic has been recognized by various authors in Indochina and the Malay Peninsula.

In Indochina megaliths of one sort or another are found along the edge of the Chaîne Annamitique from Trân-ninh in the north to the Mọi upland overlooking the Mekong delta in the south, and as far west as Roi Et in present-day Thailand. Especially prominent are the white-sandstone urns, funerary in purpose, which occur in their thousands on the Trân-ninh plateau and in the vicinity of Xieng-khouang.[51] The general opinion is that the simple schistose menhirs of Hua Phan are of earlier date than the urns, which were evidently carved with iron tools, and considerably older than the chamber-tomb of Xuân-lộc,[52] which in turn was a larger and more complex version of tombs found on the Malay Peninsula[53] and in Indonesia. In the same area as that occupied by the megaliths of Indochina there is also a series of earthworks, usually mounds and ditches enclosing circular enceintes. None of these sites has been excavated or dated, but their spatial association with megaliths has led Bernard Groslier to propose that some of them may have been the dwelling areas of the people who buried their dead in the stone urns and dolmens.[54] Groslier has also suggested that this megalithic culture, which followed broadly the axis of the Mekong, was in rough correspondence with the distribution of Mon-Khmer speakers,[55] but this interpretation would fail to account for the presence of typologically similar megaliths in areas far beyond the range of Mon-Khmer peoples. Groslier further dates the Trân-ninh and related megaliths, on the basis of the discovery of bells in Đông-sơn style in the vicinity of urns at Bang-an, to the period between the 5th and 1st centuries B.C.[56] This dating is far from secure but, for what it is worth, would assign the urns of Trân-ninh and elsewhere to the Younger Megalithic. It may be noted in passing, though, that Heine-Geldern and Quaritch Wales, on grounds that are neither more nor less trustworthy, have associated the Mon-Khmer speakers with the Shouldered Axe Culture and thus, in their schemas, with the Older

Megalithic tradition.[57]

The fundamental uncertainty inherent in any assessment of the so-called Megalithic Culture of Southeast Asia is the extent to which it constitutes a unitary category of investigation. Are the numerous types of stone structures in all their regional variations different manifestations of a single, coherent nexus of beliefs, or are they the artifactual expressions of two or more widely disparate cultures? If the former, at which points in space and time should the Southeast Asian Megalithic be separated from morphologically similar cultures in neighboring parts of Asia? Answers to these and similar questions will in turn be partly dependent on our views as to the purposes for which the megaliths were constructed. Clearly a high proportion of the urns and dolmens of the postulated Younger Megalithic were funerary in purpose, for human ashes and bones have been found in, under, or near them, but the functions of those structures assigned to the Older Megalithic are still a subject for debate. Virtually all scholars who have attempted to explain their purpose have relied on the implications of ethnographic parallels, and most have interpreted the menhirs, dolmens, pyramids, seats, terraces, and similar structures as designed to promote fertility and to reify certain eschatological notions. In generalized terms, their explications take the following line. The men of the Older Megalithic erected their dolmens and so forth not as burial chambers but as monuments to venerated ancestors, as responses to the need to express the fructifying power of the soil in concrete form so that it might thereby be rendered more accessible for intercession. A menhir thus became not merely the god's lodging but the very deified potency of the earth. The most efficacious link with the abstract god now comprehended within the menhir was the chief who, in his role as intermediary between god and man, came to partake of the divinity of the god. Even more effective as intercessor was the ancestral chieftain, the progenitor of the lineage or tribe, who, after sharing the fortunes of the group, had returned to the earth to mingle with the god of the soil. In accordance with this interpretation, the stone seats which figure prominently in the roster of Older Megalithic structures are often specified as thrones for ancestral spirits.[58]

There are several variations on this basic interpretation, but potentially the most illuminating appears to be A. H. Christie's suggestion that at least some of the Southeast Asian megalithic structures were, like those in Europe, Tibet, and

Mongolia, intended for astronomical and calendrical purposes.[59] As
Christie points out, such an interpretation would not be wholly
incompatible with the fertility roles postulated by Heine-Geldern,
Quaritch Wales, and Fürer-Haimendorf, for calendrical observations
can play an important part in the regulation of a farming cycle.
Verification of the thesis, however, would transfer the emphasis
from chthonic to uranic gods, and probably imply the possibility of
predicting astronomical events, a capability which might have been
used to enhance the prestige of a chief or "big man" in the
community. There are, however, not inconsiderable difficulties
inherent in any attempt to elicit the astronomical purposes of
structures whose dates are still matters of speculation, as well as
in establishing the value of such structures in low latitudes.

It is evident enough from the preceding paragraphs that
Groslier's characterization of a Megalithic Culture or Cultures as
still only a promising hypothesis is cautious and correct.[60] And it
will remain just that until existing theories have been tested by
excavation of new sites and known sites re-examined in the light of
new hypotheses. It is unlikely that the problem will be
satisfactorily resolved in the very near future.

Literary Evidence

The fact that only scientifically acquired archeological
evidence can be considered primary for the study of structural
change in ancient Southeast Asia does not mean that transmitted
texts are worthless, but rather that their content must always be
evaluated both skeptically and contextually, chapter by chapter,
line by line, phrase by phrase, or even word by word if necessary.
Indigenous literary sources are, of course, completely lacking for
the pre- and proto-urban phases of development, but certain foreign
literatures, if used with discrimination, can be made to yield
information of not negligible value. Although these sources are
typically fragmentary, intractable, and equivocal, they are capable
of generating inferences supplementary to those derived solely from
archeological evidence. And when this latter is, as happens in the
present instance, exiguous, then the literary sources are by that
much the more valuable.

The most useful of these bodies of evidence for present
purposes is that, predominantly annalistic in character, which can
be culled from Chinese histories, encyclopedias, and topographies.
Generally speaking, the amount of relevant information in this
class of sources diminishes from north to south, that is from the

Tong-King delta, for which it constitutes almost a primary documentation, to Java and Sumatra, for which it provides very little of significance.[61] The second corpus of foreign materials relating to ancient Southeast Asia derives from the Indian subcontinent. But the genius of Indian thought sought its fulfillment in literary genres other than those of historical or topographical writing, so that the formal chronologies, descriptions, and ostensible objectivity characteristic of the Chinese sources are lacking, and we are dependent on incidental allusions in some such medium as Sanskrit verse or Tamil court poetry.[62] The third body of evidence is to be found in the Classical literatures of the West, culminating in the spurious precision of the Ptolemaic corpus, but interpretation of the information which it purveys is controversial in the extreme.[63] None of the three classes of evidence bears on the process of urban genesis at its inception, though some of their information does relate to the earlier phases of that process. It goes without saying, therefore, that these literary sources are relevant to the pre-urban phase of sociocultural evolution only to the extent that we are prepared to ignore the organizational inputs generated by already evolving proto-urban institutions. In the following sections we shall illustrate the way in which these literary sources can be used to supplement the general picture of pre-urban Southeast Asia provided by archeology.

Local Specialization in the Northern Highlands

At the beginning of the Christian era or thereabouts, the arc of mountainous terrain half encircling the Tong-King lowland on the north presented an ethnological pattern of kaleidoscopic diversity, in which virtually each ecological zone, and sometimes niches within zones, were characterized by their own particular modes of adaptation and degrees of differentiation. The *locus classicus* for a statement on conditions in the mountainous south and west of China proper in the late centuries B.C. is two chapters in Ssŭ-ma Ch'ien's 司馬遷 *Shih Chi* 史記, written at the end of the 1st century A.D. Chüan 113, which provides an account of Nan-Yüeh 南越,[64] is not helpful in the present instance, but Chüan 116, dealing with the so-called Southwestern Barbarians 西南夷, contains a certain amount of information on adaptational modes among the tribal peoples of present-day Ssŭ-ch'uan, Kuei-chou, and Yün-nan.[65] "Among the Southwestern Barbarians," the Chüan begins, "chieftains are to be counted by tens" 西南夷君長

以什數.⁶⁶ In the vicinity of the Tien Lake 滇池, for example, a congeries of groups inhabited permanent settlements set amid cultivated plots which the text seems to imply were at least quasi-permanent: 耕田有邑.⁶⁷ What Ssŭ-ma Ch'ien did not mention was the fact, revealed by archeology, that the farmers along the lake shore supplemented the yields of their fields by intensive fishing and mollusk collecting. In fact, so casual does their cultivation appear in the archeological record, these latter may well have been swidden cultivators.⁶⁸ A similar combination of farming, fishing, and mollusk collecting characterized the ancient village at Hai-men K'ou 海門口 in the district of Chien Ch'uan 劍川 in Northwest Yün-nan, though there farming was more strongly developed, with wheat, millet, and *padi* all under cultivation.⁶⁹ To the northward of these farming communities, on the upland plains "from ***D'ung-si̯ər* (MSC T'ung-shih) eastwards to ***D'i̯ap-di̯u* (MSC Yeh-yü)," were the ***Si̯wər* 巂 (MSC Sui) and the ***Kwən-mi̯ăng* 昆明 (MSC K'un-ming), nomadic herdsmen having no fixed abodes 隨畜遷徙. Several other groups, both migratory and sedentary, are mentioned in the same section of the *Shih Chi*, but all inhabited territories farther to the north and need not concern us here.

This pattern of localized adaptations is not in conflict with such archeological evidence as we possess, of which the most dramatic is that from Shih-chai Shan 石寨山, a village situated to the southeast of the Tien Lake.⁷⁰ Although the occupation site has been much less thoroughly excavated than the famous cemetery associated with it, it is evident that, in the centuries immediately preceding the Christian era, agriculture was practiced with the aid of metal spades,⁷¹ horses were used for riding and warfare, cattle apparently for ceremonial slaughter and perhaps for meat at other times as well, while sheep, fowl, and pigs seem to have had at least quasi-domesticated status. It is noteworthy, though, that hunting, with the aid of hounds, appears to have contributed significantly to subsistence.

Farther to the northwest, in the vicinity of Lake Erh, Wu Chin-ting and his collaborators documented a change within a single cultural tradition from primitive to relatively developed agriculture.⁷² On a slope below Ma-lung Peak 馬龍峰 in the Tien-ts'ang Range 點蒼山, some two and half miles southwest of Tali city 大理府, Wu discovered ten artificial terraces cut transversely across a settlement site from the northwestern boundary to the southeastern. Wu uses the graph 台 to denote

these terraces, but does not describe them in any detail. From the
general context of his remarks and from his plan of the site (Plate
I in the report), it would appear that they were contour terraces
cut directly into the slope of the mountain, and apparently lacked
any form of stone retaining wall. Despite the presence of several
artificially excavated ditches which have been tentatively
identified as either irrigation or drainage channels,[73] Wu is
certainly correct in excluding wet *padi* from these terraces. His
own opinion is that they served for yams, vegetables, and some
dry-field cereals, notably wheat. The terraces were certainly no
younger than the (supposedly, though not certainly) walled
settlement in their midst, and that appears to have been
contemporary with the Former Han Dynasty (206 B.C. - A.D. 8).

Similar terraces were also found below Po-yün Peak 白雲
峯.[74] Indeed, Wu Chin-ting's concluding remarks seem to imply
that terracing of the type described was a feature common to a high
proportion of the thirty-six sites that he investigated.[75] "Most of
the prehistoric dwelling sites," he wrote, "were located on gentle
slopes with terraces," and he went on to suggest that members of a
particular clan or lineage may all have occupied the same slope,
with each family cultivating the terraced land around its own
dwelling as a rather extended door-yard garden.[76]

In the light of these archeologically derived
reconstructions, it is instructive to consult an account of
agricultural practices in 9th-century Yün-nan which is incorporated
in the *Man Shu* 蠻書, even though it relates to a period
considerably later than that with which we are here concerned.
This work was written by Fan Ch'o 樊綽, an officer on the staff
of the Chinese military commander in Tong-King, between A.D. 860
and 865.[77] As the account is unusually detailed for such an early
period, I shall summarize it here.[78] In the first place, Fan Ch'o
seems to have distinguished between valley-bottom and plains
farming on the one hand and hill-slope farming on the other. With
regard to the first, from Ch'ü-ching 曲靖 (*K'iwok-dz'iäng) southward
and from Tien (*D'ien) Lake westward (that is including the Tali
district discussed in the preceding paragraph), the staple crop was
wet *padi*, which was sown in April or May to coincide with the
beginning of the summer rains, and harvested in September. During
the rest of the year these padi fields were planted to barley.
Clearly the technique of wet-field bunding was known to the Man
peoples of the 9th century, and Fan-Ch'o adds that the fields were
cultivated with the aid of a plow drawn by a yoke of oxen.

Mention of a plow raises an as yet unresolved enigma in Indochinese ethnology. As long ago as 1929 Madeleine Colani reported finding, in an otherwise typically Hoabinhian (in her terminology specifically Bacsonian) artifactual assemblage in a cave in Lạng-sơn Province, a schistose ax on which was etched a clear representation of a plow.[79] Two sub-parallel lines on the other face of the pebble have since been held to represent furrows. Any type of plough would, of course, be anomalous in a Hoabinhian layer, but the type of plow itself would have been equally unusual in any period of Indochinese history. Although it fell within the general category of *aratra,* it was fitted with both an articulated beam (permitting a variation in length and a consequent increase or decrease in the traction effort required) and, most astonishing of all, a coulter. Both these features were unknown in East Asia but were characteristic of Caucasian plows at the beginning of the present century.[80] Bezacier's subsequent attribution of the etching, as distinct from the ax itself, to some time about the 1st century B.C., when the plow was allegedly introduced into the Tong-King delta by Chinese immigrants, may have assigned it to a more compatible level of ecological adaptation, but has done nothing to resolve the problem of the wholly anomalous design of the plow.[81] In my opinion, the representation remains an enigma. It is true, though, that the plow was apparently furnished with a yoke for two draft animals, which would not be unexpected as Tong-King lies in the northern part of the easternmost sector of the zone of *attelages à timon* that stretches across South Asia from the Levant to the South China Sea. For the 9th century A.D. such an arrangement was confirmed by the comment of Fan Ch'o mentioned in the preceding paragraph.

Fan Ch'o seems to imply that, in addition to the bunded *padis,* there were permanently dry fields. On ridges and hillocks whose relief or soil rendered them unsuitable for wet *padi*, wheat was planted, probably in November or December,[82] for harvest in April, and on lands immediately surrounding the houses, hemp, beans, and varieties of millets were raised. This last mode of cultivation serves to recall the terraced plots on the slopes of Tien-ts'ang, which Wu Chin-ting interpreted as the door-yard holdings of separate families; each of whom, of course, may also have cultivated land at a distance.

Fan Ch'o had less to say about hillside farming which he denoted by the phrase *shan t'ien* 山田 , though he did observe that, as the Man cultivators relied on springs to water their fields, they were not troubled by drought. Furthermore, he observed that this particular mode of cultivation was strictly controlled by a skillful and beneficent Man administration (蠻治山田殊為精好) which "everywhere ordered, supervised, watched over, pressed forward, and constrained" the farmers (遍令監守催促). It might at first glance be thought that Fan Ch'o was here referring to swidden farming, but T'ang authors usually denoted this by the graph *she* 畬. Moreover, swidden plots in Southeast Asia are by their very nature never irrigated in any way. It is presumably to be inferred, in fact, that Fan Ch'o was referring to terrace cultivation, specifically to what Spencer and Hale have categorized as linear, contour, irrigable terracing.[83]

The Lặc fields of Tong-King

In 208 B.C. the Tong-King delta was incorporated into the quasi-autonomous state of Nan-Yüeh, a territory which in 111 B.C. was itself absorbed into the Chinese empire as a protectorate administered under indirect rule. The earliest historical (as opposed to semi-legendary) information about ecological adaptation in the delta derives ultimately from these late centuries B.C.

The material relevant to our present purpose exists only in the form of quotations in later Chinese works, and those in two mutually complementary traditions. The first tradition [A], which is the earlier, is exemplified in the *Chiao-Chou Wai-yü Chi* 交州外域記, which was compiled by Yang Fu 楊孚 between the 3rd and 5th centuries A.D. This work now survives only fragmentarily in the *Shui-Ching Chu* 水經注, a commentary written by Li Tao-yüan 酈道元 early in the 6th century. The relevant passage reads as follows:[84]

> A1. 交州外域記曰交阯昔未有郡縣之時土地有雒田其田從潮水上下民墾食其田因名為雒民設雒侯主諸郡縣縣多為雒將雒將銅印青綬
>
> The *Chiao-Chou Wai-yü Chi* states: In *Kau-tśi (MSC Chiao-chih)[85] in times past, when there were neither commanderies nor prefectures, the land was in *lâk (MSC *lo*; Sino-Việt. *lặc*) fields. In these fields the [level of the] water used to rise and fall in accordance with the [rise and fall of the] tides. The folk who brought these fields into cultivation were called *Lâk (Sino-Việt. Lặc). Subsequently a *Lâk king was instituted and *Lâk lords appointed to govern commanderies and prefectures, [as well as] prefectural officials entitled to bronze seals with green ribbons.

The same tradition is expressed in abbreviated form in the *Kuang-Chou Chi* 廣州記, a work written by Ku Wei not later than the 5th century A.D. but now known only from citations in the

So-yin 索隱 commentary on Chüan 116 of *Shih Chi*:[86]

A2. 廣州記云交趾有駱田仰潮水上下人食其田名為駱侯諸縣自名為駱將銅印青綬即今之令

In *Kau-tsi there used to be *lâk (MSC lo; Sino-Việt. lạc) fields where the water rose and fell in accordance with the tides. Those who lived off these fields were called Lâk lords. Prefectural officials styled themselves *Lâk officials, [and were entitled to] bronze seals with green ribbons, in the same way as magistrates at the present time.[87]

Pierre Gourou, misunderstanding somewhat ambivalent translations by Abel des Michels and Camille Sainson of parallel paragraphs in, respectively, *Khâm-định Việt-sử thông-giám cương-mục* 欽定越史通鑑綱目 and *An-nam chí-lược* 安南志略, took the passages here reproduced to imply an irrigation system of the sort that in recent times has been in operation in the neighborhood of Hải-dương.[88] This has indeed been dependent on the rise in river levels that accompanies the diurnal movement of the tides in the Gulf of Tong-King, but it has functioned only with the aid of an ancillary, though complex, system of sluices and canals.[89] The information available on Tong-King in the early centuries of the Christian era, meager though it is, makes it doubtful if the Lạc chieftains of the time commanded sufficient technological expertise, and possibly also social power (though this last might be challenged), to undertake the construction of intricate irrigation works. It would seem more likely that the so-called *lạc* fields were deltaic terrain subject to largely uncontrolled inundation by sweet river water dammed back by the rise of the tides in the Gulf of Tong-King. It is not unlikely, though, that flood water was trapped in the fields by the raising of earth bunds. At the present time, tidal influence in the several distributaries of the Red river reaches almost to Hà-nội in the dry season, perhaps not more than half that distance in the wet season.[90] It is to be presumed that the *lạc* fields were sown to wet *padi,* most varieties of which will tolerate a minor degree of salinity, though only at the cost of reduced yields and diminished quality.[91] This interpretation implies, however, that the Chinese annalists and topographers, through ignorance or by design, treated what could never have been more than a localized particularity as symbolizing the general level of Lạc agricultural practice.

The second [B] of the two textual traditions relating to indigenous farming practice in the Tong-King lowlands is somewhat at variance with that which has just been evaluated. As in the case of Tradition A, there are a *textus amplior* and a *textus simplicior*. The former is incorporated in the Tʻai-pʻing Kuang Chi 太平廣記,

a collection of miscellaneous records assembled by Li Fang 李昉 in A.D. 981 (chüan 482, f. 4 recto et verso):

B1. 交趾之地頗為膏腴徙民居之始知播植厥土惟黑壤厥氣惟雄故今稱其田為雄田其民為雄民有君長亦曰雄王有輔佐焉亦曰雄侯分其地以為雄將 (出南越志)

The land of *Kau-tśi is of considerable fertility. Immigrants were the first to understand its cultivation. Its soil is black and rich, and its ch'i is strong (雄 **giŭng, *jiung, MSC hsiung, Sino-Việt. hùng), so that now these fields are called *jiung fields, and the people [who cultivate them] *jiung folk. There is a chief similarly styled the *Jiung King, whose aides are also called *jiung lords. The territory is apportioned among *jiung officials (Cited from Nan-Yüeh Chih).

The abridged version of this tradition occurs in the T'ai-p'ing Huan-yü Chi 太平寰宇記, where it is acknowledged as a quotation from the 5th-century Nan-Yüeh Chih 南越志:[92]

B2. 南越志云交趾之地最為膏腴舊有君長曰雄王其佐曰雄侯以其田曰雄田

The Nan-Yüeh Chih states: The land of *Kau-tśi is exceedingly fertile. In olden times there was a chieftain styled the *Jiung King. His officials were called *Jiung lords, and his fields *Jiung fields.

In the context in which these passages were written, the immigrants referred to can only have been the diverse groups of Chinese and Sinicized Yüeh who, for one reason or another, made their way into the delta after the establishment of imperial authority in the area. But Tradition B would then contradict Tradition A, which explicitly states that there were lạc fields (and thereby implies lạc cultivation) "when there were neither commanderies nor prefectures," that is prior to Chinese domination. Moreover, whereas the Tradition [A] preserved in the earlier texts refers to lạc fields, rulers, lords, and officials, the Tradition [B] incorporated in the later (Sung) texts speaks of hùng fields, rulers, lords, and officials. This raises the question of the relation between the two Traditions. Henri Maspéro resolved this problem by the expedient of reducing them to one tradition. For him hùng 雄 was simply a scribal error for lạc 雒.[94] This would be plausible enough, especially as lạc is found solely in the earlier texts and hùng in the later, if it were resorted to only once. But both the Sung texts employ the form hùng, so that if a mislection is to be postulated, it must be attributed (barring an extraordinary coincidence) not to the Sung authors but to the compiler of some earlier work from which both Li Fang and Yüeh Shih derived their information.

Emile Gaspardone has proposed an alternative interpretation which not only obviates the need to invoke a twice-perpetrated mislection but also affords a rationale for the use of the epithet hùng as applied to ch'i 氣.[95] This author accepts Tradition A as a reasonably accurate statement of conditions in the Tong-King delta prior to the Chinese immigration of the 1st centuries B.C. and A.D. The lạc fields were, according to this point of view, the creations of an indigenous folk and consequently shared their ethnic attribution. Subsequently Tong-King passed under Chinese rule and experienced an influx of Chinese and Sinicized immigrants, as a result of which agricultural practice was substantially changed. From this phase in its history, according to Gaspardone, dates Tradition B, with its ethnic attribution of hùng:

> En des temps plus calmes, les terres lointaines du Sud ont pu, mieux reconnues et déjà parsemées de Chine, recevoir l'épithète hiong, "fortes." L'application a pu s'étendre à ces parties du Kiao-tche [Chiao-chih] ou du Si-ngeou [Hsi-ou], identifiés l'un à l'autre, extérieures à la zone soumise aux marées. Deux traditions, complémentaires ou rivales, ont pu s'établir et s'exprimer en parallèle dans le même ouvrage ou en opposition dans des ouvrages et peut-être à des âges différents, embrasser pour les recueils tardifs l'ensemble, disputé, de la commanderie de Siang [Hsiang: cf. chap. 8 below] et ses nations variées, ajouter enfin à la confusion.[96]

This assignment of the two Traditions to different phases in the process of ecological adaptation in Tong-King affords a possible rationale for the ethnological oppositions in our texts, but does nothing to explain the significance of the ethnic epithet hùng as a replacement for lạc. It is possible, though not in my opinion probable, that the Chinese *Jiung was a transcription of some Việt word other than the hùng specifically denoted by the Chinese character. It is more likely, I think, that the Sung editors deliberately amended their texts to bring them into conformity with a revered classic. There can be no doubt that their principal exemplar was the ancient Shu Ching 書經, though they may have also been influenced by the attempt of Ling-hu Te-fen in the 7th century A.D. to model the official history of the Northern Chou dynasty[97] on that Classic. Both the vocabulary and the structure of certain phrases in Text B1, for instance, are clearly harking back to the Yü Kung 禹貢 section of the Shu Ching where it is written that in Chi 冀 Province 厥土惟白壤, and in Yen 兗 Province 厥土黑墳. Echoes of this phraseology are also to be heard in the Shih Chi,[98] while the Erh-ya[99] commentary on Yang Province 揚州 employs ch'i in a seemingly similar sense to that of our Text B1, and then goes on to derive the ethnic name from the character of the inhabitants: because their spirit is expansive (揚), so the province is called Yang. This again is a precise syntactic parallel to our Text B2. In a web of literary allusion of this sort, *lo* (雒駱) has no significant connotation; *hsiung* (雄) has several such connotations,[100] and for that reason might well have commended itself to consciously archaizing editors of the Sung period.

This, in turn, raises the problem of the precise meaning to be attributed to *ch'i*. Maspero translated it as "exhalaisons,"[101] Gaspardone rendered it as "air" (in its French sense) or "vapeurs,"[102] and was half-inclined to interpret it as a stereotyped literary echo of the noxious vapors which early Chinese authors were accustomed to associate with the tropical valleys of South China.[103] In both instances the authors were thinking in terms of meteorological phenomena, and it is true that the *Erh-ya* seems to use *ch'i* in the general sense of "climate," but I think that it is not impossible that in the two Sung texts it should be accorded its technical geomantic meaning of *pneuma* or cosmic breath. It was employed in this way in the *Kuan-tzŭ*, which was probably given its present form in Han times,[104] and figured, though as an unacceptable doctrine, in the writings of Wang Ch'ung during the second half of the 1st century A.D.[105] More or less contemporary references to "diviners by the canopy [of heaven] and the chariot [of earth]" 堪輿家 were almost certainly concerned with interpretation of the geomorphological manifestations of *ch'i*, as were equally certainly the *Kung Chai Ti-hsing* 宮宅地形 and the *K'an-yü Chin-kuei* 堪輿金匱 that are mentioned in the bibliography of the *Ch'ien-Han Shu*. In any case, a system of geomancy based on the analysis of morphological and spatial expressions of *ch'i* was well established by the middle of the 3rd century A.D., which is some two centuries earlier than the *Nan-Yueh Chih* which the *T'ai-p'ing Huan-yü Chi* purports to be quoting, and which Li Fang may also have been drawing from in Text B1. A *$j̑i̯ung$ (strong) *ch'i* would have gone far to meet the geomantic desideratum for prosperity of a beneficent conjunction of three-fifths *yang* and two-fifths *yin*. It is, though, a moot question whether Li Fang was responsible for linking the notion of a strong *ch'i* to the name of the people of Tong-King or whether he depended on an already existing tradition. In any case, the notion of *ch'i* as a subtle force circulating through the veins and vessels of the earth would have been alien neither to Shen Huai-yüan in the 5th century nor to Li Fang in the 10th.[106]

In this context of archaization, symbolism, and pseudo-science it is probably unwise to attempt to relate the pedological remarks in Text B1 to actual conditions in the delta.

The most strikingly prominent black soils today are the đất thịt, đất sét, or đất cái, soils traditionally described as "black as buffalo liver," which occur in seasonally inundated regions of Thanh-Hóa and elsewhere;[107] but these are characteristically heavy, sticky, and poorly flocculated, and not at all consonant with the epithet jang, signifying primarily richness and fertility but with overtones of mellowness and, in a farmer's phrase, friability.

The texts we have adduced in this section provide no definitive evidence of agricultural practices in the Tong-King delta at the time when it was coming under Chinese control, but it would seem a not unreasonable inference that a wet-land crop was being cultivated in at least limited tracts of the territory, and, in the general ecological and historical context, it is difficult to see that it could have been other than padi. At this stage of the investigation, we can only concur with Emile Gaspardone who, in concluding his own study, characterized the two sets of texts as "reliques dont il serait aussi imprudent de vouloir trop conclure qu'il serait illogique de vouloir négliger."[108]

The Uplands of Annam

Information concerning the tribal groups which in the earlier centuries of the Christian era occupied the uplands behind the coastal plains of North Annam, the Ramparts of the Sky 天障/鄣 as they were called in ancient times,[109] is, not unexpectedly, meager and equivocal. The earliest material seems to have derived ultimately from the 3rd century A.D., but is now preserved only in the form of quotations in later works. *Lji 里/俚 tribes were recorded in and to the west of Chiu-chen 九真 commandery in A.D. 36,[110] and *Ia-lâng savages 夜郎蠻 in 107,[111] but neither are described in detail. Farther south in Chiu-te 九德 prefecture were the *Luo-iwo savages 盧舉蠻,[112] with the *Kuo-lâng savages 古朗郎蠻[113] in the interior of Quảng-Bình. Among the tribes which at least notionally came within the jurisdiction of Jih-nan 日南 commandery were the *Śiək-bʻuk 式僕,[114] the *Puâ-lieu 波遼,[115] and the *Kiəu-puət-dzʻi 究不事,[116] none of whom can be either identified or located with certainty.

The ethnic groups described most fully are those within or on the borders of *Tśʻiu-nguo 朱吾[117] and *Ziang-liəm 象林,[118] prefectures which comprised the drainage basins of, respectively, the Cam Lo and Han rivers in Quảng-Tri and the Hương river in Thừa-Thiên. In a memoir which should probably be ascribed to the 4th century A.D., it is stated explicity that rice played no part in the diet of the inhabitants of *Tśʻiu-nguo, who lived solely off fish (不食米止資魚以為生).[119] Prominent among these folk were the *Miuən-lâng savages 文狼[120] 野人, who occupied the southern fringes of the prefecture.[121] They are described as "living in the forested wastes where, lacking houses, they pass the night in trees.[122] They eat flesh [partially contradicting the source just cited] and raw fish, and make a business of collecting aromatics which they trade in the markets [of *Tśʻiu-nguo and neighboring prefectures]." There is an element of literary hyperbole in this account, which a concluding remark serves to confirm: "One would say that they were a folk from mythical times" (上皇之民); but the dietary habits of the *Miuən-lâng, together with their roles as collectors of aromatics— an activity which in Southeast Asia has not usually been combined with the cultivation of permanent fields — afford strong indications that these folk were swidden cultivators: if they farmed at all, that is. This interpretation is somewhat strengthened by the report that, when a Han prefect introduced a system of taxation into these tribal territories, a group of *Mi̯uən-lâng migrated to a district known to the Chinese as *Kʽi̯uət-tuo-kuən 屈都昆 .[123] Flight is the ultimate sanction of the swidden cultivator in the face of bureaucratic tyranny, but is seldom resorted to by groups who have made the sort of investment in capital equipment that is represented by, say, wet-padi farming.

Another tribal folk, mentioned in a record deriving from the 5th century A.D., who appear to have been basically swidden cultivators were the *Zi̯wo-lâng 徐狼 (MSC Hsü-lang) on the upper reaches of the Hương river. This group was credited with two distinctive activities, namely silent barter, and the ability to scent the quality of gold at night. The second capability was obviously legendary, but neither activity was normally attributed to settled agriculturalists.[124]

These fragments of information, *analecta* from the folklore of northern Indochina incorporated in garbled Chinese literary traditions, are too ambivalent to permit the formulation of definitive conclusions, but the general context of agricultural development that they establish between, say, 200 B.C. and A.D. 500, even allowing for the Chinese cultural bias which habitually denigrated the cultural achievements of tribal peoples, points uncompromisingly towards swidden, rather than permanent-field, agriculture. However, when we turn to the archeological record, there is indisputable evidence of permanent-field farming integrated with a megalithic tradition of the type discussed in a previous section of this chapter. This highly distinctive ecosystem, which is associated with numerous villages on the Gio-Linh uplands in Quảng-Trị province, was the subject of a monograph by Madeleine Colani in 1940.[125] In the attenuated form in which this tradition exists today it comprises discrete series of stone-embanked terraces for both farming and ritual purposes, each series being combined with one or more tanks serving an irrigation system. The significant point is that each of these systems — and they are rather numerous — was designed as a complete regional scheme. Although the units involved, whether terrace, basin or flume, were of simple construction, they were combined into a complex series in such a way as to facilitate the management of an entire socio-economic unit, namely the territory and persons constituting a group of families or even a whole village. A representative system would include, at decreasing elevations, the following elements: (i) one or more dry-field terraces constructed

at the highest point of the village territory; (ii) an upper tank
serving as a reservoir for the collection of water from stream or
spring; (iii) a lower tank to serve the domestic needs of the
village or family, particularly washing and bathing; (iv) and one
or more fairly extensive wet-field terraces. Below the upper tank
water is led from level to level by a series of flumes and
channels, the whole system being the expression of a preconceived
and carefully executed plan. The integral character of each of
these systems is a sufficient indication that it did not develop
piecemeal and haphazardly.

Associated with these terrace complexes are bridges,
causeways, and staircases, all — like the terraces and tanks —
being of dry-stone construction. Moreover, the presence at various
points within the system of menhirs, stone seats, earthen pyramids
and circular mounds attests, at least in the conventional
interpretation (but see p. 62 above), the cult basis of the whole
layout. On this view, the menhir was originally a spirit-stone,
the material manifestation of a chthonic god who was himself a
divinization of the energy of the earth, "un dieu impersonal", as
Mus has aptly phrased it, "défini avant tout par une
localisation."[126] Such beliefs, it is usually contended, constituted
a basic stratum in the cultural infrastructure of Southeast Asia.
Subsequently the earth-god was apt to acquire anthropomorphic
traits, and in some areas was eventually transformed, under Śaivite
influence, into the *liṅga* that symbolized the permanent and
imperishable principal of the Hinduized state. In any case,
whatever interpretations be placed on the various forms of
megalithic structures, the folk who built these terraces and
spillways on the Gio-Linh uplands not only conceived and planned
each system as a whole, but also took care to ensure that the
ritualistic aspects of the microcosm that they were creating
received as much attention as the ecological. For them, as they
sought to ensure the welfare of their settlement by propitiation of
the earth-god from whose soil they garnered the usufruct, the use
of water for irrigation had no priority over its use for ritual
lustration and bathing, and the upper terraces at least were
probably as important for the cult of the mountain god as for the
provisioning of the settlement. In these beliefs and practices we
may perhaps see prefigured the great Khmer agro-architectural
complexes in which technology and economics were subsumed within an
all-pervading symbolism expressing the reciprocal relations between
the deity and the state. The water seeping from the sacred hill

and carrying the subtle energies of the divinity to the village
and fields below also finds analogues in other parts of Southeast
Asia and in other times. The Siemrăp river, for example, conveyed
the essence of prosperity from the sacred Kulên to Yaśodharapura,[127]
a river linked the sacred shrines of Mĩ-sơn to the capital of
Campā[128] at Trà-kiệu, the Bujang river carried the saving grace of
Maheśvara from the sacred summit of Gunung Jĕrai to the city of
Kaṭāha,[129] and there were numerous Javanese examples on a smaller
scale.

Today the Gio-Linh upland is inhabited predominantly by
Việtnamese subsistence farmers who maintain those elements in the
old systems that contribute to their economic well-being, namely
the irrigation channels and the terracing, but leave untended those
structures such as staircases, causeways and menhirs whose
significance they do not comprehend.[130] This raises the question as
to who were the authors of these sacro-economic undertakings, and
also the problem of their dating. As the systems are still in use
it has proved impossible to conduct excavations, but Mlle. Colani
has obtained provisional answers to these questions by a process of
elimination.[131] The Việtnamese have almost invariably built in
brick, earth or wood, seldom in cut stone and never in unhewn
stone, and have customarily inscribed dedicatory characters on even
the humblest construction. Consequently it would seem that the
Gio-Linh structures must be ascribed to their predecessors on the
massif. It is known that in 1572 Nguyễn-Hoàng, founder of the
Nguyễn dynasty, transported a sizable number of defeated Mạc 莫
partisans to Gio-Linh where they were settled in thirty-six
villages. It is hardly likely that he would have banished them to
a region already occupied by their countrymen, so we may assume
that the colonization of Gio-Linh by Việtnamese began with the Mạc
settlement. Who were the previous inhabitants? Prior to the Việt
southward expansion, the country had been under *Ljəm-·Təp, and later
Cam, control, but Cam irrigation technology was based on the
excavation of canals in flat alluvial terrain and had nothing in
common with the Gio-Linh systems. Moreover, the former Cam
territory is strewn with traces of their occupation in the form of
ruins, inscriptions and toponyms, all of which are lacking on the
Gio-Linh upland. The Khmer, for their part, impounded water by
means of earthen bunds rather than stone dams;[132] the Thai have
never, so far as I am aware, employed dry masonry in their
hydraulic installations, and are not much given to terracing in any
case; and there is no evidence that the *montagnards* of Indochina ever

engaged in irrigation or terracing in historic time. The only
remaining alternative is to postulate a prehistoric origin for the
Gio-Linh systems. Dr. Quaritch Wales has ascribed them to the
Older Megalithic Culture, which we have discussed in a previous
section.[133] He may well be right, but his argument depends on
diffusionist theories that are not usually countenanced at the
present time. However, the integration of stone-embanked
cultivation terraces into preconceived Megalithic sacro-economic
units would seem to provide a partial answer to one question posed
by Spencer and Hale in their investigation of the origins of
agricultural terracing, namely: is the frequently observed
association of terracing and megalithic stone works direct,
indirect, coincidental, or even in some cases illusory, the result
of faulty mapping?[134] It is difficult to deny that *in this one
instance* the relationship is direct.

Mlle. Colani has drawn attention to similar systems of
terracing in the territories of the Angami Nagas,[135] in North
Cachar,[136] Nias,[137] Java,[138] and Bali,[139] but, so far as I am aware,
integrated sacro-economic units of the Gio-Linh type have not been
demonstrated in any of these areas.[140]

It is evident from the preceding discussion that in the
early centuries of the Christian era the tribal groups of the
Annamese uplands were predominantly swidden cultivators, the
possible exceptions being the inhabitants of the Gio-Linh, who may
have grown wet *padi* in the lower basins of their irrigation
systems — though the dating of these works is still an open
question. Nor is there any strong indication that wet *padi* was at
all extensively cultivated along the narrow coastal plain. It is
true that wet-*padi* fields seem to have existed in the immediate
vicinities of the fortified city of Chʻü-su and the Lin-I capital
(pp. 385 and 389 below), but there is no reason to suppose that
they were found more than sporadically along the narrow coastal
plain between the Porte d'Annam and the Col des Nuages, which even
today is a region of extremely poor productivity.[141]

Ecological Adaptation in the Lower Mekong Valley[142]

Owing to a virtually complete absence of paleogeographical
research in Indochina, it is not at present possible to reconstruct
with any great degree of confidence local environmental systems
within the Mekong delta in immediately pre-urban times. It is
reasonably certain, however, despite assertions to the contrary by
some previous authors, that the Cà-mau peninsula had already

78   *Nāgara and Commandery*

assumed something like its present form.[143] Behind its broad fringe of glaucous mangrove, it constituted an enormous sponge of coherent muds and vegetable debris — "un cloaque de boues molles," as Bernard-Philippe Groslier has called it[144] — where a mantle of swamp forest masked such diversification as parallel-trending sand ridges (*giồng* in the vernacular) might otherwise have induced. Through this waste of swamp seeped rather than flowed an infinitude of strangulated streams, a labyrinthine network of waters whose all but insensible percolation was governed, according to a system of complex hydraulic relationships, by the two chief distributaries of the Mekong, now known as the Bassac and the Fleuve Antérieur. Only in the upper and narrower tracts of the delta, between Châu-dốc and Phnoṃ-Penḥ, was the level surface of this green sea broken by sandstone outliers from the southern foot of the Chaîne Annamitique. For the rest, the whole delta, to judge by present-day conditions, seldom exceeded three meters above sea level, and large tracts were at an elevation only insignificantly above that of the sea. Coupled with a benign tropical climate, these physiographic conditions offered a habitat suitable to a people accustomed to a semi-aquatic mode of life such as, in the light of archeological research, the folk of the Mekong delta seem to have been. Excavations at Oc-èo, for example, would seem to imply that a ciy on that site took its rise in a cultural milieu somewhat resembling that of the typesite at Saṃròṅ Sen.[145] Generally speaking, this culture gives the impression of having adapted to, rather than remodelled, its environment, and seems not to have disturbed to any great extent the balance of nature in the Mekong valley. In no instance, whether at Saṃròṅ Sen, Cùlao Rùa, Long-prao, Oc-èo, Xuân-lộc, Côn-sơn, or elsewhere has archeological excavation yielded specific evidence of developed agricultural practices, and we are left with the impression that fishing and the collection of shellfish contributed more than a little to the diet of these people at least to the beginning of the historical period, and probably long afterwards.[146]

The Chinese sources relating to the Mekong delta during the protohistoric period do not substantially modify the adaptational pattern implied by archeology. Such references to ecological matters as occur are concerned predominantly with the natural flora and fauna of the countryside, not infrequently in their role as tribute offerings,[147] rather than with subsistence crops. However, the *Chin Shu*, the earliest Chinese work to accord a discrete paragraph to the delta,[148] incorporates a brief comment on farming

practice in that area. Unfortunately the relevant phrases are
obscure and ambiguous. They run, "[The inhabitants of the region]
engage in farming. They sow [or plant] in one year [and] reap for
three" 以耕種為務一歲種三歲穫 .[149] Most previous
authors have noted this statement and passed on as if its
implications were self-evident.[150] This is far from being the case.
At their face value the phrases would seem to refer to some form of
ratooning. Southeast Asian crops commonly treated in this way
include sugar-cane and sago. So far as the first of these is
concerned, it is true that, although sugar-cane (Saccharum officinarum,
Linn.) has now virtually disappeared from the Trans-Bassac, the
environment of the Lower Mekong was not inhospitable to its
cultivation, which is mentioned at least twice in Chinese accounts
of the delta;[151] and its importance in the economy of that time has
been confirmed by the discovery of granite rollers from ancient
sugar presses in the Cambodian province of Tà Kèo and in the
Trans-Bassac.[152] It is true, too, that many observers of sugar
culture are particularly struck by the ratooning process. However,
there is nothing to connect the ratoon cultivation of sugar-cane to
a specific three-year cycle and, more important perhaps, it is
implicit in the Chinese text that the reference was to a staple
food crop, presumably a cereal, rather than to a dietary adjunct,
which is all sugar-cane ever can be. The sago palm, Metroxylon sagus,
Rottb. and *M. rumphii,* Mart., certainly provides a staple food in
many parts of Southeast Asia, and is especially suited to
marshlands, but its ratoon cycle is nearer to ten than three years.
Moreover, some familiarity with Chinese agricultural history leads
me to doubt if the Chinese envoys would have included sago
cultivation in the phrase 耕種 .

Turning specifically to cereal crops, *padi,* of course, is
ratooned in Southeast Asia, though at the present time only in a
minor way and usually where a shortage of labor causes an
involuntary ratooning, or where some pattern of shifting
cultivation induces a more or less fortuitous second crop owing to
a change in the location of the main *padi* fields. Probably in the
past ratooning was most common in tracts of deep swamp such as were
not uncommon in parts of the Mekong delta, where there would have
been adequate moisture for the regeneration of the *padi* crop, and
probably few cattle to graze the young shoots. Yet it would be
extremely unusual to take more than one crop in this way as the
yield drops sharply with the first ratoon, and subsequent crops are
inordinately meager. To this state of affairs there is a partial

exception in the case of the so-called floating rices, which are today cultivated on the margins on the Tonlé Sap and along the lower Mekong and its distributaries. These rices exhibit a high location- and maturity-specific photoperiod sensitivity, together with branching at the upper nodes, and rapid internode elongation which permits the plants to maintain their tips above a rising water-level.[153] Heading begins when the water subsides, allowing roots from the internodes to penetrate the soil. Today the plants are raised as annuals, being seeded directly into the fields in the low-water period of March or April, but it is not impossible that in ancient times they may have been treated as perennials. In fact, there is general agreement among plant geneticists that, although these rices are usually regarded as strains of *Oryza sativa*, Linn., one of the perennial races has contributed genetically to their development, namely *O. perennis* if we follow Ramiah and Ghose,[154] *O. rufipogon* in the opinion of Te-Tzu Chang.[155] That the perennial habit was dominant in Cambodian floating rices in earlier times was attested by Chou Ta-kuan 周達觀 in the 13th century. Reporting his experiences on a mission to Cambodia in 1296-7, he wrote of "natural fields where *padi* always grows without being sown; when the water rises a fathom, the *padi* grows as much."[156] Some three centuries subsequently Chou's observation was confirmed by Diogo do Couto in a recently discovered passage which, although written in about 1611, was omitted from the published version of that author's lengthy history of the Portuguese in the East. The passage in question is entitled: *Capitulo 6 da grande e admiravel cidade que se discobrio nos matos do Reino camboja e de sua fabrica e sitio*. The relevant paragraph reads as follows:

> Em hum serto tempo, sae do fundo desta alagoa [Tonlé Sap], hum anno, e outro não, grande cantidade de darros com sua casca, a que na India chamão bate [<Kanarese *bhatta* = rice in the husk; perhaps in this instance influenced by Malay *padi*[157]] en Inde, que sostenta muito parte da gente das aldeas ao redor: por onde parece que se cria em baxo como a sargaso, e que como he de ves arrebenta para cima, e naquele tempo handão muitas almadias por esta alagoa, colhendo este arros com muitas festas, bailos, e tamgeres.[158]

It is tempting to assume that this *padi* springing up from the floor of the Tonlé Sap was one of the deep-water, so-called floating, rices. The plant that Couto was describing was not strictly a perennial, and his account of its growth cycle ("it pushes upwards under the water like a seaweed, and at the proper time rises to the surface") is not an accurate description of the way in which floating rices actually rise with their tips above the flood. Nevertheless, it must be remembered that Couto was a layman reporting at secondhand: he may have been misinformed, or he may simply have failed to appreciate the botanical import of his remarks.[159] In any case, it is difficult to see what other type of rice would have matched his description more closely. Moreover, it is evident that the plants described by both Chou Ta-kuan and Diogo do Douto were not the cultivated floating rices currently grown, say, to the south of Phnom Penh, but rather the wild rices (Cambodian = *srangne*) still found à l'état naturel in the vicinity of Battambang.[160]

None of this is decisive, but if the perennial habit can be documented in Cambodia of the 13th and 17th centuries, it makes it that much easier to accept the notion of its existence in the protohistoric period. That rice of some sort did play a part in the economy of the delta during the early centuries of the first millennium A.D. is attested both by Louis Malleret's excavation of rice grains at Oc-èo,[161] and by a note in the *Wai-kuo Chuan* 外國傳, compiled in the 3rd century A.D., that rice figured in trials by ordeal in a polity in that region;[162] but whether or not it was all or partly floating rice remains a question for future research.[163]

If *padi* is held not to meet the implications of the *Chin Shu* passage, then the only alternatives are emendation of the text or extension of the meaning of the graphs beyond their normally accepted connotation. No readily apparent emendation suggests itself,[164] but, resorting to the second expedient, it is not impossible that 種 should be understood to imply cultivation in a broad sense rather than simply sowing, perhaps with some of the overtones of the phrases 種田 or 種地, meaning "to farm" or "to prepare the soil for cultivation." In this case, it may be that the text refers to a form of swidden cultivation on a three-year cycle, and should be read as, "[The inhabitants of the delta] . . . during any particular year prepare their fields [i.e. clear their *ray*] which they harvest for three years [before moving to a new *ray*]." This interpretation is not wholly inconsistent with the exiguous ecological data relating to cultures of Samroṅ Sen type.[165] In view of the archeological and literary evidence mentioned in the preceding paragraph, however, an interpretation along these lines would imply that *padi* of some sort had been incorporated into the swidden cycle. Generally speaking, the floating rice version seems, on present evidence, to be preferable.

The Diffusion of Wet *Padi* through Southeast Asia

Each of the vignettes of ecological adaptation presented in the preceding pages has raised the question of the likelihood of wet-*padi* cultivation in protohistoric Southeast Asia. Indeed, documentation of the diffusion of this crop must be regarded as a research priority in the elucidation of the cultural evolution of the region.[166] The archeological record is, as we have noted, in this respect exiguous and often of doubtful interpretation, while relevant documentary materials are both few and intractable, so that any argument must depend on circumstantial evidence and proceed by means of inference.

The earliest dated evidence for the occurrence of *padi* in Southeast Asia was obtained, in the form of carbonized rice glumes, probably from the first half of the 4th millennium B.C., by Donn Bayard during his excavations at Non Nok Tha in northeastern Thailand.*[167] It is not immediately evident from the recovered specimens whether the plants were actually cultivated forms or wild relatives, nor whether they were produced by swidden or wet-field techniques, but Bayard's assumption of "the probable presence of rice agriculture in the area prior to 3500 B.C. and perhaps extending back as far as the beginning of the fifth millennium B.C." is allegedly supported not only by carbon-14 datings from Non Nok Tha itself, but also by the thermoluminescent dating of pottery sherds obtained by Chin Yu-ti [Youdi] from the typologically similar site at Ban Chiang in neighboring Udọn Thani province.[168] However, in his own evaluation of the combined evidence from both sites, Chin is unwilling to admit the possibility of *padi* farming *before* 3500 B.C.[169] Even this later date is some fifteen hundred years prior to the earliest evidence for rice cultivation in India, namely radiocarbon determinations from Period IIIB of the Navdatoli site in the Narbadā valley,[170] but it is subsequent to the earliest evidence from China — dated to 4000-4400 B.C. at Ho-mu-tu in the Yangtzǔ valley — by at least half a millennium. Rice remains have also been excavated at a group of sites in the Han valley which are collectively known as Ch'ü-chia Ling 屈家嶺 but the experts differ in their dating of those remains. Whereas, for example, the excavators of the sites[171] and Chang Kwang-chih[172] appear to favor a

---

*Since this was written I. C. Glover has announced the possible discovery of rice, perhaps domesticated, at Ulu Leang in Sulawesi at levels attributed to the 4th or 5th millennium B.C. ["The Late Stone Age in Eastern Indonesia," *World Archaeology*, vol. 9 (1977), p. 52].

date in the neighborhood of 2500 B.C., Ho Ping-ti ascribes the rice finds to about 3 000 B.C., and is prepared to place the introduction of *padi* cultivation into the lower Han valley a whole millennium earlier even than that.[173] However, in a detailed analysis of the stratigraphic relationships of the Chʻü-chia Ling sites, Judith Treistman has proposed a considerably later date for the rice-bearing levels.[174] Restricting her analysis to securely established stratigraphical relationships, she has discriminated within the artifactual assemblages a three-fold cultural succession, the upper two levels of which were almost entirely historic in time. "The fact," she writes, "that the painted Chʻü-chia-ling pottery is all wheel-produced, the appearance of geometric stamped decoration at the type site, at I-chia-shan and Yang-chia-wan, and the presence of bronze implements or apparent imitations of bronze vessels all argue for late dating, at least post-1000 B.C."[175] Finally, Dr. Treistman (who, incidentally, was writing before the finds at Ho-mu-tu were published) was led to the conclusion that not until the 1st millennium B.C. did wet *padi* replace millet as the *staple* crop in the middle Yangtzŭ valley, whence it subsequently diffused throughout the delta.[176]*

The evidence from the Yangtzŭ valley and northeastern Thailand in no way runs counter to the implications of presently available botanical and linguistic data. Botanists have for long been disposed to view Southeast Asia *sensu lato* as one of the original locales of *padi* domestication,[177] and the geneticist Te-Tzŭ Chang has recently assigned the event specifically to the zone "between northern India and the Pacific coast adjoining Vietnam and China" (Fig. 3).[178] This interpretation, in turn, is inconsistent neither with Paul Benedict's postulated, but controversial, borrowing by the early Chinese of an Austro-Thai lexicon of terms reflecting both the cultivation of the *padi* plant and the preparation of rice grain for food nor with the implications of Robert Blust's reconstructed Proto-Austronesian vocabulary.

Within Southeast Asia, the next earliest instance of *padi* farming subsequent to that from Non Nok Tha is inferred from the discovery of stone and shell sickles and quern stones at the archeological site of Ban Kao in the foothills defining the western edge of the central plain of Thailand, the earliest levels of which

---

*While this volume was in press R. Pearson read a paper on "The Chʻing-lien-kang Culture and the Chinese Neolithic" to a symposium on *The Origin of Agriculture and Technology: West or East Asia?* (Moesgard, Denmark, 1979), in which he attributed domesticated *padi* to the lower Yangtzŭ valley as early as 5000 B.C.

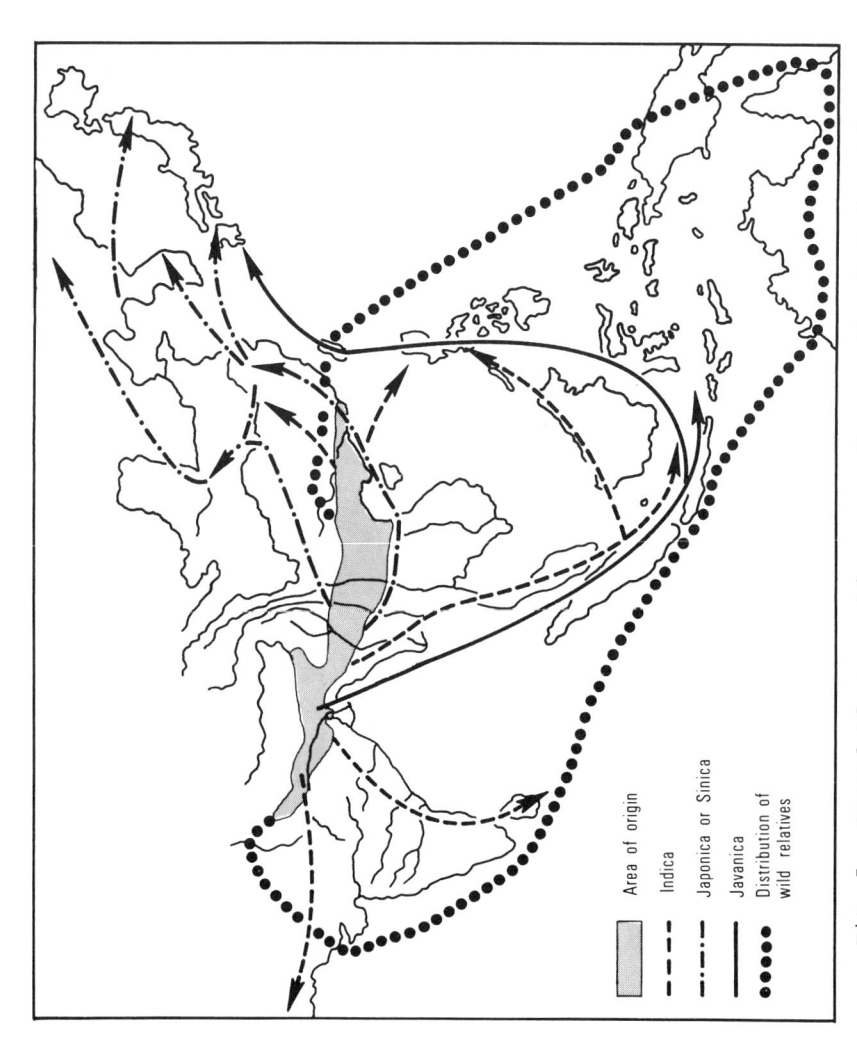

Fig. 5. Spread of geographic races of *Oryza sativa* in Asia. After Te-Tzu Chang, "The rice cultures," *Philosophical Transactions of the Royal Society of London*, Series B, vol. 275 (1976), p. 144.

have been dated by radiocarbon analysis to about 2000 B.C.[179] Thus Non Nok Tha, Ban Chiang, and Ban Kao can be postulated as representing a lower-piedmont adaptation in which *padi* was integrated into an ecosystem still based largely on vegeculture, but also including domesticated cattle. The piedmont sites, while affording a terrain suitable for experiments with primitive and localized inundation, perhaps even with irrigation properly speaking, would also have permitted access to the resources of neighboring, vertically stratified ecozones. At this time, *padi* cultivation must have been of limited extent and essentially supplemental within the piedmont ecosystem. In the opinion of the late Chester Gorman, who devoted several studies to the paleoenvironmental archeology of Southeast Asia,[180] the wet-*padi* techno-complex was elaborated and extended on to lowland alluvial plains only with the advent of an iron technology during the 1st millennium B.C., a development that was possibly in some instances facilitated by the harnessing of the tractive power of the water buffalo. The evidence on which Gorman bases this proposition derives from Thailand, where reasonably thorough surveys have failed to locate a single pre-metal age site on the central plain. Sites implying the level of sociocultural integration associated with the colonization of alluvial lowlands have been excavated at Lopburi[181] and Chansen[182] in the heart of the central plain of Thailand, while similar developments have been recorded from several localities in the broad, alluvium-floored valleys of Khorat, notably a group of three sites in the neighborhood of Roi Et.[183] In short, it is sufficiently attested that wet *padi* had become a crop of considerable importance in appropriate ecological niches in the territories now known as Thailand well before the beginning of the Christian era, though its precise extent is still a matter for speculation. Beyond the borders of Thailand, however, Gorman's model has only the status of a hypothesis to be tested by future research.

During the historical period, a reasonably reliable index of the spread of wet-padi farming would be the development of irrigation systems. The hydraulic projects not infrequently referred to in epigraphic and textual sources, apart from those constructed specifically for transportation and drainage purposes, are unlikely to have been intended for anything other than the irrigation of wet *padi*. Flooding of taro pits is commonly practiced in Polynesia and apparently to a very limited extent in Southeast Asia, but is unlikely to have been undertaken by societies capable

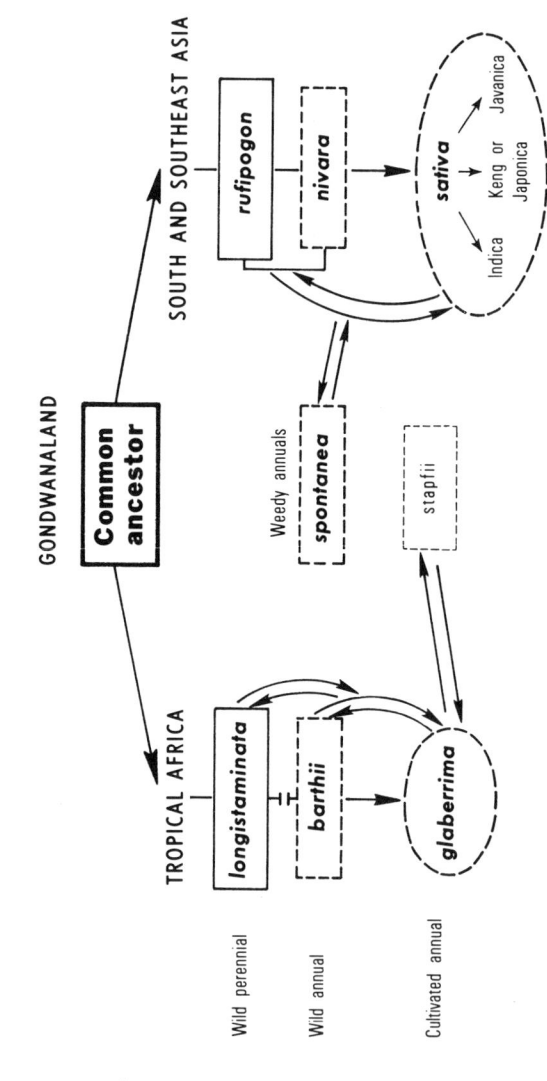

Fig. 6. Evolution of the two cultivated species of rice. After Te-Tzu Chang, "The rice cultures," *Philosophical Transactions of the Royal Society of London*, Series B, vol. 275 (1976), p. 144. Double arrows indicate introgressive hybridization.

of both supporting an hereditary elite and building *caṇḍi* and temple-mountains. The earliest epigraphic reference to water management in Southeast Asia occurs in an inscription of Pūrṇavarman of Tārūmā, a kingdom in western Java, and apparently records the construction of a watercourse nearly seven miles long by royal order in the middle of the 5th century A.D.,[184] but there is no guarantee that this canal was devised for irrigation purposes. In Professor Sarkar's (slightly amended) rendering the inscription reads as follows:[185]

1. Formerly, the Candrabhāgā, dug by the overlord of kings (*rājādhirāja*), *viz*. the strong-armed *guru*, having reached the famous city (*purī*),

2. went to the ocean. In the twenty-second year of his augmenting reign, by the illustrious Pūrṇavarman, who became the foremost (lit. banner) of the rulers of men on account of the lustre of auspicious qualities,

3-4. was dug the charming river Gomatī, of pure water, in length six thousand one hundred and twenty-two *dhanus*, having begun it on the eighth day of the dark half of the month of Phālguna and completed it in twenty-one days, on the thirteenth day of the bright half of (the month of) Caitra. (That river) having chaneled through (*vidārya*) the camping-ground (? *śibirāvani*) of the Grandfather and Royal Sage (*pitāmahasya rājarṣer*),

5. floweth forth after having been endowed by the Brāhmaṇas with the gift of a thousand cows.

By relating information in this text to past and present landscape morphologies in the vicinity of Tugu, where the inscription was found apparently *in situ,* Noorduyn and Verstappen have been able to demonstrate with a high degree of probability that what Pūrṇavarman's engineers achieved was the diversion of the channel of the Cakung river from a northerly course transverse to the beach ridges that back the coast to the east of Tanjung Priuk to a northeasterly course which entered Jakarta Bay (and still does) near Marunda.[186] It was because the new channel utilized natural depressions between beach ridges for much of its length that the undertaking could be completed, as the inscription records, in 21 days. In fact, apart from a certain amount of channel excavation close to the point of diversion, and again whenever the new channel was cut through a beach ridge separating one depression from its subparallel neighbor, the operation would have been essentially a linking of existing depressions into a continuous waterway. It is more than doubtful that a diversion of this character in this particular terrain would have had irrigation as its primary purpose. As Noorduyn and Verstappen suggest, it was probably undertaken to alleviate flooding along the lower course of the Cakung river (the Candrabhāgā of the inscription) occasioned by silting of the channel where water flow was impeded by transverse beach ridges. On this interpretation, the claim of Pūrṇavarman (or one of his forebears: the text is unclear on this point) to have excavated (*khyātā*) the Candrabhāgā river is presumably to be understood as an inflated reference to a certain amount of channel modification and, possibly, earlier attempts to cope with flooding in the lower reaches.

A Sanskrit inscription of slightly later date from Tháp-Mười in the Plaine des Joncs would seem to provide inferential evidence of wet-*padi* cultivation. It relates how a prince of the royal house of *Bʻi̭u-nậm (for which see pp. 120-7 below) was commended to the charge of a religious fief [lit. the seat of those who depend on alms] "conquered in the mud," and presumably refers to alluvial land reclaimed for agriculture.[187] There is, too, some confirmation of this interpretation if, as Coedès suggests, the sentence, ". . . by whose arm the very Ocean of Milk, drained of its water, [was] transformed into a lake of ambrosia . . ." constitutes an oblique reference to the draining of that part of the Plaine des Joncs. If this were so, it is highly probable that the main crop on the reclaimed land was wet *padi*. The rice grains, deriving from a still earlier period, which Malleret discovered at Oc-èo (p. 81) were unfortunately destroyed by the explosion of the Saigon magazine before they could be subjected to laboratory analysis, so that it is unknown whether they represented wet or dry varieties.[188] We shall subsequently have occasion to mention the networks of canals that radiated from the cities of *Bʻi̭u-nậm, and which may therefore be presumed to be earlier than the 7th century, but so far it has not been demonstrated that they were designed for irrigation. In the light of the evidence discussed in the preceding pages, it cannot be assumed with certainty that wet *padi* was grown extensively in the Mekong delta at the beginning of the Christian era, though there is considerable likelihood that it was already established on ecologically favorable terrain. It does appear, however, that it was adopted earlier, and grown more extensively, on the mainland of Southeast Asia than in the archipelago. In Kalimantan, for instance, it has achieved only a limited extension, and that mostly in recent centuries. Even on Java, where *sawah* is often counted as one of the three inevitable elements of the landscape (the other two being coconut palms and volcanoes), as late as 1800 wet *padi* was restricted to especially suitable terrain. Clifford Geertz has calculated that in 1833 the Javanese acreage of wet *padi* was only just over a third of what it is at the present time.[189] And in the Nusa Tenggara, which is rendered ecologically marginal for wet *padi* by the length of its dry season, the crop even today has hardly begun to displace the old vegecultural farming system.

* * * * * * * * *

From the preceding discussions it is evident that by the beginning of the Christian era, and in point of fact probably several millennia earlier, at least five main categories of ecotype were co-existing in Southeast Asia. These distinctive systems of energy transfers may be conveniently discriminated on the bases of their primary subsistence modes, in the inferred chronological order of their appearance, as:

(1) Nomadic hunting and foraging within — to judge from more recent ethnographic parallels — defined but shifting ranges, which probably at any particular time seldom encompassed more than two or three adjacent tributary valleys.

(2) Semi-sedentary hunting and fishing, together with foraging activities which often extended to the more or less casual tending of certain prized plants.

(3) Root horticulture in semi-permanent garden plots adjacent to dwellings, and always potentially supplementable by fishing.

(4) Developed swidden agriculture, including the cultivation of Job's tears (*Coix lachryma-jobi*, Linn.) and dry *padi*, together with fishing when possible.

(5) Relatively localized, permanent-field, wet-*padi* cultivation, with domesticated cattle for sustenance and sacrifice, and perhaps for draft purposes, and supplemented by mixed gardening and fishing.

Such archeological evidence as is presently available, especially when interpreted in the light of comparative ethnography,[190] implies that, at the dawn of the historic period, these ecotypes tended to occur in broadly catenary sequences stretching from upland interiors, both continental and archipelagic, to coastal lowlands. It also appears that earlier practices in the evolutionary sequence were not inevitably replaced by later ones which developed at lower elevations, but rather were often integrated into them. In other words, later stages in the developmental process were likely to incorporate components from

earlier phases. The unit of settlement in category 5, for
instance, was the village, often a collection of stilted houses,
dependent for a substantial part of its subsistence on the produce
of its wet-*padi* fields, but also drawing heavily on gardens and
multi-storeyed groves of fruit trees disposed around the
settlement. The highest storey comprised mainly coconut crowns,
the spreading, pinnate fronds of areca, and, usually somewhat apart
from the main groves, the graceful heads of sugar-palms. At
successively lower levels rambutans, mangosteens, bananas, bamboo,
sugar-cane, various aroids, yams, and numerous zingiberaceous
plants formed a bosky thicket of vegetation. Whereas *padi* provided
a staple grain in return for a seasonably variable investment of
labor, the fruits, tubers, and vegetables yielded throughout the
year while yet making few demands on the time or labor of the
villager. This integration of wet-*padi,* a relatively late
development, with a so-called mixed gardening[191] reminiscent of the
earlier Crystallitic phase, proved to be a remarkably stable
ecosystem, which has, in fact, survived until recent times as the
basis of the predominant subsistence economy in many parts of
Southeast Asia.[192] Among the groups who did not adopt *padi* as a
crop, however, reliance on protein-deficient vegetal culture
necessitated a continued involvement with hunting, and surely helps
to explain the importance of fishing — marine, riverine, and
field — among Southeast Asian farmers down to the present time.

  The social groups associated with ecosystems (1) through (3)
were inevitably familistic in terms of both social and cultural
organization; those practicing developed swidden agriculture
certainly exhibited at least some of the integrative devices
characteristic of "tribal" (segmentary) society; while those
undertaking wet-padi cultivation, which requires at the minimum no
inconsiderable organization of labor for leveling, bunding, and
water management, appear sometimes to have achieved the level of
integration of the chiefdom (pp.10-20 above). The evidence for
this is mainly inferential. The requisite degree of centralized
direction is implicit, for instance, in the archeological remains
of large, functionally differentiated settlements in both the
middle Irawadi and lower Mekong valleys which apparently attained
their apogee during the early centuries of the Christian era, and
whose origins are therefore presumably to be sought in still
earlier times. Charles Keyes has similarly interpreted both
archeological and legendary evidence from Khorat as implying an
advanced chiefdom level of integration late in the prehistoric

period. In fact, this author is unexpectedly explicit in his attribution, referring to the society of the time as "something of a transitional type between tribal chiefdoms (perhaps not dissimilar to those of the Tai of northern Laos and northern Vietnam), and the fully developed state system of Angkor."[193] Nor is Bronson and Dales' reconstruction of Phase I (the 2nd and 1st centuries B.C.) in the sequence they recovered at the Central-Thailand site of Chansen inimicable to such an inference, though it is true that they provide no evidence specifically diagnostic of a chiefdom level of differentiation and centralization.[194] The earlier strata of references to Southeast Asia in Indian literature are, generally speaking, equally ambivalent, though some of the tales in, say, the *Jātaka* corpus (to be discussed in Chap. 7) might be construed as implying the existence of chiefdoms in certain parts of western Southeast Asia before the rise of Indianized states proper.

The only *direct* evidence for a chiefdom degree of centralization prior to the beginning of the Christian era derives from the far north of the region, on the borders of the Sinic culture realm. The King of Tien, mentioned by Ssŭ-ma Ch'ien in *Shih Chi* and independently attested by archeology, exercised an authority over a hierarchy of neighboring rulers which was surely that of a paramount chief over subordinate chieftains, and validated his status by a spurious claim to descent from the princely house of the old Yang-tzŭ valley state of Ch'u.[195] In the Tong-King lowlands the chief who styled himself the Lạc [or Hùng] King (pp. 67-72 above) appears to have filled much the same role. But it is probably permissible to postulate chiefdoms at a still earlier period in the history of Tong-King. The later phases of the recently discovered archeological assemblages which go under the name of the Phùng-nguyên Culture afford some support for the suggestion that the so-called kingdom of Âu-Lạc 歐駱 was in fact a reasonably highly developed chiefdom. According to both Chinese and Việtnamese annals, this polity was founded in 258 B.C. when an aggressor from the northward imposed his rule on pre-existing communities known collectively in later times as the kingdom of Văn-Lang 文郎國.[196] Superimposition of status in this way is a not uncommon means of inducing rank differences of the chiefdom type, with the lineages of the more (though not necessarily highly) differentiated society monopolizing positions of power and the conquered comprising in effect an understratum of commoners. The seat of the paramount ruler of Âu-Lạc was established at Cổ-loa

92   Nāgara and Commandery

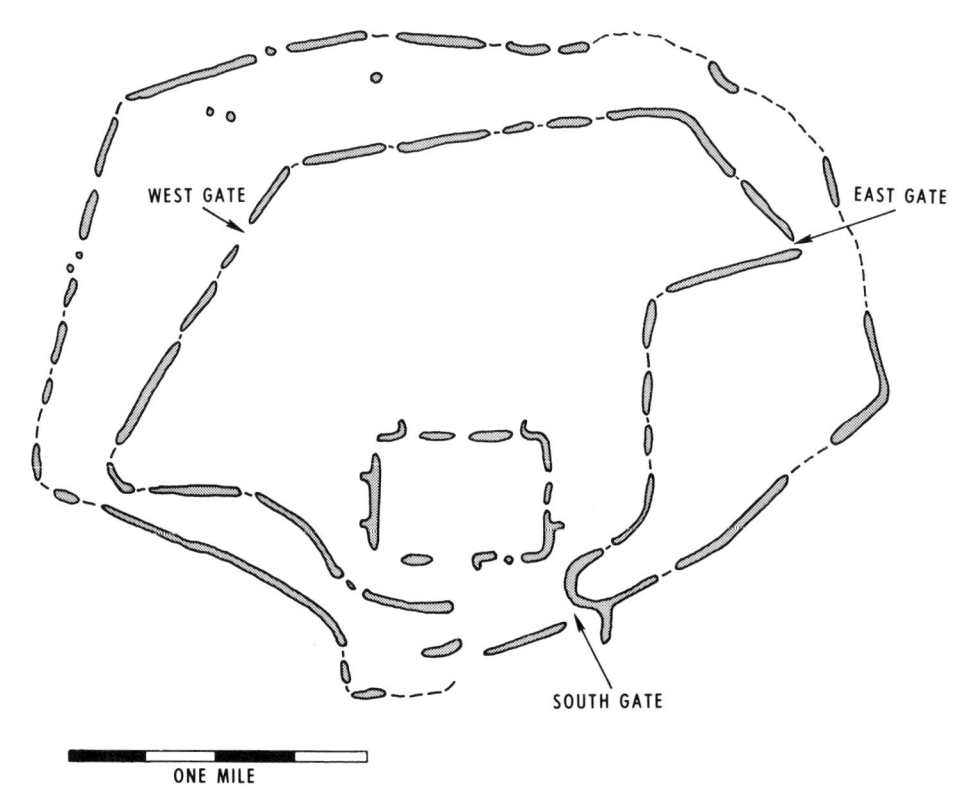

Fig. 7. Plan of the enceintes at Cổ-lõa, which almost certainly incorporate elements from the ramparts of Lõa Thành. Based on Louis Bezacier, *Le Viêt-Nam* (Paris, 1972), p. 248.

古螺, some 17 kilometers to the north of present-day Hà-nội. Tradition has it that the settlement was enclosed by nine earthern ramparts, whence it was designated Loa Thành 螺城, the City of the Conch,[197] but it is evident from air photographs of the site that there have never been more than three enceintes disposed as shown in Fig. 7.[198] And not all those are necessarily of great antiquity. Cô-loa was subsequently the site of the capital of a kingdom founded by Ngô Quyền in A.D. 939 so that, until more intensive archeological investigation has been undertaken, it will be impossible to be sure which of the constructions presently visible have in fact survived from the earlier period of occupation and which are of 10th-century date. The bricks which are occasionally found lying on the ground within and around the enceintes are certainly from the later period. However, it is usually considered — on no very good grounds, as far as I have been able to ascertain — that the course of the ramparts and at least their foundations were established in the 3rd century B.C.[199]

The implication of the preceding paragraphs is that, at about the beginning of the Christian era, Southeast Asia was occupied by a kaleidoscopic variety of societies and cultures which, although adapted to a great variety of individual environmental niches, formed part of numerous regional co-traditions which were in turn subsumed within a common, recognizably Southeast Asian trajectory of cultural evolution.[200] The strong emphasis in all the co-traditions on the manipulation of generalized ecosystems, whether in permanent polycultural gardens or swidden clearings, and even when these were combined with wet-*padi* farming, served both to reduce the demands on social and technological mobilization and to permit an unexpectedly high degree of mobility. It follows, moreover, that these differently constituted societies would have responded in correspondingly diverse ways to external influences, a supposition which is to some extent confirmed by the meager evidence to hand. We shall discover in subsequent chapters, for instance, that Indian cultural contacts appear to have operated selectively on different groups, exerting their major effects on what we perceive to have been the socially more differentiated among the constellation of Southeast Asian communities, that is those practicing wet-*padi* farming and the use of metals.

It is to the transformations induced by the establishment of cross-cultural contacts between certain groups in, respectively, India and various parts of Southeast Asia that we shall now turn our attention. In Chapters 3 through 6 we shall present sequentially the evidence for the earliest urban forms in each of the main cultural realms, to be followed in Chapter 7 by a tentative interpretation of the process by which these several urban traditions came into being.

Notes and References

1. As recently as 1967 Wilhelm G. Solheim II could assert that, "There is not a single published final report on a major prehistoric site in Southeast Asia that can be considered acceptable under present-day standards": "Southeast Asia and the West," *Science,* vol. 157, no. 3791 (1967), p. 896. The lack of firm stratigraphic controls was especially deleterious when, as not infrequently happened, long-lived artifactual forms were integrated into new cultural inventories and thereby persisted among localized groups for long periods of time. A type of heeled stone axe, for instance, which is ascribed broadly to the Indochinese Neolithic, and dated to the pre-Christian era when found at Plei-ku or Long-khánh, was apparently still in use near Phan-rang during the Earlier Lê and Later Lý dynasties (980-1225), and was recorded among the Bahnar tribes even at the beginning of the present century: cf. Olov R. T. Janse, "An archaeological expedition to Indo-China and the Philippines," *Harvard Journal of Asiatic Studies,* vol. 6 (1941), p. 255; E. Saurin, "Nouvelles observations préhistoriques à l'Est de Saigon," *Bulletin de la Société des Etudes Indochinoises,* New Series, vol. 43 (1968), p. 14, citing Verneau; Louis Malleret, *L'archéologie du delta du Mékong:* vol. 2, *La civilisation matérielle d'Oc-èo* (Paris, 1960), p. 19; Jeremy H. C. S. Davidson, "Archaeology in northern Viêt-Nam since 1954" and "Archaeology in southern Viêt-Nam since 1954" in R. B. Smith and W. Watson (eds.), *Early South East Asia* (New York and Kuala Lumpur), pp. 98-124 and 215-222. At a much more complicated level, Giang Thành, in the vicinity of Hà-tiên, for long thought to have been a pre-Aṅkorian structure, has recently been shown to be a Việt citadel constructed subsequent to 1820 on pre-existing Khmer foundations: Malleret, *L'archéologie du delta du Mékong,* vol. 1, *L'exploration archéologique et les fouilles d'Oc-èo* (Paris, 1959), p. 14, note 1.

2. As recently as 1970, not a single Neolithic site had been identified with certainty in the whole of Indonesia.

3. Robert von Heine-Geldern, "Urheimat und früheste Wanderungen der Austronesier," *Anthropos,* vol. 27 (1932), pp. 543-619; "Vorgeschichtliche Grundlagen der Kolonialindischen Kunst," *Wiener Beiträge zur Kunst- und Kulturgeschichte Asiens,* vol. 8 (1934), pp. 5-40; "The archaeology and art of Sumatra," in Edwin M. Loeb, *Sumatra: its history and people.* Wiener Beiträge zur Kulturgeschichte und Linguistik, vol. 3 (Vienna, 1935), pp. 305-331 and 339-342; "L'art prébouddique [sic] de la Chine et de l'Asie du Sud-Est et son influence en Océanie," *Revue des Arts Asiatiques,* vol. 11, no. 4 (1937), pp. 177-206; "Prehistoric research in the Netherlands Indies," in Pieter Honig and Frans Verdoorn (eds.), *Science and scientists in the Netherlands Indies* (New York, 1945), pp. 129-167; "Research on Southeast Asia: problems and suggestions," *American Anthropologist,* vol. 48 (1946), pp. 149-175. Cf. also a later paper by the same author: "Die kulturgeschichtliche Bedeutung Südostasiens," *Geographische Rundschau,* vol. 9 (1957), pp. 121-127. For evaluations of the lifetime *oeuvre* of Heine-Geldern see Count Vinigi L. Grotanelli, "Robert Heine-Geldern's contribution to historical ethnolgy," *Current Anthropology,* vol. 10, no. 4 (1969), pp. 374-376; Paul Kirchhoff, "Robert von Heine-Geldern," *Zeitschrift für Ethnologie,* vol. 94 (1969), pp. 163-168; Erika Kaneko, "Robert von Heine-Geldern: 1885-1968," *Asian Perspectives,* vol. 13 (1972), pp. 1-10. See also Wilhelm G. Solheim II, "Neue Befunde zur späten Prähistorie Südostasiens und ihre Interpretation. Ein Blick auf R. von Heine-Gelderns 'L'Art Prébouddhique de la Chine et de L'Asie du Sud-Est et son influence en Océanie' vierzig Jahre später," *Saeculum,* vol. 31, pts. 3 and 4 (1980), pp. 275-409.

4. Wilhelm G. Solheim II, "Reworking Southeast Asian prehistory," *Paideuma: Mitteilungen zur Kulturkunde,* vol. 15 (1969), p. 126.

5. Hallum L. Movius, Jr., "The Lower Palaeolithic cultures of southern and eastern Asia." *Transactions of the American Philosophical Society*, New Series, vol. 38, pt. 4 (Philadelphia, 1948), pp. 325-420; "Palaeolithic archaeology in southern and eastern Asia, exclusive of India," *Journal of World History*, vol. 2, no. 2 (1955), pp. 257-282, and no. 3, pp. 520-553; "Introduction" to Special Palaeolithic Issue of *Asian Perspectives*, vol. 2, no. 2 (1958), pp. xi-xiv; Tom Harrisson, "Tampan: Malaysia's Palaeolithic reconsidered," *Modern Quarternary Research in Southeast Asia*, vol. 1 (1975), pp. 53-70.

6. Ann Sieveking, "The Palaeolithic industry of Kota Tampan, Perak, Northwestern Malaya," *Asian Perspectives*, vol. 2, no. 2 (1958), pp. 91-102, especially pp. 92-93 and 99.

7. Madeleine Colani, "L'âge de la pierre dans la province de Hoa-Binh, Tonkin," *Mémoires du Service Géologique de l'Indochine*, vol. 14, no. 1 (Hanoi, 1927); "La civilisation hoabinhienne extrême-orientale," *Bulletin de la Société Préhistorique Française*, vol. 36 (1939), pp. 170-174; John M. Matthews, *A checklist of "Hoabinhian" sites excavated in Malaya 1860-1939* (Singapore, 1961); *The Hoabinhian in Southeast Asia and elsewhere*. Ph.D. dissertation submitted to the Australian National University (Canberra, 1964); and "A review of the 'Hoabinhian' in Indo-China," *Asian Perspectives*, vol. 9 (1966), pp. 86-95. Louis Bezacier, *Le Viêt-nam: Part I: De la préhistoire à la fin de l'occupation chinoise* (Paris, 1972), pp. 25-32. This is vol. 2 of *Asie du Sud-Est*, under the direction of George Coedès and Jean Boisselier, which itself constitutes part I of *Manuel d'Archéologie d'Extrême-Orient*, prepared under the direction of Henri Hierche. The term *Bacsonien* (after the limestone upland of Bắc-sơn in Tong-King) has been used by French-speaking archeologists to denote artifactual assemblages in which stone tools exhibit a higher degree of grinding and polishing than that customarily associated with the Hoabinhian: cf. H. Mansuy, "Stations préhistoriques dans les cavernes du massif calcaire de Bắc-sơn (Tonkin)," *Mémoires du Service Géologique de L'Indochine*, vol. 11, pt. 2 (1924); "Nouvelles découvertes dans les cavernes du massif calcaire de Bắc-sơn (Tonkin)," *loc. cit.*, vol. 12, pt. 1 (1925); "Stations préhistoriques de Keo-phay, Khắc-Kiệm, Lai-ta et Bang Mac dans le massif calcaire de Bắc-sơn (Tonkin)," *loc. cit.*, vol. 12, pt. 2 (1925); Bezacier, *Le Viêt-nam*, pp. 32-36; Mansuy and Madeleine Colani, "Contribution à l'étude de la préhistoire de l'Indochine: VII. Néolithique inférieure (Bacsonien) et néolithique supérieure dans le Haut-Tonkin (dernières recherches), avec la description des crânes du gisement de Lang-Cuam," *Mémoires du Service Géologique de l'Indochine*, vol. 12, no. 3 (1925), pp. 1-54; R. W. Brandt, "The Hoabinhian of Sumatra: some remarks," *Modern Quaternary Research in Southeast Asia*, vol. 2 (1976), pp. 49-52.

8. George Coedès, *Les états hindouisés d'Indochine et d'Indonésie* (3rd edition, Paris, 1964), p. 27. Cp. also D. G. E. Hall, *A history of South-East Asia* (London, 1955), p. 8; Victor Goloubew, "L'âge du bronze au Tonkin et dans le Nord-Annam," *Bulletin de l'Ecole Française d'Extrême-Orient*, vol. 29, pt. 1 (1929), pp. 1-46; H. R. van Heekeren, *The Bronze-Iron Age of Indonesia* ('s-Gravenhage, 1958); Prince John Loewenstein, "The origin of the Malayan Metal Age," *Journal of the Malayan Branch of the Royal Asiatic Society*, vol. 29, pt. 2 (1956), pp. 5-78.

9. Coedès is here quoting Jean Przyluski in Sylvain Lévi (ed.), *Indochine*, vol. 1 (Paris, 1931), p. 54.

10. Nicholaas J. Krom, *Hindoe-javaansche geschiedenis* (2nd edition, The Hague, 1931), pp. 47-48. In formulating these cultural inventories both Coedès and Krom were heavily indebted to J. Brandes, "Een jayapattra of acte van eene rechterlijke uitspraak van Çaka 849," *Tijdschrift voor Indische Taal-, Land- en Volkenkunde*, vol. 32 (1889), pp. 98-149.

11. A bronze model from Shih-chai Shan in Yün-nan represents a type of horizontal loom that is still encountered widely in Southeast Asia. For reference see note 70.

Of Chiefs and Chiefdoms 97

12. Here I am following Thomas S. Kuhn's interpretation of paradigm transformation: *The structure of scientific revolutions* (Second edition, Chicago, 1970), esp. chap. 6.

13. Geoffrey Benjamin, "Prehistory and ethnology in Southeast Asia: some new ideas." Working Paper no. 25, Sociology Department, University of Singapore (1974). Subsequently, but apparently independently of Benjamin's work, Karl L. Hutterer has discerned in the archeological record "two separate processes of culture change, intertwined in many ways. One of these processes may be termed a 'vertical' transformation, a change in subsistence form from a lower to a higher level of intensity and from a lesser to a greater degree of specialization, or a change from a lower to a higher level of sociopolitical complexity, i.e. an evolutionary change. The other may be characterized as a 'lateral' transformation, a change that remains on the same level of 'phylogenetic' development, akin to speciation in biology." Professor Hutterer believes that, within certain constraints, "it is still possible to construct phases of Southeast Asian cultural history. These phases cannot, however, be based on specific technological, political, or racial developments. Rather, they must be conceived on a more abstract level and should express the change in the organization of the total human environment of the area" [Hutterer, "An evolutionary approach to the Southeast Asian cultural sequence," *Current Anthropology*, vol. 17, no. 2 (1976), pp. 221-242: the quotations are from, respectively pp. 226 and 227.] In contrast to Hutterer's optimism, Professor Donn T. Bayard believes that "the time is not ripe for the formulation of an overall cultural sequence for Southeast Asia as a whole": Comment on Hutterer's paper, *ibid.*, p. 229. Cf. also H. R. van Heekeren, "Chronology of the Indonesian prehistory," *Modern Quaternary Research in Southeast Asia*, vol. 1 (1975), pp. 47-51.

14. See, for instance, Fredrik Barth, *Ethnic groups and boundaries* (London, 1969), *passim*.

15. Ian C. Glover, "Late Stone Age traditions in South-East Asia" in Norman Hammond (ed.), *South Asian archaeology. Papers from the First International Conference of South Asian Archaeologists held in the University of Cambridge* (London, 1973), pp. 51-65, and "The late prehistoric period in Indonesia" in Smith and Watson, *Early South East Asia*, pp. 167-184.

16. Bennet Bronson, "The late prehistory and early history of Central Thailand with special reference to Chansen," in Smith and Watson, *Early South East Asia*, pp. 315-336; Bronson and George F. Dales, "Excavations at Chansen, Thailand, 1968 and 1969: a preliminary report," *Asian Perspectives*, vol. 15 (1973), p. 26. Magdalene von Dewall has made much the same point in connection with Neolithic communities around the Tien Lake in Yün-nan ["The Tien culture of South-west China," *Antiquity*, vol. 41 (1967), p. 10] while H. David Tuggle, Karl L. Hutterer, and Warren E. Peterson have encountered similarly individualized technological traditions in, respectively, southwestern Samar and northeastern Luzon [Tuggle and Hutterer, *Archaeology of the Sohoton area, southwestern Samar, Philippines*, Leyte-Samar Studies no. 6; Peterson, "Summary report on two sites from northern Luzon," *Archaeology and Physical Anthropology in Oceania*, vol. 9 (1973), pp. 26-35. Cp. also Solheim's comments on the likely course of events during the Late Hoabinhian in "Reworking Southeast Asian prehistory," p. 132, and Donn T. Bayard's more specific remarks on northeast Thailand in his evaluation of Hutterer's paper in *Current Anthropology*, vol. 17, no. 2 (1976), p. 229.

17. R. B. Smith has prepared a useful summary of carbon-14 datings falling between 5000 B.C. and A.D. 1000 in "A check-list of published Carbon-14 datings from South East Asia," in Smith and Watson, *Early South East Asia*, pp. 493-507. Thirty-six radiocarbon dates from northern Vietnamese sites were published in *Khảo Cổ Học*, No. 17 (1976), pp. 94-96 and a more complete list was incorporated in William Meacham, "Continuity and local evolution in the Neolithic of South China," *Current Anthropology*, vol. 18, no. 3 (1977), pp. 419-440.

18. Wilhelm G. Solheim II, "Early bronze in northeastern Thailand," *Current Anthropology*, vol. 9, no. 1 (1968), pp. 59-62: also in *Silpākọn*, vol. 11, no. 4 (1967), pp. 44-48 [English version] and 49-60 [Thai version]; Donn T. Bayard, "Excavation at Non Nok Tha, northeastern Thailand, 1968: an interim report," *Asian Perspectives*, vol. 13 (1972), pp. 109-143; Bayard, "Early Thai bronze: analysis and new dates," *Science*, vol. 176 (1972), pp. 1411-1412; Bayard, "An early indigenous bronze technology in northeast Thailand; its implications for the prehistory of East Asia," *Proceedings of the 28th International Congress of Orientalists, Canberra, 6-12 January 1971* (Canberra). Inconsistencies in the sequence of C-14 and thermoluminescence dates for Non Nok Tha are evaluated by Bayard, "The chronology of prehistoric metallurgy in north-east Thailand: *Śilābhūmi* or *Śamṛddhabhūmi?*" in Smith and Watson, *Early South East Asia*, pp. 15-32. The nearest source of suitable copper ores to Non Nok Tha would seem to have been deposits in the valley of the Lam Pa Sak, 130 or so kilometers to the west: Richard Pittioni in Wilhelm G. Solheim II, "Northern Thailand, Southeast Asia, and world prehistory," *Asian Perspectives*, vol. 13 (1972), pp. 158-161. Note: In the reports of the 1964 and 1965 excavations the site subsequently known as Non Nok Tha was referred to as Nam Phọng 7. Cf. also Davidson's conclusion to his study of the Phùng-nguyên Culture: ". . . the astounding implication remains that a knowledge of bronze-casting existed in Viêt-Nam in the early second or late third millennium B.C." ("Archaeology in northern Viêt-Nam since 1954," p. 102).

19. Edmond Saurin, "Nouvelles observations préhistoriques à l'est de Saigon," *Bulletin de la Société des Etudes Indochinoises*, New Series, vol. 43, pt. 1 (1968), p. 3. See also Roland Mourer, "Laang Spean and the prehistory of Cambodia," *Modern Quaternary Research in Southeast Asia*, vol. 3 (1977), pp. 29-56.

20. Bennet Bronson and M. Han, "A thermoluminescence series from Thailand," *Antiquity*, vol. 46 (1972), pp. 12-15; Bronson and Dales, "Excavations at Chansen," *passim*; Wilhelm G. Solheim II, "Northern Thailand, Southeast Asia, and world prehistory," *Asian Perspectives*, vol. 13 (1972), p. 154. Iron has also been reported from 5th-century B.C. levels at Taungthaman in Upper Burma: Janice Stargardt, *L'Annuaire de L'Ecole Pratique des Hautes Etudes*, IVe Section (1978).

21. Chester F. Gorman, "Hoabinhian: a pebble-tool complex with early plant associations in Southeast Asia," *Science*, vol. 163 (1969), pp. 671-673; "Excavations at Spirit Cave, North Thailand: some interim interpretations," *Asian Perspectives*, vol. 13 (1972), pp. 79-107; "The Hoabinhian and after: subsistence patterns in Southeast Asia during the late Pleistocene and early Recent periods," *World Archaeology*, vol. 2, no. 3 (1971), pp. 300-320.

22. Carl O. Sauer, *Agricultural origins and dispersals*. Bowman Memorial Lectures, Series II (New York, 1952), chap. 2.

23. Bayard, "Excavation at Non Nok Tha," p. 135; I. W. Mabbett, "The 'Indianization' of Southeast Asia: reflections on the prehistoric sources," *Journal of Southeast Asian Studies*, vol. 8, no. 1 (1977), p. 8, citing a personal communication from Wilhelm G. Solheim II. Note also C. F. W. Higham, A. Kijngam, and B. F. J. Manly, "An analysis of prehistoric canid remains from Thailand," *Journal of Archaeological Science*, vol. 7 (1980), pp. 149-165, where it is suggested that the domestic dog was introduced into northeast Thailand by the first lowland, wet-*padi* farmers, by whom it was apparently butchered for food. In this connection it will be recalled that the dog is missing in Benedict's Austro-Thai lexicon (p. 57 above).

24. It is noteworthy, though, that Gorman, whose excavations at Spirit Cave in North Thailand have provided much of the information on which the new construction is based, interprets the development of this technological complex, or more accurately nexus of complexes as implying a movement of settlement downward from restricted upland valleys to more extensive lowland

plains. ["The Hoabinhian and after," pp. 314-316]. This reading of events is not fundamentally different in its implications, radically at variance in its chronology though it be, from Heine-Geldern's postulation of the Quadrangular Adze Culture (*Vierkantbeilkultur*) as carrying several of the same technologies from the uplands of continental Southeast Asia into the lowland and archipelagic realms ["Prehistoric research in the Netherlands Indies," pp. 138-142].

25. Wilhelm G. Solheim II, "Reworking Southeast Asian prehistory," *Paideuma: Mitteilungen zur Kulturkunde*, vol. 15 (1969), pp. 126-139, esp. p. 137. The schema is revised and amended in the same author's "Northern Thailand, Southeast Asia, and world prehistory," *Asian Perspectives*, vol. 13 (1972), pp. 145-162. Cf. also "The 'new look' of Southeast Asian prehistory," *Journal of the Siam Society*, vol. 60 (1972), pp. 1-20; "Prehistoric archaeology in eastern mainland Southeast Asia and the Philippines," *Asian Perspectives*, vol. 13 (1972), pp. 47-58. The recent developments in Southeast Asian archeology on which Solheim's reconstituted periodization is based are compendiously summarized in the regional and topical reports included in the successive issues of *Asian Perspectives* (subtitled *A journal of archaeology and prehistory of Asia and the Pacific*), 1957-, and most recently by Donn Bayard, "The roots of Indochinese civilisation: recent developments in the prehistory of Southeast Asia," *Pacific Affairs*, vol. 53 (1980), pp. 89-114. Cf. also Solheim, "Prehistoric pottery of Southeast Asia" in Noel Barnard (ed.), *Early Chinese art and its possible influence in the Pacific basin*, vol. 2 (New York, 1972), pp. 507-532. A division of Philippine prehistory into the four phases of Germinal, Formative, Incipient, and Emergent that has been proposed by F. Landa Jocano does little more than foist new names on traditional periods: "Beyer's theory on Filipino prehistory and culture: an alternative approach to the problem," in M. D. Zamora (ed.), *Studies in Philippine anthropology* (Quezon City, 1967), pp. 128-150.

26. See, for example, the developing thought of Paul K. Benedict as expressed in: "Thai, Kadai, and Indonesian: a new alignment in Southeastern Asia," *American Anthropologist*, vol. 44 (1942), pp. 576-601; "Austro-Thai," *Behavior Science Notes*, vol. 1 (1966), pp. 227-261; "Austro-Thai studies: 1, Material culture" and "2, Kinship terms," *loc. cit.*, vol. 2 (1967), pp. 203-244; "Austro-Thai studies: 3, Austro-Thai and Chinese," *loc. cit.*, vol. 2 (1967), pp. 275-336. These papers have been reprinted, together with additional material, in *Austro-Thai: language and culture, with a glossary of roots* (New Haven, Conn., 1975). Also the papers in Norman H. Zide (ed.), *Studies in comparative Austroasiatic linguistics* (The Hague, 1966); Otto C. Dahl, "Proto-Austronesian," *Scandinavian Institute of Asian Studies Monograph Series* no. 15 (Copenhagen, 1973); André G. Haudricourt, "The limits and connections of Austroasiatic in the northeast," *Indo-Iranian Monograph* no. 5 (The Hague, 1966). Cf. also the evaluations of Benedict's thesis by Soren Egerod, William J. Gedney, André G. Haudricourt, James Matisoff, and Harry L. Shorto in *Computational Analysis of Asian and African Languages*, vol. 6 (1978).

27. In the following summary I have incorporated a few interpretations not included in Solheim's own statements of his schema, as well as slightly shifting some of his emphases.

28. Cf. Robert B. Fox, "Excavations in the Tabon Caves and some problems in Philippine chronology," in Mario D. Zamora (ed.), *Studies in Philippine anthropology* (Manila, 1967), pp. 88-116; Tom Harrisson, "The Great Cave of Niah: a preliminary report on Bornean prehistory," *Man*, vol. 57 (1957), pp. 161-166, and "New archaeological results from Niah Caves, Sarawak," *Man*, vol. 59 (1959), pp. 1-8; H. R. van Heekeren and Eigil Knuth, *Sai-Yok: Stone Age settlements in Kanchanaburi Province* (Copenhagen, 1967); Wilhelm G. Solheim II and Chester F. Gorman, "Archaeological salvage program; northeastern Thailand, first season," *The Journal of the Siam Society*, vol. 54 (1966), pp. 111-209; Chester F. Gorman, "Hoabinhian: a pebble-tool complex with early plant associations in Southeast Asia," *Science*, vol. 163 (1969), pp. 671-673; P. I. Boriskovsky, "Basic problems of the prehistoric archaeology of Vietnam," *Asian Perspectives*, vol. 9 (1968),

pp. 83-85. In continental Southeast Asia the culture (or cultures) responsible for these stone-flake industries co-existed with Chopper-Chopping Tool cultures, but in Borneo and the Philippines, on the evidence currently available, it (or they) may have been the only culture(s) present at the time.

29. Gorman, "The Hoabinhian and after," p. 315. Cf. also Wilhelm G. Solheim II, "An earlier agricultural revolution," *Scientific American,* vol. 226 (1972), pp. 56-59. A reasonably close present-day analogue of the broad-spectrum hunting, fishing, and gathering ecotype discerned by Gorman in his archeological reconstruction from North Thailand could be that of the Tasaday in the interior of Mindanao, though these latter people do not hunt in the conventional sense of that term, and have acquired some familiarity with trapping only in recent years: Carlos A. Fernandez II and Frank Lynch, "The Tasaday: cave-dwelling food gatherers of South Cotabato, Mindanao," *Philippine Sociological Review,* vol. 20 (1972), pp. 279-313. Moreover, linguistic and ethnographic evidence suggests that the Tasaday constitute a reversion from a more complex to a simpler culture, having split off from a neighboring group no more than 500 years ago [F. Eggan, personal communication].

30. Wendell C. Bennett, "The Peruvian Co-tradition," in Bennett (ed.), *A reappraisal of Peruvian archaeology.* Memoir of the Society of American Archaeologists No. 4 (Menasha, Wisc., 1948), pp. 1-7. Cf. also Alfred L. Kroeber, *Peruvian archaeology in 1942.* Viking Fund Publications in Anthropology no. 4 (New York, 1944), p. 111. The applicability of the area co-tradition concept to East Asia, specifically to Southwest China, was first suggested by Kenneth Starr, "Comments on Kwang-chih Chang's 'Prehistoric and early historic culture horizons and traditions in South China'," *Current Anthropology,* vol. 5 (1964), p. 396.

31. Solheim, "Reworking Southeast Asian prehistory," p. 132.

32. Sauer, *Agricultural origins and dispersals,* pp. 24-27.

33. Notched pebbles on Late-Hoabinhian sites are commonly interpreted as sinkers for fishing nets. For a discussion of bark-cloth beaters see G. de G. Sieveking, "The distribution of stone bark-cloth beaters in prehistoric times," *Journal of the Malayan Branch of the Royal Asiatic Society,* vol. 29, pt. 3 (1956), pp. 78-85.

34. Gorman, "Hoabinhian: a pebble-tool complex," *passim,* and "The Hoabinhian and after," *passim.* The plant genera recovered from the site (Spirit Cave) were *Aleurites, Areca, Canarium, Cucumis, Lagenaria, Madhuca, Piper, Prunus, Pisum* or *Raphia, Terminalia, Trapa,* and *Vicia* or *Phaseolus.* The interpretation of Gorman's evidence presented here is that proposed by David R. Harris, "The prehistory of tropical agriculture: an ethnoecological model," in Colin Renfrew (ed.), *The explanation of culture change* (London, 1973), pp. 409-410.

35. Ian C. Glover, *Excavations in Timor: a study of economic change and culture continuity in prehistory.* Unpublished Ph.D. thesis, the Australian National University (Canberra, 1970), appendix 10, pp. 46-50. The plants in question, which were identified by D. E. Yen, included *Aleurites, Areca, Celtis, Lagenaria, Piper,* and *Arachis.*

36. Whether these early horticultural explorations were conducted in polycultural, more or less permanent garden plots adjacent to dwellings or in swidden clearings farther afield (both of which constitute manipulations of generalized ecosystems in the interests of human needs) is still a matter for debate. Solheim apparently assumes that swidden preceded fixed-plot cultivation. David Harris, on the other hand, makes a strong case for the belief that man's earliest system of proto-cultivation was developed in small domestic gardens, which he sees as affording both optimal conditions for the care of individual plants and a genetic environment especially suited to the selection and fixation of desirable characteristics in domestic variants ["The prehistory

of tropical agriculture," pp. 405-406 and 410]. For further disucssion of the role of vegecultural systems in traditional Southeast Asia consult I. H. Burkill, "The rise and decline of the greater yam in the service of man," *Advancement of Science*, vol. 7 (1951), pp. 443-448; J. Barrau, "L'humide et le sec. An essay on ethnobiological adaptation to contrastive environments in the Indo-Pacific area," *Journal of the Polynesian Society*, vol. 74 (1965), pp. 329-346; H. Li, "The origin of cultivated plants in Southeast Asia," *Economic Botany*, vol. 24 (1970), pp. 3-19. Note also I. H. Burkill's demonstration that names for yams constitute a basic stratum in virtually all the languages of the Malaysian world, which implies that they were domesticated during an early phase in the evolution of the parent language: "A list of Oriental vernacular names of the genus *Dioscorea*," *Gardens Bulletin, Straits Settlements*, vol. 3 (1924), pp. 131-244.

37. Harris, "The prehistory of tropical agriculture," p. 410. Several authors, including Sauer [*Agricultural origins*, pp. 27-28], have followed A. G. Haudricourt and Louis Hédin in suggesting that wet *padi* originated as a weed in taro fields [*L'homme et les plantes cultivées* (Paris, 1943), p. 154]. Others, including Te-Tzu Chang, see it as having been a plant of undisturbed swamps ["The rice cultures," *Philosophical Transactions of the Royal Society of London*, Series B, vol. 275 (1976), p. 145]. Cf. also Te-Tzu Chang, "Rice," in N. W. Simmons, *Evolution of crop plants* (London, 1976), pp. 98-104, and R. D. Hill, "On the origins of domesticated rice," *Journal of Oriental Studies*, vol. 14, no. 1 (1976), pp. 35-44.

38. See Note 23 above.

39. The claims by B. Klatt ["Entstehung der Haustiere," *Handbuch der Verebungswissenschaft* (Berlin, 1927)] and Sauer [*Agricultural origins*, p. 31] that all domestic pigs are derived from the Southeast Asian *Sus scrofa vittatus*, H. Boie has not been confirmed archeologically, although these animals are mentioned by C. F. W. Higham, A. Kijngam, and D. T. Bayard as occurring in their excavations in northeast Thailand, perhaps as early as 3000 B.C.

40. See note 18 above. For a late ("not much earlier than the seventh century [A.D.]") metal-working site, see Tom Harrisson and Stanley J. O'Connor, *Excavations of the prehistoric iron industry in West Borneo*, 2 vols. (Ithaca, N.Y., 1969). In another paper Harrisson concludes that the introduction of iron "produced technological acceleration throughout Borneo, rather than strictly speaking, a technological revolution": "The prehistory of Borneo," *Asian Perspectives*, vol. 13 (1970), p. 36. Cf. also Wilhelm G. Solheim II, *The archaeology of the Central Philippines: a study chiefly of the Iron Age and its relationships*. Monograph of the National Institute of Science and Technology no. 10 (Manila, 1964).

41. Harris, "The prehistory of tropical agriculture," p. 411. Cf. also Kwang-Chih Chang, "The beginnings of agriculture in the Far East," *Antiquity*, vol. 44 (1970), pp. 183-184.

42. See Note 26 above. Benedict's work has recently been complemented in archipelagic Southeast Asia by Robert Blust's investigations of Proto-Austronesian vocabulary, which apparently included terms for "rice plant", "husked rice", "cooked rice", and "millet", as well as "garden/field", "fallow land", and the verbs "to weed" and "to winnow": "Austronesian culture history: some linguistic inferences and their relations to the archaeological record," *World Archaeology*, vol. 8, no. 1 (1976), pp. 19-43.

43. Benedict, "Austro-Thai and Chinese," p. 323; p. 123 of the HRAF reprint.

44. Benedict, "Austro-Thai and Chinese," pp. 316-317; pp. 116-117 of the HRAF reprint. On the evidence provided, "sweep" would seem to be more appropriate than "oar" in the schedule of loans (p. 311 in the original, p. 111 in the reprint), and "market" is almost certainly too precise (as well as misleading) a term for the types of exchange involved (*Austro-Thai*, pp. 248-249, 282).

45. Benedict, *Austro-Thai*, pp. 139-140, 185-186; Andrew Pawley and Roger Green, "Dating the dispersal of the Oceanic Languages," *Oceanic Linguistics*, vol. 12 (1973), pp. 1-67.

46. Robert von Heine-Geldern, "Die Megalithen Südostasiens und ihre Bedeutung für die Klärung der Megalithenfrage in Europa und Polynesien," *Anthropos*, vol. 23 (1928), pp. 276-315. Cf. also the same author's "Der Megalithkomplex auf der Philippineninsel Luzon," *Anthropos*, vol. 24 (1929), pp. 318-321; and "Das Megalithproblem," *Beiträge Österreichs zur Erforschung der Vergangenheit und Kulturgeschichte der Menschheit — Symposium 1958*, Wartenstein (Wien, 1959), pp. 162-182; H. H. E. Loofs, *Elements of the Megalithic complex in Southeast Asia: an annotated bibliography* (Canberra, 1967); Tom Harrisson and Stanley J. O'Connor, *Gold and megalithic activity in prehistoric and recent West Borneo*, 2 vols. (Ithaca, N.Y., 1971); Tom Harrisson, "The prehistory of Borneo," *Asian Perspectives*, vol. 13 (1972), pp. 26-27.

47. R. [von] Heine-Geldern, "Prehistoric research in the Netherlands Indies," in Pieter Honig and Frans Verdoorn (eds.), *Science and scientists in the Netherlands Indies* (New York, 1945), pp. 129-167.

48. Robert von Heine-Geldern, "Ein Beitrag zur Chronologie des Neolithikums in Südostasiens," in W. Koppers (ed.), *Festschrift, Publication d'Hommage offerte au P. W. Schmidt* (Wien, 1928), pp. 809-843; "Urheimat und früheste Wanderungen der Austronesier," *Anthropos*, vol. 27 (1932), pp. 543-619; "Vorgeschichtliche Grundlagen der Kolonialindischen Kunst," *Wiener Beiträge zur Kunst- und Kulturgeschichte Asiens*, vol. 8 (1934), pp. 5-40; "Prehistoric research in Indonesia," *Annual Bibliography of Indian Archaeology*, vol. 9 (1945), pp. 26-38. For a more recent discussion of Southeast Asian adzes see Roger Duff, *Stone adzes of Southeast Asia*. Canterbury Museum Bulletin no. 3 (Christchurch, N.Z., 1970).

49. A. N. J. Th. à Th. van der Hoop, *Megalithic remains in South Sumatra* (Zutphen, 1932). The typology of bronze drums referred to was proposed by F. Heger, *Alte Metalltrommeln aus Südost-Asien* (Leipzig, 1902). It has since been somewhat modified. Cf. also Robert von Heine-Geldern, "Bedeutung und Herkunft der ältesten hinterindischen Metalltrommeln," *Asia Major*, vol. 8 (1932), pp. 519-537; Prince John Loewenstein, "The origin of the Malayan Metal Age," *Journal of the Malayan Branch of the Royal Asiatic Society*, vol. 29, pt. 2 (1956), pp. 5-78. Recently Anthony H. Christie has noted that the typology of the sites investigated by van der Hoop is not wholly consistent with Heine-Geldern's criteria for discriminating the Older from the Younger Megalithic, and has urged a re-analysis of the relevant materials ["The megalithic problem in South East Asia," in Smith and Watson, *Early South East Asia*, pp. 242-252]; but note also I. C. Glover, B. Bronson, and D. T. Bayard, "Comment on 'megaliths' in South East Asia" in *loc. cit.*, pp. 253-254.

50. Summarized by H. R. van Heekeren, *The Bronze-Iron Age of Indonesia* ('s-Gravenhage, 1958), chap. 2. Generally speaking, van Heekeren follows Heine-Geldern's interpretation of the Southeast Asian megaliths, though he is dubious as to the association of the Older Megalithic with the Quadrangular Adze Culture on the grounds that "no megalith of a neolithic age has been found either in Indo-China or in Indonesia" (p. 45). The truth is that for no megalith has an absolute date been established. Cf. also W. Kaudern, *Megalithic finds in Central Celebes* (Privately printed, 1938). See also Tom Harrisson, "Megalithic evidences in East Malaysia:— an introductory summary," *Journal of the Malaysian Branch of the Royal Asiatic Society*, vol. 46, pt. 1 (1973), pp. 123-139 and "The Megalithic in East Malaysia — II," *loc. cit.* vol. 47, pt. 1 (1974), pp. 105-109.

51. Madeleine Colani, *Mégalithes du Haut-Laos*. Publications de l'Ecole Française d'Extrême-Orient, nos. 25 and 26 (Paris, 1935). See also Wilhelm G. Solheim II, "Jar burial in the Babuyan and Batanes islands, and its relationship to jar burial elsewhere in the Far East," *Philippine Journal of Science*, vol. 84, pt. 1 (1960), pp. 115-148.

52. Henri Parmentier, "Vestiges mégalithiques à Xuân-lôc," *Bulletin de l'Ecole Française d'Extrême-Orient,* vol. 28, nos. 3-4 (1928), pp. 479-485; Emile Gaspardone, "The tomb of Xuân-lôc," *Journal of the Greater India Society,* vol. 4 (1937), pp. 26-35.

53. I. H. N. Evans, "On slab-built graves in Perak," *Journal of the Federated Malay States' Museums,* vol. 12, pt. 5 (1928), pp. 111-9; "A further slab-built grave at Sungkai, Perak," *loc. cit.,* vol. 15 (1931), pp. 63-64; M. C. ff. Sheppard, "Batu hidop — megaliths in Malacca Territory," *Bulletin of the Raffles Museum,* series B, no. 1 (1936), pp. 61-71; B. A. V. Peacock, "The later prehistory of the Malay Peninsula," in Smith and Watson, *Early South East Asia,* pp. 199-214.

54. Bernard Philippe Groslier, *The art of Indochina* (London, 1962), pp. 30-31.

55. Groslier, *The art of Indochina,* p. 31.

56. Groslier, *The art of Indochina,* p. 31.

57. Heine-Geldern: cf. references in note 46; H. G. Quaritch Wales, *The mountain of god* (London, 1953), pp. 135-142; *Prehistory and religion in South-East Asia* (London, 1957), pp. 128-129. It may be noted that over thirty years ago C. von Fürer-Haimendorf attributed the megalithic culture of Northeast India to speakers of Austroasiatic languages: "Megalithic ritual among the Gadabas and Bondos of Orissa," *Journal of the Royal Asiatic Society of Bengal: Letters,* vol. 9 (1943), p. 177. The distribution of shouldered axes is conveniently depicted in H. R. van Heekeren, *The stone age of Indonesia* ('s-Gravenhage, 1957), p. 122, and Anthony Christie, "The sea-locked lands," in Stuart Piggott (ed.), *The dawn of civilization* (London and New York, 1961), p. 292.

58. Essentially this point of view is advanced by, *int. al.,* Heine-Geldern, "Prehistoric research in the Netherlands Indies," p. 149; Wales, *Prehistory and religion in South-East Asia,* pp. 28-29, 46-47, and *passim;* van Heekeren, *The Bronze-Iron Age of Indonesia,* p. 45; Wheatley, *Impressions of the Malay Peninsula in ancient times* (Singapore, 1964), pp. 81-82; and, for India, Christoph von Fürer-Haimendorf, "The problem of megalithic cultures in Middle India," *Man in India,* vol. 25 (1945). Cp. also Madeleine Colani, *Emploi de la pierre en des temps reculés: Annam — Indonésie — Assam.* Publication des Amis du Vieux Hué (Hanoi, 1940), p. 35: "Les forces qui émanent des âmes des princes défunts servent à la fertilité du pays."

59. E.g., G. Hawkins, *Stonehenge decoded* (London, 1970); A. W. Macdonald, "Une note sur les mégalithes tibétains," *Journal Asiatique,* vol. 241 (1953), pp. 63-76; J. Maringer, "Gräber und Steindenkmäler in der Mongolei," *Monumenta Serica,* vol. 14 (1955), pp. 303-339. Christie's suggestion is advanced in the most recent evaluation of the status of megalithic studies: "The megalithic problem in South East Asia," p. 251.

60. Groslier, *The art of Indochina,* p. 30.

61. For a conspectus of Chinese sources relating specifically to the early history of the Malay Peninsula but more generally to Southeast Asia as a whole, consult Wheatley, "Chinese sources for the history of the Malay Peninsula in early times," in K. G. Tregonning, *Malaysian historical sources. A series of essays on historical material mainly in Malaysia on Malaysia* (Singapore, 1962), pp. 1-9. For Indonesia alone, and then mostly in later times, see Tjan Tjoe Som, "Chinese historical sources and historiography," in Soedjatmoko, Mohammad Ali, G. J. Resink, and G. McT. Kahin, *An introduction to Indonesian historiography* (Ithaca, N.Y., 1965), pp. 194-205.

62. For a brief summary of Indian sources containing references to early Southeast Asia see chap. 7 below.

63. See pp. 439-462 below. For the later phases of the process of urban genesis another corpus of foreign materials is of considerable importance, namely that provided by Arabo-Persian records. Though those relating to Southeast Asia were all compiled subsequent to the middle of the 9th century A.D., several of them incorporate material dating from earlier centuries. Details in Wheatley, "Arabo-Persian sources for the history of the Malay Peninsula in ancient times," in Tregonning, *Malaysian historical sources,* pp. 10-19.

64. Nan-Yüeh 南越 was a more or less literary name already in use during the later Chou period to denote the most southerly of the aboriginal peoples known to the Chinese. Subsequently it was adopted as the formal appellation of a quasi-autonomous territory which included most of what are today the provinces of Kuang-tung and Kuang-hsi, together with the delta of the Red River (see p. 357 below).

65. For the general context of early Chinese ecological adaptations to which the information in *Shih Chi* should be related, see Wolfram Eberhard, *Kultur und Siedlung der Randvölker Chinas: C. Die Randvölker des Sudens.* Supplement to *T'oung Pao,* vol. 36 (1942), pp. 176-372.

66. *Shih Chi,* chüan 116, f. 1 recto. Cp. also: "From Tien (**D'ien*) northwards the chieftains are to be counted by tens;" "From Sui (? S*i*wər) northeastwards the chieftains are to be counted by tens;" "From Tso (**Tsâk*) northeastwards . . . etc. [*loc. cit.,* ff. 1 recto - 2 recto].

67. *Shih Chi,* chüan 116, f. 1 verso. In Han times the graph 邑 formally denoted the seat of a subprefecture, but in Chinese writings about non-Chinese peoples was often also used for the principal settlement in a chiefdom, or even for any important village that appeared to exert some degree of control over others.

68. Wu Chin-ting, Tseng Chao-yü, and Wang Chieh-chen 吳金鼎 曾昭燏 王介忱 *Yün-nan Ts'ang-Erh ching k'ao-ku pao-kao* 雲南蒼洱境考古 報告 (Li-chuang, 1942). The relatively high density of population implied by the Chinese text is reflected in the close spacing of settlements revealed by archeology, those in the vicinity of the Tien Lake seldom being more than 6 kilometers apart, while the largest of the midden sites covers more than 65,000 sq. ft. to a depth of 3 meters. For a succinct summary of the archeology of Yün-nan see Judith M. Treistman, *The early cultures of Szechwan and Yunnan*: Cornell University East Asia Papers no. 3 (Ithaca, N.Y., 1974), chap. 4. Cf. also Magdalene von Dewall, "The Tien Culture of South-west China, "*Antiquity*, vol. 41 (1967), pp. 8-21; Michèle Pirazzoli-t'Serstevens, *La civilisation du royaume de Dian à l'époque Han d'après le matériel exhumé à Shizhai Shan (Yunnan),* Publication de l'Ecole Française d'Extrême-Orient, vol. 94 (Paris, 1974), and "The bronze drums of Shizhai shan, their social and ritual significance," in Smith and Watson, *Early South East Asia,* pp. 125-136.

69. Yün-nan Sheng Po-wu-kuan Ch'ou-pei-ch'u 雲南省博物館籌備處 "Chien-ch'uan Hai-men K'ou ku-wen-hua i-chih ch'ing-li chien-pao," *K'ao-ku T'ung-hsün* 劍川海門口古文化遺址清理簡報 考古通訊 no. 6 (1958), pp. 5-12.

70. Yün-nan Chin-ning Shih-chai-Shan ku-mu ch'ün-fa-chüeh pao-kao 雲南晉寧石寨山古墓羣發掘報告 (Peiping, 1959). See also Yün-nan Sheng Po-wu-kuan K'ao-ku Fa-Chüeh-kung tso-tsu 雲南省博物館考古發掘工 作組 "Yün-nan Chin-ning Shih-chai-Shan ku-i-chih chi mu-tsang," *K'ao-ku Hsüeh-pao* 雲南晉寧石寨山古遺址及墓葬考古學報 no. 1 (1956), pp. 43-63. Summary information on other sites in the vicinity of the Tien lake is available in "Yün-nan Tien-Chih chou-wei hsin-shih-ch'i shih-tai i-chih tiao-ch'a chien-pao," *K'ao-ku* 雲南滇池周圍新石器 時代遺址調查簡報考古 no. 1 (1961), pp. 46-49; "Wen-wu kung-tso pao-tao, *Wen Wu* 文物工作報導 文物 no. 1 (1954), p. 99; "Tsai Yün-nan K'ao-ku kung-tso-chung te-tao-te chi-tien jen-shih," *Wen Wu*

在雲南考古工作中得到的幾點認識　文物　no. 11 (1957), pp. 47-48.

71. Illustrated in *Yün-nan Chin-ning Shih-chai-Shan* . . . . plate V; Lê-Văn-Lan, Phạm-Văn-Kỉnh, and Nguyễn-Linh, *Nhữ'ng vết tich đầu-tiên của thờ'i đại đô đồng thầu ở' Viêt-Nam* (Hanoi, 1963), plates 1-6; Bezacier, *Le Viêt-Nam*, p. 175; Olov Janse, "Un groupe de bronzes anciens propres à l'Extrême-Asie Méridionale," *Bulletin of the Museum of Far Eastern Antiquities*, no. 3 (1931), Plate XVII (1), (2), and Figs. 25, 26; Kwang-chih Chang, *The archaeology of ancient China* (New Haven and London, 1963), plate XIV, *et al*. Spades of a similar type have also been found at Đông-sơn and in the vicinity of Sơn-tây. Not infrequently they have been characterized as plow-shares, but both the shape and the hafting are incompatible with such a function. It is just possible that they might qualify as pull-spades, an implement which has been reported in use among the Yao people [Wolfram Eberhard, *Untersuchungen über den Aufbau der Chinesischen Kultur:* II, *Lokalkulturen im alten China:* Part 2, *Die Lokalkulturen des Südens und Ostens*. Monumenta Serica Monograph III (Peking, 1942), p. 76] and from Korea [Paul Leser, *Entstehung und Verbreitung des Pfluges*. Anthropos Bibliothek, Vol. 3, no. 3 (St. Augustin, Germany, 1931), p. 552]. Cf. also Fritz L. Kramer, *Breaking ground. Notes on the distributions of some simple tillage tools*. Sacramento Anthropological Society Paper 5 (Sacramento, California, 1966), p. 88 and Fig. 63. A similar sort of implement, though with a share-like (rather than spade-like) blade was also in use among the Miao of Kuei-chou during the 16th and 17th centuries: cf. *Ming-jen ching-hsieh Miao-Man tʽu*, for which see Fr. Jäger, "Über Chinesische Miaotse-Alben," *Ostasiatische Zeitschrift* (1915/16), S.272; Chang-kong Chiu, "Die Kultur der Miao-tse nach älteren Chinesischen Quellen," *Mitteilungen aus dem Museum für Völkerkunde in Hamburg*, vol. 18 (1937). However, A. G. Haudricourt has pointed out that the hafting of the Đông-sơn implements was probably too weak to have withstood the stress of traction by either man or animal [Haudricourt and Jean Bruhnes-Delamarre, *L'homme et la charrue à travers le monde* (Paris, 1955), p. 88]. The first to identify these implements as spades (*pelles* in the author's language) was Victor Goloubew, "L'âge du bronze au Tonkin et dans le Nord-Annam," *Bulletin de l'Ecole Française d'Extrême-Orient*, vol. 29 (1929), pp. 18-19.

72. Wu Chin-ting *et al.*, *Yün-nan Tsʽang-Erh ching kʽao-ku pao-kao*, pp. 53-54.

73. Wu, *Yün-nan*, pp. 20-22. Recent Chinese practices that may be modern exemplars of those inferred by Wu Chin-ting are described by J. E. Spencer and G. A. Hale, "The origin, nature, and distribution of agricultural terracing," *Pacific Viewpoint*, vol. 2, no. 1 (1961), p. 22.

74. Wu, *Yün-nan*, pp. 53-54.

75. Of these, only five were excavated thoroughly, though test trenches were dug on two others.

76. Wu, *Yün-nan*, p. 74. I have observed localized terracing similar to that reconstructed by Wu Chin-ting associated with house sites of present-day Meo (Miao) tribes in northern Thailand and northern Laos, and such also seem to occur among the Chin peoples of northwestern Burma: *vide* F. K. Lehman, *The structure of Chin society*. Illinois Studies in Anthropology, no. 3 (Urbana, Ill., 1963), caption to fig. 16, p. 71.

77. The *Man Shu* was apparently lost during the Ming dynasty, but the substance of its contents was preserved under discrete rubrics in the *Yung-lo Ta-tien* 永樂大典, a massive encyclopedia compiled under the direction of Hsieh Chin 解縉 (completed 1407). In 1773 an anonymous scholar attempted to reconstitute the original work by recombining the then extant passages which, in accordance with information preserved in the *Library Catalogue* of the *Hsin Tʽang-Shu* 新唐書, he arranged in ten chapters. The reconstituted work was printed by the Wu-ying Tien 武英殿 in 1774. The account of Man (**Mwan*) farming practices is to be found in chüan 7: p. 31 of the *Tsung-shu Chi-chʽeng*

叢書集成 edition.

78. As a result of the vicissitudes mentioned in Note 77, the text of the *Man Shu* is far from perfect: even the Wu-ying Tien editors could not always fathom its corruptions. The account of Man farming is garbled, so that what follows is my interpretation of the original sense of the passage rather than a literal summary of it.

79. Madeleine Colani, "Gravures primitives sur pierre et sur os (stations hoabinhiennes, bacsoniennes)," *Bulletin de l'Ecole Française d'Extrême Orient*, vol. 29 (1929), p. 278.

80. Paul Lévy, "Notes de paléo-ethnologie indochinoise," *Bulletin de l'Ecole Française d'Extrême-Orient*, vol. 37 (1937), p. 482.

81. Louis Bezacier, "Sur la datation d'une représentation primitive de la charrue," *Bulletin de l'Ecole Française d'Extrême-Orient*, vol. 52 (1966-7), pp. 551-556.

82. The precise date of planting is not stated, but the relevant phrase runs: "by the last ten days of the 12th month, shoots are already beginning to appear."

83. Spencer and Hale, "Agricultural terracing," p. 10.

84. *Shui-Ching Chu*, chüan 37, f. 6 verso [Ssŭ-pu Ts'ung-K'an 四部叢刊 edition].

85. *Kau-tśi was established as a commandery of the kingdom of Nan-Yüeh (Note 64 above) in about 207 B.C., and the name was retained by the Han dynasty after it occupied the Tong-King delta in 111 B.C. From then until T'ang times the name was applied to an administrative region which, although its boundaries fluctuated, maintained commandery status. Under the Sui and the T'ang there were also subprefectures of the same name.

86. The So-yin Commentary was the work of Ssŭ-ma Chen 司馬貞 in the 8th century.

87. This rendering has been influenced by an alternative reading in *Shiki kaishū kōshō*, 9: 名為駱人有駱王駱侯・・・即今之令長・

88. Pierre Gourou, *Les paysans du delta tonkinois. Etude de géographie humaine* (Paris, 1936), pp. 83-84. The translations upon which Professor Gourou relied are to be found in Abel des Michels, *Annales impériales de l'Annam*, vol. 1 (Paris, 1889), p. 11, and Camille Sainson, *Mémoires sur l'Annam* (Pékin, 1896), p. 74.

89. E. Chassigneux, *L'irrigation dans le delta du Tonkin* (Paris, 1912), p. 53 and *passim*.

90. Naval Intelligence Division, *Geographical Handbook Series: Indo-China* (London, 1943), p. 11. Cf. also J. Gauthier, *Digues du Tonkin* (Hanoi, 1931), *passim*.

91. There are, of course, some races of *padi* which have been bred to grow in saline soils, but there is no reason to postulate the existence of such varieties in Tong-King at the beginning of the Christian era. The maximum encroachment of brackish water (during the dry season) does not normally extend inland for more than 10 miles in the southwestern tracts of the delta, nor for significantly upwards of 20 in the northeast [*Geographical Handbook Series: Indo-China*, p. 11]. In the remainder of the delta, it would have been sweet water which found its way into the *lăc* fields.

92. *Nan-Yüeh Chih*, by Shen Huai-yüan 沈懷遠 apud T'ai-p'ing Huan-yü Chi,

chüan 170, f. 9 recto. This latter work is a general description of the world compiled under the direction of Yüeh Shih 樂史 between 976 and 983.

93. In chüan 170, f.7 verso the T'ai-p'ing Huan-yü Chi employs a variant on this last phrase: 其地爲雄田.

94. Henri Maspero, "Etudes d'histoire d'Annam: IV, Le royaume de Van-lang 文郎國 ," Bulletin de l'Ecole Française d'Extrême-Orient, vol. 18, pt 3 (1918), p. 7.

95. Emile Gaspardone, "Champs lo et champs hiong," Journal Asiatique, vol. 243 (1955), pp. 461-477.

96. Gaspardone, "Champs lo et champs hiong," p. 477.

97. The Chou Shu 周書 was compiled on an imperial order of A.D. 629 by Ling-hu Te-fen 令狐德棻 and presented to the throne in 636.

98. Shih Chi, chüan 2, f. 4 verso.

99. Erh-ya 爾雅 , whose compiler is unknown, comprises material of Chou date which was stabilized in the late centuries B.C. It was enlarged and supplied with a commentary by Kuo P'o 郭璞 in about A.D. 300.

100. See, for example, the Shu chi fu 述羈賦 of Chien-wen Ti 簡文帝 (6th century A.D.): 孟夏首節雄氣吹匈 ; Sung Yü 宋玉 Feng fu 風賦 :   Hsiao T'ung 蕭統 Wen Hsüan 文選 (c. A.D. 530), chüan 13, f. 1. Cf. also P'ei-wen Yün-fu 佩文韻府 (1711), vol. 64, sub verbo.

101. Maspero, "Le royaume de Van-lang," p. 7.

102. Gaspardone, "Champs lo," pp. 469-476.

103. For the very real damp mists and rains encountered among the mountains of the south by the five armies of Ch'in Shih-Huang Ti in the campaign against the Hundred Yüeh between 221 and 214 B.C., as well as the high incidence of disease among the troops, which was also attributed mainly to noxious exhalations, see Ch'ien-Han Shu, chüan 64, ff. 1-3. General Ma Yüan's "poisonous airs and steaming miasmas . . . falling rain and rising mist" may have been less real but still testify to the vividness of these vapors in the Chinese imagination [Hou-Han Shu, chüan 54, f. 4 verso]. Cf. also note 48 to chap. 8 below.

104. The Kuan-tzŭ 管子 has traditionally been ascribed to the statesman Kuan Chung 管仲 but in the form in which we now know it is certainly a later compilation: cf. W. Allyn Rickett, Kuan-tzu. A repository of early Chinese thought (Hong Kong, 1965), pp. 1-37.

105. Wang Ch'ung 王充 , a sceptical rationalist (in so far as Chinese culture permitted), was the author of Lun Heng 論衡 , which he wrote probably in A.D. 82 or 83.

106. For a discussion of the implications of ch'i, together with a pertinent bibliography, see Joseph Needham, Science and civilisation in China, vol. 2 (Cambridge, 1956), p. 359 ff. and vol. 4 (1962), pp. xxiv, 131 ff. Cf. also Stephan D. R. Feuchtwang, An anthropological analysis of Chinese geomancy, Vol. 1 of Connaissances de l'Asie (Vientiane, 1974), pp. 48-56.

107. Charles Robequain, Le Thanh Hoa, vol. 2 (Paris, 1929), pp. 306-307.

108. Gaspardone, "Champs lo," p. 477.

109. E.G., Li Tao-yüan 酈道元 Shui-Ching Chu 水經注 chüan 36, ff.

108   Nāgara and Commandery

18r - 25v. *Ramparts of the Sky* was a literary name derived from the corpora of legends associated with the South-Chinese culture hero Fan Wen (see p. 387 below), some cycles of which assigned certain of his exploits to North and Central Annam. This name persisted until early in the 19th century, when Viêtnamese authors began to substitute an homophonous graph meaning "screen" (帳) for that meaning "rampart."

110. *Hou-Han Shu* 後漢書 chüan 116, f. 7r. The graph here transcribed as *Lji has traditionally been used to denote the Li/Lai/Loi tribes of Hai-nan and the Dioi of Kuang-hsi: cf. Paul Mus, review of *Monographie de Hainan* by F. M. Savina, *Bulletin de l'Ecole Française d'Extrême-Orient*, vol. 30 (1930), pp. 440-441.

111. *Hou-Han Shu*, chüan 116, ff. 7v-8r. Under the Ch'in and the Han dynasties, *Ia-lang (MSC = Yeh-lang) was an ethnonym denoting the Miao tribes of Kuang-hsi, Kuei-chou, southeast Yün-nan, and upper and middle Tong-King. Subsequently it seems to have come to denote little more than vaguely known mountain peoples on the fringes of Chinese administration. Rolf Stein has advanced reasons for believing that, by the 3rd century A.D., the name was applied to tribes inhabiting the Chaîne Annamitique as far south as central Annam ["Le Lin-yi," *Han Hiue*, vol. 2, pts, 1-3 (1947), pp. 61, 135-136, 228-229].

112. MSC = Lu-yü Man. *Shui-Ching Chu*, chüan 36, f. 21v. These tribes are otherwise unknown, but the *luo- element may be an ethno-generic not unrelated to the name of the *Luo-iwong 盧容 prefecture, which included the valley of the Nguôn Nay river. For the locations of Chiu-chen and Chiu-te commanderies see chap. 8.

113. MSC = Ku-lang Man. *Shui-Ching Chu*, chüan 36, f. 18r. -lang was a common second element in toponyms ranging from Ssŭ-ch'uan and Kuang-hsi in the north to Annam in the south.

114. MSC = Shih-p'u. *Chin Shu* 晉書 chüan 97, f. 15v. The territories of the *Śiək-b'uk were annexed in the 4th century A.D. by a ruler of the Lin-I who took the regnal name of Fan Wen (see p. 387 below). *B'uk, denoted by several different but related graphs, was used to transcribe an ethnonym widespread from the southern borders of Ssŭ-ch'uan and Yün-nan to Upper Burma.

115. MSC = P'o-liao. *T'ai-p'ing Yü-lan* 太平御覽 chüan 790, f. 9v. The name *Puā-lieu is perhaps reminiscent of the Vrlah hill tribes mentioned in the Po Nagar stele of Vikrāntavarman III (A.D. 854), but these were located far beyond the sphere of Chinese influence, let alone Chinese control: cf. Abel Bergaigne, *Notices et extraits des manuscrits de la Bibliothèque Nationale*, vol. 27 (Paris, 1885), no. XXIV.

116. MSC = Chiu-pu-shih. *Hou-Han Shu*, chuan 116, f. 7v.

117. MSC = Chu-wu.

118. MSC = Hsiang-lin. For further comments on these prefectures see chap. 8 below.

119. *Hsüan-chung Chi* 玄中記 by Master Kuo 郭氏 apud *T'ai-p'ing Yü-lan*, chüan 361, f. 5v.

120. MSC = Wen-lang.

121. *Shui-Ching Chu*, chüan 36, f. 23r.

122. "Nesting in trees" was a euphemism used elsewhere by Li Tao-yüan to denote the common Austroasiatic and Austronesoid preference for stilted houses, a custom which Chinese authors chose to regard as indicative of primitivity. Cp. *Shui-Ching Chu*, chüan 36, f. 19r where alleged Chinese exiles in *Pji-kipng 比

景 (MSC = Pi-ching) prefecture who had supposedly adapted to frontier life were said to "use nests for dwellings and to take their night's lodging in trees."

123. MSC = Ch'ü-tu-k'un. Cf. Wang Yin 王隱, Chin-Shu ti-tiao chi 晉書地道記 (beginning of the 4th century A.D.) apud Shui-Ching Chu, chüan 36, f. 23r. R. A. Stein ["Le Lin-yi," pp. 122-123] has equated *K̑'uət-tuo-kuən with the καττίγαρα of the Ptolemaic corpus [See note 21 to chap. 3 and Appendix, p. 447]; but cf. also J. J. L. Duyvendak's review of Stein's monograph in T'oung Pao, vol. 40 (1951), pp. 336-351.

124. Shui-Ching Chu, chüan 36, f. 29r. Silent barter was a subject of fairly frequent comment by early writers on Southeast Asia, particularly Arabs and Persians. Cf., for instance, the author of the 'Ajā'ib al-Hind [of uncertain date and attribution]: French translation in Gabriel Ferrand, Relations de voyage et textes géographiques arabes, persans et turks relatifs à l'Extrême-Orient vol. 2, (Paris, 1914); al-Bīrūnī (973-1048), Fī taḥqīq mā li'l-Hind min maqūlatin maqbūlatin fi'l-'aql aw mardhūlatin (edition of E. C. Sachau, Leipzig, 1925); and Marvazī, Ṭabā'i'al-hayawān [Minorsky's edition, London, 1942], each of whom alludes to this mode of exchange in the clove country of the Archipelago. In the Ḥudūd al-'Ālam of 982/3 [Minorsky's edition in the E. J. W. Gibb Memorial Series (2nd edition, London, 1970) p. 57], there is also a description of silent barter between the Zanj of Wāqwāq (Zangiyān-i Wāqwāqī) and Chinese merchants, while the Wen-hsien T'ung-k'ao 文獻通考 (chüan 331, p. 2600) mentions similar intercourse between the *Li̯əm-·I̯əp 林邑 (MSC = Lin-I: see chap. 8 below) and the *Lâ-sǎt 羅刹 (MSC = Lo-ch'a; a Chinese transcription of Skt. rākṣasa = demon).

The ability to scent the quality of gold was frequently recorded in the ancient world. That the feat was supposedly performed at night is perhaps related to the fact that gold was commonly believed to glow in the dark. Legends pertaining to this metal, which is so inextricably interwoven into Viêtnamese folklore and mythology that references to it in early writings can hardly ever be accepted at their face value, would have had an especial appeal for a writer with Taoist proclivities — as was Li Tao-yüan, author of the Shui-Ching Chu.

125. Madeleine Colani, Emploi de la pierre en des temps reculés. Annam — Indonésie — Assam. Publication des Amis du Vieux Hué (Hanoi, 1940). These villages of Gio-Linh are located in areas of unusually fertile red soils (the eminently desirable terres rouges of French pedologists) developed on basaltic lava flows.

126. Paul Mus, "Cultues indiens et indigènes au Champa," Bulletin de l'Ecole Française d'Extrême-Orient, vol. 33, pt. 1, (1933), p. 374; see also H. G. Quaritch Wales, The mountain of God: a study in early religion and kingship (London, 1953), chapters 3 - 6, and Prehistory and religion in South-East Asia (London, 1957), chapters 2 and 3.

127. Victor Goloubew, "Angkor in the ninth century," Indian Art and Letters, new series, vol. 8 (1934-5), pp. 123-129; and Journal Asiatique, vol. 231 (1939), p. 281.

128. Henri Parmentier, "Les monuments du cirque de Mĩ-sơn," Bulletin de l'Ecole Française d'Extrême-Orient, vol. 4 (1904), pp. 805-896.

129. H. G. Quaritch Wales, "Archaeological researches on ancient Indian colonisation in Malaya," Journal of the Malayan Branch of the Royal Asiatic Society, vol. 18, pt. 1 (1940); Alastair Lamb, "Report on the excavation and reconstruction of Chandi Bukit Batu Pahat, Central Kedah," Federation Museums Journal, new series, vol. 5 (1960), pp. 1-108.

130. There is, of course, no guarantee that the present-day Viêtnamese farmers put the several elements in these systems to the uses for which they were

originally constructed. In fact, Mlle. Colani's plans afford evidence to the contrary, as when higher-level terraces now support secondary-forest plant associations and lower-level padis have lapsed into stretches of marsh vegetation with stagnant pools at which cattle are watered.

131. Colani, Emploi de la pierre, pp. 37-39.

132. H. G. Quaritch Wales's proposal that the Gio-Linh systems were the work of a group of proto-Khmers who retreated northeastwards over the Ai-lao pass to escape from the control of a powerful kingdom in the middle Mekong valley, perhaps between the fourth and sixth centuries A.D., is not consonant with what we know of Khmer irrigation as practiced to the west of the Annamite mountains ["The pre-Indian basis of Khmer culture," Journal of the Royal Asiatic Society of Great Britain and Ireland (1952), pp. 117-123, and The Mountain of God, pp. 97-103 and 137-140].

133. Wales, The Mountain of God, pp. 97-103.

134. Cf. note 73 above.

135. J. H. Hutton, The Angami Nagas. With some notes on neighbouring tribes (London, 1921); and "The use of stone in the Naga hills," Journal of the Royal Anthropological Institute, vol. 56 (1926), pp. 71-82. The irrigated padi fields in this instance are almost always much more extensive than those of the Gio-Linh.

136. J. H. Hutton, Ancient monoliths of North Cachar (no date); J. P. Mills and Hutton, "Ancient monoliths of North Cachar," Journal and Proceedings of the Asiatic Society of Bengal, new series, vol. 25, no. 1 (1929), pp. 285-300.

137. E. E. W. G. Schröder, Nias, ethnographische, geographische en historische aandes keningen studien, 2 vols. (Leiden, 1917).

138. W. Stutterheim, "Oost Java en de Hemelberg," Djawa, vol. 6 (1926), pp. 333-349, and "Het zinrijke waterwerk van Djalatoenda," Tijdschrift voor Indische Taal-, Land- en Volkenkunde, vol. 77 (1937), pp. 214-250. The megalithic components in the Javanese examples, which include pyramids, stone seats, and occasional menhirs, tend to be more complex than those of the Gio-Linh, and in Heine-Geldern's view would pertain to the Older Megalithic.

139. Gregor Krause and Karl With, Bali. La population. Le pays. Les danses. Les fetes. Les temples. L'art (Paris, 1930).

140. It could, of course, be argued that the techniques of dry-stone construction evolved for purposes of strictly Megalithic ritual (bridges, causeways, staircases, menhirs, pyramids, circles, etc.) would also have proved their worth in the building of dry-stone embankments for agricultural terraces.

141. Cf. note 130 to chap. 8.

142. The substance, and some of the language, of this section have previously been incorporated in a paper entitled "The earliest cities in Indianized Indochina" in Janice Stargardt (ed.), Asia Antiqua: the archaeology of East and South East Asia (London, in press).

143. The notion that the Cà-mau peninsula is a recent formation is beloved of historians and littérateurs. Edgar Boulangier invoked it in 1881 [Revue scientifique, 28 février], Auguste Pavie adopted it in 1898 [Mission Pavie. Indochine. Etudes diverses, vol. 2 (Paris), pp. vii-xiii], and numerous subsequent writers have followed suit. Georges Groslier, for instance, considered that the whole of Cochin-China had been formed since the beginning of the Christian era [Arts et archéologie khmèrs, vol. 2 (Paris, 1924-1926), p. 168]. The investigations of Louis Malleret have now demonstrated that the

form of the peninsula has been relatively permanent for at least 2,000 years [L'archéologie du delta du Mékong: vol. 1, L'exploration archéologique et les fouilles d'Oc-èo (Paris, 1959), p. 161. M. Malleret also prepared a memoir, unpublished as far as I have been able to ascertain, in which he analysed the geomorphological processes that have tended to maintain this stability].

144. Bernard-Philippe Groslier, Angkor. Hommes et pierres (Paris, 1956), p. 17. A general discussion of the ecology of the Mekong delta is incorporated in W. J. van Liere, "Traditional water management in the lower Mekong basin," World Archaeology, vol. 11, no. 3 (1980), pp. 265-280. This author does not provide documentation of his assertion that, "During the early centuries of our era . . . the Mekong delta . . . had been settled by farmers growing broadcast rice watered by natural flooding" (p. 267).

145. Malleret, L'archéologie du delta du Mékong: vol. 2, La civilisation matérielle d'Oc-èo (Paris, 1960), pp. 17-88.

146. Archeological investigation in the Mekong delta prior to 1954 has been summarized by Louis Bezacier, Le Viêt-nam: Part I, De la préhistoire à la fin de l'occupation chinoise (Paris, 1972), passim, with summary on p. 277. [This work comprises part I of vol. 2 of George Coedès and Jean Boisselier (eds.), Asie du Sud-Est in the series entitled Manuel d'Archéologie d'Extrême-Orient, under the general editorship of Henri Hierche]. Subsequent work has been summarized by Jeremy H. C. S. Davidson, "Archaeology in southern Viêt-Nam since 1954," in Smith and Watson (eds.), Early South East Asia, pp. 215-222. [Cf. also Malleret, note 145 above]; E. Saurin, "Station préhistorique à Hang Gon près Xuan Loc (Sud-Viêt-Nam), Bulletin de l'Ecole Française d'Extrême-Orient, vol. 51 (1963), pp. 431-452, plates XXII-XXX; "La station préhistorique de Hang Gon, près Xuân-Lôc (Viêt-Nam), Asian Perspectives, vol. 6 (1963), pp. 164-167; "Nouveaux vestiges préhistoriques à Côn Son (Poulo-Condore)," Bulletin de la Société des Etudes Indochinoises, New Series, vol. 39 (1964), pp. 7-13; "Nouvelles observations préhistoriques à l'Est de Saigon," loc. cit., vol. 43 (1968), pp. 1-17.

147. E.g., tame elephants were offered as tribute to the Chinese court in 357 [Chin Shu 晉書 chüan 8, f. 4 verso, and chüan 97, f. 17 recto], a live rhinoceros in 539 [Liang Shu 梁書 chüan 3, ff. 6 recto and 9 recto]; the products of the country were listed as gold, silver, copper, tin, gharuwood, ivory, peafowl, kingfishers, and multicolored parakeets [Liang Shu, chüan 3, f. 5 verso], together with sugar-cane, pomegranates, oranges, and areca nuts [Nan-Ch'i Shu 南齊書 chüan 58, f. 12 recto]; bananas, sugar-cane, turtles, and birds were presented to the ruler by his subjects and by foreigners [Liang Shu, chüan 54, f. 7 verso]; crocodiles were recorded in city moats [Liang Shu, chüan 54, f. 7 verso], and cock-fighting was a popular sport [Nan-Ch'i Shu, chüan 58, f. 12 recto; and Hsin-T'ang Shu 新唐書 chüan 222C, f. 4 recto], etc. Note: all information relating to the Mekong delta contained in the Liang Shu is duplicated in Nan Shih 南史 chüan 78. For the dates of compilation of the works listed see note 10 to chap. 3.

148. For political conditions in the lower Mekong valley at this time see chap. 3. The Chin Shu, presented to the throne in 646, relates to the period between A.D. 266 and 420, but it is virtually certain that its information about the Mekong delta derived from the report of a Chinese embassy which visited the area in 245 [cf. p. 148 below].

149. Chin Shu, chüan 97, f. 16 verso. The same information is reported in Hsin T'ang-Shu, chüan 222C, f. 4 recto, where the phrase is 田一歲種三歲穫.

150. E.g., George Coedès, Les états hindouisés d'Indochine et d'Indonésie (3rd edition, Paris, 1964), p. 85; Lawrence Palmer Briggs, The ancient Khmer empire. Transactions of the American Philosophical Society, New Series, vol. 41, pt. 1 (Philadelphia, 1951), p. 14. D. G. E. Hall summarizes the implications of the phrases as, "They practised a primitive kind of agriculture" [A history of

South-East Asia (London, 1961 reprint), p. 26]. Anthony H. Christie renders the passage as "[They] are given to agriculture. They plant once a year and gather thrice," an expedient which is grammatically unacceptable ["The ancient cultures of Indo-China," *Asian Culture*, vol. 2, no. 2 (1960), p. 51].

151. *Nan-Ch'i Shu*, chüan 58, f. 12 recto; *Liang Shu*, chüan 54, f. 7 verso; *Nan Shih*, chüan 78, f. 7 verso. From the same locality there also came the *tśi̯wo-[?] tśi̯a 諸蔗 (MSC *chu-che*) [*Nan-Ch'i Shu*, chüan 58, f. 12 recto, and *Nan-fang ts'ao-mu chuang* 南方草木狀 compiled by Chi Han 嵇含 in the 3rd century A.D. (*Han-Wei ts'ung-shu* 漢魏叢書 edition, chap. A, f. 2 verso)]. According to another passage on the same folio of the *Nan-fang*, *tśi̯wo-tśi̯a* would appear to have been a species of sugar-cane. Berthold Laufer [*Sino-Iranica: Chinese contributions to the history of civilization in ancient Iran* (Chicago, 1919), p. 376] has offered the acceptable suggestion that the graphs represent a transcription of an Indochinese word. Paul Pelliot has also cited a reference to a strain of sugar-cane with three nodes to a *chang* 丈 (= 10 Chinese feet) that was grown in the Mekong delta in a work of the 6th-century author Wu Chün 吳均, which I have not seen: "Le Fou-nan," *Bulletin de L'Ecole Française d'Extrême-Orient*, vol. 3 (1903), p. 283. In a territory situated on the isthmus of the Malay Peninsula, during the 6th and 7th centuries, a yellowish-red wine was prepared from *tśi̯wo-tśi̯a* mixed with the root of a cucurbit [*Sui Shu* 隋書 chüan 82, f. 4v]. For the name and location of this territory, see pp. 234 and 251 below.

152. Pierre Paris, "Observations faites dans la région de Duong-hòa (Hà-tiên)," *Bulletin de la Société des Etudes Indochinoises* (1940), pp. 3-4; Louis Malleret, "Note conjointe aux observations de M. Paris," *loc. cit.*, p. 5, and *L'archéologie du delta du Mékong; vol. 3, La culture du Fou-nan* (1962), pp. 328-329.

153. The popular term "floating rice" apparently arose from the fact that the stems exhibit a tendency to mat below the water surface and ultimately to spread along it. The Cambodian name is *sróv lòn tu̇k* = "*padi* which rises with the water."

154. K. Ramiah and R. L. M. Ghose, "Origin and distribution of cultivated plants of South Asia—rice," *Indian Journal of Genetics and Plant Breeding*, vol. 11 (1951), p. 10.

155. Chang, "The rice cultures," p. 146. R. H. Richharia's view that floating rices actually belong to the *O. perennis* species has not found general acceptance, if for no other reason than that the elimination of the shattering characteristic of the perennials is most easily explained by postulating the introduction of a *sativa* component: "Origin of cultivated rices," *Indian Journal of Genetics and Plant Breeding*, vol. 20 (1960), p. 2; Hill, "On the origins of domesticated rice," p. 43.

156. Chou Ta-kuan 周達觀 *Chen-la feng-t'u chi* 真臘風土記 . Transl. by Paul Pelliot, *Oeuvres posthumes*, vol. 3: *Mémoires sur les coutumes du Cambodge de Tcheou Ta-kouan* (Paris, 1951), p. 25.

157. Cf. Anglo-Indian *bhatty*: Henry Yule and A. C. Burnell, *Hobson-Jobson. A glossary of colloquial Anglo-Indian words and phrases, and of kindred terms, etymological, historical, geographical and discursive* (London, 1903), pp. 72-74, 650.

158. Cited from Bernard P. Groslier, *Angkor et le Cambodge au XVIe siècle d'après les sources Portugaises et Espagnoles* (Paris, 1958), p. 171.

159. For an assessment of Diogo do Couto and his work see C. R. Boxer, "Three historians of Portuguese Asia (Barros, Couto and Boccaro)," *Boletim do Instituto Português de Hongkong, Seccão de Historia*, vol. 1 (1948), pp. 12-22. As Keeper of the Goa Archives from 1604 to 1616, Couto had access to an enormous volume of documentary evidence relating to Portuguese activities in the Orient. Although

he was a zealous collector of information, he was by no means infallible. Moreover, his work suffered the vicissitudes of fire, shipwreck, theft, loss, and official censorship, so it is not surprising that it should contain occasional errors.

160. For a discussion of the floating rices in present-day Cambodia see Jean Delvert, *Le Paysan cambodgien* (Paris & The Hague, 1961), pp. 323, 329-330, and map 9.

161. Malleret, *La civilisation matérielle d'Oc-èo*, pp. 87-88.

162. The *Wai-kuo Chuan* now survives only fragmentarily in the Sung encyclopedia *T'ai-p'ing Yü-lan* 太平御覽, where the reference is to chüan 786: cf. p. 149 below. For the polity to which this notice pertains, see chap. 3 of the present work.

163. It is only fair to note that at least one authority has claimed floating-rice cultivation as a relatively recent development: G.-G. Gustchin, "Le riz, origine et histoire de sa culture," *Riz et Riziculture*, vol. 12 (1938), p. 82. In any case, it is clear that it was introduced into the Cis- and Trans-Bassac as late as the 19th century: Delvert, *Le paysan cambodgien*, p. 330.

164. For the benefit of readers unfamiliar with the Chinese language it should perhaps be pointed out that the phrases in question cannot easily be amended to read, "They sow in the first year and reap in the third," Such would require a different grammatical construction.

165. Against this interpretation, however, it might be objected that the Chinese had a word for swidden cultivation which they might have been expected to use unless the Indochinese practice was so different from that employed in South China that the 3rd-century envoys failed to recognize fundamental similarities in the two systems: the word was 畬 *she*, lit. "to burn off brush and till the soil." With the pronunciation *yü*, it denotes a field in the third, or perhaps second, year of cultivation: the dictionaries differ on this point. *Vide Tz'ŭ Yüan* 辭源 p. 495; *Tz'ŭ Hai* 辭海 p. 917 [single volume edition]. Cf. *Shih Ching* 詩經 Mao CCLXXVI.

166. A start has been made on this enterprise in general terms by Ronald Provencher, *Notes on the relationship between the origin and dispersal of rice cultivation in the Southeast Asian Neolithic* (Berkeley, Cal., 1964). Mimeo; and for Malaya by R. D. Hill, *Rice in Malaya: a study in historical geography*. Unpublished Ph.D. thesis, University of Singapore (1973). Cf. also Joseph E. Spencer, "The migration of rice from mainland Southeast Asia into Indonesia," in J. Barrau (ed.), *Plants and the migrations of Pacific peoples* (Honolulu, 1963), pp. 83-89.

167. Donn T. Bayard, "Excavation at Non Nok Tha, northeastern Thailand, 1968: an interim report," *Asian Perspectives*, vol. 13 (1972), pp. 109-143; Bayard, *Non Nok Tha: the 1968 excavation. Procedure, stratigraphy, and a summary of the evidence*. Otago University Studies in Prehistoric Anthropology, vol. 4 (Dunedin, N.Z., 1971); Bayard, "An early indigenous bronze technology in North-East Thailand: its implications for the prehistory of East Asia," *Proceedings of the 28th International Congress of Orientalists, Canberra, January 1971* (in press); "The roots of Indochinese civilisation," pp. 103-105. See also Michael Pietrusewsky, "The palaeodemography of a prehistoric Thai population: Non Nok Tha," *Asian Perspectives*, vol. 17, no. 2 (1975), p. 135.

168. Nikhom Sudhirak (Suthiragsa), "Raingan kankhutkhon thang borankhadi konprawatisat thi Bān Chiang, Tambon Bān Chiang, Amphoe Nǫng Han, Čhangwat Udǫn Thani," *Silpākǫn*, vol. 16 (1972), pp. 36-57; "The Ban Chieng Culture," in Smith and Watson, *Early South East Asia*, pp. 42-52; Pisit Charoenwongsa, *Ban Chiang* (Bangkok, 1973); Chin Youdi, *Prehistoric man in Thailand* (Bangkok, 1969), and *Watthanatham Ban Chiang nai samai kǫn prawatsat* (Khonkaen, 1972). In Thai:

cited by Chester F. Gorman, "*A priori* models and Thai prehistory: beginnings of agriculture," in C. A. Reed (ed.), *Origins of agriculture* (Mouton, The Hague, 1977), pp. 322-355: C. F. W. Higham and A. Kijngam," Ban Chiang and N. E. Thailand: the palaeoenvironment and economy," *Journal of Archaeological Science*, vol. 6, no. 3 (1979), pp. 211-234. Gorman notes that a lack of evidence for the former existence of marshy habitats in the vicinity of Non Nok Tha and Ban Chiang might be held to imply the use of inundation systems similar to those employed for *padi* farming in the area today. In a decade-old summary of the Non Nok Tha evidence Wilhelm G. Solheim II seemed to accept Chin's more conservative dating of the rice glumes: "Northern Thailand, Southeast Asia, and world prehistory," *Asian Perspectives*, vol. 13 (1972), p. 145.

169. Chin Youti, "Archaeological evidence of rice in Thailand" (in Thai) *Silpākọn*, vol. 15, no. 2 (1971), pp. 39-44. Cp. also Chester Gorman and Pisit Charoenwongsa, "Ban Chiang: a mosaic of impressions from the first two years," *Expedition*, vol. 18, no. 4 (1976), pp. 14-26.

170. Vishnu-Mittre, *Plant economy in ancient Navdatoli-Maheshwar*. Technical Reports on Archaeological Plant Remains, vol. 2 (Poona, 1962), pp. 13-32; Bridget and Raymond Allchin, *The birth of Indian civilization* (Harmondsworth, Middlesex, 1968), p. 264. Cf. also H. D. Sankalia, B. Subbarao, and S. B. Deo, *Excavations at Maheshwar and Navdatoli 1952-53* (Poona-Baroda, 1958). Cf. also G. M. Buth and K. S. Saraswat, "Antiquity of rice cultivation," in A. K. M. Ghouse and Mohd. Yunus (eds.), *Research trends in plant anatomy* (K. A. Chowdhury Commemoration Volume. Bombay and New Delhi, 1972), pp. 33-38; R. N. Mehta and G. M. Oza, "Botanical identity of carbonized cereal grains from Nagara," *Current Science*, vol. 42, no. 5 (1973), p. 179.

171. Chang Yün-peng 張云鵬 (principal author), "Hu-pei Ching-Shan, T'ien-men k'ao-ku fa-chüeh chien-pao," *K ao-ku T ung-hsün* 湖北京山天門考古 發掘簡報 考古通訊 no. 3 (1956), pp. 11-21.

172. Chang Kwang-chih, *The archaeology of ancient China* (Revised edition, New Haven, Conn. and London, 1968), p. 445, Table 16.

173. Ho Ping-ti, "The loess and the origin of Chinese agriculture," *The American Historical Review*, vol. 75, no. 1 (1969), p. 19.

174. Judith Treistman, "Ch'ü-chia-ling and the early cultures of the Hanshui Valley, China," *Asian Perspectives*, vol. 11 (1968), pp. 69-91.

175. Treistman, "Ch'ü-chia-ling," p. 88. Cf. also Treistman, *The prehistory of China: an archeological exploration* (New York, 1972), pp. 63-65.

176. Treistman, "Ch'ü-chia-ling ," p. 90. As Gorman has pointed out ["*A priori* models and Thai prehistory," p. 6], Chang Kwang-chih's association of Lungshanoid-style pottery from Ch'ü-chia Ling with early bronze at the Han-valley site of P'an-lung Ch'eng [*Archaeology of ancient China*, p. 393] affords considerable support for Dr. Treistman's revised chronology.

177. E.g., N. I. Vavilov, "The origin, variation, immunity and breeding of cultivated plants." Transl. from the Russian by K. Starr Chester, *Chronica Botanica*, vol. 13, nos. 1-6 (1949-50); P. M. Zukovski, *Cultivated plants and their wild relatives* (an abridged transl. by P. S. Hudson: Farnham Royal, Buckinghamshire, 1962), p. 9; Jacques Barrau, "Histoire et préhistoire horticoles de l'Océanie tropicale," *Journal de la Société des Océanistes*, vol. 21 (1965), p. 342; Li Hui-lin, *Tung-nan-Ya tsai-p'ei chih-wu-chih ch'i-yüan*. An inaugural Lecture given at the Chinese University of Hong Kong in 1966; and "The origin of cultivated plants in South-east Asia," *Economic Botany*, vol. 24 (1970), pp. 3-19.

178. Te-Tzu Chang, "The rice cultures," pp. 143-144.

170. Per Sørensen and Tove Hatting, *Archaeological excavations in Thailand*, vol.

2: *Ban Kao,* pt. 1, *The archaeological material from the burials* (Munksgaard, Copenhagen, 1967). The excavators characterized the site at Ban Kao as representing a Neolithic phase. However, in a review of the above report, R. H. Parker [*Journal of the Polynesian Society,* vol. 77 (1968), pp. 307-313] has suggested that the skeletal material and associated grave furniture obtained from the site should be regarded as intrusive Iron Age burials, and proposed that they should be dated no earlier than 500 B.C. This is not to deny, of course, that Ban Kao was an agricultural settlement from its inception at the beginning of the 2nd millennium B.C. Cf. also Per Sørensen, "Ban Kao," *Journal of the Siam Society,* vol. 52, pt. 1 (1964), pp. 75-97.

180. See particularly, "*A priori* models and Thai prehistory." Cp. also C. F. W. Higham, "Initial model formulation in *terra incognita,*" in D. L. Clarke (ed.), *Models in archaeology* (London, 1972), pp. 453-476.

181. Even though this site (known specifically as the Lopburi Artillery site) was first excavated in 1964 by Nai Vidja Intakosai, a detailed report has yet to be published, but for summaries of the investigations and a thermoluminescence date of 700 ± 166 B.C. see Chin You-ti, *Prehistory and prehistoric excavations in Lopburi Province* (Bangkok, 1965): in Thai. The date is reported on p. 103.

182. Bennet Bronson and George F. Dales, "Excavations at Chansen, Thailand, 1968 and 1969: a preliminary report," *Asian Perspectives,* vol. 15 (1973), pp. 15-46.

183. C. F. W. Higham and R. H. Parker, *Prehistoric investigations in north-east Thailand, 1969-70: a preliminary report* (Dunedin, N.Z., 1970), pp. 23-24. Cf. also Higham and B. Foss Leach, "An early centre of bovine husbandry in S.E. Asia," *Science,* vol. 172 (1971), pp. 54-56; Higham, "The prehistory of the southern Khorat plateau, North East Thailand with particular reference to Roi Et Province," *Modern Quaternary Research in Southeast Asia,* vol. 3 (1977), pp. 103-141.

184. J. Ph. Vogel, "The earliest Sanskrit inscription of Java," *Public. Oudheidk. Dienst. Nederl. Indië,* vol. 1 (1925), pp. 15-35; Bijan Raj Chatterjee, *India and Java,* pt. 2 (Calcutta, 1933), pp. 20-27; B. Ch. Chhabra, "Expansion of Indo-Aryan culture during Pallava rule, as evidenced by inscriptions," *Journal of the Asiatic Society of Bengal,* Letters, vol. 1, no. 1 (1935), pp. 31-33; Himansu Bhusan Sarker, "Four rock inscriptions of Batavia," *Journal of the Asiatic Society,* vol. 1, no. 2 (1959), pp. 135-141.

185. Sarkar, "Four rock inscriptions," pp. 138-139 (slightly modified).

186. J. Noorduyn and H. Th. Verstappen, "Pūrṇavarman's river-works near Tugu," *BKI,* vol. 128 (1972), pp. 298-307. The symbolism associated with the inscription is not without relevance to matters discussed in subsequent sections of this book. F. D. K. Bosch has referred the ornamental figure serving to separate the beginnings from the ends of lines of text encircling the stone to the trident (*triśūla*) which in Indian mythology was used by a divine *Guru* (note that a *guru* is mentioned in the inscription) to conjure from the earth, as an act of beneficence, a spring of water. Moreover, the form of the Tugu rock simulating a phallus, a *motif* further emphasized in the shape of the trident, is almost certainly related to an episode in the *lakon Kumbayana* in which a mythical personage employed his phallus as a plough ["Guru, trident and spring" in Bosch, *Selected studies in Indonesian archaeology* (The Hague, 1961), pp. 155-170.

187. George Coedès, "Etudes cambodgiennes: XXV, Deux inscriptions sanskrites du Fou-nan," *Bulletin de l'Ecole Française d'Extrême-Orient,* vol. 31 (1931), pp. 1-8. For the kingdom of *Bʰi̯u-nậm see chap. 3 below.

188. Cp. Malleret, *L'exploration archéologique et les fouilles d'Oc-èo,* p. 241, note 1, and *La culture du Fou-nan,* p. 336, note 5 and p. 347.

189. Clifford Geertz, *Agricultural involution: the process of ecological change in Indonesia* (Berkeley & Los Angeles, 1963), p. 34.

190. The use of ethnographic parallels is, of course, not without its dangers. For a spectrum of views on the permissibility of such inferences see M. A. Smith, "The limitations of inference in archaeology," *Archaeological Newsletter,* vol. 6 (1955), pp. 3-7; R. Ascher "Analogy in archaeological interpretation," *Southwestern Journal of Anthropology,* vol. 17 (1961), pp. 317-325; L. R. Binford, "Methodological considerations of the archaeological use of ethnographic data," in R. B. Lee and I. DeVore (eds.), *Man the hunter* (Chicago, 1968), pp. 268-273; Peter J. Ucko, "Ethnography and archaeological interpretation of funerary remains," *World Archaeology,* vol. 1 (1969), pp. 262-280; and, the most recent summary of the problem, Bryony Orme, "Twentieth-century prehistorians and the idea of ethnographic parallels," *Man,* new series, vol. 9 (1974), pp. 199-212. It is probably true to say that a majority of contemporary archeologists invoke ethnographic analogy not so much in support of a particular interpretation of specific archaeological data as to suggest the range of possible factors involved in an interpretation, "to avoid over-emphasis of one's own experience based on one's own cultural conventions," as Peter Ucko has phrased it ["Australian rock art in world context," *Australian Institute of Aboriginal Studies Newsletter,* vol. 2, no. 6 (1967), p. 53].

191. Cf., for instance, G. J. A. Terra, "Mixed-garden horticulture in Java," *The Malayan Journal of Tropical Geography,* vol. 3 (1954), pp. 33-43.

192. Both of the main components in this ecosystem proved to be highly stable, but for different reasons. In the case of the wet-*padi* complex, stability derived ecologically from the medium- (i.e. water-) focused character of the regime and socially from the investment of labor in the construction of the *padi*-field, which amounts even in the simplest case to incipient terracing (often in association with feeder and drainage channels). In the case of the mixed garden, stability was achieved by maintaining the general structure as close as possible to that of climax forest, a biotic community which lives off its own decay. From the ecological point of view, of course, the *padi*-field represents a complete remodelling of the environment, a transformation of a generalized ecosystem into a specialized one devoted to human food production, while the mixed garden constitutes a generalized ecosystem (though containing only selected harvestable plants) which is to a large extent self-maintaining (though it may be fertilized more or less casually by domestic waste). For an exposition of this distinction in non-technical terms see Clifford Geertz, *Agricultural involution. The process of ecological change in Indonesia* (Berkeley and Los Angeles, 1963), chap. 2.

193. Charles F. Keyes, "A note on the ancient towns and cities of northeastern Thailand," *Tōnan Ajia Kenkyū,* vol. 11, no. 4 (1974), p. 505.

194. Bennet Bronson and George F. Dales, "Excavations at Chansen, Thailand, 1968 and 1969: a preliminary report," *Asian Perspectives,* vol. 15 (1973), pp. 25-27.

195. A gold seal inscribed "Seal of the King of Tien" was found in tomb No. 6 at Shih-chai Shan: for references see Notes 68 and 70 above. The spurious character of the ruler's claim to have descended from the ruling house of Chʻu has been demonstrated by William Watson, "Dongson and the kingdom of Tien," *Readings in Asian Topics.* Scandinavian Institute of Asian Studies Monograph Series No. 1 (Lund, 1970), pp. 45-71. For the degrees of social stratification and political centralization implied by the archeological and literary evidence relating to the Tien culture see Magdalene von Dewall, "The Tien culture of South-west China," *Antiquity,* vol. 41 (1967), pp. 8-21. See also note 68 above.

196. See chap. 8 and the accompanying references. The Phùng-nguyên Culture is discussed in English by Davidson, "Recent archaeological activity in Viet-Nam," *Journal of the Hong Kong Archaeological Society,* vol. 6 (1976), pp. 80-99 and "Archaeology in northern Viêt-Nam since 1954," in Smith and Watson, *Early South*

East Asia, pp. 99-102, which incorporates a bibliography of works in Việtnamese; Nguyễn Phuc Long, "Les nouvelles recherches archéologiques au Việtnam," Arts Asiatiques (Complément au Viêtnam de Louis Bezacier), vol. 31 (1975), pp. 1-54; Hà Văn Tấn, "Nouvelles recherches préhistoriques et protohistoriques au Vietnam," Bulletin de l'Ecole Française d'Extrême-Orient, vol. 68 (1980), pp. 113-154.

197. For references see Davidson, "Archaeology in northern Việt-Nam since 1954" and "Urban genesis in Việt-Nam: a comment" in Smith and Watson, Early South East Asia, pp. 98-124 and 304-314, citing particularly Đào duy Anh, Đất nước Việt-nam qua các đời (Hà-nội, 1964), and Lê văn Hòe, "Góp ý kiến với ông Đào-duy-Anh về vấn đề Loa-thành," NCLS, vol. 86 (1966), pp. 39-44.

198. Georges Dumoutier, Etude historique et archéologique sur Cô-loa, capitale de l'ancien royaume de Âu-lạc (réunion de Thục et de Văn-lang), 255-207 av. J.-C. Nlles. Archiv. des Missions Scient. et Litt., vol. 3 (Paris, 1892); R. Despierres, "Cô-loa, capitale du royaume d'Âu-lạc," Société de Géographie de Hanoi, vol. 35 (1940); Louis Bezacier, Le Việt-Nam: Book I. De la préhistoire à la fin de l'occupation chinoise (Paris, 1972) [which is vol. 2 of George Coedès and Jean Boisselier (eds.), Asie du Sud-Est, which is in turn Part I of Manuel d'Archéologie d'Extrême-Orient, under the general direction of Henri Hierche], pp. 247-249.

199. Jeremy Davidson ["Urban genesis in Việt-Nam," passim], elaborating the implications of the more or less standardized views of the Việtnamese archeologists who revealed the Phùng-nguyên Culture, has characterized Âu-Lạc, and even the preceding Văn-Lang, as urbanized polities. Reaction to this claim will, of course, be contingent on the reader's view of what constitutes an urban form. On the definition adopted in this study, the Âu-Lạc kingdom would not qualify as urbanized for the following reasons. A city in the full meaning of the word is the locale where, in order to minimize the friction of distance, the higher-level (mainly policy-making) institutions of government are assembled. In other words, it is the organizational focus (or at any rate one of the organizational foci) of the state. The archeological assemblages which are the material expression of Phùng-nguyên Culture and which are reported by Dr. Davidson, in my opinion, provide evidence neither of a fully state level of institutional development, nor of an articulated urban hierarchy. It is true that the transmitted texts specify an appropriate degree of centralization, but they are patently archetyped, heroized, and only too obviously modelled on Chinese exemplars. What they may perhaps preserve is an archetyped remembrance of hereditary hierarchical status arrangements that probably reflected a substantial degree of centralization. With that interpretation the archeological evidence is not in conflict. It should be borne in mind, though, that the relevant excavation reports cited in Davidson's (as well as more recent) papers are preliminary notices rather than complete evaluations, while the use of type-site names by different authors to denote both developmental stages and regional cultures, combined with an as yet necessarily imprecise chronology, make it difficult to arrive at firm conclusions.

200. Closely parallel "non-nuclear" views of East Asian prehistory emphasizing the localized regional development of cultures are expressed by William Meacham, "Continuity and local evolution in the Neolithic of South China: a non-nuclear approach," Current Anthropology, vol. 18, no. 3 (1977), p. 419-440; and Donn T. Bayard, "Recent developments in the prehistory of mainland Southeast Asia and South China." Paper presented at the Second New Zealand Asian Studies Conference, Christchurch, N.Z., May 12, 1977 [Mimeo]; "The roots of Indochinese civilisation: recent developments in the prehistory of Southeast Asia," Pacific Affairs, vol. 53 (1980), pp. 89-114; also Bayard, "Phu Wiang pottery and the prehistory of northeastern Thailand," Modern Quaternary Research in Southeast Asia, vol. 3 (1977), pp. 57-102, especially pp. 96-99.

CHAPTER 3

Cities of "The Hunter"

> The divine Maheśvara favors it as a place on which to send down his holy spirit. The princes of the country all receive [the god's] protection and the populace is tranquil. It is because the grace [of Śiva] is all-pervasive that the people submit willingly to authority.
>
> Nāgasena, A.D. 484[1]

We shall consider first the process of urban generation in one section of the so-called Indianized territories of Indochina. This was not the earliest manifestation of the process in Southeast Asia, nor even in the Indianized realms, but it is to date the most fully — though still very inadequately — documented, with archeological and literary sources partially complementing each other, and epigraphy supplementing both in the later phases. The areas with which we are particularly concerned are the lower reaches of the Mekong valley. Chinese records affirm the existence in this region from the first half of the 3rd century A.D. to early in the 7th of a polity which they refer to as Fu-nan (扶南 *$B'i̯u$-$nậm$).[2] They also preserve a dynastic myth which, despite its patently anhistorical character, claims to place the founding of this kingdom a century or two earlier.[3] The precise focus and frontiers of the polity are known only by inference, but it has been deduced on fairly strong grounds that its metropolitan territory, at least in its heyday during the 6th century, extended along the Mekong river between Châu-đốc and Phnom Penh, and there is archeological evidence for the existence of an emporium with far-ranging trade relations at Oc-èo in the Trans-Bassac, as well as for several other important settlements in the same area. Prevailing opinion holds that in its beginnings the polity known to the Chinese as Fu-nan was confined to the then half-inundated alluvial plains of the Mekong delta (here defined as the tracts of the valley below Phnom Penh).[4] From the 3rd century onwards it is possible to discern the transformation of a congeries of autonomous chieftainships into a chiefdom, whose frontiers at one time or another may have reached to Nha-trang in the east and at least to the isthmian tracts of the Siamo-Malayan Peninsula in the west, perhaps even to the Gulf of Martaban.[5]

Glimpses of an Emergent Urban Hierarchy in the Lower Mekong Valley

The origin myth of a Fu-nan dynasty that was recorded by Chinese envoys in the middle of the 3rd century[6] alluded to a settlement (i 邑) which had been ruled by a woman (女人為王) before the coming of the divinely inspired founder of the dynasty.[7] This culture hero allegedly arrived at what the text refers to as Fu-nan wai-i 扶南外邑, which Paul Pelliot translated as "en dehors de la ville du Fou-nan," adding "J'entends qu'il arriva par eau aux faubourgs de la capitale qui bordaient la rive."[8] Despite the enormous authority of Pelliot in such matters, this is not an acceptable translation, and the phrase must be construed instead as "the city outside (or on the border of) Fu-nan," implying the first city reached by the envoys, probably a port. In Han times and during the period of the Three Kingdoms, the graph 邑 was used to denote a subprefectural headquarters,[9] but in the present context of archetyped myth it probably signified no more than a projection into the past of a patterning of society from the period when the myth was formalized.

It is, unfortunately, not possible completely to isolate the several strata of information relating to Fu-nan that have been fused together in the Chinese records.[10] The basic material was provided by the report of a Chinese embassy to that country in about 245, which was presumably confirmed and supplemented by the interrogation of some, at least, of the tribute missions that appeared at the Chinese court at fairly regular intervals between 226 and 649.[11] Beyond that it is difficult to be sure of the provenance of any particular item of information, for the Chinese annalists and encyclopedists were apt to incorporate into their topographical descriptions any apposite material conveniently to hand, however dated it might be.[12] It would be unwise to assume, for instance, that all the information contained in the Nan-Ch'i Shu, relating to the period between 479 and 502, necessarily referred to a later period in the history of Fu-nan than did that in the Chin Shu, which dealt with the years from 266 to 420. There is, in fact, reason to think that at least one of the later Chinese encyclopedias, the T'ai-p'ing Yü-lan, which was not completed until 983, preserves material deriving from the very earliest stratum of information, for it acknowledges the main source of its information on Fu-nan as Wai-kuo Chuan 外國傳, a memoir believed to have been compiled by one of the envoys who visited that country in about A.D. 245,[13] and attributes a shorter paragraph to the Nan-chou I-wu Chih 南州異物志, a miscellany of mirabilia from the brush of Wan Chen 萬震, also from the 3rd century.[14]

With these provisos in mind, we may turn our attention to the emergence of urban clusters in the Mekong delta as recorded in Chinese writings. The earliest extant intimation that some sort of supra-village authority had developed in that region is to be found in the history of the Liang dynasty, a comparatively late source. This work officially records events between 502 and 556, but also includes a good deal of earlier material in its sections on foreign countries. In this instance it retells the dynastic legend of Fu-nan but also appends an item of information that is preserved in no other work, namely that the founder of the dynasty beneficed his son with seven settlements 生子分王七邑.[15] Presumably the author of the Liang Shu was here drawing on some early source now lost, probably a version of the record of the 3rd-century embassy mentioned above. Certainly the traditions current in Fu-nan at that time envisaged the establishment of centralized rule some generations, perhaps even a century or two, earlier. But the collective memory is almost invariably anhistorical and prone to project into a distant past events of quite recent occurrence,[16] so that, if it is indeed the folk recollection of the emergence of supra-village rule that is here preserved, it cannot well be dated before the 1st century A.D. at earliest. It is, too, extremely unlikely that the graph 邑 here implied anything more than a chiefly seat. Archeology has so far failed to reveal any settlement site in the Lower Mekong Valley which would have qualified for urban status in the 1st century A.D.

It is possible, though, that consolidation of the power of a developing chiefdom over a congeries of chieftaincies is reflected in the record of events in a subsequent generation, as related in the same histories.[17] No precise date can be assigned to these events, but they probably belong to the 2nd century, and perhaps to the second half of that century. Apparently a powerful chieftain (known to the Chinese as Hun P'an Huang 混盤況 (*γuən bʻuân χi̯wang) brought an unspecified number of settlements (邑) under his control and installed his male descendants (子孫) as subordinate rulers (小王) over them. Perhaps we may discern a further stage

122   *Nāgara and Commandery*

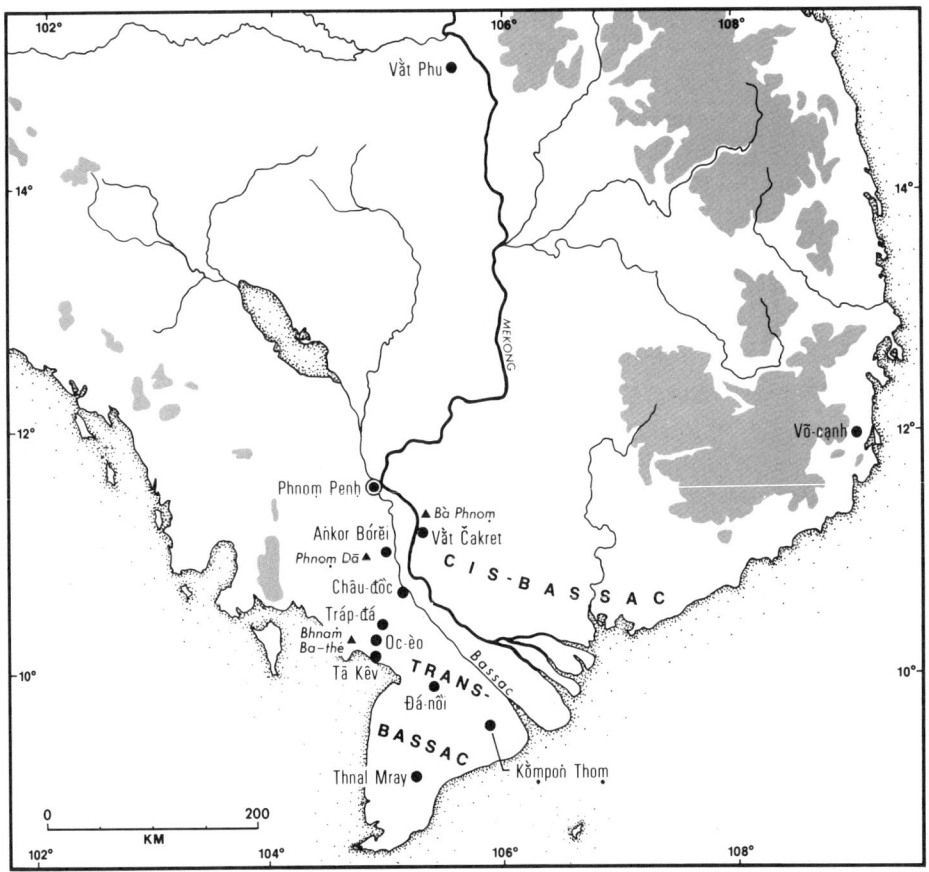

Fig. 8. Locations of archeological sites and localities mentioned in this chapter (other than those situated within the enceinte at Oc-èo, which are incorporated in Fig. 10, and those in Fig. 11).

in the expansion of the chiefdom as described straightforwardly in the phrases with which the events of a few years later were summarized. A paramount chief whose name or style was rendered in Chinese as Fan Shih Man (范師蔓 *Bʻiwɒm si miwɒn) attacked with troops and subdued neighboring territories, which all acknowledged their vassalage to him. He assumed the personal style of "Great King [sometimes taken to be a translation of the Indian style Mahārāja but perhaps more probably to be understood simply as paramount] of Fu-nan."[18] Immediately prior to his assumption of kingship this ruler had directed a maritime expedition against a dozen or more "principalities" (kuo 國) located round the shores of the South China Sea.[19] Two of these have possibly been identified in the Ptolemaic corpus, one being rubricated as a city-state,[20] and the other as a haven,[21] which might indicate that incipient urban development was not restricted to the heartland of Fu-nan. Whether or no we consider that this fact is confirmed by a remark in the Nan-Chʻi Shu to the effect that the men of Fu-nan used to raid neighboring settlements for slaves[22] will depend on the perennial question of our interpretation of the Chinese character which we have, for the interim, rendered as "settlement," namely 邑.[23] It has usually been considered that these events took place in the upper part of the Mekong delta, but this seems to reflect little more than a habit of thought induced by the knowledge that the seat of a powerful chiefdom was at one time situated some 500 li from the sea.

By the middle of the 3rd century there is every likelihood that settlements deserving to be regarded as proto-urban in the sense that they functioned as nodes of centralized control were in existence at several points in the delta. At least this is the implication of evidence contained in the Chin Shu, which, although not written until 646, almost certainly derived this particular item of information from the embassy of c. 245. The relevant phrase runs: "There are enclosed settlements, palaces and dwelling houses" 有城邑宮室,[24] which the Nan-Chʻi Shu amplifies somewhat with, "They use wooden palisades for city walls" 以木柵為城,[25] at the same time that it adds that the "king" (or perhaps more accurately paramount chief,) dwelt in some sort of storeyed edifice 國王居重閣. From the same source we learn that the populace constructed wooden houses raised on piles and thatched with the fronds of "a large bamboo 箬 having leaves from eight to nine chʻih in length,"[26] clearly a reference to the dùa nước palm, Nipa fruticans, Wurmb., whose pinnate fronds form more or less continuous stands fringing the tidal estuaries of the delta. The *T'ai-p'ing Yü-lan* draws on the *Wai-kuo Chuan* for the comment that these houses were decorated with carvings, presumably in a manner similar to that of recent times.[27]

In the passages cited so far there has been no attempt to specify any particular city or location. In fact, only two such references have been discovered in Chinese writings. The first occurs in the *Liang Shu,* and states simply that the enclosed settlement [sc. capital: *ch'eng* 城] of Fu-nan was, at an unspecified time, 500 *li* from the sea.[28] The second is from the *Hsin T'ang-Shu.*[29] The capital, we are told, used to be the city of *T'e-mu* (特牧 *D'ǝk-mi̯uk*),[30] but after the fall of that city to the neighboring polity of *Chen-la* 真臘 [31] (which is known to have occurred late in the 6th century), it was transferred southwards to the city of Na-fu-na (那弗那 *Nā-pi̯uǝt-nā*), identified by Coedès as Naravaranāgara.[32] Coedès has also recognized in the Chinese *d'ǝk-mi̯uk* a transcription of *dmāk* (or *dalmāk*), itself probably an Old Khmer translation of the Sanskrit honorific *Vyādhapura,* signifying the City of the Hunter.[33] The Hunter in question was Śiva, who is explicitly associated with the capital in the phrase *Adrivyādhapureśa* (= Śiva of Vyādhapura-on-the Mountain) which occurs in an inscription on a stele from Vǎt Čakret.[34] The city was situated at the foot of a sacred "mountain" (in reality no elevation in the lower Mekong valley could have been more than a hill), the Mahendraparvata, from which Śiva as the Divine Hunter ruled over the assembly of the Gods.[35] The mountain has usually been indentified with the Vraḥ Vnaṃ (= Holy Mountain) of inscriptions, the Bà Phnoṃ of modern times, which is a low granite hill situated a few kilometers to the southeast of Phnoṃ Penh.[36] Against this identification, however, can be adduced an apparent absence of archeological confirmation both on the ground[37] and on air photographs.[38] However, this lack of material evidence should not be regarded as conclusive until the entire vicinity of the Bà Phnoṃ has been subjected to thorough archeological investigation. In any case, it is by no means without interest that the T'ang history preserved the Old Khmer version of the name of the capital, thereby implying that the Chinese had obtained their information from Khmer-speaking officials who did not customarily use the Sanskrit honorific. Equally significant is the fact that the Chinese annalists also acquired from their informants the Tamil vocalization of the sacred mountain, namely *Mayēntiram* (instead of the Sanskrit *Mahendra*).[39] In view of the general function of

Sanskrit in the early centuries of the Christian era as the
language of literary communication both within the Indian
subcontinent and abroad, the use of a Tamil honorific in southern
Indochina in the 5th century A.D. is at first sight surprising, but
it is not the only instance of Tamil cultural influence in the
region during the Fu-nan period, not is it the earliest, for Jean
Filliozat has discerned a Tamil royal title, *MāRaN,* in the Võ-caṇh
inscription from the 3rd century.[40]

A few other *pura* are also mentioned in the pre-Aṅkor
epigraphy of the delta but none has been located with certainty.
For Tamandarapura, mentioned in a stele from the southern edge of
the Plaine des Joncs,[41] it is not even possible to hazard a guess as
to its location. Samudrapura, a mere name in a 7th-century
inscription of uncertain provenance,[42] would seem by reason of that
name — The City of the Sea — to have had a maritime location
(unless, of course, a symbolic ocean was implied), and may possibly
be represented by one of the archeological sites on the seaward
face of the delta, perhaps Kŏmpoṅ Thoṃ close to the Bassac,[43] but
more probably Oc-èo, which is discussed below. Of still another
city, Svargadvārapura, nothing is known beyond the inference that
it was in existence at the beginning of the 7th century, and a
suspicion that it may have been located in the vicinity of Thvãr
Kděi.[44]

More than a score of other *pura* outside the delta are
mentioned in pre-Aṅkor inscriptions, but very few can be located
with certainty. For some it is possible to specify if not a site,
at least a locality; but most can be assigned only a regional
designation. Śreṣṭhapura,[45] Bhavapura,[46] Īśānapura,[47] and
Śambhupura,[48] for example, were recorded as the capitals of
paramount rulers during the 5th, 6th, and 7th centuries;
Amoghapura,[49] Bhīmapura,[50] and Cakrāṅkapura[51] seem to have been
marcher chieftainships enjoying a considerable degree of
independence on the borders of the early Khmer culture realm during
the first half of the 7th century; while Ādhyapura,[52]
Aninditapura,[53] Dhanvipura,[54] Dhruvapura,[55] Indrapura,[56] Liṅgapura,[57]
Puraṇḍarapura,[58] Tāmrapura,[59] and Ugrapura[60] were clearly lesser
ritual-administrative centers to which temporary autonomy may have
fallen from time to time. To this schedule O. W. Wolters has added
the names of five chieftainships situated in northwest Cambodia
whose names are known in pre-Aṅkor times only from Chinese texts.[61]
On Fig. 9 the locations of these chiefly capitals are plotted only
as accurately as the fragmentary and ambivalent sources permit.

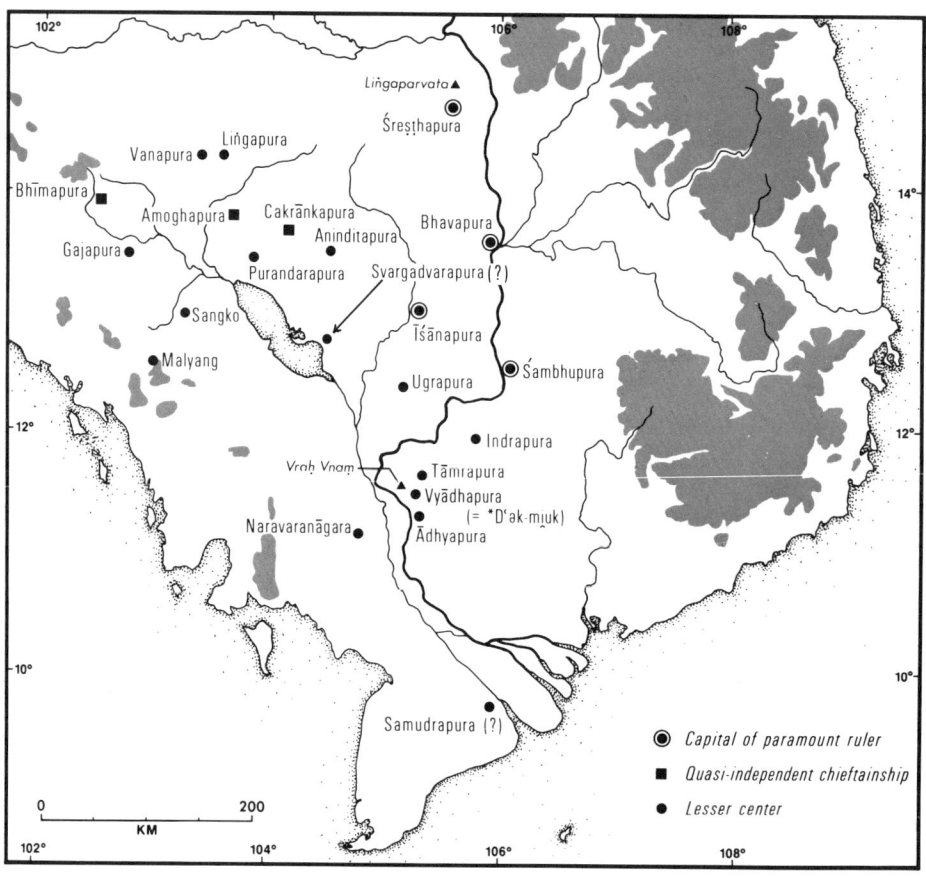

Fig. 9. Identifiable ceremonial and administrative centers mentioned in Pre-Aṅkor epigraphy.

That there were other settlements of some importance is implied by
a statement in the *Sui Shu* that early in the 7th century there were
as many as 30 enclosed settlements (*chʻeng* 城) with populations of
at least a thousand households, say perhaps 2,500 - 3,000 adult
inhabitants.[62]

The Settlement at Oc-èo

In the preceding pages attention has been focused on
evidence deriving from pre-Aṅkor epigraphy and from Chinese
literature, both of which have tended to illumine, however,
faintly, the function of urban settlements in Fu-nan. The primary
importance of the archeological evidence *sensu stricto* resides in
its contributions to our knowledge of urban morphology and only
secondarily to an understanding of function. Not that this
evidence is in any way superabundant for our present purposes, and
by far the greater part of it relates to a single site in the
Trans-Bassac that was investigated by Louis Malleret between 1942
and 1944.[63] This site has taken its name from the low knoll of
Oc-èo,[64] situated about 1,500 meters to the southeast of Bhnaṁ
Ba-thê in the former province of Rạch-giá.[65] Here, at a distance of
25 kilometers from the sea, air photographs revealed a rectangular
enclosure 3,000 meters in length by 1,500 in width, and with its
longer axis oriented approximately 27° east of north. The 450 or
so hectares thus delimited appear to have been bounded by 9
kilometers of multiple enceintes in the form of four ramparts and
five ditches, at least one of the former presumably being designed
to support wooden palisades of the sort described in Chinese annals
(p. 123 above). (That at least some Fu-nan cities were moated is
confirmed by a notice in the *Liang Shu* which states that the
crocodiles bred in these moats played a role in judicial ordeals.[66])
Through the longer axis of the city there passed a canal, now
represented by the Lung Giếng-đá (Cambodian = Aṇtūṅ Bhṭak Kay),
which constituted a major channel in the hydraulic network of the
Trans-Bassac, while four transverse arteries that may have been
either avenues or canals, but most probably the latter, divided the
enclosed area into eight quarters.

Malleret's excavations were interrupted by military and
civil disturbances while still in their exploratory stage, so that
our knowledge of the architectural configuration of the city is
dependent on a few more or less preliminary investigations. At the
moment the most that can be said is that at least two — and there
were certainly others as yet unexcavated — monumental ensembles
were surrounded by agglomerations of dwellings of wood, bamboo, and

palm fronds, these latter providing some archeological confirmation of the descriptions contained in Chinese accounts. However, by no means all the houses of the humbler folk were, as the Chinese reports might lead us to believe, raised on piles. According to Malleret, on the sandy giồng that rose a foot or two above the general elevation of the plain there was a considerable number of dwellings at ground level, while pile-raised houses seem to have been the normal type of habitation in the lower-lying, swampy lung between the giồng. Numerous remnants of these piles have been found *in situ* along the edge of the presumed water-courses that transected the ancient city, and some have shown traces of decorative carving such as is mentioned in *T'ai-p'ing Yü-lan*.[67] Whether or not these two types of dwellings were the prerogatives of distinct ethnic groups it is impossible to say.

Only one graphic representation of an ancient building has so far been discovered, and that is far from distinct. It is a *graffito* on the reverse side of a schistose mold for the casting of tin ornaments, and depicts a gabled edifice of apparently light construction carried on the back of a *makara*.[68] Presumably it was intended to represent a building of some importance, in which connexion we may recall that, according to Chinese sources, the royal palace was a wooden structure. This style of palace architecture was, in fact, common practice in later and better documented periods of Southeast Asian history — at least in so far as the Indianized realms were concerned. Malleret also concluded that two brick and stone structures, both on sandy ground slightly above the average elevation, were designed for sacred purposes, though in neither case has this been demonstrated with certainty. The first,[69] of which there now remain only imposing brick foundations oriented roughly to the southeast, was probably a *stūpa*, though certain architectural peculiarities have led Louis Malleret to suggest that it was possibly a building designed to facilitate the decarnification of the bones of the dead, a version of the Iranian *dakhma*, in fact. This interpretation appears less far-fetched when we recall the strong Indo-Scythian influence that permeated the culture of Fu-nan during and after the reign of the Candan monarch in the middle of the 4th century.[70] That decarnification was practiced in Fu-nan and neighboring countries is attested in Chinese histories.[71] However, the matter is by no means settled, and the most that can be said with any measure of assurance is that the building may have had a religious use.[72]

The second monumental edifice excavated within the confines

Cities of "The Hunter"   129

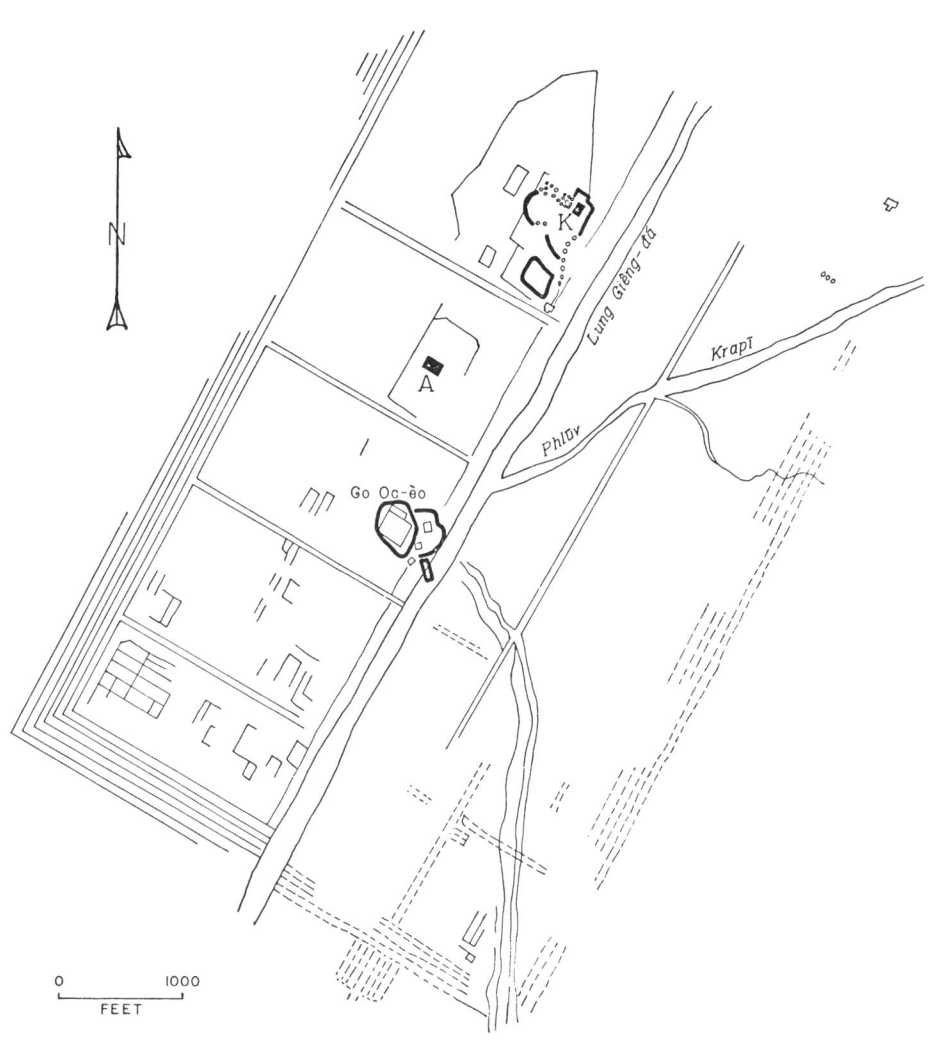

Fig. 10. The layout of the ancient city at Oc-èo in the Trans-Bassac as it appears on air photographs. Based on Plates XV, XLIX and L of Louis Malleret's *L'archéologie du delta du Mékong*, vol. 1: *L'exploration archéologique et les fouilles d'Oc-èo* (Paris, 1959). The traces of former habitation showed most clearly on photographs taken toward the end of April, when the first rains of the summer monsoon had induced a new verdure in the *lung* and other depressions in contrast to the sere vegetation of the *giồng* and similar low eminences. Even so, the clearest photographs leave much to be desired, so that there is room for argument as to the significance of the fleeting shadows that we have had no choice but to depict here as firmly printed lines. Excavations (as opposed to surveys) are indicated by heavy lines.

of the city[73] exhibited cardinal orientation, and consisted essentially of huge granite slabs mortised one to another and supporting a corbelled vault, the whole being raised on brick foundations. A brick annex comprised at least three rooms and was surrounded by a gallery on three sides. Although Malleret's suggestions that the main edifice was modelled on the famous cave-temples common in southern and central India in Gupta times and that the adjoining structure fulfilled the function of a *maṇḍapa* or *antargṛha* have not so far been formally challenged, they also remain wholly unverified. However, it is not unlikely on general grounds that the building served a religious purpose.

In the absence of a written commentary on this or any other city of Fu-nan, it is hazardous to speculate on the possible significance of the distinctive layout of the city at Oc-èo. Malleret was tempted to recognize in the four ramparts and five moats that comprised its perimeter "l'évocation d'un système cosmologique engloblant des continents et des océans périphériques."[74] If so, we must look to other than Hindu or Buddhist cosmology for the model on which the design was based. Neither the air photographs published by Malleret nor his own plan of the city show any affinity with Indian cosmology. Until the form of the enceinte as it appears on air photographs has been confirmed by archeological investigation it will be impossible to elicit its potential cosmological significance. Four ramparts and five moats[75] bear no special significance, but a total of nine defences does serve to recall the legendary City of the Conch, Loa Thành, alleged capital of the Âu-lạc of Tong-King.[76] According to Lạc tradition preserved in both Chinese and Viêtnamese histories, this city was constructed on the pattern of the mythical *axis mundi*, the Kʻun-lun mountain 崑崙山, with nine ramparts in the form of a conchshell.[77] There is no real basis for suspecting that the nine "defenses" of the city at Oc-èo were an expression of some version of this myth diffused through the folklore of Indochina, but it is a point that might stand further investigation. Rolf Stein has already drawn attention to the significance of the initials *k-* and *l-* in Tibeto-Chinese binoms denoting undulations, folds, or whorls such as those making up a conchshell.[78] These binoms in turn are related to another series of words with the same initials whose meanings are rooted in the idea of chaos or undifferentiation, and which appear to bear some at present unexplained relationship to a family of Mon-Khmer roots built around the consonantal groups *PRM-KRM*. In this connexion we may

Cities of "The Hunter" 131

recall that Rolf Stein has traced several important Proto-Khmer and Cam toponyms to this source,[79] and it is just possible that the design of an important city of Fu-nan, where this consonantal group was not unknown,[80] may have incorporated traces of this symbolism. But such speculation is premature, and a very much more sophisticated study of the folk beliefs of the cultural infrastructure of Indochina will be required before such essays become at all profitable.

If it is not possible to discern any hint of Indian symbolism in the form of the enceinte of the city at Oc-èo, it is also patently evident that the canonically prescribed cardinal orientation and axiality common in certain genres of South Asian cities are lacking. The longer axis at Oc-èo runs approximately from north-northeast to south-southwest. This is very close to the alignment of the drainage established on the constructional surface of this sector of the delta, and may represent no more than an attempt to adapt the layout of the city to the direction of its axial waterway. On the other hand, the northeastern point of the compass is not without its cosmic symbolism. In this connexion the term northeast refers not so much to the specific compass direction as to the azimuth of the sun at its rising at the summer solstice. At 10° 13' 32"N, the latitude of the hillock of Oc-èo,[81] which is at least 580 meters southwest of the geometrical center of the enceinte so far as it can be determined from aerial photographs, in the early centuries of the Christian era at the summer solstice the sun would have risen at an azimuth of 66° 4' east of north.[82] This bears no relation to the orientation of the longer axis of the city at approximately 27° east of north.[83] The effects of precession and magnetic declination (the second of which was certainly unknown in Fu-nan) have been excluded from this calculation, but in any case would be insufficient to induce any coincidence in these directions. Of course, the orientation of the city need not have been effected at the solstice. Parmentier has suggested that the alignments of certain Cam temples may have reflected the azimuth of the rising sun on particular festivals or perhaps simply on the auspicious days of their foundation.[84] Even so there is a wide discrepancy between the orientation of the city at Oc-èo and the azimuth of the sun at its rising on any day of the year. One final possibility may be mentioned, namely the adoption by the architects of Fu-nan of an alignment related to the rising sun in more northerly latitudes. It is, however, difficult to point to any particular practice that could have served as a model

132   Nāgara and Commandery

for the Fu-nan planners. Yet the fact remains that the northeastern quadrant of the compass had an important ritual significance not only in other parts of Southeast Asia but in cultures as widely disparate as those of the pre-Columbian Americas, Northwest Europe, ancient Egypt, early Mesopotamia, Vedic India, China, Korea and Melanesia.[85] In Southeast Asia in later times the northeast was the realm of Yama, god of the dead, known in his capacity as judge of the deeds of men as Dharmarāja. In classical Yaśodharapura, the crematorium of the kings and other members of the royal family is believed to have been situated on the so-called Terrace of the Leper King to the northeast of the royal palace.[86] This is, moreover, the relative position of the sites reserved for royal cremations in both Bangkok and Phnom-Penh even in recent times.[87] Coedès has further drawn attention to the role of two supplementary cavities in the northeast corners of the mortuary caskets customarily placed in the base of Khmer and Javanese portrait statues and liṅga to afford the spirit of the statue a means of escape in its migration upwards.[88] In Việtnam great importance is attached to this same compass direction during the ceremony in which an eldest son propitiates the White Tiger subsequent to the death of his father,[89] as well as in the Nam-giao ceremony.[90] Pierre Paris has also claimed to distinguish an important northeast-southwest component in the alignments of the Aṅkor complex.[91] This undoubtedly exists, but I am inclined to regard it as a fortuitous byproduct of the cardinal orientation and axiality of the numerous structures erected on the plain and of little, if any, significance to the princely "masons" who planned the complex and added to it through four centuries.

It is also noticeable that the powerful centrality induced in the later Khmer temple-city by the presence of a sacred mountain situated at the generating focus of its axes was lacking at Oc-èo, as indeed it appears to have been in all other known Pre-Khmer cities, such as Vyādhapura, (if that city was indeed at the foot of the Bà Phnom), Aṅkor Bóréi and Vắt Phu, in all of which the sacred mountain was outside the city proper. It should be noted that the most centrally situated hillock within the city at Oc-èo, the Go Oc-èo, has so far yielded no evidence of former monumental architecture.[92] It is noticeable, too, that the gates which, in a representative city of South India or classical Cambodia took the form of gopura raised in a massive architectural style consonant with the heavy burden of symbolism that they carried, appear to have enjoyed no special prominence in such sectors of the enceinte

at Oc-èo as can be reconstructed from air photographs. The one
possible exception to this statement is the trace of a structure on
the outer flank of the southwestern boundary, where a minor canal
(or avenue) once passed through, or perhaps under, the ramparts.
Whether the projecting shadows in the photographs actually betoken
a gate-tower cannot be decided until archeological excavation is
undertaken at that point. Close examination of the air photographs
also reveals a trace of what was apparently a raised avenue
bordering the axial Lung Giếng-đá, and this appears to have
extended beyond the ramparts on the southwestern side of the city.
How it negotiated the ramparts and moats again cannot be known at
this juncture. However, it must be emphasized that only
comparatively short sectors of the enceinte are decipherable on the
published photographs, and definitive statements must await further
investigation.

The dates of this settlement have not been clearly
established, but stylistic considerations combine with epigraphy to
establish the earlier and later limits of Oc-èo culture
respectively during the 2nd and 7th centuries A.D., with possibly
an early florescence during the 3rd century and an apogee in the
second half of the 5th and early in the 6th centuries.[93] This span
of time accords fairly well with the formative and mature phases in
the history of Fu-nan, though there are some stylistic indications
that Oc-èan culture survived for perhaps a century or so the
political demise of the kingdom.

Apart from a cellular arrangement that was induced in at
least part of the city by the transverse arteries, whether avenues
or canals, intersecting the axial watercourse, and apart from
certain rectangular patterns probably denoting street blocks and
temple enceintes (these are particularly noticeable in the
southwest corner: see Fig. 10), nothing is known of the internal
disposition of this city. Whether the cells delimited by the major
lines of communication were characterized to any extent by ethnic
or occupational homogeneity, whether they were in fact true urban
"quarters" or simply sectors defined fortuitously by the exigencies
of transport or hydraulics, will probably never be known, but the
presence of a flourishing artisanry is amply attested by the wealth
of material remains collected by Malleret. Potters,[94] workers in
glass,[95] gold-beaters,[96] jewellers,[97] engravers in many media,[98] and
craftsmen in bronze,[99] iron[100] and tin[101] have left abundant evidence
of their activities in the shape of their manufactures, their
tools, and their refuse, but none can at this juncture be assigned

specifically to a particular quarter of the city.[102]

Up to the present it has been the external relations of the city that have captured the imagination of historians of Southeast Asia. Items of trade originating from points strung along the length of the great South Asian trade route stretching from the Middle East to Tong-King and South China, as well as others from the archipelagic realms of the Southeast, have come to light not only at Oc-èo but in other parts of the Trans- and Cis-Bassac.[103] Perhaps those that have received most attention have been the medallions, cabochons, coins, glass, rare pieces of statuary and, above all, influences on theme, form and technique that derived immediately or ultimately from the Hellenistic world. The far-flung trade relations to which these items bear testimony lend credence to George Coedès's suggestion that certain small tin plaques bearing the caution *apramādam* (= take care) were seals for merchandise.[104]

The role of the city at Oc-èo as an important node in the web of South Asian trade cannot be divorced from its quasi-littoral site. Located some 25 kilometers from the Gulf of Siam, to which it was apparently linked by the Lung Giếng-đá, the city occupied a situation common to numerous Southeast Asian towns in early times: reaping the harvest of maritime relations without suffering the perils of maritime exposure, and combining the advantages of land and sea in a way no purely coastal city could do.[105] The Lung Giếng-đá passed through the heart of the city and afforded communication not only with the sea but, in its northeastward extension, with the master waterway in the whole hydraulic network that the people of Fu-nan had created in the delta, namely the canal running for more than 100 kilometers from Đá-nổi in the south to Aṅkor Bórĕi in the north (Fig. 11).[106] But it is doubtful if the city had been sited simply with the imperatives of commerce or the demands of defense in mind. In view of the significance of high places in the cosmology of both indigenous and "Indianized" Southeast Asia, it is unlikely that the location at the foot of Bhnaṁ Ba-thê[107] was fortuitous. It would seem more probable that the three peaks of this granite hill, none exceeding 750 feet in height but visible from all parts of the plain of Oc-èo, constituted the sacred mountain of the northwestern Trans-Bassac, at the foot of which the city was laid out. The relation of the City to the Ba-thê seems analogous to that postulated for Vyādhapura and the Vraḥ Vnaṁ,[108] demonstrable for Aṅkor Bórĕi and the Phnoṁ Dà,[109] and for Śreṣṭhapura and the Liṅgaparvata,[110] and

Cities of "The Hunter"   135

suspected for Kaṭāha and Gunung Jerai.[111] Malleret has gone so far as to suggest that the artificially constructed watercourses which surrounded the hill constituted "une véritable ceinture sacrée de voies d'eau, évoquant peut-être l'océan cosmique."[112] This is to read into Fu-nan culture a concept that has certainly been demonstrated in the symbolism of later Khmer cities, but which is also associated with an urban layout differing in fundamental ways from that at Oc-èo, a layout dominated by cardinal orientation and axiality and vitalized by an intense centrality focusing on a sacred mountain located within the urban enceinte. So far as can be ascertained from the very imperfect records at our disposal, these cosmological themes that characterized the classical Khmer cities were lacking at Oc-èo, and the sacred mountain — if that is what the Ba-thê was — lay outside the perimeter of the city. At a material level, there is no reason to doubt that the springs of the Ba-thê afforded a supply of potable water when the wells of the plain ran dry, as they often do today, towards the end of the dry season. In any case, we are not yet in a position to reject the idea that the "ceinture de voies d'eau" was anything more than a series of drainage trenches designed to control run-off from the Ba-thê.

The evidence of ancient settlement on the slopes of the Bhnaṁ Ba-thê itself, taken in conjunction with at least eighteen pieces of statuary and two inscriptions[113] that attest the sacred character of the hill, are suggestive of a cult center serving the spiritual needs, and hence in ancient times ensuring the material welfare, of the people on the plain below. It is initially tempting to see in this settlement pattern a functional and developmental phase in the evolution of city life, a phase in which contributions from the surplus productions of surrounding villages towards the maintenance of a more or less centrally situated shrine, the seat of an especially powerful or beneficent deity, were stimulating the elaboration of the redistributive sectors of the economy into an institutionalized superordinate system.[114] Unfortunately for this theory, all the statuary found on the Ba-thê has been dated to the centuries following the fall of Fu-nan,[115] which has led Malleret to suggest that the slopes of the hill provided a refuge for the inhabitants of the city at the time of its final catastrophe.[116] This might be held to imply that the disruption of the city was the result of some sort of inundation.[117] It is still possible, though, that the Ba-thê in earlier days had functioned as a cosmic axis and site of a shrine that effected the integration of the surrounding countryside into a coherent region. But all such speculation is otiose until further excavation is undertaken on Bhnaṁ Ba-thê itself.

Malleret did not restrict his investigations to the neighborhood of Oc-èo, and did in fact bring to light the existence of what appear to have been other contemporary, and inferredly proto-urban complexes in the Trans-Bassac: at Đá-nổi where air survey revealed "un véritable compartimentage du sol" that betokened a planned settlement of some size;[118] at Tráp-đá where scattered relics indicated apparently extensive habitation;[119] possibly at Tà Kêv, which seems to have been an outport for the city at Oc-èo;[120] and particularly at Thnal Mray in the heart of the Cà-mau peninsula,[121] where surface finds may one day be correlated with evanescent shadows on the shimmering vegetation that, to an attentive observer from the air, seem to betray the former presence of rectangular enceintes. All these sites await future research before their significance can be adequately evaluated.

The Role of Hydraulics

Another problem intimately related to the progress of urbanism in Fu-nan must also remain unresolved for the time being, and that is the role of the network of canals that seamed the surface of the delta (Fig. 11). Pierre Paris[122] was the first scholar to draw attention to the importance of such ancient channels in the (then) provinces of Tà Kèo and Châu-đốc,[123] and his survey was subsequently refined and extended by Louis Malleret to cover the whole of the Trans-Bassac.[124] Virtually all of the network has been built up from the study of air photographs so that most of the channels have not been dated. However, the manner in which they focus on the chief sites of Fu-nan settlement, particularly in the neighborhood of Oc-èo, combined with a striking lack of archeological finds from the Trans-Bassac relating to later centuries, afford sure guarantees that at least some of the more important elements in the network must date from the Fu-nan period.

The hydraulic system which Paris and Malleret have revealed consists of two master channels linked by numerous branches to focal districts that are presumed to have been — and can in some instances be demonstrated to have been — centers of settlement in the Fu-nan period. The most imposing of the two master strands in this web ran, with some slight changes in direction, from Aṅkor Bórěi (probably a late capital of Fu-nan) southwards between Núi Sam[125] and the Thât-Són,[126] skirted the eastern slopes of the Bhnaṁ

Ba-thê with the city at Oc-èo to its south, and proceeded in a general southerly direction to the neighborhood of Đá-nổi, another important node in the settlement pattern of the Trans-Bassac. When its trace finally peters out to the south of that settlement, it appears to be heading in the direction of Giồng-đá so that there is a presumption that it may eventually have reached as far south as 10° latitude. In any case, it can be said to have constituted a major artery whose construction and maintenance imply close relationships between Aṅkor Bórĕi and the city at Oc-èo, as well as some considerable degree of unity in the administration of the northwestern sector of the delta.

The second most important strand in this pattern of artificial waterways is today represented by the Lung Giếng-đá, the canal that constituted the longer axis of the city at Oc-èo. Thence it is visible in a northeasterly direction for at least twenty kilometers, and would seem to have been directed towards the archeological site at Tráp-đá, which represents another ancient settlement of some importance. Even more significant is the extension of the Lung Giếng-đá southwestwards for fifteen kilometers to link Oc-èo to its outport at Tā-kêv on the Gulf of Siam. This port was itself situated about ten kilometers from the sea, at a point where a canal running parallel to the coast crossed the Lung Giếng-đá. Another important channel ran parallel to the southern section of the main north-south waterway, approximately midway between Oc-èo and the sea, and was itself connected by another canal with Đá-nổi. The rest of the system was composed essentially of two elements: feeder channels linking the arteries already described, and short lengths of canal radiating from focal settlements. These last were particularly well developed in the neighborhoods of Đá-nổi and Aṅkor Bórĕi (Fig. 11) but, somewhat surprisingly, were less prominent in the vicinity of Oc-èo. Malleret's suggestion that the girdle of waterways surrounding the Bhnaṁ Ba-thê had been constructed in accordance with a cosmo-magical symbolism has been mentioned above.

It has from time to time been suggested that the hydraulic technology practiced on the Oc-èo plain may have derived from the irrigation tradition of southern India.[127] The evidence for this is slight and at best inconclusive. In the first place, South Indian practices were, generally speaking, adapted to a more diversified terrain than that of the Mekong delta and, to judge from the evidence of epigraphy, were concerned almost exclusively with the construction of tanks and feeder canals.[128] In South India emphasis

138 Nāgara and Commandery

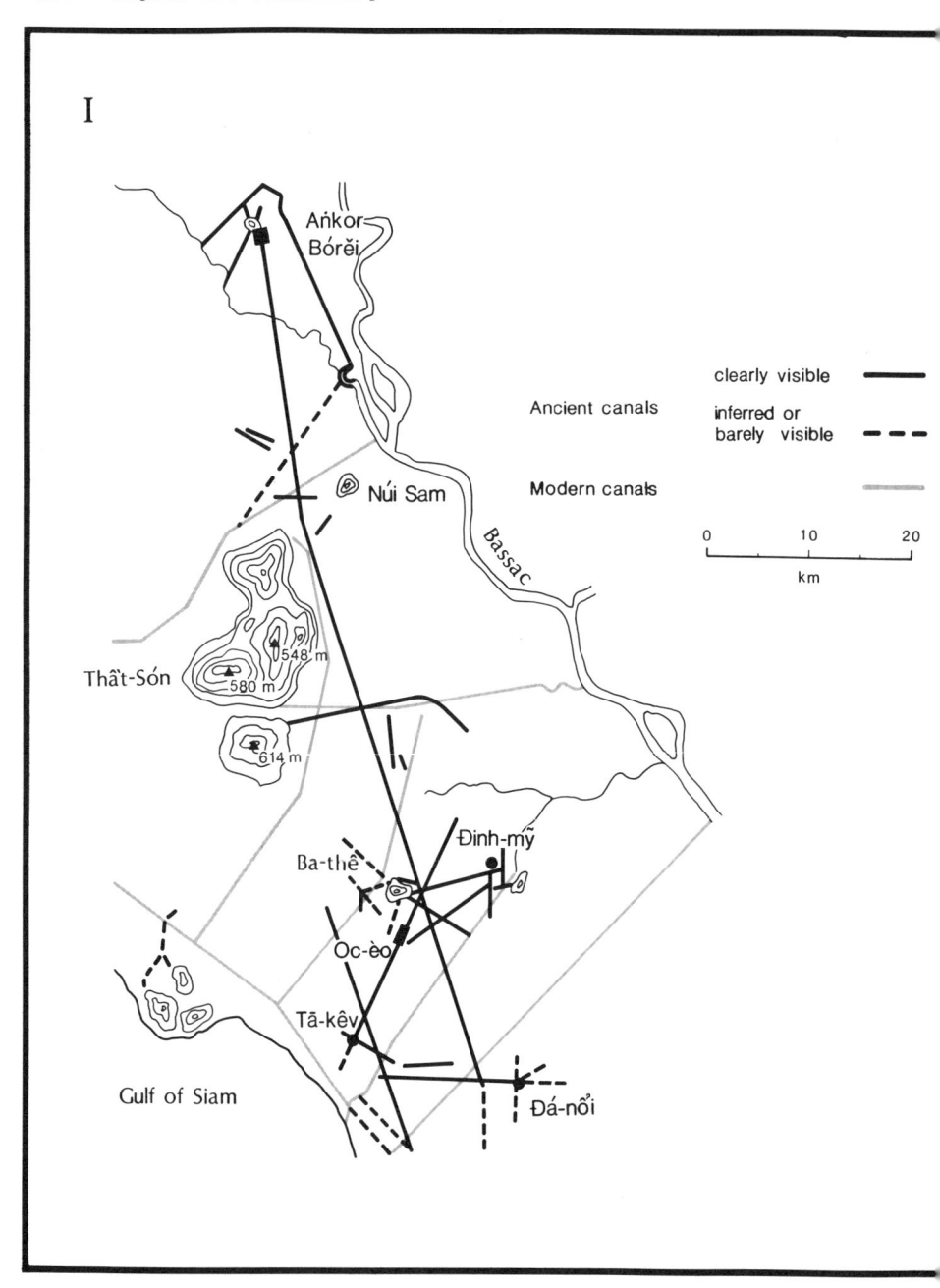

I

Ańkor Bórĕi

clearly visible ———
Ancient canals
inferred or barely visible ---

Modern canals

0   10   20
km

Núi Sam

Bassac

Thất-Sơn
548 m
580 m
614 m

Đinh-mỹ
Ba-thế
Oc-èo
Tã-kêv

Gulf of Siam

Đá-nổi

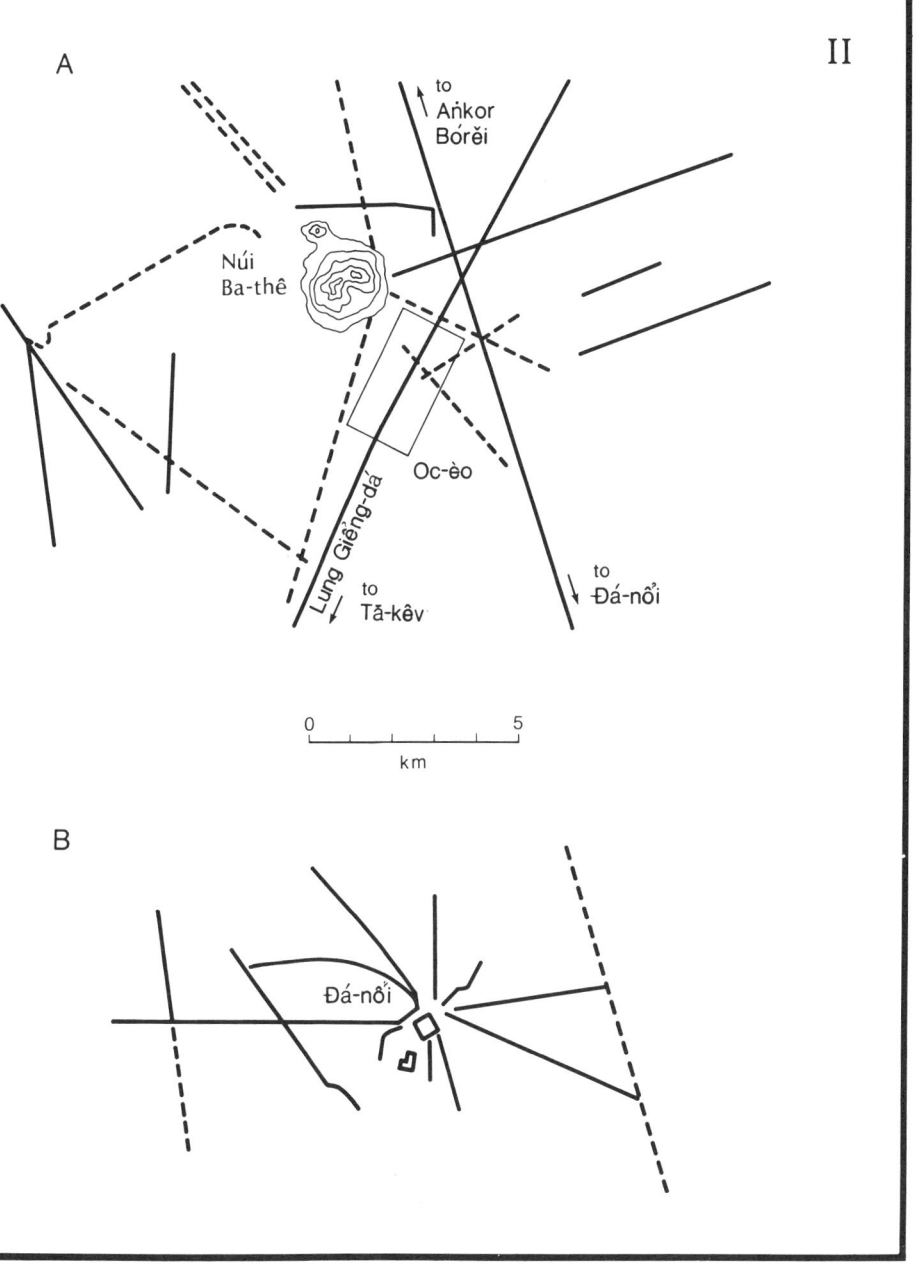

Fig. 11. I: The major channels in the hydraulic system on the Oc-èo plain as revealed by air photographs. It is virtually certain that a substantial part of the system dates from the period of Fu-nan. II: The radial arrangements of canals in the vicinity of (A) Bhnaṁ Ba-thê and (B) Đá-nổi (see pp. 137 and 145 of the text).

was clearly on irrigation, whereas in Fu-nan this has not been adequately demonstrated. Numerous ancient tanks appear on air photographs of the delta but do not seem to have been integrated into the canal system. In the second place, the earliest reference that I have been able to find to hydraulic works in the Telugu and Kanarese country dates only from the first half of the 6th century A.D.,[129] in the Pallava domains probably from the first half of the 7th century,[130] and only in the 9th century and later do such references become at all common in South Indian epigraphy.[132] If irrigation on a reasonably large scale was practiced earlier, as it almost certainly had been, then it was not recorded on copper plates. Finally, it may be seriously doubted whether hydraulic technology in Indochina in the early centuries of the Christian era was any less advanced than that of South India. In this connexion we may recall Mlle Colani's investigations of the prehistoric hydraulic systems of the Gio-linh massif.[132] These assume particular significance, in view of the symbolic role of water in the classical Khmer temple-city, and perhaps in that of Fu-nan, by reason of their comprehensiveness, domestic and agricultural purposes being combined with ritual uses to form a regionally integrated hydraulic system. None of these arguments disproves Indian influence on the hydraulic technology of Fu-nan, but it is more than likely that if it did exist it was grafted on to an already developed indigenous tradition. At this juncture it would seem that the system which we but glimpse in the shifting shadows of the Mekong delta might trace its lineage to the Gio-linh massif as easily as to India.

Despite the high degree of overall coherence and integration apparent in Malleret's reconstruction of this hydraulic system, it is certainly not complete. Numerous fragments still remain discrete from the system and, therefore, of dubious significance. Many sectors have doubtless been permanently erased by the technical expertise of large-scale agricultural colonization in this century, but there is reason to think that a continued survey from the air would reveal many links that are at present missing. A series of photographs taken at different seasons of the year would prove especially valuable in this connexion. At present, dependent as we are on an imperfect picture of the system, it is difficult to be certain of the precise role of the canals in the life of Fu-nan. Malleret was aware that a cosmo-magical significance may have attached to some of these waterways. that most of them probably served for transport purposes, and that they

almost certainly acted as drainage channels, but it is also
implicit in his résumé that they were primarily irrigation
canals.[133] Bernard-Philippe Groslier further accords them a role in
desalinization.[134] Definitive proof of an irrigation fuction would
have far-reaching implications for the study of the cultural
history of Fu-nan, and in particular would shed light on the
economic basis of the state. During the half-millennium of
Fu-nan's existence, the delta doubtless witnessed economic and
ecological changes that matched the contemporary political and
social transformations. In a Chinese text that probably drew its
information from the 3rd century A.D., we read of what is
apparently the gathering (or possibly cultivation) of so-called
floating rice, but by early in the 6th century, who can say what
technological changes had supervened? Of the five functions
suggested above, none of which is verified, ritual purposes and
drainage are contextually possible; transport purposes are strongly
supported by the manner in which the channels served to connect the
chief settlements and focused on the individual sites of Oc-èo,
Tā-Kèv, Dá-nỏi and Đinh-mỹ; irrigation is debatable but possible;
and desalinization is no more than speculative. Until more precise
answers can be given to these questions, it were profitless to
attempt to relate the role of this hydraulic system to the growth
of cities in the Mekong delta.

The Nature of the Urban Hierarchy in Pre-Aṅkor Kampuchea

Professors Wolters and Jacques have both argued against the
conception of a single state occupying the lower Mekong valley
during the early centuries of the Christian era. The former writes
of "an unknown number of independent centres of territorial
authority" and of "chiefs [who] did not understand the notion of a
'kingdom' with its supra-territorial demands on their loyalty,"[135]
while Professor Jacques has commented on the "evidence in the Khmer
country of a multitude of little realms and princedoms."[136] Whereas
Wolters implies that it was the Chinese "sense of dynasty" which
misled the chroniclers into assuming the existence of a unitary
kingdom of Fu-nan, Jacques imputes to them deliberate
misrepresentations designed to inflate the importance of the
Chinese Emperor by demonstrating that he could command tribute from
large states in the southern ocean.[137] This latter contention runs
counter to all that we know about the operation of the Chinese
bureaucracy, but Professor Wolters's view deserves consideration.
He, and indeed Professor Jacques too, are correct in their emphasis

on the multiplicity of political entities in the lower and middle reaches of the Mekong valley in early times, and it is true that the Chinese envoys to Fu-nan were attempting to convey to their countrymen the idea of a polity of a type with which they were probably unfamiliar. Yet it is evident that a "sense of dynasty" did not mislead the Chinese envoys who reported on the political situation in contemporary south Korea or among the Wa tribes of the Japanese islands,[138] and it has been claimed that, if anything, they erred in the opposite direction in their discussion of the Lạc tribes of the Tong-King delta by understating both the degree of centralized control and the continuity of dynastic rule obtaining among those groups.[139] Why, then, should they have failed to perceive the true situation in the lower Mekong valley? I would suggest that the Chinese envoys perceived the situation accurately enough but lacked a vocabulary capable of expressing it in terms immediately intelligible to a 20th-century scholar. Consequently, their inexpert and imprecise essays into sociopolitical description have to be interpreted in terms of comparative ethnography before their true import becomes apparent.

    I think that one 3rd-century Chinese author got the matter right when he wrote that, "The vassal territories [of Fu-nan] all have their own chiefs."[140] In other words, the Fu-nan polity comprised a system of chieftainships under the rule of a paramount, and as such can be appropriately designated a chiefdom. As was made clear in Chapter 1, there is a difference between a chieftainship incorporated in the pyramidal political organization of a chiefdom and a wholly independent polity. Although it is true that in the former situation a chief's control over his own community is virtually absolute as long as he does not violate tradition or contravene the interests of the paramount, yet in the last analysis he rules at the pleasure of the paramount. It should not be forgotten that the bonds that hold a chiefdom together include the exercise of largely arbitrary power as well as fragile loyalties founded on common interest. The potentiality for internal conflict is ever present, and early Kampuchea was no exception. Even from the fragmentary record available to us, it is evident that the paramountcy changed hands with a high degree of frequency. A notable series of such transfers of power between families followed the death, toward the end of the first quarter of the 3rd century, of the paramount known to the Chinese as Fan Man or Fan Shih Man (cp. p. 123 above). The *Liang Shu* reports that a nephew of Fan Man — whether classificatory or otherwise is uncertain — at the head of 2,000 followers, seized power while the designated heir was raiding to the westward. In due course a younger son of Fan Man, "who had been living among the people" (sc. among his kindred), reclaimed the paramountcy for the original line, only to be overthrown himself shortly afterwards by a warrior of repute (the Chinese called him a high-ranking general 大將) in the usurper's faction. Supreme rule thus passed finally to a competing family, an event which appears to have been commemorated by the building of a new palace complex.[141]

In my opinion the surviving evidence for political conditions in the lower Mekong valley during the first half-millennium of the Christian era implies not so much a plethora of independent centers of territorial authority as a matrix of chieftainships integrated into a continually changing pattern of chiefdoms. The Chinese envoys who visited the region in the middle of the 3rd century A.D. claimed to have heard of well over a hundred political entities (國) in Southeast Asia,[142] and the *Liang Shu* preserves an account of the manner in which, in the 3rd century A.D., Fan Man brought under his paramountcy first those in his immediate vicinity, and then from ten to twenty situated at a greater distance.[143] Two 7th-century inscriptions from Hàn Čei show King Bhavavarman (it is unclear whether I or II) doing much the same thing by conquering "the kings of the mountain [*parvatabhūpāla*, that is either rulers whose authority derived from their association with Śiva or the *liṅga* they erected: see Chap. 7, pp. 289 - 295] up to the summits of their peaks."[144] Like Fan Man several centuries earlier, "No sooner had [Bhavavarman] crossed into the territory of enemy princes than his exploits carried him beyond the confines [even] of their country."[145] That a process of political expansion on these lines should have resulted in the formation of a chiefdom occupying more or less the whole of the lower Mekong valley is by no means improbable; and it is not impossible that territories as far apart as present-day southern Burma (sometimes alleged to have been the Golden Frontier: Note 5 above) and south Việtnam (the site of the Võ-cạnh inscription: cf. Note 5) could at one and the same time have acknowledged the supremacy of an especially powerful paramount in the Kampuchea lowlands. If a tradition recorded in the *Liang Shu* is to be believed, Fan Man raided by sea at least as far west as the Siamo-Malayan isthmus.[146] It would appear, though, that territorial aggrandizement, generally speaking, signified not the extinction of a conquered chieftainship but rather its incorporation as a dependent unit within the expanding chiefdom.

In Pre-Aṅkor Kampuchea such pyramidally structured politics, dependent as they were on the paramount's ability to demonstrate the superior efficacy of his relationship with Śiva, were seldom stable over extended periods. As each chieftainship subsumed within a chiefdom was constituted as a smaller-scale replica of that chiefdom, and as often as not its ruler adopted into the established hierarchy, the dissolution of the polity usually resulted in the formation of an array of minor entities each furnished with the institutions and ceremonial trappings appropriate to a more prestigious state. Such periods of dissolution are easily recognizable in the historical record, meager though it be. One such clearly followed the death of Fan Man; another the death of Kauṇḍinya Jayavarman in 514; and another, lasting for some three decades of the 7th century, supervened between the loss of prestige by Bhavavarman's line and the assumption of power by Jayavarman I. For almost all of the 8th century, at least two paramounts, as well as an undetermined number of lesser chiefs, competed for control of the plains of the lower Mekong and, as far as is known, no ruler succeeded in again uniting that territory within a single chiefdom until Jayavarman II established a new paramountcy in the later decades of the 8th century.[147] Even during periods of only weakened central authority, chieftains remote from the seat of the current paramountcy not unnaturally tended to treat their de facto independence as de jure sovereignty. Bhavapura, Aninditapura, Śreṣṭhapura, Śambhupura, Amoghapura, Bhimapura, Liṅgapura, and Ugrapura afford examples of chieftainships all of which seem to have established their independence of any central power at one time or another (See Fig. 9). In fact, both Śambhupura and Aninditapura were seats of paramountcies in their own right, each ruling over an unknown member of subordinate chieftainships. It is probable that the same was true of Raktamṛttika, which the Chinese described, under the translated rubric "Red-Earth Kingdom," as "another kind of Fu-nan" (扶南之別種), presumably referring thereby to a territorially discrete polity based on the cult of Śaivism characteristic of the lower Mekong valley.[148] It is wholly in keeping with the chiefdom mode of political organization that the personage who, when erecting a liṅga under the vocable of Bhadreśvara, was referred to by a Sanskrit phrase appositely rendered into English as "Paramount Chief of Ugrapura" [Ugrapurādhīśas], proudly proclaimed in the Hàn Čei inscriptions the merits and glories of a still more

authoritative ruler, Bhavavarman II.[149] This is surely a timely
reminder that style and titles are hardly ever reliable guides to
status and power in ancient Southeast Asia, a point already made
for early Javanese history by F. H. van Naerssen.[150]

Although the political surface of Pre-Aṅkor Kampuchea
exhibited an unstable, sometimes volatile, arrangement of power
foci, it is possible to discern beneath the flux of dynastic
fortunes a persistent centroid of political power occupying a zone
of territory about 75 miles wide running from the neighbourhood of
Kompong Cham southward to about latitude 10°N. From this zone come
nearly three-fifths of all known Kampuchean inscriptions, in both
Sanskrit and Khmer, dating from the 5th to the 8th century
inclusive.[151] Perhaps even more strongly indicative of at least a
moderate degree of continuity of power and authority in this zone
is the network of canals which linked the main settlements between
Aṅkor Bórĕi and Đá-nỏi (pp. 136 - 141 above). The investment of
labor required to bring this hydraulic system into being bespeaks
a significant degree of centralized direction even though the focus
of power is known to have shifted within the territory.

The fragmentary and equivocal evidence discussed in the
preceding pages permits only the broadest of generalizations about
the nature of urban life in the lower Mekong valley from the 2nd to
the 7th century A.D. It would seem that at least from the middle
of the 3rd century onward palisaded and moated ceremonial and
administrative centers were situated at focal points in the
hydraulic system that consolidated the heartland of the Mekong
delta into an economic, and, at certain times, political unity.
These urban centers were apparently integrated into a three-level
settlement hierarchy, consisting of one or more paramount capitals
(such as Vyādhapura), a larger number of seats of chieftainships
(such as Tāmrapura), and a village level of settlement which has to
be inferred principally from the evidence of Khmer-language
inscriptions. Usually there were also a few settlements exploiting
anomalies in the distribution of power in order to maintain a *de
facto* and temporary autonomy. On the evidence available, it would
seem that these proto-urban centers consisted of agglomerations of
dwellings, constructed of light materials such as wood, bamboo,
and *dừa nước*, and often raised on piles, clustered about
administrative and ceremonial complexes which, on the only site
excavated, included brick and granite structures. These latter
were not situated centrally in relation to the enceinte of the
city. Integrated into this layout in a manner unknown to us was

the palace of the ruler, a double-storeyed building of wood apparently on the pattern of those customarily built by numerous Southeast Asian rulers until quite recent times. A feature of the only city plan that has been even partially revealed on the ground, and that in no great detail, is a complete absence of the symbolism associated both with the Indian city and with the cities of the Aṅkor period. Yet it is difficult to believe that the orientation of the main axis of the city at Oc-èo from northeast to southwest was fortuitous, and that the form of the enceinte carried no symbolic significance.

Notes and References

1. *The City of the Hunter* is the honorific style of the earliest capital in the Mekong valley of which the name has been preserved. The Hunter was, of course, Śiva in his abode on the Mahendraparvata: see p. 124. Nāgasena was an emissary from Fu-nan (for which see Note 2) to the court of the Southern Chʻi in 484: See *Nan-Chʻi Shu* 南齋書 chüan 58, ff. 10v - 11r.

2. *Bʻi̯u-nậm is usually believed to have been a Chinese transcription of Old Khmer [*Vrah̰*] *Vnam* = [Sacred] Mountain, an idea first suggested by Etienne Aymonier, *Le Cambodge*, vol. 1 (Paris, 1900), p. 283. Mainly on the grounds that a 7th-century inscription from Hàn Čei [ISCC, no. VIII] refers to "kings of the mountain" (*parvatabhūpāla*) and another of approximately the same date from Kūk Prăh Kŏt to a *śailarāja* [George Coedès, "On the origin of the Śailendras of Indonesia," *JGIS*, vol. 1, no. 2 (1934), pp. 67-68], both of which terms could have been rendered into Old Khmer as *kuruṅ vnaṃ*, it is conveniently assumed that this latter phrase figured in the style of the ruler of Fu-nan and was mistakenly reported by the Chinese as the name of the country [e.g., Louis Finot, "Sur quelques traditions indochinoises," *Mélanges d'Indianisme offerts par ses élèves à M. Sylvain Lévi* (Paris, 1911), p. 203 and "Séance du 14 janvier 1927," *JA*, vol 210 (1927), p. 186]. There seems no compelling reason, though, why *vnaṃ* should not have constituted an element in the name of the polity as well as in the style of its ruler. However, the term *kuruṅ vnaṃ* has not been discovered in any extant Old Khmer inscription, but *vrah vnaṃ* occurs in a 10th-century inscription from Phum Mĩen [Aymonier, *Le Cambodge*, vol. 1, p. 283; Coedès, "Etudes cambodgiennes, XXI: la tradition généalogique des premiers rois d'Angkor d'après les inscriptions de Yaçovarman et de Rājendravarman," *BEFEO*, vol. 28 (1928), p. 128]. In this inscription it appears to be used as a designation of the *adri* in the name Adrivyādhapura = the City of the Hunter on the Mountain.

The Chinese transcription customarily used to denote the name of this polity was *Bʻi̯u-nậm 扶南 but a possible *Pi̯u-nậm 夫南 occurs once, in Tso Szŭ's 左思. *San-tu Fu* 三都賦 (3rd century), and, significantly, on two occasions I Ching 義淨 used respectively the forms *Bʻuât-nậm 跋南 and Puā-nậm 跛南, while retaining the more usual transcription in a third reference [*Ta-Tʻang Hsi-yü Chʻiu-fa Kao-seng Chuan* 大唐西域求法高僧傳, part I, f. 2; *Nan-Hai Chi-kuei Nei-fa Chuan* 南海寄歸內法傳, chüan 1, f. 4 recto]. I Ching was an able philologist who, as a result of protracted labours in the precise translation of difficult *mantras*, had acquired a rare expertise in the transcription of foreign words. His experience in the translation of Buddhist texts induced him to pay particular attention to the problem of transcribing into Chinese foreign terms beginning with double or treble consonantal clusters, and it was surely not fortuitous that he selected the graphs above to represent the sound of *vnam*. I suspect that I Ching discerned an inadequacy in the accepted transcription of the word, which he then corrected by substituting *-uâ* for the received *-i̯u*. The precise value of this correction will remain obscure until a great deal more work has been done on the phonology of Old Khmer but, generally speaking, I Ching's transcriptions have proved to be more accurate renderings of Southeast Asian toponyms than those of either the Hung-lu clerks or private individuals. Of course, it must be remembered that I Ching was travelling in the *Nan Hai* between 671 and 695, several decades after Fu-nan had ceased to exist as a political entity. It is unlikely, judging from the record of his itineraries to and from India [*Hsi-yü*, f. 98 recto et verso], that I Ching ever visited the territories that had formerly constituted Fu-nan, but he was a voracious reader, and was almost certainly acquainted with the reports of Kʻang Tʻai and Chu Ying from the 3rd century A.D. His remark [chüan 1, f. 4 recto] that Fu-nan had formerly been known as the Kingdom of the Naked Men 裸人國, for example, might have been an echo of the notion, also preserved in at least two Chinese histories (*Chin Shu* 晉書 chüan 97, f. 16 verso and *Hsin Tʻang-Shu* 新唐書 chüan 222C f. 4 recto), that the men of that country went naked, an idea which appears to have derived ultimately from the reports of

K'ang T'ai's mission — though Paul Pelliot considered rather that it betokened a confusion with the Naked Savages 裸[形]蠻 whom T'ang texts located to the southwest of Ssŭ-ch'uan and west of Yün-nan ["Deux itinéraires de Chine en Inde à la fin du Vllle siècle," *BEFEO*, vol. 4 (1904), p. 227, note 2]. Finally, I suspect that I Ching's interpolation in the *Nan-hai* . . . that "*Buât-nậm was formerly called *B'įu-nậm" 跋南國舊云扶南 [chüan 1, f. 4 recto] should be understood to imply not that *B'įu-nậm was the former name of the country that was in his day called *B'uât-nậm, but merely that the toponym had previously been transcribed as *B'įu-nâm. An instance where 云 is incontrovertibly used with more or less this connotation is reported in *T'ai-p'ing Yü-lan* 太平御覽 chüan 788, f. 6 recto: "the territory of *Pien-tou*, also rendered as *Pan-tou*" 邊斗國一云班斗.

Since Louis Finot, following up a comment by Colonel Gerini (cf. Note 36), first proposed that *B'įu-nậm was a Chinese transcription of Old Khmer vnaṃ (see above), the identification to my knowledge has been questioned on only three occasions: by Pierre Dupont ["La statuaire préangkorienne," *AA*, Supplement 15 (1955), p. 10]; by Claude Jacques ["'Funan,' 'Zhenla': the reality concealed by these Chinese views of Indochina," in R. B. Smith and W. Watson (eds.), *Early South East Asia* (New York and Kuala Lumpur, 1979), pp. 371-379]; and by Eveline Porée-Maspero [*Etude sur les rites agraires des Cambodgiens*, vol. 1 (Paris, and La Haye, 1962), p. 171, note 1]. The first two authors based their doubts on uncertainty as to whether the inhabitants of Fu-nan were of Khmer stock in the first half of the 1st millennium A.D. It is true that this has not been established with certainty. On the other hand, the alleged Chinese transcription appears to have been as phonetically perfect as the Chinese language permitted, and at least one other Old Khmer toponym, namely *Dmāk*, has been recognized in Chinese transcription (p. 124). In my opinion, these two transcriptions themselves afford a not negligible indication that at least certain elements of society in the lower Mekong valley, probably the ruling class or some sections of it, were ethnically Khmer at the time with which we are concerned. The onus of proving otherwise would seem to fall on those who reject the validity of the transcriptions. Mme Porée-Maspero believes that the Kings of the Mountain belonged to the solar dynasty of Dry-Land Chen-La.

No one can write about Fu-nan without acknowledging his indebtedness to Paul Pelliot, whose collation of the relevant Chinese texts first rendered their implications apparent ["Le Fou-nan," *BEFEO*, vol. 3 (1903), pp. 248-303]. Earlier in the same year Etienne Aymonier had attempted to identify the kingdom represented as Fu-nan ["Le Founan," *JA*, 10th series, vol. 1 (1903), pp. 109-150], and incorporated in his discussion a list of authors who had previously speculated on its location. These included, more or less in chronological order, Wilford, Bowring, Garnier, Rémusat, de Guignes, de Rosny, Klaproth, Pautier, Hervey de Saint-Denis, Barth, Blagden, Schlegel, and Takakusu. Subsequently several other scholars, and notably Professor George Coedès, have made important contributions toward refining our knowledge of this ancient polity as reflected in texts and epigraphy. Some of their works will be discussed in subsequent pages. For the archeological elucidation of the role of the Trans- and Cis-Bassac in the evolution of this culture we are beholden virtually to one man, Louis Malleret, whose investigations, although interrupted by hostilities in 1945 before their harvest could be fully gathered in, have yielded a great deal of information on these two regions, and particularly on the ancient port at Oc-èo. Malleret's reports and expositions appeared between 1959 and 1963 as Publication No. 43 of L'Ecole Française d'Extrême-Orient under the general title *L'Archéologie du delta du Mékong*: Vol. I, *L'exploration archéologique et les fouilles d'Oc-èo*; Vol. II, *La civilisation matérielle d'Oc-èo*; Vol. III, *La culture du Fou-nan*; Vol. IV, *Le Cisbassac*.

3. It is virtually certain that the etiological legend of the Fu-nan dynasty that has been preserved in Chinese histories and encyclopedias was recorded by two envoys, the *Chung-lang* (senior secretary) K'ang T'ai 中郎康泰 and the *Hsüan-hua-tsung shih* (cultural relations officer) Chu Ying 宣化從事朱應, who undertook a mission to that country between A.D. 245 and 250 [*Liang Shu*, chüan 54, ff. 1 verso, 9 verso and 22 verso - 23 recto. Dated by Pelliot, "Le Fou-nan," pp. 303 and 430.] The reports of both envoys seem to have been lost during the Sung period, but not before they had served as a quarry for numerous

other writers, so that a considerable portion of their information has been preserved in quotation. At different times K'ang T'ai's work appeared under the following ascriptions:

Fu-nan Chi 扶南記 ⎫
Fu-nan Chuan 扶南傳 ⎭ .... in *Shui-Ching Chu* 水經注 (late-5th or early-6th century)

Fu-nan t'u-su 扶南土俗 ⎫
Wu-shih wai-kuo chuan 吳時外國傳 ⎭ ... in *T'ai-p'ing Yü-lan* 太平御覽 (983)

Fu-nan t'u-su chuan 扶南土俗傳 ... in ⎰ *T'ung Tien* 通典 (c.812)
⎱ *T'ai-p'ing Huan Yü Chi* 太平寰宇記 (976-983)

K'ang-T'ai wai-kuo chuan 康泰外國傳 ⎫
K'ang-Shih wai-kuo chuan 康氏外國傳 ⎭ in *Shih-chi Cheng-i* 史記正義 (8th century)

Fragments of Chu Ying's report have been preserved under the following titles:

Fu-nan i-wu chih 扶南異物志 .... in ⎰ *Sui Shu* 隋書 (656)
⎱ *Hsin T'ang-Shu* 新唐書 (1060)

Fu-nan i-nan chi 扶南以南記 .... in *Nan Shih* 南史 (659)

And possibly as *I-wu chih* 異物志 .. in ⎰ *Shih-chi Cheng-i*.
⎱ *T'ung Tien*.

In addition, *Shui-Ching Chu* and *T'ai-p'ing Yü-lan* make frequent reference to a *Fu-nan Chi* 扶南記 by an otherwise unknown Chu Chih 竺枝/芝, which probably also derived ultimately from K'ang T'ai's work.
For the bibliography of these works see Paul Pelliot, "Le Fou-nan," pp. 275-277; Wheatley, *The Golden Khersonese* (Kuala Lumpur, 1961), pp. 114-115; and Hsiang Ta 向達 "Han-T'ang-chien Hsi-yü chi Hai-nan chu-kuo ku ti-li shu hsü-lu" 漢唐間西域及海南諸國古地理敘錄 *Bulletin of the National Library of Peip'ing*, vol. 4, no. 6 (Peip'ing, 1930).
The dynastic legend itself is incorporated, in slightly varying forms, in *Chin Shu* 晉書 chüan 97, ff. 16 verso - 17 recto; *Nan-Ch'i Shu* 南齊書 chüan 58, f. 8 verso; *Liang Shu* 梁書 chüan 54, ff. 6 verso - 7 recto; *Nan Shih* chüan 78, ff. 6 recto et verso; *T'ung Tien* 通典 chüan 188, f. 1008; *T'ai-p'ing Yü-lan* 太平御覽 chüan 786, f. 7 recto and 347, f. 7 verso.

4. The Chinese annalists are explicit in their assertions that the focus of the so-called Fu-nan polity was located in a broadly littoral situation:

Chin Shu, chüan 97, f. 16 verso: "It is in a great bay of the sea" 在海大灣中.
Nan-Ch'i Shu, chüan 58, f. 8 verso; *T'ai-p'ing Yü-lan*, chüan 786, f. 6 verso; and *Wen-hsien T'ung-k'ao* 文獻通考 chüan 331, f. 2601: "in a western bay of the ocean." *Nan-Ch'i Shu* actually says "among the oceanic Western Man" 大海西蠻中 but there can be no doubt that *Man* is a mislection for 灣 *wan*, the reading of the *T'ai-p'ing Yü-lan* and *Wen-hsien T'ung-k'ao*.
Nan-Ch'i Shu, chüan 58, f. 10 recto: "bordering the sea" 邊海.
Liang Shu, chüan 54, f. 5 recto; *Nan Shih*, chüan 78, f. 5 recto: "It is on a great bay in the west[ern part] of the sea 海西大灣中.
T'ung Tien, chuan 188, f. 1008: "It is on a large island in the west[ern part] of the sea" 海西大島中.
Moreover, a familiarity with the sea is implicit in the accounts of Fu-nan

contained in these works, whether it be manifested in references to the dừa nướ́c palm fringing the estuaries (Nan-Ch'i Shu, chüan 58, f. 11 verso) or to an ambitious ruler's designs for maritime expansion (Liang Shu, chüan 54, f. 7 recto).

I Ching [Nan-Hai Chi-kuei Nei-fa Chuan, chüan 1, f. 4 recto], with his customary concern for accuracy, specifically repudiated the word "island" (and with it presumably the 島 of T'ung Tien), saying, "There is the southernmost angle of Jambu[dvīpa]; it is not an island in the sea" 斯即瞻部南隅非海洲也. In Hindu cosmography Jambudvīpa was that one of the four continents disposed round Mount Meru which lay to the southward and was the home of man. The southern tracts of this continent constituted Bhāratavarṣa (the Indian subcontinent), so it follows that I Ching presumably regarded Fu-nan as a part of the Indian cultural realm.

5. The longitudinal extent of the kingdom of Fu-nan was presumably reflected in the statements of two Chinese histories (Nan-Ch'i Shu, chüan 58, f. 8 verso, and Liang Shu, chüan 54, f. 5 verso) and at least three encyclopedias (T'ung Tien, chüan 188, f. 1008; T'ai-p'ing Yü-lan, chüan 786, f. 6 verso; and Wen-hsien T'ung-k'ao, chüan 331, f. 2601) that it was more than 3,000 li in extent. Whatever length may be attributed to the li in these times (see below), this would seem to have been an excessive distance, but undoubtedly reflects the impressions made by this country on the minds of Chinese envoys. The most easterly extension of the Vnaṃ territories seems to be evidenced by an inscription from Võ-canh in the present-day Vietnamese province of Khánh-hòa. Both the date and the implications of the text have been the subject of lively debate, but it seems now that the late George Coedès successfully sustained his claims for a date in the 3rd century A.D. Possibly, as Louis Finot suggested some fifty years ago, the Nha-trang district was constituted a tributary chieftainship as a result of the predations of the ruler of Fu-nan in the 3rd century. [The controversy as to the date and implications of this inscription can be followed in: Auguste Barth and Abel Bergaigne, Inscriptions sanscrites de Campā et du Cambodge. Académie des Inscriptions et Belles-Lettres: Notices et Extraits des Manuscrits de la Bibliothèque Nationale et autres Bibliothèques XXVII, I (Paris, 1885-93, p. 191; Louis Finot, "Notes d'épigraphie," BEFEO, vol. 15 (1915), p. 3, and "Séance du 14 janvier," JA, vol. 210 (1927), p. 186; George Coedès, "The date of the Sanskrit inscription of Võ-canh," IHS, vol. 16, pt. 3 (1940), pp. 484-488; Dines Chandra Sircar, "Date of the earliest Sanskrit inscription of Campā," JGIS, vol. 6 (1939), pp. 53-55, and "Date of the earliest Sanskrit inscription of Campā, IHS, vol. 17, pt. 1 (1941), pp. 107-110; Naojirō Sujimoto, in Kuwabara hakushi kanseki kinen Tōyō shi ronsō (Kyōtō, 1931), especially pp. 265-267; Emile Gaspardone, "La plus ancienne inscription d'Indochine," JA, tome 241 (1953), pp. 477-485, and "L'inscription de Võ-canh et les débuts du sanskrit en Indochine," Sinologica, vol. 8, no. 3 (1965), pp. 129-136; K. Kumar Sarkar, "The earliest inscription of Indochina," Sino-Indian Studies, vol. 5, pt. 2 (1956), pp. 77-87; K. Bhattacharya, "Précisions sur la paléographie de l'inscription dite de Võ-Canh," AA, vol. 24 (1961), pp. 219-224; Jean Filliozat, "L'inscription dite de Võ-canh," BEFEO, vol. 55 (1969), pp. 107-116; Claude Jacques, "Notes sur la stèle de Võ-canh," BEFEO, vol. 55 (1969), pp. 117-124. For further remarks on these eastern territories of Fu-nan see Pierre Dupont, "Tchen-la et Panduranga," BSEI, new series, vol. 24, no. 1 (1949), pp. 9-25].

The position assigned to the western boundary of the kingdom will depend on the locations ascribed to several chieftainships brought within the realm during the 3rd century, at least one of which, that known to the Chinese as Tun-sun, appears to have been situated at the root of the Malay Peninsula in what is today western Thailand (see pp. 212-214 below). Fan Shih-man, allegedly the architect of the Fu-nan polity, died while campaigning against a country which the Chinese called Chin Lin 金鄰/潾 (Liang Shu, chüan 54, f. 7 recto]. Some commentators have read these graphs as a translation of Pāli Suvaṇṇabhūmi (= Land of Gold) or Sanskrit Suvarṇakuḍya (= Wall of Gold), which they have then been led to locate in the Irawadi valley. If this argument were to be sustained, it would place the western frontier of Fu-nan somewhere on the Bay of Bengal. I am not at this juncture prepared to deny the validity of this argument, but I do consider that it is open to some doubt and other interpretations are certainly possible (For bibliographical notes on Chin Lin see Wheatley, *The Golden Khersonese*, pp. 116-117, and for additional comments consult H. H. E. Loofs, "Problems of continuity between the pre-Buddhist and Buddhist periods in Central Thailand, with special reference to U-Thong," in Smith and Watson, *Early South East Asia*, pp. 342-351).

It is not possible to define the northern boundary of the kingdom at its maximum extent beyond noting that the vassal principality that eventually overthrew Fu-nan was located to the north of the Dangrēk escarpment [George Coedès, "Etudes cambodgiennes: A propos du Tchen-la d'Eau," *BEFEO*, vol. 36 (1936), pp. 1-13]. The lie of the southernmost frontier will depend on our interpretation of the location both of some of the 3rd-century Funanese conquests and of the principality known to the Chinese as *Ch'ih-t'u*, which was characterized as "another group of Fu-nan" 扶南之別種也 : *Sui Shu*, chüan 82, f. 3 recto; *Pei Shih* 北史 chüan 95, f. 11 verso; *T'ai-p'ing Yü-lan*, chüan 787, f. 1 verso; and *Wen-hsien T'ung-k'ao*, chüan 331, f. 2602 . Some of the conquered territories can be assigned with a fair degree of certainty to the isthmian tract of the Malay Peninsula [Wheatley, *Khersonese*, pp. 16-25], and *Ch'ih-t'u* was probably in the southern part of that region. [For an analysis of the relevant texts see Wheatley, "Ch'ih-t'u 赤土 " *JMBRAS*, vol. 30, pt. 1 (1957), pp. 122-133]. Louis Malleret has already pointed out that the territories falling within the limits defined in this manner are broadly in accord with the zone of diffusion of the coins stamped with the trefoil-like *śrīvatsa* emblem that occurred in great numbers in the excavations at Oc-èo [*L archéologie du delta du Mékong*, vol. 3, p. 327]. However, as Bennet Bronson has pointed out, the presence of the *śrīvatsa* design on *other* than numismatic artifacts at Beikthano in central Burma may argue for a Burmese (presumably Pyū), rather than a Funanese, origin: review of Aung Thaw, *Report on the excavations at Beikthano* in *Asian Perspectives*, vol. 12 (1969), p. 143. The bounds here prescribed in any case would have marked the farthest extensions of the polity and there is little reason to assign them any great degree of permanence. It is more likely that there was a continual fluctuation of the frontiers during the half-millennium of Fu-nan's existence.

For a general discussion of the location of Fu-nan see Brian E. Colless, "The ancient Bnam empire: Fu-nan and Po-nan," *Journal of the Oriental Society of Australia*, vol. 9, nos. 1 and 2 (1972-73), pp. 21-31.

The *li*, in which the Chinese often specified long distances in the South Seas, has varied with time and place. Between 721 and 725 I Hsing 一行, most famous of Chinese mathematicians under the T'ang, and Nan-kung Yüeh 南宮說 used standard 8-ft. gnomons to take simultaneous measurements of shadow lengths at summer and winter solstices along a meridian line stretching from northern Shan-hsi to Annam. From the results thus obtained it was calculated that a terrestrial distance of 1° was equivalent to 351 *li*, 80 *pu*. During the eighteenth century these figures were quoted by A. Gaubil [*Histoire de l'astronomie chinoise*, vol. 1. In *Lettres édifiantes et curieuses, écrites des missions étrangères: nouvelle édition——Mémoires des Indes et de la Chine* (Paris, 1783), p. 77], and in the nineteenth century by Vivien de Saint Martin [in Stanislas Julien, *Voyages des pèlerins bouddhistes*, vol. 3: *Hsi-Yü Chi*, (Paris, 1858), p. 258]. More recently John C. Ferguson ["Chinese foot measure," *Monumenta Serica*, vol. 6 (Peking, 1941), pp. 357-382] has used standard metal *ch'ih* to determine lengths at different periods in Chinese history, and found that the *ch'ih* of the Chou, Han and Western Chin (only a few years removed from K'ang T'ai's embassy) were equivalent to 0.231 meters, that of the Liang to 0.236 meters. In *Kuo-Hsüeh Ch'i K'an*, vol. 5, no. 4, T'ang Lan 唐蘭 has prepared a table of *ch'ih* measures which provides Chou and Han examples of 0.225, 0.23, 0.231, 0.234, 0.235, and 0.24 meters, with the median falling close to 0.23. This is also close to the Liang standard, so may be taken as representative for our present purpose. A Liang *li* would then have been equivalent to 414 meters. Some confirmation that this was approximately correct was obtained by R. A. Stein in his Indochinese studies, "Le Lin-Yi," *Han-Hiue*, vol. 2, parts 1 - 3 (Pekin, 1947), p. 89. See also this author's exposition on p. 11 of the same work, but cp. Wolfram Eberhard ["Bemerkungen zu statistischen Angaben der Han-Zeit," *T'oung Pao*, vol. 36 (1940), pp. 1-25], who defines the Han *li* as 496.8 meters, and Jen Nai-ch'iang 任乃強 [K'ang-tao Yüeh-k'an 康導月刊, vol. 2, p. 14], who found from an analysis of itineraries that the T'ang li approximated to a third of the contemporary li, that is about 360 meters. More recently, Wang Kuan-cho 王冠倬 has re-examined I Hsing's meridian measurements and demonstrated that in T'ang times a "short foot" of approximately 24.7 inches co-existed with a "long foot" of approximately 29.7 inches [Wen Wu 文物, no. 6 (1964), pp. 24-29].

Finally, it should be noted that the li of 556.5 meters was adopted by the K'ang-hsi Emperor on the advice of Jesuit astronomers, and derived ultimately from their calculation that 1° of longitude at the equator was equivalent to 200 li. On this topic it is still difficult to find a more succinct account than that in F. von Richthofen's *China: Ergebnisse eigener Reisen und darauf gegründeter Studien,* vol. 1 (Berlin, 1877), p. xix.

6. See Note 10 below.

7. The precise wording varies from source to source, but the expression quoted occurs in *Chin Shu,* chüan 97, f. 17 recto; *Liang Shu,* chüan 54, f. 6 verso; *Nan Shih,* chüan 78, f. 6 verso.

8. "Le Fou-nan," p. 254 (text and Note 6).

9. In Chou times the graph i denoted a walled city, a fortified burgh, or a seignioral seat. Even in Han and later times Chinese authors writing about foreign countries seem to have used it loosely to signify almost any settlement other than a capital.

10. The main accounts of Fu-nan are to be found in the following works:

(i) *Chin Shu* 晉書 chüan 97, ff. 16 verso - 17 recto. Compiled on an imperial order of 644 by Fang Hsüan-ling 房玄齡 and others, and presented to the throne in 646; relates to the period 266-420.

(ii) *Nan-Ch'i Shu* 南齊書 chüan 58, ff. 8 verso - 12 recto. Privately compiled by Hsiao Tzǔ-hsien 蕭子顯 (489-537) at some time prior to 530; relates to the period 479-502.

(iii) *Liang Shu* 梁書 chüan 54, ff. 5 recto - 9 recto. Compiled on imperial orders of 622 and 629 by Yao Ssǔ-lien 姚思廉, and presented to the throne in 636; relates to the period 502-557.

(iv) *Nan Shih* 南史 chüan 78, ff. 5 recto - 8 verso. Privately compiled by Li Yen-shou 李延壽 in 659; relates to the period 420-589.

(v) *Hsin T'ang-Shu* 新唐書 chüan 222 C, ff. 4 recto et verso. Compiled on an imperial order of 1045 by Ou-yang Hsiu 歐陽修 and Sung Ch'i 宋祁; presented to the throne in 1060; relates to the period 618-907.

(vi) *T'ung Tien* 通典 chüan 188, f. 1008. Compiled by Tu Yu 杜佑 over a period of thirty-six years: completed in about 812.

(vii) *T'ai-p'ing Yü-lan* 太平御覽 chüan 786, ff. 6 verso - 8 verso. Compiled under the direction of Li Fang 李昉 between 977 and 983.

(viii) *Wen-hsien T'ung-k'ao* 文獻通考 chüan 331, f. 2601. Begun by Ma Tuan-lin 馬端臨 in about 1254, completed in about 1280, but not published until 1319.

For other Chinese works treating of Fu-nan in less detail or even cursorily see Pelliot, "Le Fou-nan," pp. 275-288. A comparative analysis of the information contained in (i), (ii), (iii), (iv), and (vii) has been undertaken by Eveline Porée-Maspero, *Etude sur les rites agraires des Cambodgiens,* vol. 3 (Paris and La Haye, 1969), pp. 790-800.

11. Embassies from Fu-nan to the Chinese court are recorded at the following times:

226-231	San-Kuo Chih (Wu), chüan 15, f. 7 recto.	
243-244	San-Kuo Chih (Wu), chüan 2, f. 23 verso. Chüan 47, f. 12 verso dates this embassy precisely in 243.	
268	Chin Shu, chüan 3, f. 5 verso.	
285	Chin Shu, chüan 3, f. 13 recto.	
286	Chin Shu, chüan 3, f. 13 verso.	
287	Chin Shu, chüan 3, f. 13 verso.	
357	Chin Shu, chüan 97, f. 10 recto.	
434	Sung Shu, chüan 5, f. 6 verso.	
435	Sung Shu, chüan 5, f. 7 recto.	
438	Sung Shu, chüan 5, f. 7 verso.	
484	Nan-Ch'i Shu, chüan 58, ff. 5 verso - 6 recto.	
503	Liang Shu, chüan 2, f. 4 verso	
511	Liang Shu, chüan 54, f. 5 recto.	
512	Liang Shu, chüan 2, f. 10 recto.	
514	Liang Shu, chüan 2, f. 11 recto.	
517	Liang Shu, chüan 2, f. 12 verso.	
519	Liang Shu, chüan 2, f. 13 recto.	
520	Liang-Shu, chüan 3, f. 1 recto.	
530	Liang Shu, chüan 3, f. 5 verso.	
535	Liang Shu, chüan 3, f. 8 recto.	
539	Liang Shu, chüan 3, f. 10 recto.	
559	Ch'en Shu, chüan 2, f. 6 recto.	
572	Ch'en Shu, chüan 5, f. 4 recto.	
588	Ch'en Shu, chüan 6, f. 6 verso.	
618-649	Hsin T'ang-Shu, chüan 222C, ff. 2 verso - 3 recto.	

12. An extreme instance of this practice is to be found in San-ts'ai T'u Hui 三才圖會, compiled by Wang Ch'i 王圻 in 1609 but still preserving unchanged material from K'ang T'ai's report on Fu-nan in the 3rd century A.D. To the paragraph on Tun-sun, however, Wang Ch'i added a picture of an inhabitant dressed in a manner more suitable for Central than for Southeast Asia. This is an extreme case, but the practice was general in all classes of Chinese topographical writing.

13. See Note 10 above. In ascribing the Wai-kuo Chuan to the 3rd century, I am following Paul Pelliot ["Deux itinéraires de Chine en Inde à la fin du VIIIe siècle," BEFEO, vol. 4 (1904), p. 270, note 3] who equated it with the Wu-Shih Wai-kuo Chuan 吳時外國傳, attributed by Tao Shih 道世 in his celebrated Fa-yüan Chu-lin 法苑珠林 (668) to that century. The validity of this identification has been questioned by Mme Eveline Porée-Maspero [Etude sur les rites agraires des Cambodgiens, vol. 3 (Paris and The Hague, 1969), pp. 793-794] on the grounds that the phrasing of its account of the dynastic myth of Fu-nan is, generally speaking, closer to versions from demonstrably later texts (such as the Liang Shu) than to those of earlier ones (such as the Chin Shu). However, even if this be true, there is no guarantee that earlier texts invariably preserved earlier versions of the myth. In numerous instances comparatively late Chinese authors have preserved citations from early sources

otherwise unknown but still available to them. In any case, it is known that reports prepared by the 3rd-century envoys to Fu-nan did exist for a considerable period of time under a variety of ascriptions (cp. Note 4 above), and, what must surely be accounted significant in the present context, the *Shih-chi Cheng-i* of the 8th century refers to a *Wai-kuo Chuan* under the extended titles *K'ang-T'ai Wai-kuo Chuan* 康泰外國傳 and *K'ang-Shih Wai-kuo Chuan* 康氏外國傳. It is unlikely that memoranda such as K'ang T'ai's were formally titled, so that subsequent authors had little choice but to coin titles to a greater or lesser degree indicative of a document's contents. That the compilers of the *T'ai-p'ing Yü-lan* sought out materials dating from the 3rd century is attested by their inclusion of a paragraph from the *Nan-chou I-wu Chih* by Wan Chen in the same section as that mentioning the *Wai-kuo Chuan*.

14. For information on Wan Chen see *Sui Shu*, chüan 33, f. 10.

15. *Liang Shu*, chüan 54, f. 7 recto. The passage is repeated in *Nan Shih* (chüan 78, f. 6 verso), where the account of Fu-nan is a verbatim reproduction of that in the *Liang Shu*.

16. On this topic generally see A. H. Krappe, *La genèse des mythes* (Paris, 1938), and Mircea Eliade, *Cosmos and history. The myth of the eternal return* (New York, 1959. Original French edition, *Le mythe de l'éternel retour: archétypes et répétition,* Paris, 1949). This latter work describes a striking example of the rapidity with which an event can be reduced to a category and an individual to an archetype (pp. 44-45). In this instance, set in a Rumanian village, it took less than forty years, and, most surprising of all, the event had been transmuted into legend while a principal witness was still alive and resident in the neighborhood.

17. *Liang Shu*, chüan 54, f. 7 recto; repeated in *Nan Shih*, chüan 78, f. 6 verso.

18. *Ibid.*

19. *Ibid.*

20. Chiu-chih (九稚 *$K\underline{i}\underline{\partial}u$-ḍʑ̍) for Chü-li (拘利 *$K\underline{i}u$-1ji) = κώλη[πόλις]. Cf. p. 231.

21. Ch'ü-tu-k'un (屈都昆 *$K'\underline{i}uət$-tuo-kuən = καττίγαρα [ὅρμος Σίνων]. Cp. p. 447. Literally ὅρμος denotes a roadstead or anchorage, especially the inner part of a harbor where ships lie.

22. *Nan-Ch'i Shu*, chüan 58, f. 11 verso.

23. Cf. p. 120 above.

24. *Chin Shu*, chüan 97, f. 16 verso.

25. *Nan-Ch'i Shu*, chüan 58, f. 11 verso. Cp. the reference in *Hsin T'ang-Shu*, chüan 222C, f. 4 recto to a palisade serving as a wall 柵城.

26. *Nan-Ch'i Shu*, chüan 58, f. 11 verso. *Hsin T'ang-Shu* (chüan 222C, f. 4 recto) remarks more simply, but misleadingly, that dwellings were covered with bamboo. 梽, the graph translated as "bamboo," customarily refers to a fabulous tree or a fruit, but presumably here is used instead of the more usual 若 that is employed in the *Nan-Ch'i Shu*.

27. *T'ai-p'ing Yü-lan*, chüan 786, f. 8 recto.

28. *Liang Shu*, chüan 54, f. 5 verso. Repeated in *Nan Shih*, chüan 78, f. 5 recto.

29. *Hsin T'ang-Shu*, chüan 222C, f. 4 recto et verso.

30. The expression used is: "[the king] ruled over the city of Te-mu" 治特牧城.

31. Anc. Ch. = *Tśi̯ĕn-lâp.

32. George Coedès, "Etudes combodgiennes: quelques précisions sur la fin du Fou-nan," BEFEO, vol. 43 (1943-6), p. 4. Cf. also Pelliot, "Le Fou-nan," p. 295. Coedès' argument essentially is that a certain inscription, dated 664 and recording a royal promulgation (ājñā), was brought to the neighborhood of Bà Phnom by "the sādhu residing in the city of Naravaranāgara" [A. Barth, Inscriptions sancrites du Cambodge. Académie des Inscriptions et Belles-Lettres: Notices et Extraits des Manuscrits de la Bibliothèque Nationale et autres Bibliothèques, vol. 27, fasc. 1 (1885), no. X]. Naravaranāgara, therefore, must have been the name of the capital at that time, that is during the reign of Jayavarman I. Several inscriptions cut according to the commands of this king have been found in the neighborhood of Aṅkor Bórĕi, which is accordingly regarded as his probable capital: whence it follows that Aṅkor Bórĕi was the site of Naravaranāgara. For the precise significance of ājñā, see Hubert de Mestier du Bourg, "Ājñā, praçasta, çāsana," Journal Asiatique, vol. 254, nos. 3-4 (1967), pp. 375-382, but note certain reservations stated by Sachchidanand Sahai, Les institutions politiques et l'organisation administrative du Cambodge ancien. Publications de l'Ecole Française d'Extrême-Orient, vol. 75 (Paris, 1970), p. 32, note 4.

33. George Coedès, Inscriptions du Cambodge, vol. 2 (Hanoi, 1942), p. 110, note 5, and "Quelques précisions sur la fin du Fou-nan," p. 4.

34. George Coedès, "Etudes cambodgiennes: la tradition généalogique des premiers rois d'Aṅkor," BEFEO, vol. 28 (1928), p. 127. Cp. also Vnaṃ Vyādhapura mentioned in an inscription from Kŏk Rosĕi: Coedès, Inscriptions du Cambodge, vol. 6 (Paris, 1954), pp. 176-179.

35. For the Chinese text referring to events in 484 which established Śiva (not Indra) on the Mahendraparvata see Wheatley, "The Mount of the Immortals: a note on Tamil cultural influence in fifth-century Indochina," Oriens Extremus. Zeitschrift für Sprache, Kunst und Kultur der Länder des Fernen Ostens, vol. 21, pt. 1 (1974), pp. 97-109.

36. George Coedès was the first to attempt to substantiate this identification ["La tradition généalogique," p. 128), but Colonel Gerini had come close to the same conclusion when he equated Fu-nan with Khmer phnoṃ = hill, and located the capital of the country at Bà Phnoṃ [Researches on Ptolemy's geography of eastern Asia (London, 1909), p. 209. For a possible, though not probable, alternative "mountain," see Wheatley, "The Mount of the Immortals," p. 109.

37. The vicinity of the hill has yielded no inscription earlier than the reign of Īśānavarman I, who probably succeeded to the throne of Chen-la soon after 610.

38. Louis Malleret, L'archéologie du delta du Mékong, vol. 3: La culture du Fou-nan (Paris, 1962), p. 453: " . . . en survolant la région, ni Pierre Paris, ni moi-même n'y avons jamais vu quoi que ce soit qui pût éveiller l'idée de vestiges d'une grande ville."

39. Wheatley, "The Mount of the Immortals," passim.

40. Jean Filliozat, "L'inscription dite de Vō-canh," BEFEO, vol. 55 (1969), pp. 107-116. Also Filliozat, "New researches on the relations between India and Cambodia," Indica, vol. 3, no. 2 (1966), pp. 95-106.

41. Louis Malleret, Musée Blanchard de la Brosse. Catalogue général . . ., vol. 1 (Hanoi, 1937), no. 57, p. 70; Coedès, Inscriptions du Cambodge, vol. 5, pp. 35-38.

42. Coedès, *Inscriptions du Cambodge,* vol. 2, p. 115; Malleret, *L'archéologie,* vol. 3, p. 425.

43. Malleret, *L'archéologie,* vol. 1, pp. 139-143 and 154-155.

44. Inscription found in the Mébŏn and dated Ś 874 (A.D. 952); transcribed and translated by Louis Finot, "Inscriptions d'Aṅkor," *BEFEO,* vol. 25 (1925); refers to Svargadvārapura on pp. 312 and 332. It is interesting to note that Svargadvārapura is here compared to Puraṇḍarapura (the city of Indra):

Svarggadvārapure Puraṇḍarapuraprasparddhisaṃvarddhane
sārthvaś śarvvam [for śarvvaś] atiṣṭhipat savibhavaṃ liṅgaṃ vidhānānvitam.

Cp. also Coedès, *Inscriptions du Cambodge,* vol. 1 (1937), p. 106 and vol. 6 (1954), p. 6; and "Etudes cambodgiennes: A propos du Tchen-la d'Eau," *BEFEO,* vol. 28, no. 1-2 (1928), p. 134. It is not improbable that Svargadvārapura was subsequently the birthplace of King Bālāditya of Aninditapura (dates uncertain) who, in an inscription from Práh Ěinkosěi [*ISCC*, no. 14, A, st. 6, 1. 11] is referred to as *Svargadvārapurodito.* Coedès [*loc. cit.*, p. 133] has suggested that this city may possibly be identified with Dvāravatī (= Thvăr Kděi, not the kingdom discussed in Chap. 5) where Mahendradevī established foundations in Ś 874 and 879.

45. Stele of Tà Prohm, stanzas VI-VII: *vide* George Coedès, "La stèle de Tà Prohm," *BEFEO,* vol. 6 (1906), p. 71.

46. Inscription from Pràsàt Ampĭl Rolŭ'm: Coedès, *Inscriptions du Cambodge,* vol. 6 (1954), pp. 100-106; Claude Jacques, "Etudes d'épigraphie cambodgienne: VII, Sur l'emplacement du royaume d'Aninditapura," *BEFEO,* vol. 59 (1972), p. 217; Paul Lévy, "Thala Bŏrivăt ou Stu'n̊ Trèn̊: sites de la capitale du souverain khmer Bhavavarman Ier," *JA,* vol. 258 (1970), pp. 113-129.

47. Inscription from Sambór-Prei Kŭk: Coedès, *Inscriptions du Cambodge,* vol. 4 (1952), pp. 20-24. Cf. also *Sui Shu,* chüan 82, f. 5 recto; *Pei Shih,* chüan 95, f. 14 recto (Īśāna City, under the transcription **i-śi̯a-nā* 伊奢那城); Hsüan Tsang 玄奘 *Ta-T'ang Hsi-yü chi* 大唐西域記 (Taishō edition), chüan 10, f. 51 recto (Īśānapura, under the transcription **i-śi̯ang-nā-puo-lā* 伊賞那補羅). Aerial surveys have shown that at one time, probably the beginning of the 7th century, a wall and a moat enclosed some 4 square kilometers containing both temples and dwellings: "Chronique" for 1937 and 1938 in *BEFEO,* vol. 37 (1937), p. 655 and vol. 38 (1938), p. 442. The role of Īśānapura as an administrative, religious, and cultural center has been explicated by Milton Osborne, "Notes on early Cambodian provincial history: Isanapura and Sambhupura," *France-Asie,* vol. 20 (1966), pp. 433-449.

48. Barth and Bergaigne, *ISCC,* p. 369. For the presumed functions of Śambhupura as a point of consolidation during Khmer southward expansion, and subsequently as both an outpost for interaction with the hill tribes to the east and an outer defence against Cam incursions, see Osborne, "Notes on early Cambodian provincial history," pp. 443-448.

49. For references see Coedès, *Inscriptions du Cambodge,* vol. 8 (1966), "Index des noms propres de l'épigraphie du Cambodge," *sub verbo,* p. 20. Cf. also Georges Groslier, "Amarendrapura dans Amoghapura," *BEFEO,* vol. 24 (1924), pp. 359-372; Georges Coedès and Pierre Dupont, "L'inscription de Sdŏk Kăk Thom," *BEFEO,* vol. 43 (1943-46), pp. 114-115, 117, 121, note 2; Jacques, "Sur l'emplacement du royaume d'Aninditapura," p. 200.

50. Citations as for Note 49.

51. Citations as for Note 49.

52. For citations see Coedès, *Inscriptions du Cambodge,* vol. 8 (1966), "Index

des noms propres," p. 20; Lawrence Palmer Briggs, *The ancient Khmer empire*. Transactions of the American Philosophical Society, New Series, vol. 41, pt. 1 (Philadelphia, 1951), p. 55.

53. Stele of Pràsàt Trapāṅ Run, published and translated by Louis Finot, "La stèle du Pràsàt Trapāṅ Run," *BEFEO*, vol. 28 (1928), p. 58. Cf. George Coedès, "Les traditions généalogiques des premiers rois d'Angkor d'après les inscriptions de Yaçovarman et de Rājendravarman," *BEFEO*, vol. 28 (1928), pp. 124-140; Coedès, "A propos du Tchen-la d'Eau: trois inscriptions de Cochinchine," *BEFEO*, vol. 36 (1936), p. 12; Pierre Dupont, "La dislocation du Tchen-la et la formation du Cambodge préangkorien," *BEFEO*, vol. 43 (1943-46), p. 25; Jacques, "Sur l'emplacement du royaume d'Aninditapura," pp. 194-205.

54. Barth and Bergaigne, *ISCC*, Inscription from Poñā Hòr (Ponhear Hor), pp. 21-26.

55. For citations see Coedès, *Inscriptions du Cambodge*, vol. 8 (1966), "Index des noms propres," p. 41.

56. Coedès, "Index des noms propres," p. 21; Coedès, "Les capitales de Jayavarman II," *BEFEO*, vol. 28 (1928), pp. 117-119. Indrapura, probably situated to the east of Kŏmpoṅ Cam, seems to have become the capital of Jayavarman II (802-850), but late in the 6th century had constituted a patrimonial-style benefice granted to one Narasimhagupta: see Coedès, "Etudes cambodgiennes: XXXVI, quelques précisions sur la fin de Fou-nan," *BEFEO*, vol. 43 (1943-46), pp. 5-8.

57. For citations see Coedès, "Index des noms propres," p. 55.

58. Coedès, *Inscriptions du Cambodge*, vol. 2 (1942), pp. 12 and 151, and vol. 7 (1964), p. 14.

59. Barth and Bergaigne, *ISCC*: Inscription from Vằt Căkret in the architectural group of Bà Phnoṃ, pp. 38-44; Etienne Aymonier, *Le Cambodge*, vol. 3 (Paris, 1903), p. 420; Georges Maspero, *L'empire khmer* (Phnoṃ Penḥ, 1904), p. 24, note 1. Although Aymonier and Maspero's identification of Tāmrapura with Tʻe-mu (*$D̑ǝk$-$m̯iuk$: p. 124 above), apparently on phonetic grounds, cannot be sustained, the provenance of the Vằt Căkret inscription makes it probable that Tāmrapura was located in the general vicinity of Bà Phnoṃ.

60. For citations see Coedès, "Index des noms propres," p. 22. Cf. Barth and Bergaigne, *ISCC*, inscription from Hàn Čei, pp. 8-21.

61. O. W. Wolters, "North-western Cambodia in the seventh century," *Bulletin of the School of Oriental and African Studies*, vol. 37, pt. 2 (1974), pp. 355-384. The chieftainships, which were reportedly absorbed by Chen-la during the second half of the 7th century, were:

    Seng-kao (*$Səng$-kau 僧高) = Sangko. Cf. inscription from Vằt Bàsĕt: Coedès, *Inscriptions du Cambodge*, vol. 3 (1951), pp. 5 and 9; stele from Stŭṅ Čràp: Coedès, *IC*, vol. 5 (1953), p. 209.

    Wu-ling (*$M̯iu$-$li̯äng$ 武令) = Malyāng. Cf. Coedès, *IC*, vol. 1 (1937), p. 30.

    Chia-cha (*Ka-$dẓ̑a$ 迦乍) = Gaja[pura]. Cf. inscription from Phnoṃ Pràḥ Nét Práḥ: Coedès, *IC*, vol. 3, p. 36.

    Chiu-mi (*$Ki̯ǝu$-$mi̯ĕt$ 鳩密) = *Kum——. The final element in this name has not been restored.

    Fu-na (*$Pi̯ǝu$-$nâ$ 富那) = Vana[pura]. Cf. inscription from Nong Pʻang Pʻuey: Coedès, *IC*, vol. 7 (1964), p. 139.

158   Nāgara and Commandery

The first four toponyms are mentioned in *Wen-hsien T'ung-k'ao* (Wan-yu Wen-k'u edition), p. 2602; all five in *Hsin T'ang-Shu* 新唐書 chüan 222C, f. 2r and *Ts'e-fu Yüan-kuei* 冊府元龜 chüan 970, ff. 11398v and 11402v.

62. *Sui Shu*, chüan 82, f. 6r. One city which has figured as a capital of Chen-la since its existence was first proposed by George Coedès in 1936 ["A propos du Tchen-la d'Eau," pp. 3 and 11] must now be discounted. Coedès's argument was as follows. A certain Bālāditya is mentioned in pre-Aṅkor epigraphy as ruler of Aninditapura (cf. Note 53 above) at an undetermined date. It would not have been out of character for this Bālāditya, like many other Khmer monarchs, to have founded a capital bearing his name, Bālādityapura, and Coedès claimed to see confirmation of such an action in the name under which the Chinese referred to the capital of Maritime Chen-la: *B'uâ-lâ-d'iei-b'wat 婆羅提拔 [*Hsin T'ang-Shu*, chüan 222C, f. 5r.; *Wen-hsien T'ung-k'ao*, chüan 332]. This interpretation implied, of course, that Bālādityapura was an alternative style for Aninditapura, a name which, in any case, did not occur in Khmer inscriptions until the reign of Yaśovarman (889-900) [Coedès, "A propos du Tchen-la d'Eau p. 11, note 10.]. Unfortunately for this theory, it is not possible to accept *B'uâ-lâ-d'iei-b'wat as a transcription of Bālādityapura: instead it should be restored as Baladeba or Baladeva [Note that the Buddhist transcription of Bālāditya, though not necessarily that which would have been employed by the authors of the T'ang history or the *Wen-hsien T'ung-k'ao*, was 婆羅阿迭多 *B'uâ-lâ-.â-d'iet-tâ]. What this means is that if Bālāditya did build a capital bearing his name, it has not yet been discovered in text or inscription.
Of the two restorations proposed here, Bālādeba is to be preferred. Normally -deva is rendered as — 提婆 : e.g. Mokṣadeva 木义提婆; Devavarman 提婆跋摩; Sarvajñadeva 薩婆慎若提婆; Candradeva 旃達羅提婆; Cintadeva 振多提婆; Buddhadeva 佛陀提婆; Saṃghadeva 僧伽提婆. On the other hand, the form Bālādeba occurs only once in Khmer epigraphy, and then as the name not of a ruler but of a sculptor working as late as the reign of Jayavarman VII (1181- c.1219): cf. "Inscriptions de Prāsāt Tā Kèv" in Coedès, *Inscriptions du Cambodge*, vol. 4 (1962), p. 160.

63. All the information relating to the city at Oc-èo contained in this section is derived from the four volumes in which Louis Malleret reported the results of his archeological investigations in the Mekong delta (Note 2 above).

64. In recent writing on Fu-nan there has been a tendency to refer to the city revealed by Malleret's investigations as the city of Oc-èo. This is a convenient form of reference so long as it is borne in mind that the name is recent, and that all attempts to connect it with ancient toponyms such as Κοκκο[ναγάρα] of the Ptolemaic corpus are illusory. Oc-èo appears to be a French rendering of a Việtnamese transcription of O-Kéo, a postulated dialectal form of Kampuchean Ūr-Kèv, meaning "the Canal of the Jewels." This name serves to recall the canal that ran through the longer axis of the city in ancient times and where, presumably, inhabitants of neighboring villages in more recent days were accustomed to find items of jewelry such as first drew M. Malleret's attention to the site. That the name is recent is attested by the fact that *kèo* (= "gem" or "jewel") is a Thai loan word unknown in Khmer during the Aṅkor period (Malleret, *L'archéologie*, vol. 1, p. 99 and vol. 2, 427).

65. At the time of Malleret's excavations Oc-èo was situated in Rạch-giá province, and consequently appears in this way in the literature. However, Ordinance No. 143-N.V. of 22 October 1956 reconstituted the administrative divisions of Việtnam so that the village now lies in Kiên-Giang province.

66. *Liang Shu*, chüan 54, f. 7 verso. Also *Nan Shih*, chüan 78, ff. 7 recto et verso.

67. Malleret, *L'archéologie*, vol. 1, chap. 14, "L'habitation sur pilotis." Also p. 123 above.

68. *Loc. cit.*, vol. 2, pp. 291-292 and plate XCIX.

Cities of "The Hunter" 159

69. *Edifice A* in Malleret's catalogue: vol. 1, pp. 233-251.

70. George Coedès, *Les Etats hindouisés d'Indochine et d'Indonésie* (3rd edition, Paris, 1964), pp. 92-94, and Malleret, *L'archéologie*, vol. 3, chap. 22.

71. E.g. in Fu-nan: *Liang Shu*, chüan 54, f. 8 verso, and *Nan Shih*, chüan 78, f. 8 recto; in Chen-la: *Sui Shu*, chüan 82, f. 7 recto and *Wen-hsien T'ung-k'ao*, chüan 332, f. 2605; in Tun-sun: *T'ai-p'ing Yü-lan*, chüan 788, f. 1 verso, *T'ung Tien*, chüan 188, ff. 1008-9, and *Wen-hsien T'ung-k'ao*, chüan 331, f. 2601.

72. It may be that the centrally situated well in this building was a symbolic representation of the lower pole of the axis that, in passing through Mount Meru, afforded access to the Ocean. *Vide* plate XXII of Malleret's *L'archéologie*, vol. 1.

73. *Edifice K* in Malleret's catalogue, vol. 1, pp. 258-269.

74. *L'archéologie du delta du Mékong*, vol. 1, pp. 202-203.

75. These figures assume that the form of the enceinte has been deciphered correctly, but Malleret himself cautions that, "La topographie de l'enceinte est du reste trop atténuée et trop incertaine, pour que l'on puisse en toute sécurité s'engager dans de semblables spéculations" (*L'archéologie*, vol. 1, p. 203).

76. See pp. 91-93.

77. Shen Huai-yüan 沈懷遠 *Nan-Yüeh Chi/Chih* 南越記/志 apud *T'ai-p'ing Huan-yü Chi*, chüan 165, f. 5 verso: 其城九重 ; *Ðai-Việt sử-kí toàn-thư* 大越史記全書 quyển 2, f. 6 recto.

78. Rolf Stein, "Jardins en miniature d'Extrême-Orient," *BEFEO*, vol. 42 (1942), p. 54; and "Le Lin-yi," *Han-Hiue*, vol. 2, fasc. 1-3 (Pékin, 1947), chap. 6. [In this second work the author appears as R. A. Stein.]

79. Stein, "Le Lin-yi," chap. 6. In Stein's interpretation the ethnonyms Lin-I (*Liəm-ʻiəp), K'un-lun (*Kuən-luən) and Khmer, the name of the state known to the Chinese as Chen-la (*Tśiěn-lâp), and numerous other toponyms, among them Prome and Campā, all derive by phonetic evolutions proper to their respective languages from a consonantal complex KRM or PRM.

80. E.g., the style of the king of Fu-nan incorporated the syllables *kuruṅ* [as the *Hsin T'ang-shu*, chüan 222C, f. 4 recto, puts it: "The family name of the king is *kuruṅ* (*ku-lung* 古龍)": cp. *Wen-hsien T'ung-k'ao*, chüan 331, f. 2601], as did that of its vassal Tun-sun (*T'ai-p'ing Yü-lan*, chüan 788, f. 1 verso), while the same element figured prominently in the titles of the chief ministers of the principality known to the Chinese as P'an-p'an (see p. 313 below). Stein (*loc. cit.*) has also suggested that the name Chen-la (*Tśiěn-lâp*), by which the Chinese referred to an important vassal of Fu-nan, was also a rendering of this basic element after the initial consonant had changed according to a regular and allegedly well attested evolution *kl-/pl-* or *kr-/pr-* > č/s.

81. In the French system of co-ordinates this latitude is recorded as 11 grades 362 N.

82. *Vide* P.[ierre] Paris, "L'importance rituelle du Nord-Est et ses applications en Indochine," *BEFEO*, vol. 41, fasc. 2(1941), pp. 303-333.

83. This orientation is measured off plates XII, XIII and XV of Malleret's *L'archéologie*, tome 1.

84. Henri Parmentier, *Inventaire descriptif des monuments čams de l'Annam*, vol. 2 (Paris, 1918), 27.

85. Paris, "L'importance rituelle du Nord-Est," pp. 303-333.

86. G[eorge] Coedès, "Etudes cambodgiennes: La destination funéraire des grands monuments khmers," *BEFEO,* vol. 40, fasc. 2 (1940), pp. 338-9.

87. In both Thailand and Burma the site of the royal crematorium is known by a name derived from Skt. *Meru:* Thai = T'ung P'ra Men; Khmer = Văl Práh Mén [both < *Braḥ Meru*]. In Yaśodharapura the fabulous creatures such as *nāga, kumbhanda* and *gandharva* depicted on the successive tiers of the so-called Terrace of the Leper King leave no doubt that this also was a symbolic representation of Mount Meru (Coedès, *loc. cit.,* p. 338).

88. Coedès, *loc. cit.,* p. 332. For a Javanese example see J. L. A. Brandes, "Een puzzle opgehelderd," *TBG,* vol. 47 (1904), p. 461.

89. Gustave Dumoutier, *Le rituel funéraire des Annamites. Etude d'ethnographie religieuse* (Hanoi, 1904), pp. 80 et seq.

90. L[eopold] Cadiére, "Le sacrifice du Nam-giao; La disposition des lieux," *Bulletin des Amis du Vieux Hué* (Hanoi, 1915), pp. 101 et seq.

91. Paris, "L'importance rituelle," pp. 317-324 and plate XLIII.

92. Malleret, *L'archéologie,* vol. 1, pp. 189-190.

93. Malleret, *L'archéologie,* vol. 3, chap XIX.

94. Malleret, *L'archéologie,* vol. 2, part 2.

95. *Loc. cit.,* vol. 3, chap. 17.

96. *Loc. cit.,* chaps. 1-10.

97. *Loc. cit.,* chaps. 12-16.

98. *Ibid.*

99. *Loc. cit.,* vol. 2, part 3.

100. *Ibid.*

101. *Ibid.*

102. This inability to distinguish any degree of areal specialization within the city results not only from the relatively unstable nature of the deltaic terrain in which the excavations were carried out, as well as their comparatively short duration that permitted examination of only a few selected sites within the enceinte of the city, but also from the fact that the ground was greatly disturbed by clandestine treasure seekers both before and during Malleret's investigations. In fact, a considerable proportion of the materials from Oc-èo that are now housed in the Ho Chi Minh City museum were acquired by purchase from such treasure hunters. With the collapse of governmental control after 9 March 1945 the site became subject to looting on a grand scale, so that it is doubtful if it would repay further archeological investigation. Malleret reports that, "Quand nous l'avons survolé en 1946, il donnait l'impression d'un terrain qui semblait avoir été soumis, pendant des semaines, à un bombardement d'artillerie et, comme l'on était à la fin de la saison sèche, l'illusion d'une certaine altitude était celle d'un paysage lunaire" (Malleret, *L'archéologie,* vol. 1, p. 225).

103. Malleret, *L'archéologie,* vol. 3, chaps. XXII-XXIV and vol. 4, *passim.*

104. George Coedès, *apud* Malleret, *L'archéologie,* vol. 3, p. 311. See also

vol. 2, pp. 335-342. It is known that superficially similar objects were used as seals in Roman times, but Malleret points to a possible Buddhist implication in the term *apramādaṃ*, in which case the plaques may have served as amulets. It is well established that Buddhism was strongly represented in Fu-nan from the 2nd century A.D. until the dissolution of the kingdom.

105. Several Trans-Gangetic cities in the Ptolemaic corpus seem to have been similarly situated: Καττίγαρα, Ἀσπίθρα, Ταμάρα, Ἀγιμοίθα; the city known to the Chinese as Tun-sun was 10 *li* from the sea; the capital of the Lin-I 40 *li*; Lion City, capital of the Red-Earth Country, was probably a day's journey from the coast (assuming that "month" 月 in the relevant text, an impossible time in the circumstances, should be emended to read "day" 日). See p. 252; if Lo-yüeh (*Lâ-jiwat 羅越) is indeed to be identified with Sĕluyut, as J. L. Moens has suggested (which involves the emendation of "thousand" to "ten"), then it was located in a similar situation [Moens, "Srīvijaya, Yāva en Katāha," *TBG*, vol. 77 (1937), p. 337].

106. See pp. 137-141.

107. Also known as Núi Ba-thé. To the Cambodians it is Bhnaṃ Pá Thê or Pā Dhê, or even occasionally Bhnaṃ Pād Saṃnêr.

108. P. 124 above.

109. Cp. Note 32.

110. George Coedès, "Le site primitif de Tchen-la," *BEFEO*, vol. 18 (1918), pp. 1-3.

111. Wheatley, *The Golden Khersonese*, chap. XVIII.

112. Malleret, *L'archéologie*, vol. 1, p. 200.

113. Malleret, *L'archéologie*, vol. 1, chap. 4.

114. Cf. Wheatley, *The pivot of the four quarters* (Edinburgh and Chicago, 1971), chap. 3.

115. Malleret, *L'archéologie*, vol. 1, p. 92.

116. *Ibid*.

117. Such an inundation features prominently in the folklore of Indochinese hill tribes such as the Bahnar, Stieng and Rhadé. Cp., *int. al.*, T. Gherber and L. Malleret, "Quelques légendes des Moï de Cochinchine," *BSEI*, (1946); B. Y. Jouin, "Les traditions des Rhadés: *loc. cit.*, vol. 25, pt. 1 (1950), pp. 357-400; *France-Asie*, nos. 49-50, pp. 21-24; Jean Cassaigne, "Les montagnards de la région de Djiring," *loc. cit.*, no. 74 (1952), pp. 352-359 and no. 75 (1952), pp. 504-512; P. Guerlach, *Annales des Missions Catholiques*, vol. 19 (1887).

118. Malleret, *L'archéologie*, vol. 1, pp. 125-131.

119. Malleret, *loc. cit.*, pp. 110-113. It is significant that Tráp-đá signifies "stony swamp," presumably with reference to the granite blocks, vestiges of former settlement, lying on its surface. The site is also known locally as Brai Aṅgrūṅ or Thma Aṇtêt (= protruding stone).

120. Malleret, *loc. cit.*, pp. 102-106.

121. Malleret, *loc. cit.*, pp. 163-169. Thnal Mray = "hundred avenues," whence the French translation Cent Rues by which this location is usually known. Certain sites in the vicinity are known as Liếp-đá (= mound of stones), Liếp-bàn (= earth mound), Liếp-vườn (= garden mound), Đền Công Chúa (= princess's palace)

and Nền Công Chúa (= foundations of the princess's palace).

122. P.[ierre] Paris, "Anciens canaux reconnus sur photographies aériennes dans les provinces de Tà Kèv et de Châu-đốc," BEFEO, vol. 31 (1931), pp. 221-4; "Notes et mélanges: anciens canaux reconnus sur photographies aériennes dans les provinces de Takeo, Châu-Đốc, Long-Xuyên et Rach-giá," BEFEO, vol. 41 (1941), pp. 365-370; and "Autres canaux reconnus à l'Est du Mékong par examen d'autres photographies aériennes," loc. cit., pp. 371-373.

123. As a result of the reconstitution of the provinces in 1956 (see Note 47), the former province of Châu-đốc is now incorporated in An-giang province.

124. L'archéologie, vol. 1, pp. 117-124.

125. Also known as Bhnaṁ Svām.

126. Also known as Bảy Núi, and on French maps optionally as Massif de Triton and Sept Montagnes.

127. Recent advocates of this point of view include Louis Malleret, L'archéologie, vol. 3, p. 324, note 3 and Bernard-Philippe Groslier, The art of Indochina (London, 1962), p. 56.

128. V. Venkayya, "Irrigation in southern India in ancient times," Archaeological Survey of India, Annual Report 1903-04 (Calcutta, 1906), pp. 202-211.

129. F. Kielhorn, "Talagunda pillar inscription of Kakusthavarman," Epigraphia Indica, vol. 8 (Calcutta, 1905), pp. 24-36. In verse 33 it is related that the Kadamba king Kākusthavarman constructed a tank at Talagunda in the Shimoga district of Mysore State.

130. E. Hultzsch, "Mahendravadi inscription of Gunabhara," Epigraphia Indica, vol. 4 (1896-97), pp. 152-3. This inscription refers to a tank built by the Pallava king Mahendravarman I at Mahendrāvaḍi in North Arcot. See also District Manual of North Arcot, vol. 2, pp. 438-439.

131. Venkkaya, "Irrigation in southern India," passim.

132. Madeleine Colani, Emploi de la pierre en des temps reculés: Annam — Indonésie — Assam. Publication des Amis du Vieux Hué (Hanoi, 1940), especially pp. 13-14.

133. See particularly Malleret's comments on the implications of the canals for land tenure, population density, and urban concentration in ancient Fu-nan on p. 123 of vol. 1 of L'archéologie.

134. Bernard-Philippe Groslier, The art of Indochina (London, 1962), p. 56: "It therefore seems likely that the canal network was so arranged by skilful adjustments of the gradients that it both carried the water of the Bassac to the sea, and washed the salt out of the ground, making possible intensive cultivation of floating rice."

135. Wolters, "Khmer 'Hinduism'," pp. 428 and 429.

136. Claude Jacques, "'Funan,' 'Zhenla': the reality concealed by these Chinese views of Indochina," in R. B. Smith and W. Watson, Early Southeast Asia: essays in archaeology, history and historical geography (New York and Kuala Lumpur, 1979), p. 376. On this topic see also Jacques, Annuaire, 1971-1972, pp. 609-610; Wolters, "North-western Cambodia in the seventh century," pp. 379-383; and I. W. Mabbett, "The 'Indianization' of Southeast Asia: reflections on the historical sources," Journal of Southeast Asian Studies, vol. 8, no. 2 (1977), p. 154.

137. Wolters, "Khmer 'Hinduism'," p. 429; Jacques, "'Funan', 'Zhenla'," pp. 375-376.

138. *Hou-Han Shu* 後漢書 chüan 115; *San-Kuo Chih* 三國志 chüan 30. For an analysis of the situation in the latter area see Paul Wheatley and Thomas See, *From court to capital* (Chicago, 1978), pp. 18-36.

139. P. 367 below.

140. Wan Chen, *Nan-chou I-wu Chih apud T'ai-p'ing Yü-lan*, chüan 786, f. 12.

141. *Nan-Ch'i Shu*, chüan 58, ff. 8v - 9r; *Liang Shu*, chüan 54, f. 7r and v.

142. *Liang Shu*, chüan 54, f. 1 r and v.

143. *Liang Shu*, chüan 54, f. 7r.

144. Door-pillar inscription from Hàn Čei: Auguste Barth, "Inscriptions sanscrites du Cambodge," *Journal Asiatique*, ser. 7, vol. 20 (1882), pp. 223 and 229, st. v. Cp. also pp. 219 and 226, st. x.

145. Barth, "Inscriptions sanscrites," p. 226, st. xi.

146. *Liang Shu*, chüan 54, f. 7r. For a commentary on this text see Wheatley, *The Golden Khersonese*, chap. 2.

147. George Coedès, "Etudes cambodgiennes, XX: Les capitales de Jayavarman II," *BEFEO*, vol. 28 (1928), pp. 113-123; Pierre Dupont, "La dislocation du Tchen-la et la formation du Cambodge angkorien (Vlle - IXe siècle)," *BEFEO*, vol. 43 (1943), pp. 17-55, and "Le début de la royauté angkorienne," *BEFEO*, vol. 46 (1952), pp. 119-176; O. W. Wolters, "Jayavarman II's military power: the territorial foundation of the Angkor empire," *JRAS*, no. 1 (1973), pp. 21-30; Claude Jacques, "Etudes d'épigraphie cambodgienne: VIII: La carrière de Jayavarman II," *BEFEO*, vol. 59 (1972), pp. 205-220. There is some likelihood that at least one of the competing chiefdoms during the Chen-la period was considered a tributary of the Javanese Śailendra dynasty: see Coedès, "A possible interpretation of the inscription at Kĕdukan Bukit (Palembang)," in John Bastin and R. Roolvink (eds.), *Malayan and Indonesian studies. Essays presented to Sir Richard Winstedt on his eighty-fifth birthday* (Oxford, 1964), pp. 24-32, and *Etats hindouisés*, pp. 176-177.

148. Cf. Chap. 6, p. 234 and Note 24.

149. Barth, "Inscriptions sanscrites du Cambodge," pp. 222 and 228, st. xxxii.

150. F. H. van Naerssen, "Sovereignty in early Hindu-Java," in Himansu Bhusan Sarkar (ed.), *R. C. Majumdar felicitation volume* (Calcutta, 1970), pp. 164-178.

151. These inscriptions have been plotted on a map of the Indochinese Peninsula by Dr. Judith M. Jacob in Smith and Watson, *Early South East Asia,* map at end of volume. This map relates to Dr. Jacob's paper placed earlier in the volume: "Pre-Angkor Cambodia: evidence from the inscriptions in Khmer concerning the common people and their environment," pp. 406-426.

CHAPTER 4

Cities of the Pyū

The preta in the form of a monitor lizard with a double tongue . . . signifies that the people of the kingdom shall not till the land but shall live by merchandise, selling and buying . . .

Prophecy of Gautama Buddha.
Cited in *The Glass Palace Chronicle*:
English translation by Pe Maung Tin and G. H. Luce.

It has already been pointed out that parts of the isthmus of the Malay Peninsula, together with the southern reaches of the Čhao Phraya, may have come under the nominal control of one of the *parvatabhūpāla* of Fu-nan, perhaps as early as the 3rd century A.D., and it is not impossible that the lower Irawadi valley may also have been brought under his sway. At the same time the Chinese were extending their control southwestwards from Ssŭ-ch'uan. In A.D. 69[2] they established the prefecture of Yung-ch'ang 永昌 to watch over the Ai-lao (哀牢 *·âi-lâu) in the high country between the Mekong[3] and the Salween.[4] Although it was abolished in 342,[5] this temporary salient of Chinese political power served as a window on to the great valleys beyond. From time to time various tribal groups from beyond the frontiers offered tribute at Yung-ch'ang[6] and it would appear that in the early centuries of the Christian era Upper Burma afforded a route — though difficult and apparently not used all that frequently — between India and the Chinese realm. However, the monk I Ching 義淨 preserved the memory of more than a score of Chinese Buddhist pilgrims who, during the 7th century, made their way to India by the Tsang-k'o 牂牁 road, that is through Ssŭ-ch'uan and Yün-nan to the Upper Irawadi and Chindwin and so to Assam or Bengal.[7] Concurrently, disconnected fragments of information about kingdoms in the far west of peninsular Southeast Asia began to filter into the Chinese world. Chin-lin (金隣 *Ki̯ǝm-li̯ĕn), Lin-yang (林陽 *Li̯ǝm-i̯ang), and the Nu-hou (奴後 *Nuo-ɣǝu) are mentioned vaguely in

165

166   *Nāgara and Commandery*

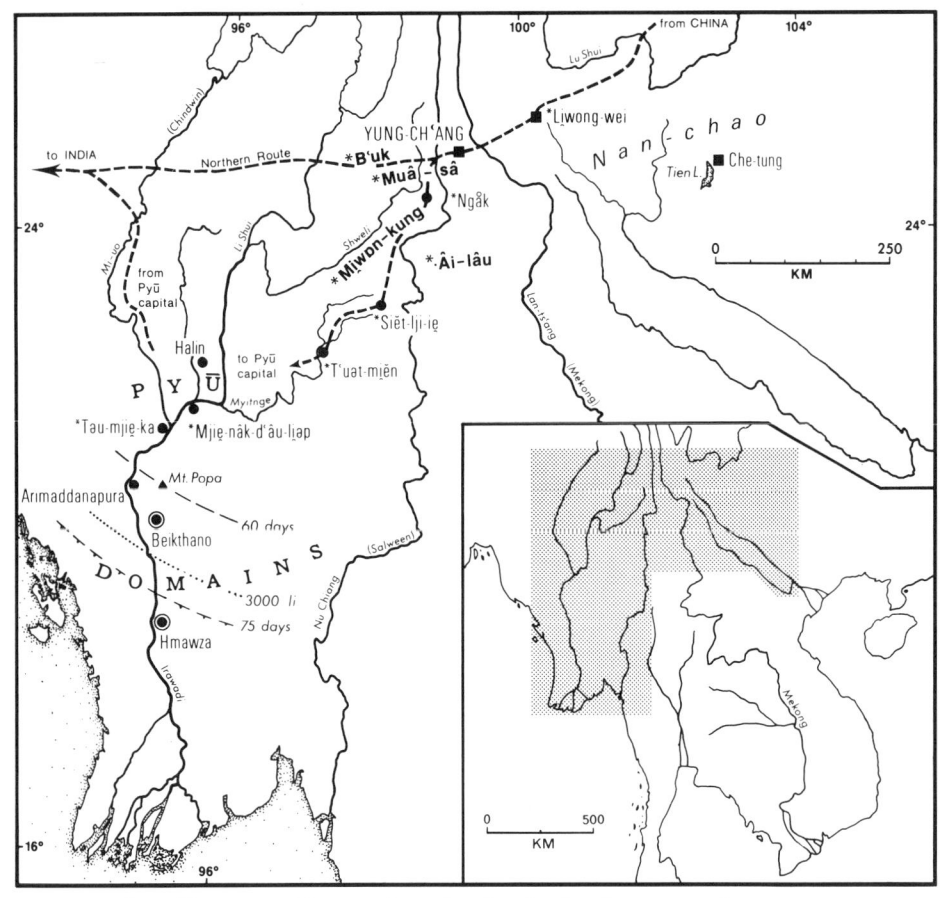

Fig. 12. Locations of archeological sites, ancient toponyms and ethnonyms mentioned in this chapter. The arcs in the southwestern sector of the map indicate the distances, in *li* and days' travel from Yung-ch'ang, that are discussed on p. 179 and in Note 67.

surviving works,[8] and, though they cannot be identified with
certainty, may be assigned with some confidence to the vicinity of
modern Burma. With the Pʻiao (剽 *Pʻi̯äu) we are on firmer ground.
They are described as living beyond the cannibalistic Pʻu (濮 *Bʻuk)
tribes in the vicinity of what is now the Sino-Burmese frontier,
and at a distance of 3,000 *li* from Yung-chʻang.[9] That the Chinese
considered the Pʻiao to have attained some degree of civilization is
evident from the remark of the author of the *Hou-Han Shu* that they
acknowledged the Confucian proprieties.[10] There can be no doubt that
these *Pʻiao* are the people who, though known to the Burmese as Pyū,
called themselves *Tirčul* or something similar.[11] Archeological and
epigraphic evidence of Pyū settlement has been found as far south
as Prome and as far north as Halin, so that it is safe to say that
they were at one time the dominant ethnic group in the middle
Irawadi valley. They are usually said to have been ethnically
proto-Burman, but this categorization is of dubious value, and the
point has little significance for our present study.

The City at Beikthano

The earliest evidence of Pyū culture, which is at the same
time the earliest manifestation of urban — or at least
proto-urban — form anywhere in the Indianized realms of Southeast
Asia, has been acquired from archeological excavations at
Beikthano, a site some 12 miles west of Taungdwingyi.[12] There
U Aung Thaw and his collaborators investigated a trapezoidally
shaped enceinte of some 3 1/2 sq. miles enclosed by a wall of baked
brick (Fig. 13) which on the north and south sides even today
attains an average height of six feet. The east wall now survives
only as a low ridge, while the west wall is no longer visible,
having presumably been eroded away by floodwaters from the Yan Pe
stream and from the Ingyi and Gyogyakan lakes which abut against
the course that this section of wall presumably once took. The
original height of the wall is unknown.[13] The east wall is aligned
13° west of north,[14] and the west wall was probably inclined at
about 16°. The south wall and the eastern half of the north wall
run within a degree or two of a true east-west direction, but the
western half of the north wall swings to more than 20° to the south
of a latitudinal line. Whereas the eastern wall is almost exactly
2 miles in length, the north and south walls are each some two
furlongs less, while the west wall, because of the southerly
inclination of the western half of the north wall, was probably
even shorter. It is noticeable, moreover, that, whereas the walls

168 Nāgara and Commandery

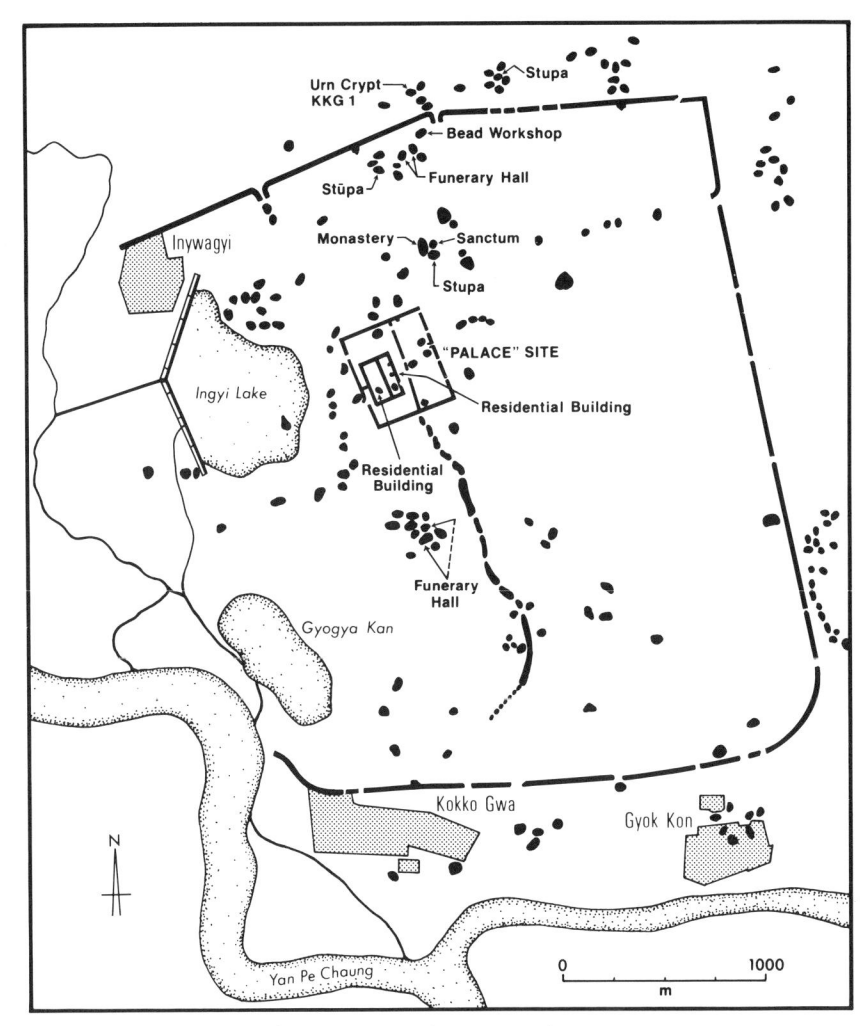

Fig. 13. Remains of the city at Beikthano. Based on Aung Thaw, *Report on the excavations at Beikthano* (Rangoon, 1968), Fig. 1. The numbers attached to sites are those of Aung Thaw's KKG (for Kokkogwa Village Tract) serial numeration.

at the northeast corner meet sharply at an angle of 92°, both southern corners are rounded. Nevertheless, the general impression afforded by the enceinte is of an approach to square shape and orientation to the cardinal compass directions. Internally, an irregular, though generally north-south trending, wall divided the city into eastern and western sectors.[15] No traces of a moat were observed, though a natural channel may have served that purpose along at least part of the north wall.[16]

Situated somewhat to the north-northwest of the geometrical center of the enceinte, and astride the dividing wall, is a brick-walled enclosure, departing only slightly from the rectangular and with sides 513 yards from north to south by 413 yards from east to west. It also is divided lengthwise by a partition wall into two unequal areas, the western (larger) one of which contains yet another rectangular enclosure that is itself divided into two by its own partition wall. All six longer walls within this inner complex are aligned about 17° west of north, which means that they diverge from a cardinal orientation by more than the deviation of the east wall of the city or the presumed run of the west wall. In other words, from the standpoint of overall design, the city comprised three more or less rectangular enceintes at successively reduced scales, each being internally divided by a partition wall. The inner two enceintes together have traditionally been known as the Palace Site, a usage followed by Aung Thaw in his report.

The perimeter wall of the outer city was pierced by twelve gates, apportioned three to each side[17] in what may have been an approach to the cosmomagically sanctioned manner mentioned in a subsequent paragraph. Two of these gates were excavated, both in the north wall (KKG 13 and 15 in Aung Thaw's serial numeration of excavated sites). Each was formed by projections from the main city wall curving inwards for a distance of more than 80 feet to form a passage 20 feet wide, within which a double-leaf, wooden gate reinforced with iron was hung on iron sockets. The passageway was floored with rammed earth and sand on a foundation of brickbats. Guardrooms were incorporated within the arms immediately behind the gates. A smaller gateway was also excavated, this time near the midpoint of the east wall of the Palace Site. It was designated by Aung Thaw as the principal entrance to that complex. Unlike the practice in the perimeter gates, the arms of the palace wall turned inwards abruptly at right angles, and projected only to a distance of 35 feet. The resulting passageway was 14 ft. 9 in. wide and floored with the same materials as were the outer gateways. Sentry recesses were provided in the arms. No traces of a gate were recovered, but two huge sandstone blocks, positioned outside the enclosure wall and bearing pairs of human feet in high relief, were interpreted by the excavators as indicating the former presence of larger than life-size *dvārapāla* guarding the main entrance to the "palace" complex.[18] Architecturally similar fortified gateways have also been discovered at Hmawza and Halin.

An extremely important aspect of the investigations at Beikthano, and one which distinguishes the site from others of comparable date in Southeast Asia, was the discovery of nearly a hundred substantial brick structures within and around the city. These seem to have included buildings for religious, funerary, probably ceremonial and administrative purposes, and in at least one instance a workshop — though Aung Thaw is at pains to emphasize the predominantly tentative nature of his classification of architectural functions.[19] The population at large, by contrast, and probably its rulers as well, dwelt in houses of perishable materials such as timber and bamboo, none of which was recovered during the excavations.

Among the structures excavated were apparent residential buildings both within and outside the palace complex (KKG 5 and 7), a postulated religious building containing an inner cella interpreted as a sanctum and surrounded by a circumambulatory corridor (KKG 4), *stūpas* (KKG 3, 14, 18), funerary halls (KKG 9, [ascribed on radiocarbon evidence to the 1st century A.D.], 11, 12, 24), a bead-making workshop (KKG 17), and what appears to have been the living quarters of a community of Buddhist monks (KKG 2). This last, situated about 300 yards north of the palace complex, comprised a two-storey building of approximately 100 x 35 ft., excluding an entrance hall projecting from the east side (Fig. 14). Its residential function was deduced from the presence of an abundance of domestic pottery and the recovery of personal ornaments.[20] Like the structure of undetermined "residential" use revealed at Site KKG 5,[21] this building followed the orientation of the palace complex.[22] And like several other structures excavated within the city confines, it showed the influence of the Buddhist architects of Nāgārjunakoṇḍa in the Kṛṣṇa valley of South India. Among other structures exhibiting similar influence were a cylindrical building at site KKG 3 which resembled the typical Āndhra type of *stūpa,* with *āyaka* platforms at the cardinal points,

Cities of the Pyū   171

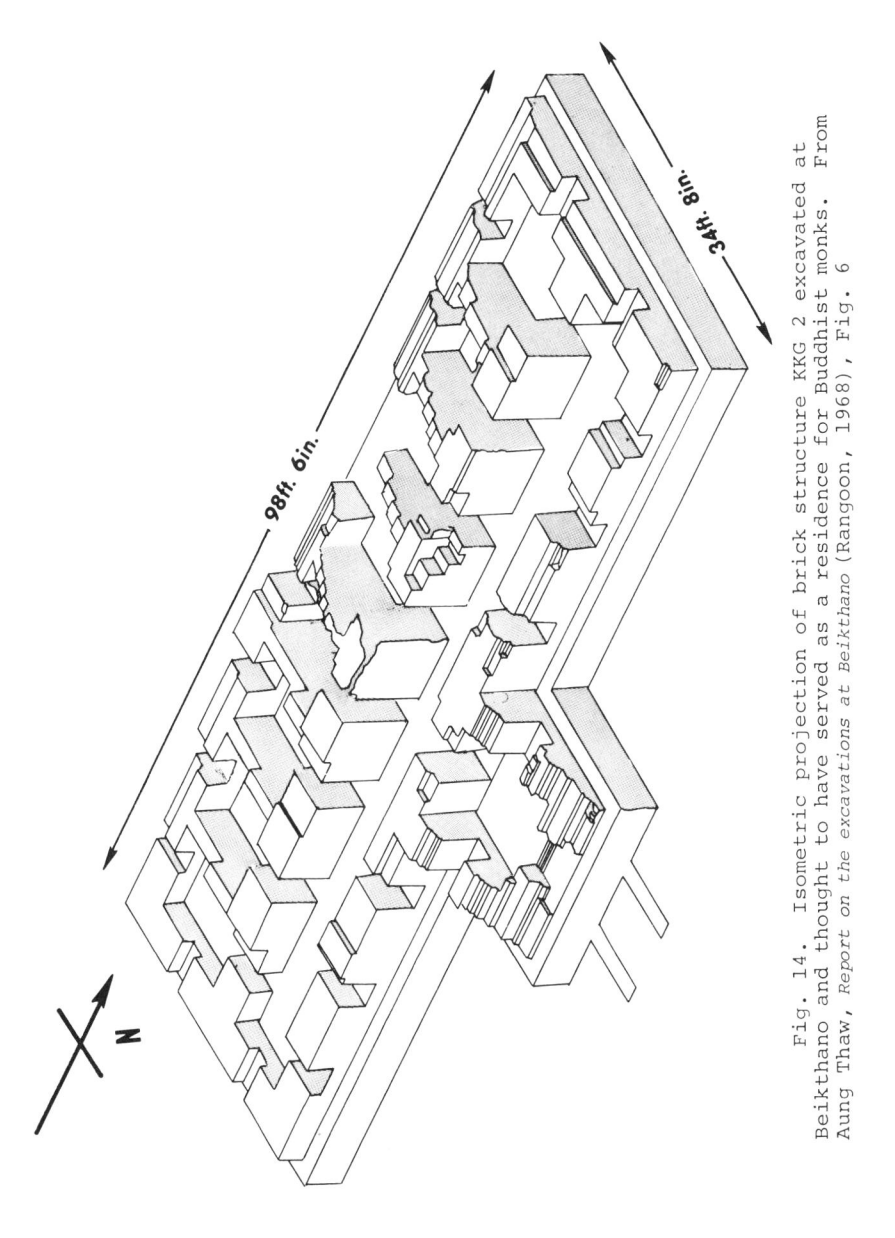

Fig. 14. Isometric projection of brick structure KKG 2 excavated at Beikthano and thought to have served as a residence for Buddhist monks. From Aung Thaw, *Report on the excavations at Beikthano* (Rangoon, 1968), Fig. 6

at Amarāvatī and Nāgārjunakoṇḍa;[23] three cylindrical structures standing on square bases and probably surmounted by low, hemispherical domes, which resemble the *uddeśika stūpas* of Nāgārjunakoṇḍa (KKG 6, 14, 18);[24] and oblong buildings (KKG 9 and 11) which had parallels at Nāgārjunakoṇḍa in the form of pillared assembly halls attached to monastic establishments.[25] The absence of artistic and ritual objects on these sites (even allowing for the centuries of pillaging that undoubtedly preceded the excavations: one site [KKG 21] is currently known to local villagers as *Shwegyingon*, meaning "Gold-sifting Mound") has led Aung Thaw to suggest that these architectural forms were introduced into the middle Irawadi valley by monks of the original Apara-mahāvina-seliya and Mahīsāsaka sects of Āndhradeśa, who refused to accede to the practice of worshipping the Buddha image.[26] It follows, of course, that the structures exhibiting these features from Nāgārjunakoṇḍa cannot antedate the very end of the 3rd century A.D., while it is equally evident that the earliest structures on the site — the halls mentioned above — manifest no Indian influence at all.

Most notable among other cultural affinities observed by the excavators of Beikthano are the correspondences with the Pyū sites at Hmawza and Halin as established by the presence of elaborately flanged and ridged burial urns, uninscribed coins (popularly known as Pyū coins),[27] large bricks with finger marks, and beads of clay and semi-precious stones. Despite the close architectural resemblances of the religious structures at Beikthano to Buddhist monuments at Nāgārjunakoṇḍa, the mass burials in urns both within the precincts of religious buildings and in brick crypts outside the city walls are a distinctively Pyū characteristic.

In spite of the wealth of cultural information yielded by the site, the most significant result obtained from the excavations at Beikthano concerns the dating of the settlement. Four radiocarbon dates assign sites KKG 9 and KKG 11 respectively to the 1st or 2nd century and the 3rd or early-4th century A.D.,[28] which establishes Beikthano both as the earliest Pyū site so far discovered and as the earliest possible urban (perhaps more accurately proto-urban) form yet known in western Southeast Asia. The earliness of the attribution is wholly in accord with the letters in Brāhmī script of the 2nd century A.D. on a seal impression found outside the residential building at site KKG 2;[29] with the imprint on the seal of a donor's name ending in *-siri*, a practice common in Amarāvatī inscriptions of the 1st century A.D.;[30]

with the occurrence of certain pottery types having analogues at early historic sites in India and mainland Southeast Asia;[31] with the imprint of auspicious symbols on pottery sherds and the so-called Pyū coins in a manner common at early Buddhist sites in India; and with the evident influence of Āndhra practice on Beikthano architectural forms. The city was apparently destroyed by fire in the 4th or 5th century A.D.

In Aung Thaw's view, then, the city flourished from the 1st to the 5th century A.D. However, in a perceptive review of *The Excavations,* Bennet Bronson has pointed out that the primary reason for terminating the occupation of Beikthano in the 5th century is that its artifactual assemblage appears to be earlier than that of the other large central-Irawadi settlement of Hmawza.[32] Aung Thaw has given his opinion that the last phase at Beikthano coincided with the beginning of the earliest phase at Hmawza.[33] But the dating of Hmawza is not precise in its limits and, in Bronson's opinion, it should not be assumed that "all Period I material at Beikthano necessarily dates as early as A.D. 500." Bronson has further remarked that the excavators of the city did not relate their artifactual typologies to the stratigraphy of the sites in an entirely satisfactory manner, so that their *Report* tends to imply that the material culture of the city was homogenous and unchanging through at least four centuries of its existence. Needless to say, this assumption makes for difficulties in effecting precise comparisons with other sites.

The City at Hmawza

The only literary mention of the Pyū contemporaneous with the period of Beikthano as defined by Aung Thaw is an uninformative reference in the *Hua-yang-Kuo Chih* 華陽國志 of A.D. 347.[34] The earliest archeological finds made so far outside the vicinity of Beikthano have been fragments of the Pāli Buddhist canon, dateable paleographically no earlier than about A.D. 500, from the neighborhood of Hmawza, or Old Prome.[35] It was in this general area that in the 7th century the Chinese monks Hsüan Tsang 玄奘 and I Ching 義淨 located a kingdom which they called Śrī Kṣetra,[36] an honorific previously associated with the city of Puri in Orissa, and presumably indicative of a desire by the Pyū rulers of Śrī Kṣetra to share in the traditions of that city.[37] It was probably at the end of this century and the beginning of the 8th that there reigned the only two known Pyū dynasties, one associated with a *-vikrama* style, the other with a *-varman* style. In a Sanskrit

174   *Nāgara and Commandery*

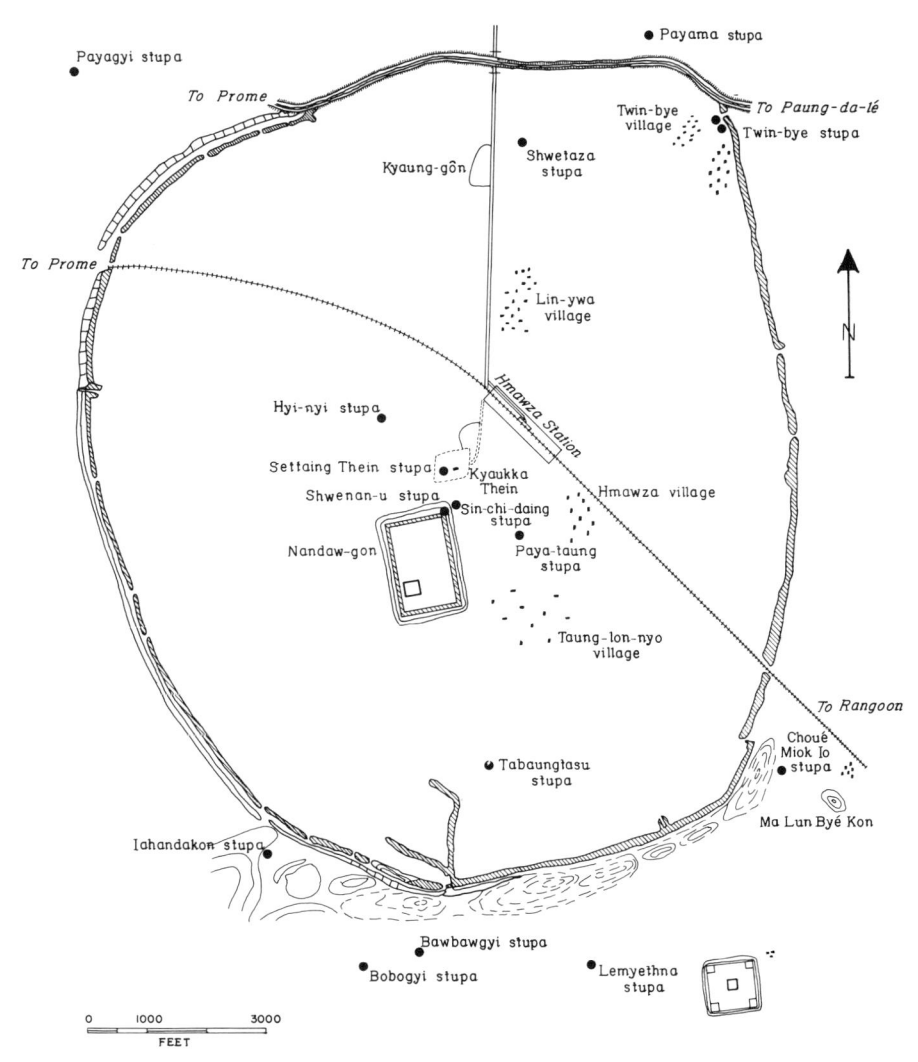

Fig. 15. Surviving traces of the ancient enceinte at Hmawza, which is believed to have been the Pyū capital of Śrī Kṣetra. Redrawn from a map by the Archaeological Survey of Burma for General L. de Beylié and published in his *Prome et Samara* (Paris, 1907), Fig. 55. The plan was subsequently published in the *Report of the Superintendent of the Archaeological Survey of Burma for the year ending 31st March, 1925* (Rangood, 1925).

inscription dated paleographically to about the 7th century, representatives of the two dynasties are depicted as ruling over twin cities (*puradvayam*) between which a treaty of friendship had been negotiated under the auspices of a religious teacher (*ārya*).[38] It has usually been assumed that one of these cities was Śrī Kṣetra (Burmese = Thayekhettayā), but this is by no means securely established: the prestigious style is not mentioned in the inscription. That the two cities were not of equal status in the eyes of the author of the inscription is evident from the fact that Jayacandravarman referred to the ruler of the other city, a certain Harivikrama, as his "younger brother" (*tasyānuja*), thereby signifying that the latter was his tributary.[39] The statement in the inscription that the two cities were both built in one day (*ekaika divase*) presumably signifies only that the geomantic and ritual procedures associated with their founding were completed on a certain day, or possibly that both were of comparable antiquity. On the basis of urn inscriptions from Hmawza, it is usually contended that the -*vikrama* dynasty ruled at Śrī Kṣetra. If that were indeed so, and if the tribute-offering Harivikrama were the prince mentioned in an urn inscription as dying in 695, then in the last decade of the 7th century Śrī Kṣetra could not have been the most powerful of the Pyū kingdoms. This is, however, the only Pyū site dateable to the 7th and 8th centuries which has been investigated with any degree of thoroughness, and it is not impossible that the identification may eventually prove to be spurious. Certainly the vestiges surviving to the present day indicate that a settlement of impressive size formerly occupied the site, and epigraphic and sculptural remains attest that Pyū at some time occupied this region. So far as I have been able to discover from the published reports of excavations at Hmawza,[40] the walls of the city have not been dated specifically to the Pyū period, but in the context outlined above it is reasonably certain that this was a Pyū foundation, and probably a capital. Luce is inclined to believe that the city originally occupied a tract of land in a fork of the river, with "one shallow branch of the Irrawaddy (or perhaps the Nawin Chaung) flowing across the north and east sides of the city into the Myitmaka."[41] The most striking features of the ruins are the sections of massive brick wall that demarcate a roughly circular perimeter of some eight and a half miles (Fig. 15). In Burmese legend the Nāga King described this perimeter, in the presence of the assembled gods, with the aid of a rope one end of which was held steady by Śakra[42] at the center of the circle.

Within the area meted by the Nāga in this manner Śakra built "the golden city . . . noble and glorious as Sudassana city, his own abode; marvellously graceful it was, having all the things needful for a city, namely: main gates thirty-two, small gates thirty-two, moats, ditches, barbicans, machicolations, four-cornered towers with graduated roofs over the gates [meaning, I presume, that the gates were surmounted by four-cornered towers . . .], turrets along the walls, and so forth; the whole being one *yojana*[43] in diameter and three *yojana* in circumference."[44] The implications of this legend are many and varied, but it is sufficient here to note that the spatial deployment of institutions and features of city morphology in multiples of four pertains to a genre of symbolism designed to ensure the harmony of man and his works with the patterned rhythms of the universe. To what extent the symbolism was notional and to what extent it was carried into practice in the Pyū capital, is impossible to say. It would seem virtually certain that the majority of the gates would have been depicted symbolically, perhaps by false doors or even niches in the wall, but, on the other hand, the traces of moats, both external and internal, are apparent today. The architectural prominence of the gate-towers also belongs to the complex of symbolism just mentioned.[45] What is usually believed to have been a palace complex comprised a rectangular precinct set within a rectangular enceinte with dimensions of 650 x 350 meters. The whole arrangement was situated some distance south of the geometrical center of the city and, as at both Beikthano and Halin, orientated with its longer axis slightly west of north.

Curious, and so far unexplained, features of the layout of this city are the isolated, moated enceintes that are still discernible both inside and outside the walls. Those within the city limit serve to recall the morphologically similar "Western Quarter" situated within the capital of the Lin-I (p. 389 below), but even if this is a valid comparison, no one has been able to suggest the functional role of such enclosures. Those outside the wall present an even more difficult problem which is unlikely to be solved except by archeological investigation. Also outside the walls, there still survive three *stūpas* of a style that took its origin on the coast of Orissa, and which, together with several vaulted and *śikhara*-crowned chapels inspired by structures in the same part of India, confirm that association of Śrī Kṣetra with the pilgrimage city of Puri which is implicit in the name of the capital. This is all that it is possible to say about the morphology of the city, but it is evident that in literary descriptions it was held to incorporate elements of a symbolism founded upon a pentad of cosmic forces. Only further archeological research will determine if this symbolism was more than notional in the material form of the city. Other supposedly Pyū settlment sites are known, but none has been investigated archeologically except Halin, and that only cursorily, so that it is uncertain whether they date from the earlier or later periods of Pyū history.[46]

In 802 and 807 Pyū envoys accompanied an embassy from Nan Chao 南詔 to the Chinese court, as a result of which paragraphs on their homeland were incorporated in both T'ang histories and sundry other annals and encyclopedias.[47] Included in these accounts are items of information about the capital city: the city wall, bordered by a moat, was 160 *li* in circumference,[48] faced with glazed tiles of greenish hue 青甓 and pierced by twelve gates (presumably three to each side, though this is not stated explicitly). A subsequent phrase notes that "the four corners took the form of pagodas" 四隅作浮圖, but it is not entirely clear whether this remark refers to the corners of the gates or those of the walls: I am inclined to prefer the former alternative. The city encompassed more than a hundred wats, decorated with gold and silver, cinnabar and gum-lac, and furnished with embroidered rugs. A brief remark in the *New T'ang History* adds that the dwelling of the king was similar to the wats, meaning, I take it, that its architectural style and decoration were on the same pattern. The tiles used in the city (or perhaps those on the pagodas at the four corners: the phrasing is unclear) were of lead and tin, and the timbering of *li-chi*.[49] A final sentence observes that the populace lived wholly within the city, but I am uncertain as to the precise implications of this statement. The *Old T'ang History* includes an additional note to the effect that the inhabitants actually residing within the city (城內) numbered several tens of thousands of families,[50] which implies a population of from 60 - 100,000. This seems an unlikely magnitude in view of what little we know about the populations of early Southeast Asian cities.

The reader will have noticed that this description of the Pyū capital provided by the Chinese annalists differs from that of Burmese legend. It differs in the length accorded the perimeter (160 *li* versus 3 *yojana*), for example, though this is probably not very significant, the Chinese estimate deriving from a Pyū embassy, the Burmese from legend. More important is the difference in the number of gates — twelve as against the thirty-two main and thirty-two minor gates of the *Glass Palace Chronicle*. Twelve gates, in the context of the symbolism by which urban space was subsequently sacralized through much of East Asia, implied a square enceinte,[51] whereas both legend, and probably archeology (if Śrī Kṣetra was indeed at Hmawza), attest a roughly circular wall. It is, of course, not impossible that Śrī Kṣetra, despite the apparent agreement of archeology and tradition, is not represented by the ruins at Hmawza, but even so the testimony of the *Glass Palace Chronicle* implies a memory of a circular enceinte. An alternative resolution of the discrepancy between the accounts would be to postulate a change in the location of the capital city so that, whereas Burmese legend would have preserved the rememberance of an earlier urban tradition, the Hung Lu clerks and others would have described a later foundation. This interpretation, in fact, accords with evidence marshalled by Gordon Luce which may be held to imply a movement of the capital from Hmawza in the south (if we accept the tradition that this was at one time a Pyū capital) to somewhere in Upper Burma.[52] In the first place, both the *Hsin T'ang-Shu* and the *Man Shu* speak of "sandhills 沙山 devoid of vegetation" 不生草 in the vicinity of the capital,[53] terrain that is more consonant with the seasonal drought of Upper Burma than with the perpetually humid climate of the lower Irawadi valley. In the second place, an itinerary prepared by Chia Tan 賈耽, Duke of Wei and Prime Minister under Emperor Te-tsung 德宗 at the end of the 8th century,[54] outlined a route leading southwestwards from Yung-ch'ang into the valley of the Myitnge (or perhaps the Shweli) and on to the Pyū capital, whence a continuation turned northwestwards up the Chindwin[55] and so by way of present-day Manipur to Kāmarūpa. Luce has queried whether a trade route between China and India would have diverged so far southward, and is inclined to see in this itinerary evidence of a capital located in Upper Burma. Against this interpretation, it might be argued that Chia Tan was not necessarily charting a main route of travel from China to India so much as a route from Yung-ch'ang to the Pyū capital, whence it was also *possible* to go to India. The direct route between China and India in any case passed far to the north.

It is unfortunate for our present purpose that the T'ang histories do not name the Pyū capital in the 8th century, although the *Old T'ang History*[56] notes that in Pyū tradition it was supposed to

be the native city of Śariputra (rendered as 舍利佛), one of
Gautama's foremost disciples, who actually hailed from Rājagṛha in
Magadha. On the basis of this text, Luce has suggested that the
Pyū capital may also have received the honorific Rājagṛha.[57] Even
if this were so, Śrī Kṣetra could also have figured in the full
style of the city since city honorifics often showed a tendency to
comprehensiveness.[58]

Finally Fan Ch'o, in the *Man Shu*,[59] located the Pyū capital
seventy-five days' journey from Yung-ch'ang which, to judge from
other itineraries preserved in the same work, would place the
capital in Upper Burma — though not necessarily to the north of the
Chindwin-Irawadi confluence. If we seek a possible site in that
region, it is Halin (Hanlaṅ) that immediately comes to mind. In
this neighborhood remains of irregular walls, spaced over a
distance of two miles but apparently part of one complex, are still
visible, and sculptures, coins, and Pyū inscriptions have come to
light, one incorporating, significantly, the styles of a king and
queen.[60] However, nothing has so far been found to link these
remains specifically to a Pyū capital, and there are some
indications that the artifactual assemblage from Halin implies a
rather earlier date than that with which we are here concerned.
Moreover, it should be remembered that this is the only Pyū site in
Upper Burma subjected to systematic investigation, and that but
superficially. Speculation on the role of Halin in the Pyū polity
will therefore be premature until more intensive excavation is
undertaken.

The identities of the twin cities mentioned in the
(apparently) 7th-century inscription referred to in a previous
paragraph remain as a continuing problem in Pyū historiography. On
the basis of currently available archeological and epigraphic
evidence, the balance of probability would appear to incline
towards identifying one of the cities as Śrī Kṣetra and, such is
the consensus of tradition, locating it at Hmawza. However, the
theme of twin cities also figures prominently in Burmese mythology.
According to the mythologized annals known as the *Taungdwingyi
Thamaing*,[61] Śrī Kṣetra and Beikthano were once ruled by,
respectively, King Duttabaung and Princess Panhtwar, both of whom
were descended through the folk heroes Mahāthambawa and
Sulathambawa from a ruler of Tagaung. Ultimately Duttabaung
signalled his defeat of the Princess in war by marrying her. What
is significant in this tale for present purposes is that, whereas
Duttabaung (Pyū = Great King) was credited with possession of a

third, divine eye, and therefore assimilated to the god Śiva, Princess Panhtwar was styled *Beikthano* [= Viṣṇu] *Minthami*. It has been suggested, therefore, that the tale of these two cities is a mythologized remembrance of the establishment of a Śaivite ascendancy over a Vaiṣṇavite community.[62] If the protagonists were indeed the rulers of Śrī Kṣetra and Beikthano, then it need occasion no surprise that the latter city plays no further part in the Burmese chronicles. It will be recalled, moreover, that Beikthano was destroyed by fire, allegedly in the 4th or 5th century A.D.[63]

The chief impediment to this reading of the *Taungdwingyi Thamaing* is, of course, the disparity in the chronologies assigned to Beikthano and Śrī Kṣetra: respectively the 1st to 5th centuries A.D. as against the 5th to 7th centuries. It is true that some scholars[64] have taken the dates of the *-vikrama* dynasty of Śrī Kṣetra as having been reckoned by the Śaka Era, which was initiated in A.D. 78, rather than by the Burmese Era (Cf. Note 38). By placing the dynasty in the 2nd century instead of from the 5th to the 7th, this change in chronology would render Śrī Kṣetra and Beikthano partly contemporaneous but would raise formidable problems of representational, stylistic, symbolic, and epigraphic attribution. A more acceptable resolution of the disparity in the chronologies of the two cities would be to rely on Bronson's opinion, cited on p. 173 above, that all Period I material from Beikthano does not necessarily antedate the beginning of the 6th century. On this view, the later phases at Beikthano would have overlapped with the earlier phases at Hmawza/Śrī Kṣetra, and a triumphant Śaivism would have supplanted Vaisnavism before itself yielding precedence to Theravāda Buddhism employing both the Pāli and Sanskrit (Sarvāstivāda) canons.[65] However, all this is speculation which may be subverted by archeological research at any moment.

Intimations of a Developing Urban Hierarchy

The capital or capitals, as the case may be, are the only Pyū cities of which we know more than the name. Although even in these cases the available information is meager in the extreme, the aura of symbolism that pervades the fragments of evidence makes it virtually certain that these cities fell within the broad category of ceremonial-administrative complexes. It is known that there were other urban or proto-urban foci in the Pyū territories, but it is impossible to suggest locations for more than one or two. The *New T'ang History*,[66] for example, lists nine what it calls garrison towns 鎮城 within the Pyū dominions, of which three can be assigned approximate locations, namely those known to the Chinese as Hsi-li-i (悉利移 *Si̯ĕt-lji-i̯e), T'u-min (突旻 *T'uət-mi̯ĕn), and Mi-no-tao-li (彌諾道立 *Mji̯e-nāk-dʻâu-li̯əp).⁶⁷ The same work also records eighteen alleged "dependencies" 屬國 and thirty-two of the "best known tribes" 部落 . . . 以名見者 subject to Pyū overlordship. If a substantial number of these transcriptions could be restored to their native forms it would probably provide us with a fair idea of the extent of the Pyū kingdom. As it is, although some of the names sound vaguely familiar, rather like echoes of places once visited but long forgotten, none has been located with certainty. A few, such as Chan-p'o (瞻婆 *Tśi̯äm-bʻuâ), P'o-li (婆梨 *Bʻuâ-lji), She-p'o (闍婆 *Dzʻi̯a-bʻuâ), Fo-tai (佛代 *Bʻi̯uət-dʻậi), and Lo-yü (羅聿 *Lâ-i̯uĕt), may, if they be transcribed — as seems inevitable — respectively as Campā, Bali, Java, Vijaya, and Seluyut, represent no more than the received geographical knowledge of the Pyū court. *Źi̯wän-lâ-bʻuâ-dʻiei 磚羅婆提 should presumably be emended to read *Dʻuâ-lâ-bʻuâ-dʻiei 陏羅婆提 or Dvāravatī (p. 203 below). At least one so-called dependency, *Mji̯e-źi̯ĕn 彌臣, almost certainly constituted a part of the contemporary Mōn world.

It is impossible to say which of the other settlements mentioned in T'ang sources as existing within or on the frontiers of present-day Burma formed part of the Pyū polity or polities. *Təu-mji̯e-ka-muk stockade 兜彌伽木柵 (or perhaps *Təu-mji̯e-ka wooden stockade)⁶⁸ on a sandbank in the *Mji̯e-nāk river (possibly on the elongated island that divides the channel of the Irawadi immediately below its confluence with the Chindwin), may be safely assigned to the Pyū domain. The city of *Ngåk (or *Lâk 樂), on the other hand, although featuring in the southernmost of Chia Tan's trans-Irawadi itineraries, was clearly situated beyond the Pyū frontiers on two counts. In the first place, Chia Tan locates it on the Nan Chao side of the frontier. Second, it is certainly the settlement which the Man Shu categorized as "*Ngåk (or *Lâk) city of the *Muâ-sâ 磨些樂";⁶⁹ that is, it was within Nan Chao tribal territory.

Arimaddanapura

One other city, which is not cited in either the official T'ang histories or the Man Shu, requires mention. In some respects, it may be the most significant Pyū foundation of which we have record. This was Arimaddanapura[70] or, popularly, Pagan. According to Burmese legend,[71] at an undetermined date Arimaddana was formed by a process of synoecism very similar to that which Thukydides envisaged at the consolidation of Athens.[72] There were originally, so runs the legend, nineteen villages[73] in the area, each with its own *nat* or local guardian spirit. In the course of time, one *nat* came to dominate, and in some ways to subsume, the others, and that one *nat* was situated on the summit of Mount Popa, the cone of an extinct volcano on the northwestern flank of the Pegu Yoma. Here were enshrined Min Mahāgiri,[74] the Lord of the Great Mountain, and his sister Taunggyi-shin,[75] both martyred by order of a rival monarch. According to the legend, these events were purposefully willed by King Thinlikyaung in an attempt to build a nation in Upper Burma. From the vantage point of comparative studies, we see it as a classic instance of the formation of a dispersed ceremonial city, with an especially efficacious and powerful shrine functioning as the organizing principle.[76] Important for its specifically Southeast Asian context is the fact that the cult of the *nat* was established on a mountain, and that the presiding spirits were referred to as Lords of the Mountain. According to Burmese chronicles, Arimaddana became a compact city in A.D. 849 when King Pyinbya enclosed the discrete settlements with a wall. However, there is no epigraphic reference to the city earlier than a Cam inscription of c.A.D. 1000-1050,[77] and the first Mōn record relates only to 1093.[78] It is certain that the city became important only in the later days of the Pyū hegemony, probably after "*Mwan rebels" 蠻賊 , in reality Nan Chao armies, sacked the capital in 832, and carried off 3,000 inhabitants to Che-tung (柘東 *Tśi̯a-tung) city, just north of the Tien 滇 Lake.[79] Legend tells of a period of strife between Pyū, Mōn and Myamma (*Mranmā*, i.e. Burmese), and between different branches of the Pyū themselves, as a result of which the capital was moved at least three times (to Taungnyo, Padaung Thettha, and Mindon) before the nineteen villages at Yonhlukkyun were constituted a city below the national shrine on Mount Popa.[80] After this time the Pyū are no more mentioned in Chinese annals (apart, of course, from the inevitable repetitions of earlier passages), though they continued to feature in Burmese inscriptions for some centuries, and notably in King Kyanzittha's palace inscription of 1101.

It would appear that at the beginning of the 9th century one or more fairly well developed urban hierarchies existed in the middle Irawadi valley. It is not entirely clear how the Chinese account of the structure of the principal (if not at that time the

Cities of the Pyū 183

only) Pyū polity should be interpreted, but the most reasonable view would seem to be as follows. At the apex of the hierarchy was a capital and court which even Chinese officials accustomed to the urban life of the Tʻang dynasty saw no cause to disparage. The so-called garrison towns, I suspect, were fortified posts within the territory controlled directly by the Pyū paramount (styled Mahārāja in the *Chiu Tʻang-Shu*). That one of them was described by the Chinese as being governed by a close male relative of the Pyū ruler (Note 67) in no way subverts this conclusion. The eighteen dependencies mentioned in the Chinese account sound very much like subordinate chieftainships ruled in the manner of patrimonial benefices, perhaps by heads of junior lineages, while reference to the "thirty-two best known tribes" probably reflects an attempt to organize village settlements around an administrative center on the pattern of the *pañcanāgara* that is documented in Burma in later times. If this were so, then the settlement hierarchy would seem to have taken the three-fold form that was inferred for the Mekong valley, namely a paramount capital; a series of regional capitals comprising in this instance seats of both governorships and benefices; and a village level, consisting — according to a Tʻang account — of 298 settlements, of which 32 were named.

There is at present no way of knowing how the obviously important settlements at Hmawza and Halin were integrated into this hierarchy other than what may be inferred from the traditional identification of the former with the Pyū capital of Śrī Kṣetra. Luce has suggested that Halin succeeded Śrī Kṣetra, but many Burmese scholars persist in regarding Halin as the earlier of the two sites. Nor is there any way of determining the relation of the city at Beikthano to either of the other major sites beyond the fact that its origins appear to be considerably earlier. It is significant, though, that certain architectural features, particularly the use of brickwork, the design of palace complexes, and the construction of gateways, are common to all three sites; yet, while two have approximately rectangular enceintes, the third is roughly circular, as if it had indeed been meted by the nāga's tail in the manner recounted in Burmese legend. The notion of twin cities that occurs in both epigraphy and legend may have derived from the sort of inter-city relationship depicted in the *Taungdwingyi Thamaing* or perhaps from the internal division of the site at Beikthano into two halves. Although the chronological relationship of Beikthano and Hmawza permits the drawing of certain inferences with regard to the evolution of Pyū urban forms, nothing at all is at present known about either the morphology of less important settlements or the development of the settlement hierarchy prior to the 8th century.

Temple-cities of Early Arakan

A part of Burma which has received no mention in this chapter is Arakan. Late chronicles from the region preserve long dynastic lists, which cannot be relied on for toponymy or chronology,[81] and a number of inscriptions and coins have come to light, but archeological exploration on a significant scale, let alone excavation, has until recently proved beyond the slender resources of the Burmese Archaeological Survey. As late as the nineteen-thirties (and probably today), the brick walls of a large enceinte were still visible on the bank of a tidal creek some six miles from Mrohaung,[82] and it has usually been considered that this was the site of Vaiśālī,[83] according to the chronicles the ancient Arakanese capital. It may also have been the capital whose embellishment and fortification by the first king of a Candra dynasty is mentioned in a *praśasti* of uncertain provenance but datable to the beginning of the 8th century A.D.[84] Professor E. H. Johnston has assigned the founding of this dynasty to the middle of the 4th century A.D., and it is possible that the same inscription contains less reliable information going back even as far as the last quarter of the 2nd century A.D.[85] Just prior to the time at which the *praśasti* was cut a settlement of some sort, probably a shrine, had been established at a place called Pīlakkavanaka, "formerly named Domagha (?)"[86] Other ritual and/or ceremonial centers recognized by Professor Johnston in this inscription are Pureppura,[87] apparently flourishing in the 6th century A.D., and Śrī Tāmrapaṭṭana [or Śrī Paṭṭana].[88] Somatirtha, Ḍaṅkaṅgamargaṅgaḍuvāra, and Bhūrokanaulakkalavāraka were shrines which may also have been in process of developing incipient urban functions.

The fragmentary remains so far available from early Arakan are insufficient for anything other than the broadest of generalizations: namely that temple-cities appear to have existed as early as the middle of the fourth century A.D., and possibly earlier. Epigraphy and paleography afford conclusive evidence that northern Arakan owed its Buddhist (and Hindu) traditions to India, whereas there is a strong presumption that those of southern Arakan derived from the states of the Irawadi valley, or perhaps even farther eastward from Dvāravatī, a kingdom which will be discussed

Cities of the Pyū   185

in Chapter 5. This, perhaps, is not unexpected when we recall that the T'ang histories defined the western boundary of Dvāravatī as the ocean.[89]

Cities of the Pyū   187

Notes and References

1. Anyone who writes on the history of early Burma must be indebted to Gordon H. Luce who, over a period of fifty years, labored to decipher and collate the obscure texts still remaining to us. It was from Luce's writings that I learned of these sources, and, though I have re-read the important Chinese, and the only marginally relevant Arabic and Western Classical texts (Old Mōn, Old Burmese, and Pāli I cannot read), it is within Luce's general framework that I am attempting to fit the interpretations of this chapter. Among Luce's more important papers on the Pyū are (1) "Names of the Pyu," JBRS, vol. 22, pt. 2 (1932), p. 89; (2) "The ancient Pyu, " loc. cit., vol. 27, pt. 3 (1937), pp. 239-253; (3) with Pe Maung Tin, "Burma down to the fall of Pagan" [Pt. I only published], loc. cit., vol. 29, pt. 3 (1939), pp. 264-282; (4) "Old Kyaukse and the coming of the Burmans," loc. cit., vol. 42 (1959), pp. 75-112. Numbers (2) and (3) have been republished in the Burma Research Society Fiftieth Anniversary Publication No. 2 (Rangoon, 1960), pp. 307-321 and pp. 385-403 respectively.

2. This is the date recorded by the Hou-Han Shu 後漢書 chüan 2, f. 4 recto, but in chüan 33, f. 2 recto the date is given as A.D. 59.

3. Anciently and at present known to the Chinese as the Lan-ts'ang river 蘭滄江.

4. Anciently and at present known to the Chinese as the Nu (*Nuo) river 怒江.

5. Chin Shu 晉書 chüan 14, f. 37 verso; Nan-Chʻi Shu 南齊書 chüan 15, f. 27 recto.

6. E.g., in addition to the *Âi-lao themselves, who submitted to Chinese jurisdiction in A.D. 51 and 69, two chiefs of the Tun-jen-i (敦忍乙 *Tuən-ńźiĕn-i̯ĕt) offered a rhinoceros and a large elephant as tribute [Hou-Han Shu, chüan 116, f. 5 recto]; in 107 the Lu-lei (陸類 *Ljuk-ljwi) and other pygmoid "savages" offered an elephant's tusk, a water-buffalo, and a humped ox in token of their submission [loc. cit.]; in A.D. 97 and 120 the *Źiän 撣 : MSC = Shan [the Han history states that the graph is vocalized in this way, that is as 檀, instead of as the more usual *tān] offered "precious things from their country," together with music and conjurors [loc. cit., f. 3 verso]. There has been some debate as to the exact location of the *Źiän: vide E. H. Parker, Burma, with special reference to her relations with China (Rangoon, 1893), p. 6; Paul Pelliot, "Deux itinéraires de Chine en Inde à la fin du VIIIe siècle," BEFEO, vol. 4 (1904), pp. 266-268; G. H. Luce, "The 撣 Tan (97-132 A.D.) and the 哀牢 Ngai-lao," JBRS, vol. 14 (1925), pp. 100-137; R. A. Stein, "The Lin-yi," Han-hiue 漢學 vol. 2, fasc. 1-3 (1947), pp. 136-142. Parker and Luce, and perhaps Pelliot, seem to have been disposed to seek the *Źiän somewhere beyond the frontiers of Burma, but I see no reason to dissociate them from the web of ethnonomenclature of which present-day Shan is the most familiar exemplar.

7. I Ching, Ta-Tʻang Hsi-yü Chʻiu-fa Kao-seng Chuan 大唐西域求法高僧傳 Jap. Trip., vol. 51, f. 5. Tsang-kʻo was, in Tʻang times, a county seat (chün 郡) in western Kuei-chou.

8. Shui-Ching Chu 水經注 chüan 1, f. 7 verso and chüan 36, f. 29 verso; Liang Shu 梁書 chüan 54, f. 7 recto; Tʻai-pʻing Yü-lan 太平御覽 chüan 787, f. 4 recto and chüan 790, ff. 9 verso - 10 recto; Tʻai-pʻing Huan-yü Chi 太平寰宇記 chüan 177, f. 7 verso; I Ching, Nan-Hai Chi-kuei Nei-fa Chuan 南海寄歸内法傳 chüan 1, f. 6 recto. The implications of the name Chin-lin are touched on in Note 5 to Chapter 3.

188   *Nāgara and Commandery*

9. T'ang texts use the form 驃 to denote the P'iao, which has somewhat more complementary overtones than the graph used in Chin times.
E. R. Leach is inclined to locate the *B'uk in the Kachin Hills, where modern Maru still call Jinghpaw speakers p'ok and where the Shans of Hkamti Long used to refer to their Kachin serfs as kha-p'ok (Shan kha- = serf): *Political systems of highland Burma* (London, 1954), p. 239. Hkamti Shan tradition also records Kha-p'ok among the pre-Shan inhabitants of the area. Modern Chinese refer to the Kachins as P'u Man 濮蠻 : J. Siguret, *Territoires et population des confins du Yunnan* (Peiping, 1937), p. 122.

10. *Hou-Han Shu*, chüan 116, f. 18 verso [Commentary, citing *Kuang Chih* (see below); *Fa-yüan Chu-lin* 法苑珠林 by Tao Shih 道世 (A.D. 668), chüan 49, f. 16 verso [*Ssu-pu Ts'ung-k'an* edition]; *Kuang Chih* 廣志 by Kuo I-kung 郭義恭 [4th century. *Apud Yü-han Shan-fang Chi-i-shu* (1853) chüan 74]; *T'ai-p'ing Yü-lan*, chüan 353, f. 2 verso; chüan 359, f. 3 recto; chüan 956, f. 4 verso; chüan 981, f. 7 recto; and chüan 982, f. 3 verso; *Hua-yang-Kuo Chih* 華陽國志 by Ch'ang-Ch'ü 常璩 (A.D. 347), chüan 4, f. 16 recto [This is probably the earliest extant reference to the P'iao]; *T'ang Hui-yao* 唐會要 chüan 100, ff. 17 verso - 18 recto; *T'ai-p'ing Huan-yü Chi*, chüan 179, ff. 16 recto - 17 recto, quoting *Hsi-nan I-fang Chih* 西南異方志. and *Nan-chung Pa-chün Chih* [both of uncertain date and authorship]. It will be observed that none of the texts containing these early [i.e., Chin, A.D. 266-420] references to the P'iao survives other than in quotation.

11. In the *Hsin T'ang-Shu* 新唐書 chüan 222C, f. 9 recto it is stated that "the *P'iäu refer to themselves as *T'uət-lā-tśiu 突羅朱 , the people of *Dźia-b'uā 闍婆 call them *Siɛ-lji-g'iuət 徙里掘 ". The *Chiu T'ang-Shu* (chüan 197, f. 17 recto) has the *P'iäu styling themselves *T'uət-lā-źiäng 突羅成 , which, in view of the relationship between the *Old* and *New T'ang Histories*, can probably be accounted a scribal error. Over forty years ago Gordon Luce ["Names of the Pyu"] equated *T'uət-lā-tśiu with an Old Mōn word *Tirčul* occurring in King Kyanzittha's palace inscription of c. 1101/2 from Pagan [*Epigraphia Birmanica*, vol. 3, pt. 1 (Rangoon, 1928), Inscription IXB, l. 42, edited by C. O. Blagden]. It would appear from the context that *Tirčul* was here intended as an ethnonym: " . . . singing of the Burmese (jiñjeh mirmā), singing of the Mōn (jiñjeh rmeñ), singing of the Tirčul (jiñjeh tirčul)." Subsequently V. Minorsky has discerned the same name in both Persian and Arabic texts. In Marvazī's *Tabā'i' al-hayawān* [c. 1120, V. Minorsky, *Sharaf al-Zamān Tāhir Marvazī on China, the Turks and India*, vol. XXII of the James G. Forlong Fund of the Royal Asiatic Society (London, 1942), p. 49] mention is made of a king called [? the] Ṭ.rshūl طرشول who ruled over a kingdom [eastwards] beyond the Ganges valley. In Yaʿqūbī's *History*, c. 875 [Th. Houtsma, *Ibn-Wādhih qui dicitur al-Jaʿqūbī Historiae* . . . (Leyde, 1883), vol. 1, p. 201; Gabriel Ferrand, *Relations de voyage* (Paris, 1913), vol. 1, p. 48] there is a reference to a kingdom under the same orthography, which is a reasonably accurate transcription of the Old Mōn form. The anonymous *Ḥudūd al-ʿĀlam*, which was begun in 982, and whose chapters on East Asia are derived mainly from the Sāmānid wazīr Abū ʿAbdullāh Muḥammad ibn Aḥmad Jayhānī's *Kitāb al-mamālik wa'l-masālik*, speaks of the same kingdom under the name Ṭusūl طوسول [V. Minorsky (ed.), *Ḥudūd al-ʿĀlam* (London, 1937), p. 87].

Before we leave this topic one other point deserves mention. In a passage comparable to that of the *Ṭabā'i'* mentioned above, the *'Akhbar al-Ṣīn wa'l-Hind* (851) substitutes Tanlwing تنلونج for *Ṭ.rshūl, a reading that Jean Sauvaget has equated with Tanluiñ, an ancient form of Talaiñ, the name by which the Mōn are now known to the Burmese [*Relation de la Chine et de l'Inde* (Paris, 1948), p. 54]. It is true that Tanluiñ is not attested epigraphically until 1204 [G. H. Luce, "Note on the peoples of Burma in the XIIth-XIIIth. cent. A.D.," *Burma Census Report* (Rangoon, 1931), Appendix F. Reprinted, with slight changes in the references, in *JBRS*, vol. 42, pt. 1 (1959), pp. 52-112 ; C. O. Blagden, "Notes and reviews: Etymological notes, I:Talaing," *JBRS*, vol. 4, pt. 1 (1914), p. 57], but inscriptions prior to this date are so few that it would be unwise to reject this equation on that ground alone. Why the *Ḥudūd*, and the *Ṭabā'i'* which copied it, should have replaced the earlier mention of the Pyū (Tirčul) by a reference to the Mōn (Talaiñ) I am unable to say. Possibly it might be argued that the

Persian geographers were more concerned with the interiors of the several
subcontinental realms of Asia than was the author of the ᵓAkhbār, itself one of a
large genre of anonymous "Enquiries" which drew their local color primarily from
reports of sailing voyages along the South Asian littoral. The Persian authors,
perhaps attempting to equate information obtained from travelers along the land
route between Kāmarūpa and China (which crossed the upper Irawadi valley) with
that current among Arabo-Persian mariners, may have "corrected" a reference to
the Talaiṅ to read Tirčul, a people with whom they were possibly more familiar.
Such an interpretation would account for the fact, otherwise difficult to
explain, that the earlier Arabic text made mention of the Mōn, who occupied the
Irawadi delta, whereas the later Persian authors referred to the Pyū in the
middle and upper reaches of the valley.

The broad similarity in Modern Standard Chinese pronunciation between the
name by which the Pyū referred to themselves and that by which the *Dźʿi̯a-bʿuā
knew them (Tʿu-lo-chu: Tʿu-li-chʿü) led Luce to treat them as versions of the same
ethnonym, "the latter probably the more corrupt" ["Names of the Pyu"; "Burma
down to the fall of Pagan"]. However, in their Ancient Chinese vocalizations
these names are by no means so similar, and the form attributed to the
*Dźʿi̯a-bʿuā should probably be restored as Śrī Kṣetra, the name by which Hsüan
Tsang and I Ching knew the capital of the Pyū [In fact, as long ago as 1904
Pelliot ("Deux itinéraires," p. 175) had proposed to equate *Si̯e-lji-gʿi̯uət with
Thayekhettayā, the Burmese rendering of Śrī Kṣetra; but the phonetic
correspondence with the Burmese form is imperfect and in any case the texts
seemingly relate to a period prior to the establishment of the Burmese in the
Irawadi Valley].

The name Pyū is today written as Prū by the Burmese, but the Chinese forms
mentioned above sufficiently attest the authenticity of the epigraphic Pyū
(though Prū does occur once [Luce, "Names of the Pyu"]. For references to the
form Pyū see Inscriptions of Burma (Oxford, 1933-1957), Plate 31, 1. 7; plate
144, 1. 23; plate 233, 1. 5; plate 294, 1. 33; plate 297, 1. 12; and A list of
inscriptions found in Burma, part I (Rangoon, 1921), no. 701B; lines 1 and 3
[Information from Luce, "Burma down to the fall of Pagan"]. Fairly lengthy
sections are devoted to the Pyū, under the transcription *Pʿi̯äu 驃, in Chiu
Tʿang-Shu 舊唐書 chüan 197, ff. 16 verso-17 verso, and Hsin Tʿang-Shu, chüan
222C, ff. 9 recto et seq., with supplementary accounts, in addition to the early
references listed in Note 10, in Man Shu 蠻書, chüan 10, pp. 45-46; Tʿang
Hui-yao, chüan 33, ff. 25 verso - 26 recto; Tʿai-pʿing Yü-lan, chüan 567, f. 8
verso, chüan 789, ff. 3 recto - 4 recto; chüan 813, f. 5 verso; chüan 961, f. 8
recto; Wen-hsien Tʿung-kʿao 文獻通考 chüan 330, f. 2588; Tsʿe-fu Yüan-kuei 冊
府元龜 chüan 957, f. 13 recto et verso; chüan 960, ff. 5 verso and 10 recto;
chüan 972, f. 5 recto et verso; as well as sundry later works which need not be
listed here as they yield no new information.

The Pyū language has been only partially deciphered, and that mainly owing
to the efforts of C. O. Blagden ["A preliminary study of the fourth text of the
Myazedi inscriptions," JRAS, (1911), pp. 365-388]; see also Epigraphia Birmanica,
vol. 1, pt. 1, pp. 59-68; Epigraphia Indica, "The 'Pyu' inscriptions", vol. 12,
no. 16 (1913-14), pp. 127-132 (reprinted in JBRS, vol. 7, pt. 1 (1917), pp.
37-44; Archaeological Survey of Burma (1912), pp. 11-12; (1913), pp. 13-15,
21-23; (1915), pp. 21-23; (1917), pp. 24-25; George Coedès, review of Blagden's
paper in JRAS (1911), BEFEO, vol. 11 (1911), pp. 435-436; paragraph by Paul
Pelliot in "Quelques transcriptions chinoises de noms tibétains," TP, vol. 16
(1915), p. 25; Robert Shafer, "Further analysis of the Pyu inscriptions," HJAS,
vol. 7, no. 4 (1943), pp. 313-366 [This paper contains a bibliography of works
concerned with the quadrilingual Myazedi inscriptions, c. A.D. 1113, which
provided the key to the decipherment of the Pyū language]. It is apparent from
these studies that the Pyū language belonged to the Tibeto-Burman family. The
significance and etymology of the name Pyū itself is still unknown, but it is
tempting to speculate on a possible relationship between this ethnonym and
several phonetic — and semantic — series in other Tibeto-Burman languages. Paul
Benedict ["Semantic differentiation in Indo-Chinese," HJAS, vol. 4, nos. 3 and 4
(1939), p. 223] has drawn attention to the close connexion between the words for
"silver" and "white" (the former being derived from the latter root) in the
Loloish languages, e.g. Old Burmese pʿru = white; Pʿunoi pʿiu = silver; Akha pʿlu,

pʻiu = silver, pʻju = white; Pyen plu = silver; Lahu plu, pʻfu = silver, pʻu = money, white; Lolopho pʻi = white, silver; et al. To these we may add Li-so pʻu = silver, white, and Ma-hei pʻu-tzö = silver, pa = white [Cp. also the following words for "white" which apparently have no connexion with the word for "silver": Aʻchang pʻor; A-si pʻyu; Ma-ru pʻyu; La-shi pʻyu; Kachin pʻraw; Pʻön pʻru [H. R. Davies, Yün-nan. The link between India and the Yangtze (Cambridge, 1909), appendix]. Wen Yu 聞宥 has listed the words for "white" in the several dialects of Chiang 羌 ["Chʻuan-hsi Chiang-shuo-chih chʻu-pu fen-hsi," Chung-Kuo Wen-hua Yen-chiu-so Chi-kʻan 川西羌說之初步分析 中國文化研究所集刊 (English title = Studia Serica) vol. 2 (1941), pp. 66-68]: 白 — = 水 pʻie; 色如 pʻsi; 半坡 pʻci; 牛山 pʻzi; 嘉山, pʻsi; 龍溪 pʻue; 下白水 pʻiɔ; 里坪 pɟi; and has compared them with Jyarung prɔm, Menyak pʻri. Cp. J. Huston Edgar, "English-Giarung vocabulary," Journal of the West China Border Research Society, vol. 5, Supplement (1932): white, whitewash = ki prom. Rolf Stein ["Le Lin-yi," p. 214] has added other examples to this list. Now, the similarity between the elements of these series and the name of the Pyū would probably be ascribed to coincidence were it not for two circumstances that together would seem to pass beyond the bounds of random chance. In the first place, it is in the vicinity of present-day Lower Burma that Classical authors of the West, especially Ptolemy (but including Pomponius Mela, the Elder Pliny, Solinus, Martianus Capella, and Isidore of Seville) located Αργυρα, the Silver Country [The Ptolemaic information relating to Southeast Asia will be discussed in an appendix, so textual references to the corpus will be omitted at this point]. Perhaps, as the academic Muslim geographers derived so much of their world schema from Ptolemy, this is also the region intended by the Jazīrat al-fiḍḍa جزيره الفضة [= Silver Island] of the Ḥudūd al-ʻĀlam (Minorsky's edition, p. 56), Ibn Saʼīd's Basṭ al-arḍ and other such works. These are often phrased so equivocally that they may perhaps sometimes refer to ʼΑργυρη, capital of the Ptolemaic ʼΙαβαδίου, but the mention of teak and ebony in the Ḥudūd, taken together with a city "considered as belonging to Chinistān" [az shumār-i Chīnistān], point to the Burmese rather than the Javanese Land of Silver.

In the second place, Marvazī [op. cit., p. 46] described the T.rshūl (see above) as white, and I am inclined to take this adjective as a literal translation of Pyū. The association of whiteness and silver in the territory of an ethnic group whose name subsumed those two concepts can hardly be fortuitous.

I can make nothing of the statement in the Hsin Tʻang-Shu, 222C, f. 9 recto that the *Pʻiäu were formerly *Tśju-puâ 朱波 (MSC = Chu-po).

12. The site at Beikthano was excavated during six field seasons between 1959 and 1963 under the direction of U Aung Thaw and U Myint Aung. The final site report, written by U Aung Thaw and published under the title Report on the Excavations at Beikthano (Rangoon, 1968), constitutes the first such report to be prepared by the archeological service of a Southeast Asian country. In earlier publications the name of the site, which signifies "Viṣṇu [City]," was transcribed as Peikthano, often with the suffix -myo (in this case = township) appended. Cf. Taw Sein Ko, "Annual Report of the Superintendent," Archaeological Survey of Burma (1905-06), pp. 7-10; L. de Beylié, Prome et Samara (Paris, 1907), p. 85; Archaeological Survey of India (1929-30), pp. 151-155. See also Ba Shin, Ancient Peikthano and its history (Rangoon, 1966), [in Burmese].

13. The volume of debris remaining on either side of the wall was insufficient to induce the excavators to postulate a really formidable original height, though they did make the point that it is impossible to estimate the depredations that have occurred through the centuries by villagers and others in search of building materials and brick ballast: Aung Thaw, Excavations, p. 8.

14. Aung Thaw, Excavations, p. 7. The author does not state whether this particular alignment is recorded in relation to true or magnetic north, but in light of the comment in Note 22 below, the latter seems the more likely.

15. The northern sector of this partition wall is not depicted on Fig. 2, but Aung Thaw's remark that "the continuation of this ridge on the north of the palace area could hardly be traced" presumably implies that it did exist: Excavations, p. 2.

16. Aung Thaw, *Excavations*, p. 8.

17. This conclusion is, of course, inferred from investigation of the three sides of the enceinte that still remain. No gates have been physically located in the west wall.

18. Aung Thaw, *Excavations*, pp. 12, 52.

19. Aung Thaw, *Excavations*, p. 12. Janice Stargardt has concluded from a study of the structures on sites KKG 9 and 11 that their brick architecture was modelled on a pre-existing constructional tradition using only wood.

20. Aung Thaw, *Excavations*, pp. 13-16.

21. Aung Thaw, *Excavations*, pp. 16-17. In the report this structure is classified as "residential" only because it is situated within the palace complex and exhibits no features that would imply a religious or manufacturing function.

22. Aung Thaw specifies a longitudinal alignment of "about 13° to the west of the magnetic north" for this building, and of "about 13° westwards" for the structure at site KKG 5 (*Excavations*, pp. 13 and 16). This is, in fact, in accord with the alignment of the east wall of the city, but some 3 or 4 degrees less than the westward orientation of the palace complex as depicted on Aung Thaw's plan of the city (Fig. 1). Cp. Fig. 13 of the present volume.

23. Aung Thaw, *Excavations*, pp. 18-19. For the significance of āyaka (= worshipful) pillars and platforms see A. H. Longhurst, *The Buddhist antiquities of Nāgārjunakoṇḍa*. Archaeological Survey of India Memoir no. 54 (Delhi, 1938), p. 12.

24. Aung Thaw, *Excavations*, pp. 20, 23-24.

25. Aung Thaw, *Excavations*, pp. 20-21, 22.

26. Aung Thaw, *Excavations*, p. 66. Cf. also H. Sarkar, "Some aspects of the Buddhist monuments at Nāgārjunakoṇḍa," *Ancient India*, no. 16 (1960: published 1962), pp. 65-84.

27. Aung Thaw, *Excavations*, Plate LVIII. It is unlikely that these silver disks, bearing symbols such as the śrīvatsa, baddhapitha, svastika, and twin fishes were used as currency. The occurrence in many of them of one or two holes for stringing would seem to imply that they were worn as pendant ornaments or medallions, probably to ward off evil.

28. Aung Thaw, *Excavations*, p. 62.

29. Aung Thaw, *Excavations*, pp. 50-51.

30. C. Sivaramamurti, "Amaravati sculptures in the Madras Museum," *Bulletin of the Madras Government Museum*, New Series: General Section vol. 4 (1942), Appendix III.

31. Aung Thaw, *Excavations*, chap. 3.

32. Bennet Bronson, Review of Aung Thaw, *Report on the excavations at Beikthano* in *Asian Perspectives*, vol. 12 (1969), pp. 142-143.

33. Aung Thaw, *Excavations*, p. 62. The period of occupation referred to is that officially designated as Period I: a subsequent, and quantitatively unimportant, occupation assigned to the 11th century is not relevant to the present discussion.

34. Note 10 above.

35. Tun Nyein, "Maunggun gold plates," *Epigraphia Indica*, vol. 5 (1898-9), pp. 101-102; Louis Finot, "Un nouveau document sur le bouddhisme birman," *JA*, 10th series, vol. 20 (1912), pp. 131-135, and (1913), p. 193; Charles Duroiselle, "Excavations at Hmawza," *Archaeological Survey of India, Annual Report, 1926-1927* (1927), p. 175, *1927-1928* (1928), pp. 127-135, *1928-1929* (1929), pp. 105-109, and *1929-1930* (1930), pp. 155-156; *Report of the Archaeological Survey of Burma, 1938-1939* (1939), pp. 12-22. There is a short summary of the Pyū remains in Reginald Le May, *The culture of Southeast Asia* (London, 1954), pp. 45-49. See also Nihar-Ranjan Ray, *Sanskrit Buddhism in Burma* (Amsterdam, 1936), pp. 3-4.

36. Hsüan Tsang 玄奘 used the form *śiĕt-lji Tṣ'a-tât-lâ 室利差呾羅 in *Ta-T'ang Hsi-yü Chi* 大唐西域記, chüan 10, f. 51 recto. I Ching 義淨 used the Chinese transcription *śiĕt-lji Tṣ'at-tât-lâ 室利察呾羅 in *Nan-hai Chi-kuei Nei-fa Chuan*, chüan 1, f. 3 verso; but 怛 is substituted for 呾 in *Ta-T'ang Ta-tzŭ-en-ssŭ San-ts'ang Fa-shih Chuan* 大唐大慈恩寺三藏法師傳 by Hui Li 惠立, chüan 2053, f. 240, which includes a parallel passage.

37. The honorific Śrī Kṣetra occurs at least once elsewhere in Southeast Asia as the name of a pleasance established by King Jayanāsa near Palembang in 684 [Talang Tuwo inscription: B.Ch. Chhabra, "Expansion of Indo-Aryan culture during Pallava rule, as evidenced by inscriptions," *Journal of the Asiatic Society of Bengal, Letters*, vol. 1 (1935), p. 29].

38. The inscription, in Sanskrit verse with Pyū glosses, was discovered at Kan-wet-khaung-kon in Hmawza in 1927-28 and, as far as I know, has not been published, although several authors have made use of the information contained in it. Vide Luce, "Ancient Pyu," pp. 311-312 and "Burma down to the fall of Pagan," p. 389 (both in the reprinted edition of 1960); George Coedès, *Les états hindouisés d'Indochine et d'Indonésie* (3rd edition, Paris, 1964), pp. 164-165. The chief difficulty in establishing an absolute chronology of the *-vikrama* kings resides in the fact that, although the dates of their deaths are recorded, there is no mention of the era involved. It is usually assumed, however, that the dates were calculated according to the Burmese (Khaccapañca) Era, which took its origin in A.D. 638 [May Oung, "The Burmese Era," *JBRS*, vol. 2, pt. 2 (1912), pp. 197-203]. On this reckoning a Sūryavikrama died in A.D. 688, a Harivikrama (whether or not the ruler mentioned below as the tributary of Jayacandravarman is uncertain) in 695, and a Sīhavikrama in 710. For information relating to the *-varman* dynasty, the dates of which are unknown, consult Ch. Duroiselle, *Arch. Survey India, 1926-1927* (1927), p. 176 and *1927-1928* (1928), pp. 128, 145, and Plate LIV.

39. The literal interpretation of some earlier scholars according to which the two rulers were at least classificatory (and possibly biological) kin must now be abandoned: cf. Maung Htin Aung, *A history of Burma* (New York and London, 1967), p. 14.

40. E. Forchhammer was the first to describe the visible remains at Hmawza in the *Reports of the Administration of British Burma*, pt. 2 (1882-3), p. 155; (1883-4), pp. 94-95; (1884-5), p. 70. Subsequently the site was investigated by General L. de Beylié, who incorporated his findings in, among other publications, *Prome et Samara* (Paris, 1907) and *L'architecture hindoue en Extrême-Orient* (Paris, 1907), and continued excavations were undertaken by Messrs. Taw Sein Ko and Charles Duroiselle, whose reports appeared in the *Archaeological Survey of India* between 1926 and 1930, and in the *Archaeological Survey of Burma* during the same period. For a complete bibliography of this topic, which includes numerous short notes not directly relating to the specifically urban characteristics of Hmawza, see Luce and Pe Maung Tin, "Burma down to the fall of Pagan," p. 399, note 19 (reprinted version). See also Sein Maung U, *Ancient Thayekhettaya* (Rangoon, 1968), [in Burmese].

41. Luce, "The ancient Pyu," p. 313 (reprinted version).

42. One of Indra's many names.

43. Like the Chinese *li* and the English league in their respective cultures, the *yojana* has varied in length with successive periods of Indian history. The explicit statements most commonly invoked take it as equivalent to 4 *krośa*, each of 2,000 *daṇḍa*, or about 9 miles. The *Arthaśāstra*, however, equates it with 4 *krośa* of only 1,000 *daṇḍa*, or a distance of about 4 1/2 miles. There is some evidence that the shorter distance was in more general use for practical, as opposed to literary, purposes. If we assume that it was this unit that was incorporated in the Burmese myths relating to Śrī Kṣetra, then the perimeter of the city would have been in the neighborhood of thirteen or fourteen miles. The ruins of the wall at Hmawza are about 8 1/2 miles in circumference.

44. *The Glass Palace Chronicle of the Kings of Burma*, translated by Pe Maung Tin and G. H. Luce (London, 1923. Reprinted with identical pagination, Rangoon, 1960), p. 14. This chronicle is a collation (a "sifting" as its authors called it), with lengthy disquisitions on debatable points incorporated in the text, of earlier Burmese chronicles. It was compiled by a committee of "learned monks, learned brāhmaṇs, and learned ministers" at the command of King Bagyidaw, and takes its name of *Hman Nan Yazawin* or *Glass Palace Chronicle* from the fact that the committee carried out its task in the front chamber of the Palace of Glass. The work was started in 1829, and presented to Bagyidaw in 1832. It treats of the history of Burma from the time of Gautama to 1821. [Aldous Huxley's characterization of this "chronicle" as "the most learned edition of a fairy tale that has ever been published . . . as though a committee of Scaligers and Bentleys had assembled to edit the tales of the nursery" is not grossly inapt: *Jesting Pilate* (London, 1957)]. Pe Maung Tin's translation is based on the Mandalay edition of 1908 in three volumes. For a short exposition of the character of Burmese chronicles see U Tet Htoot, "The nature of the Burmese chronicles" in D. G. E. Hall [ed.], *Historians of South-East Asia* (London, 1961), pp. 50-62. The *Hman Nan Yazawin* is treated on pp. 54-55.

45. See, for example, Wheatley, *The pivot*, p. 435.

46. Myin Aung, *Ancient Halin* (Rangoon, 1968); U Kan Hla (nom de plume of the Soviet scholar Sergey S. Ozhegov), "Ancient cities in Burma," *Journal of the Society of Architectural Historians*, vol. 38, no. 2 (1979), pp. 95-102.
Walter Liebenthal ["The ancient Burma road — a legend?," *JGIS*, vol. 15, no. 1 (1956), pp. 4 and 15] has denied that the ethnonym *P'iäu used in the earlier stratum of Chinese texts necessarily refers to the kingdom of the Vikrama dynasty of Śrī Kṣetra. "The tribes of P'iao," he says, "must be distinguished from the kingdom of P'iao", and, pointing out that in the *Nan-Chao Yeh-shih* 南詔野史 [Bk. I, chüan 15] the *P'iäu are located beyond the southern frontiers of Nan Chao (南詔 *Nâm-tśiäu), he suggests that their homeland may have been in present-day Laos. But the *Nan-Chao Yeh-shih* belongs to a genre of historiography, "unconventional histories" as Gardner has called them, that is as much fiction as fact, and its unsupported testimony cannot be held to overrule the consensus of the texts enumerated in Note 10:" beyond the P'u tribes and some 3,000 *li* from Yung-Ch'ang." In any case, the directions recorded in Chinese historical writings are often somewhat imprecise. It also seems probable that Dr. Liebenthal is envisaging the Pyū polity in terms of the nation-state of the modern West, whereas the traditional "kingdom" of Southeast Asia consisted of a core-area, a sort of city-state controlled directly from a temple-city, surrounded by tracts of territory that paid tribute only when the ruler of the city-state was powerful enough to exact it.

47. See Note 10 above.

48. In T'ang times the *li* appears to have approximated to 360 meters (Cp. Note 5 to Chap. 3). For 160 *li*, the reading of the T'ang history, the *Man Shu*, chüan 10, p. 45, substitutes "a day's march" 周行一日程. This is a curious alternative, because a day's march was usually reckoned at about 50 *li*. In *T'ai-p'ing Huan-yü Chi*, chüan 171, f. 7 recto, for example, the distance from

Huan Chou 驩州 to the capital of the kingdom of Huan-wang 環王國 is stated to be ten days' journey or about 500 li. Ch'ien-Han Shu (chüan 64B, f. 7 recto) provides information that is in agreement with this rate of march, stating specifically that the Chinese Emperor made 50 li a day when travelling with his retinue, but only 30 when leading his army. I can offer no suggestion as to the significance of this discrepancy.

The likelihood that it was the gateways that carried pagoda-like structures is somewhat enhanced by the discovery of charcoal in the passages at Beikthano. It is of little significance which site, already or yet to be discovered, the Chinese were here describing as one architectural style appears to have been common to major settlements.

49. 荔支 Nephelium litchi, Camb. Burmese = kyetmauk. The timber of this tree is virtually indestructible.

50. Chiu T'ang-Shu 舊唐書 chüan 197, f. 17 recto.

51. This is also true of thirty-two (or even sixty-four) gates, a number that is simply a canonically sanctioned multiple of four, itself symbolic of the cardinal directions. Yet thirty-two (let alone sixty-four) functional gates would have been vitually impracticable in any city, whereas twelve could have been integrated into a rectilinear layout without difficulty (as evidenced by the settlement at Beikthano and several important Chinese cities).

52. G. H. Luce, "The ancient Pyu," pp. 316-317, and "Burma down to the fall of Pagan," p. 392 (both papers in the reprint edition of 1960).

53. As these remarks are phrased in Man Shu, chüan 10, p. 45, they might be held to apply to a city called Śāri . . . (Śi̯a-lji 舍利) in India, but in the Hsin T'ang-Shu, chüan 222C, f. 10 verso they clearly relate to the Pyū capital.

54. Hsin T'ang-Shu, chüan 43B, f. 29 recto.

55. Anciently the *Mji̯e-nâk river (MSC Mi-no 彌諾江). Luce ("The ancient Pyu," p. 316 of 1960 reprint, note 6) has suggested that these graphs could perhaps be a transcription of Old Burmese mlac = river: but see also Note 67 below.

56. Chiu T'ang-Shu, chüan 197, f. 17 recto; see also Ts'e-fu Yüan-kuei, chüan 957, f. 13 verso; T'ai-p'ing Yü-lan, chüan 789, f. 18 recto; T'ang Hui-yao, chüan 100, f. 18 verso; T'ai-p'ing Huan-yü Chi, chüan 177, f. 15 recto; Wen-hsien T'ung-k'ao, chüan 330, f. 2588.

57. Luce, "Ancient Pyu," p. 317; "Burma down to the fall of Pagan," p. 392 (both from reprint edition of 1960); André Migot, "Un grand disciple du Buddha, Śariputra," BEFEO, vol. 46 (1954), pp. 405-550. Some Burmese scholars have identified this city with Yāzagyo, situated midway between Mōlaik and Kalemyo in the Chindwin valley.

58. H. L. Shorto has suggested, for instance, that the most plausible explanation of the style Thado Dhammaraza borne by kings of Prome in later times is that Sudharmanāgara featured among the classical honorifics of Śrī Kṣetra ["The 32 myos in the medieval Mon kingdom," BSOAS, vol. 26 (1963), p. 590].

59. Man Shu, chüan 10, p. 45.

60. Archaeological Survey of Burma (1905), pp. 7-10; (1906), p. 7; Charles Duroiselle, "Excavations at Halin," Archaeological Survey of India (1929-1930), pp. 151-155. A legendary account of Halin is summarized in the Shwebo District Gazetteer (Rangoon) and Charles Duroiselle, Archaeological Survey of India, 1914-15, pp. 44-45. At various times the city seems to have been known under the following honorifics: Haṁsavatī, Haṁsanāgara, Pachchhimanāgara, and Kāmavatī. According to a local legend, the city was founded by a King Karabho, son of the

famous Mahāsammata. Subsequently 798 kings supposedly reigned at Halin, followed by a monarch styled Pyū-bhandhava [Duroiselle, *Archaeological Survey of India*, 1929-30, p. 152].

61. Cited by Aung Thaw, *Report on the excavations at Beikthano* (Rangoon, 1968), pp. 2-4. *Thamaing* are *mélanges* of legendary and authentic information, often relating to temples and other religious institutions, though occasionally referring to towns. In their pastiches of legend, history, biography, and *curiosa*, they bear some resemblance to the earlier examples of European so-called topographical writing often presented under the title *History and Antiquities*. The *Taungdwingyi Thamaing* is a 19th-century example of such compilations.

The version of events retailed in the *Glass Palace Chronicle* (Note 44 above) and other similar works differs on many points but the general thrust of the argument is much the same.

62. Taw Sein Ko, cited by Aung Thaw, *Excavations*, p. 5.

63. Aung Thaw, *Excavations*, p. 6.

64. Notably U Po Lat, U E Maung, Daw Mya Mu, *Thuriya* U Thein Maung, and Maung Htin Aung. It is the views of this school of thought which are incorporated in the earlier chapters of Maung Htin Aung, *A history of Burma* (New York and London, 1967).

65. Nihar-Ranjan Ray, *Sanskrit Buddhism in Burma* (Amsterdam, 1936), chap. 1; and *An introduction to the study of Theravāda Buddhism in Burma* (Calcutta, 1946), chap. 1 (VI - IX).

66. *Hsin T'ang-Shu*, chüan 222C, f. 9 recto.

67. *Siĕt-lji-iĕ* 悉利移 is listed in *Hsin T'ang-Shu* among the garrison towns of the Pyū, and appears in the same work (chüan 222C, f. 6 verso) as being governed by the Pyū king's brother, who was sent as an envoy to the Chinese court in 802. *Chiu T'ang-Shu*, chüan 197, f. 7 verso erroneously recorded *Siĕt-lji-iĕ* as the name of the envoy (which the revised T'ang history more reliably reported as *Śiwo-nān-t'ā* 舒難陀 ; *Ts'e-fu Yüan-kuei*, chüan 972, f. 5 not only repeated this error but also substituted *i* 夷 (= foreigner, barbarian) for *ie* 移 and made the envoy a son of the Pyū king. The *Tien-nan tsa-chih* 滇南雜誌 , chüan 15, f. 1, in addition to copying this last error, also introduced an additional syllable into the name of the royal envoy: *Śiwo-nān-t'ā-nā* 舒南陀那 , which might or might not have been an improved transcription. *T'ang Hui-yao*, chüan 100 f. 17 verso, *T'ai-p'ing Yü-lan*, chüan 789, f. 18 recto, *T'ai-p'ing Huan-yü Chi*, chüan 177, f. 14, verso and *Wen-hsien T'ung-k'ao*, chüan 330, f. 2588 all copied their [mis]information from *Chiu T'ang-Shu*. In any case, it is virtually certain that the toponym under discussion is the same as the *Siĕt-lji* which featured in the southernmost of Chia Tan's itineraries through the Irawadi valley (*Hsin T'ang-Shu*, chüan 43C. ff. 13 recto - 16 verso), and it is additional information in that itinerary which enables us to assign an approximate location to this garrison town. From *Tśiwo-kāt-liang* 諸葛亮 on *Kāu-liei-kiwong* mountain 高黎共山, the route turned southwards for 200 *li* to the city of *Ngǎk* [or *Lǎk*] 樂 ; 700 *li* farther on, and beyond the *Miwɒn-kung* tribes, lay the city of *Siĕt-lji*. The route recorded by Chia Tan is leading southwards towards the Pyū capital, so that we need not expect any major permanent change in direction before *Siĕt-lji* is reached. Turning to Chüan 1 of the *Man Shu*, we find there displayed several itineraries which illustrate the order of distance implied by 900 *li* in these mountainous territories during the 9th century. From *Źiäng-tuo* 成都 to the *Ngâ-γwǎi* Range 俄淮嶺 is about 1,500 *li* [The totals of Fan-Ch'o and the Wu-ying Tien editors do not agree, and I am here following the latter, whose figure is in accord with the text as we now have it]; from the *Ngâ-γwǎi* Range to *Iang-tsʻiwo-iang* 陽直咩 city is about 1,000 *li* [the author and his editors again fail to agree on their totals, and again I am accepting the text in the form in which it has been preserved]. Each of these totals is made up of smaller distances e.g., from *Źiäng-tuo* to

196   Nāgara and Commandery

G'i̯wong-tśi̯əu 邕州 is 250 li. Other stages are recorded in terms of days' journey, and some in terms of both distance and time (li and day's march), which sometimes offers the opportunity of cross-checking in cases of ambiguity or uncertainty. The nine days recorded for the journey from Tśia-tung city 柘東城 to *I̯ang-tsʻi̯wo-i̯ang, for example, accord fairly well with the best estimate of the Tʻang li (Note 48 above), with the fact that post-stations were spaced at intervals of approximately 40 li [Man Shu, chüan 1, p. 2], that 30 of them accounted for 1,495 li [ibid.], and that, say, *Li̯wong-mjwei city 龍尾城 was a single day's journey from *I̯ang-tsʻi̯wo-i̯ang. In other words a day's march may be confidently defined as between 40 and 50 li (cp. Note 48 above). On this basis it is possible to locate *Si̯et-lji [-i̯e̯] (? = Śrī . . .) in the general vicinity of present-day Lashio.

*Tʻuət-mi̯en was situated at an unspecified distance beyond *Si̯et-lji-i̯e̯ but still on the route towards the Pyū capital. Pelliot ("Deux itinéraires," pp. 176-177), locating the capital at Hmawza, identified *Tʻuət-mi̯en with Pagan, supposedly the most important settlement between the Chindwin-Irawadi confluence and Hmawza. However, this city had been known to the Chinese under the transcription *Bʻuo-kâm 蒲甘 since the time of the Liu Sung dynasty, A.D. 420-479 [Sung Shih 宋史 chüan 489, f. 5 recto], and no one so far has been able to connect the name *Tʻuət-mi̯en with this foundation. Moreover, if the Pyū capital was by this time located in Upper Burma (see p. 178), *Tʻuət-mi̯en must have been still further north along the route to *Si̯et-lji-i̯e̯, probably in the Myitnge valley. I am unable to suggest an original for this toponym (perhaps something akin to *Turmi[n]), but in the form in which Chia Tan recorded it, it is phonetically not too dissimilar to the *Tʻuət-mjie 突彌 which the I-chʻieh-Ching Yin-i 一切經音義 chüan 81 [originally by Hsüan-Ying 玄應 in c. 649; enlarged by Hui-Lin 慧琳 in c. 730] included in a list of Kʻun-lun 崑崙 countries, together with *Tsəng-gʻjie 僧祇 , *Kuət-dʻâng 骨堂 , and *Kâp-miet 閣蔑 (= Qmar = Khmer) [Pelliot has already drawn attention to this text in another connexion: Etudes Asiatiques, vol. 2 (1925), pp. 261-262]. *Tsəng-gʻjie, although involved in linguistic ramifications that would lure us as far as the coast of East Africa, may here be an alternative transcription of the name of the particular Pyū tribe (部落) that the Tʻang history lists as *Tsəng-ka 僧迦 . *Kuət-dʻâng may not be unrelated to the Pyū tribe elsewhere transcribed as *Kân-dʻang 乾唐 . In any case, *Tʻuət-mjie is clearly associated with other Southeast Asian toponyms which seem likely to have been located on the mainland.

*Mji̯e̯-nâk dʻâu li̯əp market town 彌諾道立鎮城. According to the Man Shu, chüan 2, p. 9, this garrison town [here termed a stockade (柵 cha), the character customarily used to denote the timbered enceintes of Southeast Asian settlements] bordered the Li river 麗水 (= Upper Irawadi). As the Chindwin was known as the *Mji̯e̯-nâk river 彌諾江 , it is likely that the garrison town was close to the confluence of these two rivers. G. H. Luce has suggested a location in the neighborhood of Mingin ["Sources of early Burma history," in C. D. Cowan and O. W. Wolters (eds.), Southeast Asian History and Historiography. Essays Presented to D. G. E. Hall (Ithaca, N.Y., 1976), p. 35. Nor is it easy to dissociate this town from the *Mji̯e̯-nâk kingdom, even though this is described by the Man Shu as a seaboard territory "lacking walls and suburbs" (國無城郭 : chüan 10, p. 45). According to the same source this kingdom was 60 days' journey southwest of Yung-chʻang which, on the principles enunciated above, would locate it in Upper Burma, far from the sea. (For comparison, the Pyū capital was 75 days' journey from Yung-chʻang: loc. cit.)

The other garrison towns of the Pyū, which I have been unable to identify, were: *Dʻâu-li̯əm-ji̯wang 道林王 ; *Sâm-tʻâ 三陀 ; *Tiei-gʻi̯ät 帝偈 ; *Tʻât-lji-mi̯əu 達棃謀 ; Kân-dʻang 乾唐 ; and *Muât Reach 末浦 . This last would be identified with *Muât stockade (末柵), were it not that the latter occurs in a Man Shu itinerary leading from the *Ngâ-ɣwǎi Range to *I̯ang-tsʻi̯wo-i̯ang. However, it is by no means unlikely that the Pyū envoys stretched a point or two when they were interviewed by officials of the Hung Lu.

The complete list of Pyū dependencies as transcribed in the Hsin Tʻang-Shu is as follows: 迦羅婆提 *Kâ-lâ-bʻuâ-dʻiei; 摩禮烏特 *Muâ-liei-uo-dʻək; 迦棃迦 *Kâ-liei-ka; 半地 *Puân-dʻi; 彌臣 *Mji̯e̯-zi̯en; 坤朗 *Kʻuən-lâng; 偈奴 *Gʻi̯ät-nuo; 羅聿 *Lâ-i̯uĕt; 佛代 *Bʻuət-dʻậi; 渠論 *Gʻi̯wo-li̯uĕn; 婆棃

*Bʻuâ-lji; 偈陀 *Gʻiät-tʻâ; 多歸 *Tâ-kjwei; 摩曳 *Muâ-i̯äi; 餘郎 *I̯wo-lâng; 合衛 *Si̯a-ji̯wäi; 贍婆 *Tśi̯äm-bʻuâ; 闍婆 *Dẓʻi̯a-bʻuâ. The names of the "best-known tribes" were transcribed as: 萬公 *Mi̯wɒn-kung; 充兹 *Tśʻi̯ung-ńźi̯ak; 羅君潛 *Lâ-ki̯uən-dzʻi̯äm; 彌緾 *Mjie̯-tśʻi̯ak; 道雙 *Dʻâu-sång; 道襲 *Dʻâu-·ung; 道勿 *Dʻâu-mi̯uət; 夜半 *I̯a-puân; 不悉姿 *Pi̯əu-·âk-dʻuât; 莫音 *Muo-i̯əm; 龍映 *Ka-li̯wong-dʻâm; 阿黎吉 **â-lji-ki̯ět; 阿棃闍 **â-lji-dźʻi̯a; 阿棃怛 **â-lji-mwâng; 達歷 *Tʻât-muâ; 水潘 *Gʻi̯əu-pʻuân; 僧塔 *Tsəng-tập; 提黎 *Dʻi̯ei-lji-lâng; 望朦 *Mi̯wang-dʻəng; 擔泊 *Tâm-bʻâk; 祿烏 *Luk-·uo; 乏毛 *Bʻi̯wɒp-mâu; 僧迦 *Tsəng-ka; 提追 *Dʻi̯ei-ṫwi; 阿米運 **â-mjwei-lâ; 迦越 *Źi̯äi-ji̯wɒt; 騰陵 *Dʻəng-li̯əng; 歐咩 *·əu-i̯ang; 碑羅婆提 *Pʻuo-lâ-bʻuâ-dʻi̯ei; 祿羽 *Luk-ji̯u; 隨蠻 *Ləu Mwan 磨地勃餘 *Muâ-dʻi-bʻuət-i̯äu.

68. Or possibly the graph 木 is simply a dittography perpetrated by a clerk who paused in the drawing of 册.

69. *Man Shu*, chüan 6, p. 30. In *Chiu Tʻang-Shu*, chüan 197, f. 7 verso this name has inadvertently been abbreviated to *Sâ-ngâk/lâk 些樂, but is explicitly located on the Nan Chao side of the frontier. Cp. also *Tʻai-pʻing Huan-yü Chi*, chüan 177, f. 15.

70. The Pyū form, which appears in the Myazedi inscription (c. A.D. 1113), is *Rimadhanabū*. The honorific signifies Trampler of Enemies.

71. J. S. F. [John Sydenham Furnivall], "The foundation of Pagan," *JBRS*, vol. 1, pt. 2 (1911), pp. 6-9; Maung Htin Aung, "The Lord of the Great Mountain," *JBRS*, vol. 38, pt. 1 (1955), pp. 75-82; George Coedès, *Les états hindouisés d'Indochine et d'Indonésie* (3rd edition, Paris, 1964), pp. 197-199, and *Les peuples de la péninsule indochinoise* (Paris, 1962), p. 110. The legend itself is preserved in *The Glass Palace Chronicle*, pp. 28-29. Luce ["Burma down to the fall of Pagan," p. 402] gives another reference that I am unable to read: *Mahā Yazawin Gyi*, I, 163 (Burma Research Society Publication, series no. 5, 1926). See also Maung Maung, "A History of Lower Burma," *JBRS*, vol. 11, part 2 (1921), p. 83.

72. C. Foster Smith, *Thucydides* (London, 1919), pp. 288-291.

73. The names of the villages were: *Nyaung-u, Nagabo, Nagakyit, Magyigyi, Tuti, Kyaussaga, Kokkèthein, Nyaungwun, Anurada, Tazaunggun, Ywamon, Kyinlo, Kokko, Taungba, Myegèdwin, Tharekya, Onmya, Yonhlut*, and *Ywasaik*. The *Glass Palace Chronicle*, p. 29, notes that there is some doubt as to whether [*Nga*] *Singu* should be included in place of *Onmya*.

74. A Burmese-Pāli phrase: *Min* (B.) = lord; *Mahāgiri* (P.) = great mountain.

75. A purely Burmese style: *Taunggyi* = great mountain.

76. For a discussion of this type of urban morphology in the traditional world see Wheatley, *The Pivot*, pp. 305-311 and 389-390.

77. Etienne Aymonier, "Première étude sur les inscriptions tchames," *Journal Asiatique*, 8th series, vol. 17 (1891), p. 29; Louis Finot, "Notes d'épigraphie," *BEFEO*, vol. 3 (1903), p. 633.

78. *Epigraphia Birmanica*, plate 6, l. 25.

79. *Hsin Tʻang-Shu*, chüan 222C, f. 17 verso; *Man Shu*, chüan 10, p. 45.

80. *Glass Palace Chronicle*, pp. 28-29.

81. Phayre, *History of Burma*, pp. 8 and 293-304.

82. M. S. Collis and U San Shwe Bu, "Arakan's place in the civilization of the Bay," *JBRS*, vol. 15, pt. 1 (1925), pp. 34-52. Reprinted in *Burma Research*

Society Fiftieth Anniversary Publications No. 2 (Rangoon, 1960), p. 486.

83. Burmese = Wethali.

84. The *praśasti*, in honor of a king Ānandacandra, is inscribed on the west face of a pillar that at some time or other has been re-erected in the Shitthaung pagoda at Mrohaung. It was described by Hirananda Sastri in the *Annual Report of the Archaeological Survey of India* (1925-1926), p. 146, and read by the late Professor E. H. Johnston, "Some Sanskrit inscriptions of Arakan," *BSOAS*, vol. 11, pt. 2 (1944), pp. 357-385. The verse relevant to the capital is not entirely clear, but Professor Johnston has translated it as: "He [Dveñ Candra], strong of arm because of righteousness, conquered 101 kings, and built a compact (?) city furnished with walls and moat . . . which laughed at the beauty of Paradise." Johnston has suggested that *Dveñ* may = Sanskrit *Tuiñ* < *Taing*, an honorific prefixed to the style Candra for the first nine kings of the line in Burmese chronicles (p. 368).

85. Johnston, *loc. cit.*, pp. 359 and 368.

86. The reading is uncertain. The text says specifically ". . . there have been constructed streets, various pleasances, causeways and passages" [Johnston, *loc. cit.*, p. 382].

87. Johnston, *loc. cit.*, pp. 369 and 376.

88. Johnston, *loc. cit.*, pp. 372 and 379.

89. Note 28 to Chapter 5.

CHAPTER 5

Cities of the Rmañ

At the beginning of the Christian era the deltas of the Irawadi and Salween rivers, the plains of the lower Čhao Phraya, and at least the northern parts of the isthmian tract of the Malay Peninsula appear to have been ethnically Mōn.[1] In the earlier centuries of this era these territories may possibly at times have been incorporated into one or the other of the Fu-nan chiefdoms,[2] but from the 6th century A.D. at latest, they seem to have afforded bases for the development of independent polities. Concerning these there are two main traditions, which we shall call Western Mōn and Eastern Mōn, and which it will be convenient to examine separately, although it is by no means improbable that both stem from a common series of events. Both traditions are unfortunately involved in an historical paradox which in the present state of knowledge cannot be resolved. According to later traditions, both written and oral, of the Burmese and Thai — indeed of the Mōn themselves — the hearth of Mōn culture was situated in Lower Burma, particularly in the neighborhood of the cities of Thatōn and Pegu, which might have been expected as a consequence to yield a rich harvest of Mōn remains. The opposite is the case. Even allowing for a paucity of excavations, it is safe to say that archeology and epigraphy afford only exiguous glimpses of the settlement hierarchy in Lower Burma prior to the 9th or 10th century A.D.[3] Moreover, whereas Mōn, Burmese and Thai[4] chronicles all depict a strongly Theravādin state in that area in early times, such meager archeological vestiges as have come to light are uncompromisingly Hindu.[5] In central Thailand, by contrast, the elements of the paradox are reversed. The fairly abundant archeological remains available for investigation, and which bear witness to the existence of temple-cities of considerable cultural sophistication during the period from the 6th to the 11th century, have left no discernible impress on the written and oral traditions of any ethnic group.

In an attempt to resolve this incompatibility between archeological evidence on the one hand and literary records and folklore on the other, the Thai scholar Prince Damrong Rajanubhab proposed to locate the culture hearth of the Mōn wholly within the territories of present-day Thailand.[6] Most subsequent scholars have found themselves unable to accept the radical disruption of traditional Mōn toponymy which this thesis necessarily involves. Dr. Quaritch Wales sought to evade this dilemma by delaying the Mōn adoption of the Pāli canon until the first half of the 11th century, that is until immediately before the Burmese conquest of Thatōn by Aniruddha in 1057.[7] This interpretation is, of course, in direct contradiction to the record of the chronicles, and substitutes one incompatibility for another. But this time the variance may prove less intractable. More than two decades ago the late Pierre Dupont called in question the integrity of the whole Burmese tradition upon which the notion of an early Mōn state in the delta country has been based.[8] The earliest epigraphic reference to Theravāda tenets in this region dates only from the 15th century, when the legend of an Aśokan (3rd century B.C.) proselytizing mission was included in the Kalyāṇī inscriptions of King Dammazedi.[9] The *loci classici* for this mission are the Singhalese chronicles *Dīpavaṃsa* and *Mahāvaṃsa*,[10] and it may be significant for the present argument that during the 15th century Mōn Buddhism was allegedly reformed on the basis of Singhalese practice. As earlier documents are entirely lacking, it is impossible to tell whether a pseudo-memory of such a mission derived from some independent Mōn source or was adopted as a result of the 15th-century mission to Ceylon. In this connexion, though, it should be noted that the Kalyāṇī inscriptions contain a good deal of frankly mythical material, as well as some anachronisms,[11] and that they have nothing to say about the Mōn polity for some fourteen centuries subsequent to the Aśokan mission. Professor Dupont was, therefore, led to suggest that the Mōns of the 15th century had recast aspects of their past, about which they probably knew little in any case, in a form that would bestow the dignity of age on their newly purified faith. This interpretation implied that the strong oral tradition existing among both Mōns and Burmese derived from the period of Kalyāṇī inscriptions, perhaps actually stimulated by those epigraphs and others like them now lost.[12] Certainly all the Burmese chronicles in the form in which we know them are considerably later than the inscriptions. The Thai

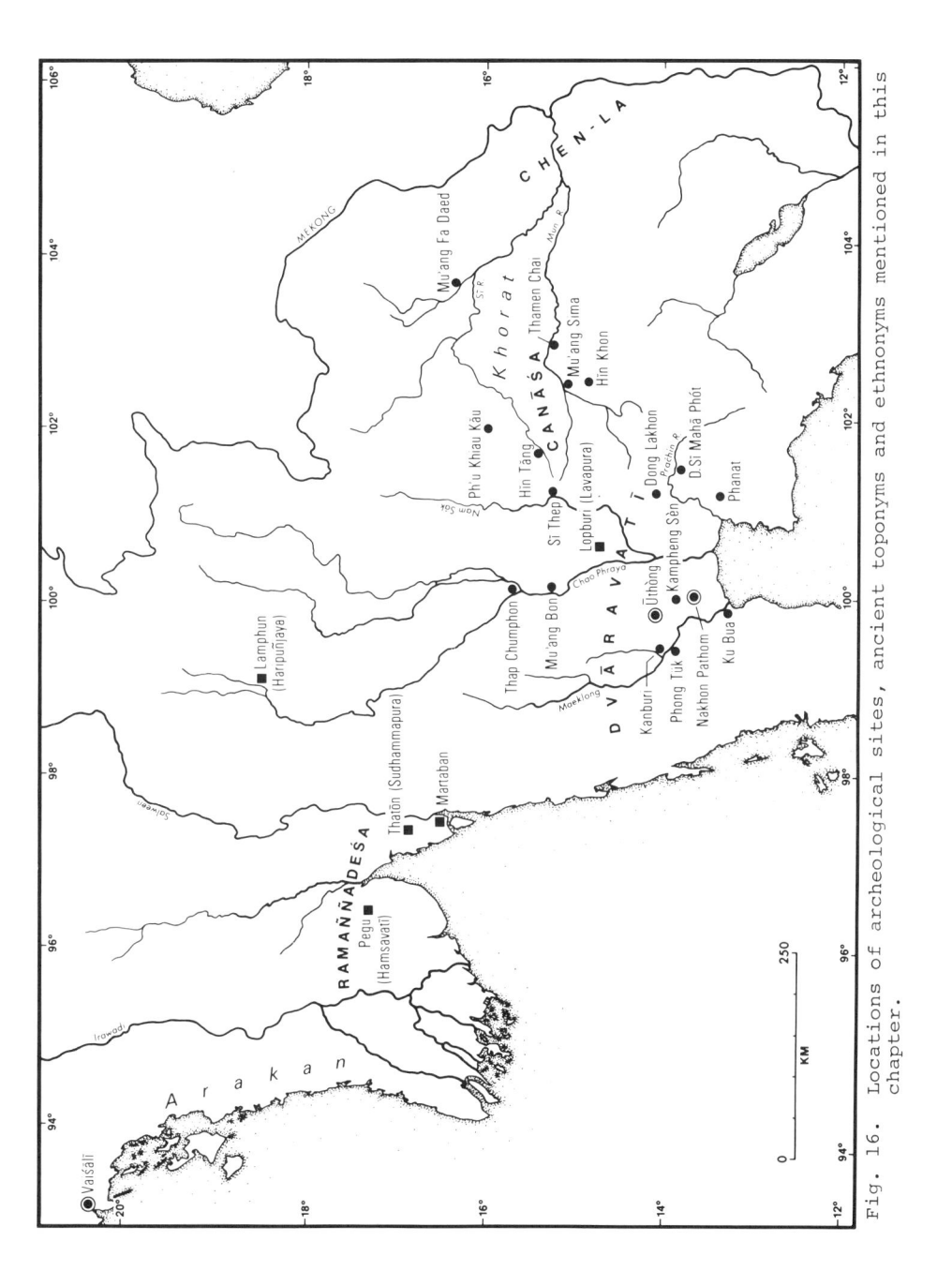

Fig. 16. Locations of archeological sites, ancient toponyms and ethnonyms mentioned in this chapter.

written tradition, and without doubt the oral as well, were, in this interpretation, accounted for by the well-attested migration of Mōn refugees eastwards between 1581 and 1824.[13]

Subsequently George Coedès, while acknowledging the late development of Buddhism in Lower Burma, proposed that the Theravāda faith had been introduced into the Delta not from Ceylon in the 15th century (as Dupont had supposed), but by refugees fleeing from a cholera epidemic in Haripuñjaya in the 11th century.[14] The disappearance of literary records relating to central Thailand was attributed by Coedès, not implausibly, to the successive conquests by Khmers and Thais which followed early indigenous state developments in the region. The continued presence of Mōns in Lower Burma, by contrast, together with the not inconsiderable part they played in the political and cultural history of Burma, ensured the preservation of their traditions virtually down to the present time. Coedès's interpretation, though still only an hypothesis, accords more closely with the received chronology of events than does Dupont's, and is certainly the most probable resolution so far advanced of the incompatibility between archeological evidence and tradition in the Mōn territories.

The Western Mōn Tradition

We have seen that Burmese, Mōn and Thai chronicles claim to trace classical Mōn culture to a hearth closely associated with ancient capitals at Sudhammapura (Thatōn[15]) and Haṃsavatī (Pegu[16]), yet archeological confirmation of this is lacking. It is possible that parts of the walls of both cities antedate the 11th century, as may also the ruins of several shrines within the enceintes, and there are some half-dozen other sites in the neighborhoods that appear to be earlier than the Burmese conquest of 1057.[17] The few epigraphical remains so far discovered are still unedited and unpublished,[18] and it is far from certain that all are pre-eleventh century in date. It appears that the rulers of the time did not practice the custom common in other parts of Southeast Asia of placing dated dedicatory inscriptions in their shrines, a lack only partially compensated for by the fact that schedules of offerings were occasionally inscribed on statuary. One such inscription in Old Mōn, of age unknown but probably pre-eleventh century, mentions a queen (possibly of Martaban, though the reading is very uncertain) residing in the city of Duwop.[19] The name of this city occurs twice more, once in a faint duplicate of this inscription and once in a separate inscription, both of which are in the

Shwezayan pagoda at Thatôn.[20] Finally, in yet another Shwezayan
inscription, Pierre Dupont[21] has tentatively discerned a reference
to Tāmbāviseya,[22] the Land of Bronze, a name which is reminiscent of
other toponyms of western mainland Southeast Asia (such as
Tāmraliṅga on the isthmus of the Malay Peninsula,[23] Tāmpadīpa in
Upper Burma[24]), of Śrī Tāmrapaṭṭana, a kingdom neighboring
Arakan,[25] and of the legendary cities of bronze that feature in the
folklore of Southeast Asia.

It is unfortunate that external sources relating to Lower
Burma in the days before the Burmese conquest are exiguous,
obscure and unreliable. The Ptolemaic corpus locates several *poleis*
and *emporia* in this general area, and these will be discussed
subsequently. So far as the Chinese were concerned the Mōn country
was poorly reported, for it lay off both land and sea routes to
India. The former passed across Upper Burma en route to Kāmarūpa,
the latter followed a course over the open ocean from the northern
end of Melaka Strait to the Nicobar Islands, and thence either to
Tāmraliptī in the Ganges delta or to the ports of South India.
Some scholars have located Mi-chen (彌城 *Mjie-źiĕn), a maritime
territory mentioned in T'ang and later works, on the Gulf of
Martaban,[26] but it lacked "cities with walls and suburbs"[27] and so
is of no direct concern to us at the moment.

The Eastern Mōn Tradition

Once across the mountain ridge into what is today Thai
territory, the archeological record becomes more ample (though
certainly not adequate to answer more than a small proportion of
the questions that suggest themselves). Generally speaking, the
productive sites are distributed in an arc round the outer edge of
the Bangkok plain. Although systematic excavation has so far been
restricted to the western sector of this arc, sufficient evidence
has accumulated in the form of shrine foundations still protruding
through the soil, enceintes still discernible as faint undulations
on its surface, and statuary discovered fortuitously throughout the
area, to support the notion of a Mōn polity or polities of some sort in
existence from the 6th to the 11th century. For nearly a century
it has been inferred that this was the region known in Chinese
records as Dvāravatī,[28] a name incorporated in the honorific applied
to the much later Thai capital of Ayutthaya, and even in that of
present-day Bangkok, but conclusive evidence of this association
has come to light only very recently in the form of two coins from
Phra Pathom, each bearing the royal style of *Śrī Dvāravatīśvara*.[29]

On the western sector of the arc mentioned above the most productive archeological sites have proved to be in the neighborhood of — from north to south — the present-day towns of Ū Thòng, Nakhon Pathom, Ratburi (Ku Bua), Kampheng Sèn, and Phong Tük, with Kanburi Kao also contributing remains possibly from this same period. These sites have between them yielded a fairly wide range of archeological evidence[30] but relatively little of it relates directly to city life. At least two of these settlements have been suggested as possible capitals of a Dvāravatī kingdom, namely Ū Thòng and Phra Pathom. Although the complete site report for Ū Thòng has not yet been published, partial reports summarizing the results of excavations by H. G. Quaritch Wales, Prince Subhadradis Diskul, and Jean Boisselier make it clear that the site was occupied uninterruptedly from protohistoric times down to the 11th or 12th century A.D.[31] The artifactual assemblages from the earlier levels are said to attest a Funanese style of culture focused on "un des sites les plus anciens et les plus riches de toute l'Asie du Sud-est."[32] By Dvāravatī times, say the 7th century, the main settlement at Ū Thòng was enclosed within a moat that defined an elongated oval having diameters of some 1850 yards from north to south and 920 from east to west (Fig. 17A). What gives some plausibility to the suggestion that Ū Thòng was at this time the capital of Dvāravatī is the substance of an inscription, written in pre-Aṅkorian characters, on a copper plate found at the northern end of the enceinte.[33] The inscription commemorates a gift to the liṅga Āmrātakeśvara by a certain Śrī Harṣavarman who "had ascended by regular succession to the lion throne," and who is further described as a grandson of King Śrī Īśānavarman. The political and dynastic import of this relationship turns on whether or no the Īśānavarman referred to was the ruler who succeeded to the throne of Chen-la in about 615. If so, and if his grandson were a Khmer king, then a new name would have to be inserted into the received list of 7th-century Chen-la rulers either before or after Bhavavarman II, whose only established date is 639. This would not today be such a desperate expedient as it might have appeared a few years ago. However, there is also the possibility that Harṣavarman (or perhaps his father) was a Khmer prince who, on being beneficed, in typical patrimonial fashion, with territories in the Čhao Phraya valley, had there introduced one of the more popular Khmer cults of Śiva. A third possibility is to regard both Īśānavarman and Harṣavarman as members of a local Dvāravatī dynasty. This would avoid the necessity of postulating

Cities of the Rmañ   205

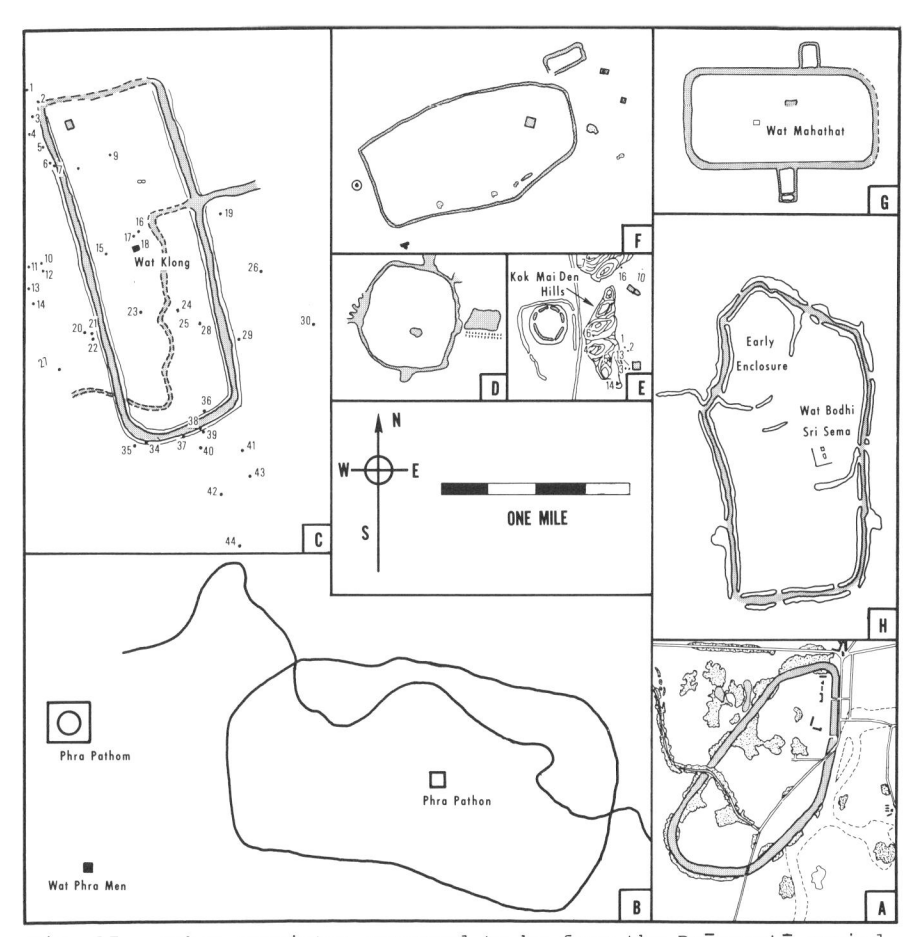

Fig. 17. Urban enceintes presumed to be from the Dvāravatī period.

A. Ū Thòng. Based on a plan prepared by the Fine Arts Department, Bangkok.
B. Nakhon Pathom. Based on a sketch in H.G. Quaritch Wales, *Dvāravatī* (London, 1969), p. 15.
C. Ku Bua and associated archeological sites, a high proportion of which appear to be *stūpa,* and perhaps *caitya,* bases. Based on a plan prepared by the Fine Arts Department, Bangkok.
D. Chansen. Based on an outline plan in Bennet Bronson and George F. Dales, "Excavations at Chansen, Thailand, 1968 and 1969," *Asian Perspectives,* vol. 15 (1973), p. 19.
E. Mu'ang Bon and associated archeological sites, more than a dozen of which are *stūpa* bases. Based on a plan prepared by the Fine Arts Department, Bangkok.
F. Dong Sī Mahā Phót. Based on a sketch in Wales, *Dvāravatī,* p. 89.
G. Phanat. Based on a sketch in Wales, *Dvāravatī,* p. 94.
H. Mu'ang Fa Daed. Based on a plan prepared by the Fine Arts Department, Bangkok.

that the inscription was brought to Ū Thòng from Chen-la for some unknown reason, and would circumvent the inconvenient fact that engraving on copper plates, though current in India and Indonesia at the time, was not practiced in the Khmer homeland. Coedès has also pointed out that certain peculiarities of the script may betoken Mōn influence. The implications of the inscription cannot be adequately evaluated on the evidence currently available, but whether or not Ū Thòng was ever a capital of a kingdom, still uncompleted archeological investigations attest that it was a city of considerable importance in the Dvāravatī period, with a landscape diversified by both Theravāda Buddhist and Brāhmaṇical foundations.

The other settlement which has been claimed as a possible capital of Dvāravatī was on the site of present-day Nakhon Pathom, where a roughly rectangular enclosure of some 2 x 1 1/4 miles is bounded by rampart and moat (Fig. 17B).[34] In this case the claim to capital status is based primarily on the discovery beneath a ruined sanctuary within the enceinte of two silver coins, each of which bears on its reverse, in a script assigned to the 7th or 8th century, an inscription reading: "The meritorious work of the King of Śrī Dvāravatī (śrīdvāravatīśvarapuṇya)."[35] It is thought that the meritorious work referred to was probably the building of the Chula Pathon, a huge *caitya* erected almost in the geometrical center of the city, and forming the chief structure of the group that included the much smaller shrine beneath which the coins were found. The earlier aspects of the archeological assemblage from Nakhon Pathom conform reasonably closely to the dating implied by the script previously mentioned, with the notable exception of a structure excavated at Wat Phra Men, situated just over three-quarters of a mile to the west of the city wall, where the earliest architectural affinities are not entirely clear.[36] From the central sector of the main enceinte a causeway led to a satellite sanctuary at Non Phra some 3 1/2 miles to the south.[37] It is noticeable that at both Nakhon Pathom and Ū Thòng the medium of architectural construction was invariable a brick of unusually large size and a texture which has been compared to that prevalent in Orissa at the time.[38] Decorative features were mainly in terracotta during the 7th century, but in stucco thereafter. Stone was apparently reserved for the principal cult images.

At Kampheng Sèn, about a third of the way along the road from Nakhon Pathom to Ū Thòng, a moat and two low ramparts enclose a rectangle with rounded corners and extreme measurements of 857 x

804 yards.[39] A Pāli inscription in Pallava characters found there apparently dates from the 8th century, and Dupont has characterized stucco Buddha images discovered outside the eastern gate as of late-Dvāravatī origin.[40] However, the sparseness of the potsherd deposits would seem to imply a small population. Wales has suggested (he characterizes his remark as a guess) that the settlement was "an early outpost towards the sea which stagnated rather than developed with the establishment of a definitive seaside capital ot Nak'on Pathom."[41]

Another roughly rectangular enclosure has been investigated at Ku Bua, 11 miles south of Ratburi in the lower Maeklong valley.[42] It is about 1 3/4 miles from north to south by half a mile from east to west, and is bounded by the remains of two ramparts separated by a moat 55 yards in width, all of which have been erased on the north side. Centrally situated within this enceinte are the remains of a large rectangular structure which Wales is inclined to interpret as a *caitya* on the general pattern of the Phra Pathon at Nakhon Pathom. Unfortunately the site is now partially occupied by Wat Klong, so that further excavation will be impracticable for the foreseeable future. More than forty *stūpas* and other structures, mostly still unexcavated, occur both inside and outside the enceinte (Fig. 17C), and in the base of one a quinquncially compartmented ritual deposit box was found of a type not uncommon in other parts of South and Southeast Asia.[43] Quaritch Wales, on no very strong grounds, has assigned the settlement to the 8th century, after which it was apparently supplanted by Ratburi, possibly as a result of a shift in the main channel of the Maeklong.

An arresting feature of the archeological assemblage from Ku Bua is the hoard of stucco figures and decorative fragments which, wholly unexpectedly, have come to light on the sites, particularly those numbered 39 and 40, both of which are located immediately outside the south wall of the settlement. These stuccoes include vegetal motifs, animals, *garuḍas, gandharvas,* a *yakṣa,* apparently royal personages, servants, musicians, dancers, warriors, prisoners, and seemingly foreigners, probably traders[44] — in short a cross-section of court life. Most significant of all, however, were certain *bodhisattvas* in a style close to the tradition of Ajanta, which betoken the presence of a non-Tantric Mahāyāna Buddhism in the heart of what has previously been regarded as Theravāda and brāhmaṇical territory. The antelope skin worn by one such Avalokiteśvara, a feature which appeared at Ajanta and Ellora late

in the Gupta period, presumably implies that these figures, and in
all probability the structures into the facades of which they were
incorporated, were not earlier than the beginning of the 8th
century.[45] The truth is, of course, that we have no idea of the
manner in which the individual figures were integrated into
coherent compositions, nor of the appearance of the facades that
they decorated. These uncertainties are exacerbated by the
circumstance that the terracottas acquired from Sites 39 and 40
were too numerous to have been appropriately employed in the
decoration of structures of those sizes. Dr. Quaritch Wales's
purely hypothetical, though nonetheless plausible, explanation of
these hoards envisages a monastery of Mahāyāna monks on the
outskirts of the town declining for lack of popular and
governmental support in a predominantly Theravāda kingdom. When
the monks finally departed, either their followers or superstitious
townspeople loath to anger the Mahāyānist deities collected the
unwanted terracottas in a place where they would be either safe or
unnoticed.[46]

At Phong Tük, higher up the Maeklong valley than Ku Bua,
archeological remains, as yet only partially excavated, are
sufficiently extensive to indicate that, in the context of the
time, they represent at least an incipiently urban focus rather
than an isolated shrine.[47] Wales inclines to a date no earlier than
the second half of the 8th century for the *floruit* of the
settlement, and interprets its role as that of a small market
center located between larger and more prestigious cities. Its
lack of a defensive rampart, unique among the settlements
discussed, he attributes to its relatively late development in the
heart of a region already fairly densely settled.

On the northern edge of the Bangkok plain numerous but
scattered surface finds in the vicinity of Lopburi represent the
material remains of the city known to Pāli and Chinese chronicles
alike as Lavapura.[48] Subsequent settlement has inhibited
archeological investigation to such an extent that the plan of the
ancient city is unknown, but the site has produced some of the
finest extant Dvāravatī images and not a few inscriptions, the
earliest of which is a single line of Mōn, probably dating from the
6th century. The majority of the finds point to the 8th century or
later. A relatively short distance farther north, near the modern
village of Chansen, is a moated enclosure, approximately square in
shape, though with rounded corners, oriented roughly to the
cardinal compass directions, and with sides of about 700 yards

(Fig. 17D).[49] A large trapezoidal tank is situated outside the eastern boundary of the enclosure, and a causeway projects axially from the same side. The excavators inferred from the several-fold increase in potsherd densities between about A.D. 600 and 800 that the settlement experienced a very sizeable increase in its population during Dvāravatī times, but, although two brick structures were located, they were not identified. The earthworks appear to date from the same period but the role of the site in the settlement hierarchy even at that time is wholly obscure.

Still farther north, on the left bank of the Čhao Phraya, is the double enceinte known as Mu'ang Bon.[50] The assumed nucleus of this settlement was a circular, ramparted enceinte situated at the northern end of an outer enclosure with a perimeter of about 1,000 yards. The inner rampart was 20 yards broad at its base and still stands 6 feet above the level of the ground within the enclosure. Both ramparts were flanked by moats averaging perhaps 35 yards in width. Whereas the depth of pottery sherds was roughly the same in both the inner and outer enclosures, the concentration of sherds within a given horizon was less in the outer than in the inner enceinte, implying (1) that both enclosures were constructed at much the same time, but that (2) population was focused in the inner citadel. Altogether more than a dozen *stūpa* bases have been excavated on the slopes of the neighboring Kok Mai Den hills and even farther afield (Fig. 17E), several of which provided information, lacking at both Ū Thòng and Phra Pathom, of the way in which stucco relief figures were utilized in the decoration of monuments. At two sites an actual scene from the *Caddanta Jātaka* is depicted, specifically the Elephant King being confronted by the hunter Sonuttara. Quaritch Wales had discerned in these assemblages tendencies to both crudity in the stucco figures and simplification in architectural design which he plausibly equates with provincialism. The artifacts and the style of the letters in a very badly mutilated inscription place the settlement between the 8th and 10th centuries.

Thap Chumphon,[51] three miles north of Nakhon Sawan, and Sī Thep[52] in the Nam Săk valley appear to have been relatively prosperous settlements at the threshold of urban status during Dvāravatī times. The former is acribed to the 7th or 8th century and gives every indication that it was a Mōn foundation, but the categorization of Sī Thep is a more complicated matter. While an inscription of Bhavavarman I of Chen-la discovered less than 8 miles from the settlement at Sī Thep attests Khmer control of the locality late in the 6th or early in the 7th century,[53] it is clear that Mōn culture prevailed in the region then and until the end of the 10th century. Certain Mahāyānist sculptures from the neighboring Thamorat Hill, the significance of which in this border region between Mōns and Khmers has not been adequately explored, seem to indicate that in the 8th century or thereabouts the hill was a pilgrimage center for a lay community in the settlement below.[54] Finally, the early 15th-century Pāli chronicle *Cāmadevīvaṃsa* attributes to a queen of Lavapura the founding of the city of Haripuñjaya (modern Lamphun) during the 8th century.[55] The tradition is apparently reliable.

Several of the archeological sites enumerated thus far, and particularly the important ones at Nakhon Pathom and Lopburi, have afforded bases for later settlements, so that a great deal of the morphological evidence of interest to the student of city life has been obliterated. The eastern fringe of the plain, by contrast, appears to have witnessed relatively fewer such superimpositions after the dissolution of Dvāravatī, with the result that the traces of at least three former settlements in the Prachin valley are still clearly visible on the surface of the ground. At Dong Si Mahā Phót, close to Prachinburi, a (possibly double) rampart and a moat form a trapezoidal figure with extreme measurements of 1,640 x 875 yards (Fig. 17F).[56] Entrances are not readily apparent in the currently degraded state of the ramparts, but seem to have been spaced at irregular intervals. Archeological finds chanced upon fortuitously over the years and acquired during systematic excavation by the Fine Arts Department in 1968-69 indicate the coexistence of Brāhmanical and Theravāda Buddhist cults characteristic of Dvāravatī sites. At Phanat (Fig. 17G), immediately behind the coast of the Gulf of Bangkok and not far from the estuary of the Prachin river, is a rectangularly shaped enceinte with rounded corners defined by a double rampart enclosing a moat. Its dimensions are approximately 1,520 x 760 yards.[57] Small projections extend from both eastern and western sides. Trial excavations undertaken by Quaritch Wales revealed only a late and relatively brief Dvāravatī occupation. According to Lajonquière, both these sites were until recently known locally as Mu'ang Phra Rot, or the City of the Sacred Chariot. An indication of some former relationship between them is possibly provided by alleged traces of an avenue linking the two enceintes,[58] but Wales would regard road construction of this type as characteristically Khmer rather than Mōn, and therefore to be assigned to the post-Dvāravatī

Cities of the Rmañ 211

period.⁵⁹ The third enclosure still visible in the Prăchin valley, at Dong Lakhon, has not been excavated, but Lajonquière published a plan showing double enclosing walls separated by a moat forming a cardinally oriented square with sides of 500 meters.⁶⁰ However, subsequent inspection of the forest-covered site has rendered this plan highly suspect. Meager surface finds tend to imply a Dvāravatī occupation.

Rather surprisingly, evidence of Dvāravatī cultural influence, if not political control, has also come to light on sites as far afield as Khorat. In 1950 the late Major P. D. R. Williams-Hunt published an air photograph of Mu'ang Sima showing what appears to be a roughly square enceinte with rounded corners, to which has been added a large, irregularly shaped, northern enclosure, while a small irregular enclave has subsequently been partially superimposed on the original enceinte.⁶¹ From this site had already come two inscriptions. One, in Sanskrit and dated not later than the 7th century, recorded gifts made to a Buddhist community by a ruler of Śrī Canāśa.⁶² An incomplete list of the members of a dynasty of this kingdom has been preserved in a Śaivite inscription of 937, in Sanskrit and Khmer, which was found in the ruins of the Court Brāhmaṇas' temple at Ayutthaya.⁶³ It is also likely that a king Jayasiṃhavarman mentioned in a Buddhist Sanskrit inscription of the 7th or 8th century which was found at Ph'u Khiau Kău, to the north of Chăiyăph'um, was a ruler of Canāśa.⁶⁴ As none of the names in the list occur in the extant epigraphy of Cambodia, it is to be assumed that Canāśa enjoyed at least nominal independence during at least part of the Dvāravatī period. In fact, the second of the Mu'ang Sima inscriptions, in Sanskrit and Khmer and dated 868, commemorates the establishment of a *liṅga* at a place, evidently Mu'ang Sima itself, which is specifically stated to have been outside the domain of Kambudeśa (*Kambudeśāntare*).⁶⁵ It is, moreover, significant that the Khmer language employed in two bi-lingual (Sanskrit and Khmer) 8th-century inscriptions from Hĭn Khōn, just over 20 miles south of Khorat (and therefore probably within the territory of Canāśa), shows traces of Mōn influence.⁶⁶ Like the inscription from Ph'u Khiau Kău and another from Hĭn Tăng,⁶⁷ the Hĭn Khōn dedication provides testimony to the presence of the Sanskrit Buddhist canon in Khorat during the 7th or 8th centuries: unexpected perhaps but, as we have seen, also attested at Ku Bua in the very heart of Dvāravatī. Coedès's conclusion, after study of these several inscriptions, was that, "Ces divers documents épigraphiques assez disparates ont pour caractère commun d'être étrangers au Cambodge, même s'ils emploient la langue khmère. Certains d'entre eux émanent peut-être de pays ayant fait partie, ou ayant reconnu la suzeraineté, du royaume de Dvāravatī."[68] Quaritch Wales's subsequent trial excavations at the circular, multi-ramparted sites of Thamen Chai and Mu'ang Phet tended to support that conclusion.[69]

The farthest eastward that elements of Dvāravatī influence (though not necessarily, or even probably, of Mōn cultural provenance) have been discerned is the site of Mu'ang Fa Daed (Fa Dēt), situated in relatively undifferentiated country near the Phau tributary of the Si river, that is in northeast Khorat. The existing surface morphology appears to indicate that the settlement grew from a very roughly oval nucleus by two successive extensions towards the south. The outermost enclosure is broadly rectangular, with dimensions of approximately 1 1/2 x 3/4 miles.[70] Stūpa bases and stucco ornamentation from the now collapsed superstructures exhibit typically Dvāravatī characteristics, but the features that have attracted most attention are the numerous sēmā stones, some up to 4 ft. high and often bearing Buddhist scenes in relief. One such scene, depicting in orthodox fashion the Buddha's return to Kapilavastu, includes a sāla which affords a distant glimpse of what Dvāravatī wooden architecture must have been, while in the foreground a city wall and storeyed gate-tower guarded by armed men are presumably reasonably accurate renderings of urban defenses of the time. The sēmā stones themselves must be accounted survivals from the Southeast Asian Megalithic which were put to a new use in the local culture of 8th-century northeast Khorat, without losing completely all the associations previously attributed to menhirs. Of course, sēmā stones were normally incorporated in Dvāravatī Buddhist architecture, being placed singly or in pairs at the cardinal and subcardinal compass points of sacred enclosures, but never in the heartland of Mōn culture were they employed in the manner or on the scale evident at Fa Daed.

The "Five Cities"

It is probable that at least the northern parts of the Siamo-Malayan isthmus were also Mōn territory. Isolated and sporadic finds seem to indicate as much,[71] but the whole region is inadequately explored from the archeological point of view, and excavations are practically non-existent. However, it is to these territories that we should almost certainly assign what appears to be the earliest Mōn settlement of which there may have survived a record. This is the city known to the Chinese as Tun-Sun (頓遜

*Tuən-suən), which features in a schedule of territories (國) allegedly incorporated in the kingdom of Fu-nan during the 3rd century A.D.[72] It was situated in the sort of position favored by numerous other Southeast Asian emporia, namely 10 *li* from the coast (and, though this is not stated explicitly, probably a short distance up a river), accessible from the ocean yet protected from it. I have elsewhere argued that the site of Tun-Sun should be sought in the far north of the Siamo-Malayan isthmus,[73] an hypothesis that has been considerably strengthened by H. L. Shorto's suggestion that the Chinese graphs were a transcription of a Proto-Mōn *ḍuñ sun, meaning "five cities."[74] This interpretation itself receives strong support from a remark in the *Liang Shu* to the effect that there were five princes (王) in the kingdom. As Shorto has pointed out, we are here almost certainly dealing with an early instance of the *pañcanāgara* or five-unit system that was widely diffused through both mainland and archipelagic Southeast Asia in later times.[75]

It is impossible at this juncture to point to a precise location for Tun-Sun. Among the sites described above, Ū Thòng is the only one that has yielded an appreciable quantity of remains earlier than the seventh century. At present it is a good deal more than 10 *li* from the coast, but the delta is currently building seaward at an estimated rate of from fifteen to twenty feet a year.[76] It is unlikely that this rate of accretion has been constant over the previous two millennia, but it can be safely assumed that in the 3rd century A.D. Ū Thòng was nearer to the shore than at present. The implications of the artifactual remains and epigraphic evidence attributable to the 7th century are not at all incompatible with a notice in the 5th-century *Fu-nan Chi* which recorded the presence in the city of both Brāhmaṇical and Buddhist adherents.[77] Nakhon Pathom, Ku Bua, or Phong Tük would seem to offer locations more consonant with the Chinese evidence, but none of those sites has yielded artifacts earlier than the 7th century. In any case, wherever *Tun-Sun* may eventually prove to have been located, it was virtually unique among the cities of Indianized Southeast Asia in the emphasis that the Chinese records (as opposed to archeology) placed on its commercial functions. Because of its advantageous location where the land "curves round and projects into the sea for more than a thousand *li*," says the *Liang Shu*, "all the countries beyond the frontier [i.e. the Chinese frontier: hence is implied 'all the countries of Southeast Asia'] come and go in pursuit of trade . . . . At this mart East and West meet together, so that every day there are great crowds there. Precious goods and rare merchandise—they are all there." According to the *Liang Shu*, in the 6th century Tun-Sun's trading relations extended [north]eastward to Tong-King, westward to India and Parthia,[78] a circumstance which recalls to mind the Semitic traders identified by Elizabeth Lyons among the terracotta figurines (probably of the 8th or 9th centuries) from Ku Bua.[79] If traders from the western fringes of Asia were temporarily resident in the relatively small city of Ku Bua (though one which may have functioned as an outpost for a metropolis farther inland), then it is not impossible that they were also to be found in the major settlements of Dvāravatī. And the fact that they featured in the terracotta decoration of a structure in Ku Bua probably signifies that these foreigners donated, or at least contributed to the building of, the monument on which they appeared, and thereby left us an enduring record of their continuing, rather than transient, involvement in the affairs of the town.

* * * * * * * * * *

The evidence assembled in the preceding pages provides the fullest, though still woefully inadequate, documentation of the evolution of urban form in any part of Southeast Asia (though not of the underlying social processes). The apparent lack of archeological confirmation of urban forms in the Mōn territories of Lower Burma prior to the 9th century is puzzling, but may be at least partly illusory, the result of insufficiently thorough survey. The existence of an at least proto-urban/chiefdom level of organization in that region in the 8th century is surely implied by the seemingly reliable record in the *Jinakālamālī* of a matrimonial alliance between the ruling houses of Lavapura (Lopburi) and Ramaññanāgara.[80] In the eastern Mōn territories the situation is clearer, with a fairly close network of ritual and administrative centers spread through the plains of the lower Čhao Phraya and extending eastwards on to the Khorat upland. At the apex of this hierarchy was the still unidentified capital of the Śrī Dvāravatīśvara, from which was governed a polity of considerable power and prestige.[81]

This simple statement of urban conditions in the Mōn and immediately neighboring culture realms does not venture beyond a narrow interpretation of the archeological, epigraphic, and literary evidence. However, Quaritch Wales has gone farther and attempted to elicit developmental sequences in both the integration of the urban hierarchy and the morphology of individual cities.[82] In the first place he infers that the focus of the urban system shifted from an earlier capital at Ū Thòng to a later capital at Nakhom Pathom in response to progressive seaward extension of the delta (This interpretation presumably implies some maritime concerns on the part of the rulers of Dvāravatī). Dr. Wales believes that this migration of the capital probably took place during the last quarter of the 7th century, when the political weakness of Chen-la supposedly afforded an opportunity for Dvāravatī both to consolidate its control over its nuclear territories and to extend its frontiers. In the two succeeding centuries, not only were new towns established in the lower Čhao Phraya and Maeklong valleys, but Dvāravatī-style settlement expanded into the Prachin valley, as well as into the lands bordering the middle reaches of the Čhao Phraya, and, ultimately, to Lamphun in the far north. Not all these foundations were wholly successful. In contrast to the prosperity that is evident in the archeological remains from Ku Bua, the settlement at Kampheng Sèn seems to have been but meagerly populated and to have declined during the 8th century, in Wales's view possibly as a result of its functions being usurped by the more strategically sited city at Nakhon Pathom. In both the middle Čhao Phraya and Prachin valleys settlements allegedly manifested a predictable degree of cultural provincialism. Finally, the northeasterly thrust of Dvāravatī settlement reached on to the Khorat upland, probably by way of the important, but only cursorily investigated, site at Mu'ang Sima, which was in a position to control the main pass through the western rim of the plateau. There are reasons for believing that the political units which encompassed settlements exhibiting Dvāravatī cultural traits in Khorat, even during the period of Dvāravatī pre-eminence, were largely, or even totally, autonomous.

Wales's interpretation of the development and elaboration of the eastern Dvāravatī settlement hierarchy is plausible enough in its own terms. Our objection is primarily to its implicit conceptualization of the nature of statehood in early Southeast Asia and of the role of the city in the polity. We shall take up these objections in a subsequent section. From Wales's postulated morphological development of Dvāravatī cities we see no reason to dissent. Though the sequence is not proved, it does not, in its main outlines, constitute an unreasonable proposition. In the author's own succinct summary:

What we find in Dvāravatī is an improvement [I would dissent from that particular phrase] from irregular, more or less circular or oval, nuclei, which we also find forming the village sites of the K'orat plateau and the unsuccessful town of Kamp'eng Sèn, by the grafting on of a secondary enclosure, as at Śī T'ep, Fa Daed and no doubt U T'ong, or by the enclosing of the original circular site by a wider area of land with new ramparts and moats, as at Müang Bon and Putthai Song. Sometimes the addition, as at Fa Daed and Śī T'ep . . . has a somewhat more regular shape. It is only when we come to . . . cities like Nak'on Pathom, Śī Mahā P'ot and P'anat, that we find the approximately rectangular construction *ab initio* . . . Multiple moats and ramparts were not needed in the towns of central Dvāravatī where there was sufficient population to guard against the danger of surprise attack, but they are a feature of the K'orat plateau villages.[83]

Mention of these Khorat settlements is a reminder that thirty years ago Peter Williams-Hunt discerned on air photographs of this region approximately 200 "small defended towns characterized by multiple, concentric earthworks," as well as a variety of other more irregular constructions.[84] Subsequently Charles Keyes placed the number of sites enclosed by earthworks as high as 300,[85] and still more recently N. Saengwan has published an atlas of all known moated sites on a scale of 1:50,000.[86] Several of these sites have yielded accumulations of late-prehistoric pottery and other finds implying a period of occupance extending from about 500 B.C. to A.D. 1000, while scenes engraved on *sēmā* stones at Mu'ang Fa Daed and on silver votive plaques from Kantarawichae include depictions of apparently princely personages, together with divinities and *stūpas*, the latter being ascribed to the 9th or 10th century.[87] Saenqwan's atlas, in turn, has permitted Higham, Kijngam, and Manly to calculate the areas of moated sites in Khorat, which, they found, ranged from 3 to 171 hectares. In one particular part of Mahasarakham Province abutting on the Chi river, these authors were further able to use data from the same source to establish the statistical likelihood of a settlement hierarchy having existed in the first millennium A.D., possibly focused on the relatively large, circular site of Ban Chiang Hian.[88] It is not without interest that the same statistical techniques implied the absence of such a hierarchy farther north in the vicinity of Lake Kumphawapi. These same authors were also able to show that the mean area of 1300 sq. kilometers enclosed by Thiessen polygons[89] constructed around all sites of more than 30 hectares accorded with the range proposed by Colin Renfrew for what he terms the Early State Module.[90] This is essentially a geometricized expression of the chiefdom focused on a "central place" which, in its mediation of both economic and informational exchanges, corresponds to the seat of a paramount chief. As such, it is an

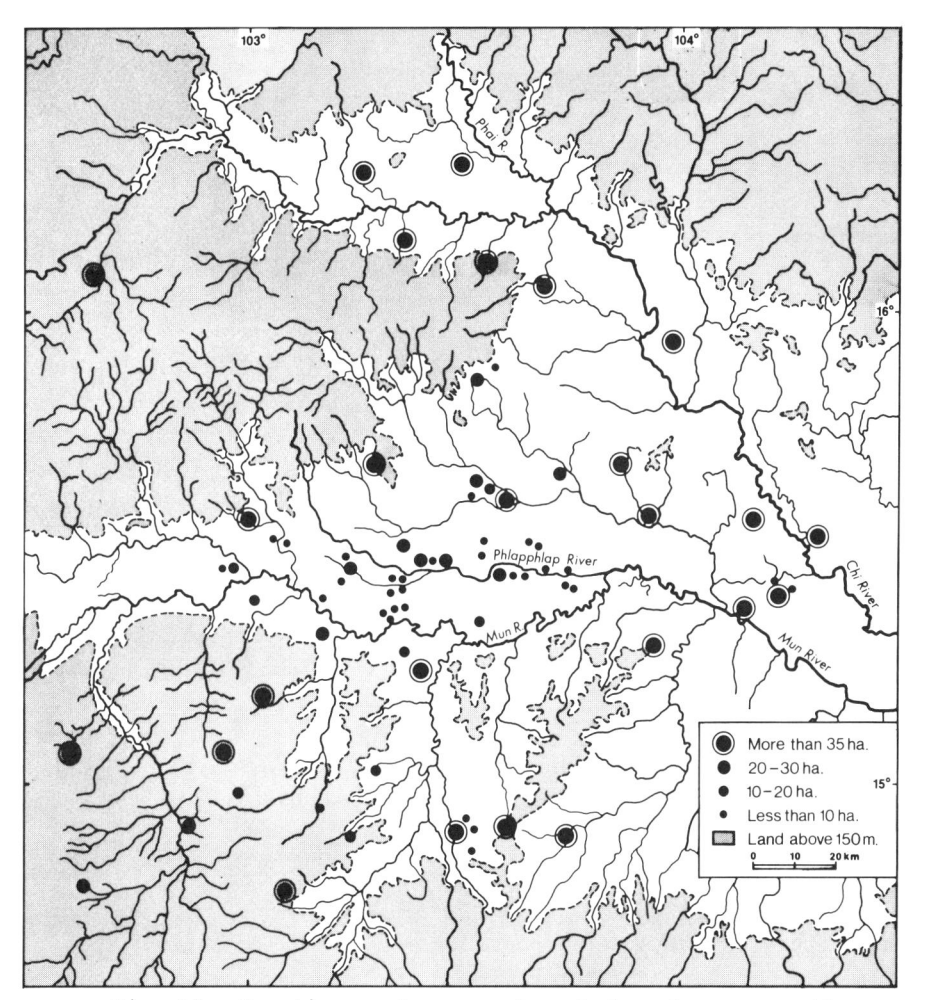

Fig. 18. Locations and areas of moated enclosures on the Khorat plateau. Based on C.F.W. Higham and Amphan Kijngam, "Irregular earthworks in N.E. Thailand: new insight," *Antiquity*, vol. 56 (1982), pp. 102-110.

abstraction of the spatial aspects of a middle-range chiefdom (as defined in Chapter 1), useful to the archeologist in his attempts to reconstruct the territorial basis of emergent statehood but lacking the overtones of social differentiation, chiefly hierarchy, centralized direction, and economic centripetality characteristic of the concept of chiefdom.

The mean distance between major moated centers (as represented by larger sites) in Khorat, that is 24 km, also conformed to the Renfrew model. It is noticeable though that, whereas the larger sites were distributed fairly evenly through the Mun and Chi river basins, smaller sites were restricted to the Mun valley and its tributaries (Fig. 18), a circumstance which Higham and Kijngam attribute to the latter valley's "greater proximity to the Khmer, the relative aridity of the region, or their location near the Mun flood plain, either singly or in some combination."[91] These authors ascribe at least part of the settlement dynamic of this region in the first millennium A.D. to traffic over a route which was described in a topographical memoir compiled by Chia Tan 賈耽, a high Chinese official, between A.D. 785 and 805. The itinerary is recorded as passing from the neighborhood of present-day Hà-tinh southwestwards across the Annamite mountains to the "Small Sea" 小海, probably the Gulf of Siam.[92] This route, however tortuous its windings and deviations, can hardly have avoided crossing the Khorat and may well have descended into the Chao Phraya valley by way of the site at Mu'ang Sima (p. 211 above).

The rationale of the multiple moats, and in some instances ramparts, characterizing these Khorat settlements is still a matter of inference. Whereas Williams-Hunt and Quaritch Wales assumed they were constructed for defensive purposes, Srisakra Vallibhotama believes that they served primarily as reservoirs designed to store water against the long dry seasons.[93] On this view, construction of the outer earthworks of a settlement is presumably to be construed as a response to increases in its population. To these reasons Higham and Kijngam have added the possibilities of the moats having served as diversionary conduits for flood water or having had a ritual significance,[94] while there is no reason to doubt that in times past they provided, as such bodies of water almost invariably do today, both fish and plant foods.

Although available information about the broad outlines of the morphology of Dvāravatī settlements is slightly fuller than that for any of the other main culture realms of Southeast Asia, the nature of the settlement hierarchy and its evolution are still obscure. However, the most effective way of integrating the disparate fragments of evidence into a reasonably convincing framework would seem to be once again to invoke the pyramidal political organization of the chiefdom. There is every likelihood that the site of the paramount's capital changed from time to time, and probably the ruling line as well, although the sources are silent on this point. In the neighborhood of Khorat, Dvāravatī rulers appear to have competed with Khmer paramounts for the allegiance of chieftainships, and even chiefdoms such as Canāśa. Although Mōn cultural influences can be detected in the region, it is unlikely that the power of the Śrī Dvāravatīśvara extended that far for other than relatively brief periods. There is little evidence relating to the number of levels in the settlement hierarchy even as late as the 10th century, but it is unlikely to have exceeded three or at most four.

Notes and References

1. Mōn is the current orthography of this ethnonym, though the form Mān was used as late as the 19th century [C. O. Blagden, "Notes and reviews: II: Mon and Ramaññadesa," *JBRS*, vol. 4, pt. 1 (1914), p. 60], being in turn derived from Middle Mōn *Rman* < *Rmañ* (attested in Khmer epigraphy of the 7th century A.D.), which appears to have coexisted with an alternative form *Rmeñ* (referred to an unspecified inscription by Blagden, *ibid.*, and attested in a Javanese inscription of 1021). On this topic generally see Pierre Dupont, *L'archéologie mône de Dvāravatī*. Publications de l'Ecole Française d'Extrême-Orient, vol. 41 (Paris, 1959), pp. 2-4.

    By the Burmese the Mōn are usually called *Talaiṅ* < **Tanluiṅ* (Cp. the Arabic transcription *Tanlwing* from A.D. 851: see Note 11 to Chap. 4), a form which may have been constructed from a stem *tluiñ* and the ancient infix *-in-* or *-an-*. It has usually been considered that such a stem was in some way related to the name *Teliṅgā[na]*, applied to the Madras district [Blagden, *loc. cit.*, pp. 57-59], but this interpretation has recently been strongly challenged by Louis-Charles Damais, "Etudes sino-indonésiennes. III: La transcription chinoise *Ho-ling* comme désignation de Java," *BEFEO*, vol. 52, fasc. 1 (1964), pp. 97-100. It is interesting to note that the Mōn designate by the term *Talaiṅ* a despised group among themselves, presumably an attempt on the part of the majority to shift the obloquy of a disparaging epithet on to the shoulders of the class least able to repudiate it.

2. Chap. 3.

3. The history of scholarship in the neighboring territory of Thailand, in Campā, Cambodia, and Java demonstrates that even before archeological investigation had begun, fortuitous discoveries of statuary on the surface of the ground or preserved in shrines and temples had led scholars to an appreciation, albeit imperfect, of these vanished civilizations. In the Mōn country of Lower Burma such statuary is exiguous.

4. For statements on the nature of these chronicles see H. L. Shorto, "A Mon geneology of kings: observations on the *Nidāna Ārambhakathā*," in D. G. E. Hall (ed.), *Historians of South East Asia* (London, 1961), pp. 63-72; U Tet Htoot, "The nature of Burmese chronicles," *loc. cit.*, pp. 50-62; Klaus Wenk, "Prăchum Phongsāwadān historischen Quellen," *Oriens Extremus*, vol. 9, pt. 2 (1962), pp. 232-325.

5. Dupont, *L'archéologie mône*, pp. 7-11; H. G. Quaritch Wales, "Anuruddha and the Thaton tradition," *JRAS* (1947), p. 152; Nihar-Ranjan Ray, *Brahmanical gods in Burma* (Calcutta, 1932).

6. Prince Damrong Rajanubhab, "History of Siam in the period antecedent to the founding of Ayuddhya by King Phra Chao U Thong," *JSS*, vol. 13, pt. 2, pp. 30-31. In a version of this paper published in *Selected Articles from the Siam Society Journal* (Bangkok, 1959), the reference occurs on pp. 64-66.

7. Wales, "Anuruddha and the Thaton tradition," pp. 152-156.

8. Dupont, *L'archéologie mône*, pp. 13-15.

9. C. O. Blagden, *Epigraphia Birmanica*, vol. 3, pt. 2.

10. Wilhelm Geiger (assisted by Mabel H. Bode), *The Great Chronicle of Ceylon* (London, 1912); Hermann Oldenberg [ed. and trans.], *Dīpavaṃsa* (London, 1879), VIII, 12. The mission of Aśoka is also related in the *Samanta-pāsādikā*, Buddhaghosa's commentary on the five *Vinaya*.

11. The story is replete with 500 *rākṣasa* in the form of lions and a *rākṣasī*

that fed on children; the style of the king of Thatōn, Sīrimāsoka (presumably for Siridhammāsoka) is suspiciously reminiscent of the Mauryan Aśoka, instigator of the missionary enterprise with which the Kalyāṇī inscription begins its account of ancient Burma; whichever territories were comprised within the realm of Suvaṇṇabhūmi in later days (and it is unlikely that the toponym was ever restricted to the Mōn country), when applied to Lower Burma in the 3rd century B.C. the term is an anachronism.

12. As far as I have been able to ascertain there is no evidence other than that of the chronicles for the existence of a Mōn state, subsuming and transcending individual chieftainships, in the delta lands of Lower Burma in early times. It is true that Buddhist monks at some time coined the clerkly Pāi term *Ramaññadesa,* but it seems to have been employed as much as a cultural term as one denoting a political entity. Its earliest epigraphic use occurs in the Kalyāṇī inscriptions from the end of the 15th century, but the orthography indicates that it was modelled on a form *Rman,* which is attested as early as the 7th century A.D. (cp. Note 1). In fact, a Sanskrit version, *Rāmaṇya,* occurs in a Khmer inscription of Rājendravarman, 944-968 [George Coedès, *Inscriptions du Cambodge,* vol. 5 (Paris, 1953), pp. 99 and 101; Dupont, *L'archéologie mône,* p. 3]. In all probability it is *Rman* that is transcribed by Marvazī [Minorsky's edition (cf. Note 11 to Chap. 4), p. 39 of the Persian text, pp. 52 and 153 of the English translation] under the orthography *al-Arh.n* الا رهن which must surely be a mislection of the *al-Arm.n* الا رمن located in a similar situation by Ibn Rustah in c. 903 [*al-Aʿlaq al-nafīsah,* edited by M. J. de Goeje, *Bibliotheca Geographorum Arabicorum,* vol. 7 (Leyden, 1892), p. 133]. It is interesting that Marvazī [*loc. cit.*] noted that the women of this country were "white and pleasant-looking." Is this perhaps an echo of the white-silver-Pyū-Argyre complex of ideas discussed on p. 190?

In connection with this theme of the re-casting of early Mōn history, it can hardly be without significance that the names of the twin founders of Haṃsavatī (Pegu), Wimala and Thamala, can be traced in the dynastic lists of the Indian state of Vijayanāgara, 1336-1565 [Sir Arthur P. Phayre, *History of Burma* (London, 1883), p. 30], that a tradition preserved in the *Lik Smiṅ Asaḥ* brings Vijayanāgara merchants to Haṃsavatī, and that men from that kingdom allegedly disputed with the twin Mōn culture-heroes for possession of the ground on which the city was built [R. Halliday, *JBRS,* vol. 7, pt. 3 (1917), p. 206].

13. Cp. G. E. Harvey's remarks in *History of Burma* (London, 1925), p. 100, note 3: "Talaing [= Mōn] exoduses were so frequent that the kings of Siam used to appoint special frontier guards to watch for them, and to maintain granaries along their route. The Talaings addressed the king of Siam as 'the Lord of the Golden Pyathat, the Righteous King of Ayuthia, the Haven of the Mon people,' who on every occasion saved their lives." See also R. Halliday, "Immigration of the Mons into Siam," *JSS,* vol. 16 (1922).

14. George Coedès presented an initial outline of this proposal in a review of *L'archéologie mône de Dvāravatī* by Pierre Dupont in *Arts Asiatiques,* vol. 23 (1960), p. 235, and a refined version in "Les Môns de Dvāravatī," in Ba Shin, Jean Boisselier, and A. B. Griswold (eds.), *Essays offered to G. H. Luce,* vol. 1: *Artibus Asiae,* Supplement XXIII (Ascona, 1966), p. 116.

For Haripuñjaya see p. 210 below.

15. Thatōn = the Burmese form of Mōn *Sadhuim* < **Sudhuim* < Pāli *Sudhamma* [*-pura, -nāgara, -vatī*]. Cp. Skt. *Sudharmā* = the hall of Indra [Blagden, "Notes and reviews: VI. Thaton, "*JBRS,* vol. 5, pt. 1 (1915), pp. 26-27]. According to local legend, this was the city where Buddhaghosa, the founder of Singhalese Buddhism, lived and died—surely an additional indication of the reconstruction of Mōn history postulated above.

16. Pegu < O. Burm. *Payku,* Middle Mōn *Pago.* Cp. the transcription of Ṣadīq Iṣfahānī (admittedly late-17th century): *Fāygū* [Gabriel Ferrand, *Relations de voyages et textes géographiques arabes, persans et turks relatifs à l'Extrême-Orient,* vol. 2 (Paris, 1914), p. 560]. According to a Mōn chronicle,

the city was founded in A.D. 825 by twin sons of the first ruler of Suvaṇṇabhūmi (which in chronicles is usually synecdochistically and anachronistically equated with Thatōn). Legend has it that Indra himself described the circuit of the city with the aid of a rope attached to an *indakhīla* pillar, a veritable *axis mundi* that subsequently served as the Meru or axial mountain of the city [J. S. Furnivall, "Notes on the history of Hanthawaddy," *JBRS*, vol. 3, pt. 2 (1913), p. 167; H. L. Shorto, "The 32 myos in the medieval Mon kingdom," *BSOAS*, vol. 26 (1963), p. 577, note 1]. This is, of course, essentially the same story that is told of the founding of the Pyū capital of Śrī Kṣetra, but whether the Mōn borrowed it from the Burmese, or the Burmese from the Mōn, or both from a third source, it is impossible to say. It is noteworthy, though, that the territory of Pegu was known as *Ussa* (< Oḍra = Orissa), a nomenclature which parallels that of Śrī Kṣetra (= Puri, also in Orissa). In the case of the Pyū capital, the connexion is substantiated by archeological evidence of architectural borrowings, but these are absent at Pegu.

For sketch plans of early Thatōn and Pegu see U Kan Hla, "Ancient cities in Burma," *Journal of the Society of Architectural Historians*, vol. 38, no. 2 (1979), Figs. 1 and 2.

17. J. A. Stewart, "Excavation and exploration in Pegu," *JBRS*, vol. 7, pt. 1 (1917), pp. 13-26. The meager yield of early antiquities from the Mōn country of Burma has been summarized by G. H. Luce, "Mons of the Pagan dynasty," *JBRS*, vol. 36, pt. 1 (1953), pp. 1-19, and still more recently by Pierre Dupont, *L'archéologie mône*, pp. 7-11.

18. The only source of information available on the few epigraphic records so far discovered consists of a page or two in Luce's paper, "Mons of the Pagan dynasty," with critical comment, in so far as the unpublished state of the texts permit, by Dupont, *loc. cit.*

19. Luce, "Mons of the Pagan dynasty," p. 5.

20. *Ibid.*

21. Dupont, *L'archéologie mône*, pp. 8-9.

22. Doubtless inspired by the Pāli *Tāmbaviṣaya*. Cp. Skt. *Tāmraviṣaya*.

23. The considerable literature relating to this toponym is summarized in O. W. Wolters, "Tāmbraliṅga," *BSOAS*, vol. 21 (1958), pp. 587-607.

24. According to the Burmese chronicles, it was in Tāmpadīva that in the 11th century the Mōn reformer, the Shin Arahan, began his mission, so that the name was presumably applied to the country around Pagan. Cp. Nihar-Ranjan Ray, *Theravada Buddhism in Burma* (Calcutta, 1946), p. 77.

25. E. H. Johnston, "Some Sanskrit inscriptions of Arakan," *BSOAS*, vol. 11, pt. 2 (1944), p. 372. It is tempting to associate this kingdom either with Tāmralipti, near the mouth of the Hooghly river, or with the Tāmraviṣaya mentioned above.

26. *Man Shu*, chüan 2, p. 9 and chüan 10 p. 45; *Hsin T'ang-Shu*, chüan 222C, f. 9 verso; *T'ang Hui-yao*, chüan 33, f. 26 recto, chüan 100, f. 19 recto; *T'ai-p'ing Yü-lan*, chüan 567, f. 8 verso, chüan 789, f. 5 recto [citing *Man Shu* under the title *Nan-i chih* 南夷志]; chüan 961, f. 8 recto, chüan 971, f. 5 recto; *Ts'e-fu Yüan-kuei*, chüan 965, f. 10 verso, chüan 972 f. 5 verso. In the T'ang history, Mi-chen appears among the vassal states of the Pyū, but in 805 it sent an embassy to the Chinese court, as a result of which the Emperor accorded formal recognition to its king. In 835 the state was invaded by those whom the Chinese called *Man* barbarians, certainly meaning the armies of Nan-Chao, as a consequence of which two or three thousand of the inhabitants were transported to wash for gold in the Upper Irawadi.

The only significant information bearing on the location of *Mjie̯-ẓie̯n is the remarks in the *Man Shu* that it was (i) a maritime state (ii) bordering the *Mjię-nâk* (Chindwin-Irawadi) river. In 1904 Pelliot ["Deux itinéraires de Chine en Inde à la fin du VIIIe siècle," *BEFEO*, vol. 4 (1904), p. 172, note 1, and pp. 222-3] located it in the Irawadi delta. Subsequently, Gordon Luce expressed a preference for the estuary of the Sittaung [Review of Gabriel Ferrand's "L'empire sumatranais de Çrīvijaya," *JBRS*, vol. 13, pt. 2 (1923), pp. 154-155, and "Sources of early Burma history": in C. D. Cowan and O. W. Wolters (eds.), *Southeast Asian History and Historiography. Essays Presented to D. G. E. Hall* (Ithaca, N.Y., 1976), p. 35.

The original word which the Chinese transcribed as *Mjię-źięn* has not so far been restored, and at present there is no way of establishing a more precise location. The element *mjię* occurs in at least four other toponyms associated with the region of present-day Burma: *Mjię-tśʿiak* 彌緉, one of the best known tribes of the Pyū (cp. p. 197 above); *Mjię-nâk* river (= the Chindwin-Irawadi), together with *Mjię-nâk-dʿâu-lịəp* stockade 彌諾道立柵, one of the garrison towns of the Pyū, probably located close to the Chindwin-Irawadi confluence [See *Man Shu*, chüan 2, p. 9]; and *Mjię city* 彌城. If the element for "city" (*źịäng*) be included, this last name is suspiciously similar to *Mjię-źięn*, but both *Man Shu* (chüan 6, p. 30) and *Hsin Tʿang-Shu* (chüan 45) agree in locating it in Upper Burma. These several combinations incorporating *mjię* tend to imply that this element is a transcription of an ethnonym of fairly wide occurrence and varied application.

27. *Man Shu*, chüan 10, p. 45. The same phrase is used to denigrate the settlements both of *Mjię-nâk* [*ibid.*] and of the *Mwâng Mwan* aborigines 芒蠻部落 [*Man Shu*, chüan 4, p. 20].

28. As early as 1884 Samuel Beal restored a Chinese transcription employed by Hsüan Tsang (see below) as Dvāravatī [*Si-yu-ki: Buddhist records of the Western World, translated from the Chinese of Hiuen-Tsiang (A.D. 629)*, vol. 2 (London, 1884), p. 200]. In due course the identification was adopted by Edouard Chavannes [*Mémoire composé à l'époque de la grande dynastie Tʿang sur les religieux éminents qui allèrent chercher la loi dans les pays d'Occident* (Paris, 1894), p. 59], Junjirō Takakusu [*A record of the Buddhist religion as practised in India and the Malay Archipelago (671-695 A.D.) by I-Tsing* (Oxford, 1896), p. 10], and Paul Pelliot ["Deux itinéraires de Chine en Inde à la fin du VIIIe siècle," *BEFEO*, vol. 4 (1904), p. 223], but it was not until 1925 that the archeological remains of Central Thailand associated with Dvāravatī were recognized by George Coedès, on the basis of inscriptions in the Old Mōn language from Nakhon Pathom and Lopburi, as being ethnically Mōn ["Documents sur l'histoire politique et religieuse du Laos occidental," *BEFEO*, vol. 25 (1925), p. 17, note 1; "Tablettes votives bouddhiques du Siam," in G. Van Oest (ed.), *Etudes Asiatiques*, vol. 1 (1925), p. 152, note 1; "Les collections archéologiques du Musée National de Bangkok," *Ars Asiatica*, vol. 12 (1928), *passim*].

Dvāravatī [or Dvāraka] = the City of Gates, Kṛṣṇa's capital in Gujarāt. The earliest date associated with the Mōn Dvāravatī in Chinese records is 638 [*Chiu Tʿang-Shu*, chüan 197 f. 3 verso and 4 recto], in which year *Dʿuâ-γuâ-lâ* 墮和羅 [=Dvāra] sent an embassy to the Chinese court, to be followed by another in 649. Other significant references to Dvāravatī in Chinese records are as follows:

Chiu Tʿang-Shu, chüan 197, f. 4 verso: *Dʿuâ-γuâ-lâ* adjoins *Bʿuân-bʿuân* 盤盤 [a kingdom in the neighborhood of Bandon: cp. pp. 252-253] on the south, *Kâ-lâ-śia-bʿịuət* 迦羅舍佛 (Kalaśapūra) on the north, *Tśịen-lâp* 真臘 [a Khmer chiefdom in the Mekong valley] on the east, and the ocean on the west.

Hsin Tʿang-Shu, chüan 222C, f. 6 recto: *Dʿuâ-γuâ-lâ* 墮和羅, also called *Dʿuk-γuâ-lâ* 獨和羅, has the boundaries enumerated above; but in a subsequent passage [chüan 222C, f. 9 recto] it is located to the southwest [*sic*] of the Pyū.

Hsüan Tsang 玄奘 *Ta-T'ang Hsi-yü Chi*
大唐西域記 chüan 10, f. 51r

Hui Lin and Yen Sung, *Ta-T'ang Ta-tzǔ-en-ssŭ San-ts'ang Fa-shih Chuan*
大唐大慈恩寺三藏法師傳
Taishō edition, no. 2053, chüan 4, p. 240

Duâ-lâ-puâ-tiei 墮羅鉢底 is east of Kāmalaṅkā 迦摩浪迦, which in turn is southeast of Śrī Kṣetra [cp. p. 173 above].

I Ching 義淨 *Nan-hai Chi-kuei Nei-fa Chuan* 南海寄歸內法傳 chüan 1, f. 3 verso: *Źi̯a-ɣuâ-puâ-tiei* 社和鉢底 [which G. H. Luce emends to *D'uâ* 杜 ——: "Countries neighbouring Burma," *JBRS*, vol. 14 (1925), p. 160] is located approximately as stated by Hsüan Tsang. In another paragraph in the same work I Ching used the orthography *D'uâ-ɣuâ-lâ* 杜和羅 and in his *Ta T'ang Hsi-yü Ch'iu-Fa Kao-seng Chuan* 大唐西域求法高僧傳 the extended form *Duâ-ɣuâ-lâ-puâ-tiei* 杜和羅鉢底 (biographies of I Lang 義朗 and Ta Ch'eng-teng 大乘燈).

This, or similar information, is also incorporated in several encyclopedias, notably *T'ung Tien* 通典 chüan 188, p. 1010; *Ts'e-fu Yüan-kuei* 冊府元龜 chüan 971, f. 8 verso; *T'ai-p'ing Yü-lan* 太平御覽 chüan 788, f. 7 recto, in all of which works the form *D'uk-ɣuâ-lâ* 獨和羅 is used.

The above texts make it clear that Dvāravatī occupied the plains of Central Thailand, with perhaps on occasion an extension across the Burmese deltas to the Bay of Bengal (Cp. *Chiu T'ang-Shu* above), but it was Professor George Coedès who first associated these fragments of information with archeological remains from the Bangkok plain [*Recueil des inscriptions du Siam*, pt. 2 (Bangkok, B.E. 2472 = A.D. 1929), pp. 1-4]. For subsequent reviews of the evidence consult G. H. Luce, "Countries neighboring Burma," *JBRS*, vol. 14, pt. 2 (1925), pp. 178-182, pp. 279-283 of 1960 reprint; Hsü Yün-ts'iao 許雲樵, "T'o-lo-po-ti k'ao," *Nan-yang Hsüeh-pao* 墮羅鉢底攷 南洋學報 vol. 4, pt. 1 (1947), pp. 1-7; L. P. Briggs, "Dvaravati, the most ancient kingdom of Siam," *JAOS*, vol. 65, no. 2 (1945), pp. 98-107; George Coedès, "A la recherche du royaume de Dvāravatī," *Archéologie et Civilisation*, vol. 1 (1964); H. G. Quaritch Wales, "Some notes on the kingdom of Dvāravatī," *Journal of the Greater India Society*, vol. 5 (1938), pp. 24-30; "Dvāravatī in South-east Asian cultural history," *Journal of the Royal Asiatic Society* (1966), pp. 40-62; *Dvāravatī, the earliest kingdom of Siam* (London, 1969); Elizabeth Lyons, "Dvāravatī, a consideration of its formative period," in R. B. Smith and W. Watson, *Early South East Asia* (New York and Kuala Lumpur, 1979), pp. 352-359.

The *Hsin T'ang-Shu* (chüan 222C, f. 6 recto) lists two dependencies of Dvāravatī: *T'ân-li̯əng* island 曇陵洲 which I am strongly inclined to equate with *Tanluiñ*, the ancient name by which the Burmese referred to the Mōns (cf. Note 1 above), and *T'â-ɣuǎn* 陀洹 for which I can offer no identification. It is true that the *Tanluiñ* country was not an island (the Chinese used the phrase 在海洲中), but *chou* was frequently employed in Chinese sources in the general sense of "land" or "country," and the graphs in question offer a satisfactory transcription of *Tanluiñ*.

It is just possible that the *Svargadvārapura* which later Khmer epigraphy traces back to the 7th century may have been in some way connected with Dvāravatī (though this is not the interpretation proposed on p. 156 above), but it is not unlikely that the honorific was bestowed on more than one Southeast Asian city. It is alleged, for instance, that Sandoway in Arakan was formerly known by this name [Charles Duroiselle, *Report of the Superintendent, Archaeological Survey, Burma* (1923), p. 19, and G. H. Luce, "Countries neighbouring Burma," p. 179: p. 280 of 1960 reprint; also San Shwe Bu, "The legend of the early Aryan settlement of Arakan," *JBRS*, vol. 11, pt. 2 (1922), p. 69; Sir Arthur Phayre, *History of Burma* (London, 1882), *passim*].

29. George Coedès, *Les états hindouisés d'Indochine et d'Indonésie* (3rd edition, Paris, 1964), p. 145, note 5; J. J. Boeles, "The king of Śrī Dvāravatī and his regalia," *JSS*, vol. 52, pt. 1 (1964), pp. 99-110.

30. Summarized, for the period prior to 1959, by Dupont in *L'archéologie môn̄e*, *passim*, and *in toto* by Wales, *Dvāravatī*, *passim*.

31. Wales, "Some notes on the kingdom of Dvāravatī," *passim*; Jean Boisselier, "Ū-Thòng et son importance pour l'histoire de Thailande," *Silpākǫn*, vol. 9, no. 1 (1965), pp. 27-30; "Récentes recherches archéologiques en Thailande:" Rapport préliminaire de Mission (25 juillet-28 novembre 1964), *Arts Asiatiques*, vol. 12 (1965), pp. 125-174; *Nouvelles connaissances archéologiques de la ville d'Ū-Thòng* (Bangkok, 1968), p. 23 [In Thai and English]; H. H. E. Loofs, "Problems of continuity between the pre-Buddhist and Buddhist periods in Central Thailand, with special reference to U-Thong," in Smith and Watson, *Early South East Asia*, pp. 342-351.

32. Boisselier, "Ū-Thòng," p. 28. The artifacts ascribed to the so-called Fu-nan period, which appear to have been predominantly chance surface finds, include beads, tin ear-rings, medallions, seals, and amulets, stone moulds for their manufacture, gold ornaments, a fragment of a terracotta lamp, a number of seals depicting naturalistic and human figures, and a 3rd-century Roman coin (whose chronological implications are ambivalent), together with certain figurines of a type not encountered at Oc-èo but believed to be of Indian inspiration, if not provenance. In addition, fragments of stucco and terracotta architectural decoration in Amarāvatī style are held to imply the existence of architectural structures dating from the 3rd or 4th centuries [Wales, *Dvāravatī*, pp. 10-11]. See also Loofs, "Problems," *passim* and "Funanese cultural elements in the lower Menam basin," *Journal of the Oriental Society of Australia*, vol. 8, nos. 1 and 2 (1971), pp. 5-8.

33. George Coedès, "Nouvelles données épigraphiques sur l'histoire de l'Indochine centrale," *Journal Asiatique*, vol. 246 (1958), pp. 129-131. Although in 1928 Coedès proposed to locate the capital of Dvāravatī at Ū Thòng, he seems subsequently to have abandoned the idea, which has only recently been tentatively revived by Quaritch Wales (*Dvāravatī*, p. 20) and Jean Boisselier ("Ū-Thòng, p. 29).

34. The claim to capital status has been advanced most explicitly by Wales, *Dvāravatī*, pp. 32-49, and implicitly by Boeles, "The king of Śrī Dvāravatī," p. 102. See also Lucien Fournereau, *Le Siam ancien*, vol. 1 (Paris, 1895), pp. 117 *et seq.*; Dupont, *BEFEO*, vol. 39, pp. 355 *et seq.*, and *L'archéologie môn̄e*, *passim*. Nakhon Pathom (< Skt. Nāgara Pattana) = "the city of the chief sanctuary," was the name given to the settlement when it migrated from a location farther east consequent upon the construction, on the site of a much earlier shrine, of the highest *stūpa* in Siam during the reigns of kings Mongkut (1851-1868) and Chulalongkorn (1868-1910). Both town and *stūpa* are, therefore, in their present form recent foundations, but it is significant that the local governor holds the title of Phya Sī Vichai, in which it is possible to discern the honorific Śrī Vijaya, widespread through Indianized Southeast Asia in early times [Dupont, *BEFEO*, vol. 39, p. 355]. See also Jean Boisselier, "Récentes recherches à Nakhon Pathom," *JSS*, vol. 58, pt. 2 (1970), pp. 54-65.

35. P. 203 above.

36. Dupont, *L'archéologie môn̄e*, chap. 2; Wales, *Dvāravatī*, p. 38. Cedi Chula Pathon was known to Dupont and some other writers as Wat Phra Pathon.

37. Dupont, *L'archéologie môn̄e*, pp. 117-8.

38. Boisselier, "Récentes recherches archéologiques," p. 141.

39. Reginald Le May, *A concise history of Buddhist art in Siam* (Cambridge, 1938), pp. 27-28, and *The culture of South-East Asia* (London, 1954), p. 70; Pierre Dupont, "Chronique: rapport de M. P. Dupont sur sa mission archéologique (18 janvier - 25 mai 1939)," *BEFEO*, vol. 39, fasc. 2 (1939), p. 364. Boisselier, "Récentes recherches," p. 150; Wales, *Dvāravatī*, pp. 49-51.

Cities of the Rmañ 227

40. Dupont, *L'archéologie môn̄e,* pp. 199 ff. and Figs. 401-403.

41. Wales, *Dvāravatī,* p. 51.

42. Boisselier, "Récentes recherches," pp. 148-149; Wales, *Dvāravatī,* pp. 51-63; Fine Arts Department, *Guide to antiquities found at Ku Bua, Ratburi* . . . (Bangkok, 1961).

43. Stanley J. O'Connor, "Ritual deposit boxes in Southeast Asian sanctuaries," *Artibus Asiae,* vol. 28, pt. 1 (1966), pp. 53-60.

44. At least this is how certain very un-Dvāravatī-like figures are interpreted by Elizabeth Lyons, "Traders of Ku Bua," *Archives of the China Art Society* (1965), pp. 52-56.

45. Wales, *Dvāravatī,* p. 61.

46. Wales, *Dvāravatī,* pp. 62-63.

47. George Coedès, "The excavations at P'ong Tük and their importance for the ancient history of Siam," *JSS,* vol. 21, pt. 3 (1928), pp. 195-209, and "Excavations at P'ong Tük in Siam," *Annual Bibliography of Indian Archaeology* (1927), pp. 16-20; H. G. Quaritch Wales, "Further excavations at P'ong Tük," *Indian Art and Letters,* vol. 10 (1936), pp. 42-48; Wales, *Dvāravatī,* pp. 63-67; Dupont, *L'archéologie môn̄e,* pp. 102-114.

48. Dupont, *L'archéologie môn̄e,* pp. 114-117; Jean Boisselier, "Un fragment inscrit de Roue de la Loi de Lop'buri," *Artibus Asiae,* vol. 24, pts. 3 and 4 (1961), pp. 225-240; Wales, *Dvāravatī,* pp. 68-70. For the role of Lavapura in the *Jinakālamālī* of Phra Ratanapañña (first composed in A.D. 1516, but now incorporating an extension to 1527), see George Coedès "Documents sur l'histoire politique et religieuse du Laos occidental," *BEFEO,* vol. 25 (1925), *passim.* There are Chinese references to this same city, under the transcription *Lā-ɣuk* 羅斛 in *Sung Shih* 宋史 chüan 489, f. 23 recto, and in *Wen-hsien Tʻung-kʻao,* chüan 332, p. 2612. In Cambodian epigraphy both place and people are referred to as *Lvo.*

49. Bennet Bronson and George F. Dales, "Excavations at Chansen, Thailand 1968 and 1969: a preliminary report," *Asian Perspectives,* vol. 15 (1973), pp. 15-46.

50. Fine Arts Department, *Some recently discovered sites of Dvāravatī period* (Bangkok, 1965); H. G. Quaritch Wales, "Müang Bon, a town of northern Dvāravatī," *JSS,* vol. 53, pt. 1 (1965), pp. 1-7; Wales, *Dvāravatī,* pp. 70-80.

51. Wales, *Dvāravatī,* pp. 80-81.

52. H. G. Quaritch Wales, "The exploration of Śrī Deva, an ancient Indian city in Indochina," *Indian Art and Letters,* vol. 10 (1936), pp. 61-99; *Dvāravatī,* pp. 12-14, 81-85; B. Ch. Chhabra, "Expansion of Indo-Aryan culture during Pallava rule, as evidenced by inscriptions," *Journal of the Asiatic Society of Bengal, Letters,* vol. 1 (1935), p. 54; George Coedès "Note sur quelques sculptures de Śrīdeb (Siam)," *Etudes d'orientalisme (Mélanges Linossier),* vol. 1 (Paris, 1932), pp. 159-164; Boisselier, "Récentes recherches," p. 154; Charernsupkul Anuvit, "Dating the two brick monuments at Muang Si Thep: a style analysis," *Muang Boran,* vol. 5, no. 4 (1979), pp. 102-104.

53. George Coedès, *Inscriptions du Cambodge,* vol. 7 (Paris, 1964), pp. 156-158.

54. Wales, *Dvāravatī,* p. 84.

55. George Coedès, "Documents sur l'histoire politique et religieuse du Laos occidental," *BEFEO,* vol. 25 (1925), p. 19. For variant versions of the story of the founding of Haripuñjaya, and for an evaluation of the texts on which they

are based, see Donald K. Swearer, "Myth, legend and history in the northern Thai chronicles," *JSS*, vol. 62, pt. 1 (1974), pp. 67-88. Swearer also points out that the founder's role attributed in all versions to Cāmadevī should not be taken as necessarily implying a predominantly Mōn population in Haripuñjaya in the 8th century.

56. R. P. Juglar, "Note sur l'existence de ruines khmères dans la province siamoise de Mɯang Phanom Sarakam" *BEFEO*, vol. 5 (1905), pp. 415-416; Lunet de Lajonquière, "Rapport sommaire sur une mission archéologique (Cambodge, Siam, Presqu'île malaise, Inde, 1907-1908)," *BCAI*, (1909), pp. 212-215, and "Essai d'inventaire archéologique du Siam," *loc. cit.* (1912), pp. 22-27; E. A. Voretzsch, "Über altbuddistische Kunst in Siam," *Ostasiatische Zeitschrift*, vol. 5, pt. 2 (Berlin 1916/7), Fig. 25; George Coedès, "Les collections archéologiques du Musée National de Bangkok," *Ars Asiatica*, vol. 12 (1928), plate IX, and *BEFEO* (1927), pl. 51A; Dupont, "Chronqiue: mission de M. Pierre Dupont au Siam (23 juillet - 22 août 1937)," *BEFEO*, vol. 37 fasc. 2 (1937), pp. 690-693, and *L'archéologie mône*, pp. 118-120; Wales, *Dvāravatī*, pp. 88-93.

57. Lunet de Lajonquière *BCAI* (1909), p. 212 and (1912), pp. 27-30; Wales, *Dvāravatī*, pp. 93-96. Lajonquière's plan of Phanat depicting a lance-head shape for the perimeter has no basis on the ground.

58. This avenue is mentioned in both of Lajonquière's reports (1909, p. 212, and 1912, pp. 27-28) but receives no comment in Dupont's more recent survey.

59. Wales, *Dvāravatī*, p. 96.

60. Lajonquière, *BCAI* (1909), pp. 216-217, and (1912), pp. 30-32; Wales, *Dvāravatī*, pp. 96-97.

61. P. D. R. Williams-Hunt, "Irregular earthworks in eastern Siam: an air survey," *Antiquity*, vol. 24 (1950), p. 35 and Plate VIII B. Both this author and Quaritch Wales [*Dvāravatī*, pp. 101-102] interpret the curious arrangement of enclosures as denoting an original southern nucleus to which were added on the north side two successive lateral extensions of increasing size. The archeologists of the Fine Arts Department, who surveyed the site in 1959, presumably subscribed to my interpretation for they restricted their investigations to what I regard as the original (central) enclosure and made no mention of the others: Fine Arts Department, *The survey and excavations in Northeast Thailand, 1959* (Bangkok, 1960), p. 61.

62. George Coedès, "Nouvelles données épigraphiques sur l'histoire de l'Indochine centrale," *JA*, vol. 246 (1958), p. 127.

63. George Coedès, "Une nouvelle inscription d'Ayuthya," *JSS*, vol. 35 (1944), p. 73; "Nouvelles données," p. 127. The origin of this inscription, which finally found its way to Ayutthaya, is unknown.

64. Coedès, "Nouvelles données," p. 128: but note that Pierre Dupont suggested that Jayasiṃhavarman was a ruler of Chen-la [*BEFEO*, vol. 42 (1942), p. 46].

65. Coedès, "Nouvelles données," p. 127.

66. Coedès, "Nouvelles données," pp. 127-128. George Coedès, *Inscriptions du Cambodge*, vol. 6 (Paris, 1954), pp. 73-79.

67. Coedès, "Nouvelles donnés," pp. 131-132.

68. Coedès, "Nouvelles données," p. 128.

69. Wales, *Dvāravatī*, pp. 103-105.

70. Erik Seidenfaden, "Kanŏk Nakhon, an ancient Mön settlement in northeast Siam (Thailand) and its treasures of art," *BEFEO*, vol. 44, pt. 2 (1954), pp. 643-647; M. C. Subhadradis Diskul, "Mueng Fa Daed, an ancient town in northeast Thailand," *Artibus Asiae*, vol. 19 (1956), pp. 362-367; Wales, *Dvāravatī*, pp. 105-113. None of the enclosures has been dated with any degree of precision, and some scholars regard it as likely that the outermost is not older than the 11th century [R. B. Smith, "Mainland South East Asia in the seventh and eighth centuries A.D.," in Smith and Watson, *Early South East Asia*, p. 456. For a summary and discussion of a legend relating to the origins of Mu'ang Fa Daed which currently circulates in Northeast Thailand see Charles F. Keyes, "A note on the ancient towns and cities of northeastern Thailand," *Tonan Ajia Kenkyū*, vol. 11, no. 4 (1974), pp. 497-506.

71. Summarized by Dupont, *L'archéologie mône*, p. 21.

72. *Liang Shu* 梁書 chüan 54, f. 5 verso; *Nan Shih* 南史 chüan 78, f. 5 recto et verso; *Nan-chou I-wu Chih*, apud *T'ai-p'ing Yü-lan* 南州異物志． 太平御覽 chüan 788, f. 1 verso; *Fu-nan Chi* 扶南記 apud *TPYL*, chüan 788 f. 1 recto et verso; *T'ung Tien* 通典 chüan 188, pp. 1008-9. Additional brief references to this city are noted in Wheatley, "Tun-sun (頓遜)," *JRAS*, pts. 1 and 2 (1956), pp. 17-30.

73. Wheatley, *loc. cit.*

74. Shorto, "The 32 *myos* in the medieval Mon kingdom," *Bulletin of the School of Oriental and African Studies*, vol. 26 (1963), p. 583. In later times ḍuṅ might signify either the capital, or a provincial city, or a district town.

75. See, for example, F. D. E. van Ossenbruggen, "De oorsprong van het javaansche begrip Montjå-pat in verband met primitieve classificaties," *Verslagen en Mededeelingen der Koninklijke Akademie van Wetenschappen*, Afd. Letterkunde, 5de Reeks, deel 3 (1918), pp. 6-44; A. W. Macdonald, "Notes sur la claustration villageoise dans l'Asie du Sud-Est," *JA*, vol. 245, fascicule 2 (1957), pp. 185-210.

76. Robert L. Pendleton, *Thailand* (New York, 1962), p. 37. For a brief discussion of the problems involved in determining past positions of the seaward face of the Chao Phraya delta see Larry Sternstein, "An 'Historical Atlas of Thailand,'" *JSS*, vol. 52, pt. 1 (1964), pp. 11-12.

77. I am here translating *fo-t'u* (佛圖 *b'i̯u̯ət-d'uo*) as *stūpa*, though the phrase might have denoted a Buddha image. In either case a shrine is implied. Cf. also p. 299 below.

78. *Liang Shu*, chüan 54, f. 5v.

79. Lyons, "The traders of Ku Bua," *passim*.

80. Coedès, "Documents sur l'histoire politique et religieuse du Laos occidental," pp. 75-76.

81. This, at any rate, is the view of George Coedès, *Les états hindouisés*, pp. 146-147: ". . . des vestiges archéologiques et épigraphiques, d'origine bouddhique, présentant entre eux assez d'affinités pour qu'on soit amené à les considérer comme des vestiges d'un même Etat."

82. Wales, *Dvāravatī*, pp. 116-117.

83. Wales, *Dvāravatī*, pp. 116-117. We see no basis for Boisselier's remark that "Toutes [plans des villes], sauf Ku Bua de plan sensiblement rectangulaire et qui semble un cas particulier, sont de plan plus ou moins elliptique . . .: "Récentes recherches," p. 141.

84. Williams-Hunt, "Irregular earthworks in eastern Siam," *passim*.

85. Charles F. Keyes, "A note on the ancient towns and cities of northeastern Thailand," *Tōnan Ajia Kenkyū*, vol. 11, no. 4 (1974), p. 497. Cf. also Thiva Supajanya and Srisakra Vallibhotama, "The need for an inventory of ancient sites to anthropological research in northeastern Thailand," *Journal of Southeast Asian Studies*, vol. 10 (1972), pp. 284-297.

86. N. Saengwan, *Ancient cities in N.E. Thailand* (N.E. Thailand Archaeological Project, Khon Kaen, 1979).

87. P. 212 above and M. C. Subhadradis Diskul, "The development of Dvāravatī sculpture and a recent find from North-east Thailand," in Smith and Watson, *Early South East Asia*, pp. 360-370. See also Srisakra Vallibhotama, "The sema complex of the northeast," *Muang Boran*, 2, vol. 1 (1975), pp. 79-117.

88. C. F. W. Higham, Amphan Kijngam, and B. F. J. Manly, "Site location and site hierarchy in North-East Thailand," *Proceedings of the Prehistoric Society*, vol. 48 (1982).

89. The construction of Thiessen polygons, a method of bounding a set of points by lines which divide a region into a set of areally homogeneous units, has been widely used in the study of market hinterlands [Cf., for example, Peter Haggett, *Locational analysis in human geography* (London, 1965), pp. 247-248]. While it is true that all points within a particular Thiessen polygon lie nearer to the enclosed center than to any other center, the procedure is based on the by no means universally applicable assumption that a center controls all the area geometrically closest to it. Thiessen polygons are also known as Dirichlet regions and Voronoi polygons.

90. Colin Renfrew, "Trade as action at a distance: questions of integration and communication," in Jeremy A. Sabloff and C. C. Lamberg-Karlowsky (eds.), *Ancient civilisation and trade* (University of New Mexico Press, Albuquerque, N. Mex., for the School of American Research, 1975), pp. 3-60.

91. C. F. W. Higham and Amphan Kijngam, "Irregular earthworks in N. E. Thailand: new insight," *Antiquity*, vol. 56 (1982), pp. 102-110.

92. *Hsin T'ang-Shu*, chüan 43B, ff. 29v - 30r.

93. Srisakra Vallibhotama, review of H. G. Quaritch Wales, *Dvāravatī, the earliest kingdom of Siam* in *JSS*, vol. 58, pt. 1 (1970), pp. 135-136.

94. Higham and Kijngam, "Irregular earthworks in N. E. Thailand," p. 109.

CHAPTER 6

Cities of the Early Malaysian World

As has not infrequently happened in other realms of Southeast Asia, extravagantly early dates have sometimes been attributed to cities of the Malaysian world. It has been stated, for example, that Surabaya was founded "long before the coming of the Hindus."[2] In so far as the evidence permits an opinion, it seems that even proto-urban centers cannot be documented before the 2nd century A.D., and, since these were situated on the isthmian tract of the Malay Peninsula, it is not unlikely that they were Mōn rather than Malaysian, or at least an amalgam of Mōn, Khmer and Malaysian elements. However, it is possible that the absence of centralized control in the archipelagic realm proper may be more apparent than real, for the Chinese texts that provide our earliest information on continental Southeast Asia are silent on conditions farther south. Most of the information in these texts derives from a Chinese embassy to Fu-nan in about A.D. 245[3] which, although reasonably well informed about peninsular territories, collected very little material relating to the archipelago. The absence of archeological evidence in the south need occasion no surprise, as it is completely lacking even on the isthmian tracts prior to the 4th or 5th century A.D. — and some scholars would refer even these meager finds to the 6th or 7th century.

The Earliest Literary and Epigraphic Evidence

Among the dozen or more "kingdoms" (國) reportedly incorporated in the chiefdom of Fu-nan during the 3rd century A.D.,[4] at least two or three were probably located on the Siamo-Malaysian isthmus. One of these, Tun-sun, has been discussed above.[5] Perhaps Chiu-chih (九稚 *$Ki̯ə u$-$\hat{d}$'i̯), mentioned in the same context,[6] was another. Subsequent Chinese texts preserve a tradition that the kingdom of Langkasuka, prominent on the Malayan isthmus in later times, was founded more than four centuries prior to the rule of the Southern Liang sovereigns in China, which would place the event early in the 2nd century A.D.[7] In the light of developments in Fu-nan, this date at first sight seems fairly plausible, but this may be no more than coincidence. The *Liang Shu*, earliest of the texts relating to Langkasuka, was not presented to the throne until 636 and refers to a dynasty that reigned from 502 to 557, so that it was at least four centuries removed from the event it purports to describe. It claims to be reporting local tradition (國人說立國以來四百餘年), but in Southeast Asian society the popular memory has been predominantly anhistorical, unable to retain specific events except in so far as it has transformed them into archetypes, and thus subordinated their chronological relationships to the requirements of atemporal heroic myth. It is extremely unlikely that the traditions of Langkasuka in the 6th century A.D. preserved historical truth about events that took place four centuries previously.[8] It is just possible, however, that despite the phrasing of the *Liang Shu*, the founding of the kingdom of Langkasuka was linked in legend in some way to a particular dynasty or to some event in Chinese history which enabled the Chinese themselves to supply the chronological framework. This need not have been too explicit a reference. Possibly a phrase such as "long before (interpreted rightly or wrongly as an interval of a century) the embassy of K'ang T'ai and Chu Ying"[9] would have been sufficient to indicate a date in the 2nd century. This is all speculation, and it would surely be prudent to treat the Chinese text with reserve until it is confirmed or disproved by archeological investigation.

Possibly the earliest epigraphic records from the Malaysian world consist of fragments of Buddhist votive inscriptions from the state of Kedah.[10] They cannot be older than the 4th century A.D., and some scholars incline to a later date. Sundry pieces of statuary and divers archeological finds from subsequent centuries attest varying degrees of Indian influence in settlements ranging from as far north as Takuapā to Perak in the south,[11] but none bears directly on the problem of urban origins. In Kalimantan, *yūpa* (sacrificial post) inscriptions from the Kutai valley have been dated to the beginning of the 5th century,[12] and in western Java brāhmaṇical inscriptions bear witness to the existence of the kingdom of Tārŭmā half a century or so later.[13] Noorduyn and Verstappen have given cogent reasons for locating "the famous city" of the Tugu inscription, perhaps the capital of Tārŭmā, in the two

miles or so of country between Tugu village and Tanjung Priok.[14]
Early in 414 the monk [Shih] Fa Hsien (釋)法顯 visited the
kingdom of *Ia-bʻuâ-dʻiei 耶婆提 which, like the Ptolemaic
'Ιαβαδίου, is a phonetically adequate transcription of the Prākrit
Yāvadiu (= Java Island).[15] There can be no doubt that this form
relates to an island of Java, but the course followed by Fa Hsien's
vessel after leaving *Ia-bʻuâ-dʻiei and the winds encountered on the
voyage have led some scholars to speculate (not very profitably, I
think) that this particular island may have been situated to the
north of the equator, say in western or northern Kalimantan.
However that may be, it seems likely that the capital of the
kingdom, known as Αργυρα in the Ptolemaic corpus, merited at least
proto-urban status.[16] Ten years later the monk Guṇavarman is said
to have proselytized in *Dźʻia-bʻua 闍婆,[17] a country which sent
envoys to the Chinese court in 433 and 435.[18] This name seems to
have been a transcription of the indigenous form Jāva, in
contradistinction to Fa Hsien's Sanskritized Yāva. Among the
kingdoms on this island was one known to the Chinese as Ho-lo-tan
(訶羅單 *Xâ-lâ-tân), which first presented tribute to the
Chinese court in 430.[19] In 434 a king of this polity who had
adopted the style Śrī Vijaya again sent a mission to China.[20]
Between 454 and 464 a King Śrī Varanarendra of Kan-tʻo-li
(*Kân-tʻâ-lji 干陀利), a kingdom probably located in Sumatra,
dispatched an envoy with the Indian name of Rudra to China.[21]
Little is known about these polities beyond their names and a record
of their embassies to the Chinese court, but the prevalence of
Sanskrit honorifics is indicative of Indian influence that most
probably manifested itself, as elsewhere in Southeast Asia, in the
formation of kingdoms whose organs of government were dignified by
Indian administrative terms.

Peninsular Evidence Subsequent to the 5th Century

From the beginning of the 6th century Chinese knowledge of
the Siamo-Malaysian isthmus becomes a little more detailed, and the
evidence of centralized control unmistakable. By the second decade
of the century at latest, the capital of Langkasuka was a fortified
(perhaps signifying "palisaded") enceinte with double gates, towers
and tiered buildings (其國累樓為城重門樓閣).[22]
It is significant that the use of the graph 國 to mean "capital" or
simply "city" (it cannot in this context signify "kingdom" or
"country" or "state") reflects the nature of the political unit: a
polity in which a focally situated settlement exercised direct
control over a restricted peripheral territory and exacted whatever
tribute it could from an indefinite region beyond. Very similar

was *Siṁhapura, capital of the Red-Earth Kingdom, which was protected by walls with triple gates more than 100 paces apart 有門三重相去各百許步. Within the enceinte the palace consisted of a complex of storeyed structures, all with their doors facing north.[23] The report of two Chinese envoys who visited the kingdom in 607-8 makes it fairly certain that this city was situated somewhere on the Siamo-Malaysian isthmus, probably in the neighborhood of Songkhlā.[24]

This century also witnessed the *floruit* of the polities known to the Chinese as *B'uân-b'uân* 槃槃 and *Tân-tân* 丹丹, although the former was in existence certainly as early as the 5th century and the latter continued well into the third quarter of the 7th. *B'uân-b'uân* seems to have occupied that sector of the isthmus fronting the Bay of Bandon.[25] The Chinese notices of this state are explicit in referring to a maritime people, who lived mostly by the water-side and, in default of city walls, depended entirely on palisades (百姓多緣水而居國無城皆豎木為柵), a description that recalls the stockaded settlements of the Pyū and the Mōn. It is not certain that *Tân-tân* was on the peninsula,[26] and an alternative location in eastern Java has been suggested; but wherever it may have been, it provides one of the few estimates of population available for early Southeast Asian cities. *T'ung Tien* and later texts attribute somewhat more than 20,000 families to the capital, which implies a population of the order of 50-80,000 people. Judging from such estimates as we have of the size of urban settlements in Southeast Asia in the early colonial period, it is difficult not to regard this figure as an exaggeration — though it was doubtless intended to include all the people in the territories controlled by the city. It is not known if Chinese envoys ever visited this kingdom. Probably the estimate of population was prepared by Chinese officials from information provided by the *Tân-tân* embassies which came to China fairly frequently during the sixth and seventh centuries.[27]

During the 7th century a city recorded by Arabs and Persians under the transcription *Kalāh*,[28] and situated on the west coast of the isthmus, sent its earliest recorded embassy to the Chinese court, though several texts state that it had first become known to the Chinese during Han times. Subsequently both Chinese and Arab authors commented on the walls of the city with their storeyed gate-towers.[29] Within the enceinte all buildings, even the palace, were roofed with *atap*, which implies the wooden construction that would be expected on other grounds. Abū Dulaf,

Fig. 19. Locations of archeological sites and ancient toponyms mentioned in this chapter.

a moderately reliable reporter, referred explicitly to the numerous gardens and springs within the city, which, incidentally, he claimed to have visited.[30] It is curious — and perhaps significant as reflecting the cultural biases that informed the writings of Chinese and Arabo-Persians — that, whereas the former made no mention of trading activity in Kalāh, this constituted the main theme in the works of several Arab authors. Abū Zayd, for example, in the second decade of the 10th century, wrote that, "Kalāh is the center of commerce for aloeswood, camphor, sandalwood, ivory, tin, ebony, baqqam (بقم),[31] spices of all kinds, and a host of objects too numerous to count. It is thither that the trading expeditions which start from ʿUmān make their way, and thence set out for [i.e., to return to] the land of the Arabs."[32] A quarter of a century later Masʿūdī referred to Kalāh as the "general rendezvous of the Muslim ships of Sīrāf and ʿUmān, where they meet the ships of China."[33]

A few other urban nuclei mentioned from time to time in Tʿang and contemporary texts must also be assigned to the peninsula. Kaṭāha,[34] famous in Indian literature as "the Seat of all Felicities" and probably represented by the archeological remains at the southern foot of Gunung Jerai,[35] was, according to I Ching, the point of departure for vessels setting out to cross the Bay of Bengal and also the port where pilgrims boarded ship for the voyage down the Strait of Melaka on their return voyage. The remains of more than thirty shrines on the southern flank of Gunung Jerai attest the existence of an important settlement during a period of centuries. The precise dates are still a subject of dispute. Dr. Quaritch Wales, who carried out an archeological survey of the area late in the nineteen-thirties, concluded that recorded settlement began as early as the 5th or 6th century; more recently professor Alastair Lamb has postdated this event by several centuries.[36] Archeology has yielded no specific information as to the morphology of Kaṭāha and the texts are silent on this point, but the disposition of shrines below the sacred peak of Jerai, itself crowned by a sanctuary, is in accordance with a pattern common to ceremonial centers (and probably village settlements as well, if we had records of them) in Southeast Asia.[37] So far no settlement enceinte has been discovered. However, it must be remembered that alluviation has been heavy round the Merbok estuary, and the site of a compact nucleus may have been long since buried. On the opposite side of the Peninsula it is possible that Tāmraliṅga was already in existence as a city-state in the vicinity of Chaiyā, for

Sylvain Lévi has recognized the name in its Pāli form, Tambaliṅga, in the *Mahāniddesa* of the 2nd or 3rd century A.D.[38] There is no guarantee, of course, that it referred to the Tāmraliṅga on the Malayan isthmus, though in view of the locations of the other toponyms mentioned in the same context,[39] it is not unlikely. Finally, in the far south of the peninsula T'ang texts locate the trading station of *Lâ-ji̯wɒt 羅越, some 50 *li* from the northern shore of a strait known in the vernacular as *Tśi̯ĕt 質. This last was probably, as Pelliot suggested, a transcription of Malay *selat* (meaning "strait"),[40] and *Lâ-ji̯wɒt may have been, as Moens proposed, a transcription of Seluyut, now a river, hill and district at the head of the Johor estuary, though an adequate phonetic correspondence can be achieved only by means of drastic aphaeresis.[41] In any case, the strait referred to can hardly have been other than all or a sector of the Melaka Strait and its continuation through Singapore Main Strait,[42] and a location at the southern end of the Malay Peninsula accords well with the statement of the T'ang history that "traders passing back and forth meet there."[43]

Javanese Evidence Subsequent to the 5th Century

Writing about events that took place during the last quarter of the 7th century, I Ching enumerated the political entities of which he was cognizant in the Malaysian world. From west to east these read as follows: Barus (*B'uâ-luo-ṣi 婆魯斯),[44] Malayu (*Muât-lâ-i̯ǝu 末羅遊), *Muo[k]-Xâ-si̯ĕn (莫訶信),[45] Walaiṅ (*Xâ-li̯ǝng 訶陵)[46] in Java, *Tân-tân and *B'uǝn-b'uǝn, both of which may have been located on the Malay Peninsula and which are noted above, probably Bali (婆利),[47] and Gurun (*G'i̯uǝt-li̯uĕn 掘倫).[48] Each of these he termed an "island" (洲), but it is likely that each constituted a kingdom so focused on a capital city that it would almost have merited the term city-state. Four of these kingdoms were accorded paragraphs in the T'ang histories and encyclopedias, namely *Tân-tân,[49] *B'uǝn-b'uǝn,[50] Bali[51] and Walaiṅ, but only for the last of these is there the slightest hint of the character of the city; and then it is a simple statement that it was surrounded by a palisade and that it contained a large two-storeyed edifice, probably a palace, roofed with fronds of the *lontar* palm (檂欄)[52]—or, as another history put it, even the largest buildings are roofed with palm fronds.[53] So far as the Chinese were concerned, the capital of Walaiṅ was called Java [*Dźǎ-b'uâ 闍婆] City.[54] Between 742 and 755, according to a Chinese record, it was transferred to *B'uâ-luo-ka-si̯ɛ 婆露伽斯

some distance to the eastward.⁵⁵ T'ang texts provide a sprinkling of additional toponyms which should probably be assigned to Java or the eastern sectors of the archipelago,⁵⁶ though their precise locations are at best in dispute, at worst wholly obscure. Possibly *B'uət-niei 勃泥, which has usually been identified with Berunei, may also have been in existence in the seventh century, although the earliest reference in Chinese sources is no earlier than the second half of the ninth century,⁵⁷ and no embassy is recorded before 977.⁵⁸

Prior to the 8th century, archeology contributes little in support of these meager literary allusions to possible urban foci in Java. An inscription from the foot of Gunung Merbabu in the central part of the island has been attributed to the 7th century, but does little more than attest Indian mythology and the possible existence of a Vaiṣṇavite shrine associated with the Tuk Mas (the Golden Spring), comparable in its purifying powers to the Ganges.⁵⁹ Perhaps an inscription from the Diëng plateau, whose paleography, although the meaning is undecipherable, has been dated to the 7th century, is witness to the beginnings of monumental architecture on that upland whose very name is evidence of its sacred character in early days.⁶⁰ In 732 a king Sañjaya erected a śivaliṅga in a sanctuary on the Wukir hill bordering the Kĕḍu plain,⁶¹ all or part of which was then known as the land of Kuñjarakuñja.⁶² It is customary also to ascribe to the late-7th or early-8th century the exclusively Śaivite monuments that betoken the former existence of a temple complex on the Diëng plateau, though the earliest inscription dates only from 809.⁶³ Here, at a height of 6,000 feet, set amid solfataras and suphurous lakes in a sediment-filled volcanic crater, is all that remains of the earliest Javanese temple complex that has survived in the archeological record. Today this amounts to eight small caṇḍi more or less intact, together with the foundations of other temples and of several pĕṇḍapa or wooden halls. The crater was approached by means of stone staircases, and a stone drainage channel may also have been contemporary with the temples. Farther eastwards, in the upper Brantas valley, a similar developmental pattern was recurring at least as early as 760, when one of a dynasty of Śaivite kings ruling over Kañjuruha styled himself protector of a liṅga called Pūtikeśvara, in which was concentrated the subtle essence and validation of royalty.⁶⁴ This appearance of the organizing principle of statehood in East Java can probably be related to the eastward movement of the capital of Walaiṅ from Java City to

*Bʻuâ-luo-ka-siɛ,⁶⁵ which is itself to be correlated with the rise to dominance in Central Java of a Mahāyāna Buddhist dynasty styling itself Śailendra or Kings of the Mountain.

Developments in Sumatra Subsequent to the 5th Century

In the second half of the 7th century the monk I Ching visited an enclosed settlement (廓 for 郭), located somewhere on the southern shores of the South China Sea, which he designated by the honorific Śrī Vijaya (*Si-lji Bʻi̯uət-żi̯äi 尸利佛逝). He observed that it was a center of Buddhist scholarship, where more than a thousand monks were engaged in study and exposition of their canon "exactly as in Mādhyadeśa (India)."⁶⁶ Since 1880, when the equation was first proposed, early Śrī Vijaya has usually been located in the neighborhood of Palembang, a regional ascription for which the evidence of literary and epigraphic sources affords considerable support.⁶⁷ However, a recent archeological survey failed to elicit evidence of any substantial residential site in the immediate vicinity of Palembang which could be dated prior to the 14th century.⁶⁸ Possibly the relatively dense habitation in the present-day city is obscuring archeological vestiges of such a settlement, but more likely is Professor O. W. Wolters's suggestion, proposed after an exhaustive study of available literary, epigraphic, and physiographic evidence, that the early city was probably situated somewhere to the south of modern Palembang, in the drainage basins of the Ogan, Rambang or Kumering rivers.⁶⁹ In any case, the long-accepted sacrality of the neighboring Bukit Seguntang, the Mahameru of Malay legend, remains unimpaired, at least from the 14th century onward.

Archeological and epigraphic evidence from this formative phase of the Sumatran settlement pattern is meager, but a series of Old Malay inscriptions — four from the vicinity of Palembang, one from the upper reaches of the Batang Hari, one from Kota Kapur on the island of Bangka, and one discovered very recently at Palas Pasemah, close to the Sunda Strait⁷⁰ — seemingly attest the transformation of the Śrī Vijayan polity from local chiefdom to thalassocracy during the last quarter of the 7th century. By 686 Śrī Vijaya apparently held sway over the southern half of Sumatra, the island of Bangka, and possibly part of western Java. Once having established this territorial base, she was in a position to reap the fruits of her nodality with regard to the maritime trade routes of Southeast Asia. But in an age of speculative, adventurous commerce, when prosperity was virtually synonymous with monopoly, one region was of crucial importance in Śrī Vijaya's attempt to consolidate her position as the premier power in the archipelago. This was the isthmian sector of the Malay Peninsula, at least part of which had been brought within the Śrī Vijayan realm by the end of the 7th century. Kedah seems to have been incorporated in the developing thalassocracy by 689,[71] and the famous Ligor stele attests the power of Śrī Vijaya on the east coast of the isthmus by 775.[72] This expansion of the kingdom has been documented and discussed by a succession of able scholars[73] and it is not necessary to elaborate on this theme here, particularly as it contributes practically nothing to our knowledge of the mechanics of the process of urban genesis. However, the general course of Śrī Vijayan history would seem to imply that, although both I Ching and the 7th-century inscriptions placed their emphasis exclusively on the roles of groups of officials, religious devotees and literati, trade played an important part in the burgeoning of the polity, a point which was in fact emphasized by Arab and Persian authors from the 9th century onward; but of this neither texts nor archeology afford any confirmation during the formative phase of the kingdom.

* * * * * * * * * * *

The information available about the origins of urban life in the Malaysian world is the least satisfactory of that for any major culture realm of Southeast Asia. This is partly because the archipelago was more remote from the Middle Kingdom than was continental Southeast Asia, so that notices relating to it in Chinese annals and encyclopedias began a century or two later, and even then tended to be less specific, than those for more northerly territories. The deficiencies also stem from the circumstance that until recently archeologists working in the region have been overwhelmingly concerned with either prehistoric investigation or the interpretation and preservation of the monumental architecture of the great shrines of later days. As a result, many parts of the area have been but poorly prospected archeologically. Moreover, the equatorial environment is perhaps the most inimical of the world's major natural regions to the preservation of archeological evidence. Doubtless some ancient monuments are still engulfed in a green sea of vegetation, while others have been swept away by flood-water, entombed by alluvium, corroded by soil acids, or devoured by insects. Still others were probably destroyed by religious fanaticism or, quite certainly, expunged by the blind spade of ignorance. In recent times, governmental apathy has allowed not a few known sites to disintegrate and their artifacts to be misappropriated. The equatorial rain forest, too, is not conducive to the easy recognition of ancient sites on air photographs. For all these reason it may not be too surprising that archeological investigation has so far yielded only meager evidence of early urban development. Yet, when all is said and done, some parts of the area have been relatively well explored archeologically, but even in those territories almost no evidence of proto- or early historical settlements has come to light.

On the other hand, the usual Chinese sources attest the existence in the region of political entities typically characterized as *kuo* 國 . In Chinese historiography this term had a broad connotation ranging in meaning from a vague implication of "country" through the somewhat more specific concepts of "state" or "kingdom" to the relatively precise signification of "capital." What was common to all these meanings was the implication of centralized leadership (here often in the hands of rulers and officials proclaiming Sanskrit names or titles) and socio-economic differentiation at least equal to those of a chiefdom. On the Siamo-Malaysian isthmus, such polities appear to have been in existence by at latest the 3rd century A.D., and possibly their origins should be carried back even earlier. One of them, Langkasuka, was accorded the equivalent of a paragraph in the *Liang Shu* (relating to the period 502-557); another, the Lion City, was described in the *Sui Shu* (relating to 581-618), and accounts of others were incorporated in various Tʻang dynasty (618-907) texts. The isthmus has also yielded a considerable number of first-millennium artifacts, at least four earthwork enceintes of uncertain date (at Yarang, Wieng Sra, Old Songkhla, and Satingphra), and from time to time extremely small quantities of residential debris. For the archipelago from the 5th century onward Chinese sources provide similar information couched in the same terminology. In central Java and, to a lesser extent, South Sumatra the implications of the texts are partially confirmed by epigraphic documents, which begin to appear in the second half of the 7th century, and thereafter — in Java at any rate — become increasingly common, nearly always, as would be expected, in association with monumental architecture and statuary. However, outside these areas, archeological finds are exiguous, perhaps the most notable being the *yūpa* inscriptions from eastern Kalimantan. What is seemingly anomalous in the archeological record of the archipelago is the virtually complete absence of any indication of large, or indeed small, proto- and early historical residential sites. Neither substantial deposits of residential debris nor enclosing walls such as are a feature of many mainland settlements have so far come to light. Even Śrī Vijaya and Walaiṅ (Java City) seem to have left no traces from which posterity might reconstruct their morphologies. Of Palembang, for long the presumed site of Śrī Vijayapura, where in the 7th century more than a thousand monks were studying the Buddhist canon, Bronson and Wisseman write that, "The entire vicinity . . . does not contain enough pre-14th century domestic artifacts to make one small village."[75] The same authors go on to point out that the earliest "substantial settlement" (by which they appear to imply an urban form) so far discovered in Indonesia is at Kota Cina in northern Sumatra, which cannot antedate A.D. 1000.[76]

This discrepancy between the implications of literary and epigraphic sources on the one hand and the results of archeological research in the archipelago on the other has been discussed at some length by Bronson and Wisseman and by Wolters. As a means of resolving this apparent paradox, the former authors have postulated early loci of authority that were flimsily built, devoid of durable ceremonial foci, existing in what the authors call comparative isolation from their hinterlands, and situated close to the sea, which would have provided both access to trade routes and a possible means of disposing of domestic refuse in a way that would not immediately attract the attention of archeologists in later times.[77] This prescription is certainly devised on the right principles, but I would suggest that the conceptualization of some of the components be modified somewhat. For flimsy construction I would substitute "structures of easily perishable materials," of which wood, bamboo, and ratan are the obvious exemplars. Although the dwellings of commoners in many parts of Southeast Asia could properly be described as flimsy, as could in some instances those of rājas and even sultans — as was made clear in Sir Frank Swettenham's account of the settlements at Langat and Lukut in the 1870's — many houses in, say, the Minangkabau or Batak territories or in Kelantan were of sturdy construction; nevertheless, they disintegrated readily enough in the equatorial climate, leaving few traces to alert the archeologist.

The second postulate, namely ceremonial foci constructed of readily degradable materials, is not difficult to accommodate to the historical record of later times. Even rulers in times past in the Malaysian world have resided, with a few notable exceptions, in palaces of carved timbers. In the specific case of Śrī Vijaya, Dra. Satyawati Suleiman has pointed out that the monks would have lived in monasteries of wood, bamboo and palm thatch such as are still in existence in Bali or at the Purba Baru pesantren in South Tapanuli. The only structures not of timber would have been brick *stūpas*, foundations for which have been reported by Bronson and others from Bukit Seguntang and elsewhere in Sumatra.[78] The perimeter of the settlement would probably have been delimited by a wooden palisade, as was explicitly noted to be the case in *B'uān-b'uān (p. 234 above). It is not without interest in this connection that no outer wall has yet been found surrounding the capital of Majapahit, even though brick walls are known to have enclosed the constituent compounds.[79] In any case, in the Malaysian culture realm the ruler was often identified with the axis of the universe, a conception expressed explicitly in the style Paku Buwono, Nail of the World, assumed by the Susuhunans of Surakarta in more recent times.[80] Where the ruler dwelt, there was the quintessentially sacred enclave that sustained the laws of space, direction, and time and whence power flowed out toward the cardinal compass points. Professor Wolters is both correct and perceptive when he remarks that the distinguishing signs of a ruler's court were those of behavior and rank expressed in terms of deference, raiment, and relative position, whether vis-à-vis the ruler in court ceremonial or in the location of a courtier's residence with respect to the palace.[81] Hence the preoccupation of Malaysian courts with protocol and ritual, a feature that seldom failed to impress foreign travelers from Ch'ang Chün's embassy to the Red Earth Kingdom in 607[82] to 18th-century visitors to Javanese keratons, and an account of which pre-empted a substantial section of the *Sejarah Melayu*.[83] At the very heart of court ceremony and protocol were the regalia, the symbols of sovereignty that validated a ruler's claim to supreme authority. It was presumably the symbolism of these palladia that gave rise to the tales of supernaturally endowed head-dresses which found their way into Chinese accounts of a country whose name was transcribed as *San-fo-ch'i* 三佛齋 [84] and of Dragon-teeth Strait,[85] and which also figured prominently in the *Sejarah Melayu*.[86] The point is that in the Malaysian world sovereignty was not customarily expressed in perduring monumental architecture but inhered in the person of the ruler by virtue of his possession of the palladia of the state.

The implications of the third characteristic of the ancient

settlement pattern postulated by Bronson and Wisseman, that important centers existed in comparative isolation from their hinterlands (They subsequently refer to a "city without a hinterland"), are not entirely clear. The choice of 15th-century Melaka as an archetypical example of such a center is perhaps misleading, for the rulers of that city maintained close cultural and economic relations with a hinterland which, as a matter of record, encompassed most of Southeast Asia and certainly the full extent of the Malaysian world as far east as Banda and Ternate.[87] It is true that the territory immediately surrounding the city produced few cereals (although it was prodigal of fruits and other forest products[88]) but that was only a minute fraction of the total hinterland. Although rice was imported from as far afield as Java and Siam, it was mainly on her directly controlled territories and benefices on the Malay peninsula and the east coast of Sumatra that Melaka relied for her provisioning. Moreover, as will be explained below, the rivers and coasts even in the close vicinity of the city produced a breed of men whose life style and skills were of particular value to the rulers of Melaka. I would suggest that the prescription be rephrased to read "not primarily dependent on surpluses generated by the labors of a subject farming population in the immediate vicinity." Political power in Southeast Asia in premodern times derived from control over labor (even though in the indigenous view dense populations, like fertility, stability, prosperity, and glory, were probably regarded as manifestations, rather than sources, of power). In the agrarian-based kingdoms of the mainland and Java, the labor pool took the form of a self-supporting peasantry which in time of need could be summoned for corvée or as military levies; in the archipelago it was often a highly mobile force of seamen capable of undertaking a wide range of assignments, naval, military, trading, and ceremonial, on both sea and land. In at least the early days of Melaka and in the Johor empire these general-purpose mariners were mostly so-called Orang Laut,[89] a group who may have performed similar functions for their rulers in earlier times. When summoned by their sovereign they would put out in their *perahus,* and sometimes larger vessels, from the rivers, creeks, and inlets throughout the kingdom and, suitably accoutered, converge on a designated meeting place. Wolters cites as instances of such gatherings the assembling of Śrī Vijayan maritime and land forces at Mināña Tāmvan as recorded in the Kedukan Bukit inscription of 682, the administering of an oath to levies who had come from a distance as related in the more or less contemporary Sabokingking inscription, the tradition preserved by Abū Zayd in the 10th century that the Mahārāja of Zābag (= Jāvaka) had ordered the readying of a thousand vessels in preparation for a raid on Kampuchea, and the statement by Chao Ju-kua that in time of war the people of the country he knew as San-fo-ch'i would assemble under their chiefs, each of whom would furnish equipment and provisions for his own followers.[90] The pyramidal political structure of early Malaysian kingdoms seems not to have differed greatly from those characteristic of the mainland states, but their ecological bases (except those of Java) elicited different modes of exploitation.

Commenting on these aspects of the problem, Professor Wolters has suggested that "the significant spatial unit in Śrīvijayan history [He could have generalized his remarks to many other parts of the archipelago] . . . would not have been a lonely 'city,' distinguished by material 'urban' signs and exercising coercive power over a distant hinterland" but rather "a network of settlements up and down the river, from which people sallied forth to participate in the ruler's adventures and provided him with key members of his entourage, sometimes bound to him by marriage alliances."[91] This latter pattern of settlement is, of course, widespread through ecosystems developed on the Sunda platform. In both narrow valleys of the uplands and along rivers and sea faces of the alluvium that mantles much of the lowlands, physiographic constraints prescribe a linear arrangement of dwellings interrupted, typically, at infrequent and irregular intervals only by spatially restricted nuclei of administrative, religious, and service facilities.[92] As settlements of this type are common on the coastal lowlands of the Malay world and can be documented at least as far back as the beginning of the colonial period, it is not unreasonable to suppose that they existed in still earlier times.

Bronson and Wisseman claim that a settlement meeting their postulates "does not seem abstractly impossible."[93] In my opinion they could have gone farther and, with the modifications suggested above, have specified it as the observable norm in the coastal tracts of Malaysia and Indonesia. However, the question remains as to how the domestic refuse from these habitation sites was disposed of so as not now to be readily discernible by the enquiring eye of the archeologist. The fact that they were predominantly in riparian or coastal situations probably accounts for the apparent disappearance of some domestic, and to a minor extent industrial, waste, especially where the houses were constructed on rafts or

piles actually over the water. Today villages built partly over
water are common throughout the coastal zones of Malaysia and
Indonesia, and sizable settlements almost wholly of this type were
reported in the past. The earliest extant record of such a
settlement is a description of *Bʻuān-bʻuān probably deriving from the
6th or 7th century (p. 234 above). In 1225 Chao Ju-kua commented
that, even though the capital of San-fo-chʻi [usually believed at this
time to have been in the vicinity of Jambi] was enclosed by a brick
wall, "The people lived scattered about outside the city [in the
network of dwellings discussed above] or on reed-covered wooden
rafts floating on the water."[94] From early in the 16th century
comes Pigafetta's description of Berunei,

> entirely built on foundations in the salt water, except the
> houses of the king and some of the princes: it contains
> twenty-five thousand fires or families. The houses are all of
> wood, placed on great piles to raise them high up. When the tide
> rises the women go in boats through the city selling provisions
> and necessaries.[95]

In more recent times both Banjarmasin and Palembang have attracted
attention as largely floating cities. Alfred Wallace, who visited
the latter city in 1861, wrote an account of it so apposite to the
present discussion that I quote it *in extenso*:[96]

> The city is a large one, extending for three or four miles along
> a fine curve of the river [Musi] . . . The stream is, however,
> much narrowed by the houses which project into it upon piles, and
> within these, again, there is a row of houses built upon great
> bamboo rafts, which are moored by rattan cables to the shore or
> to piles, and rise and fall with the tide. The whole river-front
> on both sides is chiefly formed of such houses, and they are
> mostly shops open to the water, and only raised a foot above it,
> so that by taking a small boat it is easy to go to market and
> purchase anything that is to be had in Palembang. The natives
> are true Malays, never building a house on dry land if they can
> find water to set it in, and never going anywhere on foot if they
> can reach the place in a boat.[97]

Wallace's further remark that for many miles both upstream and
downstream of Palembang the banks of the Musi and its tributaries
were flooded in the wet season suggests another reason why domestic
refuse may sometimes have left few traces, especially in situations
where alluviation has been unusually heavy. In this connection it
should be borne in mind that over much of the Malaysian Peninsula
and the Indonesian Archipelago the last two centuries must be
considered geomorphologically anomalous in that denudation and
accretion rates have multiplied several fold as a result of
extensive deforestation in the course of agricultural and mining
operations.[98] How many early settlements suffered the fate of Kuala
Kubu in the valley of the Sungai Selangor, which was completely

buried by alluvium in the 19th century as a result of uncontrolled mining around the headwaters of the river, is a matter for speculation.

There is, too, I think, another reason why the domestic refuse from ancient settlements is not overly prominent in the archipelagic realm, even in the vicinity of surviving monuments. As dwellings were of perishable materials, so also were domestic utensils and other household wares. Dra. Suleiman has noted, for instance, that the monks who followed their calling in Śrī Vijaya in the 7th century would have eaten off large leaves, drunk from coconut husks and gourds, and used bamboo utensils, just as did the populace at large.[99] Of the country known to the Chinese as *Teng-liu-mei* 登流眉 in the 13th century, it was explicitly recorded that palm leaves served as dishes, but in this case "fingers were used for eating instead of spoons or chopsticks."[100] As a matter of fact, it was not only the common folk who took their repasts off palm fronds. At the banquet in honor of the Chinese envoys who visited the Lion City in 607, leaf-platters, each 15 feet square, and containing a great variety of foods, were placed before the King and his guests.[101] The use of leaves, bamboo, and sometimes wood for these purposes has been customary throughout the Malaysian world at all times, including the present. In fact it has been so commonplace as to excite comment only from foreigners accustomed to different dining arrangements. In any case, it needs no emphasis that receptacles and utensils of this type survive for only a minimal length of time in the highly acid soil solutions of the equatorial environment.[102] The gold and silver plate sometimes affected by the ruling classes[103] would, of course, have been removed by its owners in time of disaster or perhaps buried, carried off by a conqueror, or appropriated by survivors at the first opportunity. The rapidity with which traces of human occupance can be erased in the equatorial zone is attested by the paucity of domestic refuse (other than imported Chinese pottery) in the residential sectors at Johor Lama. This settlement is known to have been the capital of the Johor kingdom from about 1540 to 1587, during which time it was visited by Portuguese. Yet, in spite of a nearly contemporary description of the city by Diogo do Couto,[104] the surviving remains are insufficient to permit the reconstruction of the settlement in any detail.[105] A similar situation obtains at Beretam, where the founder of Melaka established his court and which served as a royal retreat at least until the beginning of the reign of Sultan Alau'd-din (1477-88), and perhaps until the fall of

248   *Nāgara and Commandery*

the city to the Portuguese in 1511.[106] But inspection of the ground in the vicinity of the present-day village yields no trace of the old settlement, nor, as far as I know, has any artifact of the period ever been reported from the neighborhood.

It is evident, upon reflection, that the apparently anomalous paucity of archeological evidence for early settlement in the Malaysian culture realm is a less intractable problem than it at first appears. The preceding arguments, which can be reduced effectively to the proposition that ancient settlements were not greatly dissimilar to indigenous (that is excluding colonial) ones in recent times, does not entirely resolve the anomaly, but it does imply that the remains of early settlements are not likely to be overly prominent in the present-day landscapes of Malaysia or Indonesia.

Notes and References

1. By this term I intend to denote those realms of Southeast Asia, predominantly archipelagic (though including the southern half of the Malay Peninsula), where Austronesian languages of one sort or another are spoken today, and where Malay runs as a *lingua franca*. Used in this way the term includes the present-day states of Malaysia and Singapore, several provinces in southern Thailand, Berunei, and Indonesia (together with the Philippines, though these will not concern us here), and is, therefore, broader in connotation than the political unit of Malaysia, but roughly equivalent to the region known to Dutch ecologists and some American archeologists as Malesia. The location of the boundary between Mōn and Malay culture at the beginning of the Christian era is obscure and it is possible that some of the isthmian kingdoms discussed in this section should have been included in the preceding study of Mōn urbanism.

2. G. H. von Faber, *Oud-Soerabaia. De Geschiedenis van Indie's eerste koopstad van de oudste tijden tot de instelling van de gemeente raad* (Soerabaia, 1931), chap. 1

3. P. 148 above.

4. P. 123 above.

5. P. 212 above.

6. Chiu-chih is almost certainly a graphic error for Chiu-ya (九雅 *Kiəu-nga) which *T'ai-p'ing Yü-lan* 太平御覽 (chüan 788, f. 6 recto et verso) locates "across the Great Bay of Chin-lin (Note 5 to Chap. 3 above) from Fu-nan and 3,000 *li* southwards" [*TPYL* claims to be quoting *Sui Shu* 隋書 but the information is lacking in that work in the form in which we now know it. The substance of this passage does occur, however, in *T'ung Tien* 通典 , chüan 188, f. 1010, and *T'ai-p'ing Huan-yü Chi* 太平寰宇記, chüan 177, f. 7 verso]. TPYL also notes that Chiu-ya was an alternative [perhaps erroneous is implied] form of Chü-li (拘利 *Kiu-lji), the name of a kingdom mentioned in *Shui-Ching Chu* 水經注 (chüan 1, f. 12 verso) and *Liang Shu* 梁書 (chüan 54, f. 22 verso) as a port on the route from Fu-nan to India, and which has sometimes been identified with the κωλη [πολις] of the Ptolemaic corpus (p. 439 below). These and related matters are discussed in Wheatley, "An early Chinese reference to part of Malaya," *MJTG*, vol. 5 (1955), pp. 57-60.

7. *Liang Shu*, chüan 54, f. 14 recto uses the transcription *Lâng-nga-siəu 狼牙修 ; *T'ung Tien* (chüan 188, f. 1009), *T'ai-p'ing Huan-yü Chi* (chüan 176, f. 12 recto et verso, and *Wen-hsien T'ung-k'ao* 文獻通考 (chüan 331, f. 2602) reproduce the passage from *Liang Shu* with a few alterations, but use a slightly different transcription: 狼牙修 . For an analysis of these and related texts, with references to previous literature, see Wheatley, "Langkasuka," *TP*, vol. 44 (1956), pp. 387-412. A different interpretation of these texts is advanced by Mom Chao Chand, "Lang-Ya-Shu and Langkasuka: a reinterpretation," *Nusantara,* no. 2 (1972), pp. 277-284. See also H. G. Quaritch Wales, "Langkasuka and Tambralinga: some archaeological notes," *JMBRAS*, vol. 47, pt. 1 (1974), pp. 13-40.

8. This is not to say, of course, that social and political forms may not be transmitted with substantial accuracy through the medium of epic myth. The *Iliad* and the Norse sagas, for instance, depict ways of life that existed long before these epics were given their present form; the *Sějarah Mělayu*, although its characters are frequently larger than life, records with a reasonably high degree of fidelity the customs of a port city at least a century before its composition; and Serbian epics depict the hazards of life on the Turkish frontier before the Peace of Karlowitz in 1699 with a comparable degree of verisimilitude

[Matthias Murko, *La poésie populaire épique en Yougoslavie au début du XXe siècle* (Paris, 1929), p. 29].

9. Cp. Note 3 to Chap. 3.

10. Summarized in H. G. Quaritch Wales, "Archeological researches on ancient Indian colonization in Malaya," *JMBRAS,* vol. 18, pt. 2 (1940), pp. 1-85, "Malayan archaeology of the 'Hindu period': some reconsiderations," *JMBRAS,* vol. 43, pt. 1 (1970), pp. 1-34, and (with D. C. Wales) "Further work on Indian sites in Malaya," *JMBRAS,* vol. 20, pt. 1 (1947), pp. 1-11; B. Ch. Chhabra, "Expansion of Indo-Aryan culture during Pallava rule, as evidenced by inscriptions," *JASB, Letters,* vol. 1 (1935), pp. 14-20; Wheatley, *The Golden Khersonese* (Kuala Lumpur, 1961) pp. 273-278, and *Impressions of the Malay Peninsula in ancient times* (Singapore, 1964), Appendix 1; Stanley J. O'Connor, Jr., *Hindu gods of peninsular Siam.* Artibus Asiae Supplementum XXVIII (Ascona, 1972), *passim*; George Coedès, *Les états hindouisés d'Indochine et d'Indonésie* (3rd edition, Paris, 1964), pp. 99-101; Alastair Lamb, "Miscellaneous papers on early Hindu and Buddhist settlements in northern Malaya and southern Thailand," *Federation Museums Journal,* New Series, vol. 6 (Kuala Lumpur, 1961). Each of these works contains references to early publications of this material, not all of which were adequate by present standards of epigraphic interpretation, so that it is all the more regrettable that some of the fragments have been lost (cp. Chhabra, "Expansion," p. 14).

11. See Note 10 above and, additionally, Alastair Lamb, "Report on the excavation and reconstruction of Chandi Bukit Batu Pahat, Central Kedah," *Federation Museums Journal,* New Series, vol. 5 (1960), pp. 1-108; F. E. Treloar, "Chemical analysis of some metal objects from Chandi Bukit Batu Pahat, Kedah: suggested origin and date," *JMBRAS,* vol. 41, pt. 1 (1967), pp. 193-198; Janice Stargardt, "The extent and limitations of Indian influences on the protohistoric civilizations of the Malay Peninsula," in Norman Hammond (ed.), *South Asian archaeology* (London, 1973), pp. 279-303. Cf. also F. E. Treloar and G. J. Fabris, "Evidence for the contemporary existence of two Kedah sites," *JMBRAS,* vol. 48, pt. 1 (1975), pp. 74-77; B. A. V. Peacock, "Pillar base architecture in ancient Kedah," *JMBRAS,* vol. 47, pt. 1 (1974), pp. 68-86.

12. Cf. Note 168 to Chapter 7.

13. Cf. Note 189 to Chapter 2. Since Pelliot's paper of 1904, Tārŭmā has usually been equated with the **Tâ-lâ-muâ* 多羅磨 of *T'ung Tien,* chüan 188, p. 1010 and other T'ang texts, but two decades ago Dr. L. C. Damais rejected this identification on the grounds of the imperfection of the phonetic correspondence between the toponym and the transcription [Review of Poerbatjaraka's *Riwajat Indonesia, BEFEO,* vol. 48 (1957), p. 611], but if the middle syllable of the name is short and unstressed, I am inclined to regard 羅 as a not unsatisfactory transcription of *-ru-*. N. J. Krom [*Hindoe-Javaansche Geschiedenis,* p. 78] derived the name Tārŭmā from Malay *tarum* = indigo, but it also occurs as a toponym in the vicinity of Cape Comorin and, as Tārumāpura, in an inscription from Cōḷapuram in the same district [*South Indian Inscriptions,* vol. 3, pt. 2 (Madras, 1902), p. 159]. In view of the fact that the two streams mentioned in the inscription bore the names of rivers found in both North and South India and in Ceylon — Candrabhāgā (now Chenab) and Gomatī [Chhabra, "Expansion," p. 32] — it would seem that the name Tārŭmā was also probably adopted from the subcontinent, although the process may not have been uninfluenced by the existence of a local toponym.

14. J. Noorduyn and H. Th. Verstappen, "Pūrṇavarman's river-works near Tugu," *BKI,* vol. 128 (1972), pp. 305-306.

15. Wheatley, *The Golden Khersonese,* pp. 39-40.

16. The significance of the Ptolemaic corpus for the study of urban origins in Southeast Asia is examined in an Appendix, pp. 439 - 462.

17. *Kao-Seng Chuan* 高僧傳, compiled by Hui Chiao 慧皎 between 519 and 554, chüan 3, ff. 15-16. In this text Guṇavarman is transcribed as *G‛i̯əu-nâ-bʽuât-muâ 求那跋摩 .

18. *Sung Shu* 宋書 chüan 5, f. 5 recto; *Tŭ-shu Chi-chʻeng*, "Pien-i tien," chüan 97.

19. *Sung Shu*, chüan 97, f. 5 recto. In chüan 5, f. 8 recto the transcription 呵羅單 is used, and in various other texts the following forms: *Xâ-lâ-tʽâ 訶羅陁/陀, ——— 軍 (evidently a graphic error for 單), ——— 且 (an error for 旦), and probably ——— 單單 (presumably a simple dittography). [For a succinct summary of what is known about this kingdom see O. W. Wolters, *Early Indonesian commerce. A study of the origins of Śrīvijaya* (Ithaca, N.Y., 1967), pp. 151-153, and "Studying Śrīvijaya," *JMBRAS*, vol. 52, pt. 2 (1979), p. 28]. In this last paper Professor Wolters has sought to connect the Chinese transcription with *Ciruton* (*ci* = river), the present-day name of a stream in western Java. The phonetic correspondence is imperfect in so far as Ruton is concerned (the *ci* can presumably be disregarded in discussing the name of the country), but it should perhaps be noted that the name of the stream in question is today sometimes vocalized as Arutön (*vulgo* Ciaruten or Ciaruteun) [e.g. Himansu Bhusan Sarkar, *Corpus of the Inscriptions of Java*, vol. 1 (1971), pp. 3 and 10, note 11], a circumstance which renders the transcription a good deal more accurate.

20. *Tʻai-pʻing Yü-lan*, chüan 787, f. 7 recto. Śrī Vijaya is here transcribed as *Si-lji bʽji-tśi̯a-i̯a 尸梨毘遮耶.

21. *Liang Shu*, chüan 54, f. 13 recto. Cp. *Kien-tʽâ-lji 斤陀利) in *Sung Shu*, chüan 97, f. 4 verso. In the Chinese record Śrī Varanarendra is transcribed as *Śiak bʽuâ-lâ-nâ-lien-tʽâ 釋婆羅那憐陀; [the Indian] Rudra as [*Tuok] *Li̯əu-tʽâ [笁] 留陀. Traditional Chinese historiography since the Ming dynasty has located the capital of this kingdom at Palembang, but this is no guarantee of a continuous tradition from Liang to Ming times. There are numerous examples of able Chinese annalists who clung to traditional but erroneous identifications long after they had become incompatible with contemporary knowledge. It has been suggested that *Kân-tʽâ-lji represented an original name close to *Kandārī* or perhaps *Gandhārī*, and Gabriel Ferrand drew attention to a passage in Ibn Mājid's *Ḥāwīyah* (A.D. 1462. Bibliothèque Nationale, *MS Arabe 2292*, f. 110 verso) which may have referred to a district of Kandārī كندارى in northeast Sumatra ["Le K'ouen-louen et les anciennes navigations interocéaniques dans les mers du sud," *JA*, 11th series, vol. 13 (1919), pp. 238-241]. Senarat Paranavitana has similarly suggested that the Chinese form was a transcription of Sanskrit *kandara* (etymologically meaning "torn away or broken by water" and therefore signifying a strait), which he claims to read as a place of shipwreck in the *Sīhaḷavatthuppakaraṇa* (for which see p. 266 below): *Ceylon and Malaysia* (Colombo, 1966), pp. 4-5. Unsupported by other evidence, this suggestion can only be treated with reserve.

22. For references see Note 7 above.

23. Cp. the houses of the Lin-I, in which doors allegedly opened toward the north [p. 391 below], but *cave* the overtones of symbolism in the Chinese accounts of this ethnic group, and which may not be entirely absent in the description of the Red-Earth Kingdom.

24. The most detailed account of the Red-Earth Kingdom occurs in *Sui Shu*, chüan 82, ff. 3 recto - 5 verso, in which is incorporated the report of the Chinese envoys who travelled thither in 607-8. Parallel passages also occur in *Pei Shih* 北史 chüan 95, ff. 11 verso - 14 recto; *Tʻai-pʻing Yü-lan*, chüan 787, ff. 1 verso - 3 recto; and *Wen-hsien Tʻung-kʻao*, chüan 331, ff. 2602-3, and similar but not identical accounts in *Tʻung Tien*, chüan 188, ff. 1009-1010 and *Tʻai-pʻing Huan-yü Chi*, chüan 177, ff. 1 verso - 3 recto. The passage in question has been translated and evaluated in its historical context by Wheatley, *JMBRAS*, vol. 30, pt. 1, pp. 122-133.

The transcription employed by Kʻung-Ying-ta 孔頴達, compiler of the *Lieh Chuan* 列傳 chapters of the *Sui Shu*, as well as by all subsequent authors, is *Tśʻi̯äk-tʻuo 赤土, which may possibly illustrate the Chinese penchant for choosing transcriptions that not only reproduced foreign toponyms phonetically but also translated or interpreted them. *Tśʻi̯äk Tʻuo, meaning "Red Earth," may just possibly have been intended as a transcription of Skt. *rakta* = "red". It is not unlikely that this is the country which features, under the name Raktamṛttika, in a votive inscription erected by a shipmaster (*mahānāvika*) in Kedah, perhaps as early as the middle of the 5th century A.D. [Cf. Note 10 above]. A note added to the paragraphs on *Tśʻi̯äk-tʻuo in *Tʻung Tien* and *Tʻai-pʻing Huan-yü Chi* states that the king "resided in *Səng-gʻi̯e̯* (僧祇 = Skt. Siṁha = lion) City, which "was also called the City of the Lion 獅子城 ." All of which suggests that possibly Malay Singora (Thai = Songkhlā) may be a contracted form of Siṁhapura. The evidence as to the location of the Red-Earth Kingdom is certainly not opposed to such a situation: its northern boundary was the ocean; it lay beyond Langkasuka from the Chinese point of view; and it was ten days' voyage from *Tśʻi̯äk-tʻuo to Campā. All the texts state that the capital was more than a month's journey from the point where the envoys first met their native escorts, presumably at the sea coast. Only the interior of the Malay Peninsula can meet this exigency, and I have elsewhere suggested the upper Kelantan basin as a possible site for the capital. On re-reading the texts, however, I am inclined to think that, despite the unanimity of the Chinese authors, which in any case is likely to be misleading as they probably all borrowed from the now lost *Chʻih-tʻu Kuo Chi* 赤土國記 [Vide *Hsin Tʻang-Shu* 新唐書 chüan 58, f. 19 recto], 月 (month) should be emended to read 日 (day). A site a day's journey from the coast was much favored in early Southeast Asia: cf. Note 105 to Chap. 3.

The neighborhood of Singora further recommends itself as the general vicinity of the Red-Earth Kingdom as it would have permitted the journey of a day and more to have taken the form of a voyage through the skein of waterways, both natural and artificial, that extended northwards from the city. Perhaps the Chinese envoys who reported on this journey traversed the lake that is now known as Thale Sap Songkhlā, or, possibly, in view of the fact that a metal cable was used as a hawser for their vessel (金鑠以覽 : *Sui Shu*, chüan 82, f. 4v) — which probably implies towing in a situation where sails were impracticable — they were hauled along the canal whose vestiges are today called the Klong Ō, and which has recently been revealed by Dr. Janice Stargardt ["Southern Thai waterways: archeological evidence on agriculture, shipping and trade in the Śrīvijayan period," *Man*, vol. 8, no. 1 (1973), pp. 5-29]. An alternative route might have been by way of the Kok Tong canal which, crossing the Satingphra peninsula at its northern end, was bordered by monumental structures that are unfortunately too degraded to allow even their groundplans to be recovered [Stargardt, *op. cit.*, pp. 12-16]. For archeological investigations on the Satingphra peninsula see H. G. Quaritch Wales, "A stone casket from Satiṅpra," *JSS*, vol. 52, pt. 2 (1964), pp. 217-223; Alastair Lamb, "A stone casket from Satiṅpra: some further observations," *JSS*, vol. 53, (1965), pp. 191-195; Lamb, "Notes on Satingpra," *JMBRAS*, vol. 37, pt. 1 (1964), pp. 74-87; Stanley J. O'Connor, "Satingphra: an expanded chronology," *JMBRAS*, vol. 39 (1966), p. 137-144; O'Connor, "An early brahmanical sculpture at Soṅkhlā," *JSS*, vol. 52, pt. 2 (1964), pp. 163-169; Janice Stargardt, "The Srivijayan civilization in southern Thailand," *Antiquity*, vol. 47 (1973), pp. 225-229; "Man's impact on the ancient environment of the Satingpra Peninsula: South Thailand. I: The natural environment and natural change," *Journal of Biogeography*, vol. 3, no. 3 (1976), pp. 211-228 and II: "Ancient agriculture," *ibid.*, vol. 4, no. 1 (1977), pp. 35-50. Dr. Stargardt's discovery at Kok Tong of Fu-nan style pottery accords well with the remark in the *Sui Shu*, chüan 82, f. 3r that "Chʻih-tʻu was another kind of *Vnam*" 赤土國扶南之別種也. The main settlement on the Satingphra peninsula occupied a rectangular area of 1,600 meters by 900 meters; its longitudinal axis was inclined 13° west of north, the precise orientation of the east wall at Beikthano (p. 167 above).

25. Fairly detailed paragraphs relating to *Bʻu̯ân-bʻu̯ân are included in *Hsin Tʻang-Shu*, chüan 222C, ff: 3 recto-4 recto; *Tʻung Tien*, chüan 188, f. 1009;

T'ai-p'ing Huan-yü Chi, chüan 176, ff. 12-13; and Wen-hsien T'ung-k'ao, chüan 331, f. 2602 (this being the most detailed of all). The Liang Shu, chüan 54, f. 10 recto and the Chiu T'ang-Shu 舊唐書 chüan 197, f. 2 recto use the transcription 盤盤, while I Ching's *B'uən-b'uən 盆盆 (I Ching, Nan-Hai Chi-kuei Nei-fa Chuan 義淨南海寄歸內法傳 chüan 1, f. 3 verso) almost certainly represents yet a third form. The relevant passages are translated and analysed by Wheatley, Khersonese, pp. 47-51.

The essential information relating to the location of this polity is as follows: it lay to the southwest of the Lin-I on a bay of the sea; it was south of Dvāravatī but adjoined [i.e., presumably was north of] Langkasuka. The only site capable of meeting these exigencies is that part of the isthmus in the vicinity of Bandon, which suggests a possible connection of the name with the Phumpin of earlier European maps. It is interesting to note that *B'uân-b'uân was the only one among such isthmian kingdoms as can be identified in which the royal style and the titles of the chief ministers were couched in a language other than Sanskrit. The royal style in this case, beginning with *i̯ang- 楊, may have incorporated Cam yaṅ (=god) or, more probably, Malay yang (a prefix in titular honorifics), or even an Old Mōn form. Of the titles of the four ministers, three included the Old Khmer kuruñ.

26. Material relating to *Tān-tān is to be found in Pei Shih, chüan 95, f. 15 recto; Sui Shu, chüan 82, ff. 7 verso et 8 recto; Hsin T'ang-Shu, chüan 222C, f. 8 verso; Nan-hai Chi-kuei Nei-fa Chuan, chüan 1, f. 3 verso; T'ung Tien, chüan 188, f. 1010; T'ung Ch'ih 通志 chüan 198, p. 3177; T'ai-p'ing Huan-yü Chi, chüan 177, f. 7 recto et verso; Wen-hsien T'ung-k'ao, chüan 332, f. 2607. The relevant passages are analysed by Hsü Yün-ts'iao; "Notes on Tan-tan," JMBRAS, vol. 20, pt. 1, pp. 47-63, and translated and annotated by Wheatley, Khersonese, pp. 51-55. Hsin T'ang-Shu employs the transcription 單單 which may be read as *tān or *źi̯än, but I Ching's use of 呾呾, together with the commonest form 丹, support the first reading.

Available information about the location of this kingdom is contradictory and obscure. The fact that it is described once as northwest, and once as west, of *Tâ-lâ-muâ 多羅磨, here identified with the Tārumā of Pūrṇavarman's inscription from Tugu [Cp. Note 13 above], although Damais has called this equivalence in question [BEFEO, vol. 48 (1957), p. 611], and the circumstance that in several texts it is linked with *B'uân-b'uân and Tś'i̯äk-t'uo, afford some indication that Tân-tân was situated on the Malayan isthmus. However, this is not wholly consonant with the production of white sandalwood, obtained from Santalum album, Linn., which is not native to the isthmus, nor even to the peninsula. Two alternatives present themselves. Either the Chinese were mistaken, or Tân-tân was in the eastern part of the archipelago (certainly not farther west than Central Java) where Santalum album is indigenous. There are two points on which the Chinese may have been mistaken. In the first place, the wood may have been a re-export. Second, the Malays often apply the term cendana puteh to the wood of Eurycoma, Jack, and it is possible that this was the sandalwood reported on in this instance. O. W. Wolters [Early Indonesian commerce: a study of the origins of Śrīvijaya (Ithaca, N.Y., 1967), pp. 201-206] has argued forcefully for a location in Central Java, mainly on the grounds that I Ching's list of countries in the South Seas (in which *Tân-tân occurs) excludes all but archipelagic locations, and that the products of *Tân-tân are more consonant with those of Java than with those of the peninsula. Presumably Wolters is here thinking specifically of the white sandalwood. I do not think that the first point has been adequately demonstrated, but there is considerable weight in the second. The location of *Tâ-lâ-muâ is clearly crucial to the solution of this problem, and the choice of site for *Tân-tân depends on our acceptance or rejection of Damais's argument. At the moment I rest with a non liquet. In any case, wherever *Tân-tân may have been situated, it seems to have been within the broadly Malaysian realm.

27. E.g., in 530, 531, 535, 571, 581, 585, c. 616, 666/7 and 668/9. See Wheatley, "Desultory remarks on the ancient history of the Malay Peninsula," in John Bastin and R. Roolvink, Malayan and Indonesian Studies. Essays presented to Sir Richard Winstedt on his eighty-fifth birthday (Oxford, 1964), pp. 52-53

and 71-72.

28. Kalāh appears under a variety of orthographies in both Chinese and Arabo-Persian texts. The main Chinese source is *Hsin T'ang-Shu*, chüan 222C, ff. 3 verso - 4 recto and chüan 176, f. 2 verso, with parallel passages in *T'ung Tien*, chüan 188, f. 1007; *T'ai-p'ing Huan-yü Chi*, chüan 176, f. 2; and *Wen-hsien T'ung-k'ao*, chüan 331, f. 2600. The usual transcription is *Kā-lā 哥羅, but the *Hsin T'ang-Shu* adds the alternative 箇羅 (also rendered in Anc. Ch. as *Kā-lā) and the extended form *Kā-lā-piəu-sa-lā 哥羅富沙羅. This latter was interpreted by Gabriel Ferrand ["Le K'ouen-louen et les anciennes navigations interocéaniques dans les mers du sud," *JA*, 11th series, vol. 14 (1919), pp. 236-238] as a mislection for *Kā-lā-ṣa-piəu-lā = Kalaśapūra, the capital of Suvarṇadvīpa, which was mentioned in the *Kathāsaritsāgara* (p. 264 below) and known to the Chinese under other transcriptions, e.g., *Ka-lā-śịa-bịuət 迦羅舍佛 (*Chiu T'ang-Shu*, chüan 197, f. 3 recto) and 迦羅舍弗 (*Hsin T'ang-Shu*, chüan 222C, f. 6 recto); and *Kā-lā-śịa-pịuən 哥羅舍分 (*Hsin T'ang-Shu*, chüan 222C, f. 7 verso and *Wen-hsien T'ung-k'ao*, chüan 332, f. 2608). In Arabo-Persian texts this toponym, always in its abbreviated form, occurs as Kalāh كله et var. كله, كلا, كلاه, قلعة [*Vide* Wheatley, "Desultory remarks," pp. 68-70]. I have elsewhere discussed the tangled skein of evidence relating to the location of Kalāh [*ibid.*] and argued for a position in the neighborhood of Mergui. Several previous authors have preferred Kedah (summarized in Wheatley, *Khersonese*, pp. 55-59 and 216-224), and Professor S. Q. Fatimi has sought to justify a site in the vicinity of Kelang ["In quest of Kalah," *JSEAH*, vol. 1, no. 2 (1960), pp. 62-101], a point of view subsequently espoused with enthusiasm by Brian E. Colless, "Persian merchants and missionaries in medieval Malaya," *JMBRAS*, vol. 42, pt. 2 (1969), pp. 10-47, especially pp. 21-34.

Whether or not they refer to ancient Kalāh, the following remarks of Commandant E. Lunet de Lajonquière are not without relevance to this chapter:

> Mes prospecteurs birmans m'ont donné un renseignement que j'ai eu le gros désappointement de ne pouvoir contrôler. Il y aurait, dans l'île de Kisseraing [Kittha-reng] (une des grandes îles de l'archipel de Mergui), au débouché de la Lanya, une ancienne grande ville abandonnée et en ruines. L'île est maintenant absolument déserte, infestée de tigres et de serpents et je n'ai pu trouver personne pour m'y accompagner. Il aurait fallu organiser une petite expédition, cela ne m'était pas possible pour diverses raisons.

["Rapport sommaire sur une mission archéologique (Cambodge, Siam, Presqu'île Malaise, Inde, 1907-1908]," *Bulletin de la Commission Archéologique de l'Indochine* (Paris, 1909), p. 185].

In attempting to locate isthmian toponyms such as those discussed here, we should remember that the earliest archeological remains in peninsular Thailand have come from Chaiyā and Nakhon Sithammarat, both of which have yielded statues of mitred Viṣṇus in a style closely comparable to that characteristic of the later days of Fu-nan, and therefore probably to be dated to the 6th century A.D. In the Wat Mahātat in Nakhon Sithammarat there is also an inscription in an early Pallava script which J. G. de Casparis dates not later than the 6th century, while a small brick Śaivite shrine in the same town still houses a *liṅga* very similar to some of those discovered by Louis Malleret in his investigations in the Trans-Bassac. This information is derived from a report by Alastair Lamb, *Federation Museums Journal*, New Series, vol. 6 (1961), pp. 70-72. One particular Viṣṇu image from Chaiyā has been dated to the 5th (or possibly the 4th) century, and is therefore older than a closely similar Viṣṇu from Oc-èo. It is, in fact, to be accounted the most ancient Hindu image so far discovered in Southeast Asia; *vide* Stanley J. O'Connor, Jr., *Hindu gods of peninsular Siam*. Artibus Asiae Supplementum XXVIII (Ascona, 1972), p. 39.

29. *Hsin T'ang-Shu*, chüan 222C, f. 3 verso; Abū Dulaf (c. 940) *apud* Yāqūt's *Mu'jam al-Buldān*, Wüstenfeld's edition, vol. 3, p. 302.

30. Abū Dulaf, *loc. cit.*

31. *Baqqam* = brazilwood (*bresil, brezile, bersi*, etc.), a name superseded by sapan[wood] not later than the 17th century. It is the product of *Caesalpinia sappan*, Linn. Cf. Ibn al-Bayṭār, *al-Jāmiʿ fi al-Adwiyah al-Mufradah* (Lucien Leclerc's version in *Notices et extraits des manuscrits de la Bibliothèque Nationale*, vol. 23 (Paris, 1877), no. 314.

32. Abū Zayd, in J. T. Reinaud's edition of the text, *Relations des voyages faits par les Arabes et les Persans dans l'Inde et à la Chine dans le IXe siècle de l'ère chrétienne* (Paris, 1845), p. 92.

33. ʿAlī al-Masʿūdī, *Murūj al-Dhahab wa-Maʿādin al-Jawhar* (943); in text of C. Barbier de Meynard and Pavet de Courteille, *Les prairies d'or* (Paris, 1861), p. 307.

34. Tamil = Kaḍāram.

35. For discussions of the archeological remains in the neighborhood of Gunung Jerai see Notes 10 and 11 above, together with three papers dealing with Candi Bukit Batu Pahat in *Malaya in History*, vol. 4, no. 2 (1958), pp. 2-9, vol. 5, no. 1 (1959), pp. 13-20, and vol. 5, no. 2 (1959), pp. 5-21. I Ching 義淨 in *Ta Tʿang Hsi-yü Chʿiu-fa Kao-seng Chuan* 大唐西域求法高僧傳 f. 98 transcribed Kaṭāha as *γât-tsʿât 羯茶. For a summary of references in Indian literature see Wheatley, *Khersonese*, pp. 278-280.

36. Cf. Notes 10 and 11 above. For a discussion of early settlements on the west coast of the Siamo-Malay peninsula see Brian E. Colless, "The early western ports of the Malay Peninsula," *JTG*, vol. 29 (1969), pp. 1-9.

37. Cf. pp. 10 and 11 above; Wheatley, *Khersonese*, p. 276.

38. Sylvain Lévi, "Ptolémée, le Niddesa et la Bṛhatkathā," *Etudes asiatiques*, vol. 2 (Paris, 1925), p. 26.

39. E.g., Vesuṅga, Verāpatha, Java, ——, Vaṅga, Elavaddhana, Suvaṇṇakūṭa, Suvaṇṇabhūmi, Tāmbapaṇṇi.

40. Paul Pelliot, "Deux itinéraires de Chine en Inde à la fin du VIIIe siècle," *BEFEO*, vol. 4 (1904), p. 232. *Lâ-jiwpt is mentioned in Chia Tan's itinerary in *Hsin Tʿang-Shu*, chüan 433, f. 30 recto, and in the same history, chüan 222C, f. 8 verso it is described as being 5,000 *li* northwards from the sea 北距海五千里, a distance that Pelliot was certainly justified in emending to 50 *li* 五十里 (the graphic difference in the characters is small). Chia Tan located *Lâ-jiwpt on the northern shore of the strait and Vijaya (*Bʿiuət-ẓiäi 佛逝), presumably Srī Vijaya—although this honorific was not uncommon in Indianized Southeast Asia and may conceivably here have referred to another settlement—on the southern shore. *Lâ-jiwpt is also mentioned in the *Sung Shih*, chüan 489, f. 23 recto, and occurs in a Japanese account relating to the 9th century A.D. [Nanjō Bunyū 南條文雄 and Takakusu Junjirō 高楠順次郎 *Futsuryē Indo-Shina* 佛領印度支那 (Tōkyō, 1903), p. 34, and J. Takakusu, *A record of the Buddhist religion as practised in India and the Malay Archipelago* (Oxford, 1896), p. xlv].

41. J. L. Moens, "Srīvijaya, Yāva en Kaṭāha," *TBG*, vol. 77, pt. 3 (1937), p. 337. Cf. also N. J. Krom, "De Naam Sumatra," *BKI*, vol. 100 (1941), p. 10. No archeological evidence of ancient settlement at Seluyut has so far come to light, but it was later the site of a capital of the Johor empire. An alternative identification formerly espoused by George Coedès [Review of Gabriel Ferrand, "L'empire sumatranais de Çrīvijaya," *BEFEO*, vol. 23 (1923), p. 470] and adopted by Paul Pelliot [*Notes on Marco Polo*, vol. 2 (Paris, 1963), p. 766] equates *Lâ-jiwpt with the Malay *laut* = "the sea," a designation that would be analogous to *Samudra* (= Ocean) > Sumatra. The name also occurs, under the

transcription *Lâ-i̯ŭĕt 羅 聿 in the *Hsin T'ang-Shu* as a Pyū dependency (Note 67 to Chap. 4 above).

42. According to Chia Tan (*Hsin T'ang-Shu*, chüan 43B, f. 30 recto), the strait was "100 *li* from south to north." It was probably this same Malay word *sĕlat* that gave rise to Arabic *Shalāhiṭ* لهايط, *Salāhaṭ* لهاط et var., applied to an island and a strait in archipelagic Southeast Asia. In the *'Akhbār aṣ-Ṣīn wa'l-Hind* (c. A.D. 851) [Sauvaget's edition, p. 4] the sea of *Salāhaṭ* or *Salāhṭ* is said to border one side of the island of *Lambri* [< Lampurī = roughly the territory of present-day Aceh], the other side fronting on to the sea of Harkand [the Bay of Bengal and those ocean tracts to the southward]. Mas'ūdī [*Murūj*, p. 330: for text see Note 32] writes of the sea of Kalāh-bār كلابار in much the same context as the *'Akhbār* refers to the sea of *Salāhaṭ*. Later Arab and Persian authors are, generally speaking, less precise in their usage, and *Salāhaṭ* becomes either a distant sea celebrated for its ambergris or an island producing sandalwood, nard, and cloves, a schedule of exports deriving originally from a remark by Ibn Khurradādhbih [*Kitāb al-masālik wa'l-mamālik* (first draft prepared in 846, a second in 885), p. 46 of de Goeje's edition]. For other references to *Salāhaṭ*, see the works of Ya'qūbī, Ibn al-Faqīh, Ibn Rustah, al-Idrīsī, al-Dimashqī, and *Alf Laylah wa Laylah* [conveniently collected in Gabriel Ferrand's *Relations de voyages et textes géographiques, arabes, persans et turks relatifs à l'Extrême-Orient du VIIIe au XVIIe siècles*, 2 vols. (Paris, 1913-14)] and the *Ḥudūd al-'Ālam*, p. 57 of Minorsky's edition.

43. *Hsin T'ang-Shu*, chüan 222C, f. 8 verso.

44. A Sumatran port frequently mentioned by both Chinese and Arab authors from the 7th century onwards. It has usually been identified with the modern port of the same name, but O. W. Wolters has argued for a location in the vicinity of present-day Aceh ["Śrīvijayan expansion in the seventh century," *AA*, vol. 24 (1961), pp. 419-422. Arab and Persian writers consistently praised the quality of the camphor exported from the hinterland of the port, the great authority Ibn al-Bayṭār declaring it to be the best grade of all [No. 1868 of Leclerc's text].

45. Since the publication of a paper entitled "Was Malaka emporium vóór 1400 A.D. genaamd Malajoer?" [*BKI*, vol. 77 (1921), pp. 359-569] by G. P. Rouffaer, Malayu has been identified with present-day Jambi. This kingdom sent its first tribute mission to China in 644/5 [*Hsin T'ang-Shu*, chüan 221D, f. 7 recto; *T'ang Hui-yao* 唐會要 chüan 100, f. 13 verso; *Ts'e-fu Yüan-kuei* 冊府元龜 chüan 970, f. 10 recto].

Professor O. W. Wolters has recently reconstructed the indigenous form of which **Muo-χâ-si̯en* was a transcription as Mukha Asin = "Briny Face" or "Briny Surface" ["Studying Śrīvijaya," p. 30]. The phonetic correspondence is adequate and a river called Banyu Asin (= "Briny Water") flows into the sea to the northwest of the Musi estuary; but I doubt if *mukha* would have been used in the literal sense of water "surface" (although it has been used to denote "the upper side"). However, the dictionaries also cite the derived sense of "estuary" [e.g., Monier-Williams, *A Sanskrit-English dictionary* (New edition, 1970), p. 819, col. 3] and, if Professor Wolters's reconstruction is valid, I would suggest that this is the sense in which *mukha* should be contrued here. The Air Banyu Asin does in fact enter Bangka Strait by means of a wide embouchure which constitutes a very prominent feature on the east-Sumatran littoral.

46. Identified by Louis-Charles Damais, "Etudes sino-indonésiennes: III La transcription chinoise 訶陵 Ho-ling comme désignation de Java," *BEFEO*, vol. 52, fasc. 1 (1964), pp. 93-141. Walaiñ, a name which occurs in several Javanese inscriptions, was probably the seat (*kaḍatuan*) of one of the premier dynasties of Java from the middle of the 7th century to about the middle of the 9th. According to J. G. de Casparis, it was located on the Ratu Båkå plateau [*Prasasti Indonesia*, vol. 2 (Bandung, 1956), p. 255].

47. The equation of **B'uâ-lji* with the present-day island of Bali has been accepted by a preponderance of scholars since Pelliot placed his imprimatur on

de Rosny's suggestion in 1904 ["Deux itinéraires," pp. 270 and 282; L. de Rosny, *Les peuples orientaux connus des anciens Chinois* (2nd edition, Paris, 1886), p. 141], but recently Professor O. W. Wolters has proposed a location in southeastern Java [*Early Indonesian Commerce*, pp. 200-201]. Paragraphs are devoted to *Bʻuā-lji in *Liang Shu*, chüan 54, f. 15 recto; *Nan Shih*, chüan 78, f. 14 verso; *Sui Shu*, chüan 82, f. 8 recto; *Chiu Tʻang-Shu*, chüan 197, f. 4 recto; *Hsin Tʻang-Shu*, chüan 222C, f. 4 recto; *Tʻung Tien*, chüan 188, pp. 1010-11; *Wen-hsien Tʻung-kʻao*, chüan 331, p. 2602. The significant locational information is (1) *Bʻuā-lji was two months' voyage southeast of Kuang-Chou; (2) it was east of Walaiṅ (cf. Note 46 above). This kingdom sent its first tribute mission to China in A.D. 517, but was known to the Chinese in the first half of the 5th century [Paul Pelliot, "Meou-tseu ou les doutes levés," *TP*, vol. 19 (1920), pp. 267 and 433].

48. This was the identification proposed by Gabriel Ferrand, though he read 堀 *kʻuət- for 抾 *gʻi̯uət- ["Le Kʻouen-louen," pp. 301-302]. The name *Gurun* occurs twice in Prapañca's *Nāgara-Kĕrtāgama* (A.D. 1365) [Theodore G. Th. Pigeaud's edition of the text, *Java in the 14th century*, vol. 1 (The Hague, 1960), canto 14, stanzas 3 and 4], but this work is too remote in time from I Ching's *Memoir* for the equation, in the absence of supporting evidence, to command much confidence. Van Eerde identified the first *Gurun* (stanza 3), with its capital of Sukun, as the island of Nusa Penida [apud N. J. Krom, "De eigennamen in den Nāgarakṛtāgama," *TBG*, vol. 56 (1914), pp. 491-552]; and Rouffaer equated the second place of the same name with the Gurung Archipelago [quoted in Pigeaud, *op. cit.* vol. 4 (1962), p. 34 and Ferrand, *loc. cit.*, p. 301]. In default of any better suggestion, I have adopted Ferrand's identification, without necessarily endorsing Van Erde and Rouffaer's locations.

49. Note 25 above.

50. Note 24 above.

51. Note 46 above.

52. *Chiu Tʻang-Shu*, chüan 197, f. 4 verso. The *lontar* is the palmyra palm (*Borassus flabellifera*, Linn., Javanese *lontar* by metathesis < *ron-tal* = leaf of the [Skt.] *tala*). The use of this palm affords some indication that Walaiṅ was in the eastern half of the island of Java, for it only becomes at all abundant in the drier east.

53. *Hsin Tʻang-Shu*, chüan 222C, f. 5 verso.

54. It is interesting to note that perhaps a century later, in Ś 833 [= A.D. 911 (-12)], the Cams — another foreign people — referred to the Javanese capital in a similar manner: *Yāvadvīpapūra* = City of the Island of Java [E. Huber, "Etudes indochinoises, XII, 8," *BEFEO*, vol. 11 (1911), pp. 303 and 309].

55. *Hsin Tʻang-Shu*, chüan 222C, f. 5 verso; *Wen-hsien Tʻung-kʻao*, chüan 332, p. 2608; *Yüan-shih lei-pien*, chüan 42, f. 37 recto; Hsü Chi-yü 徐繼畬 *Ying-huan Chih-lüeh* 瀛環志略 (1848), chüan 2, f. 16 recto. These last two works, compiled at much later periods, assign this event to the Tʻien-pao period, i.e., 742-755; the Tʻang *History* makes no mention of a date.

In another section of the *Hsin Tʻang-Shu* (chüan 222C, f. 10 recto) the new capital appears under the orthography *Bʻuā-Xuai̯-kā-luo 婆賄伽盧, which seems to be no more than a farrago of substitutions and transpositions. Gabriel Ferrand ["Le Kʻouen-louen," pp. 304-5] has restored the first form as Javanese *waruh grĕsik* = sandy beach, a common phrase and place-name, but so far it has not been discovered in Javanese epigraphy. It seems unlikely that the name of the ancient capital was connected with the Waruh Grĕsik (*vulgo* Gresik) of more recent times. For *Bʻuā 婆 as a transcription of Javanese -wa- see Damais, *BEFEO*, vol. 52 (1964).

56. E.g., *Ki̯u-li̯u-mi̯ĕt 拘蔞蜜, a month's voyage to the southeast of Kalāh

258   Nāgara and Commandery

and ten days' journey from *Bʻuā-lji [Hsin Tʻang-Shu, chüan 222C, f. 4 recto; Tʻang Hui-yao, chüan 100; Tʻung Tien, chüan 188, p. 1007; Wen-hsien Tʻung-kʻao, chüan 331, p. 2600]: *Pi̯ə u-dźʻi̯uĕt 不 述 , five days' from *Ki̯u-li̯u-mi̯ĕt [loc. cit.]; *Dʻuā-bʻuā-təng 驃 婆 登 , situated to the east of Walaiñ [Chiu Tʻang-Shu, chüan 197, f. 4 verso]; *Miei-liei-ki̯wo 迷 黎 車 , still farther eastward [ibid.].

57. Man Shu, chüan 6, p. 29.

58. Wen-hsien Tʻung-kʻao, chüan 332, p. 2610.

59. H. Kern, BKI, vol. 65 (1911), pp. 334-336, and Verspreide Geschriften, vol. 7 ('s Gravenhage, 1917), pp. 199-204; N. J. Krom, Hindoe-Javaansche Geschiedenis, (2nd edition, 's Gravenhage, 1931), p. 103; Bijan Raj Chatterjee, India and Java, pt. 2 (Calcutta, 1933), p. 28; Chhabra, "Expansion of Indo-Aryan culture," pp. 33-34; Himansu Bhusan Sarkar, Corpus of the inscriptions of Java, vol. 1 (Calcutta, 1971), pp. 13-14.

60. Krom, Hindoe-Javaansche Geschiedenis, p. 102; Chhabra, "Expansion," p. 33. Diĕng < Di Hyang = seat of the gods, Cp. Skt. Devālaya [L. C. Damais, BEFEO, vol. 48 (1957), p. 627].

61. For references see Note 59 above.

62. W. F. Stutterheim, "Note on cultural relations between S. India and Java," TBG, vol. 79 (1939), pp. 73-84; J. Ph. Vogel, "Aanteekeningen op de inscriptie van Tjanggal," BKI, vol. 100 (1941), p. 445. In India Kuñjarakuñja is the name of a district on the border between Travancore and Tinnevelley where there is a well known sanctuary dedicated to Agastya, and the presence of this place-name in Java is probably also related to the legendary activities of this sage. Cf. L. C. Damais, BEFEO, vol. 48 (1957), pp. 628-631.

63. The archeological remains on the Diĕng plateau are described by N. J. Krom in Inleiding tot de Hindoe-Javaansche Kunst, vol. 1 (2nd edition, 's Gravenhage, 1926). For a general discussion of central Java in early times see Soekmono, "The archeology of Central Java before 800 A.D." in Smith and Watson, Early South East Asia, pp. 457-472.

64. F. D. K. Bosch, "De Sanskrit inscriptie op den steen van Dinaja (682 çaka)," TBG, vol. 57 (1916), pp. 410-444, and "Het Lingga-Heiligdom van Dinaja," loc. cit., vol. 64 (1924), pp. 227-286; Chatterjee, India and Java, pt. 2, pp. 35-40; Sarkar, Corpus, pp. 25-33. J. G. de Casparis finds the name Kañjuruha persisting in that of the present-day village of Kejuron, located to the west of Malang ["Nogmaals de Sanskrit-inscriptie op den steen van Dinojo," TBG, vol. 81 (1941), p. 499].

65. The first stirrings in this emergence of centralized rule in East Java may go back somewhat earlier than 760, for W. F. Stutterheim has drawn attention to a short undated inscription from Jember which paleographically appears to be older than that of Dinaya ["Oudheidkundige aanteekeningen," BKI, vol. 95 (1937), pp. 397-401].

66. Mūlasarvastivāda-ekaśatakarman, Taishō Tripiṭaka, vol. 24, no. 1453, 477c.

67. The location of Śrī Vijaya at Palembang was first proposed by W. P. Groeneveldt in 1880, though the name was then restored as Śrī Bhoja [Notes on the Malay Archipelago and Malacca compiled from Chinese sources (Batavia), pp. 68-76, especially p. 76], and subsequently adopted by Samuel Beal, "Some remarks respecting a place called Shih-li-fo-tsai" in P. A. van der Lith and Marcel Devic (eds.), Livre des merveilles de l'Inde (Leyden, 1883-86), pp. 251-253, and, most notably, by George Coedès, "Le royaume de Çrīvijaya," BEFEO, vol. 18, fasc. 5 (1918), pp. 1-36. The identification has been queried or denied by H. G. Quaritch Wales, "A newly explored route of ancient Indian cultural expansion,"

IAL, vol. 9 (1935), pp. 1-31 [For comments on this paper see Coedès, " A propos d'une nouvelle théorie sur le site de Çrīvijaya," *JMBRAS*, vol. 14 (1936), pp. 1-9]; by J. L. Moens, "*Šrīvijaya, Yāva en Katāha*," *TBG*, vol. 77 (1937), pp. 317-487. Abridged English translation by R. J. de Touché, *JMBRAS*, vol. 17, pt. 2 (1940), pp. 1-111 [Critique by K. A. Nilakanta Sastri, "Notes on the historical geography of the Malay Peninsula and Archipelago," *JGIS*, vol. 7 (1940), pp. 15-42]; and most recently by M. C. Chand Chirayu Rajani, "Background to the Sri Vijaya story—Part I," *JSS*, vol. 62, pt. 1 (1974), pp. 174-211. See also J. Ph. Vogel, "Het koninkrijk Çrīvijaya," *BKI*, vol. 75 (1919), pp. 626-637; C. O. Blagden, "The empire of the Mahārāja, King of the Mountains and Lord of the Isles," *JSBRAS*, no. 81 (1920), pp. 23-28; R. Soekmono, "Tentang lokalisasi Çrīwijaya," *Laporan Kongres Ilmu Pengetahuan Nasional Pertama* (1958), pp. 245-258. The preferred alternative site for the capital of Śrī Vijaya has been one on the Siamo-Malaysian isthmus.

68. The survey, undertaken jointly by the Lembaga Purbakala dan Peninggalan Nasional [of Indonesia] and the University of Pennsylvania Museum in 1974, has been reported by Teguh Asmar and Bennet Bronson, *Archeological research in Sumatra 1974: a preliminary report* [mimeo]. Cf. also Bronson, "A lost kingdom mislaid: a short report on the search for Srivijaya," *Field Museum of Natural History Bulletin*, vol. 46, no. 4 (1976), pp. 16-20; Jan Wisseman, "Archeology in Sumatra—1974," *Indonesian Circle*, no. 6 (1975), pp. 6-8; Bronson, "The archeology of Sumatra and the problem of Srivijaya," in R. B. Smith and W. Watson (eds.), *Early South East Asia* (New York and Kuala Lumpur, 1979), pp. 395-405; Bronson and Wisseman, "Palembang as Śrīvijaya: the lateness of early cities in southern Southeast Asia," *Asian Perspectives*, vol. 19, no. 2 (1978), pp. 220-239.

69. O. W. Wolters, "Landfall on the Palembang coast in medieval times," *Indonesia*, no. 20 (1976), pp. 1-58. In this paper Wolters is concerned primarily with the location of later settlements in the vicinity of Palembang, and the conclusion cited here is implicit, rather than explicit, in his analysis. Much the same point was made by F. D. K. Bosch, "Verslag van een Reis door Sumatra," *Oudheidkundig Verslag uitgegeven door het Koninklijk Bataviaasch Genootschap van Kunsten en Wetenschappen* (1930), p. 156. Recently Wolters has outlined an agenda for the investigation of the many problems involved in arriving at an understanding of the nature of the Śrī Vijayan polity: "Studying Śrīvijaya," *passim*. See also Wolters, "A note on Sungsang village at the estuary of the Musi River in Southeastern Sumatra: a reconsideration of the historical geography of the Palembang region," *Indonesia*, vol. 27 (1979), pp. 33-50.

70. George Coedès, "Les inscriptions malaises de Çrīvijaya," *BEFEO*, vol. 30 (1930), pp. 29-80; Coedès, "A possible interpretation of the inscription at Kĕdukan Bukit (Palembang)," in John Bastin and R. Roolvink, *Malayan and Indonesian Studies* (Oxford, 1964), pp. 24-32; Gabriel Ferrand, "L'empire sumatranais de Çrīvijaya," *JA*, vol. 20 (1922), pp. 1-104 and 161-246; "Quatre textes épigraphiques malayo-sanskrits de Sumatra et de Banka," *JA*, vol. 221 (1932), pp. 271-326; J. W. J. Wellan, "Çrīwijaya, 1250 jaren geleden gesticht," *Tijdschrift van het Koninklijk Aardrijkskundig Genootschap*, vol. 51 (1934); J. G. de Casparis, *Prasasti Indonesia*, vol. 2 (Bandung, 1956), pp. 1-46. The Palas Pasemah inscription is still unpublished, but its substance has been briefly reported by Kenneth R. Hall in Hall and John K. Whitmore (eds.), *Explorations in early Southeast Asian history: the origins of Southeast Asian statecraft*. Michigan Papers on South and Southeast Asia No. 11 (Ann Arbor, Mich., 1976), pp. 69 and 99. Cf. also F. M. Schnitger, *The archaeology of Hindoo Sumatra* (Leyden, 1937); N. J. Krom, "Antiquities of Palembang," *Annual Bibliography of Indian Archaeology* (1931), pp. 29-33, and "De Heiligdommen van Palembang," *Mededeelingen der Koninklijke Akademie van Wetenschappen*, Afdeeling Letterkunde, new series, vol. 1, no. 7 (1938); Jean Przyluski, "Indian colonization in Sumaṭra before the seventh century," *JGIS*, vol. 1 (1934), pp. 92-101; R. B. Slametmuljana, *Kerajaan Sriwijaya* (Singapore, 1963).

For a discussion of Chinese transcriptions of other early toponyms in what is today western Indonesia which either cannot be identified or at best can be assigned only regional locations, among them Ko-ying (哥 營 *Kâ-i̯wäng*),

P'u-lo-chung (蒲羅中 *B'uo-lâ-ṭi̯ung) and Fo-shih-pu-lo (佛逝補羅 *B'i̯u ət-ẓi̯äi-puo-lâ = Vijayapura), see Wolters, Early Indonesian commerce, passim, but especially maps on pp. 353-355, and "Studying Śrīvijaya," p. 29.

71. O. W. Wolters, "Śrīvijayan expansion in the seventh century," AA, vol. 24 (1961), pp. 417-424.

72. George Coedès, "Le royaume de Çrīvijaya," BEFEO, vol. 18, fasc. 5 (1918), pp. 29-31, and Recueil des inscriptions du Siam, vol. 2 (Bangkok, 1929), pp. 35-39; Chatterjee, India and Java, pt. 2, pp. 40-44; Chhabra, "Expansion," pp. 20-27; K. A. Nilakanta Sastri, "Śrī Vijaya," BEFEO, vol. 40 (1940), pp. 252-254.

73. See Coedès, "Le royaume de Çrīvijaya;" Nilakanta Sastri, "Śrī Vijaya;" and particularly Wolters, "Śrīvijayan expansion."

74. For a very full discussion of the commercial milieu within which the Śrī Vijayan polity developed see O. W. Wolters, Early Indonesian commerce. A study of the origins of Śrīvijaya (Ithaca, N.Y., 1967), passim. The earliest extant mention of merchants in Śrī Vijaya appears to be that in the Telaga Batu inscription, c. 686. Cited by Jan Wisseman in Jeremy A. Sabloff and C. C. Lamberg-Karlovsky, Ancient civilization and trade (Albuquerque, N. Mexico, 1975), p. 267.

75. Bronson and Wisseman, "Palembang as Śrīvijaya," p. 233.

76. Bronson and Wisseman, "Palembang as Śrīvijaya," p. 221. For the results of investigations at Kota Cina see E. E. McKinnon, "Kota Tjina — a site with T'ang and Sung period associations: some preliminary notes," Sumatra Research Bulletin, vol. 3, no. 1 (1973), pp. 46-52, and (with Tengku Luckman Sinar S. H.), "Kota China: notes on further developments at Kota China," Sumatra Research Bulletin, vol. 4, no. 1 (1974), pp. 63-86.

77. Bronson and Wisseman, "Palembang as Śrīvijaya," pp. 234-237.

78. Satyawati Suleiman, "A few observations on the use of ceramics in Indonesia," cited by Wolters, "Studying Śrīvijaya," p. 19. I have not been able to consult this paper.

79. Cf. W. F. Stutterheim, "De Kraton van Majapahit," Verhandelingen van het Koninklijk Instituut vóór de Taal-, Land- en Volkenkunde van Nederlandsch-Indië, vol. 7 (1948), pp. 1-131; Theodore G. Th. Pigeaud, Java in the 14th century. A study in cultural history, vol. 4 (The Hague, 1962), chap. 2.

80. Robert Heine-Geldern, "Conceptions of state and kingship in Southeast Asia," Far Eastern Quarterly, vol. 2 (1942), p. 22.

81. Wolters, "Studying Śrīvijaya," p. 19. Wolters cites in support of his comment the Cornell University doctoral dissertation of A. C. Milner, The Malay raja: a study of Malay political culture in East Sumatra and the Malay Peninsula in the early nineteenth century (1977), a work which I have not consulted. There is much on court protocol from the 16th to the 19th century in Soemarsaid Moertono, State and statecraft in Old Java. Modern Indonesia Project Monograph, Cornell University (Ithaca, N.Y., 1963). For the symbolic significance of residential locations in Majapahit, see Pigeaud, Java in the 14th century, vol. 4, chap. 2.

82. Wheatley, The Golden Khersonese, pp. 26-30.

83. Sir Richard Winstedt (ed.), "The Malay Annals or Sejarah Melayu," JMBRAS, vol. 16, pt. 3 (1938), pp. 84-88; C. C. Brown (transl.), "Sějarah Mělayu or 'Malay Annals'," JMBRAS, vol. 25, pts. 2 and 3 (1952), pp. 54-59.

84. Chao Ju-kua 趙汝适, *Chu-fan Chih* 諸蕃志 (Feng Ch'eng-chün's 馮承鈞 edition, Shanghai, 1938), p. 13; Friedrich Hirth and W. W. Rockhill, *Chau Ju-kua* (St. Petersburg, 1911), p. 61.

85. Wang Ta-yüan 汪大淵, *Tao-i Chih-lüeh* 島夷誌畧, transl. in Wheatley, *The Golden Khersonese*, p. 82.

86. Winstedt, "The Malay Annals," pp. 60-61; Brown, "Sějarah Mělayu," p. 30.

87. See, *int. al.*, Kernial Singh Sandhu and Paul Wheatley (eds.), *Melaka*, vol. 2 (Kuala Lumpur, 1981), Chap. 46, Figs. 2 and 3.

88. Sandhu and Wheatley, *Melaka*, vol. 2, pp. 520-3. Cp. the comment of Tomé Pires: (transl.), "Eredia's description of Malaca, Meridional India, and Cathay," *JMBRAS*, vol. 8, pt. 1 (1930), p. 22.

89. Sandhu and Wheatley, *Melaka*, vol. 2, p. 509. Cp. the comment of Tomé Pires: "They [the *Celates* = Orang Laut] serve as rowers when they are required by the King of Melaka, without payment, just for food, and the 'governor' of Bintan brings them when they have to serve for certain months of the year": Armando Cortesão (ed.), *The Suma Oriental of Tomé Pires*, vol. 2: Hakluyt Society, Second Series, no. XC (London, 1944), pp. 264 and 492; Leonard Y. Andaya, "The structure of power in seventeenth century Johor," in Anthony Reid and Lance Castles (eds.), *Pre-colonial state systems in Southeast Asia*, Monograph of the Malaysian Branch of the Royal Asiatic Society No. 6 (Kuala Lumpur, 1975), p. 7, and *The Kingdom of Johor 1641 - 1728* (Kuala Lumpur, 1975), pp. 46-48.

90. Wolters, "Studying Śrīvijaya," p. 18; Coedès, "A possible interpretation of the inscription of Kědukan Bukit," pp. 25 and 29; J. G. de Casparis, *Prasasti Indonesia II: Selected inscriptions from the 7th to the 9th century A.D.* (Bandung, 1956). pp. 15-46; Abū Zayd, in Gabriel Ferrand, "L'empire sumatranais de Çrīvijaya," *JA*, vol. 20 (1922), p. 60, and *Relations de voyages et textes géographiques arabes, persans et turks relatifs à l'Extrême-Orient du VIIIe au XVIIe siècles*, vol. 1 (1913), p. 86; Chao Ju-kua, *Chu-fan Chih*, p. 13; Hirth and Rockhill, *Chau Ju-kua*, p. 60.

91. Wolters, "Studying Śrīvijaya," p. 21.

92. See, for example, E. H. G. Dobby, "Settlement patterns in Malaya," *The Geographical Review*, vol. 32 (1942), pp. 211-232, and "Padi landscapes of Malaya," *The Malayan Journal of Tropical Geography*, vol. 6 (1955), Parts I and II and vol. 10, Parts I, II and III; Norton Ginsburg and Chester F. Roberts, Jr. (eds.), *Malaya* (Seattle, 1958), maps 8 and 9; cp. also p. 81: "The Malay unit of settlement is the village . . . sited along or near streams or along the coast, usually in relatively narrow ribbonlike groupings . . . The structures are not closely clustered but are widely dispersed;" Ooi Jin-bee, *Land, people and economy in Malaya* (London, 1963), Fig. 35; cp. also p. 159: "The houses are set well apart from one another, and there is little tendency for Malay kampongs to assume a compact form . . .;" Zaharah binti Hj. Mahmud, "The period and the nature of 'traditional' settlement in the Malay peninsula," *JMBRAS*, vol. 43, pt. 2 (1970), pp. 81-113; *Atlas van Tropisch Nederland* (Amsterdam, 1938), Plate 6b, maps 6 (Banjarmasin) and 7 (Location not specified): Plate 8e, maps 4 (Jember), 8 (Kerawang), and 12 (Palembang). Archetypical representations of these linear types of settlement can be studied on almost any large-scale map of a coastal tract in Malaysia or Indonesia. In the technical literature such a settlement is often categorized, according to its origin and situation, as a *Strassendorf*, *Marschhufendorf*, or *Waldhufendorf*. For a classic analysis of village form see Albert Demangeon, *Problèmes de géographie humaine* (Paris, 1947), pp. 159-205.

93. Bronson and Wisseman, "Palembang as Śrīvijaya," p. 236.

94. Chao Ju-kua, *Chu-fan Chih*, p. 13; Hirth and Rockhill, *Chau Ju-kua*, p. 60.

Chao took this information from Chou Ch'ü-fei 周去非, *Ling-wai Tai-ta* 嶺
外代答 (1178).

95. Lord Stanley of Alderley, *The first voyage round the world by Magellan*.
Hakluyt Society, First Series, vol. 52, (London, 1874), p. 114.

96. Alfred Russel Wallace, *The Malay Archipelago* (First published by Macmillan
& Co., 1869. The quotation is from the Tenth Edition 1890), p. 94.

97. Cp. Wolters's reference to "a paddle-based culture" in "Studying
Śrīvijaya," p. 18.

98. Cp. H. Th. Verstappen, "On palaeo climates and landform development in
Malesia," *Modern Quaternary research in Southeast Asia*, vol. 1 (1975), p. 16.

99. Cited in Wolters, "Studying Śrīvijaya," p. 19.

100. Chao Ju-kua, *Chu-fan Chih*, p. 10; Hirth and Rockhill, *Chau Ju-kua*, p. 57.

101. *Sui Shu*, chüan 82, f. 5v. On a previous occasion when the envoys were
served food in their lodging, the leaf-platters were 10 feet square.

102. It has been demonstrated experimentally that under certain Malaysian
conditions human bone can decompose and vanish without trace in as short a time
span as forty years [Personal communication from Mr. John Matthews, formerly
Curator of Museums, Federation of Malaya].

103. In the Mekong valley, probably in the 3rd or 4th century A.D., many of the
utensils used for eating (presumably among the ruling class) were of silver
[*Chin Shu*, chüan 97, f. 16v.], and golden goblets played their part at a
banquet in honor of Chinese envoys to the Lion City in 607 (cf. Note 101),
despite the use of leaf-platters for the food courses.

104. Diogo do Couto, *Ásia* (Lisboa, 1778-88), década 21, pp. 469-470.

105. G. de G. Sieveking, Paul Wheatley, and C. A. Gibson-Hill, "Recent
archaeological discoveries in Malaya: 1952-53: the investigations at Johore
Lama," *JMBRAS*, vol. 27, pt. 1 (1954), pp. 224-233; Gibson-Hill, "Johore Lama and
other ancient sites on the Johore river," *JMBRAS*, vol. 28, pt. 2 (1955),
reprinted for the Singapore Historical Society and the University of Malaya
Archaeological Society (Singapore, 1957), n.p; B. A. V. P[eacock], *Guide to
ancient monuments and historic sites*, Part I (Kuala Lumpur, 1959), pp. 7-14;
Wilhelm G. Solheim II and Ernestene Green, "Johore Lama excavations, 1960,"
Federation Museums Journal, New Series, vol. 10 (1965), pp. 1-78.

106. Sandhu and Wheatley, *Melaka*, vol. 2, p. 497.

CHAPTER 7

Urban Genesis in the Indianized Territories

> Continuing to advance, he saw a city with walls of gold, with gardens, groves, and lotus ponds, and [permeated with the aroma of] burning incense.
>
> Mahākarmavibhaṅga xxxii.

In documenting the rise of the city in the western territories of Southeast Asia, we have had frequent occasion to mention the presence in the region of Indian institutions, languages, scripts, architecture, iconographical idioms, mythologies, and religions. Indeed, by the end of what we judge to have been the formative phase of state and urban evolution (which, incidentally, varied considerably in time of appearance and duration between the major culture areas), hierarchies of settlement nodes of a recognizably urban character had been integrated into kingdoms formally subscribing to (though perhaps not always implementing) Indian principles of polity. It would appear likely, therefore, that the maturation, if not the origin, of these states and urban hierarchies may have been in some way connected with the acculturation process by which selected Indian values and norms were adopted by certain individuals, groups, and classes in Southeast Asia.[1] When this process began is presently unknown, but references in early Indian literature would seem to carry it back into the late-prehistoric period.

The Realms of Gold

In the earliest extant stratum of Indian literature in which references to Southeast Asia have been recognized, the region figures merely as a vaguely known realm of wealth and abundance beyond the sunrise, much in the manner in which, in Iberia of the 15th century, El Dorado was perceived as a land of opportunity beyond the sunset. These early references have been analyzed in considerable detail on numerous occasions,[2] and need only be summarized here.

Perhaps the most commonly employed designation was one which incorporated the notion of "gold" or "golden," as in Suvarṇadvīpa, Suvarṇabhūmi (both signifying Land of Gold), or Suvarṇakuḍya (meaning Wall or Frontier of Gold).[3] The earliest mention of *Suvarṇadvīpa* occurs in the *Rāmāyaṇa*, in popular estimation India's "first ornate poem" (*ādikāvya*), which, although traditionally ascribed to the sage Vālmīki, supposedly a contemporary of Rāma, probably did not assume its present form prior to the 2nd or 3rd century B.C.[4] Subsequently the same toponym is mentioned fairly frequently in both Hindu and Buddhist literature. A source for many tales in the former tradition was Guṇāḍhya's *Bṛhatkathā*, said to have been written in the Paiśāchī Prākrit, perhaps in the 1st century A.D. Although long since lost, this work supplied themes for numerous later collectanea, notably Budhasvāmin's 8th-century verse abridgment known as *Bṛhatkathā-ślokasaṁgraha*, which included the story of Sānudāsa, a merchant's son, who penetrated into the interior of Suvarṇabhūmi.[5] From the same source came tales of several voyages to Suvarṇadvīpa which were eventually incorporated in Somadeva's *Kathāsaritsāgara*, including those of the Princess Guṇavatī[6] and the merchants Rudra[7] and Samudraśūra, the last of whom was credited with a visit to Kalaśapura, the capital of Suvarṇadvīpa.[8] It is noteworthy that all three voyagers experienced shipwreck. Also narrated in the *Kathāsaritsāgara* were the odyssey of the brāhmaṇa Candrasvāmin, who sailed to Suvarṇadvīpa in search of his lost children,[9] together with accounts of trading expeditions to the same country mentioned in tales, respectively, of the merchant Iśvaravarman[10] and of King Yaśaḥketu.[11] Nor were references to Suvarṇadvīpa restricted to the *kathā* literature, for the name is cited in none other than the *Arthaśāstra* as the source of a particular class of aloeswood (*agaru*),[12] while Varāhamihira (d. A.D. 587) listed it in his *Bṛhatsaṁhitā* as a country in the eastern sector of the known world.[13] Of a similar type to the tales featuring in the compendia mentioned above is a story included in the corpus of Jain tales known as the *Kathākośa*, in which the King of Suvarṇadvīpa rescued the fleet of Nāgadatta, scion of an Indian merchant family, from "the hollow of the snake-encircled mountain."[14]

This fabled Land of Gold figured equally prominently in ancient Buddhist literature. Probably the most familiar reference is the passage in the *Milinda-pañha* in which Suvaṇṇabhūmi occurs in a schedule of ports "where shipping congregates."[15] Often coupled with this schedule is another in the *Mahā-Niddesa*, dating from the 2nd or 3rd century A.D. and therefore the oldest surviving Pāli commentary. In a gloss on the word *parikissati (parikilissati)*, or "torment," the hazards of ocean voyaging to a series of foreign lands, including Suvaṇṇabhūmi, are listed as heat and cold, gadflies and mosquitoes, wind, sun, serpents, hunger, and thirst[16]— to which might have been added shipwrecks such as were experienced by Princess Guṇavatī and the merchants mentioned in the previous paragraph. The difficulties and vicissitudes of the journey to Suvaṇṇabhūmi are taken up again in one of the collection of Buddhist stories known as the *Divyāvadāna*, dating probably from the 4th century A.D. Here one particular traveller is reported to have approached the country (or more likely a part of its interior) by scaling a mountain range with the aid of rattan ladders.[17] These "calamities of foreign travel" *(deśāntaravipāka)* are illustrated in the *Mahākarmavibhaṅga* specifically with reference to the experiences of merchants sailing to Suvarṇabhūmi from Tāmraliptī, one of India's premier ports situated at the mouth of the Hooghly river.[18]

The *Jātakaṭṭhavaṇṇanā* is another relatively prolific source of citations. In fact, this great compendium of tales, which are so diverse in form and substance that the only characteristic they have in common is their adaptation to a Buddhist purpose, appears to picture an established pattern of trade relations between certain Indian ports and Suvaṇṇabhūmi. As at least the core of the corpus already existed in the late centuries of the pre-Christian era, while a good deal of the material derived from an even earlier period, it is evident that these commercial bonds must have been forged initially before the end of the prehistoric period in Southeast Asia. Generally speaking, the type of tale in which Suvaṇṇabhūmi is mentioned is not greatly different from those in the Hindu collectanea which we have already cited. One such story, for example, tells how Prince Mahājanaka joined with a company of merchants bound for the Land of Gold.[19] Another relates the trading ventures of the brāhmaṇa Śaṁkha in the same part of the world,[20] and two others involve voyages thither from Bharukaccha (modern Broach).[21] In the *Jātakamālā*, a Sanskrit version of the Jātaka tales composed by Ārya Śūra probably in the 3rd or 4th century A.D., Śūrpāraka, also on the northwestern coast of the Deccan, is specified as a port-of-call for merchants trading to Suvaṇṇabhūmi,[12] a commerce which is depicted as reasonably regular and regularized — in its eastern sectors, at least — in Dhammapāla's (probably) 5th-century *Paramatta-Dīpanī*.[23] A similar emphasis on

Suvaṇṇabhūmi as a goal of South Asian traders is evident in several Siṅhalese collections of edifying tales. On at least two occasions in the *Sīhaḷavatthuppakaraṇa*, a corpus which includes stories that were apparently current in southern Asia at the beginning of the Christian era, Suvaṇṇabhūmi is cited as a region where enterprising men, in one case a Buddhist lay-devotee, in the other a goldsmith, might recoup depleted fortunes.[24] A similar tale of a Siṅhalese voyaging to Suvaṇṇabhūmi in search of wealth is to be found in the *Rasavāhinī*, a Pāli text from the first half of the 12th century which, like the *Kathāsaritsāgara* and other "oceans of story," incorporates material from much earlier periods.[25]

It was not only as a milieu for profitable exchange of material goods that Suvarṇadvīpa was perceived in India of the Mauryan and Classical ages, but also as a field for Buddhist proselytization. The *Mahākarmavibhaṅga* attributes the conversion of *Suvarṇabhūmi* to the *Arhant* Gavāmpati,[26] whose voyage to the Land of Gold is actually related in the *Sāsanavaṃsappadīpikā*. This last work also perpetuates a myth of alleged missionary activities in Suvaṇṇabhūmi by the Aśokan *theras* Soṇa and Uttara soon after the Third Buddhist Council, held in the middle of the 3rd century B.C.,[27] a topic which also figures, often with considerable elaboration, in the Siṅhalese ecclesiastical chronicles *Mahāvaṃsa* and *Dīpavaṃsa*[28] and in such works as *Sāmanta-Pāsādikā, Mahābodhivaṃsa, Thūpāvaṃsa,* and *Pūjāvalī*.[29] Even Tibetan sources contribute tardily and in a minor way to the Suvarṇabhūmi corpus. Bu-ston's *Čhos-'byuṅ* (c. 1322), for example, as well as other similar works, have the great Dharmapāla of Kāñcī visiting that region in the 7th century A.D., to be followed some four centuries later by the celebrated Dīpaṅkara Atīśa.[30]

It is unfortunate that none of the texts which are so liberal in their references to Suvarṇadvīpa specifies precisely which territories were included in its bounds, an omission which has left modern authors free to propose their own delimitations. Nor have these invariably been free of national bias. It cannot be random chance that has induced a preponderance of Burmese historians to locate the Golden Land in Burma and a majority of Thai historians to find it in Thailand. By no means unrepresentative is Maung Htin Aung's confident assertion that, "The capital city of Suvarṇabhūmi was Thatōn in Lower Burma"[31] or M. C. Chand Chirayu Rajani's no less peremptory declaration that it was at Chaiya in peninsular Thailand.[32] Certain scraps of evidence gleaned from the works we have enumerated are not incompatible with such opinions, but others — particularly the voyages of the Princess Guṇavatī and Candrasvāmin, and the distinction in at least one passage of the *Mahākarmavibhaṅga* between Suvarṇabhūmi and Dvīpāntara (the archipelago)[33] — could equally plausibly be held to imply that either a part or the whole of Sumatra was intended. This, indeed, appears to have been the prevailing view among Arabo-Persian authors, though al-Bīrūnī seems to have subsumed under the term most of the western part of the Malaysian world. At any rate, in his discussion of India he wrote, "The islands of Zābaj زابج [in the 11th century still vocalized in Southern Arabic as *Zābag* ‹ *Jāvaka*, apparently signifying all or some parts of the Malaysian culture realm] are called *Sūwarn dīb* سُورن ديب (=Suvarṇadvīpa) by the inhabitants of India."[34] Incidentally, this was also the view of the Siṅhalese Buddhist exegete Subhūti, one of the foremost Pāli scholars of the 19th century.[35] In any case, whatever the name signified to those who braved the perils of the ocean, it is more than doubtful if the Indians of the Classical period in general entertained any conception of Suvarṇadvīpa more precise than that of a beckoning eldorado beyond the ocean.[36]

The Dvīpāntara mentioned in the preceding paragraph is another toponym with broad regional implications which appears to have come into use during the earlier centuries of the 1st millennium A.D. The significance of the term was first pointed out by Sylvain Lévi[37] when he noted that a Sanskrit-Chinese lexicon compiled in the 7th or 8th century by a Central-Asian monk Li Yen 禮言 employed Dvīpāntara as a synonym for the Chinese *K'uən-luən 崑崙, itself a generalized term for the various maritime peoples of Southeast Asia.[38] Several references in the *Purāṇas* may be older than Li Yen's work, but all these collections of "old tales" are cumulative texts, so that it is difficult to be certain of the date of any particular piece of information.[39] The name also occurs again in the *Kathāsaritsāgara*,[40] in the *Mahākarmavibhaṅga*,[41] and in Kālidāsa's 5th-century epic *Raghuvaṁśa,* where breezes from Dvīpāntara are described as wafting the scent of cloves over Kaliṅga.[42] A particular passage in the *Guruparamparai, Arāyirappaḍi*, one of the earliest hagiologies of Tamil Vaiṣṇavism, is phrased in such a way as to lead Nilakanta Sastri to conclude that Dvīpāntara denoted the Siamo-Malay Peninsula.[43] However, the prevailing impression left by the suite of references as a whole is of a broad regional designation for the archipelago, probably including at least the southern tracts of the Siamo-Malay Peninsula. This was, in fact, Sylvain Lévi's conclusion.

Occasionally it is also possible to elicit from the rich matrix of early South Asian literature references to nebulous territories apparently located within the capacious bounds of Suvarṇadvīpa or Dvīpāntara. One such reference belongs to the very earliest stratum of extant Southeast Asian toponyms, for it occurs in the Fourth Book of the Bombay Recension of the *Rāmāyaṇa*, as Sugrīva, king of the monkeys, commands his followers to search for Sītā in "Yāvadvīpa embellished with seven kingdoms (*yāvadvīpam saptarājyopaśobhitam*)" and furnished with mines of gold and silver (*suvarṇarūpyakadvīpam; suvarṇākaramaṇḍitam*).[44] There has been considerable, and probably unnecessary, discussion of the location of the territory denoted by this name. There seems no good reason to doubt that it at least included the island of Java, though a case might be made for extending its coverage into the neighboring territories of Kalimantan and/or Sumatra.[45] At least one other name cited in the *Purāṇas* referred to a part of Southeast Asia, namely Kaṭāhadvīpa, modern Kedah; while a second name, Malayadvīpa, has been plausibly assigned to Sumatra. The locations of Kaserudvīpa and Barhiṇadvīpa in Sumatra, however, are more dubious attributions.[46] Ramachandra Dikshitar, an authority on the Purāṇas, is not disposed to admit anything more than that both localities were within the bounds of *Bhāratavarṣa*.[47] Generally speaking, though, the constituent territories within the broadly designated framework of Suvarṇadvīpa were mentioned more frequently in writings of progressively later dates as conceptions of the geography of the area became more formalized. Among such names were Suvarṇakudya (not necessarily to be distinguished from Suvarṇadvīpa),[48] Suvarṇapura,[49] Karpūradvīpa (the Camphor Land),[50] Jāva, Tamaliṁ (which Sylvain Lévi has equated with the Tāmbraliṅga of later times),[51] Takkola,[52] and Kaṭāha, which the *Kathāsaritsāgara* described with engaging hyperbole as "the seat of all felicities" (*ketanaṁ sarva-sampadāṁ*).[53] A number of other possible references to Southeast Asia in ancient Indian literature have been proposed from time to time, but add little to the picture presented here.[54]

The references cited in the preceding paragraphs have already carried us beyond the period with which we are primarily concerned in this volume and, indeed, many of the toponymic traditions which we have touched upon persisted down to quite recent times.[55] If any one theme is to be regarded as dominant in this corpus of references to Southeast Asia in early Indian literature, it is the speculative trading voyage, undertaken at considerable risk and at the hazard of *deśāntaravipāka* but yielding

high profit if brought to a successful conclusion. Kauṭilya, it
will be recalled, in his famous manual of stratagems for worldly
success, ranked the pursuit of profit above all other goals of
life, above even the pursuit of virtue or of love. As the *Rās Mālā*
put it in a later age,

> Who goes to Jāva
> never returns
> If by chance, he returns,
> Then, for seven generations, to live upon
> Money enough, he brings back.[56]

In short, as Majumdar has written in recent times, "If literature
can be regarded as a fair reflex of popular mind, trade and
commerce must have been a supreme passion in India in the centuries
immediately preceding and following [the beginning of] the
Christian era."[57]

The Development of Long-distance Trade to and through Southeast Asia

By the beginning of the Christian era the sea-lanes of
Southeast Asia had already been incorporated into the great
maritime trade route that ultimately came to extend from the Red
Sea to South China. More accurately it should be described as a
series of trade routes, for during this period no one group of
merchants operated throughout its length and no one class of
merchandise travelled from end to end. The only characteristic
common to all its commodities was their status as luxury articles.
The western sectors of this trade route are, generally speaking,
better documented than the eastern. Until the end of the 1st
century A.D. the trade of the Arabian Sea was a virtual Arab
monopoly, but from about that time Greek and Egyptian mariners
began to compete for shares of the Indian cargoes that brought
rich rewards when sold in the cities of the Roman empire. However,
there is no reason to believe that these Mediterranean and Egyptian
merchants penetrated far beyond the cape that they knew as *Komar* or
Komaria, present-day Comorin, the southernmost point of the Indian
subcontinent.[58] Even the author of the *Periplus Maris Erythraei*,
apparently a seaman of wide practical experience, had not voyaged
much beyond Nelkynda on the Malabar coast.[59] Beyond that point the
commerce of the Bay of Bengal seems to have been mainly in the
hands of Indian merchants, with Southeast Asian mariners perhaps
pre-empting an unknown, but almost certainly minor, share of the
cargoes. Many of the former intruded deep into the waters of the
Southeast Asian archipelago, but the bulk of the carrying trade
both in Malaysian (*au sens ethnique*) waters and in the South China Sea

seems to have been controlled by various seafaring peoples referred to collectively by the Chinese of the time as *Mwan-i [蠻夷 Modern Standard Chinese Man-i], or "barbarians."[60] No extant source specifies the precise identities of these Southeast Asian traders, but it may be plausibly inferred that they were the folk subsequently known to the Chinese as *Kʽuən-luən, an ethnikon which, as we have indicated on p. 267 above, apparently subsumed a succession of peoples ranging from Malays in the archipelago to Cams along the coasts of Indochina.[61] From the second half of the 5th century onwards, a group of shippers known to the Chinese as *Puâ-się (波斯 MSC Po-ssŭ) were prominent in the trade between Southeast Asia and China, but have not so far been identified.[62] In the Gulf of Tongking and along the South China coast the carriers of both merchandise and merchants were *Jiwɒt [越 MSC Yüeh] sailors. The final, but very attenuated, sector of this trade route was defined by a trickle of commodities high in value but small in bulk which were transported from South China overland to the capital at Lo-yang.[63] It was presumably over the several stages of this trade-route that the relatively numerous Mediterranean artifacts unearthed in Southeast Asia had travelled eastwards,[64] and doubtless along this route in the reverse direction that had passed the tales of the land of *Thin* (or perhaps *Thina*) "below Ursa Minor" which the author of the *Periplus* had incorporated in his trade manual.[65] It is surely significant, though, that the archeological evidence for Chinese trade goods having been shipped westward along this route is unexpectedly meager, even in excavations conducted in neighboring countries such as Indochina.[66]

When Indian merchants first explored the seaways of Southeast Asia is presently unknown, but it is certain that by the early centuries of the Christian era they were already trading with various groups both on the mainland and in the archipelago. Among the various explanations that have been proposed to account for this intensification of Indian trading activity at about the beginning of the Christian era, perhaps the most credible is that formulated by George Coedès, who attributes the reorientation of Indian commercial interests to changing political conditions in the Mediterranean and Central Asia.[67] Vespasian's (A.D. 69-79) prohibition of the export of precious metals from the Roman empire aggravated a scarcity of gold that had obtained in India since nomadic disturbances in Central Asia during the two centuries preceding the Christian era had closed the Bactrian trade routes over which Siberian gold had hitherto found its way to South Asia.

In default of other readily accessible sources of this metal, it is suggested, Indian merchants turned eastwards to the half-legendary regions beneath the sunrise where not only could gold — allegedly but hardly truthfully — be picked up from the surface of the ground, but where other profitable cargoes, notably spices and aromatics, could be obtained. Southeast Asia has never been one of the world's major gold-producing regions, but in ancient times this metal was a much rarer commodity than at present, so that primitive methods of working it were proportionately more profitable. In any case, and for whatever reason, the motive for a large proportion of the voyages described in the several genres of Indian literature relating to this period was, as we have seen, commercial profit.

Two developments appear to have facilitated the undertaking of voyages to Southeast Asia at this time. The first was of a technological nature. The early centuries of the Christian era witnessed innovations in ship construction which, taking their origins in the Persian Gulf, spread rapidly round the shores of the Indian Ocean. Perhaps the most significant of these technical improvements was the use of a rig which allowed vessels to sail closer to the wind. Ships were also built on a larger scale, among them the κολανδια which the *Periplus* described as sailing directly from South India to Chryse, and which were probably the *k'uən-luən tân* [崑崙單 MSC k'un-lun tan] of a 6th-century Chinese commentary.[68] Other vessels that sailed the Indian Ocean at least as early as the 3rd century A.D., and probably a good deal earlier, were known as *k'uən-luən bɒk*, [崑崙舶 MSC k'un-lun po]. Allegedly they measured 200 feet from stem to stern, and were capable of transporting some 6 or 700 men and more than 300 tons of cargo from South China to Southwest Asia[69] in about two months.[70] These dimensions and capacities may appear unrealistic, particularly in view of Pliny's regarding an Indian ship of 75 tons as large, but the consensual testimony of a considerable corpus of texts and traditions in East and South Asia is not to be rejected casually. It is known, for example, that in the 3rd century A.D. a Central-Asian people rubricated by the Chinese as *Ngiwɒt-źiɐ̯* (月氏 MSC Yüeh-chih) exported horses by ship even as far as Indochina, which implies vessels of substantial displacement,[71] while in A.D. 414 the monk Fa Hsien [釋] 法顯 made the voyage from Ceylon to China on two vessels each of which carried more than 200 souls.[72]

The second development which tended to facilitate, perhaps even encourage, overseas travel by Indians was the expansion of

Buddhism. Brāhmaṇism had paid at least some heed to the laws of Manu which formally prohibited such voyages,[73] while the *Baudhāyana Dharmasūtra* placed them at the head of *patanīyanī* and prescribed a three-year penance.[74] Although in practice the prohibition seems to have been frequently flouted, there is no doubt that it exerted some restraint on foreign voyages.[75] Buddhism, by contrast, by rejecting brāhmaṇical ideas of racial purity and the ensuing fear of pollution through contact with *mleccha*, did much to dispel the Indian repugnance to travel. The greater freedom of movement associated with Buddhist beliefs is reflected not only in the prominence accorded the merchant in the *Jātaka* tales but also in the fact that in several realms of Southeast Asia the earliest material evidence of Indian culture is a statue of the Buddha Dīpaṁkara, "Calmer of the Waters," a favorite talisman of Indian seamen.[76] Standing Buddhas of this type have come to light on sites in Thailand,[77] Việtnam,[78] Sumatra,[79] eastern Java,[80] and Sulawesi. Nor should it be overlooked that one of the earliest artifacts displaying Indian influence so far found in Southeast Asia is an ivory comb engraved with Buddhist emblems that was found at Chansen in Central Thailand, and which may be as old as the first century A.D.[81]

There has been considerable debate as to the regional provenance of the Indian traders who voyaged to Southeast Asia in early times, with the historians of North and South India arguing predominantly as committed protagonists on behalf of their respective homelands. Both regions are, in fact, represented in Southeast Asia by scripts, plastic arts, architecture, literature, toponymy, and ethnological characteristics, while the topographic texts at our disposal testify to sailing routes from virtually the whole length of the Indian littoral. Whereas the *Periplus Maris Erythraei* (para. 60) mentioned Kamara (Ptolemaic Khabêris, i.e. Kāviri[paṭṭinam]), Podoukē (probably close to Pondichéry), and Sōpatma, all on the Coromandel coast, as the points from which *kolandia* set sail for Chryse, Ptolemy (VII, i, 15) located his port of departure (ἀφετήριον) farther north, either in the composite delta of the Kṛṣṇa and Godāvarī rivers or possibly in the neighborhood of present-day Śrīkākulam. Whereas the Chinese pilgrim I Ching in the 7th century, as well as several of the monks whose biographies he recorded,[82] both arrived at, and embarked from, Tāmraliptī at the mouth of the Hooghly, others passed through Nāgapaṭṭinam and the ports of Ceylon, as indeed had Fa Hsien nearly three centuries previously. Nor was this traffic restricted to east-coast ports, for as we have noted, the *Jātaka* tell of voyages to Suvaṇṇabhūmi from Bharukaccha (Ptolemaic Barygaza: modern Broach), Śūrparaka (Ptolemaic Souppara) and Muchiri (Ptolemaic Mouzêris, usually located in the neighborhood of Kranganur), all on the western side of the peninsula. However, during the past quarter of a century it has become increasingly evident that the preponderant cultural influence on Southeast Asia in the earlier phases of Indianization emanated from southern India, with not negligible contributions from the western part of the subcontinent.[83] Without doubt, though, the region whose contribution has been most underrated is Ceylon, one of the two islands that were particularly identified with the cult of the Buddha Dīpaṁkara (the other being Yāvadvīpa — the Island of Java, and possibly neighboring parts of the Malaysian world),[84] and the style center for at least three of the erroneously ascribed "Amarāvatī" Buddhas that feature among the earliest South Asian archeological finds in Southeast Asia.[85]

To summarize briefly: by the beginning of the Christian era Indian merchants had worked their way through the sea-lanes of Southeast Asia and familiarized the inhabitants of certain strategically situated territories with a range of material products, and probably also with some of the less tangible features, of Indian civilization. Within a century or two, in the same territories there would emerge kingdoms whose governance was based on Indian (Hindu or Buddhist) conceptions of social order (Chaps. 3-6), and it is our present task to elicit from exceedingly intractable evidence the mechanisms of that transformation; in part to explain why, when at the beginning of the Christian era the type-representative of Indian civilization in Southeast Asia was the seasonally visiting merchant-mariner, some seven centuries or so later it had become the divine monarch claiming to rule over the four *varṇas*, to follow the Veda, observe the *dharma*, and generally behave according to the prescriptions of the Smṛti canon.

The Formation of the Southeast Asian *Nāgara*

> To understand the negara is . . . to elaborate a poetics of power, not a mechanics.
>
> Clifford Geertz, *Negara*, p. 123.

It would be right and proper at this point to describe the ethnological and ecological situation in Southeast Asia at the time when Indian voyagers first began to probe its seaways. However, this is not a practicable proposition. In the first place, it is not possible to ascribe a date to those earliest explorations. Although some of the references to Southeast Asia in the *Purāṇas*, the *kathā* literature, and the *Jātakas* almost certainly derive ultimately from the pre-Christian era, there is no way in which their information can be assigned a precise date in terms even of centuries. In the second place, the only available periodizations of Southeast Asian prehistory are of so gross a character — in Solheim's schema, for instance, the Extensionistic Period runs from 10,000 to 2,000 B.P. — that they afford only an insecure basis for the investigation of local or short-term changes, even if the latter be conceived as encompassing millennia. In these circumstances, our only practicable expedient is to relate our interpretation of the role of the earliest Indian voyagers to the ethnographic pattern which we have in part reconstituted, in part postulated, for the beginning of the Christian era, being careful to bear in mind, of course, that this is probably subsequent, by an undetermined length of time, to the period when Indians first established links with Southeast Asia.

The third impediment to reconstructing the world of Southeast Asia as it was at the time of the earliest Indian voyages is physiographic in character. The localities where Indian influence subsequently became important were predominantly lowlands (Java being the significant partial exception), and often those developed on the mantle of coastal alluvium which peripherally mitigates the starkness of the region's tectonic skeleton. Depositional forms of this type are liable to rapid (geologically speaking) physiographic change. The Irawadi delta, for instance, is currently building seaward at a rate of more than 60 yards a year, that of the Mekong at between 60 and 80 yards, and the Ci Manuk and Solo deltas at as much as 100 yards annually. And it is not only the structural forms of these sedimentation features which are subject to change, but also the courses of the distributaries which flow over their surfaces. One of the most extensive of these marshy lowlands fringes virtually the whole length of the eastern seaboard of Sumatra. Here prolonged sedimentation under equatorial conditions has produced, and is still augmenting, some 60,000 square miles of alluvium which already account for roughly a third of the area of the island. There is no reason to suppose that the accretion rates of sediments of this type have remained constant in the past, but there have been relatively few attempts to reconstruct changes in alluvial morphologies during the last four

or five millennia. Some years ago Louis Malleret prepared an
apparently unpublished study of the evolution of the Cà-mau
peninsula,[86] Larry Sternstein has summarized available information
about the past positions of the seaward face of the Čhao Phraya
delta,[87] several authors have discussed changes in coastal
morphology in Sumatra,[88] and there have been sporadic investigations
of similar phenomena elsewhere; but for the most part the historian
seeking to reconstruct the physiographies of the past is dependent
on inferences, and not always well founded ones at that. For these
reasons, and because paleoclimatic reconstructions for the past
5,000 years in Southeast Asia are extremely rare, while
extrapolations of results achieved in other parts of the world
(which in any case are usually outside the equatorial zone) are
fraught with unacceptable risks, we shall be forced to locate the
climacteric social transformations which we shall seek to explicate
in the following pages in physiographic settings with rare
exceptions not very different from those of the present time.[89]

Even when we have made these unavoidable concessions to
expediency, we still face the problem of explaining the relatively
high degree of differentiation which characterized Southeast Asian
ethnography at the beginning of the Christian era. Geoffrey
Benjamin has suggested a mechanism, namely ecological
specialization, by which groups at significantly different levels
of sociocultural integration could have evolved in close
juxtaposition to each other while yet maintaining a high degree
of isolation and self-sufficiency,[90] but his exposition sheds little
light on the actual processes of differentiation. What
constellation of factors, for instance, initiated the
centralization processes which led to the emergence of chiefdoms in
several parts of prehistoric Southeast Asia? In Flannery's terms,
which were the socio-environmental stresses that selected for the
evolutionary mechanisms of centralization and segregation in those
distant, unrecorded times? Archeology may ultimately provide clues
to the answers to these questions, and ethnographic parallels aid
our understanding of the processes, but at present we can no do
more than speculate.

It is a commonplace that so-called tribal societies are
characterized by a variety of leveling mechanisms which tend to
restrain variables within the subsystems of society to goal ranges
consonant with an egalitarian life style. Some of these
instruments for the preservation of equality are evident in
present-day Southeast Asian societies. Among certain groups, for

instance, it is incumbent on a local lineage producing a substantial surplus to prepare a feast at which accumulated food resources are distributed to the entire community.[91] Although the donating lineage, and especially the lineage head, derive prestige from their ability to provide the feast, they do not necessarily thereby acquire preferential access to resources or means of production. In other words, the lineage does not, by repeated feast-giving, inevitably come to constitute itself as a superior class within society. However, it is also true, as Flannery has pointed out,[92] that, in appropriate adaptive contexts, nominally equilibrating instruments can be manipulated in such a way as to induce the emergence of hereditable privileged rights over strategic resources. This is presumably what Morton Fried had in mind when he implied that the potential for stratification *in a propitious environmental context* was always present in egalitarian society.[93] For the period with which we are here concerned, which lacks a written record and is furnished with wholly inadequate archeological documentation, we can only suggest possible stress-inducing agents which, in the context of the time, may have effected a limited degree of centralization and differentiation.

One particular instrument favored by numerous authors in times past can be discounted at the outset, namely conquest of one segmental society (or tribe) by another. The ethnographic record testifies that such conquests are seldom permanent, and that, in the absence of a pre-existing measure of centralization, the conquerors do not cohere as a ruling class. This means, of course, that the evolutionary pressures towards stratification must be sought within society, rather than adduced from the operation of hypothetical exogenous factors. Another commonly invoked agent of social change is population increase. In fact, Netting has characterized it as "the critical variable, the engine which sets in motion adaptive changes in a set of related technological and social variables among subsistence cultivators."[94] If this be so, it is still not at all clear how the engine operates and precisely which adaptive processes it selects for. In the classic Malthusian view, population growth is regarded as a dependent variable contingent on changes in the availability of food, which in turn are a function of advances in technological expertise.[95] To this, Ester Boserup nearly two decades ago opposed the view that, at least under conditions of primitive agriculture, population growth is an independent variable; the final determinant of productivity, and therefore of the food supply, in her view being availability of

labor.[96] In this formulation, agricultural technology is most
likely to change when population pressure (which, of course, is not
at all the same thing as population density) exceeds a particular
critical level. From this point onward, continued increases in
population may induce changes in farming practices designed to
enhance productivity. If they do this successfully, they almost
inevitably augment gross yields.[97] Hence Netting's conclusion cited
earlier in this paragraph. Inherent in this model is the
implication that farming systems, far from constituting enduring
phases of evolutionary adaptation reflected in particular patterns
of population and settlement, are in fact themselves sensitive and
reasonably rapid responses to the changing impact of demographic
pressures on natural resources. It follows from this line of
reasoning that, in regions of high physiographic diversity, where
population densities and pressures are also often subject to great
variation, contrasting land-use systems (ecotypes) are likely to
occur in close juxtaposition; which is precisely the situation that
we inferred from the archeological evidence in Chapter 2. Indeed
Boserup's model may not implausibly be characterized as supplying
the demographic and economic dimensions to Benjamin's cultural and
ethnographic interpretation which we had occasion to mention in the
same chapter.

This rationale of developments in prehistoric Southeast Asia
at present can be no more than a suggestion, one expedientially
conceived possibility from among many. Even the grosser
demographic characteristics of the region such as population sizes,
densities, and rates of growth are to be inferred only from
archeological data which are totally inadequate in both type and
quantity, even when supplemented by ethnographic analogy, while the
subtler measures of age and sex ratios, life expectancies and
mortalities are wholly unknown, perhaps with rare exceptions
unknowable. But the concept of population pressure can be defined
adequately, and therefore employed effectively, only with reference
to specific patterns, and at least potentially measurable
intensities, of land utilization. Consequently, although the
notion has been invoked fairly frequently by writers on Southeast
Asian prehistory,[98] it must be regarded as a component in a so-far
untested, and indeed presently untestable, hypothesis.

Another possible cause of socio-environmental stress which
has sometimes been invoked as an agent of social change in
Southeast Asia in early times is agricultural innovation,
potentially in the form of a new crop or combination of crops, a

new tool, or a new technology involving both. In this context, it
is the adoption of wet *padi* as a staple grain crop which comes most
readily to mind. We have already seen in Chapter 2 that this crop
probably diffused from the piedmont zone into certain ecologically
favorable localities on the alluvial lowlands during the 1st
millennium B.C. Such a transduction often necessitates the
adoption of new technological aids, and it may have been in these
or similar circumstances that the spade-like implements discovered
at Shih-chai Shan and Đông-sơn (Note 71 to Chap. 2) were replaced,
so far as *sawah* cultivation was concerned, by simple types of *aratra*.
This last suggestion is pure speculation, but in any case the
wet-*padi* techno-complex represented an intensification of
cultivation and a greater relative investment in agricultural
labor. And what is equally important, by inducing significant
differentiation in the productivity, and hence inequalities in the
value, of farm land, it may well have encouraged the development
of social stratification. Furthermore, as the relatively
restricted acreage of land subject to the new technology came
increasingly to assume the character of a capital asset, so it
would have tended to stimulate competition for a scarce resource,
thereby reinforcing the trend towards social stratification and not
improbably leading ultimately to the expansionism customarily
associated with the chiefdom.[99]

One particular agricultural innovation deserves special
mention, namely irrigation. There is, of course, no question of
the construction of large-scale hydraulic systems of the type to
which Karl Wittfogel ascribed the power of generating coercive,
bureaucratic controls.[100] Schemes on this scale, which reconstitute
an ecosystem by wholesale remodelling of the landscape, in any case
are a result more than a cause of the institutionalization of
centralized leadership. Small-scale, localized irrigation, by
contrast, does little more than modulate a given ecosystem.
Although it involves the construction of dams, reservoirs, flumes,
wells, and short feeder canals, and not infrequently provides for
the disposal of flood water, it requires no elaborate social
organization, and demands no labor resources beyond those available
through reciprocal arrangements to family or neighborhood groups.
As such, it is capable of acting as one of a nexus of functionally
interrelated factors operating to augment agricultural
productivity: to which extent its potential efficacy as a generator
of social change is on a par with that of any other agricultural
innovation inducing inequalities in land values. That such

localized irrigation schemes existed in various parts of Southeast Asia at about the beginning of the Christian era has been established in Chapter 2, and some of them may well have been initiated in somewhat earlier times. Construction of even the simplest wet-*padi* field involves at least a minimal control of water, even if it amounts only to provision of a means of removing excess rainfall at certain seasons of the year. And that technology, it is inferred, was introduced into the alluvial lowlands during the 1st millennium B.C. (see Chap. 2).

The socio-environmental stresses which have been adduced in the preceding paragraphs as potential selectors for mechanisms of centralization and segregation all offer the possibility of archeological confirmation at any time in the future. A model of chiefdom formation recently devised by Jonathan Friedman, by contrast, relies for its interpretative power almost exclusively on ethnographic analogy explicated in terms of Marxist social theory. Starting from the observed properties of a single, currently existing, tribal society, Friedman attempts to deduce the properties of a spectrum of derivative societies some of which ultimately attain the integrative level of full statehood.[101] The society in question, that of the Kachins, swidden cultivators of dry *padi* and other crops on mountain slopes in the so-called Triangle region of Upper Burma,[102] is characterized by an apparent oscillation between two political forms, one egalitarian (*gumlao*) without any sort of chiefs, the other hierarchical (*gumsa*), with certain individuals laying claim to hereditary rank.[103] The point of departure for Friedman's exposition is the prevalence of generalized exchange[104] among Kachin lineages. The resulting unidirectional circulation of women establishes the structural necessity of a flow of prestations in the opposite direction, thereby permitting the valuation of women, alliances, and, indeed, of whole lineages, in terms of bridewealth goods. By discriminating between wife-givers (*mayu*) and wife-takers (*dama*), this generalized exchange system induces a hierarchy of statuses which affords a structural basis for, but does not prescribe, the emergence of relative social rank. This is achieved through claims on the supernatural, which are affirmed when a chief represents his lineage as a corporate entity before the spirits of fertility at a community feast. Both chief and lineage thereby acquire prestige which is subsequently translated into absolute rank during the generalized transfer of women between lineages — the prestige of a lineage being reflected, of course, in the value of its daughters.

In short, the surplus which makes the feast possible in the first instance is converted into prestige, which in turn generates affinal ranking. Friedman summarizes the internal logic of the argument, in Kachin (that is "emic") terms, as follows:[105]

> 1. A wealthy lineage head, A, who can afford to give great feasts to the entire village, can only do so because he has good harvests.
> 2. But the way in which the lineage head ensures good harvests is by sacrificing to the local and celestial spirits. That is, wealth is not the product of labor and control over others' labor but the "work of the gods."
> 3. Thus, if A is successful, it must be because he has more influence with the spirits.
> 4. But influence can only be the result of a closer genealogical relationship.
> 5. Therefore, A must be more closely related to the local spirits, which is where the chain of supernatural communication begins.
> 6. The claim that A's lineage is the same as that of the local spirit, and that his ancestor is therefore the territorial deity, thus becomes perfectly natural.

From the external ("etic") point of view, a chiefly lineage is thus simply one which has succeeded in inserting itself at a higher segmentary level in the genealogical structure of the community. In Flannery's terms (Chap. 1, p. 26), this is a classic case of usurpation, in which the whole regulatory agency of a tribe passes under the control of a subsystem, here a lineage, which it formerly regulated. Phrased in a different idiom, relative affinal ranking has been converted into absolute social age in relation to a common ancestor. Moreover, as the common ancestor, the progenitor of the community, is also the territorial spirit, the chiefly lineage in the direct line of descent is automatically senior to all others in the territory, and those who take its wives are classed together as sibling lineages. In other words, the community in this phase of its evolution constitutes a conical clan, a relatively extensive common-descent group which ascribes absolute rank according to genealogical distance from the main line of descent.[106]

In proposing the term "conical clan," Paul Kirchhoff emphasized the flexibility of such stratified kin groupings in the face of change, as well as their potentialities for the evolution of socially and politically differentiated hierarchies.[107]

Subsequently this capacity for aggrandizement has been documented in numerous ethnographic reports and, in the case of the Kachin, analysed in some detail by Friedman. Internally, the status of the chief is continually reinforced by his developing capacity to translate economic surplus first into prestige and subsequently into rank, by virtue of which he is able to impose new exactions (in the form of tribute and other obligations) on members of subordinate lineages. But the increased demand for surplus leads to an inflation of all prestige goods (Kachin = *hpaga*), which in turn threatens every level of the conical-clan hierarchy with indebtedness. In these circumstances, a progressive differentiation of rank, by exacerbating debt inflation, induces an increased verticalization in the flow of wealth.[108] However, the degree of hierarchization ultimately attainable is determined by the rate of surplus accumulation. For the process to continue, either technology must be capable of augmenting productivity to keep pace with accelerating demand (which is unlikely to happen except in very unusual circumstances), or there must be currently uncultivated land open to colonization. In either event, the hierarchization of rank and verticalization of flows of wealth can, in Friedman's view, continue to the point at which, in Marx's terms, an "Asiatic" state comes into being.[109] A progressive increase in absolute surplus would certainly appear to be capable of rendering vertical relations dominant throughout the community, and even an increase in relative surplus might well effect the same result. In which connection, we can add that such increases could plausibly have been engendered by the previously postulated movement of Southeast Asian farmers from the piedmont zone down to alluvial lowlands, with the concurrent adoption of wet *padi* as a major crop. In any case, the timing would have been consonant with such an interpretation, and Friedman has actually specified examples of this type of development in later times: Kachin groups which migrated down to the plains of Assam did, in fact, develop small polities in the chiefdom mode.[110]

If territorial aggrandizement continues at a rate sufficient to maintain productivity, the polity will sooner or later exceed the direct governmental capacity of the chief's household, so that he will be constrained to delegate authority in the form of grants of patrimonial benefices in return for stipulated administrative services in the manner described in Chapter 1, accompanied in all probability by the delegation of responsibilities for the performance of certain public duties to liturgical associations.[111]

By this phase in the interacting processes of differentiation (segregation in Flannery's terminology) and centralization, lineage rank is established by descent without reliance on either wife-giving or feasting. In fact, women are now transferred centripetally upwards either as tribute or by means of hypergamous unions,[112] and feasts come merely to symbolize the ritual, political, and economic power inherent in rank. At the same time, the patrimonial-style assignment of particularized administrative duties to genealogically determined ranks tends to extend the power and authority of a ruling lineage to a whole quasi-sacred aristocracy. As Friedman puts it, "A sacred segmentary hierarchy whose function is to control the reproduction of the society through its access to the supernatural emerges as a class which is identical with the state."[113] And ultimately,

> With the continued growth of surplus and the emergence of the state, the political hierarchy which had formerly been generated by the economic flows of horizontal exchange comes, finally, to dominate that flow. The chief who becomes a sacred king naturally appropriates all of the community rituals . . . The head of state climbs a good deal further up the ancestral hierarchy — he is no longer the representative of the community to the gods, but descends from the heavens as the representative of the gods to the community.[114]

Or, looked at from another point of view:[115] whereas in the earlier phases of development authority had been validated by association with the sacred, authority now manipulated sanctity as an instrument for the acquisition and retention of power.

Friedman's analysis makes it clear that the structural transformation envisaged in the preceding paragraphs does not invariably run its full course. More often than not, an increasing demand for surplus with which to acquire prestige and thereby to establish control over the disposal of labor and materials, allied with associated increases in population density and population pressure, lead to a progressive deterioration of the ecosystem, with a concomitant decline in yields, and a decreasing *relative* surplus. This last the chief alone is in a position to counteract, specifically by using his control of a growing proportion of the total available surplus labor to enlarge his *absolute* surplus. But, as the chief's appropriations come to comprise an ever larger proportion of a diminishing surplus, dissension arises between debtors and creditors in all sectors of the system: in the horizontal circuits between affines, and in the vertical hierarchy between superior and subordinate chiefs and lineages. In the case of the Kachin, these stresses result, it is alleged, in periodic popular revolts which devalue both prestige goods and social status, thereby suppressing social rank and restoring an egalitarian political form.[116] But this symmetrical oscillation between egalitarian and stratified orders is possible only when opportunities for migration combine with the demographic dispersion that sometimes follows on revolt to permit the regeneration of the swidden ecosystem. When the ecosystem turns more or less permanently maladaptive, however, the restored egalitarian society is required to adapt to an ecosystem substantially different from that in which the stratification process had been initiated. In other words, the oscillatory, short-term cycle is displaced through a unidirectional, long-term cycle, each segment of which is characterized by distinctive political and social forms. In this way Friedman attempts to account not only for the reversibility of Kachin *gumlao-gumsa* social integrations at one end of the political spectrum and for the formation of "Asiatic" states at the other end, but also for a series of hierarchical sociopolitical systems (Kachin, Chin, Haga, Wa) allegedly resulting from the devolutionary process which we have just described, and which Friedman himself defines as "the structural transformation that occurs when a social formation reproduces itself in continually deteriorating conditions of production."[117]

The formulation outlined in the preceding paragraphs is an ambitious attempt to generate within a single deductive model a continuum of polities whose order of appearance in eastern Asia is, in Friedman's words, "determined by the evolution or degradation of the conditions of production."[118] It involves, of course, an application to specific circumstances of the Lévi-Straussian conception of kinship terminology as a branch of semiology, and concerns itself, therefore, primarily with the internal logical structures of the meanings of sets of symbols. Lévi-Strauss himself goes even further, at least in his later works, and strongly implies that events and structures are perceived in terms of binary oppositions which constitute a universal attribute of the human mind. Although the Lévi-Straussian line of argument is consistent with the "formal ethnography" of Floyd G. Lounsbury and some others in the United States,[119] it is by no means universally accepted as the most profitable approach to kinship studies. Any of the other currently favored approaches, functionalist, cross-cultural inductionist, evolutionist, cognitive, or whatever would almost certainly lead to different conclusions. Most British functionalist anthropologists, for instance, probably regard systems of kinship terminology as responses to different patterns of social organization, and Edmund Leach has in fact explicated the oscillation between Kachin *gumlao* and *gumsa* orders essentially in these terms, with the invocation of the additional factor of strong influence by external political factors.[120] For this author, who has undertaken extensive field investigations in the Burma highlands (an advantage denied to Friedman), *gumsa* stratification is a kind of imitation of the political order of neighboring Shan groups. *Gumsa* organization, he writes, "was adapted to fit with Shan political ideas, so that Shan princes who wanted to employ Kachins as mercenaries employed only *gumsa* Kachins, and this led to the absorption of the lesser hill tribes into the *gumsa* system."[121] By which I take it he means that Kachin *gumsa* chiefs were absorbed as subordinate rulers into Shan chiefdoms, in which status they received the support of Shan centralized power. Difficulties would have arisen, in Leach's words, "only when external factors led to a decay of Shan power. It is then that Kachin chiefs would get the chance to assume powers close to that of a *saohpa* [Shan prince], and it is only then that a *gumlao* revolt [was] likely to ensue."[122] And at least partly for the following reason:

> The Kachin chief who aspires to the position of a Shan *saohpa* cannot consolidate his position . . . He cannot accept women from his Shan adherents without prejudice to his position as a Kachin; he cannot go on giving women to his Kachin adherents . . . without prejudice to his status as a Shan prince. Or, to put it in another way, the Kachin chief can "become a Shan" without loss of status but his commoner Kachin followers cannot. Therefore, in becoming a Shan, the Kachin chief tends to isolate himself from the roots of his power, he offends against the principles of *mayu-dama* [wife-giver/wife-receiver] reciprocity, and encourages the development of *gumlao* revolutionary tendencies. Then with the first shift in the economic and political wind his power collapses altogether. In his rise to power a Kachin chief depends upon the support of his relatives; but, if over-successful he can retain his position only with the aid of external authority.[123]

Even if Friedman's model is accepted on its own terms, it still incorporates certain structural ambivalences. In the first place, by no means every anthropologist will subscribe to Lévi-Strauss's claim, espoused in the present instance by Friedman, that generalized exchange can be developed into a principle capable of explaining the evolution of egalitarian society into a society of hierarchically ordered classes. Leach, a prominent opponent of Lévi-Strauss in this particular arena, characterizes the latter author's elaborate explication of this principle as follows:

> Thus reduced, the theory sounds preposterous, and even when presented at full length it is still open to all kinds of criticism of the most destructive sort, and yet there *is* an odd kind of fit between some parts of the theory and some of the facts on the ground even though, at times, the facts on the ground perversely turn Lévi-Strauss's argument back to front![124]

Furthermore, some scholars might well take issue with Friedman's somewhat simplistic view of the functioning of swidden ecosystems, and of the relations of short-term oscillations to their envelope curve. Nevertheless, the model is surely the most encompassing interpretation of state formation yet devised for any part of the world, and, as such, it throws additional light on numerous topics discussed in earlier chapters of this volume. It is unfortunate that the specific basis of the theory somewhat restricts its application in the present instance, mainly because generalized exchange is by no means universal in Southeast Asia. Lévi-Strauss has discerned an axis of "privileged territory for generalized exchange" running in archaic times from western Burma northeastwards through China[125] to eastern Siberia, and today a preferential rule of matrilateral cross-cousin marriage is not unknown in Sumatra, the Nusa Tenggara, Maluku, and elsewhere in Indonesia.[126] However, restricted exchange (*échange restreinte*)[127] has been postulated for Java in pre-Indian times, and is presently found in both developed and vestigial forms in communities virtually throughout the rest of Indonesia.[128] Unless one is prepared to resort to the functionalist expedient of invoking a transformation of certain systems of kinship terminology in historic time in response to changes in social organization, the Friedman formulation, whatever its potentialities as a normative model in the northern territories of Southeast Asia, appears to be of doubtful applicability to much of the archipelagic realm.

The truth of the matter, stark and inescapable, is that we cannot reconstruct with confidence the processes of societal differentiation in prehistoric Southeast Asia. The possibilities which we have been discussing are just that, neither more nor less, supported though they may be in varying degrees by ethnographic analogy. In these circumstances, we shall simply assume that a spectrum of hierarchical political and jurisdictional organizations, ranging from some of Philippine *barangay* type[129] through more highly differentiated systems of the order of Kachin gumsa societies and Chin chiefdoms[130] to strongly developed and centralized paramountcies such as the Kingdom of Tien (p. 91 above), had already come into existence in parts of Southeast Asia at the time, which is at present undetermined, when Indian culture first diffused into those regions.

For an earlier generation of historians of precolonial Southeast Asia, carrying among their intellectual baggage the categories and attitudes of 19th-century imperial politics, the causal relationship between trade and state was obvious and direct: the polities that first became visible in the early centuries of the Christian era were empires of conquest strung along the eastern sectors of the South Asian, maritime, trade route and were ruled by Indian dynasts *au sang pur*. Political power had reached out along the trade routes to the East as European flags were to follow in the wake of commerce during the 18th and 19th centuries. At a slightly later phase in the interpretative process the emphasis shifted from colonies of conquest to colonies of settlement comprising communities of Indians planted amid aboriginal tribes to whom they brought the blessings and benefits of a superior civilization. This was the theme that permeated several books by the Indian historian R. C. Majumdar[131] and, with few exceptions, the works sponsored by the Greater India Society. It was also espoused from time to time by Indian public figures who were not primarily historians, notably by Rabindranath Tagore, who once referred in good Ratzelian terms to "that age when she [India] realised her soul, and thus transcended her physical boundaries."[132] Subsequently one particular variant of this theme attributed the initiation of the process of state formation to the organizing skills of a relatively small number of Indians, primarily traders, who by precept and action, often aided by intermarriage with indigenous women, established Indian cultural traditions on the soil of Southeast Asia. Perhaps this point of view received its most imaginative expression in the writings of Gabriel Ferrand,[133] but it was carried to its logical conclusion in the magistral expositions of Nicholaas Krom.[134] Nor was it entirely absent in the works of George Coedès,[135] doyen of historians of this period, and author of the most comprehensive theory of so called "Indianization" to date, who, in a metaphor reminiscent of *Manu* IX:35-40, categorized Indian culture in Southeast Asia as a transplant rather than a graft: "l'Inde . . . a exporté partout la même plante qui, suivant la nature du terrain où elle s'est développée, a produit des fruits de saveur différente."[136]

The interpretations cited thus far have all attached considerable importance to the activities of Indian traders in Southeast Asia, either as precursors or agents of political control or as themselves transmitters of Indian cultural traits. Almost alone in denying traders any significant role in this momentous transformation was Jacob Cornelis van Leur, who constructed his theory of Indianization around the ritualistic and consecratory roles of the brāhmaṇa priesthood.[137] It is apparent that none of

these explanations is completely satisfying. In fact, the conquest
interpretation is no longer viable, while various objections can
be, and often have been, advanced against any particular version of
the alternative hypotheses: that traders would, generally speaking,
have been incapable of transmitting the subtler concepts of Indian
thought, that Hinduism was not a missionary religion, that it would
have been difficult to integrate non-Indians into the Hindu social
system except as *mleccha*, that the culture which had defined itself
in Southeast Asia by the 7th century A.D. was one of literati
rather than of merchants or warriors, and so forth. The truth of
the matter is, I suppose, that each hypothesis contains some truth,
some elements that should be included in any reinterpretation of
what was indubitably one of the most momentous instances of
large-scale acculturation in the history of the world. My own
opinion is that the available evidence, both archeological and
literary, is so meager and obscure that several internally
consistent hypotheses might be devised to account for it, and that
a number of analytically discrete though continually interacting
processes were in fact involved in the transformation. What
follows is an interpretation that seems, given the inchoate state
of the investigation, to offer a reasonably coherent, though
generalized and inevitably partial, explanation of events in
Southeast Asia during the first half of the first millennium A.D.

The Hinduization of Western Southeast Asia

We have seen that, by the beginning of the Christian era,
Indian merchants were weaving an intricate web of trade relations
with communities both on the mainland and in the archipelago. It
has also been suggested that Southeast Asian voyagers to India were
equally effective intermediaries between the two great culture
realms.[128] Owing to the nature of the evidence currently to hand,
however, it is not practicable to arrive at an informed estimate of
the importance of such contacts. That "Malaysians" in the broadest
ethnic sense reached Madagascar and the east coast of Africa in
early times is not in dispute,[139] and they were allegedly reported
in Baṣrah in the 7th century,[140] but archeological testimony to the
presence of Southeast Asians in India in early times is lacking and
references in Indian literature are extremely rare. In fact, I
have noted only two, and both are illustrative of conditions at an
undetermined period in an archetyped past rather than records of
actual events. The first is a bare mention of the departure from
Bharukaccha of Suvarṇabhūmi merchants (*vaṇijā*), presumably setting

sail for their homeland;[141] the second is a reference in the *Kathāsaritsāgara* to the presence in India of four merchants from Kaṭāha. It is possible, though, that towards the end of the 2nd century B.C. at least one Yüeh expedition voyaged as far as India, while in about the middle of the 3rd century A.D. a ruler in the lower Mekong valley dispatched an envoy to a counterpart somewhere in the subcontinent.[142] But that is all the evidence at present available. Yet, despite the paucity of primary documentation, whether archeological, epigraphic, or literary, it is not unreasonable to infer on general grounds that, by the beginning of the Christian era, certain Malayo-Polynesian peoples, others of whom in all probability had already reached at least as far west as Madagascar and as far east as Tonga and Samoa, had raised landfalls in South Asia. They were members of a maritime culture whose representatives were capable, as one author has said, "of traversing immense distances in accordance with the laws of their environment, of wind systems, currents and the migratory patterns of the animals upon which they were dependent, and [of] discovering islands, not as Europeans discover them, by chance, but naturally where birds and fish led them."[143] And the stretches of ocean sailing involved in crossing the Bay of Bengal were considerably less intimidating than those known to have been traversed by the eastern wing of the Malayo-Polynesians in their colonization of the Pacific. Nevertheless, it must be admitted that, as matters stand at present, the notion that Southeast Asians traded in the ports of South Asia in prehistoric times is almost wholly inferential. Equally undocumented but difficult to disregard in the culturally diversified context of the time is the virtual certainty of the existence within prehistoric Southeast Asia of trading networks willing and able to respond to commercial opportunities afforded by external contacts of whatever sort.

We have already adduced evidence attesting the existence of a degree of political centralization and social ranking consonant with a chiefdom level of societal integration at least along the northern rim of Southeast Asia in prehistoric times, while in the protohistoric period polities apparently of this type are implicit in Chinese accounts of the region and in the archeological remains of relatively highly differentiated settlements in the Mekong and Irawadi valleys, as well as in Java and what is now central Viêṭnam. It is in these pre- and protohistoric chiefdoms, we believe, that the dynamism of the Hinduization process should be sought. In systems of graded sociopolitical priorities of this

type, a paramount ruler (and, indeed, lesser chiefs in their
several degrees) are first and last concerned to maximize the
vertical flows of commodities and services (that is to strengthen
instruments of redistribution and mobilization such as tribute and
corvée) as compared with the horizontal flows of prestations that
stem from differences in affinal ranking. The wealth that is
thereby channelled into the coffers of paramount and subordinate
chieftains enables them, each according to his rank in the chiefdom
hierarchy, to undertake construction of the monumental complexes,
to commission the high-wrought art and, in the more advanced
chiefdoms, the high-flown inscriptions, to sustain the elaborately
ritualized style of life, and to mount the lavish ceremonial
spectacles that collectively designate their capitals as seats of
power. On the paramount, as he represents his community before the
gods, devolves responsibility for the prosperity of the whole
chiefdom, and from this role derives the authority which enables
him to extract from his followers the surplus necessary to
propitiate the territorial deity, who will then ensure still more
ample returns from the annual cycle of plant and animal life for
the entire community.

It is more than probable that a paramount chief in western
Southeast Asia at about the beginning of the Christian era, perhaps
caught in a spiralling process of territorial aggrandizement as the
only means of maintaining his status in a flux of competing,
nascent polities, perhaps merely seeking augmented authority with
which to appropriate a larger share of the profits of a burgeoning
commerce, would have benefited from any expedient that enhanced his
own sanctity and thereby affirmed his possession of power. One
such course of action that appears, intentionally or adventitiously,
to have produced precisely these effects was for the chief to
identify himself with an Indian deity potentially more efficacious
than the traditional territorial spirit of the tribe. A favorite
choice was Śiva, whose numerous attributes subsumed aspects of an
ancient South Asian fertility deity of a type by no means unknown
in Southeast Asia. As early as the second half of the 4th century
A.D., inscriptions cut to the order of a King Bhadravarman attest
the dominance of the cult of Śiva-Umā at the royal court of
Campā.[144] In 484 an emissary from Fu-nan to the court of the
Southern Ch'i dynasty at Chien-k'ang reported that Śiva worship was
prominent in the former country and that the god manifested himself
at regular intervals on Mount Mayēntiram (Tamil:Sanskrit =
Mahendra).[145] Subsequently the capital of a paramount ruler of

Fu-nan was known as the City of the Hunter (Skt. *Vyādhapura*; O. Kh. *Dalmāk*) in honor of Śiva in his hierophany as the divine Hunter on the Mahendraparvata,[146] while on a stele from Vằt Čakret the Sanskrit honorific was combined with *adri* (= mountain) in the Śaivitic phrase *Adrivyādhapureśa*, signifying Lord (Śiva) of Vyādhapura-on-the-Mountain.[147] In a passage which probably relates to the reign of Kauṇḍinya Jayavarman at about the beginning of the 6th century, a Chinese history records that among the statuary of Fu-nan were bronze figures with two faces and four arms that can only have been representations of Harihara, a syncretism of Śiva and Viṣṇu. A century or so later, both Khmer epigraphy and a Chinese history located a *svāyambhuvaliṅga* (natural *liṅga*) near present-day Bassac in the middle Mekong valley. It was surmounted by a temple dedicated to the god Bhadreśvara and was known as *Liṅgaparvata* (*Liṅga* Mountain). In the second half of the 7th century a minister of Jayavarman I venerated a similar natural manifestation of Śiva's potency bearing the honorific Kedareśvara.[148] More or less contemporaneously, *liṅga* were being set up in various parts of the country under a variety of vocables such as Śambhu, Tryambaka, Tribhuvaneśvara, Giriśa, and Gambhireśvara. Indeed, in the pre-Aṅkorian kingdom known to the Chinese as **Tś'i̯ĕn-lâp* (MSC = Chen-la), Śaivism was sufficiently prominent to be properly regarded as the state religion. Although even before the end of the 6th century the royal brothers Bhavavarman and Citrasena-Mahendravarman were, in Kamaleswar Bhattacharya's phrase, "de fervents adorateurs de Śiva,"[149] the earliest explicit statement of Śaivite doctrine in ancient Kampuchea is incorporated in an epigraphic invocation to the god recovered from Phnoṃ Bàyaṅ and dated 526 Śaka (A.D. 604).[150]

The broad outlines of the situation in ancient Kampuchea are clearer than elsewhere but Śaivism can be documented in lesser detail in other cultural realms of Southeast Asia at comparably early phases of state development. The dedication of a shrine to Śiva Bhadreśvara at Mĩ-sơn, near the Cam capital, in the second half of the 4th century has already been mentioned. In the Mōn territories during the 7th century, in a settlement on the site of present-day Ū-Thòng gifts were being made to a *liṅga* bearing the honorific Āmrātakeśvara (p. 204). It has been inferred from numismatic evidence that in Arakan at much the same time a reigning Candra-style dynasty was Śaivite.[151] In the Irawadi valley, however, traces of Śaivism are very sparse and of uncertain implication. In central Java the earliest surviving temple complexes, those of

the Diëng and Gedong Songo groups, are purely Śaivite, but there
may be even earlier evidence of Śaivite devotionalism in Java, for
Kern has suggested that the "heretical brāhmaṇas" 外道婆羅
門 mentioned by Fa Hsien early in the 5th century may have been
Pāśupatas, adherents of the oldest form of sectarian Śaivism. More
certainly, in 732 a King Sañjaya commemorated the carving of a *liṅga*
in what his inscription calls "a holy and wonderful shrine
dedicated to Śiva for the good of the world, set in the prosperous
country of Kuñjarakuñja, and surrounded by Gaṅga and other holy
rivers." The *liṅga* was actually raised on Gunung Wukir on the edge
of the Kĕḍu plain. Nearly three decades later, at least two
members of a royal lineage exercising authority in the upper
Brantas valley were protectors of a *liṅga* known as Pūtikeśvara
(p. 238).[152] In eastern Kalimantan, the name Vaprakeśvara may have
implied the practice of Śiva worship at the beginning of the 5th
century (pp. 232 above and 296 below). Although in the instances
we have cited Śaivism was the court religion, both Buddhism and
other Hindu cults, notably from the 5th century onward Vaiṣṇavism,
coexisted in the territories concerned; but it was clearly Śaivism
which was most commonly linked to royal authority.

In a recent prescient exposition of the nature of authority
in 7th-century Kampuchea, Professor O. W. Wolters has demonstrated
that the chiefly hierarchy in the lower Mekong valley and on the
plains bordering the Tonlé Sap was founded on relative intensities
of Śaivite devotionalism, each chieftain seeking to reinforce his
claims to intimate association with the divine through the practice
of *bhakti*.[153] Wolters describes the way in which this ecstatic
piety, almost invariably manifested in personal asceticism,
pervaded what he calls the Khmer or princely elite,[154] and his
observations are confirmed by the frequency with which the term
bhakti occurs in ancient inscriptions.[155] Although the earliest
expressions of *bhakti* in South Asia — as exemplified, for instance,
in the *Bhagavad Gītā* sections of the *Mahābhārata* — appear to have been
fairly restrained in their expression and inspired by sentiments of
respect rather than of passionate devotion, all stressed the merits
of worship over sacrifice and adopted the devotional path
(*bhakti-marga*) to salvation in preference to the path of rites and
ceremonies (*karma-marga*) or that of gnosis (*jñāna-marga*). In
Kampuchea, the *Mahābhārata,* which is the earliest document to
preserve a record of the *bhakti* sect of Pāśupatas, was known as
early as the second half of the 5th century A.D., while one of the
purāṇas (the literature of devotionalism *par excellence*) was cited in

a 7th century inscription.[156] The earliest epigraphic evidence of *bhakti* occurs in connection with Viṣṇu worship in a 5th-century inscription,[157] and is attested in relation to a Śaivite cult early in the 7th century,[158] by which time Sanskrit devotional terms were being incorporated in even Khmer-language inscriptions.[159]

Professor Wolters has also drawn attention to epigraphic records of ascetic practices undertaken by both paramount and subordinate rulers in the 7th century as a measure of their devotion to the god Śiva, the archetypical ascetic,[160] and has documented the presence at Khmer courts during the same century of *bhakti* specialists, particularly Pāśupatas.[161] For all these, ruler and teacher alike, *bhakti* asceticism was the chosen path to spiritual power. A passionate desire for union with the Lord Śiva, utter submission to his will and devotion to his service were conjoint means of participating in the divine reality through the agency of the affections, and thereby of sharing in the god's spiritual potency (*śakti*). Bhavavarman I, founder of *Chen-la*, was explicitly credited with having attained the kingship by virtue of his personal *śakti*, while both Īśānavarman I (reigning in the first half of the 7th century) and Bhavavarman II (reigning in 639) possessed it in abundance, and Jayavarman I (acceded to the throne in about 650) actually claimed to incarnate an aspect of Śiva.[162]

Professor Wolters seems to view the ecstatic piety and mysticism of Khmer chiefs primarily as a means of personal achievement in a world of competing, would-be hegemons. For instance, he writes that:

> The process of 'Hinduisation' . . . was one of empathy, and, because it was possible through the cultivation of mental aptitudes taught by devotional pedagogy, was essentially one of self-Hinduisation. It was a matter of imaginative intention, and the intention which supplied the underlying impulse was that of tapping cosmic power for personal ends.

And:

> Political allegiance, expressed by personal loyalty, was no more than the sum total of the personal religious concerns of the territorial chiefs who believed that an overlordship was providing them with additional means of earning merit and satisfying their death wishes.
>
> . . . 'kingship' remained essentially a personal achievement.[163]

No doubt Professor Wolters is essentially correct in this interpretation so far as it concerns the way in which a Khmer chief understood his relations with Śiva: his motive was indeed to draw on cosmic power for personal ends. But intentions breed actions, and actions consistently informed by a common purpose are likely to produce effects transcending the original intention. One such probably unintended result of merging a chief's *ātman* with that of Śiva would have been to enhance the prestige of his kindred or descent group within the political and/or genealogical structure of the chiefdom. And, as the chiefly ranks controlled the resources with which to construct larger temples and commission more impressive statues and liṅga wherewith to demonstrate their devotion to Śiva, so the vast preponderance of the merit acquired in this way would have inhered in the senior members of the senior kindreds and descent groups, thus tending to create a class endowed with privileged access to the sacred and supernatural. A member of this class, so the argument runs, would have attracted a following of kinsmen and others anxious to share in both the spiritual and material rewards of his exceptional qualities, which constituted in fact a true charisma or gift of grace.

Professor Wolters characterizes a leader capable of attracting followers in this way as a "man of prowess," which the context makes clear is his more felicitous rendering of the concept that certain Melanesian groups and contemporary anthropologists denote by the term "big man," or a "man with a name," in the Biblical phrase "a fisher of men," he who, by force of personality, harnesses other men to the wheel of his ambition and thereby integrates an atomistic tribal system into a temporary consensual unity.[164] But although such a leader enjoys influence and prestige, he does not exercise a true authority. He does not inherit or otherwise come to fill an already existing office or wield ascribed power, but instead achieves his status anew through qualities of personal leadership. And when he dies, his status effectively dies with him. Although certain incidental advantages may accrue to his sons if they seek to emulate their father, they do not inherit his status. It follows that, on this reading, Professor Wolters's interpretation leaves unanswered the question as to how the high achieved status of the "man of prowess," described in one instance as "ablaze with śakti" ("Khmer 'Hinduism'," p. 431), was ultimately transformed into an office that continued beyond the competency of an individual incumbent. We are left to speculate that perhaps a "man of prowess," by virtue of a charismatic personality, a propitious location, and an abundance of pertinent material resources, on occasion succeeded in underpinning his prestige with an especially effective and durable redistributive system. Because the authority structure of the community would also have served as the redistributive structure, the situation might well have proved tolerably stable, perhaps even to the point of surviving the "big man's" demise. In which case the community might have come to perceive its survival as

contingent on the system and, hence, on the continuity of the
leadership, possibly first in the form of an offspring of the "big
man" but ultimately in terms of an office to be filled rather than
a status to be achieved. In this way there would have been created
a continuing position of authority ready to be pre-empted by an
enterprising leader of the next generation. Of course, other paths
to the same end could be proposed but at present they would all be
as speculative as the one I have just suggested.

However, I am inclined to suspect that, by the time when
Śiva-intoxicated paramounts were first recorded in Kampuchea, the
process of state formation was somewhat more advanced than the
preceding argument implies. In my view, neither epigraphy nor
contemporary Chinese accounts of the region are inimical to the
idea that paramountcy ("kingship" in the conventional terminology)
was a more or less permanent office — even though probably as often
as not filled successively by hegemons from competing factions — as
early as the second half of the 4th century. That Śrī Bhadravarman
of Campā (p. 396 below) may have created the style *Dharmamahārāja* for
himself (though there is no compelling reason to suppose so) is no
impediment to the possibility that he succeeded, hereditarily or
by stratagem unknown, to an already existing office. And the same
sort of argument could be made in connection with Pūrṇavarman's
assumption of the style *Rājādhirāja* of Tārūmā in the middle of the
5th century (p. 87 above). Moreover, it is evident that the
settlement at Oc-èo (pp. 127-137), and that at Beikthanomyo perhaps
even more so (pp. 167-173), both of which existed for centuries,
were not created and sustained by a single leader, however
charismatic and powerful. In fact, it is difficult to conceive of
their persistence in the absence of permanent, and probably
ascribed, positions of power and authority. The construction and
support of even Aṅkor Bórĕi as revealed by archeology or of
Īśānapura as described in a contemporary Chinese history would seem
to imply a degree of continued centralized control beyond the
capabilities of a "big man." I have already commented on the
implications of the hydraulic network in the Mekong delta for a
continuity of power and authority in early times, at least in the
territory lying between Aṅkor Bórĕi and Đá-nôi (p. 145 above). If
this interpretation holds and reasonably durable offices exercising
centralized power already existed in the so-called Fu-nan period,
then the era of the "big man" will have to be pushed even farther
back into the mists of prehistory (if it occurred at all), and the
Śiva-worshiping paramounts will have practiced their *tapas* and other

devotions within a framework of institutionalized offices.

The evidence on which to resolve this issue is so meager and ambivalent that it will certainly provoke further discussion but, whatever the outcome, it is clear that devotional asceticism was a powerful means of intensifying chiefly charisma without necessarily effecting radical change in the religious and ethical conceptions of early Khmer society. This low degree of perceived change in the acculturation process was emphasized by Paul Mus half a century ago (although in terms of a rather different argument), when he wrote that, "Ainsi s'est-il fait que lorsque l'hindouisme, avec sa littérature sanskrite, a eu gagné l'Extrême-Orient, c'est avec lui surtout à une expansion des vieilles idées asiatiques que l'on assiste: idées aussitôt reconnues, comprises et endossées par des peuples qui n'ont peut-être pas eu toujours conscience de changer tout à fait de religion en adoptant celles de l'Inde . . . L'hindouisme, dans ses marches lointaines, se résorbe en ce dont, dans l'Inde même, nous l'avions vu sortir."[165]

Available documentation elsewhere in Southeast Asia does not permit analyses of the depth and quality of that undertaken by Professor Wolters for ancient Kampuchea, so that it is debatable to what extent the ramifications of his model of Hinduization are applicable to the other cultural realms of the mainland and the archipelago. However, the prominence of Śaivite cults among the religions of the region in early times affords considerable inferential support for such an interpretation, particularly in Campā and Java; while the prevalence through much of the area in later times of a more developed form of state Śaivism focused, as in the beginning, on the cult of the royal *liṅga* presupposes a preceding widespread phase of religious organization and symbolism that may not have differed markedly in its broader structural outlines from that described by Professor Wolters.

In the phase of sociopolitical development reached in our discussion thus far, certain Southeast Asian paramounts have been able to merge their inner selves with the *ātman* of an Indian divinity, who has replaced the old fructifying territorial spirit of former times. In other words, they have attained the threshold of a divine kingship couched essentially in Hindu terms, although not modeled on a specifically Indian cultural pattern. In this connection, it is germane to our present purpose to note than an instrument for the validation of royal authority already existed in India in the form of the *vrātyastoma*, the brāhmaṇic rite by which indigenous chieftains could be inducted into the *kṣatriyavarṇa*,[166] and it is this stage in the acculturation process that seems to be reflected in Southeast Asian epigraphy by the Sanskritization of dynastic styles in successive generations. By early in the 3rd century A.D., we have seen (p. 147 above), at least one ruler in the lower Mekong valley had assumed the style "King of the Mountain" (Śailarāja, Parvatabhūpāla), thereby identifying himself with the god Śiva on Mount Mahendra.[167] Even more significant assumptions of Indian titularies are recorded from the archipelagic territories. According to a sacrificial inscription from Muara Kaman in eastern Kalimantan dated to about A.D. 400, the reigning king of a small principality bore the name Mūlavarman, and was the son of "the renowned Aśvavarman," founder of the dynasty (vaṁśakartri). Both these names are good Sanskrit, but an apparently predynastic ruler, father of Aśvavarman, was referred to as "the famous prince Kuṇḍuṅga," which seems to have been an Indonesian, or perhaps a Tamil, name.[168] Another and later inscription, this time from Javanese Matarām and dated to 732, records that Sañjaya, founder of his line and bearer of a Sanskrit name, was nephew and successor to Sannaha, who bore a Javanese name in Sanskritized form;[169] while the styles of the first two rulers of Arakan's Candra dynasty would seem to imply a similar process of Sanskritization of indigenous names. Here surely is revealed one of the devices of an emergent political elite seeking to legitimize its authority on an Indian pattern.

It is virtually certain that the process outlined above was not the only way in which elements of Indian culture were diffused through Southeast Asia in the early centuries of the Christian era (although it may have made the major contribution to state formation). It is by no means improbable, for example, that the settlements of kṣatriyan adventurers and their followers and the trading factories of merchant corporations played a part in the transformation. The alleged role of the former has been emphasized by Mukerji,[170] Berg,[171] Moens,[172] and others, but although it is the high-caste entrepreneur who predominates as ship-owner, investor, and speculator in the more popular literature of classical and medieval India,[173] scientifically attested records of kṣatriyan settlement (by which is meant evidence acquired through controlled excavation) are almost totally lacking. Not a single praśasti recording a digvijaya that might have resulted in the establishment of a kṣatriyan-led colony, not a single vaṁśāvali ascribing high birth to ancestors has come to light on any archeological site in Southeast Asia dating to the earlier centuries of the so-called

Indianization process.¹⁷⁴ Yet in the mythologized literature such kṣatriyan enterprises are not unknown. According to the traditional chronicles of Burma, for instance, the earliest kingdom in the Irawadi valley, centered on Tagaung, was founded by a prince who had been deprived of his lands in India,¹⁷⁵ while in the Javanese Pañji narrative-cycle the dispossessed prince from beyond the sea who founds a kingdom is a familiar theme. And, if Filliozat is correct in his interpretation of the Võ-caṇh stele, either the petty dynast MāRaN (Sanskritized in the inscription as Śrī Mara) or one of his descendants may have been a scion of the Pāṇḍyan royal house who, for reasons unknown, settled in southern Indochina.¹⁷⁶ It may possibly be another enterprise of this type that appears, transmuted in the collective memory of Kedah folklore, in the Hikayat Marong Mahawangsa, late though that text be.¹⁷⁷ This event, and others like it, have only too patently been archetyped into heroic situations, and the personalities transformed into culture heroes, so that the reality they mask is now probably lost irretrievably. Nevertheless, they may be transmitting if not echoes of actual events, then resonances of those echoes.

For Indian commercial settlements in Southeast Asia in early times there is epigraphic evidence in the form of inscriptions recording the presence of Tamil merchant corporations. The first, in Tamil and dated to the 9th century A.D., was discovered at Takuapa on the isthmus of the Siamo-Malay peninsula.¹⁷⁸ It records the placing of a tank constructed in the locality under the protection of the Maṇigrāmam, a powerful mercantile corporation from South India.¹⁷⁹ The second inscription, from Labu Tua in western Sumatra, dated 1088, and also in Tamil, similarly refers to a so-called merchant corporation, the Aiññuṛṛuvar, well known in South India,¹⁸⁰ while a third was found in Pagan and still others come from the Pasisir of Java.¹⁸¹ Although it is likely that South Indian medieval mercantile associations should be regarded less as guilds and corporations than as dispersed communities bound by a common code of conduct, and although the evidence is relatively late in time, these inscriptions do imply a mode of cultural transference that may possibly have operated in much earlier periods, and which has in fact been postulated as of primary importance by van Naerssen.¹⁸² Kṣatriyan settlement and mercantile corporation alike would have been potentially able to expand and diversify the habituated means and goals of neighboring communities. Those individuals with the most compelling reasons to change the old order of society — presumably those members of the chiefly class who, by acting as spokesman for their respective groups, came to function as intermediaries between local folk and intrusive aliens — would have been likely to manipulate the new alternatives or inconsistencies thus created in the indigenous value system in an effort to enhance their own prestige and ultimately to achieve some degree of freedom from what they increasingly came to regard as the restrictive bonds of custom. But all such interpretations are at present speculative and inferential.

We have seen that Śaivite devotionalism was a cultural borrowing which, from early in the Christian era, began to consolidate and elaborate the structure of authority relationships in certain strategically situated parts of Southeast Asia, and which ultimately led to the emergence of divine kingship. This, in turn, involved a relation of mutual but asymmetrical dependence between two principles — "the two forces" as they were often called — of Indian social and political organization, namely Brāhmaṇ and Kṣatra.[183] In the Indian formulation, the Brāhmaṇ, being the source from which the Kṣatra springs, is ontologically the prior of the two principles, and consequently the superior; it could exist, though in the political domain it never does, in the absence of the Kṣatra.[184] The human incarnations of these two principles stand in a similar hierarchical relationship to each other, but although the brāhmaṇa is spiritually superior to the kṣatriyan ruler, in the temporal world he is by force of circumstance subject and dependent. Although the brāhmaṇa, who teaches the sacred lore, is, in the words of the Śatapatha Brāhmaṇa, a human god,[185] yet he walks in the suite of retainers behind the kṣatriyan king, and accepts that the role of purohita (king's chaplain) is his livelihood.[186] Whereas the brāhmaṇa's efficacy relates to a realm of values, specifically to the dharma (universal order) of the Brāhmaṇ, the kṣatriya's functions pertain to the particularized realm of artha (interest or advantage). As Louis Dumont has put it, "Temporal authority [exercised by the ruler] is guaranteed through the personal relationship in which it gives preeminence over itself to spiritual authority incarnated in the purohita."[187] Of especial relevance to the concerns of the present chapter is the fact that the elaborate ceremony of consecration, a prerequisite for kingship on the Indian pattern, was a jealously guarded prerogative of the brāhmaṇavarṇa.

The presence of brāhmaṇas in Southeast Asia was attested probably as early as the 3rd century A.D., specifically in the

Kingdom of Five Kings, rubricated by Chinese envoys as *Tuən-suən (pp. 212-214 above), where more than a thousand brāhmaṇas "devoted themselves solely to study of their sacred texts, purified themselves with fragrant flowers, and practiced tapas 精進 by day and night."[188] It is surely significant that these brāhmaṇas were reported in a state whose commercial relations with places as far distant as Parthia in the west and with Tong-King in the east were stressed by the Chinese annalist.[189] Nor was it fortuitous, I think, that there were some 500 Persian and/or Sogdian (*γuo 胡 :MSC = hu) households in the kingdom.[190] Even though Pelliot's suggestion — likely enough on general grounds — that the Chinese distinction between brāhmaṇa and *γuo implies that the latter constituted a merchant community still awaits verification, it is sufficiently evident that the brāhmaṇas in *Tuən-suən had voyaged along the seaways pioneered by the merchant fraternity.

Another state in which brāhmaṇas were in evidence from a comparatively early date, probably the 5th or 6th century, was that known to the Chinese as *B'uân-b'uân (MSC = P'an-p'an), which appears to have been located in what is today southern Thailand (pp. 252-253 above). Of this kingdom it was recorded that, "numerous brāhmaṇas from India have sought out the King to entreat for support: they stand high in the royal favor."[191] At the beginning of the 7th century Chinese envoys to a polity which they called the Red-Earth Kingdom, and which was apparently another chiefdom on the Siamo-Malay isthmus, described the important ceremonial and ritual functions of a corps of several hundred brāhmaṇas, who, they observed, commanded greater respect than did the Buddhists in the same kingdom.[192] These are literary references: the earliest epigraphic mentions of brāhmaṇas in Southeast Asia occur in five of the seven sacrificial inscriptions of King Mūlavarman that we have already mentioned as dating from about the beginning of the 5th century A.D. In one inscription, for instance, we read of a munificent gift of cattle to "the twice-born resembling fire" (brāhmaṇas) attached to the shrine of Vaprakeśvara in the Kutai valley of eastern Kalimantan; in another of brāhmaṇas "who have come here [from] different [parts]" to erect a yūpa.[193] Half a century later, brāhmaṇas in the kingdom of Tārumā in western Java were performing rituals associated with the completion of a hydraulic project.[194] From that time onward epigraphy and literature both bear unequivocal witness to the role of brāhmaṇas at the royal courts of Southeast Asia as purveyors and conservators of the siddhânta, esoteric knowledge, necessary for stable government. Some of the clearest evidence for this comes from classical Kambujadeśa, where numerous Sanskrit inscriptions testify that the varṇāśramadharma was adapted, although in very attenuated form, to Khmer sociopolitical needs, with Khmer kings as kṣatriyas consecrated by and receiving the advice of brāhmaṇa purohitas.

There has been considerable debate among historians of Southeast Asia as to whether the brāhmaṇas mentioned in Chinese texts and Southeast Asian epigraphy were actual immigrants from South Asia and their descendants or merely signified the adoption by indigenous courts of an Indian institution. For some brāhmaṇas of classical Kampuchea the answer is not in doubt, for their careers were summarized in inscriptions. One named Divākarabhaṭṭa, for instance, was born in Kalindī, that is in the country of Mathurā, Vṛndāvana and the Yamunā. Others traced their birth to the Āryadeśa, perhaps here to be understood as the Āryāvarta, the territory that, extending from the western to the eastern ocean, lay between the Vindhya and Himālaya mountains (Manu II, 22, 23). And still another brāhmaṇa came to Kampuchea from the Dakṣiṇāpatha.[195] These migrants were all mentioned subsequent to the 8th century, but it is not unreasonable to suppose that, if Indian brāhmaṇas traveled to Southeast Asia during later centuries, then they may well have done so in earlier periods. But this raises the question of the Smṛti prohibition of foreign travel, which is often held to have applied with especial force to brāhmaṇas. According to the purists, a sea voyage in particular vitiated brāhmaṇical status. In evaluating this argument it must be remembered that the Smṛti canon tended, generally speaking, to become more authoritative with the passing of time, a fact reflected in the lack of opprobrium attaching to those brāhmaṇas whose journeys to Suvarṇadvīpa were recorded in Sanskrit literature such as the Vetālapañcaviṁśatikā.[196] Furthermore, Coedès,[197] citing a personal communication from Robert Lingat, has drawn attention to a passage in the Baudhāyana Dharmaśāstra (I, i, ii, 4) in which sea-voyaging (samudrasaṁyānam) is cited as a custom peculiar to brāhmaṇas of North India. There is, however, abundant evidence that South Indian brāhmaṇas also played prominent roles in early Southeast Asian statecraft. In any case, as Filliozat has pointed out, even Manu (III:158) merely excluded the sea-voyager (samudrāyayin) from the śrāddhas, but did not expel him from his varṇa. This is confirmed indirectly by a passage in the Ādityapurāṇa (preserved in the Dharmasindhu) which takes it to be the part of wisdom to abstain from communication with the dvija who crosses the ocean as a precaution against loss of *dharma* (*dharmalopabhayāt*), but which makes no reference to an automatic loss of caste by such a traveller.[198]

It has also been objected from time to time that, since it is highly improbable that Indian women traveled overseas in these early days, the great brāhmaṇa ministerial families that are epigraphically attested in some states could never have come into being, let alone have prospered, had their founders been Indian immigrants. To Indian brāhmaṇas the very idea of miscegenation, it is alleged, would have been abhorrent. Yet at least one Chinese text reports that in the kingdom known to the Chinese as *Tun-sun*, probably in the 3rd century A.D., the local folk espoused the Hindu faith and gave their daughters to the brāhmaṇas in marriage. And then the text adds significantly, "Consequently numerous of the brāhmaṇas remain there."[199] Presumably these brāhmaṇas, and numerous others like them employed for their consecratory powers and magical skills at the courts of Southeast Asian rulers, would have invoked in justification of the brāhmaṇic status of their offspring the text of *Manu* (IX:35-40) according to which the *jāti* of a tree is determined by the seed rather than the field. In other words, the offspring of a brāhmaṇa by any mother retains the *varṇa* of the father.[200]

In the present context it is pertinent to note that the *brāhmaṇavarṇa* was not solely and invariably a caste of *clercs* performing ritual services. That brāhmaṇas engaged professionally in commerce is evident from numerous records from medieval India,[201] while it is beyond dispute that in later times the Dayśasta Marāthā brāhmaṇas of Mahārāṣṭra traditionally pursued careers in trade and intermarried with merchant communities. If these things happened in medieval and later times when the Smṛti rules had come to constitute an unimpeachable authority, then it is not unlikely that they also happened in ancient times when Smṛti precepts were less restrictive. Moreover, in India itself it appears that Dravidian shamans were occasionally assimilated to the *brāhmaṇavarṇa*, and there is no reason why, when the process of brāhmaṇization extended across the ocean, such inductions could not also have occurred in Southeast Asia. In this connection we may recall Max Weber's remarks on the Kammalars, the skilled craftsmen in metal, wood, and stone who, claiming descent from the artisan god Viśvakarma, "gerufen von den Königen, weithin nach Birma, Ceylon, Java verbreitetin und den Rang vor den Priestern, auch den zugewanderten Brahmanen, beanspruchten. Sie wurden, offenbar als

Träger magischer Kunst, auch von andern Kasten als guru's, geistliche Seelenleiter, in Anspruch genommen: » der Kammalar ist der Guru aller Welte « ".[202] The possibilities of brāhmaṇa interaction with Southeast Asian societies in transition were numerous. What is certain is that the Smṛti texts are an inadequate guide to the intricacies of the so-called Hinduization process in South India, let alone to events on the farthest frontiers of Āryadeśa.

The discussion thus far has been concerned mainly with generalities that would have been applicable to brāhmaṇas voyaging overseas at any time during the first millennium A.D. In the particular case of pre-Aṅkor Kampuchea, however, and probably throughout much of the rest of Southeast Asia during the period of state formation, two additional factors must be borne in mind. In the first place, as George Coedès pointed out half a century ago, there are reasons to believe that *brāhmaṇa* was effectively a generic term for members of any and all Śaivite sects;[203] while more recently Kamaleswar Bhattacharya has concluded that, upon initiation, every Śaivite, whatever his caste at birth, was considered a brāhmaṇa.[204] It follows that, given the prevalence of Śiva worshipers in parts of early Southeast Asia, at least a proportion of the brāhmaṇas mentioned in Chinese texts and indigenous epigraphy were probably Śaivite devotees who had crossed a caste boundary when they were initiated into the cult. Among the Śaivite communities in pre-Aṅkor Kampuchea, probably Java, and almost certainly elsewhere were Pāśupata ascetics, who not infrequently enjoyed royal favor.[205] Although reckoned as brāhmaṇas, they were, in Professor Wolters's words, "wayward brahmans who . . . believed that Śiva's grace prevailed over the laws of *karma*."[206] It would not be altogether surprising if these doctrinally deviant brāhmaṇas evinced few scruples about travelling abroad, especially as the rigors of ocean voyaging could be construed as hardships endured for Śiva's sake.[207]

Nor were these the only differences between brāhmaṇa functions in South and in Southeast Asia. In India, brāhmaṇas were traditionally honored because of the rituals that they performed on behalf of society and for which they were rewarded with gifts. As a result, by Gupta times brāhmaṇas had become wealthy landowners in some parts of the subcontinent. In ancient Kampuchea, by contrast, gifts of land were made to Śiva, not to brāhmaṇas, whose function apparently was to guard and interpret the *siddhānta*. On this view the support sought by the brāhmaṇas of P'an-p'an (p. 299

above) would have been that incidental to the management of temples and the performance of family, or even personal, rituals rather than simply royal largess. In the Kutai valley of Kalimantan in the 5th century, however, "The Most Excellent King [Mūlavarman] did [actually] bestow on brāhmaṇas the gifts of water, *ghṛta*, tawny cows, and sesame seeds, as well as eleven bulls" — all, incidentally in accord with the injunctions of the *Manusmṛti* IV, 229, 233, etc. The early date of this inscription may possibly imply that brāhmaṇas in at least some parts of Southeast Asia were originally treated in the Indian manner and only later came to assume different roles. However that may be, the crystallization of the concept of divine kingship threatened from a comparatively early date to subvert the Indian clarity of the distinction between the human incarnations of the two great principles of *Brāhmaṇ* and *Kṣatra*. Brāhmaṇa status in Southeast Asia, generally speaking, was relatively less exalted than in India, the majesty of the king tending to overshadow the religiosity of the priest, (a relationship that even in these formative times foreshadowed the situation which Clifford Geertz, with more and better quality evidence at his command, has described for 19th-century Bali: "The court-connected Brahmana was not ambassador to the gods for a secular ruler; he was celebrant-in-chief for a sacred one." *Negara*, p. 126).

The Nature of the Nāgara

In the preceding pages we have suggested ways in which the spiritual potency of a Southeast Asian chieftain could have been intensified to the point where he attained the threshold of thearchic kingship. However, although power was derived from proximity to the sacred and accumulated through personal austerities, to be effective its concentration had to be signified in terms of political stability, glory, prosperity, fertility, and control over large populations, especially over men mustered as the followers of ritually subordinate chiefs. Consequently a chieftain involved in the transformation would have had a strong incentive to extend his authority so as to draw on labor rights in as many different settlements as possible (in other words, to attract as many subordinate groups as might be practicable to the umbrella of his particular descent group). It is equally probable that opposition to this expansion developed at an early stage in the process, provoked at first by less thoroughly acculturated chieftains and in a later phase by competing, nascent god-kings who would have regarded, correctly enough, a diminution in their labor forces as a premonitory indication of a decline in their power. At the same time, the maintenance of a ceremonial state appropriate to a divine ruler and his priesthood demanded the ministrations of increasing numbers of craftsmen and artisans, the more highly skilled of whom were probably accommodated within the enceinte of the royal capital. Equally necessary was the labor of cultivators, an incipient peasantry, who could contribute the surplus produce of their fields for the support of the royal court, as well as — given the prevailingly unstable political situation — a band of armed retainers who could act as household guards and generally enforce the will of the ruler throughout the demesne lands that he personally controlled. In short, there had evolved the *nāgara* in the form of an advanced level of chiefdom, organized on essentially indigenous (but sometimes elaborated) principles of polity that were framed in a Sanskrit nomenclature, and which focused on the capital of a monarch affecting a Sanskrit style and other honorifics. Where there had been a tribal paramount descended from a territorial spirit, there was now an incarnation of Śiva (or other Indian deity); where there had been a shaman, there was now a brāhmaṇa learned in the *siddhānta*; where there had been a tribesman, there was now a peasant, a cultivator bound to the emergent ceremonial center in an asymmetrical structural relationship that required him to produce in one form or another a fund of rent.[208] At the same time key Indian institutions were adopted in form but given new substance and meaning, while indigenous custom was broadened within the framework of the *Dharmaśāstra*. Concurrently, already existing redistributive and mobilizative modes of economic integration were elaborated and formalized as instruments of tribute exaction and inchoate taxation. These institutional transformations, in turn, were manifested morphologically in the elaboration of the paramount's abode into a royal palace; the transformation of the old spirit house into a temple ornamented with purely Indian architectural motifs that were yet combined in an entirely original (and "un-Indian") way; the conversion of the spirit stone into the *liṅga* that was to become the palladium of the state, and the boundary marker at the entrance to the village into the city wall or palisade (as well, incidentally, as the boundary spirits into the Lokapālas presiding over the cardinal compass directions). In other words, the *kampung* had become the *nāgara* (or in Java the *keraton*) through a series of social, political, and economic transmutations that collectively signified a transition from culture to civilization.

The evidence on which to base an interpretation of the formative phase in the evolution of these nāgara is very unevenly distributed so that there is an almost irresistable tendency to rely primarily on the relatively more abundant Kampuchean data, supplemented mainly by materials, including literary descriptions, from Campā (pp. 394-397 below) and the isthmian tract of the Siamo-Malaysian peninsula. One is tempted, dangerously but perhaps inevitably, to treat the Kampuchean (which means in effect the Fu-nan and Chen-la) experience as an ideal-typical paradigm against which to evaluate the sequence of events in other parts of Southeast Asia.

Whatever may be inferred from the wholly inadequate archeological evidence currently available, the surviving literary and epigraphic texts leave no doubt that during the first five centuries of the Christian era each of the principal culture realms of western Southeast Asia witnessed the emergence of a plurality of polities, "an expanding cloud of localized, fragile, loosely interrelated petty principalities" as Clifford Geertz has characterized a similar multiplicity of statelets in later times.[209] Yet it would appear that the political structures of these regions were seldom completely atomized. Usually a varying proportion of their territories were integrated into a relatively small number of composite, pyramidal kingdoms apparently of the advanced-chiefdom type, which may have been structured on principles of segmentation (as in the classically studied cases of the Polynesian high islands or Pre-Islāmic Arabia[210]), of differentiation (as in the 19th-century Balinese dadia, which has been likened to a set of nested Chinese boxes[211]), or on combinations of both. Not infrequently, but usually for a limited period of time, a cluster of competing polities was subsumed into a single paramountcy occupying all or most of a core region. There is reason to think, for example, that many of the Kings of the Mountain in the lower Mekong valley were temporarily united in such a pyramidally structured polity in the middle of the 3rd century A.D., and perhaps again during the second half of the 6th century and the second half of the 7th, as well as on several intervening occasions which are less well documented. However, for almost all of the 8th century at least two paramounts, and sometimes as many as five, are known to have competed for control of the plains of the lower Mekong.[212] In eastern Indochina a number of Cam groups from

Quảng-nam south to Phú-yên Province had apparently been integrated into the kingdom of Amarāvatī well before the beginning of the 5th century, while, according to a Chinese account, in the 8th century the Pyū tribes of the Irawadi valley were organized in a tiered political hierarchy that is most readily construed as a chiefdom. In the lower Čhao Phraya valley the paramountcy of the kingdom of Dvāravatī seems to have migrated between princely capitals (and perhaps between descent groups or kindreds, although that aspect of the rulership is ignored by all available evidence) which were probably sometimes incorporated into a single major kingdom but which at other times competed among themselves for control of the region. A similar chiefdom-style polity bearing the honorific Śrī Canāśa apparently existed in the Khorat during the 7th and 8th centuries, while a series of lesser kingdoms flourished on the Siamo-Malaysian isthmus from the 3rd to the 8th century and later. The probability is that at least some of these small polities were included in the more powerful kingdoms to the north when the latter were strong (This certainly happened in the 3rd century) but lapsed into quasi-independence when politically centripetal forces were weak. In the archipelago, at the beginning of the 5th century Śrī Mūlavarman likened the absorption of neighboring "kings" (sc. chieftains) into his chiefdom in the Kutai valley of eastern Kalimantan to the exploits of Yudhiṣṭhira, a legendary hero of the *Mahābhārata*, and signified his status as a paramount by designating himself "the Lord of Kings." In the 7th century the Śrī Vijayan thalassocracy carried the stamp of a composite kingdom held together by the ritual authority of a charismatic ruler and, although contemporary evidence for Java is meager in the extreme, it is worth recalling van Naerssen's conclusion to his study of the island's early administrative history: "As reflected by the oldest known inscriptions up to about 873 . . . it is hard to imagine that one *kraton* ruled with a centralised administration over a large territory as Central Java . . . That there were struggles for the hegemony and attempts to centralize the *kratons* is certain [*The economic and administrative history*, p. 39]. In any case, the polities mentioned above are probably only a small proportion of those which actually existed at one time or another during the first half-millennium of the Christian era. It is likely that the names of most of the major paramountcies, those which exercised authority over relatively extensive tracts of territory during that period, have survived either in epigraphy or Chinese annals but, from among the swarms of petty principalities that formed and dissolved, were reconstituted and dissolved again, probably the names of only a handful have survived the chance winnowing of time. And, even allowing for the fact that the historical record tends to become somewhat fuller with the passage of time and for that reason alone is liable to impart an impression of increasing complexity, it is still evident that the secular political trend was toward an ever more differentiated form of patrimonial statehood structured about a slowly maturing urban hierarchy.

The representative *nāgara* in both continental and archipelagic Southeast Asia in, say, the 7th century A.D. was governed formally according to the precepts of the *Smṛti* canon, especially the *Mānava Dharmaśāstra*, or lawbook of Manu, which was probably given its present form in the 2nd or 3rd century A.D., and the *Arthaśāstra*.[213] The terms *dharmaśāstra* and *arthaśāstra* both occur in a Khmer text of A.D. 668 as the respective spheres of expertise of two ministers,[214] while Manu is cited in a Javanese inscription of 732.[215] In one Pre-Aṅkorean inscription even a slave is named Mānudharma.[216] It may be remarked in passing that the two great Hindu epics, the *Mahābhārata* and the *Rāmāyaṇa*, were both known in Kampuchea from very early times. An inscription from the second half of the 5th century, for instance, quotes four verses from the *Araṇyaparvan*;[217] in the 6th century a manuscript of the *Śambhavaparvan* was donated to the temple now known as the Pràsàt Prăḥ Thát; and in the 7th century complete copies of both epics were presented to the god Tribhuvaneśvara.[218] Vālmīki, traditionally regarded as the author of the *Rāmāyaṇa*, was the recipient of an official cult in 7th-century Campā.[219]

The source of authority in virtually all these early kingdoms seems to have been a thearchic kingship. In several of the realms discussed above the king was represented as an incarnation of Śiva, a circumstance often to be inferred but made explicit in an inscription from Tăṅ Kraṅ which eulogized Jayavarman I (c. 650) of Chen-la as "an incarnate part" of Śrī Piṅgaleśa (Śiva).[220] In later times Khmer kings were sometimes compared to Viṣṇu in the splendor of their rule but were never in any extant text regarded as an incarnation of that god. Similarly they were likened to Indra in their function of ensuring the prosperity of their kingdoms.[221] In Kampuchea, where such matters are best documented, two dynasties, a lunar and a solar, were in subsequent centuries held to have competed for control of the lower and middle Mekong valley. The lunar dynasty of Fu-nan appears to have been a later codification on an Indian pattern of an indigenous descent group.²²² It was replaced for a while by the solar dynasty of Chen-la, but the known kings of this line soon reverted to the lunar mythology. A late (10th-century) inscription unites these two dynasties, but there can be little doubt that this union, and indeed the very notion of lunar and solar lines, were imposed on Khmer history by status-conscious genealogists attempting to invest their rulers with the aura of a prestigious Indian tradition.²²³ It is worthy of note that in Pre-Aṅkor times a Kampuchean ruler had no style distinguishing him from grand officers of state. Sanskrit *deva*, certainly in later times and probably in earlier, was shared by the king, high officials and brāhmaṇas, while Khmer *vraḥ kamratāṅ aṅ* in the Pre-Aṅkor period was used indifferently for royalty, brāhmaṇas and gods.²²⁴ Contrariwise, in earlier times (but as late as the reign of Yaśovarman I, 889-900), posthumous titles intended to emphasize divinity were the prerogative of kings, and only subsequently were accorded to high officers of state.²²⁵

In the Aṅkor period, the principal duty of the king was to defend the rule of right conduct, to restore to the bull symbolizing *Dharma* the three hoofs it had lost in preceding ages of confusion and declining moral standards. This was almost certainly also true in earlier centuries, in which connexion it is pertinent to recall that the style of King Bhadravarman I of Campā included the component *Dharmamahārāja*. It is clear enough that the power on which the ruler relied to effect this was regulatory rather than legislative.²²⁶ Generally speaking, Aṅkor monarchs tended to emphasize the more authoritarian aspects of the Hindu conception of royalty, casting the ruler in the role of a master (*guru*) among servants rather than as a father to his children, but the evidence for the earlier period is too meager to warrant the drawing of conclusions. According to the *Liang Shu*, one of the *bnaṃ* rulers in the Mekong valley gave three or four audiences each day, but the *Sui Shu* records that the ruler of the kingdom known to the Chinese as Chen-la gave audiences only on every third day, while reclining on a couch in a pavilion in his capital.²²⁷

In Campā and Fu-nan, the styles of the paramount rulers prior to the second half of the 4th century that have been preserved were cast in indigenous forms (Or perhaps, to be pretentiously accurate, we should say they were recorded in that way: it is just possible, although not very likely, that some of these rulers also laid claim to Sanskrit styles. A chief of the Lin-I, it may be noted, had himself eulogized in what appears to have been an Indian script and probably, therefore, in an Indian

language, from which it would have been but a short step to the
assumption of a Sanskrit title).[228] From that time onward, all the
known royal styles in use in the bnaṃ polities and many of those in
Campā were in a Sanskrit idiom. Among the rulers of kingdoms on or
near the Siamo-Malaysian isthmus, the high king of Tun-sun in the
3rd century apparently assumed the Old Khmer style of *kuruṅ* (rendered
as *kʻun-lun* 崑崙 by Chinese reporters),[229] while as late as the
4th or 5th centuries the dynastic style of the rulers of Pʻan-pʻan
incorporated an element *yang* that may have been of Cam, Malay, or
Old Mōn origin. The other known honorifics from the isthmus, in so
far as they can be restored from Chinese transcriptions, appear to
have been Sanskrit titles: Gautama ———— (unrestored) in the
Red-Earth Land, Bhagadatta in Langkasuka, and Śrī Parameśvara in
Ko-lo.[230] In Sumatra, Sanskrit styles were in evidence from the 5th
century, when a King Śrī Varanarendra dispatched a mission to China.
In western Java the earliest evidence of such titularies dates from
about the same time (Pūrṇavarman, with the style Rājādhirāja of
Tārumā, and the king of Ho-lo-tan), while in the Kutai valley of
eastern Kalimantan and in Arakan epigraphy actually permits a
glimpse of the process of Sanskritization of indigenous names
perhaps as early as the beginning of the same century. In eastern
Java, by contrast, a similar transformation of styles was still
taking place some three and a half centuries later.[231] Among the
Pyū, Sanskrit styles are probably attested first toward the end of
the 7th century, but it may not be without significance that in
Burmese mythology the culture hero Duttabaung, although assimilated to
Śiva, had a Pyū style.[232] In the Mōn territories two Sanskrit
titles, seemingly from the 7th century, were the prerogatives of
the rulers of, respectively, Dvāravatī and Ū-Thòng. Farther
eastwards, the paramounts of Canāśa had seemingly assumed Sanskrit
styles by the end of the 7th century.[233] In short, Sanskrit
titularies first appeared in Southeast Asia in about the middle of
the 4th century A.D. and became increasingly common thereafter (The
Śrī Mara of the Võ-canh inscription, which probably dates from the
3rd century A.D., was apparently a *Sanskritization* of a Pāṇḍyan royal
style).

Although kings of the type we have been discussing made both
executive and judicial decisions, they customarily delegated
certain responsibilities to ministers and officials of their
courts, a high proportion of whom were *brāhmaṇas*. Although these
official hierarchies were well documented in later times, available
information from the formative centuries of the Indianization

process is so fragmented and ambivalent as to prevent the
presentation of a connected and comprehensive account. With one
regional exception, the general pattern of administration has to be
inferred from chance references in epigraphy and Chinese histories.
The single exception is provided by the Telaga Batu inscription,
which takes the form of an imprecation in Old Malay directed
against those who would subvert the fortunes of the king and the
polity of Śrī Vijaya. Although no date can be discerned in the
text, modern commentators agree that the inscription should be
assigned to the later decades of the 7th century.[234] A substantial
portion of the text is occupied by a roster of persons in the
service of the state which in its totality affords a rare glimpse
of the organization and administration of a Southeast Asian kingdom
prior to the 8th century.

Next to the king in precedence in Srī Vijaya was a group of
royal princes: *yuvarāja, pratiyuvarāja,* and *rājakumāra,* thought to have
been respectively the heir-apparent, the next in line to the throne
after the heir-apparent, and lesser princes of the royal blood.
Sharply distinguished from all three of these classes of princes
were the *rājaputra,* technically also princes but probably those born
of concubines (and therefore excluded from succession) or, less
likely, powerful benefice holders or other dependent rulers.[235]
Also within the privileged circle of the court were *daṇḍanāyaka* (high
justiciaries), *nāyaka* and *pratyaya* (seemingly stewards, reeves, or
bailiffs in charge of properties belonging to the royal family),[236]
hājipratyaya (royal sheriffs),[237] *kumārāmātya* (certain minor
officials),[238] *kāyastha* (palace clerks), *sthāpaka* (priestly
construction supervisors), relatively low-ranking *cāthabhaṭa* (cutlers)
and *adhikaraṇa* (inspectors), supervisors of various sorts (*tuhā an vatak
vuruḥ; addhyākṣī nījavarṇa = adhyakṣa nīcavarṇa*), *marṣī hāji* (perhaps the
king's washermen),[239] and *hulun hāji* (probably palace retainers).
Three ranks of military commanders, *parvāṇḍa, pratisāra,* and *senāpati,*
also figure in the list of state servants, of whom only the first
two appear to have been closely associated with the court, perhaps
as, respectively, higher- and lower-ranking commanders of royal
troops.[240] Also attached to the court in some undisclosed way were
puhāvaṃ (ships' captains) and *vaṇiyāga* (for *vaṇyāga* = merchants).

Outside the court and the territories under the king's
direct control, authority was apparently delegated to a hierarchy
of benefice holders and their dependents. *Bhūpati* seem to have been
among the more important of these, with *dātu* either holding lesser
benefices (*maṇḍala*) or perhaps being sub-beneficed by *bhūpati.* Royal

princes could evidently be beneficed as *dātu*, as could high-ranking commoners.[241] Local chieftains, or persons exercising a similar type of authority over unspecified groups either within or outside the court (the point is not clear), were known as *mūrddhaka*.

Despite the heterogeneity of the occupations and ranks specified, the inscription clearly does not furnish a comprehensive schedule of officials and ministrants in the service of the Mahārāja, listing as it does only those perceived to be strategically placed to subvert the authority of the ruler. Nevertheless, the roster provides fuller documentation than is available for any other Southeast Asian polity at a comparably early phase in its development. For Kampuchea, Sachchidanand Sahai has assembled a good deal of information relating to the Fu-nan and Chenla periods incidentally to his comprehensive study of the Aṅkor era, but the result, even when supplemented by additional Pre-Aṅkorian materials from Coedès's *Inscriptions du Cambodge*, amounts to little more than a series of chance and unconnected references to office holders of one sort or another, who were often also benefice holders[242] and who appear to have come exclusively from "noble" (sc. chiefly) families. Sahai is of opinion that, among the most noble personages, there may have been two grades of *rājaputra*, those born into the royal kindred, and who were therefore eligible to succeed to the paramountcy, and those on whom the title was conferred.[243] An inscription from the reign of Jayavarman I (657-681) affords a graphic illustration of the involvement of one particular patrician family in the administration of a kingdom.[244] First a certain Dharmasvāmin, lord of Dharmapura, claims that his forebears "have never ceased to occupy the office of *hotar*." Then it is recorded that his elder son, after being appointed successively to the "highly desirable" post of Marshall of the [King's] Horse (*mahāśvapati*) and the lordship of Śreṣṭhapura, has been beneficed with the territory of Dhruvapura which, from its description as "covered with dreadful forests inhabited by savages," seems to have been a frontier region. In other words, the elder son in question had been inducted as a marcher lord. A younger son of the same Dharmasvāmin began his career in what the inscription calls the "very distinguished office of *parigrāha*" (perhaps recruiter or even commandant) of the royal guard, and subsequently became successively comptroller, with the title of *samantasarāla*, of the retainers charged with the care of the personal royal insignia (*upabhoga*) at the court of Jayavarman I, supervisor of the royal oarsmen, with the title *samantanauvāha*, and finally commander of a thousand-strong military levy at Dhanvipura, a temple-city in the extreme south of the Khmer territories.[245] Jayavarman also appointed a retainer as governor of Ādhyapura "according to the succession established in his descent group," but the text in which this is commemorated does not make clear if the succession was hereditary with respect to the royal service or to the governorship.[246] Sahai has also drawn attention to a third family which provided ministers and government servants for the best part of a century and whose service spanned the transition from the lunar dynasty of Fu-nan to the solar dynasty of Chen-la, specifically from the reign of Rudravarman, who succeeded to the throne in 514, to the time of Jayavarman I.[247] In fact, the continuity of this family's service affords a valuable commentary on the manner in which power may have passed from one "dynasty" (sc. descent group) to the next.

A few Pre-Aṅkorian texts specify the public insignia (*bhoga*) that accompanied appointment to an administrative office. In the 7th century, for instance, whereas a lord of Ugrapura received a "spendid parasol with an embroidered underside and surmounted with a gold sphere," a chariot fitted with gold ornaments, and strings of horses and elephants,[248] the lord of Śreṣṭhapura mentioned above had to be satisfied with a white parasol.[249] At about the same time a functionary of Jayavarman I who was appointed president of the royal assembly (*rājasabhāpati*) was awarded, among other insignia, a gold vase (*kalaśa*), a goblet in the shape of a skull, and a white parasol.[250]

Inadequate for the restoration of Pre-Aṅkorian political and administrative systems as are these snippets of information and others like them in the inscriptional corpus, they are still superior to those available for contemporary kingdoms other than Śrī Vijaya. Elsewhere we are dependent on isolated comments such as the circumstance that the chief minister of the Pyū kingdom at the turn of the 9th century bore the title *mahāsena*;[251] that there were five high ministers of state in the polity known to the Chinese as Chen-la, namely — in their Chinese transcriptions — *kuo-lâk-tśie* 孤落支, *kâu-siang-piəng* 高相憑, *bʻuâ-ɣâ-tâ-liəng* 婆何多陵, *śia-muâ-liəng* 舍摩陵 and *ńźiäm-tâ-liu* 髯多婁, of which none has been satisfactorily restored to its original form;[252] that governmental officials in the Red-Earth Land included a *sārdhakāra*, two *dhanada* (a title which also occurs on a seal from Oc-èo), three *karmika* (charged specifically with the handling of political affairs), and a *kulapati* administering criminal law (掌刑法);²⁵³ that each town (城) in the same kingdom was under the authority of a nāyaka and ten pati;²⁵⁴ that the chief ministers of the kingdom whose name was transcribed by the Chinese as Pʻan-pʻan bore the titles *Bʻuət-laŋ-sâk-lâm 勃郎索濫, *Kúən-luən-tiei-ia 崑崙帝也, *Kúən-luən-bʻuət-γuâ 崑崙勃和, and *Kúən-luən-bʻuət-tiei-sâk-kâm 崑崙勃帝索甘, all of which seem to be indigenous rather than Sanskritic;²⁵⁵ that in the polity which the Chinese rubricated as Tan-tan there were eight high officers of state, all brāhmaṇas, known as the Eight Seats or Thrones (八座/坐);²⁵⁶ and so on: other offices are mentioned or implied in epigraphic texts but almost invariably without explicatory comment. Yet it is sufficiently evident from the more or less randomly preserved instances cited above that by the 7th century Sanskrit titles had become attached to administrative offices in kingdoms throughout western Southeast Asia, and actually prevailed in many states. The notable exception was Pʻan-pʻan, where both the royal style and ministerial titles appear to have been cast in indigenous form.

A feature of interstate relations in these early kingdoms which is mentioned in Chinese annals at least three times (and one which continued into later ages) was the employment of members of ruling families as envoys to foreign countries. In the 3rd century, for example, a paramount in the lower Mekong valley sent a kinsman as envoy to a ruler in the Indian subcontinent;²⁵⁷ in 753 the son of the king of one of the so-called Chen-la polities led an embassy to the Chinese court;²⁵⁸ and in 801/2 an embassy from the Pyū kingdom included either the son or the brother of the Mahārāja.²⁵⁹ On at least two occasions, both relatively early in the Hinduization process, envoys were designated specifically as "Indian". At some time during the decade 454-464 an emissary from Kan-tʻo-li to the Chinese court was described as "the Indian Rudra",²⁶⁰ and in 484 an Indian Buddhist named Nāgasena was employed by a ruler of Fu-nan in a similar capacity.²⁶¹

Epigraphy leaves the clear impression that the component units of the various kingdoms that have been discussed in earlier sections of this work were constituted as personal benefices held by dependent princes and territorial magnates, theoretically if not always in fact, at the king's pleasure. However, Chinese envoys to these countries, accustomed as they were to a bureaucratically administered hierarchy of local government units, on at least two occasions treated these units as administrative divisions controlled directly by the central government. Of the polity known to the Chinese as Tan-tan, for example, it was reported in the 8th century that chou 州 and hsien 縣 (presumably implying larger and smaller administrative areas) had been established in the interests of military efficiency,[262] while at much the same time the country rubricated as Ko-lo was described as divided into twenty-four chou. In this latter case, though, it was explicitly noted that there was no further subdivision of territory into hsien.[263] It is to be assumed that in these two instances Chinese envoys were imposing their own cultural perceptions of local government on alien societies. The Sui Shu came closer to the truth, perhaps, when its authors noted that in the Chen-la of Īśānavarman (first half of the 7th century) there were thirty palisaded settlements (城), each under the jurisdiction of a "governor" (部帥),[264] that is presumably a subordinate chieftain.

About the social composition of these early kingdoms little can be said with certainty. Royalty and courtiers and priests, and even the more prestigious servants of the king, figure in Sanskrit inscriptions but rarely is there mention of ordinary farmers, artisans, and craftsmen. It is, incidentally, remarkable that in the Telaga Batu schedule of offices and occupations, which included the humble cutler and washerman, only mariners were recorded under Indonesian rubrics. Only for Pre-Aṅkor Kampuchea is there anything approaching a corpus of materials relating to the common folk, in this case 139 inscriptions in the Khmer language preserving information about various religious foundations, and fortunately these have been analysed by Dr. Judith M. Jacob.[265] Even in these inscriptions free but humble people appear only infrequently, although this class is known to have included religious personnel (paṁnos) in charge of shrines, as well as families of officials. The two classes most in evidence in these Khmer inscriptions are the dignitaries who made gifts to temples and the kñuṁ they donated. There has been some debate as to the precise significance of the term kñuṁ, Dr. Jacob opting for the translation "slave" but Professor Claude Jacques and Monsieur le Bonheur objecting that this rendering is inappropriate for dancers, musicians, or cooks, especially when they were associated with temples.[266] What is certain is that kñuṁ could be bought, sold, and bestowed, and that their duties included grinding, spinning, grooming the royal elephants, moulding statues, singing, playing musical instruments, heating water for ceremonial ablutions, various domestic chores, trapping, and, of course, laboring in the padi fields and orchards. A kñuṁ vraḥ (slave of the god) probably enjoyed special privileges. For those who worked in the fields the designation "serf" might have been more apposite than "slave," although the precise status of these people is still very obscure.[267] What is surprising is that, although kñuṁ seem not to have been far removed from chattels, they often bore Sanskrit names, which were, of course, normal among the elite. Dr. Jacob suggests that some kñuṁ names may imply a non-Khmer origin.

There is no way of knowing to what extent the Khmer social system in Pre-Aṅkorian times may have been replicated in other contemporary culture realms of Southeast Asia, for none of which is there a comparable corpus of inscriptions in an indigenous language. Nor is it possible to discover the exact function of the varṇa that are sometimes mentioned in early Southeast Asian epigraphy: even for Pre-Aṅkor Kampuchea available materials are totally inadequate. It may be worth noting, however, that Dr. Mabbett has demonstrated very convincingly that varṇa in Aṅkor Kampuchea were not, as in India, divisions of the population at large, but instead elite groups attached to the court or state ceremonial apparatus.[268] It was apparently the terminology rather than the endogamous practice of Indian caste that was adopted into Khmer society. Even where the Khmer practice of varṇa conformed most closely to the Indian paradigm, that is within the ruling class, there were, as we have noted on p. 302 above, substantial differences between South and Southeast Asia in the relations of king (kṣatriya) and brāhmaṇa.

Although extant sources furnish little substantive information about the modes of economic integration that prevailed during the formative phases of these early Southeast Asian polities, the general impression that emerges of pyramidal political polities of the advanced-chiefdom type implies the existence of strong vertical flows of commodities of a redistributive and mobilizative character.[269] The mode of exchange that, in both early and later times, figured least prominently in epigraphic and literary records, and which is also the most difficult to recover from archeological excavations, was that conducted, figuratively speaking, in the market-place. The biases of all three bodies of evidence militate against the preservation of information about those economic mechanisms (as opposed to volumes of commodities and the routes they travelled) that operated outside the institutional nexuses supportive of social stratification (redistribution), political authority (mobilization), and kinship (reciprocity). When market exchange was mentioned, it was not daily domestic provisioning that was implied but rather wholesaling transactions between merchants. In Quảng-trị, for example, a tribal people known to the Chinese as *Mi̯uən-lâng (文狼: MSC = Wen-lang) were trading aromatics for unspecified commodities at least as early as the 6th century, while at much the same time in a market in Jih-nan (see the next chapter) traders were bartering "all [kinds of] fragrant substances,"[270] and some three centuries later in the Irawadi valley the Pyū were trafficking with neighboring peoples in "river pigs" (perhaps Irawadi dolphins), cloth, and glazed jars.[271] In addition to the implications of long-distance trade in the archeological record at Oc-èo, Chansen, Beikthano, Ku Bua and elsewhere, literary sources report similar activities from at latest the 3rd century A.D., when Chinese envoys to the South Seas commented on the number of traders and the volume and variety of merchandise in the capital of Tun-Sun (p. 213 above). Apparently the mart at Seluyut, "where traders passing back and forth meet together," was not very different,[272] but even these few references tell us only that exchange was taking place without specifying the precise form that it took. The principal evidence of coinages in the formative phases of state development that I have encountered includes the śrivatsa-stamped, symbolical coins mentioned in Note 5 to Chapter 3, the coins bearing the style Śrī Dvāravatīśvara that have been noted on p. 206, a late and unexpanded reference to both silver and gold coins in use among the Pyū at the beginning of the 9th century, and coins of six of Arakan's Candra rulers.[273]

As would be expected of such a relatively early phase in state development, evidence pertaining to the evolution of legal concepts is extremely meager. The five serious crimes (mahāpātaka) of the Hindu code, namely murder of a brāhmaṇa, drunkenness, theft, adultery with a master's wife, and complicity in any of the above, were recognized in Kampuchea during the Fu-nan period,[274] and the Liang Shu adds that the guilt or innocence of an accused was determined by means of a judicial ordeal. There were no prisons, the guilty presumably either dying during the ordeal or being punished by other than incarceration.[275] The same text asserts that in the half-legendary and so far unidentified kingdom of *Bi̯i-kʻi̯än (毘騫 : MSC = Pʻi-chʻien) the guilty were eaten (by whom is not specified) in the presence of the chief (王).[276] Among the Pyū at the turn of the 9th century, minor offences incurred corporal punishment but murder demanded the death penalty. The Chinese also appear to have perceived an incipient distinction between different branches of law among the Pyū, in this case criminal and civil law, when they reported that litigants engaged in meditation before a colossal Buddhist statue raised in front of the royal palace.[277] However, this is a late reference and no other text affords evidence of such discrimination. As Sahai points out, it is highly probable that, even during the Aṅkor period, Khmer law did not distinguish between a felony and a misdemeanor.[278] In fact, the clear implication of both epigraphy, especially the Telaga Batu inscription, and literary texts is that throughout early Southeast Asia public order was maintained by administrative fiat rather than by a unified body of public law. And the source of this regulative power was, of course, the king, contravention of whose ordinances was categorized as *doṣa*, that is an offence or transgression. According to a Pre-Aṅkorian inscription from Thăm Lekh, for instance, the desecration of a shrine on the slopes of Mount Bhadreśvara (Vằt Ph'u) would have constituted just such a *doṣa*.[279] In the legal jargon of the Aṅkor period crimes of violence against a person were designated *sāhasa*, one of the eighteen classes of *vyavahāra* defined by Manu as "appropriation of something involving the use of violence against the owner,"[280] but there is no evidence of this usage in Pre-Aṅkorian times. However, the ineluctability of royal ordinances under the Aṅkor monarchy is evident enough from a 10th-century inscription that castigates those who flout them as offending not only against the king and their *guru* but also and supremely against Śiva.[281] In any case, condign punishment, either at the instigation of divine powers or at the hands of royal servants, and often inflicted by both, would be the lot of those who were apprehended transgressing the king's commands, as is sufficiently attested by the Telaga Batu inscription, the Mĩ-sơn stele inscription of Bhadravarman,[282] and numerous other epigraphs throughout Indianized Southeast Asia that freeze in stone the terrifying imprecations of rulers who realized only too well the fickleness of ministers and tributaries. Sanctions there were in abundance, but they lacked attachment to enduring ordinances and seldom survived the ruler who promulgated them. When formal judgments (as opposed to commands) were pronounced, they appear to have been based on collections of doom-like decisions rather than on a corpus of true customary law.

It is apparent even from the fragments of evidence available that sanctioned custom and fiat played the major roles in maintaining social control. The four attributes required of a truly legal decision (p. 14 above) were present only individually, sporadically, and in inchoate form, and indeed remained so to a greater or lesser degree in most parts of Southeast Asia until the

19th century. For the period with which we are here concerned we can glimpse darkly no more than the uncertain beginnings of the framework that the *Dharmaśāstra* would ultimately provide for the codification of predominantly indigenous customs.[283]

On at least one occasion kingdoms of the type just described have been categorized as feudal.[284] This I believe to be a misreading of the evidence. The general tenurial configuration that underlies the disparate epigraphic and literary documents at our disposal would seem to point convincingly in the direction of a patrimonial rather than a feudal order. It is true that both types of domain focus on rulers who grant rights in return for military and administrative services, but beyond that the contractual character, social and legal aspects, and ideologies of the two systems are analytically distinct. Whereas patrimonial government, as has been explained in Chapter 1, is an extension of the principles of paternal authority obtaining within the (usually extended) royal family, feudal government is founded on a contractually ordered fealty structured upon a basis of knightly militarism. Feudalism has been aptly characterized as "domination by the few who are skilled in war," patrimonialism as "domination by one who requires officials for the exercise of his authority."[285] This having been said, it must be admitted that at the institutional level the two systems are not always entirely distinct. The extension of patrimonial rule over extrapatrimonial territories may induce the emergence of political structures which appear morphologically similar to others arising from the centripetal orientation of independent status groups under stress of external factors such as war. It may then be difficult to distinguish the personal obedience of a dependent ruler from the public duties of a political subject. In fact, patrimonial governments exhibit feudal aspects whenever a ruler grants territorially based benefices on an hereditary basis, and feudal regimes equally exhibit patrimonial aspects whenever fiefs are subject to a strong central administration. Recognizing this ambivalence in his analysis, Max Weber was constrained to admit that the two modes of government could sometimes be discriminated only after the personal positions of patrimonial officials and landed notables had been traced historically.[286]

At the heart of the distinction between the two modes of government is the circumstance that, whereas a patrimonial retainer is essentially a personal dependent of the ruler, a vassal entering the service of his king preserves his independence. In so far as

the evidence permits an opinion, it would seem that in western
Southeast Asia prior to, say A.D. 800 (and for many centuries to
come, although they do not concern us here) we are dealing with
personal benefices granted to retainers rather than with impersonal
contractual relationships between rulers and vassals. The Telaga
Batu imprecation, for instance, clearly implies sacred loyalties
rather than secular contractual arrangements. A feudal monarch
does not need to bribe his vassal with the promise of an
"immaculate *tantra*" (*tantrāmala*), as the Śrī Vijayan ruler was
constrained to do.[287] The very expression *huluntuhānku*, literally "my
commoners and lords,"[288] by which the Mahārāja referred to his
kingdom, reflects a characteristically patrimonial predisposition
to treat the whole polity as a simple extension of the royal court;
while the appointment of the brāhmaṇa Dharmasvāmin's elder son to
the post of Marshall of the [King's] Horse in 7th-century Kampuchea
(p. 311 above) nicely illustrates the way in which the patrimonial
mode of government tends to amalgamate affairs of state with
corresponding functions of the court. The Telaga Batu, Kota Kapur,
and Karang Berahi inscriptions are unambiguous in their combined
inplication that the Śrī Vijayan polity was held together not by
freely negotiated contractual relationships sealed by an instrument
comparable to the *commendatio* of medieval Europe but rather by
magical rites performed at an oath-taking ceremony that seemingly
partook of the nature of an *exequatur*.[289] It is of more than passing
interest that the maledictions invoked in these three inscriptions
were directed against internal components of the Śrī Vijayan
kingdom, not against external enemies.

The patrimonial king legitimates his rule in terms of the
welfare of his subjects and, ideally at any rate, his subjects
should express their satisfaction with his performance. On at
least two occasions Chinese envoys to the Nan Yang picked up what
were probably popular tales claiming to preserve a record of such
appreciation. The first account relates events in Langkasuka
probably at about the turn of the 6th century A.D.

> In the King's household there was a man of virtue to whom the
> populace turned [in the absence of royal leadership]. When the
> King heard of this he imprisoned the man but his chains snapped
> unaccountably. The King took him for a supernatural being and, not
> daring to injure him, exiled him from the country; whereupon he
> fled to India. The King of India gave him his eldest daughter in
> marriage. Not long afterwards, when the King of Langka[suka] died,
> the high ministers of state welcomed the exile's return as King.
>
> [*Liang Shu*, chüan 54, f. 14v].

The other example of a charismatic leader being raised to
power by popular acclaim, also reported by the Chinese and no doubt

equally apocryphal in its details, derived from one of the early
Bnaṃ kingdoms, where toward the end of the fourth or the beginning
of the 5th century A.D.,

> *Kjäu-ḏ'i̯ĕn-ńźi̯wo (憍陳如 : customarily read as a transcription of
> Kauṇḍinya) was originally an Indian brāhmaṇa. A divine voice
> commanded him to assume the kingship of Bnaṃ (Fu-nan). Rejoicing in
> his heart, *Kjäu-ḏ'i̯ĕn-ńźi̯wo arrived in P'an-p'an (Cp. p. 234 above)
> to the south, where he became known to the people of Bnaṃ. All [the
> people of] the kingdom welcomed him with jubilation and installed
> him [as their ruler].   [Liang Shu, chüan 54, f. 8r].

Needless to say, it is this type of essay in legitimation
that directs a historian's thoughts toward the likelihood of
usurpation. But other events in early Kampuchean history related
by Chinese annalists are less difficult to accept at their face
value. Even the mythologized statement that the founder of one
"dynasty" in the region beneficed his son with seven cities (p. 121
above) is not inherently unbelievable if we regard it as a
projection into the past of the sort of administrative procedure
that had become common enough when the Chinese record was
compiled.[290] And Hun P'an Huang's installation of his male
descendants as rulers of conquered settlements (p. 121) is entirely
credible in a patrimonial context, as is the beneficing of Prince
Guṇavarman, probably a son of Kauṇḍinya Jayavarman, with a domain
(bhojakapada) on the alluvial terrain of the lower Mekong.[291] Not
infrequently a powerful chieftain would hold more than one benefice.
Narasiṃhagupta, for instance, who was described as a "subordinate
ruler" (sāmanta-nṛpati) to the first three kings of Chen-la, was lord
of both Indrapura and another benefice the name of which has not
survived.[292] In 627 the lord of Tāmrapura was rewarded by
Īśānavarman I with the overlordship of Tamandarpura for his services
in "extinguishing the hostile pride of the despicable king" of that
city. In the shrine erected at Vát Čăkret to commemorate this
event, the new benefice holder is described as already possessed of
the overlordships of Cakrāṅkapura, Amoghapura, and Bhīmapura.[293]
Other benefices mentioned in Pre-Aṅkor epigraphy include that of
Maleṅ which, in 680, was in the hands of a dignitary (kuruṅ) who
endowed a shrine to the god Kedareśvara,[294] and similar territorial
holdings that have been described on p. 125 above. Sachchidanand
Sahai was close to the truth when he wrote that, " . . . dans le
royaume pré-angkorien, constitué par un certain nombre de
principautés vassales, l'autorité centrale n'était effective que
sur un territoire limité, et l'unité politique du royaume devait
dépendre de la capacité du roi, et non d'une organisation

administrative bien précise."[295] It is precisely this pyramidal political organization, its cohesiveness dependent on a web of fragile loyalties deriving from a combination of kinship ties, shared economic interests, and the ever-present threat of coercion, that we have denoted by the term "chiefdom," and we dissent from Sahai's specification only in his use of the feudal category of "vassal." Although some of the tenurial arrangements mentioned in the preceding pages are vague enough to be ascribable to either feudal or patrimonial domain, the overall configuration of the political order in western Southeast Asia during the first half-millennium of the Christian era was archetypically patrimonial in style.

* * * * * * * * * *

An apparent synchronism between the earliest evidence of long-distance trade to and through western Southeast Asia and the first indications of state and urban levels of sociocultural integration in the region has long been recognized. Except on the far northern fringe of the area, which had already been absorbed into the cultural sphere of the Han empire well before the beginning of the Christian era, no state or urban form has been documented prior to the appearance of South Asian artifacts. The earliest of these included an ivory comb, engraved with Buddhist emblems and dated between the 1st and 3rd centuries A.D. (with the balance of probability inclining to the 1st or 2nd century), which was excavated at Chansen in Central Thailand;[296] a fineware sherd from Bukit Tengku Lembu in Peninsular Malaysia which now seems to be securely assigned an Indian or Sri Lankan provenance and dated to the 1st or 2nd century A.D.;[297] and three "rouletted" fine bowls of Romano-Indian inspiration from northwest Java, dated to the same period.[298] In this connection we should also note the suggestion by Bronson and Dales that the pottery from Phase II (c. A.D. 1-250) at Chansen "looks rather like pottery from early historic sites in India and not at all like the earlier indigenous forms."[299] Only slightly later are the statues of Buddha Dīpaṁkara mentioned on p. 272 above, certain architectural structures at Beikthano which incorporated features deriving from Nāgārjunakoṇḍa building practice (p. 170), a bronze Buddha head of Gandhāran inspiration from the Bhnaṁ Ba-thê,[300] a bronze lamp with a *makara* ornament from Oc-èo,[301] and sundry artifacts deriving ultimately from the Mediterranean and the Roman Orient, presumably through the agency of Indian intermediaries.³⁰² Contemporary items of material culture from East Asia, by contrast, are unexpectedly rare: the earliest appear to be certain Han-period ceramics found in Java and Sumatra³⁰³ and possibly some mirror fragments of Han type from Oc-èo (although this style of mirror continued in use through most of the 3rd century A.D.).

As against this cumulatively convincing evidence of contacts of some sort between Southeast Asia and parts of the Indian subcontinent as early as the 1st or 2nd century A.D., and almost incontrovertibly the actual presence of Indians in Southeast Asia at the same period, the earliest explicit testimony to Indian terms for governmental and administrative institutions is encountered only in about the middle of the 4th century, when Sanskrit royal styles were recorded epigraphically in Campā³⁰⁴ and Kampuchea. However, if a 3rd-century date for the Vŏ-cạnh inscription can be sustained (Note 5 to Chap. 3), then the Sanskritization of a Tamil dynastic style can be documented in a presumed dependency of Fu-nan a century or so earlier than a Sanskrit royal title is recorded in the paramountcy itself — probably a distortion of the record induced by the chance preservation of evidence.³⁰⁵ However, if the style of Great King (大王) assumed by Fan Shih Man in the first half of the 3rd century is, as has sometimes been supposed, a translation of Sanskrit *mahārāja*, the missing evidence for an Indian titulary in the Lower Mekong valley is supplied and the apparent paradox resolved. As some assurance that a Sanskrit titulary would not have been wholly anachronistic during the reign of Fan Shih Man, it should be noted that a *Hu*, or in a broad sense "Indian," script may have been in use in Fu-nan as early as the 3rd century A.D. (depending on the provenance of information in the *Chin Shu*), presumably for ritual and chancellery purposes. If the 3rd century is inadmissible, then such a script was certainly reported in the 4th century.³⁰⁶ In Campā the Indian basis of statehood implied by a Sanskrit royal style is also confirmed as early as the 4th century by the epigraphically attested existence of a cult in which a paramount ruler indentified himself with a particular aspect of Śiva in the form of a *liṅga* by compounding his style with that of the god (p. 397 below). It was also towards the end of the 4th century, or perhaps a little later, that, according to the *Liang Shu*, the Indian brāhmaṇa of the Kauṇḍinya *gotra* whom we have already had occasion to mention (p. 320) as an example of a charismatic, though partly mythologized, ruler in the Mekong valley "restored the conduct of government in accordance with Indian *dharma*" (復改

制度用天竺法).[307] In a generally highly perceptive paper on
the dating of the Hinduization process, Dr. Anthony Christie has
taken this comment in the *Liang Shu* to signify an initial
introduction of Indian principles of statecraft into Kampuchea.[308]
However, this interpretation takes account neither of the idea of
resumption or restoration (復) explicit in the Chinese report nor
of the context in which the passage occurs. The Kauṇḍinya ruler is
described in the *Liang Shu* rather vaguely as "one of the successors"
of the Indian Caṇḍana (竺旃檀), who is known to have been
ruling in 357. It would seem likely, therefore, that Indian
influence on the style, if not the substance, of government was not
negligible at that time. Kindred and descent were matters of
supreme importance to both actual and would-be rulers in early
Southeast Asia, yet the Chinese apparently learned nothing they
considered worth recording from their informants about the
half-century or so intervening between the Caṇḍana and Kauṇḍinya
paramounts. Nor was the fact concealed that the Kauṇḍinya ruler
was a "usurper," or at least a pre-emptor, of authority, albeit at
the behest of a divinity. The inference is that the second half of
the 4th century was a time of political and social disorder,
possibly occasioned by a resurgence of indigenous values, to which
the Kauṇḍinya brāhmaṇa put an end by *restoring* the authority of the
dharmaśāstra. This reading of the text would imply that at least
some Indian elements were playing a part in Funanese statecraft as
early as the middle of the 4th century. But it is not certain that
the Caṇḍana ruler was the first to bear an Indian title and
possibly to base his sovereignty on Indian principles: only that
he was the first *recorded* paramount to do so. For all that is at
present known, the practice might have been initiated as early as
the end of the 3rd century A.D., following the hegemony of the last
paramount of a *Bnaṃ* kingdom known to have preserved an indigenous
style, namely he whose title or office was transcribed by the
Chinese as *$B'i̯wɒm$-$Zi̯əm$ 范尋 (MSC = Fan Hsün) and who was in power
as late as A.D. 287. In arguing for a considerable measure of
Indian cultural influence in the Bnaṃ polity a little earlier than
Dr. Christie is prepared to admit, it may be recalled that the *Chin
Shu*, formally chronicling events between 266 and 420 but in the
case of Fu-nan perhaps relying on the reports of an embassy to the
Mekong valley in the middle of the 3rd century, notes the existence
in the territory of "archives and [other] governmental depositories"
(書記府庫).[309] No trace has ever come to light of a
Pre-Indian, indigenous script in Kampuchea so the presumption has

to be that the records maintained in the depositories were written in the *Hu* script mentioned above, a circumstance which must surely imply a not negligible Indian contribution to the practice of religion and the conduct of government (the two were never disassociated in early Southeast Asia) perhaps during the 3rd century and certainly during the 4th.[310] In any case, it is not in doubt that these early adoptions of Indian administrative practices were substantially augmented at about the turn of the 5th century for it is from that point in time that the cult of the Śiva *liṅga* became established, together with the use of the so-called Pallava script[311] and the Śaka era,[312] incorporation of the element *-varman*, signifying "protected by," in the styles of rulers,[313] and adoption, with modifications, of the myth of the *nāginī* Somā and the origin of the Lunar Dynasty.[314] It is to be inferred, though, that whatever date may ultimately be ascribed to the earliest appearance of polities based explicitly on Indian principles of government, kingdoms of this type were not the instant creations depicted in mythology. After Southeast Asian chieftains first acquired some familiarity with the generalized configuration of Indian culture, there must have been a considerable period of adjustment before they succeeded in patterning their rule at all closely on the prescriptions of the *dharmaśāstra*. It would seem not unreasonable to postulate that, on the plains of the Lower Mekong valley and in Campā, where indigenous rulers appear to have been adapting their administrative practices to these principles at latest by the middle of the 4th century A.D., the leaven of Indian religious and political ideas had been working for at least a century previously, and possibly a good deal longer. In other words, the origins of the Hinduized state in Kampuchea and Campā is to be sought not in its earliest epigraphic records, but in the tenuous and uncertain implications of still earlier and even more fragmentary evidence. Whether this transformation did indeed occur later in other parts of Southeast Asia or only appears to have done so because of a lack of documentation contemporary with that of Kampuchea and Campā cannot be decided on the evidence at present available. However, despite the ready accessibility of southern Indochina to Chinese envoys and the obvious likelihood of it figuring in Chinese records at an early date, it should be remembered that the region also bordered the South Asian maritime trade route. Dr. R. B. Smith and Professor William Watson have drawn attention to the position of Oc-èo at the intersection of one cultural axis running from the *Bnaṃ* country to Ū-Thòng, Chansen, and Beikthano with another linking

Campā, the *Bnaṃ* kingdoms, and Java.[315] And through this same intersection also passed the just mentioned, venerable trade route from the Red Sea to China. This focusing of cultural and commercial concerns in the general area of southern Indochina in the early centuries of the Christian era is suggestive, but its true significance will only be elicited by a great deal of further archeological investigation.

It is evident that the interpretation proposed here does not fit precisely any of the models of urban generation described in Chapter 1, although the general concept of tribal and state (or village and urban) societies as distinct but interpenetrating levels of socio-cultural integration has been retained. And although western Southeast Asia was evidently a realm of secondary urban and state formation, the preceding account bears only the broadest generic resemblance to Barbara Price's explanatory model of secondary state development.[316] The present exposition starts from a largely inferential reconstruction of conditions late in the prehistoric period when Southeast Asia was occupied by a mosaic of cultures and societies ranging in their modes of ecological adaption from nomadic hunting and foraging to complex ecosystems based on wet-*padi* cultivation combined with mixed gardening, fishing, and stock raising. Typically these communities exhibited relatively high degrees of self-sufficiency, possessed distinctive artifactual traditions, and exploited ecologically complementary natural environments, while manifesting a fairly wide spectrum of social and political differentiation. At the lower end of the scale were small bands of a few loosely integrated families. At a more complex level were people caught up in the constellations of kin groupings and communities that we call tribes; while at the top of the scale were political entities approaching the threshold of true statehood, being characterized by a relatively high degree of centralized direction, hereditary hierarchical statuses, and a prevailing redistributive mode of economic integration. It is inferred that in the more advanced of these communities, dependably stable productivity based at least in part on wet-*padi* cultivation was permitting the exaction of surpluses for the support of hereditary chiefs who competed among themselves for control over labor rights in as many neighboring settlements as possible. By exalting the power of the deity with whom he himself was intimately associated, which meant in the context of the time replacing the old tribal god with an Indian deity, such a chief first "promoted" (in Flannery's terminology) the subsystem of his kindred to the highest level in the control hierarchy of the chiefdom, and then, by maintaining it in an essentially "self-serving" (general purpose) posture at that level, allowed it to "usurp" (Flannery again) the regulation of the entire polity. By merging his ātman with that of the deity, usually but by no means exclusively Śiva, the paramount came — intentionally or adventitiously is of no consequence — to establish himself as a fully fledged thearchic ruler. He was also able to fill the limited roster of positions of theocratic authority and prestige available in the chiefdom with high-ranking members of prominent kin groups, thereby creating a class-like stratum of prestigious court officers within a society still deriving much of its cohesion from ties of kinship.

In a compendious evaluation of the role of theocracies in the development of state-type institutions, Professor David Webster stresses their function "as a strategic political ploy in the *absence* of the potential for effective centralization, especially of coercive force."[317] The record of continuous political flux which not even the meagerness of our sources can conceal is powerful testimony to the relative weakness of centralized leadership in the earliest Southeast Asian states, as is the almost total absence of Flannerian-style "linearization," let alone its pathology of "meddling" (pp. 24-6 above). Very seldom is there any reason to infer higher-order administrative controls permanently bypassing lower-order controls in order to intervene in the functioning of socio-environmental variables. And the fuller the record — as, for isntance, in the case of the *Bnaṃ* polities as compared with, say, Java — the more evident the weakness of centralizing forces other than the institution of thearchic kingship. In the period with which we are here concerned, although sanctity was a functional equivalent of political power, the wielders of power were still not entirely confident in their use of sanctity to validate the use of force. By and large such power as the political center did possess seems to have been exercised in the control of local notables, those officials, governors, benefice holders, headmen, and so forth who, because they retained traditional ties to districts and provinces, were able to translate central policy directives into social action.[318] Although paramounts rewarded notables with land, commodities, privileges, official status, and grandiloquent titles,[319] a powerful supplementary integrative force in these early polities was surely that which has been designated, infelicitously it is true, "culturological attraction."[320] In the Southeast Asian case (as in numerous other instances), this integrative mechanism took two forms, specifically a consensus among all groups within the population as to the validity of the central leadership's claim to sanctified status, and an attraction to the ritualized life of the court that presented in liturgical form symbolic statements about the nature of society, as well as offering opportunities of privileged access to the fruits of a redistributive system that creamed off economic surpluses at successive levels of the administrative hierarchy. Of course, the cement binding together the different entities within these early polities did not always resist the effects of countervailing centrifugal forces, but revolt and secession were invariably undertaken with the intention not of changing the political structure but of replacing particular leaders. Largely because of the congruence, and consequent mutual reinforcement, of authority and redistributive structures, the instability characteristic of these early kingdoms (and indeed of most others down to quite recent times) involved only access to high-status positions, not the institutional frameworks which, generally speaking, proved remarkably stable and persistent.

There is reason to think that at different times and in different localities the process outlined here, or something like it, was supplemented by the arrival of kṣatriya-led expeditions and the establishment of trading colonies. As is suggested on p. 296 above, both types of settlements could have served as channels for the transmission of aspects of Indian culture from South to Southeast Asia within the general framework of the religious and political transformations that have been proposed in this chapter. It is virtually certain that the relative contributions of the several modes of acculturation involved in the so-called Indianization process varied both regionally and temporally, but the outcome in all instances was the emergence of a ritual and administrative complex, a *nāgara*, that constituted the uppermost level of a three- or occasionally four-tier settlement hierarchy. While offering symbolic statements about the nature of society, providing assurances of cosmic certainty, and serving as theaters for display of the iconography of power, these ceremonial centers also functioned as nodes in a superordinate redistributive and mobilizative economy and as foci of craft specialization. However, while the consequences are evident enough, the processes that produced them are not equally clear in all parts of Indianized Southeast Asia. If the Kampuchean experience is to be taken as the paradigm of the Hinduization process — as at the present time it must by virtue of the preponderance of the evidence — then Campā (to be discussed in Chapter 8), at least some of the Mōn territories, and probably Java can fairly safely be construed as more or less regular declensions. For Arakan, Sumatra, and particularly the Pyū culture realm, however, the evidence is too meager and fragmented to permit the reconstruction of most of the inflectional forms. Yet there is no doubt that, whatever the combination of cultural devices involved in the transformation, the states and cities that resulted manifested in both form and function a Eutychian-style fusion of South and Southeast Asian cultures so blended together as to constitute but a single type distinct from either of its components. All in all, there is no cause to dissent from L. de la Vallée Poussin's view, subsequently espoused by George Coedès, of the Indianization of western Southeast Asia as being essentially the continuation across the Bay of Bengal of that brāhmaṇization which, taking its origin in northwest India, spread eastwards and southwards through the centuries, and which is still continuing in some of the remoter parts of the subcontinent.[321] The studies of Professor Chie Nakane on the borders of South and Southeast Asia are of especial interest in this connection, for she has documented the manner in which brāhmaṇas, both authentic and *soi-disant*, were beginning to assume important economic and social roles in village society in Tripura State as recently as the 1950s.[322] An instance of the recent adoption of Buddhism by a Burmese hill people has been described by E. R. Leach,[323] while David Sopher has drawn attention to a similar process operating among the Mru in the Chittagong uplands.[324] It would seem that in the hill tracts that now separate Burman from Bengali we are witnessing the latest stages of the acculturation process which, some two thousand years ago, began to transform the political, social, and economic life of western Southeast Asia. It would be unwise to assume that the process has been unvarying throughout its long history, that there has been no ebb and flow on the frontiers of Āryadeśa, or that the contemporary phases, working themselves out in a world of shrunken distances and burgeoning technologies, are precise repetitions of those that unfolded in the dawn of Southeast Asian history, but the correspondences between present-day observations and historical reconstructions are close enough to leave no doubt that the ancient and modern modes of acculturation belong to the same genre of historical events. The meagerness of available information renders it inevitable that the interpretation proposed here should be no more than a cartoon, outlining clusters of interacting processes and congeries of

interrelated problems but devoid of animating detail, of delicate
distinctions in social status, of intricacies in exchange
arrangements, of subtle strategems in the competition for power,
of polysemicity in religious symbolism, in fact of complexity and
subtlety in just about everything pertaining to the emergent *nāgara*.
This state of affairs is inherent in the study of origins, and
therefore irremediable; but just how subtle and complex these
crosscutting interrelationships could become in the developed *nāgara*
is amply attested in Clifford Geertz's sensitive study of
19th-century Bali to which reference has already been made (Note
209).

Notes and References

1. *Values* (conceptions of desirable types of actions and social systems) regulate the ordering of commitments by social units, and therefore take primacy in the pattern-maintenance functioning of social systems. *Norms*, which are specific to particular social functions and types of social situations [Talcott Parsons, *The system of modern societies* (Englewood Cliffs, N.J., 1971), p. 7], serve primarily to integrate social systems. They fall into two classes: those prescribing positive obligations, which may be termed *relational*, since they specify the positive content of relations between role occupants and between subgroups; and those prescribing the limits of permissible (rather than obligatory) action, which are properly termed *regulative*. These latter do not differentiate between roles and between subgroups to the same extent as do relational norms.

2. Cf., *int. al.*, Ramesh Chandra Majumdar, *Ancient Indian colonies in the Far East*, vol. 2: *Suvarṇadvīpa*. Part I, *Political history* (Dacca, 1937); Part II, *Cultural history* (Calcutta, 1938); Majumdar, *Hindu colonies in the Far East* (Calcutta, 1944); Majumdar, *Ancient Indian colonization in South-East Asia*. The Maharaja Sayajirao Gaekwad Honorarium Lectures, 1953-54 (Baroda, 1955); George Coedès, *Histoire ancienne des états hindouisés d'Extrême-Orient* (Hanoi, 1944), chap. 2 [Subsequently revised under the title *Les états hindouisés d'Indochine et d'Indonésie* (Paris, 2nd edition 1948, 3rd edition 1964)]; Wheatley, *The Golden Khersonese* (Kuala Lumpur, 1961), chap. 11; Wheatley, *Impressions of the Malay Peninsula in ancient times* (Singapore, 1964), chap. 3; Kernial Singh Sandhu, *Early Malaysia. Some observations on the nature of Indian contacts with pre-British Malaya* (Singapore, 1973), pp. 1-11.

3. These are Sanskrit forms, but the names also occur in Pāli versions such as Suvaṇṇabhūmi and Suvaṇṇakūṭa. *Dvīpa* (Pāli *dīpa*) strictly connotes land with water on two sides, i.e. peninsula or island, but in ancient writings was often used, after the manner of Pāṇini, in a general sense to mean simply "land": see V. R. Ramachandra Dikshitar, *Some aspects of the Vāyu Purāṇa* (Madras, 1933), pp. 17-18; A. A. Macdonnell, *A Sanskrit grammar* (London, 1927), p. x.

4. S. S. Katti Mudholkara (ed.), *Rāmāyaṇa* (Bombay, 1915), Book IV, *sarga* 40, *śloka* 30; Hari Prasad Shastri, *The Rāmāyaṇa of Vālmīki*, 3 vols. (London, 1952-59), vol. 2, pp. 272-4.

5. A. M. Tabard, *Lacôte's essay on Guṇāḍhya and the Bṛhatkathā* (Bangalore, 1923), p. 131.

6. *Kathāsaritsāgara*, *taraṅga* 123, *ślokas* 105ff; C. H. Tawney, *The ocean of story*, (London, 1925-8), vol. 9, pp. 50. ff. This compendium of tales was compiled in c. A.D. 1070 by the Brāhmaṇa Somadeva for the amusement of Sūryavatī, wife of King Ananta of Kāshmir, at whose court the author was a poet. It may be regarded, in fact, as a Kāshmirī recension of the Bṛhatkathā.

7. *Kāthasaritsāgara*, t. 54, ś. 86ff; Tawney, vol. 4, p. 190.

8. *Kathāsaritsāgara*, t. 54, ś. 97ff: Tawney, vol. 4, pp. 191 ff. Samudraśūra was a native of Harṣapura.

9. *Kathāsaritsāgara*, t. 56, ś. 55-64; Tawney, vol. 4, pp. 220-251.

10. *Kathāsaritsāgara*, t. 57, ś. 72 ff; Tawney, vol. 5, pp. 5 ff.

11. *Kathāsaritsāgara*, t. 86, ś. 33 ff; Tawney, vol. 7, pp. 13ff.

12. *Arthaśāstra*, Adhikaraṇa II, prakaraṇa xi, paras. 78-79; R. Shamasastry,

Kauṭilya's Arthaśāstra (Bangalore, 1915), pp. 79-80, 90-91; R. P. Kangle (ed.), The Kauṭilīya Arthaśāstra, Part II (Bombay, 1963), p. 117. What is probably the best opinion holds that the Arthaśāstra was an immediately pre-Guptan elaboration of an original Mauryan compilation: hence its traditional attribution to Kauṭilya, chief minister to Candragupta Maurya. [See H. C. Raychaudhuri in R. C. Majumdar (ed.), The history and culture of the Indian people, vol. 2: The age of imperial unity (2nd edition, Bombay, 1953), pp. 285-287; V. Kalyanov, "Dating the Arthaśāstra," Papers presented by the Soviet Delegation at the 23rd International Congress of Orientalists (Cambridge, 1954) [In Russian, with English abridgment]. Aloeswood, also known as eaglewood and gharuwood, is a pathologically diseased, fragrant wood yielded by about half the trees comprising the genus Aquilaria. For specification of the Southeast Asian regions known to have provided this aromatic in later times see Wheatley, "Geographical notes on some commodities involved in Sung maritime trade," Journal of the Malayan Branch of the Royal Asiatic Society, vol. 32, pt. 2 (1959), pp. 68-72.

13. Bṛhatsaṁhitā, chapter V, śloka 38; IX, 15, 29; X, 15, 18; XIV, 31; XVI, 1, 133; XXXII, 15; J. F. Fleet, "The topographical list of the Bṛhatsaṁhitā," Indian Antiquary, vol. 22 (1893), pp. 169-195.

14. C. H. Tawney, Kathākośa: the treasury of stories. With notes by E. Leumann (London, 1895), pp. 28-31. The Kathākośa was compiled by Jineśvara at an undetermined date, but the tales themselves are sometimes of considerable antiquity.

15. V. Trenckner (ed.), Milinda-pañha (London, 1880), Book VI, p. 359; T. W. Rhys Davids, The questions of King Milinda, Part II. The Sacred Books of the East, vol. 36 (Oxford, 1894), p. 269; Sylvain Lévi, "Ptolémée, le Niddesa et la Bṛhatkathā," in G. Van Oest (ed.), Etudes asiatiques publiées à l'occasion du vingt-cinquième anniversaire de l'Ecole Française d'Extrême-Orient, vol. 2 (Paris, 1925), p. 53; Wheatley, The Golden Khersonese, p. 181; Sandhu, Early Malaysia, p. 5. The Milinda-pañha purports to be a discussion between King Milinda of Sāgala (Greek Menander) and Thera Nāgasena on disputed points of Buddhist doctrine. The original text, written in Sanskrit or some North-Indian Prākrit at about the beginning of the Christian era, is no longer extant, and the work now known as the Milinda-pañha is a Pāli translation made in Ceylon in about A.D. 400.

16. L. de la Vallée Poussin and E. J. Thomas (eds.), Mahā-Niddesa (London, 1916-17), pp. 154-155; Lévi, "Ptolémée, le Niddesa, et la Bṛhatkathā," pp. 1-2; Wheatley, The Golden Khersonese, p. 181; Sandhu, Early Malaysia, p. 5.

17. E. B. Cowell (ed.), Divyāvadāna (Cambridge, 1886), p. 107; Majumdar, Suvarṇadvīpa, Part I, p. 45.

18. Sylvain Lévi (ed. and transl.), Mahākarmavibhaṅga (La grande classification des actes) et Karmavibhaṅgopadeśa (Discussion sur le Mahā Karmavibhaṅga) (Paris, 1932), section XXXII, paras. a-j (pp. 50-64 and 123-133).

19. V. Fausböll (ed.), Jātakaṭṭhavaṇṇanā, 6 vols. Index as vol. 7 by D. Andersen (London, 1877-97), vol. 6, book xxii, no. 539; E. B. Cowell, The Jātaka: stories of the Buddha's former births, 7 vols. (Cambridge, 1895-1907), vol. 6, pp. 19-37.

20. Fausböll, vol. 4, book x, no. 442; Cowell, vol. 4, pp. 9-13.

21 Fausböll, vol. 3, book v, no. 360, and vol. 4, book ix, no. 463; Cowell, vol. 3, pp. 124-125 and vol. 4, pp. 86-90.

22. H. Kern (ed.), Jātaka-mālā (Boston, 1891), no. XIV, sarga 1; J. S. Speyer, The Jātakamālā: or garland of birth stories (London, 1895), pp. 125ff.

23. E. Hardy (ed.), Paramatta-Dīpanī (London, 1894), Book I, gāthā 10 and IV, 11; G. P. Malalasekara, Dictionary of Pāli proper names, vol. 2 (London, 1938),

pp. 1262-1263. The Indian emporia which figured most prominently in this eastern trade, according to the *Paramatta-Dīpanī*, were Pāṭaliputta (Skt. Pāṭaliputra) and Sāvatthī (Skt. Śrāvastī), both far up the Ganges valley.

24. Aggamahāpaṇḍita Buddhadatta Thera (ed.), *Sīhaḷavatthuppakaraṇa* (Colombo, 1958), pp. 91ff. and 107ff: the 34th and 40th tales respectively. The *Sīhaḷavatthuppakaraṇa* is a translation from Old Sinhalese into an archaic style of Pāli verse by Ācariya Dhammadinna, a native of Kaṇṭakasolapaṭṭana who resided in the monastery called Paṭṭakoṭṭi-vihāra. Cf. Senarat Paranavitana, *Ceylon and Malaysia* (Colombo, 1966), pp. 3-5. It may be noted that in the 40th tale, the dishonest goldsmith echoes the theme of *deśāntaravipāka* mentioned above when he laments that, "Many are the obstacles on the journey to Suvaṇṇabhūmi:" *Sīhaḷavatthuppakaraṇa*, p. 107; Paranavitana, *op. cit.*, p. 5.

25. Cited by *Paranavitana*, pp. 5-6.

26. Lévi, *Mahākarmavibhaṅga*, section XXXII, lines a-j. It was this Gavāmpati who was adopted as the patron saint of the Mōns.

27. Mabel H. Bode (ed.), *Sāsanavaṃsappadīpikā* (London, 1897), Book III, pp. 36-41; B. C. Law, *The light of the history of the Buddha's religion* (London, 1952), pp. 41-46.

28. W. Geiger (ed.), *Mahāvaṃsa* (London, 1908), Book XII, gāthās 1-7 and 44-54; Geiger, *The Mahāvaṃsa or the Great Chronicle of Ceylon* (London, 1912), pp. 82, 86-87; H. Oldenberg (ed.), *Dīpavaṃsa* (London, 1879), Book VIII, gāthās 1-13.

29. W. Geiger, *The Dīpavamsa and Mahāvamsa and their historical development in Ceylon* (Colombo, 1908), p. 115.

30. *bDe-bar gçegs-pa'i bstan-pa rigs-'byed čhos-kyi 'byuṅ-gnas gsuṅ-rab rin-po-čhe'i mjod.* Tōhoku Catalogue No. 5197. Transl. by E. Obermiller, *History of Buddhism* (Heidelberg, 1932); Anton Schiefner (transl.), *Tāranāthas Geschichte des Buddhismus in Indien* (St. Petersburg, 1869), p. 160, but note that F. D. K. Bosch has questioned the validity of this evidence ["Een oorkonde van het Groote Klooster te Nālandā," *Tijdschrift voor Indische Taal-, Land- en Volkenkunde*, vol. 65 (1925), p. 559, note 80]. On the Tibetan sources generally see Sarat Chandra Das, *Indian pandits in the Land of Snow* (London, 1893), p. 50, and "Indian pandits in Tibet," *Journal of the Buddhist Text Society of India*, vol. 1, no. 1 (1893), pp. 1-38; B. R. Chatterjee, "Indian culture in Java and Sumatra," *Bulletin of the Greater India Society*, vol. 3 (1927), pp. 25-26; Giuseppe Tucci, "The validity of Tibetan historical traditions," in *India Antiqua: a volume of oriental studies presented by his friends and pupils to Jean Philippe Vogel* . . . (Leiden, 1947), pp. 309-322. The sojourn of Dīpaṅkara Atīśa in Suvarṇadvīpa is depicted graphically in the colophon of an illustrated Nepalese manuscript dating probably from the 11th century: A. Foucher, *Etudes sur l'iconographie bouddhique de l'Inde, d'après des textes inédits*, vol. 1 (Paris, 1900), pp. 79, 189, plate XI, 2; H. B. Sarkar, "The cultural contact between Java and Bengal," *Indian Historical Quarterly*, vol. 13 (1937), pp. 596-598.

31. Maung Htin Aung, *A history of Burma* (New York, 1967), p. 5. For the sake of conformity with the rest of this chapter, I have added the diacritical marks in the quotation. A more recent affirmation of the same view is propounded by Sao Sāimöng Mangrāi, *The Pādaeng Chronicle and the Jengtung State Chronicle translated.* Michigan Papers on South and Southeast Asia No. 19 (Ann Arbor, Mich., 1981), p. 18.

32. M. C. Chand Chirayu Rajani, "Background to the Sri Vijaya story — Part II," *Journal of the Siam Society*, vol. 62, pt. 2 (1974), p. 304. Cp. also Jean Boisselier's suggestion that the capital of Suvaṇṇabhūmi is represented by the ruins at Ū Thòng: *Nouvelles connaissances archéologiques de la ville d'Ū-Thòng* (Bangkok, 1968), p. 26.

33. Lévi, *Mahākarmavibhaṅga*, p. 123.

34. Abū Raiḥān al-Bīrūnī, *Fī taḥqīq mā li'l-Hind:* ed. by E. C. Sachau (London, 1887); English transl. in 2 vols. by Sachau under the title *Alberuni's India. An account of the religion, philosophy, literature, geography, chronology, astronomy, customs, laws and astrology of India* (London, 1910), where the reference to *Sūwarn dīb* occurs on p. 210 of vol. 1.

35. R. C. Childers, *A dictionary of the Pāli language* (London, 1875), p. 492; Sandhu, *Early Malaysia*, p. 8.

36. Col. G. E. Gerini's attempt to discriminate between Suvarṇadvīpa (Island of Gold) and Suvarṇabhūmi (Land of Gold) [*Researches on Ptolemy's geography of Eastern Asia*. Asiatic Society Monographs, vol. 1 (London, 1909), pp. 77-78] has been sufficiently refuted by Majumdar, *Suvarṇadvīpa*, Part I, pp. 42-44.

37. Sylvain Lévi, "Kouen Louen et Dvīpāntara," *Bijdragen tot de Taal-, Land- en Volkenkunde van Nederlandsch-Indië*, vol. 88 (1931), pp. 621-627.

38. See Gabriel Ferrand, "Le K'ouen-louen et les anciennes navigations interocéaniques dans les mers du sud," *Journal Asiatique*, 11th series, vol. 13 (1919), pp. 239-333, 431-492, and vol. 14 (1919), pp. 6-68, 201-241. Cf. also Note 61. O. W. Wolters believes that by the 7th century A.D. this ethnonym had become restricted to the peoples of present-day Indonesia: *Early Indonesian commerce. A study of the origins of Śrīvijaya* (Ithaca, N.Y., 1967), p. 153.

39. R. Mitra (ed.), *Agni Purāṇa* (Calcutta, 1873-79), chap. 118, ślokas 1-5 and chap. 119, ślokas 27-28; *Vāmana Purāṇa*, ch. 13, ślokas 1-11; O. C. Gangoly, "Relation between Indian and Indonesian culture," *Journal of the Greater India Society*, vol. 7 (1940), pp. 58-60; Sandhu, *Early Malaysia*, p. 3. In their present recension the *Purāṇas* are not earlier than the Gupta period, but some of the material had been current in oral tradition for several centuries previously.
The ancient kingdom of Kaliṅga occupied the territories lying between the Mahānadī and Godāvarī rivers, that is the eastern tracts of present-day Orissa and northern Andhra.

40. *Kathāsaritsāgara*, taraṅga 58, ślokas 28ff; Tawney, vol. 9, pp. 35ff.

41. *Mahākarmavibhaṅga*, section 32, line a; also pp. 50-53 and 123-125 of Lévi's translation.

42. S. Rangachariar and V. S. Aiyar (ed.), *Raghuvaṁsa* (Tanjore, 1891), canto VI, śloka 57 [pp. 39, 56-57]; K. A. Nilakanta Sastri, "Dvīpāntara," *Journal of the Greater India Society*, vol. 9 (1942), p. 3.

43. Nilakanta Sastri, "Dvīpāntara," pp. 3-4. Although the *Guruparamparai, Arāyirappadi* (also known as *Harisamayadīpam*) was not put into its present form by Ṣaṭhakāpa-rāmānuja Mudaliyār until some time between the 12th and 17th centuries, it incorporates material at least as old as the 6th century A.D. It has been edited by S. Muttu-Krishna Nayudu and K. Ramasami Nayudu (Madras, 1904). The reference to Dvīpāntara is to be found in the narration of the life of the saint and scholar Tirumaṅgai Āḻvār who, significantly, journeyed thither in the 8th century in an attempt to acquire the wherewithal to renovate a temple in his homeland.

44. Katti Mudholkara, *Rāmāyaṇa*, Book IV, sarga 40, śloka 30; Prasad Shastri, *The Rāmāyana*, vol. 2, pp. 272-274.

45. Paul Pelliot, with his customary good sense, accepted the identification with present-day Java ["Deux itinéraires de Chine en Inde à la fin du VIIIe siècle," *Bulletin de l'Ecole Française d'Extrême-Orient*, vol. 4 (1904), p. 317], as did Jean Philippe Vogel [*The relation between the art of India and Java* (London, 1925), p. 15], Majumdar [*Suvarṇadvīpa*, Part I, p. 103, note 1], and

Coedès [*Les états hindouisés d'Indochine et d'Indonésie*, 3rd edition, pp. 104-105]; but Gabriel Ferrand preferred a Sumatran locale ["L'empire sumatranais de Çrīvijaya," *Journal Asiatique*, vol. 20 (1922), pp. 202-206], an opinion in which Ananda K. Coomaraswamy concurred [*History of Indian and Indonesian art* (London, 1927), p. 198], as did Gerini [*Researches on Ptolemy's geography of Eastern Asia*, pp. 547-548]. Hirananda Shastri ["The Nalanda copper-plate of Deva-pala-deva," *Epigraphia Indica*, vol. 17, pt. 7 (1924), p. 312], Edouard Chavannes ["Guṇavarman," *T'oung Pao*, 2nd series, vol. 5 (1904), pp. 193-206], and H. Kern ["Java en het Goudeiland volgens de oudste berichten," in *Verspreide Geschriften*, vol. 5 (1916), p. 314] were prepared to countenance a combined identification with both Java and Sumatra, while Dato Sir Roland Braddell argued strongly for a location in Kalimantan ["An introduction to the study of ancient times in the Malay Peninsula and the Straits of Malacca," *Journal of the Malayan Branch of the Royal Asiatic Society*, vol. 19, pt. 1 (1941), pp. 31-72].

Some scholars believe that the *Yāmadvīpa* mentioned in the *Vāyu Purāṇa* [R. Mitra (ed.), Calcutta, 1880-88] was a variant form of Yāvadvīpa [see K. A. Nilakanta Sastri in Braddell, "An introduction," *Journal of the Malayan Branch of the Royal Asiatic Society*, vol. 15, pt. 3 (1937), pp. 115-116]; while D. R. Mankad [*The Kiṣkindhākāṇḍa: the fourth book of the Vālmīki-Rāmāyaṇa* (Baroda, 1965), pp. xxxv-xli] has advanced a similar claim for the *Javaṇadīpa* visited by Cārudatta, as reported in Saṅgharājagavi's 5th-century *Vasudevahiṇḍi*. [For the influence of the *Bṛhatkathā* on this work see A. Alsdorff, *Aprabhraṁśa-Studien* (Leipzig, 1937)].

46. *Mārkaṇḍeya Purāṇa*, chap. 57, ślokas 5-7; *Agni Purāṇa*, chap. 118, ślokas 1-5 and chap. 119, ślokas 27-28; *Vāmana Purāṇa*, chap. 13, ślokas 1-11; *Matsya Purāṇa*, chap. 114; Gangoly, "Relations between Indian and Indonesian culture," pp. 57-60. On Kaṭāhadvīpa see K. A. Nilakanta Sastri, "Kaṭāha," *Journal of the Greater India Society*, vol. 5 (1938), pp. 128-146, and Vasudeva S. Agrawala, "Some references to Kaṭāha Dvīpa in ancient Indian literature," *Journal of the Greater India Society*, vol. 11 (1944), pp. 96-97: also Note 53 below; and for the location of Malayadvīpa, Datuk Sir Roland Braddell, "Malayadvīpa," *The Malayan Journal of Tropical Geography*, vol. 9 (1956), pp. 1-20. For attempts to place Kaserudvīpa in Southeast Asia see S. Majumdar Sastri, *Cunningham's ancient geography of India* (Calcutta, 1924), Appendix I; K. P. Jayaswal, *History of India, 150 A.D. to 350 A.D.* (Lahore, 1933), p. 154.

47. V. R. Ramachandra Dikshitar, *The Purāṇa index*, vol. 1 (Madras, 1951), p. 340, and vol. 2 (1952), p. 459.

48. George Coedès, "Séance du 14 janvier 1927," *Journal Asiatique*, vols. 210-211 (1927), p. 186; Louis Finot, review of Maspero's *Le royaume de Champa* in *Bulletin de l'Ecole Française d'Extrême-Orient*, vol. 28 (1928), pp. 286-287; Coedès, *Les états hindouisés*, p. 82. Suvaṇṇakūṭa and Jāva figure in the *Māha-Niddesa* (see Note 16 above). Jāva also occurs in the form *Śāvaka[=Jāvaka]-nadu* in the Tamil epic *Maṇimekhalai* of Kūlavāṇikaṇ Śittalai Śāttaṉār [U. V. Sāmaināth-aiyar (ed.), *Maṇimekhalai* (Madras, 1898), canto 25; G. U. Pope (transl.), *Mani-mekhalai* (Madras, 1911), pp. 55-58; Ramachandra Dikshitar, *Studies in Tamil literature and history* (Madras, 1936), p. 83], in the *Mañjuśrī-mūla-kalpa* [Edited for the Trivandrum Sanskrit Series Nos. LXX and LXXVI by T. Ganapati Śāstri (1920-22): Chatterjee, "Indian culture in Java and Sumatra," p. 25], and the Prākrit *Rās Mālā*, a collection of old Gujarāti ballads [Gujarāti transl. by Ranchhodbhai Udayarama, 2 vols. (Bombay, 1869-70); English transl. by A. K. Forbes, *Rās Mālā or Hindoo annals of the Province of Goozerat in western India*, 2 vols. (London, 1856)]. Although the date of this collectaneum is unknown, it has been established that some of its materials go back to the 5th century A.D. Finally, in the *Sūrya-Siddhānta*, one of the five astronomical treatises which ranked as authoritative in about the 6th century A.D. and whose core went back at least to A.D. 400, there is reference to a Yāvakoṭi, which supposedly denoted all or part of eastern Java [Ed. by F. E. Hall and B. D. Sastrin, *Bibliotheca Indica* (Calcutta, 1859); Eng. transl. by E. Burgess, *Sūrya Siddhānta: translation of a textbook of Hindu astronomy* (Calcutta,

1860; reprinted Calcutta, 1936); Chatterjee, "Indian culture in Java and Sumatra," p. 14; Kern, *Verspreide Geschriften*, vol. 5 (pp. 246-254); K. A. Nilakanta Sastri, *South Indian influence in the Far East* (Bombay, 1949), p. 12]. Suvarṇakuḍya is mentioned in both the *Arthaśāstra* [*Adhikaraṇa* II, *prakaraṇa* xi, para. 78; Shamasastry, pp. 79-80, 90-91; Kangle, Part II, p. 117] and the *Bṛhatsaṁhitā* [chap. XIV, śloka 9; Fleet, p. 179] under a variety of orthographies.

49. Suvarṇapura was mentioned in the first half of the 7th century by Bāṇabhaṭṭa, usually accounted the greatest of Indian prose-writers, in his *Kādambarī*: M. Ramachandra Kale (ed.), *Kādambarī* (Bombay, 1895-96), paras, 234, 238-241; C. M. Ridding, *The Kādambarī of Bāṇa* (London, 1896), pp. 89-91; K. A. Nilakanta Sastri, "The Tamil land and the eastern colonies," *Journal of the Greater India Society*, vol. II (1944), pp. 26-27.

50. Karpuradvīpa is mentioned in the *Kathāsaritsāgara*, t. 56, ś. 55-64; Tawney, vol. 4, p. 244; Lévi, "Kouen Louen et Dvīpāntara," p. 627; K. A. Nilakanta Sastri, *History of India* (Madras, 1950), pp. 168-169: but note that Ferrand characterized the name as a fiction of folklore ["Le K'ouen-louen," p. 185, note 3], while S. K. De castigated it as a late Kāshmirī interpolation [in S. N. Dasgupta and S. K. De, *A history of Sanskrit literature* (Calcutta, 1947), pp. 98-99].

51. Lévi, "Ptolémée, le Niddesa et la Bṛhatkathā," pp. 26-27. For Tāmbraliṅga in later times see O. W. Wolters, "Tāmbraliṅga," *Bulletin of the School of Oriental and African Studies*, vol. 21, no. 3 (1958), pp. 587-607.

52. Wheatley, "Takola emporion: a study of an early Malayan place-name," *The Malayan Journal of Tropical Geography*, vol. 2 (1954), pp. 35-47.

53. In some *Purāṇas, Kaṭāha* was substituted for the names Saumya and Gāndharva (probably at a relatively late date). The same name is mentioned twice in the Jain Prākrit religious tale (*dharmakathā*) composed by Haribhadra under the title *Samarāicca-kahā* during the 8th century [Edited by H. Jacobi, *Bibliotheca Indica* (Calcutta, 1908), pp. 195-206 and 585], in both instances in connection with voyages thither from Tāmraliptī. It also occurs several times in the *Kathāsaritsāgara*: e.g., t. 123, ś. 110; t. 60, ś. 2-6; probably (under the orthography Kaṭakṣadvīpa) in the *Bṛhatkathā Mañjari* of the poet Kṣemendra [V. S. Agrawala, "Some references to Kaṭāha Dvīpa in ancient Indian literature," *Journal of the Greater India Society*, vol. 11 (1944), pp. 96-97]; in the Sanskrit drama *Kaumudīmahotsava*, of uncertain date [Ed. by M. R. Kavi and S. K. Ramanatha Sastri (Madras, 1929), Eng. transl. by Sakuntala Rao Sastri (Bombay, 1952)]; and in the Tamil form Kadāram in the epic *Śilappadikāram*, composed by Ilango-Aḍigal at some time between the 3rd and 7th centuries A.D. [Ed. by Mahamahopadhaya V. Swaminatha Aiyar (Madras, 1892), Eng. transl. by V. R. Ramachandra Dikshitar (Oxford, 1939)]. See also K. A. Nilakanta Sastri, "Kaṭāha," *Journal of the Greater India Society*, vol. 5 (1938), pp. 128-146; Dato Sir Roland Braddell, "Takola and Kataha," *Journal of the Malayan Branch of the Royal Asiatic Society*, vol. 22, pt. 1 (1949), pp. 1-16, and "Ilangasoka and Kadaram," *loc. cit.*, pp. 16-24; Wheatley, *The Golden Khersonese*, chap. 18, especially pp. 278-280.

54. Summarized in Sandhu, *Early Malaysia*, pp. 1-10.

55. See, for instance, Sandhu, *Early Malaysia*, p. 4.

56. Forbes, *Rās Mālā*, vol. 2, p. 79. The archetypical theme of these early Indian voyages to Southeast Asia is encapsulated in part of the passage in the *Mahākarmavibhaṅga* cited on p. 263 above, and which has been rendered into French by Sylvain Lévi as follows:

> Avec mes cinq cents camarades je me rendis sur la plage. Je fis voeu d'observer le Jour sabbatique avec les huits Commandements et je partis sur mer. Comme nous faisions route vers la Terre d'Or [Suvarṇabhūmi], notre navire battu par des vents capricieux se perdit. Tout le monde

périt. Moi seul, après bien des journées, tant bien que mal, je m'en tirai. Je sors de l'eau, épuisé de fatigue, et voilà que j'aperçois une ville avec des murailles d'or, des jardins, des bosquets, des étangs de lotus; l'encens y fumait . . .

Mahākarmavibhaṅga, pp. 125-6.

57. Majumdar, *Suvarṇadvīpa*, Part I, p. 61. Cf. also Sylvain Lévi, writing in the more restricted context of the *Jātaka*: "Un grand nombre de récits du Jātaka ont trait à des aventures de mer; la mer et la navigation tenaient manifestement une grande place dans la vie de l'Inde à l'époque où ces récits furent imaginés." ["Maṇimekhalā, divinité de la mer," *Bulletin des Lettres de l'Académie Belgique* (1930), p. 282: see, in addition, Lévi, "On Maṇimekhalā 'the guardian deity of the sea,'" *The Indian Historical Quarterly*, vol. 7 (1931), p. 173, and "More on Maṇimekhalā," *loc. cit.*, p. 371; also Madan Mohan Singh, "India's oversea trade as known from the Buddhist canons, "*The Indian Historical Quarterly*, vols. 2 and 3 (1961), pp. 177-182].

58. Wilfred H. Schoff, *The Periplus of the Erythraean Sea. Travels and trade in the Indian Ocean by a merchant of the first century* (London, 1912), p. 46; J. I. H. Frisk, "Le Périple de la Mer Erythrée," *Göteborgs Högskolas Årsskrift*, vol. 33 (1927), pp. 18, 19, 22; G. W. B. Huntingford, *The Periplus of the Erythraean Sea*. The Hakluyt Society, Second Series No. 151 (London, 1980), p. 53; Louis Renou, *La Géographie de Ptolémée, L'Inde (VII, 1-4)* (Paris, 1925), p. 6, line 8.

59. Cp. also Procopius's remark that, even as late as the 6th century A.D., Persian merchants "always locate themselves at the very harbors where the Indian ships make their landfall" (*History of the Wars*, I, xx, 12: Loeb Classical Library, 1914). Beyond Cape Comorin the character of the information in the *Periplus* changes, losing its customary precision and becoming increasingly speculative, as if picked up casually from Eastern traders encountered in the ports of Malabar. The *Periplus* is usually ascribed to about the middle of the 1st century A.D., though Jacqueline Pirenne has argued persuasively for a date early in the 3rd century ["La date du 'Périple de la Mer Erythrée,'" *Journal Asiatique*, vol. 249 (1961), pp. 441-459].

60. *Ch'ien-Han Shu* 前漢書, chüan 28B, f. 32 recto et verso; Wheatley, "Possible references to the Malay Peninsula in the Annals of the Former Han," *Journal of the Malayan Branch of the Royal Asiatic Society*, vol. 30, pt. 1 (1957), pp. 115-116.

61. To the references specified in Note 38 to this Chapter, add R. A. Stein, "Le Lin-yi, sa localisation, sa contribution à la formation du Champa et ses liens avec la Chine," *Han-Hiue*, vol. 2, pts. 1-3 (1947), pp. 209-311; A. Christie, "An obscure passage from the Periplus: κολανδιοφωντα τὰ μέγιστα," *Bulletin of the School of Oriental and African Studies*, vol. 19 (1957), pp. 345-353.

62. Although *Puâ-się was the standard Chinese transcription of *Parsa*, it is evident that the shippers of *Puâ-się cargoes were not specifically or exclusively Iranians, and that the commodities they transported were not necessarily, or even primarily, of Persian provenance, though they may have borne that generalized classification because they were of actual or supposedly "Persian type." In fact several of the commodities customarily categorized as *Puâ-się goods were Southeast Asian substitutes for Middle Eastern resins: vide *int. al.*, Berthold Laufer, *Sino-Iranica: Chinese contributions to the history of civilization in ancient Iran*. Field Museum of Natural History Publication 201 (Chicago, 1919), pp. 468-487; Wolters, *Early Indonesian commerce*, chaps. 9 and 10.

63. Cf., *int. al.*, *Huai-nan Tzŭ* 淮南子 chüan 18, f. 27; *Shih Chi* 史記, chüan 129, ff. 8v - 9v; *Ch'ien-Han Shu*, chüan 28B, f. 31v.

64. Cf. Louis Malleret, *L'archéologie du delta du Mékong: III, La culture du Fou-nan* (Paris, 1962), chap. 23. The artifacts of Mediterranean provenance that

have been excavated at the port city of Oc-èo in southern Indochina include
medallions, intaglios, beads, coins, and even a bronze bust of the Roman Emperor
Maximinus (A.D. 235-8). Techniques and ideas from the Mediterranean and the
Roman Orient are manifested most clearly in Hellenistic and Roman influences on
a few items of representational art from Indochina, notably in a Lysippan-style
figurine excavated at Trà-vĩnh [Charles Picard, "A figure of Lysippan type from
the Far East: the Tra Vinh bronze 'dancer'," *Artibus Asiae*, vol. 19 (1956),
pp. 342-352], in the Dionysian motifs discernible in a statuette recovered from a
Han-dynasty tomb in Thanh-hóa [Olov. R. T. Janse, "Dionysos au Vietnam," *Viking*
(1957-58), pp. 36-50], and a bronze Alexandrian lamp probably of the 2nd century
A.D. from the lower Maeklong valley [Charles Picard, "La lampe Alexandrine de
P‘ong Tuk [Siam]," *Artibus Asiae*, vol. 18 (1955), pp. 137-149].

65. Schoff, *The Periplus of the Erythraean Sea*, p. 48; Frisk, "Le Périple,"
p. 126; Huntingford, *Periplus*, p. 56. For the irregular declension of accusative
Θίνα, genitive Θινός, which occurs in the *Periplus*, para. 64 (as opposed to
Θίναι in Ptolemy [Renou, *La Géographie de Ptolémée*, p. 62] and Martianus of
Heraclea [*Periplus of the Outer Sea*, I, 16]), see Frisk, *op. cit.*, p. 126, and
Paul Pelliot, *Notes on Marco Polo*, vol. 1 (Paris, 1959), pp. 266-267. However,
Pelliot rejects Frisk's hypothesis of a nominative *Θίς. "Either," he says, "the
name was Θίνα in the nominative (with a final -α, which was not necessarily
etymological) and the declension is irregular and due to analogy [cp. Θίς =
sand-heap, acc. Θίνα, gen. Θινός]; or the nominative was *Θίν, with a regular
declension due perhaps to the attraction of the model of Θίς [also the name of
an Egyptian town]."

66. Malleret, *La culture du Fou-nan*, p. 395.

67. George Coedès, *Les états hindouisés d'Indochine et d'Indonésie*, pp. 44-49.

68. *Shui-Ching Chu* 水經注 chüan 23B [For this work see p. 384 below.
Although it was not compiled until the beginning of the 6th century A.D., it
seems often to have incorporated information from earlier periods]. George
Coedès has related the term *kolandia* to the *kola* mentioned in certain Sanskrit
Buddhist texts and the *kalam* of Tamil Saṅgam literature [*Textes d'auteurs grecs
et latins relatifs à l'Extrême-Orient, depuis le IVe siècle av. J. C. jusqu'au
XIVe siècle* (Paris, 1910), p. XVII, note 1, and *Les états hindouisés*, p. 63. Cf.
also Pierre Meile, "Les Yavana dans l'Inde tamoule," *Journal Asiatique*, vol. 232
(1940), pp. 90-92; Christie, "An obscure passage," *passim*.

69. Lit. "to the kingdom of Ta Ch‘in 大秦 [the Roman Orient]": K‘ang T‘ai 康
泰 *Wu-shih Wai-kuo Chuan* 吳時外國傳 apud *T‘ai-p‘ing Yü-lan* 太平御
覽 chüan 771.

70. *T‘ai-p‘ing Yü-lan*, chüan 769, f. 6r, citing the 3rd-century *Nan-Chou I-wu
Chih* 南州異物志 by Wan Chen 萬震 ; Paul Pelliot, "Quelques textes
chinois concernant l'Indochine hindouisée," in G. Van Oest (ed.), *Etudes
Asiatiques publiées à l'occasion du vingt-cinquième anniversaire de l'Ecole
Française d'Extrême-Orient*, vol. 2 (1925), pp. 255-257; Hsiang Ta 向達
"Han-T‘ang-chien Hsi-yü chi Hai-nan chu-kuo ku ti-li-shu hsü-lu," *Kuo-li Pei-p‘ing
T‘u-shu-Kuan K‘an* 漢唐間西域及海南諸國古地理書叙錄
國立北平圖書館刊 vol. 4, no. 6 (1930), pp. 27-28; Stein, "Le
Lin-yi," pp. 65-66; Joseph Needham, *Science and civilisation in China*, vol. 4,
pt. 3: *Civil engineering and nautics* (Cambridge, 1971), pp. 458-460.

71. *T‘ai-p‘ing Yü-lan*, chüan 359, f. 15r, citing *Wu-shih Wai-kuo Chuan*; *Liang Shu*
梁書 chüan 54, f. 22v.

72. John Legge (transl.), *A record of Buddhistic kingdoms: an account by the
Chinese monk Fa-Hsien of his travels in India and Ceylon (A.D. 399-414) in search
of the Buddhist books of discipline* (Oxford, 1886); H. A. Giles, *The travels of
Fa-hsien (399-414 A.D.)* (Cambridge, 1923); Wheatley, *The Golden Khersonese*, chap.
4.

It is probably vessels of the kʻuən-luən bʻɒk type that constitute the majority of those sculptured in bas-relief on the galleries of the great stūpa of Borobudur in Java, which dates from about A.D. 800 [J. Nicholaas Krom and T. van Erp, Barabudur; archaeological and architectural description, 3 portfolios and 3 volumes (The Hague, 1927-31), Ser. Ib, pl. XXVII, fig. 53; pl. XLIII, fig. 86; pl. XLIV, fig. 88; pl. LIV, fig. 108; and Ser. II, pl. XXI, fig. 41; Radhakamud Mukerji, Indian shipping; a history of the sea-borne trade and maritime activity of the Indians from the earliest times (Bombay and Calcutta, 1912), frontispiece, pp. 48, no. 3; 46, no. 1; 48, no.'s 5 and 6; J. Hornell, Water transport: origins and early evolution (Cambridge, 1946), pl. XXXIIIB, and "Sea trade in early times," Antiquity, vol. 15 (1941), fig. 5; A. J. Bernet Kempers, Ancient Indonesian art (Cambridge, Mass., 1959), pl. 78; Needham, Science and civilisation in China, vol. 4, pt. 3, fig. 973), and elsewhere.] From these representations, and from Hui Lin's 慧琳 8th-century commentary on the Vinaya Canon (I-chʻieh Ching Yin-i 一切經音義, Japanese Tripiṭaka, Wei sectn. IX, f. 155r), which incorporates a paragraph or two on Southeast Asian shipping in a textual gloss, it appears that kʻuən-luən bʻɒk hulls were sewn rather than nailed, the reason offered by Hui Lin being that "the heating of the iron would cause fires." In any case, the mode of construction produced a resilient ship well adapted to withstand the stress of monsoon storms and the jarring shock of rock and reef. The vessels depicted on the Borobudur also displayed large outriggers and the elongated, canted square-sails characteristic of certain classes of Indonesian boats in more recent times, the latter being especially significant because, as Needham as demonstrated [Science and civilisation, vol. 4, pt. 3, p. 458], canting was in all probability the first stage in the development of fore-and-aft sailing. The pʻɒk of Hui Lin and the Borobudur were some four centuries later than those of Wan Chen, so the comparison between them must not be pushed too far. But sailing technology in South Asia seems not to have changed all that rapidly, and the vessels described by Wan Chen were clearly of substantial size.

73. Manu-smṛti, Adhyāya III, śloka 158; G. Bühler, Manu-smṛti: the laws of Manu (Oxford, 1886), p. 105; R. Chanda, "Early Indian seamen," The Sir Asutosh Mookerjee Silver Jubilee Volumes, vol. 3 (Calcutta, 1922), pp. 105-106.

74. Baudhāyana Dharmasūtra, Praśna II, adhyāya 1, kandikā ii, śloka 2; G. Bühler, The sacred laws of the Āryas as taught in the schools of Āpastamba, Gautama, Vāsishṭha and Baudhāyana, Part II (Oxford, 1882), p. 217.

75. A passage in the Mṛgendrāgama actually considers sea voyages for conquest or profit to be permissible [N. R. Bhatt, Mṛgendrāgama. Publication de l'Institut Français d'Indologie No. 23 (Pondichéry, 1962), p. 76].

76. Sylvain Lévi, "Les 'marchands de mer' et leur rôle dans le bouddhisme primitif," Bulletin de l'Association Française des Amis de l'Orient (1929), pp. 19-39; Alfred Foucher, Etude sur l'iconographie bouddhique de l'Inde, d'après des textes inédits, vol. 1 (Paris, 1900), pp. 77-84.

77. George Coedès, "Excavations at Pʻong Tük in Siam," Annual Bibliography of Indian Archaeology (1927), pp. 16-20; Coedès, "The excavations at Pʻong Tük and their importance for the ancient history of Siam," Journal of the Siam Society, vol. 21 (1928), pp. 204-207.

78. Virgile Rougier, "Nouvelles découvertes chames au Quang-nam," Bulletin de la Commission Archéologique de l'Indochine (Paris, 1912), pp. 212-213; Ananda K. Coomaraswamy, History of Indian and Indonesian art (New York, 1927), p. 197.

79. F. M. Schnitger, The archaeology of Hindoo Sumatra (Leiden, 1937), plate I. This statue is probably of later date than the others, perhaps belonging to the late-7th or early-8th century: see Nik Hassan Shuhaimi, "The Bukit Seguntang Buddha: a reconsideration of its date," JMBRAS, vol. 52, pt. 2 (1979), pp. 33-40.

80. W. Cohn, Buddha in der Kunst des Ostens (Leipzig, 1925), p. 28.

81. Frederik D. K. Bosch, "Het bronzen Buddha-beeld van Celebes westkust, *Tijdschrift voor Indische Taal-, Land- en Volkenkunde*, vol. 73 (1933), pp. 495-513; Bosch, "Summary of archaeological work in Netherlands India in 1933," *Annual Bibliography of Indian Archaeology*, vol. 8 (1933), p. 35. Originally these statues were ascribed to the Amarāvatī school of Buddhist art, but subsequent examination has shown that most, if not all, of them were of Gupta date [Mirella Levi d'Ancona, "Amarāvatī, Ceylon and the three 'imported bronzes'," *The Art Bulletin*, vol. 34 (1952), pp. 1-17; Pierre Dupont, "Les Buddha dits d'Amarāvatī en Asie du Sud-Est," *Bulletin de l'Ecole Française d'Extrême-Orient*, vol. 49 (1954), pp. 631-636; Senarat Paranavitana, *Ceylon and Malaysia* (Colombo, 1966), pp. 191-195]. Dīpaṁkara has been interpreted as signifying "Island-Maker," because "it is a support to people in the sea which is devoid of all support" [Paranavitana (*loc. cit.*, p. 176), citing verbatim King Kassapa V in his *Dampiyā-aṭuvā gäṭapada*, D. B. Jayatilaka's edition, p. 6]. Paranavitana (*ibid.*) also mentions the existence in Anurādhapura in the 6th century A.D. of a corporation of bankers who had taken the Buddha Dīpaṁkara as their patron, indicating thereby that they were financing overseas trade, almost certainly with Southeast Asia partly if not wholly.

The ivory comb is described by Bennett Bronson and George F. Dales, "Excavations at Chansen, Thailand, 1968 and 1969: a preliminary report," *Asian Perspectives*, vol. 15 (1973), pp. 28-30.

82. I Ching 義淨 *Ta-T'ang Hsi-yü Ch'iu-fa Kao-seng Chuan* 大唐西域求法高僧傳 f. 98 r et v, and *passim*; Edouard Chavannes, *Mémoire composé à l'époque de la grande dynastie T'ang sur les religieux éminents qui allèrent chercher la Loi dans les pays d'occident* (Paris, 1894), *passim*; Wheatley, *The Golden Khersonese*, pp. 41-45.

83. L. de la Vallée Poussin, *Dynasties et histoire de l'Inde depuis Kanishka jusqu'aux invasions musulmanes* (Paris, 1935), p. 293; Coedès, *Les états hindouisés*, pp. 58-69; Wheatley, *The Golden Khersonese*, pp. 189-193; Jean Filliozat, "New researches on the relations between India and Cambodia," *Indica*, vol. 3 (1966), pp. 95-106; Anthony Christie, "The provenance and chronology of early Indian cultural influences in South East Asia," in Himansu Bhusan Sarkar (ed.), *R. C. Majumdar Felicitation Volume* (Calcutta, 1970), pp. 1-14.

84. Cf. p. 273 above. Foucher [*Etude sur l'iconographie bouddhique*, vol. 1, pp. 189-209] reproduces two miniature paintings of the Buddha Dīpaṁkara from Ceylon (Siṁhaladvīpa) and two from *Yāvadvīpa* which are included in an illuminated palm-leaf manuscript of the *Prajñāpāramitā* from Nepal, now preserved in the University Library at Cambridge. Cf. also Paranavitana, *Ceylon and Malaysia*, pp. 176-177, 191-198.

85. Levi d'Ancona, "Amarāvatī, Ceylon and the three imported bronzes," *passim*; Dupont, "Les Buddha dits d'Amarāvatī," *passim*. For further details of the relations between Ceylon and Southeast Asia in early times see J. G. de Casparis, "New evidence on cultural relations between Java and Ceylon in ancient times," *Artibus Asiae*, vol. 24 (1961), pp. 241-248, and, with caution, Paranavitana, *Ceylon and Malaysia*, *passim*. For predominantly skeptical evaluations of this last work, see K. Indrapala, review in *Journal of the Ceylon Branch of the Royal Asiatic Society*, new series, vol. 16 (1967), pp. 101-106, and R. A. L. H. Gunawardana, "Ceylon and Malaysia: a study of Professor S. Paranavitana's research on the relations between the two regions," *University of Ceylon Review*, vol. 25, nos. 1 and 2 (1967), pp. 1-64.

86. Cf. Note 143 to Chapter 2.

87. Cf. Note 76 to Chapter 5.

88. A high proportion of the investigations of coastal change in Sumatra have been undertaken in connection with attempts to locate the site of the capital of Śrī Vijaya (See Chapter 6, pp. 239-240): e.g., B. Obdijn, "Zuid-Sumatra volgens de oudste berichten," *Tijdschrift van het Koninklijk Nederlandsch Aardrijkskundig*

Urban Genesis in the Indianized Territories   341

Genootschap, vol. 58 (1941), pp. 190-216, 322-341, 476-507; and "Den geografische kennis omtrent Sumatra in de Middeleeuwen," *ibid.*, vol. 59 (1942), pp. 46-75 and vol. 60 (1943), pp. 102-110; Dinas Purbakala Republik Indonesia, "Garis pantai Sriwidjaja," *Amerta: Warna Warta Kepurbakalaan*, vol. 3 (1955), pp. 30-32; R. Soekmono, "Geomorphology and the location of Çriwijaya," *Madjalah Ilmu-Ilmu Sastra Indonesia*, vol. 1 (1963), pp. 79-92. Works of, in varying degrees, broader scope include H. D. Tjia *et al.*, "Coastal accretion in western Indonesia," *Bulletin of the National Institute of Geology and Mining*, vol. 1 (1968), pp. 15-45; H. Th. Verstappen, "The geomorphology of Sumatra," *The Journal of Tropical Geography*, vol. 18 (1964), pp. 184-191, and *A geomorphological reconnaissance of Sumatra and adjacent islands (Indonesia)* (Groningen, 1973); M. J. G. Chambers and A. Sobur, *The rates and processes of recent coastal accretions in the Province of South Sumatra: a preliminary survey* (Mimeo.). An unpublished paper presented to the Regional Conference on the Geology and Mineral Resources of South East Asia, Jakarta, 1975; John N. Miksic, "Archaeology and palaeogeography in the Straits and Malacca," in Karl L. Hutterer (ed.), *Economic exchange and social interaction in Southeast Asia: perspectives from prehistory, history, and ethnography*. Michigan Papers on South and Southeast Asia No. 13 (Ann Arbor, Mich., 1977), pp. 155-175. Excellent examples of ways in which geomorphological concepts can be invoked in the solution of historical problems are: J. Noorduyn and H. Th. Verstappen, "Pūrṇavarman's river-works near Tugu," *Bijdragen tot de Taal-, Land- en Volkenkunde*, vol. 128 (1972), pp. 298-307; O. W. Wolters, "Landfall on the Palembang coast in medieval times," *Indonesia*, vol. 20 (1975), pp. 1-58.

89. Additional studies bearing on this suite of problems include J. B. Scrivenor, "Geological and geographical evidence for changes in sea level during ancient Malayan history and late pre-history," *Journal of the Malayan Branch of the Royal Asiatic Society*, vol. 12, pt. 1 (1949), pp. 107-115; Herman Theodoor Verstappen, *Djakarta Bay. A geomorphological study on shoreline development*. Publicatie No. 8 uit het Geographisch Instituut der Rijks Universiteit te Utrecht ('s-Gravenhage, 1953), pp. 39-63; J. J. Nossin, "Relief and coastal development in north-eastern Johore (Malaya)," *The Journal of Tropical Geography*, vol. 15 (1961), pp. 27-38, "Coastal sedimentation in northeastern Johore (Malaya)," *Zeitschrift für Geomorphologie*, vol. 6, pts. 3 & 4 (1962), pp. 293-316, and "The geomorphic history of the northern Pahang delta," *loc. cit.*, vol. 20 (1965), pp. 54-64; R. D. Hill, "Changes in beach form at Sri Pantai, northeast Johore, Malaysia," *loc. cit.*, vol. 23 (1966), pp. 19-27. For possible, but apparently still unsubstantiated, changes in the morphology of the Annamite coast see R. A. Stein, "Le Lin-yi," *Han-Hiue*, vol. 2, fascicules 1-3 (1947), p. 57, note 39. What is known about paleoclimates in the archipelagic realms of Southeast Asia is summarized, with a pertinent bibliography, in H. Th. Verstappen, "On palaeo climates and landform development in Malesia," *Modern Quaternary Research in Southeast Asia*, vol. 1 (1975), pp. 3-35.

90. Cp. p. 49 above.

91. Cf., for example, E. R. Leach, *Political systems of highland Burma* (Cambridge, Mass., 1954), *passim*; F. K. Lehman, *The structure of Chin society. A tribal people of Burma adapted to a non-Western civilization*. Illinois Studies in Anthropology No. 3 (Urbana, Ill., 1963), *passim*; Frederick J. Simoons, *A ceremonial ox of India. The mithan in nature, culture, and history* (Madison, Wisc., 1968), which incorporates an extensive bibliography; A. Thomas Kirsch, *Feasting and social oscillation: a working paper on religion and society in upland Southeast Asia*. Data Paper No. 92, Southeast Asia Program, Cornell University (Ithaca, 1973), *passim*.

92. Kent V. Flannery, "The cultural evolution of civilizations," *Annual Review of Ecology and Systematics*, vol. 3 (1972), p. 415.

93. Morton H. Fried, "On the evolution of social stratification and the state," in Stanely Diamond (ed.), *Culture in history: essays in honor of Paul Radin* (New York, 1960), pp. 713-731.

94. R. M. Netting, "Ecosystems in process: a comparative study of change in two West African societies," in D. Damas (ed.), *Contributions to anthropology: ecological essays*. Bulletin of the National Museums of Canada, vol. 230 (Ottawa, 1969), p. 109.

95. Thomas R. Malthus, *An essay on population*. Everyman's Library, 7th edition, 2 vols. (New York and London, 1952). First edition 1798, second edition 1817.

96. Ester Boserup, *The conditions of agricultural growth. The economics of agrarian change under population pressure* (London, 1965).

97. Boserup does not assert that these adaptations *will* take place: only that conditions will be propitious for their adoption. In actual fact, it is not unknown for groups to accept a decline in living standards as a result of rising population pressures, while others resort to such expedients as population control and migration. Paula Brown and Aaron Podolefsky have, in fact, suggested that "the relationship between population density and agricultural intensity is interactional and that neither can be consistently antecedent to the other": "Population density, agricultural intensity, land tenure, and group size in the New Guinea Highlands," *Ethnology*, vol. 15 (1976), p. 229, note 5. However, correlation analysis of one particular sample of contemporary, tropical, subsistence farmers has revealed a strong positive association (although not, of course, a necessarily causal relationship) between population densities and agricultural intensities, the variation in the former accounting for 58% of the variation in the logarithm of the latter: B. L. Turner II, Robert Q. Hanham, and Anthony V. Portararo, "Population pressure and agricultural intensity," *AAAG*, vol. 67, no. 3 (1977), pp. 384-396.

98. The notion of population increase, if not of population pressure, was implicit in the expositions of virtually all the Indologists and epigraphers who provided the first syntheses of the early history of Southeast Asia and of its constituent culture realms. More recently, it has been invoked by, *int. al.*, Wilhelm G. Solheim II, "Reworking Southeast Asian prehistory," *Paideuma*, vol. 15 (1969), p. 133; Chester F. Gorman, "A priori models and Thai prehistory; a reconsideration of the beginnings of agriculture in Southeastern Asia." Paper presented to the Conference on *The origins of agriculture* at the Ninth International Congress on Ethnography and the Anthropological Sciences (Chicago, 1973), p. 28. The only attempt I know of rigorously to deduce paleodemographic data from Southeast Asian archeological evidence is Michael Pietrusewsky, "The palaeodemography of a prehistoric Thai population: Non Nok Tha," *Asian Perspectives*, vol. 17, no. 2 (1975), pp. 125-140.
For discussions of the nature of anthropological and archeological inferences concerning population densities and pressures, see Philip E. L. Smith, "Land-use, settlement patterns and subsistence agriculture: a demographic perspective," in P. J. Ucko, R. Tringham, and G. W. Dimbleby, *Man, settlement and urbanism* (London, 1972), pp. 409-425., and "Changes in population pressure in archaeological explanation," *World Archaeology*, vol. 4, no. 1 (1972), pp. 5-18; and the papers brought together in Brian J. Spooner (ed.), *Population growth: anthropological implications* (Cambridge, Mass., 1972).

99. An often cited instance of a transformation such as is here envisaged is provided by Ralph Linton and Abram Kardiner, "The change from dry to wet rice cultivation in Tanala-Betsileo," in *The individual and his society* (New York, 1939). Reprinted in T. M. Newcomb and E. L. Hartley (eds.), *Readings in social psychology* (New York, 1952). After the Tanala had adopted techniques of wet-*padi* cultivation from their Betsileo neighbors, Linton was able to document the following changes in the structure of their society: the gradual emergence of a group of landowners; the disruption of the joint family, endogamy, and self-sufficiency; the founding of settlements; modifications in the patterns of warfare; the attachment of an economic value to slaves and an associated formulation of ransom procedures; and the institutionalization of kingship. A comparable sequence of socio-economic changes induced by a transition from swidden to wet-*padi* farming among tribesmen in Tripura State has been described

by Chie Nakane ["Tripura . . .," *Minzokugaku Kenkyū*, vol. 19, pt. 2 (1955), pp. 58-99]. There, too, Professor Nakane observed a progressive dissolution of cooperative institutions and the individualization of swidden cultivation by those farmers who continued to practice it perforce in the socio-economic context of predominant wet-*padi* farming. Miss Nakane's paragraphs on this transition are so similar to those of Linton that each could be substituted for the other without doing violence to the conclusions of either paper. David E. Sopher has also reached similar conclusions as a result of his analysis of the change during the past century from swidden to plow agriculture among groups such as the Chakma and Mogh inhabiting valleys in the Chittagong hill tracts ["The swidden/wet rice transition zone in the Chittagong hills," *Annals of the Association of American Geographers*, vol. 54, no. 1 (1964), pp. 107-126].

For general discussions of the possible implications of ecosystemic diversity and dependability see Robert McC. Adams, *The evolution of urban society: early Mesopotamia and Prehispanic Mexico* (Chicago, 1966), chap. 2; Wheatley, *The pivot of the four quarters* (Edinburgh and Chicago, 1971), pp. 268-275.

100. Karl A. Wittfogel synthesized a quarter of a century of theorizing about the role of hydraulic construction in the formation of bureaucratic states in *Oriental despotism: a comparative study of total power* (New Haven, Conn., 1957). He also distilled the essence of his formulation into a paper in William L. Thomas, Jr. (ed.), *Man's role in changing the face of the earth* (Chicago, 1956), pp. 152-164. Although we discount the existence of very large irrigation schemes in prehistoric Southeast Asia, it is only fair to note that, at the swamp site of Kuk in the New Guinea Highlands, Jack Golson has discovered extensive drainage systems (some drains running uninterruptedly for as much as 3 km.) dating from at latest 4000 B.C. [Golson, "Recent discoveries in the New Guinea Highlands: simple tools and complex technology," in R. V. S. Wright (ed.), *Stone tools as cultural markers* Canberra, 1977), pp. 154-161.

101. The most compendious statement of Jonathan Friedman's deductive formulation is presented in "Tribes, states, and transformations," in Maurice Bloch (ed.), *Marxist analyses and social anthropology*. Association of Social Anthropologists Studies No. 3 (London and New York, 1973), pp. 161-202. Other of the author's works which have a bearing on the argument are *System, structure and contribution in the evolution of "Asiatic" social formations*. Unpublished Ph.D. dissertation, Columbia University (New York, 1972), and "Marxism, structuralism and vulgar materialism," *Man*, vol. 9, no. 3 (1974), pp. 444-469.

102. Cf. H. J. Wehrli, "Beitrag zur Ethnologie der Chingpaw (Kachin) von Ober-Burma," *Internationales Archiv für Ethnographie*, vol. 16 (Leiden, 1904), supplement; C. Gilhodes, *The Kachins: religion and customs* (Calcutta, 1922); O. Hanson, *The Kachins: their customs and traditions* (Rangoon, 1913); H. F. Hertz, *A practical handbook of the Kachin or Chingpaw language . . . with an appendix on Kachin customs, laws and religion* (Rangoon, 1915); Marcel Granet, "Catégories matrimoniales et relations de proximité dans la Chine ancienne," *Annales Sociologiques*, Série B, fasc. 1-3 (1939); Claude Lévi-Strauss, *Les structures élémentaires de la parenté* (First published 1949; Revised edition, Paris, 1967), chaps. 15 and 16; E. R. Leach, *Political systems of highland Burma* (London, 1954), *passim*.

103. Leach actually goes no farther than asserting that "there is a very strong suggestion that [the oscillation between *gumlao* and *gumsa* structures] is sometimes and indeed often the case" [*Political systems*, p. 210], but a recent analysis of the ethnographic literature on the peoples of upland Southeast Asia has led A. Thomas Kirsch to conclude that an actual oscillatory process similar to that postulated for the Kachin is widespread throughout the mainland territories: *Feasting and social oscillation: a working paper on religion and society in upland Southeast Asia*. Data Paper No. 92, Southeast Asia Program, Cornell University (Ithaca, 1973), pp. 2 and 35.

104. Generalized exchange (*échange généralisé*) is Lévi-Strauss's term for a preferential rule of matrilateral cross-cousin marriage (*Les structures*

élémentaires, Part 2; cp. also Robin Fox, *Kinship and marriage* (Harmondsworth, Middlesex, 1967), chapter 8). Friedman prefers to define generalized exchange as a proscription of endogamy and reciprocity (i.e., bilateral and patrilateral marriage): "Tribes, states, and transformations," pp. 168-169.

105. Friedman, "Tribes, states, and transformations," p. 173. Cp. Kirsch ["Feasting and social oscillation," p. 8]: "As in true markets, each unit is trying to maximize its position relative to all other units in the system; however, the wealth which accrues is not 'money' but an enhanced ritual status, increased control of the ritual rights, and an increment of imputed 'innate virtue'. The operation of the hill tribes 'market', i.e. the feasting system, tends to equalize actual standards of living, but to increase relative differences in ritual status."

106. Cf. Note 38 to Chap. 1.

107. Paul Kirchhoff, "The principles of clanship," in Morton H. Fried (ed.), *Readings in anthropology*, vol. 2 (New York, 1959), pp. 260-270. Cf. also Note 38 to Chap. 1.

108. In "Tribes, states, and transformations," pp. 183-186, Friedman pursues this analysis in considerably greater detail than is possible here. In evaluating his argument it must be borne in mind that, as all local lineages during this phase of societal evolution are integrated into networks of wife-givers and wife-takers, any augmentation of prestige at the summit of the hierarchy engenders a concomitant increase in brideprices (and indeed all other obligations) through all levels of the system. In other words, the rate of inflation of prestige goods depends directly on the rate of appropriation by chiefs.

109. In our opinion, the Marxian so-called "asiatic" state is nothing other than a particular functional and developmental phase in the evolution of the polity, and can be discerned in appropriate eras in virtually all realms of pristine state formation.

110. Friedman, "Tribes, states, and transformations," p. 194. This author actually refers to these polities as "small class-structured states." See also J. Butler, *A sketch of Assam with some account of the hill tribes by an officer in the Hon. East India Company's Bengal Native Infantry* (London, 1846), p. 126; S. F. Hannay, *Sketch of the Singphos or Kakhyens of Burmah, the position of this tribe as regards Bhamo and the inland trade of the Irrawaddy with Yunnan and their connection with the northeastern frontier of Assam* (Calcutta, 1847), p. 44; E. R. Leach, *Cultural change with special reference to the hill tribes of Burma and Assam*. Unpublished Ph.D. thesis submitted to the London School of Economics and Political Science in the University of London (1946), p. 481.

111. Cf. p. 14 above.

112. Even among stratified (*gumsa*) Kachin groups, hypergamy occurs in some secondary marriages. In more advanced chiefdoms and states, where all rank differences have become absolute, hypergamy often becomes generalized among aristocratic lineages.

113. Friedman, "Tribes, states, and transformations," p. 195.

114. Friedman, "Tribes, states, and transformations," p. 196.

115. Specifically the point of view adopted by Paul Wheatley and Thomas See, *From court to capital. A tentative interpretation of the origins of the Japanese urban tradition* (Chicago, 1977), esp. pp. 14-17.

116. Leach, *Political systems of highland Burma*, chap. 8.

117. Friedman, "Tribes, states, and transformations," p. 186.

118. Friedman, "Tribes, states, and transformations," p. 197.

119. Cf., for example, H. W. Scheffler, "Structuralism in anthropology" in Jacques Ehrmann (ed.), *Structuralism*. Yale French Studies Nos. 36 and 37 (New Haven, Conn., 1966), pp. 75 ff.

120. Leach, *Political systems of highland Burma, passim*.

121. Leach, *Political systems*, p. 252.

122. Leach, *Political systems*, p. 257.

123. Leach, *Political systems*, pp. 223-224.

124. Edmund [R.] Leach, *Lévi-Strauss* (London, 1970), p. 109.

125. Note, though, that K. C. Chang has recently demonstrated that in ancient China either patrilateral or matrilateral cross-cousin marriage tended to be emphasized in accordance with the political rank of the intermarrying parties. Whereas the patrilateral version was more or less customary between political equals, the matrilateral mode "tended to take place as a contributing factor in the delicate and dynamic equilibrium of political power between parties of unequal status." *Early Chinese civilization. Anthropological perspectives* (Cambridge, Mass. and London, England, 1972), p. 89.

126. Edwin M. Loeb, "Patrilineal and matrilineal organization in Sumatra: the Batak and the Minangkabau," *American Anthropologist*, vol. 35 (1933), pp. 16-50; B. Ter Haar, *Adat law in Indonesia* (New York, 1948); Ward Goodenough, "Malayo-Polynesian social organization," *American Anthropologist*, vol. 57 (1955), pp. 71-83.

127. Characterized by Lévi-Strauss as "Where an X man marries a Y woman, a Y man must always be able to marry an X woman," thereby including all varieties of directly reciprocal sister exchange. It is Lévi-Strauss's contention that so-called harmonic systems (patrilineal-virilocal or matrilineal-uxorilocal) of restricted exchange have provided the nexuses from which have evolved harmonic systems of generalized exchange.

128. C. T. Bertling, "Huwverbod op grond van verwantschapsposities in Middle Java," *Indisch Tijdschrift van het Recht*, vol. 143 (1936), pp. 119-134; R. Kennedy, "A survey of Indonesian civilization," in G. P. Murdock (ed.), *Studies in the science of society presented to A. G. Keller* (New Haven, Conn., 1937), p. 290, and "The 'Kulturkreislehre' moves into Indonesia," *American Anthropologist*, vol. 41 (1939), p. 167. Generally speaking, in terms not those of Lévi-Strauss, it is possible to recognize in Indonesia two main modes of social organization: unilineal systems, often with ranked lineages in the form of an asymmetrical connubium, in Sumatra and the Nusa Tenggara; and bilateral systems, also on occasion with ranked lineages, of the so-called ambilateral type in Kalimantan, Java and some of the eastern islands.

129. Cf. A. L. Kroeber, *Peoples of the Philippines* (New York, 1928), pp. 134-137.

130. W. R. Head, *Handbook on Haka Chin custom* (Rangoon, 1917); H. N. C. Stevenson, *The economics of the central Chin tribes* (Bombay, 1943); F. K. Lehman, *The structure of Chin society. A tribal people of Burma adapted to a non-Western civilization*. Illinois Studies in Anthropology No. 3 (Urbana, 1963).

131. Ramesh Chandra Majumdar, *Ancient Indian colonies in the Far East*, vol. 1: *Champā* (Lahore, 1927), vol. 2: *Suvarṇadvīpa*. Part 1, *Political history* (Dacca, 1937); Part II, *Cultural history* (Calcutta, 1938); *Hindu colonies in the Far East* (Calcutta, 1944); "Colonial and cultural expansion in South-East Asia," in

Majumdar (ed.), *The history and culture of the Indian people*, vol. 3: *The Classical age* (Bombay, 1954), chap. 24; *Ancient Indian colonization in South-East Asia*. The Maharaja Sayajirao Gaekwad Honorarium Lectures, 1953-54 (Baroda, 1955). Note the words "colonization" and "colonies" in these titles.

132. Rabindranath Tagore, "Foreword" to *JGIS*, vol. 1 (1934), no pagination.

133. E.g., La réalité a du être à peu près ceci: deux ou trois navires de l'Inde naviguant de conserve arrivent de proche en proche jusqu'à Java. Les nouveaux venus entrent en relation avec les chefs du pays, se les rendent favorables par des présents, par des soins donnés aux malades et par des amulettes. Dans tous les pays de civilisation primitive où j'ai vécu, du golfe d'Aden et de la côte orientale d'Afrique à la Chine, les seuls moyens efficaces de pénétration pacifique restent partout les mêmes: cadeaux de bienvenue, distribution de médicaments curatifs et de charmes préventifs contre tous les maux et dangers, réels et imaginaires. L'étranger doit être et passer pour riche, guérisseur et magicien. Personne n'est à même d'employer de tels procédés aussi adroitement qu'un Hindou. Celui-ci se pretendra sans doute d'extraction royale ou princière, ce dont son hôte ne peut qu'être favorablement impressionné.

Immigrés en cette *terra incognita*, les Hindous ne disposent pas d'interprète. Il leur faut donc apprendre la langue indigène qui est si différente de la leur et surmonter ce premier obstacle pour acquérir droit de cité chez les *Mleccha*. L'union avec des filles de chef vient ensuite, et c'est alors seulement que l'influence civilisatrice et religieuse des etrangers peut s'exercer avec quelque chance de succès. Leurs femmes indigènes, instruites à cet effet, deviennent les meilleurs agents de propagande des idées et de la foi nouvelles: princesses ou filles nobles, si elles en affirment la supériorité sur les moeurs, coutumes et religions héritées des ancêtres, leurs compatriotes ne pourront guère y contredire [Gabriel Ferrand, "Le K'ouen-louen et les anciennes navigations interocéaniques dans les mers du sud," *JA*, 2e série, vol. 14 (1919), pp. 15-16]. Cf. R. O. (later Sir Richard) Winstedt, "A history of Malaya," *JMBRAS*, vol. 13, pt. 1 (1935), pp. 18-19. The passage also occurs in modified form in the revised version of *A history of Malaya* (Singapore, 1962), p. 29.

134. Nicholaas J. Krom, *Inleiding tot de Hindoe-Javaansche kunst* ('s-Gravenhage, 1923), and *Hindoe-Javaansche geschiedenis* (Second edition, 's-Gravenhage, 1931).

135. George Coedès, "Le substrat autochtone et la superstructure indienne au Cambodge et à Java," *Cahiers d'Histoire Mondiale*, vol. 1, no. 2 (1953), pp. 368-377, and "L'osmose indienne en Indochine et en Indonésie," *loc. cit.*, vol. 1, no. 4 (1954), pp. 827-838 [N.B. The author has disclaimed responsibility for the title of the first of these papers, which is not consonant with the views of the Indianization process expressed in the text]; *Les états hindouisés d'Indochine et d'Indonésie* (Third edition, Paris, 1964).

136. Coedès, "Le substrat autochtone," p. 377.

137. Jacob Cornelis Van Leur, *Eenige beschouwingen betreffende den ouden Aziatischen handel*. Doctoral dissertation defended before the University of Leiden, 5 October 1934. Published at Middelburg, 1934. Reprinted in English translation in Van Leur, *Indonesian trade and society. Essays in Asian social and economic history* (The Hague and Bandung, 1955), pp. 1-144.

138. This thesis has recently been vigorously restated by Keith Taylor, "Madagascar in the ancient Malayo-Polynesian myths," in Kenneth R. Hall and John K. Whitmore (eds.), *Explorations in early Southeast Asian history: the origins of Southeast Asian statecraft*. Michigan Papers on South and Southeast Asia No. 11

(Ann Arbor, Mich., 1976), pp. 25-60, especially p. 49. For previous enunciations of this point of view see Frederik D. K. Bosch, "'Local Genius' en Oud-Javaanse kunst," *Mededeelingen der Koninklijke Nederlandske Akademie van Wetenschappen*, new series, vol. 15 (1952), pp. 1-25; George Coedès, *Les états hindouisés d'Indochine et d'Indonésie* (Third edition, Paris, 1964), pp. 56-57; Anon., Review of Wheatley, *The Golden Khersonese* in *The Times Literary Supplement*, September 21, 1961.

139. See, for example, Otto Christian Dahl, *Malgache et Maanjan*. Avhandlinger utgitt av Egede-Instituttet, vol. 3 (Oslo, 1951); Isidore Dyen, Review of Dahl, *Malgache et Maanjan* in *Language*, vol. 29 (1953), pp. 578-591; George Peter Murdock, *Africa: its peoples and their cultural history* (New York, 1959), chaps. 26 and 27; A. M. Jones, *Africa and Indonesia* (Leiden, 1964); J. Innes Miller, *The spice trade of the Roman empire 29 B.C. to A.D. 641* (Oxford, 1969), passim; Pierre Vérin, "Austronesian contributions to the culture of Madagascar: some archaeological problems" in H. Neville Chittick and Robert I. Rotberg (eds.), *East Africa and the Orient: cultural syntheses in pre-colonial times* (New York and London, 1975), pp. 164-191; Aidan Southall, "The problem of Malagasy origins," *loc. cit.*, pp. 192-215; Taylor, "Madagascar in the ancient Malayo-Polynesian myths," passim. It has also been suggested that the 13th-century *Tārikh al-mustabṣir* of Ibn al-Mujāwir may preserve a confused remembrance of the presence of Malaysians at ʿAden in the early centuries of the Christian era: see Ferrand, "Le K'ouen-louen," pp. 469-475. Cp. also Dahl, *Malgache et Maanjan*, p. 364.

140. To Muslim chroniclers these Indonesians, who were employed by the Sāsānians to combat piracy in the Persian Gulf, were known as Sayābijah, sing. Saibajī, Saibagī, Sābagī, Sābag (=Zābag < Jāvaka). Cf. Gabriel Ferrand, *Encyclopaedia of Islam*, sub verbo.

141. *Jātakamālā* no. XIV. See also Majumdar, *Suvarṇadvīpa*. Part I, p. 37, note 3; S. Chaudhari, *Jātakamālā* (Kathatiya, Bihar, 1952), p. 205.

142. *Kathāsaritsāgara*, t. 13, ś. 73 ff. See also Tawney, *The ocean of story*, vol. 1, pp. 156 ff; V. A. Velgus, "Some problems of the history of navigation in the Indian and Pacific Oceans" in Yu. V. Maretin and B. A. Valskaya (eds.), *The countries and peoples of the East* (Moscow, 1974), pp. 50-63. The embassy from Fu-nan to India is recorded in *Liang Shu* 梁書 chüan 54, f. 22 verso.

143. Jack Golson (ed.), *Polynesian navigation: a symposium on Andrew Sharp's theory of accidental voyages* (Wellington, N.Z., 1963), p. 63.

144. Auguste Barth and Abel Bergaigne, *Inscriptions sanscrites de Campā et du Cambodge*. Notices et Extraits des Manuscrits de la Bibliothèque Nationale XXVII (Paris, 1885-93), p. 199; Louis Finot, "Notes d'épigraphie, I: Deux nouvelles inscriptions de Bhadravarman Ier, roi de Champa," *BEFEO*, vol. 2 (1902), pp. 185-187, and "L'inscription de Chiêm-son," *loc. cit.*, vol. 18 (1918), pp. 13-14; R. C. Majumdar, *Ancient Indian colonies in the Far East, I: Champa* (Lahore, 1927), Book III, pp. 4-9; B. C. Chhabra, "Expansion of Indo-Aryan culture during Pallava rule," *Journal of the Asiatic Society of Bengal: Letters*, vol. 1 (1935), pp. 47ff.; George Coedès, "La plus ancienne inscription en langue chame," *New Indian Antiquary*, Extra Ser. I (1939), pp. 46-49.

145. Hsiao Tzŭ-hsien 蕭子顯 *Nan-Chʻi Shu* 南齊書 (completed before 530), chüan 58, ff. 10v - 11r. Sanskrit texts which ensconce Śiva (instead of Indra) on Mount Mahendra include the *Kaśyapaśilpa*, the Tantric *Niśvāsatathasaṃhitā*, the *Svacchandatantra*, and several Gaṅga inscriptions ranging in time from the 6th (or perhaps 7th) century to the 13th or 14th; but the most explicit passages in this vein occur in the *Tiruvācakam*, the "Sacred Utterances" that constitute a veritable spiritual autobiography of the Tamil saint Māṇikkavācakar, perhaps the greatest of all exponents of the Śaivasiddhānta, who lived probably during the 9th century. For these and other references see Wheatley, "The Mount of the Immortals. A note on Tamil cultural influences in fifth-century Indochina,"

Oriens Extremus, vol. 21, pt. 1 (1974), pp. 97-109.

146. George Coedès, "Etudes cambodgiennes XXI: les traditions généalogiques des premiers rois d'Aṅkor," BEFEO, vol. 28 (1928), p. 127: Inscriptions du Cambodge, vol. 2 (Hanoi, 1942), p. 110, note 5; "Etudes cambodgiennes XXXVI: quelques précisions sur la fin de Fou-nan," BEFEO, vol. 43 (1943-46), p. 4.

147. Barth and Bergaigne, Inscriptions sanscrites, no. LXIII. In a passage in the 3rd-century Fu-nan t'u-su by K'ang T'ai (see Chap. 3, p. 149), which is now preserved only in the T'ai-p'ing Yü-lan, a king of Fu-nan is said to have captured and tamed mighty elephants as a means of inducing the submission of neighboring kingdoms (Wolters in Coedès, Les états hindouisés p. 75, note 1). Possibly the implication was that the king, by identifying himself with Śiva as the divine Hunter on the Mahendraparvata, was able to subdue his rivals in the same way as the god hunted and tamed the wild animals on his mountain.

148. Liang Shu, chüan 54, f. 8v; Pierre Dupont, La statuaire préangkorienne. Artibus Asiae, Supplement XV (Ascona, 1955), p. 21; Coedès, Les états hindouisés, p. 120; Sui Shu, chüan 82, ff. 7v - 8r; Coedès, Inscriptions du Cambodge, vol. 1, p. 14, v. VII and p. 15, v. VII.

149. Kamaleswar Bhattacharya, Les religions brahmaniques dans l'ancien Cambodge d'après l'épigraphie et l'iconographie. Publication de l'Ecole Française d'Extrême-Orient No. XLIX (Paris, 1961), p. 13. Mahendravarman actually erected a series of liṅga (the form in which Śiva is most frequently worshiped) along the Mekong in the vicinities of Kratié and Stung Treng and in the region between the Mun river and the Daṅrêk upland [Louis Finot, "Notes d'épigraphie, IV: Inscription de Thma Krê (Cambodge)," BEFEO, vol. 3 (1903), p. 212; Adhémard Leclère, "Une campagne archéologique au Cambodge," loc. cit., vol. 4 (1904), p. 739; Erik Seidenfaden, "Complément à l'inventaire descriptif des monuments du Cambodge pour les quatre provinces du Siam oriental," loc. cit., vol. 22 (1922), pp. 57-58, and "Chronique," loc. cit., p. 385.

150. Barth and Bergaigne, Inscriptions sanscrites, no. 5. Cf. also Kamaleswar Bhattacharya, "La secte des Pāçupata dans l'ancien Cambodge," JA, vol. 243 (1955), pp. 479-490. For a compendious statement on Śaivite thought in early Kampuchea see Bhattacharya, "Religious speculations in ancient Cambodia: Śaiva speculations," in Himansu Bhusan Sarkar, R. C. Majumdar felicitation volume (Calcutta, 1970), pp. 79-97.

151. Nihar-Ranjan Ray, Brahmanical gods in Burma (Calcutta, 1932), p. 52 and p. 184 above.

152. Hendrik Kern, Verspreide Geschriften, vol. 7 (1917), pp. 137 ff. The Wukir inscription is transcribed and translated by, int. al., Himansu Bhusan Sarkar, Corpus of the inscriptions of Java, vol. 1 (Calcutta, 1971), pp. 15-24. For Śaivism in ancient Java generally see A. Zieseniss, "Studien zur Geschichte des Śivaismus: die śivaitischen Systeme in der altjavanischen Literatur, I," BKI, vol. 98 (1939), pp. 75-223.

153. O. W. Wolters, "Khmer 'Hinduism' in the seventh century," in R. B. Smith and W. Watson, Early South East Asia: essays in archaeology, history and historical geography (London, 1979), pp. 427-442.

154. Wolters, "Khmer 'Hinduism'," pp. 427, 430, and 431.

155. E.g., from among many such references, Coedès, Inscriptions du Cambodge, vol. 1 (Hanoi, 1937), inscription from Tûol Prāḥ Thāt, A.D. 673, pp. 14, v. VII and 15, v. VII; vol. 2 (Hanoi, 1942), inscription from Čaṃnôm, 7th century, p. 27, v. 4 (bis); vol. 4 (Paris, 1952), inscription from the north tower of Sambôr-Prei Kŭk, c. middle of the 7th century, p. 32, v. 5 (bis); vol. 5 (Paris, 1953), inscription from Kôk Roka, early 7th century, p. 29, v. III (bis); also ISCC, p. 19, v. 32.

For an earlier discussion of the role of Śaivite devotionalism in the
Hinduization of Indonesia see F. D. K. Bosch, "The problem of the Hindu
colonisation of Indonesia." An inaugural address delivered at the University of
Leiden, March 15, 1946; reprinted in Bosch, *Selected studies in Indonesian
archaeology* (The Hague, 1961), pp. 3-22, especially 16-18. On the
Śaiva-Siddhānta generally see H. W. Schomerus, *Der Çaiva-Siddhānta, eine Mystik
Indiens* (Leipzig, 1912); and, with particular relevance to early Southeast Asia,
R. Goris, *Bijdrage tot de kennis der Oud-Javaansche en Balineesche theologie*
(1926) and Jean Filliozat, "New researches on the relations between India and
Cambodia," *Indica*, vol. 3, no. 2 (1966), pp. 95-106.

156. Claude Jacques, "Notes sur l'inscription de la stèle de Vat Luong Kau," *JA*,
vol. 250, (1962), pp. 249-256 and *ISCC*, p. 31, verse 4.

157. George Coedès, "Deux inscriptions sanskrites du Fou-nan," *BEFEO*, vol. 31
(1931), p. 7.

158. Bhattacharya, "Les religions brahmaniques dans l'ancien Cambodge,"
pp. 57-58. Cf. also Bhattacharya, "La secte des Pāçupata," pp. 479-490.

159. Wolters, "Khmer 'Hinduism'," pp. 431-432, citing instances of the use of
pūjā (homage), *pradāna* (donation), *satra* (offering), *yajamāna* (donor of gifts to
a god), and *punya* (merit).

160. Wolters, "Khmer, 'Hinduism'," p. 432.

161. Wolters, "Khmer 'Hinduism'," pp. 432-433. For Pāśupata doctrine see
H. Chakraborti, *Pāśupata Sūtram with Panchārtha-bhasya of Kauṇḍinya* (Calcutta,
1970).

162. Wolters, "Khmer 'Hinduism'," p. 432, citing, respectively, *ISCC*, p. 69,
verse 5; *Inscriptions du Cambodge*, vol. 4, p. 9, v. 9; *IC*, vol. 2, p. 70, v. 1;
and *IC*, vol. 1, p. 10, v. 3.

163. Wolters, "Khmer 'Hinduism'," pp. 440-441 and 429.

164. See K. E. Read, "Leadership and consensus in a New Guinea society,"
American Anthropologist, vol. 61 (1959), pp. 452-466; Paul Bohannan,
"Extra-processual events in Tiv political institutions," *American Anthropologist*,
vol. 60 (1958), pp. 1-12; Douglas L. Oliver, *A Solomon Island society* (Cambridge,
Mass., 1955), pp. 422-439; Marshall D. Sahlins, *Tribesmen* (Englewood Cliffs,
N.J., 1968), pp. 21-22 and 88-90; Elman R. Service, *Origins of the state and
civilization. The process of cultural evolution* (New York, 1975), pp. 72-73.
The appositeness of the Biblical phrase to the role of the "big man" was first
noticed by Marshall Sahlins, *Tribesmen*, p. 22.

165. Paul Mus, "Cultes indiens et indigènes au Champa," *BEFEO*, vol. 33 (1933),
pp. 393-394. More recently Professor Wolters has also speculated on these
possibilities in "Khmer 'Hinduism'," pp. 436-437.

The precise manner in which either a "big man" amassed what Bronislaw
Malinowski called his "fund of power" or a chief or paramount consolidated his
control over his people would have been in large measure contingent upon the
kinship system prevailing within the group; but about this in ancient Kampuchea
there has been considerable dispute. George Coedès was confident that the
evidence of Khmer royal genealogies betokened a rule of succession by
primogeniture through the male line ["Les règles de la succession royale dans
l'ancien Cambodge," *BSEI*, new series, vol. 26 (1951), pp. 117-130, and *Les états
hindouisés*, p. 223, note 1]. Eveline Porée-Maspero was equally certain that
succession within royal and priestly families followed a matrilineal principle
["Nouvelle étude sur la Nāgī Somā," *JA*, vol. 238 (1950), pp. 237-267, and *Etude
sur les rites agraires des Cambodgiens*, vol. 1 (Paris, 1962), pp. 152-182].
Subsequently Kevin O'Sullivan attempted to reconcile these seemingly incompatible
views by postulating a mixed descent system in which a tendency to matrilineality

became increasingly prominent with proximity to the sacred. Hence, whereas the office of *purohita* almost invariably descended from a mother's brother to a sister's son (that is exclusively through a female line), the kings, who sustained both sacred and profane modes of existence, often promulgated mixed genealogies in which actual patrilineal descent was sometimes suppressed in favor of a desirable, legitimizing matrilineality, while the populace at large followed a cognatic (bilateral) form of kinship reckoning, as indeed they do today ["Concentric conformity in ancient Khmer kinship organization," *Chung-yang Yen-chiu Yüan: Min-ts'u-hsüeh Yen-chiu-so Chi-k'an* 中央研究院民族學研究所集刊] (English title: *Bulletin of the Institute of Ethnology, Academia Sinica*), No. 13 (1962), pp. 87-96]. Most recently A. Thomas Kirsch has reinterpreted the available evidence to show that Khmer royalty also reckoned kinship cognatically ["Kinship, genealogical claims, and societal integration in ancient Khmer society: an interpretation," in C. D. Cowan and O. W. Wolters (eds.), *Southeast Asian history and historiography. Essays presented to D. G. E. Hall* (Ithaca, N.Y., 1976), pp. 190-202]. Only in some priestly families, according to this interpretation, was matrilineal descent a prerequisite for succession to high sacerdotal office, probably as an expediential means of circumventing the effects of celibacy among holders of exceptionally prestigious positions in the prelacy. Professor Kirsch also offers the suggestion that, in this context of cognatic descent combined, on the evidence of inscriptions, with the socially integrative institution of royal polygamy, the dynastic genealogies that figure so prominently in Khmer epigraphy were "not simply . . . attempts to establish legitimacy to rule by demonstrating purity of descent but . . . efforts to mobilize political support through emphasizing a ramifying network of kinship to a number of powerful families" ["Kinship . . ." p. 201]. The point at issue, if I understand Professor Kirsch correctly, is not, as has sometimes been maintained, that the cognatic principle cannot be effectively employed to form descent groups, even clearly specified lineages — the extended Maori genealogies compiled in terms of a cognatic ideology are a good illustration — but that the Khmers (and we too if we wish to understand their society as they understood it) tended to emphasize degrees of relationship to an ego rather than to an ancestor. In other words, for some purposes at any rate, they were concerned less with corporate *groups* established through descent than with the *categories of persons* who constitute kindreds. (A "kindred" can be broadly defined as "ego's relatives up to a certain stipulated degree" and, as among, say, the Gilbert Islanders, certain peoples in the northern Philippines, or in former times the Scottish clans, can coexist with descent groups in a single society). For early Khmer society, the significance of the kindred is, first, that it often tends to be a latent concept for much of the time and to be activated only for special purposes such as raiding, land or crop apportionment, or the regulation of marriage; and second, that when ego dies (counting siblings as a collective ego), the kindred ceases to exist (whereas if a member of a cognatic descent group dies, the group still survives). From these two salient characteristics may have derived a good deal of the instability of the classical Khmer political system, but more close analysis of the relevant texts will be required before the precise relationship of kinship to polity can be specified in all its ramifications. And it is more than doubtful if the political functions of kinship in the protohistoric period will ever be known other than inferentially. Elsewhere in Southeast Asia the situation in ancient times is even more obscure than in Kambujadeśa, although it should be remarked that cognatic descent prevails today among the Malays, Burmans, and Thais, as well as among other lowland ethnic groups.

166. L. de la Vallée Poussin, *Indo-Européens et Indo-Iraniens jusque vers 300 av. J.C.* (Paris, 1924), pp. 168, 169, 174, 178, and *Dynasties et histoire de l'Inde depuis Kanishka jusqu'aux invasions musulmanes* (Paris, 1935), p. 361; Sylvain Lévi, *Le Népal. Etude historique d'un royaume hindou*, vol. 1 (Paris, 1905), p. 220; Louis Renou, *Bibliographie védique* (Paris, 1931), pp. 143, 334; Coedès, *Les états hindouisés*, pp. 53-54.

167. Wheatley, "The Mount of the Immortals," pp. 97-109.

Urban Genesis in the Indianized Territories   351

168. Hendrik Kern, "Over de Sanskrit-opschriften van (Muara Kaman, in) Kutei (Borneo). (+400 A.D.), Verspreide Geschriften onder zijn Toesicht Verzameld, vol. 7 (1917), pp. 55-76; Jean-Philippe Vogel, "The yupa inscriptions of King Mulavarman from Koetei (East Borneo)," BKI, vol. 74 (1918), pp. 167-232; Bijan Raj Chatterjee, India and Java, Part 2 (Calcutta, 1933), pp. 8-19; B. Ch. Chhabra, "Expansion of Indo-Aryan culture during Pallava rule, as evidenced by inscriptions," JASB, Letters, vol. 1 (1935), pp. 1-64, and "Three more yupa inscriptions of King Mulavarman from Koetei (E. Borneo)," JGIS, vol. 12 (1945), pp. 14-17 [Reprinted, with a postscript by J. G. de Casparis, in TBG, vol. 83 (1949), pp. 370-374]; J. G. de Casparis, "Yūpa inscriptions," India Antiqua (1947), pp. 77-82; Joseph Minattur, "A note on the King Kundungga of the East Borneo inscriptions," JSEAH, vol. 5, no. 2 (1964), pp. 181-183.

169. Hendrik Kern, "De Sanskrit-inscriptie van Canggal (Keḍu), uit 654 Cāka," Verspreide Gescriften onder zijn Toesicht Verzameld, vol. 7 (1917), pp. 115-128; Chatterjee, India and Java, Part 2, pp. 29-34; Chhabra, "Expansion of Indo-Aryan culture," p. 37.

170. Radhakamud Mukerji, Indian shipping; a history of the sea-borne trade and maritime activity of the Indians from the earliest times (Bombay and Calcutta, 1912), p. 40.

171. C. C. Berg, Hoofdlijnen der Javaansche litteratuurgeschiedenis (Groningen, 1929), p. 12.

172. J. L. Moens, "Srīvijaya, Yava en Katāha," TBG, vol. 77 (1937), p. 317. For general comments on what is sometimes called the kṣatriya theory of Indianization, see I. W. Mabbett, "The 'Indianization' of Southeast Asia: reflections on the historical sources," Journal of Southeast Asian Studies, vol. 8, no. 2 (1977), pp. 143-144 and 155-156.

173. This conclusion drawn from Indian literary records is not necessarily in conflict with Van Leur's assertion (actually a projection into earlier times of conditions in the 16th century) that the vast majority of the traders were what he termed populo minuto, peddlers, each with a few dozen pieces of silk cloth in his single chest, a few corges of porcelain, a few dozen bags of pepper, a few bahar of cloves or nutmeg, a few hundredweight of mace (Indonesian trade and society,   pp. 133, 135-137, 197-200). Until very recently even popular literature drew its heroes from the elite classes. The humble peripatetic trader, unless he demonstrated picaresque proclivities, was not likely to figure in even the kathā literature.

174. Frederik D. K. Bosch, Selected studies in Indonesian archaeology (The Hague, 1961), p. 8.

175. Sir Arthur [P.] Phayre, History of Burma including Burma Proper, Pegu, Taungu, Tenasserim, and Arakan, from the earliest times to the end of the first war with British India (London, 1883), pp. 3-5.

176. Jean Filliozat, "L'inscription dite de Vỏ-cạnh," BEFEO, vol. 55 (1969), pp. 115-116. Of course, the title MāRaN may have been assumed by a ruler, indigenous or foreign, intent simply on exploiting the prestigious titulary of the Pāṇḍyan dynasty, in which case the inscription would testify only to the presence of Tamil influence in eastern Indochina.

177. English translation by James Low ["A translation of the Keddah Annals," Journal of the Indian Archipelago and Eastern Asia," vol. 3 (1849), pp. 1-23, 162-181, 253-270, 314-336, 467-488; summary in Sir Richard Winstedt, "A history of classical Malay literature," JMBRAS, vol. 31, pt. 3 (1958), pp. 1-261; Rumi transliteration by A. J. Sturrock, "Hikayat Marong Maha Wangsa or Kedah Annals," JSBRAS, no. 72 (1916), pp. 37-123. In this potpourri of myths, Marong Mahawangsa is said to have come with a band of followers from beyond the Sea of Hindustān to impose himself as ruler over the aboriginal inhabitants in the vicinity of Gunung

Jerai in Kedah. Although this text in its present form dates from early in the 19th century, and incorporates events that occurred as late as the 18th century (Winstedt, *loc. cit.*, p. 134), it appears also to include material from much earlier periods.

178. George Coedès, *Recueil des inscriptions du Siam*, vol. 1 (Bangkok, 1924), p. 50; K. A. Nilakanta Sastri, "Mahīpāla of the Caṇḍakauśikam," *Journal of Oriental Research*, vol. 6 (1932), pp. 191-198, and "Takuapa and its Tamil inscription," *JMBRAS*, vol. 22 (1949), pp. 25-30.

179. In the conventional view, the Maṇigrāmam was a corporation of "men of different *jāti* doing business like men of the same *jati*" [K. R. Venkatarama Ayyar, "Medieval trade, craft, and merchant guilds in South India," *Journal of Indian History*, vol. 25 (1947), p. 272], but recently K. Indrapala ["Some medieval mercantile communities of South India and Ceylon," *Journal of Tamil Studies*, vol. 2, no. 2 (1970), p. 29] has suggested that South Indian medieval mercantile associations should be regarded less as guilds and corporations than as dispersed communities bound by a common code of conduct. Indrapala (p. 30) notes pertinently that "even in modern times, the business community of Cettis have their own fiscal year, stick to their own system of book-keeping and follow their own type of business practices and customs. But they could hardly be called a corporation on these grounds." In any case, whatever their precise nature may have been, Maṇigrāmams were widespread in Peninsular India. Tālakkāḍ and Kollam on the Kēraḷa coast, and Tittāṇḍattānapuram and Kāvēripaṭṭanam on the east coast were well known Maṇigrāmam cities, as were, for instance, Kuttālam in the far south and Baligāmi in the Dekkān.

180. K. A. Nilakanta Sastri, "A Tamil merchant guild in Sumatra," *TBG*, vol. 72 (1932), pp. 314-327.

181. E. Hultzsch, "A Vaishnava inscription at Pagan," *Epigraphia Indica*, vol. 7 (1902), pp. 197-198; Jan Wisseman, "Markets and trade in Pre-Majapahit Java," in Karl L. Hutterer (ed.), *Economic exchange and social interaction in Southeast Asia*. Michigan Papers on South and Southeast Asia No. 13 (Ann Arbor, Mich., 1977), p. 208.

182. F. H. van Naerssen, *Culture contacts and social conflicts in Indonesia*. Occasional Papers of the Southeast Asia Institute No. 1 (New York, 1947); "De aanvang van het Hindu-Indonesische acculturatie-proces," in *Orientalia Neerlandica* (Leiden, 1948); "Het sociaal aspect van acculturatie in Indonesia," *Zaire*, vol. 2 (1948), pp. 625-638.

183. I am here following the exposition of Louis Dumont, "The conception of kingship in ancient India": chap. 4 of *Religion, politics and history in India: collected papers in Indian sociology* (Paris, 1970). Cf. also *Manu* IX, 322; W. Caland, *Pañcaviṃśa Brāhmaṇa*, XII, ii, 9; Keith, *Aitareya and Kausītaki Brāhmaṇas*, VII, 19 *et seq*.

184. As is evident in the circumstance that, although both brāhmaṇa and kṣatriya can offer a sacrifice, only the brāhmaṇa can effectuate it.

185. Julius Eggeling, *Śatapatha Brāhmaṇa* (Oxford, 1882-1900), II, 2, 2, 6.

186. Cf., for example, Keith, *Aitareya*, VIII, 17.

187. Dumont, "The conception of kingship in ancient India," p. 65.

188. *T'ai-p'ing Yü-lan* 太平御覽 chüan 788, f. 1 verso, citing the 3rd-century *Fu-nan Chi* 扶南記 by Chu Chih 竺芝 . For a certain inconsistency in the text of the cited passage in different editions of the *T'ai-p'ing Yü-lan* see Paul Pelliot, "Le Fou-nan," *BEFEO*, vol. 3 (1903), p. 279, note 7; G. H. Luce, "Countries neighbouring Burma," *JBRS*, vol. 14, pt. 2 (1924), p. 149, note 6; Wheatley, *The Golden Khersonese*, p. 17, note 4.

189. See p. 213 above.

190. T'ai-p'ing Yü-lan, chüan 788, f. 1 v. In 1903 Paul Pelliot ["Le Fou nan," p. 279, note 4] took the term *γuo to refer to Mongol and Tartar tribes of Central Asia, but was prepared to include Indians "au sens large." Certainly under the Han it subsumed Turkic tribes, for the Hsiung-nu (*Xiwong-nuo 匈奴) are so categorized in the Shih Chi 史記, and this seems to have been the sense in which most of the northern dynasties understood the term. Cf., for example, R. B. Mather's references in Biography of Lü Kuang. University of California Chinese Dynastic Histories Translations No. 7 (Berkeley and Los Angeles, 1959), index p. 130. But note also T. D. Carroll's Account of the T'u-Yü-Hún in the History of the Chin Dynasty. University of California Chinese Dynastic Histories Translations No. 4 (Berkeley and Los Angeles, 1953), p. 35: "The term is . . . extended, in a general sense, to all the states of the Western Regions." Berthold Laufer [Sino-Iranica. Field Museum of Natural History Publication 201 (Chicago, 1919), pp. 194-195] introduced a refinement in the ascription when he claimed that "From the fourth century onward [hu] relates to central Asia and more particularly to peoples of Iranian extraction." Edouard Chavannes and Paul Pelliot expressed agreement with this interpretation, describing hu in principle as "une designation des Iraniens et en particulier des Sogdiens ["Un traité manichéen," JA, 10e série, vol. 18 (1911) and 11e série, vol. 1 (1913), passim]. More recently Edward Schafer has categorized the hu of T'ang times as being in his experience "mainly Iranians, that is to say, Persians, Sogdians, and natives of western Turkestan" ["Iranian merchants in T'ang dynasty tales," in Walter J. Fischel (ed.), Semitic and Oriental Studies. A volume presented to William Popper, being University of California Publications in Semitic Philology, vol. 11 (1951), p. 409.] Finally, it may be noted that surviving quotations from the now lost pharmaceutical codex Hu Pen-ts'ao 胡本草, compiled by Cheng Ch'ien 鄭虔 in the 8th century A.D., dealt mainly with Persian medicines. See also Ishida Mikinosuke, "Toro no koki," Chōan no haru 當壚の胡姫　長安の春 (Tōkyō, 1940), pp. 53-75. Expanded English version under the title "The Hu-chi 胡姫, mainly Iranian girls found in China during the T'ang period," Memoirs of the Research Department of the Tōyō Bunko, no. 20 (Tōkyō, 1961), especially pp. 35-40.

191. Wen-hsien T'ung-k'ao, chüan 331; commentary in Wheatley, The Golden Khersonese, pp. 47-51.

192. Ch'ih-t'u Kuo Chi 赤土國記, preserved in Sui Shu 隋書 chüan 82, ff. 3r-5v. Translation and commentary in Wheatley, "Ch'ih-t'u (赤土)," JMBRAS, vol. 30, pt. 1 (1957), pp. 122-133. Cf. also pp. 251-2 above.

193. For references see Note 168 above.

194. Cf. pp. 87-88 above, and associated references.

195. Jean Filliozat, "New researches on the relations between India and Cambodia," Indica, vol. 3 (1966), p. 98, citing relevant passages from Auguste Barth and Abel Bergaigne, Inscriptions sanscrites de Campā et du Cambodge (Paris, 1885-93).

196. Filliozat, "New researches," p. 97.

197. Coedès, Les états hindouisés d'Indochine et d'Indonésie, p. 68, note 2.

198. Filliozat, "New researches," p. 97; Cf. also P. V. Kane, History of Dharmaśāstra, vol. 3 (Poona, 1946), corresp. to Note 1803.

199. Cf. pp. 212-214 above, and associated references.

200. For a discussion of the brāhmaṇas, tracing their spiritual lineage to the kailāyaparamparai (Skt. kailāsaparamparā) and professing the doctrine of the Śaivasiddhānta, who are still active in Bangkok, and until recently in Phnom

Penh, see Filliozat, "New researches on the relations between India and Cambodia," pp. 98-100. According to the Śaivasiddhānta and the Āgamas, which are believed to have been revealed by Śiva himself, the rites are not reserved solely to brāhmaṇas. Consecration is, in fact, available to all varṇas by dīkṣā, though the rites do differ from varṇa to varṇa. Dīkṣā is bestowed according to the anuloma system. It follows, therefore, that the priests are not necessarily, or even customarily, brāhmaṇas. It is not suggested that these modern Thai and Cambodian "brāhmaṇas" are the descendants of those of ancient times — indeed it is known that they came from several different parts of India probably as recently as the Ayutthaya period (1350-1767) or perhaps even later. All have intermarried with the local community: H. G. Quaritch Wales, Siamese state ceremonies: their history and function (London, 1931), chap. 5.

201. K. R. Venkatarama Ayyar, "Medieval trade, craft, and merchant guilds in South India," Journal of Indian History, vol. 25 (1947), pp. 269-270.

202. Max Weber, Gesammelte Aufsätze zur Religionssoziologie II: Hinduismus und Buddhismus (Tübingen, 1923), p. 64, note 1.

203. George Coedès, "Etudes cambodgiennes: À la recherche du Yaçodharāçrama," BEFEO, vol. 32 (1932), p. 107.

204. Bhattacharya, Les religions brahmaniques dans l'ancien Cambodge, pp. 45-46.

205. E.g., Louis Finot, "Nouvelles inscriptions du Cambodge," BEFEO, vol. 28 (1928), p. 46, verse xii and Coedès, Inscriptions du Cambodge, vol. 4 (Paris, 1952), pp. 17-19: Inscription from Sambôr-Prei Kŭk: Īśānavarman (first half of the 7th century) appointed a Pāśupata as officiant in a temple in perpetuity; Coedès, Inscriptions du Cambodge, vol. 1 (Hanoi, 1937), pp. 4 and 5, verses IV and VIII: Inscription from Phnoṃ Prāḥ Vihār: Bhavavarman (I or II is uncertain) supported a Pāśupata community on the Tuṅgīśaparvata.

206. Wolters, "Khmer 'Hinduism'," p. 433.

207. Cp. Wolters, "Khmer 'Hinduism'," p. 433.

208. For this usage of the terms tribesmen and peasant, see Robert Redfield, Peasant society and culture (Chicago, 1956); Eric R. Wolf, Peasants (Englewood Cliffs, N.J., 1966); Marshall D. Sahlins, Tribesmen (Englewood Cliffs, N.J., 1968).

209. Clifford Geertz, Negara. The theatre state in nineteenth-century Bali (Princeton, 1980), p. 4.

210. Cp. Note 48 to Chapter 1.

211. Geertz, Negara, chapter 2.

212. Pierre Dupont, "La dislocation du Tchen-la et la formation du Cambodge angkorien," BEFEO, vol. 43 (1943), pp. 17-55.

213. Cf. Note 12 above.

214. A. Barth, Inscriptions sanscrites du Cambodge (Paris, 1885), p. 67, st. vi.

215. Sarkar, Corpus, vol. 1, pp. 18 and 20.

216. Sachchidanand Sahai, Les institutions politiques et l'organisation administrative du Cambodge ancien (VIe - XIIIe siècles). Publications de l'Ecole Française d'Extrême-Orient, vol. 75 (Paris, 1970), p. 4, note 4.

217. Claude Jacques, "Note sur l'inscription de la stèle de Vằt Luong Kằu," JA, vol. 250 (1962), p. 250.

218. Barth, Inscriptions, p. 30, st. iv.

219. Sahai, Les institutions politiques, pp. 9-10.

220. Coedès, Inscriptions du Cambodge, vol. 1, p. 8, v. III and p. 10, v. III. Cp. vol. 5, pp. 73 and 74; vol. 6, p. 32. In Kampuchea the name Piṅgaleśa is found only in Pre-Aṅkor epigraphy. Cp. also Kamaleswar Bhattacharya, "Hari Kambujendra," AA, vol. 27 (1964/65), p. 78.

221 For these comparisons see Sahai, Les institutions politiques, pp. 35-36.

222. For the probable indigenous names of the mythical founders of this line see Christie, "The provenance and chronology of early Indian cultural influences in South East Asia," p. 8.

223. Coedès, Inscriptions du Cambodge, vol. 4, p. 90, v. XI and p. 95, v. XI. Cp. also Eveline Porée-Maspero, "Nouvelle étude sur la Nāgī Somā," JA, vol. 238 (1950), p. 237; George Coedès, "Les règles de la succession royale dans l'ancien Cambodge," BSEI, new series, vol. 26 (1951), pp. 117-130.

224. Sahai, Les institutions politiques, pp. 19-20. For the significance of vraḥ kamratāṅ and kingship generally in the Aṅkor period see George Coedès, Le culte de la royauté divinisée, source d'inspiration des grands monuments khmèrs, Serie Orientale, Roma, No. 5 (1952), and "Le véritable fondateur du culte de la royauté divine au Cambodge," in Sarkar, R. C. Majumdar Felicitation Volume, pp. 55-66; Nidhi Aeusrivongse, "The Devarāja cult and Khmer kingship at Angkor," in Hall and Whitmore, Explorations in early Southeast Asian history, pp. 107-148; I. Mabbett, "Devaraja," JSEAH, vol. 10 (1969), pp. 202-223.

225. Sahai, Institutions, p. 38.

226. Sahai, Institutions, pp. 32-33 and 149.

227. Liang Shu, chüan 54, f.7v; Sui Shu, chüan 82, f.6v, reproduced by Ma Tuan-lin, Wen-hsien Tʻung-kʻao, chüan 232, p. 2605.

228. See p. 396 below.

229. Tʻai-pʻing Yü-lan, chüan 788; English transl. in Wheatley, The Golden Khersonese, p. 17. The Liang Shu, chüan 54, f.7r specifies that there were five "kings" or "princes" in the country, all subject to Fu-nan. Cp. pp. 212-214 above.

230. For translations of Chinese records relating to the isthmian kingdoms see Wheatley, The Golden Khersonese, Part I and Chapter 16.

231. The early archipelagic kingdoms are discussed in Chap. 6. It is possible that a king with a Sanskrit style was reigning in Java in 424, the year when the monk Guṇavarman sailed for China, if the Chinese *Bʻuâ-tâ-ka 婆多加 (MSC = Pʻo-to-chia/chʻieh) be accepted as a transcription of the patronymic Vātakya [Cf. p. 233 above].

232. Cf. pp. 179-180 above.

233. Cf. p. 211 above.

234. George Coedès, "Les inscriptions malaises de Çrīvijaya," BEFEO, vol. 30 (1930), pp. 29-80; Gabriel Ferrand, "Quatre textes épigraphiques malayo-sanskrits de Sumatra et de Banka," JA, vol. 221 (1932), pp. 271-326; J. G. de Casparis, Prasasti Indonesia, vol. 2 (Bandung, 1956), pp. 15-46 [This work includes a list of other significant contributions to the study of South Sumatran epigraphy: p. 1, note 1]; Kenneth R. Hall, "State and statecraft in early Srivijaya," in Hall and John K. Whitmore, Explorations in early Southeast Asian history: the

origins of Southeast Asian statecraft. Michigan Papers on South and Southeast Asia No. 11 (Ann Arbor, Mich., 1976), pp. 69-79. This last work presents a systematization of the administrative hierarchy of the Śrī Vijayan thalassocracy on the basis of information in the Telaga Batu inscription.

235. Casparis [Prasasti Indonesia, p. 19] characterizes them as possibly "vassals," implying a feudal context, but I interpret the dependency involved as patrimonial.

236. Perhaps "seneschal" would be the term conveying an appropriately elevated yet archaic sense, at least for nāyaka. Hall defines nāyaka as revenue collectors, pratyaya as managers of royal properties ("State and statecraft in early Srivijaya," p. 71); Casparis is inclined to regard pratyaya as "administrators of the property of deceased persons" (Prasasti, p. 19, note 16). Possibly the property in question was personal possessions which, under certain circumstances, reverted to the state at death. In Chen-la, for instance, the property of deceased parents whose children were already married was sequestrated by the court: Sui Shu, chüan 82; Sahai, Les institutions politiques, pp. 125-126.

237. Hājipratyaya is a highly unconventional Tatpuruṣa compound of Indonesian hāji = "king" and Sanskrit pratyaya, perhaps influenced by the term rājapratyaya. It probably implied that the official was directly responsible to the king.

238. The position of this term in the roster of officials after cutlers and inspectors makes it very unlikely that it here preserved its purely Indian meaning of a minister not of royal blood who, by royal decree, enjoyed the status of a prince.

239. Casparis, Prasasti, p. 37.

240. This is Hall's interpretation of the text: "State and statcraft," pp. 74-75.

241. Hall, "State and statecraft," pp. 75-76. For the apointment of Kampuchean princes as governors of cities and provinces, see p. 311 below.

242. Sahai, Les institutions politiques, passim. There is, of course, a relative abundance of information bearing on the administrative organization of the Khmer state in the Aṅkor period but it cannot with confidence be projected back into earlier times.

243. Sahai, Les institutions politiques, pp. 51-52. The Sui Shu, chüan 82, f. 6v notes that in Chen-la during the reign of Īśānavarman only sons of the principal wife of the ruler were eligible to succeed to the throne.

244. Coedès, Inscriptions du Cambodge, vol. 1, pp. 7-12.

245. Coedès, Inscriptions, vol. 1, p. 8, note 2 and vol. 2, p. 10, note 3. In ancient Kampuchea, the term upabhoga denoted insignia worn on the king's person, such as his crown, ear pendants, bracelets, and saltires: see Coedès, Inscriptions, vol. 1, p. 11, note 2.

246. Barth, Inscriptions sanscrites du Cambodge, p. 54, note 1 and p. 59, note 4.

247. Sahai, Les institutions politiques, p. 53.

248. Barth, Inscriptions, p. 14, v. XXIV.

249. Coedès, Inscriptions, p. 9, v. XII and p. 11, v. XII.

250. Coedès, Inscriptions, vol. 1, p. 13, v. VI and p. 15, v. VI.

251. *Chiu T'ang-Shu*, chüan 197, f. 16v.

252. *Sui Shu*, chüan 82, f. 6r. The MSC vocalizations of these titles are, respectively, *ku-lo-chih, kao-hsiang-ping, p'o-ho-to-ling, she-ma-ling*, and *jan-to-lü*. The passage is repeated in *Wen-hsien T'ung-k'ao*, chüan 332, p. 2605, where (in MSC) *ku-lo-chih* reads *ku-lo-yu* (*jiə̯u 夊), *kao-hsiang-ping* reads *hsiang-kao-ping*, and *jan-to-lü* reads *jan-lo*[*lâ 羅]-*lü*. Both texts add that there were numerous lesser officials.

253. *Sui Shu*, chüan 82, ff. 3v-4r; *Pei Shih*, chüan 95, f. 12v; *T'ai-p'ing Yü-lan*, chüan 787, ff. 1v-3r; *Wen-hsien T'ung-k'ao*, chüan 331, p. 2603. In Kampuchean epigraphy *kulapati* denotes the superior in a religious community.

254. Whereas *Sui Shu, Pei Shih*, and *T'ai-p'ing Yü-lan* assign ten *pati* to each town, *Wen-hsien T'ung-k'ao* specifies only one. *Nāyaka* also occurs in an inscription from Lopburi: Georges Coedès, *Recueil des inscriptions du Siam*, vol. 2 (Bangkok, 1929), p. 14. On these titles generally see Coedès, *Les états hindouisés*, p. 135 and Gabriel Ferrand, "Le K'ouen-louen et les anciennes navigations interocéaniques dans les mers du sud," *JA*, 11th series, vol. 13 (1919), p. 257.

255. *Wen-hsien T'ung-k'ao*, chüan 331, p. 2602. The **K'uən-luən* component in three of these titles is almost certainly a transcription of Old Khmer *kuruṅ*.

256. *T'ung-Tien*, chüan 188; *Hsin T'ang-Shu*, chüan 222C, f. 5v. Cp. Balinese *linggih*, literally "seat," but with implications of rank, status, title, etc.

257. *Liang Shu*, chüan 54.

258. Wang Ch'in-jo 王欽若 and Yang I 楊億 (eds.), *Ts'e-fu Yüan-kuei* 冊府元龜 (A.D. 1013), chüan 976, f. 6v.

259. See Note 67 to Chapter 4.

260. Cf. p. 233 above.

261. *Nan-Ch'i Shu*, chüan 58, ff. 10v-11r.

262. Cf. p. 234 above.

263. Cf. p. 234 above. Ma Tuan-lin also reported the existence of a three-tiered administrative hierarchy (*chou, chün*, and *hsien*) in a kingdom the name of which he transcribed as **D'əu-ɣuâ* (投和 ; MSC = T'o-ho), situated to the south of Chen-la and 100 days' sail from Kuang-Chou [*Wen-hsien T'ung-k'ao*, chüan 332, p. 2606]. Possibly the kingdom of Dvāra[vatī]: cf. p. 203. It sent embassies to Chinese courts in 583 [*Ch'en Shu*, chüan 6, f. 3v] and again between 627 and 649 [*Hsin T'ang-Shu*, chüan 222C, f. 4r-v].

264. *Sui Shu*, chüan 82, f. 6r. Cp. also *Wen-hsien T'ung-k'ao*, chüan 332, p. 2605.

265. Judith M. Jacob, "Pre-Angkor Cambodia: evidence from the inscriptions in Khmer concerning the common people and their environment," in Smith and Watson, *Early South East Asia*, pp. 406-426.

266. See the summary of this debate in Jacob, "Pre-Angkor Cambodia," pp. 423-426.

267. Strictly, a serf is bound to the soil rather than to his master and can be sold only with the land to which he is attached, but in Pre-Aṅkor Kampuchea *kñuṃ* could be exchanged for land: cf. Jacob, "Pre-Angkor Cambodia," p. 412. For "slavery" in Aṅkor Kampuchea see Y. Bongert, "Notes sur l'esclavage en droit khmer ancien," in *Etudes d'histoire du droit privé offertes à Pierre Petot* (Paris, 1959); A. K. Chakravarti, "Sources of slavery in ancient Cambodia," in D. C. Sircar (ed.), *Social life in ancient India* (Calcutta, 1971), pp. 121-142.

268. I. W. Mabbett, "*Varṇas* in Angkor and the Indian caste system," *JAS*, vol. 36, no. 3 (1977), pp. 429-442. For the conflicting view that *varṇa* were coextensive with Khmer free society see, *int. al.* K. Kishore, "Varṇas in early Kāmbuja inscriptions," *JAOS*, vol. 85 (1965), pp. 566-569; A. K. Chakravarti, "The caste system in ancient Cambodia," *Journal of Ancient Indian History*, vol. 4 (1970-71), pp. 14-59. Cf. also Leonid A. Sedov, "K voprosu o varnakh v angkorskoi Kambodzhe," *Kasty v Indii* (Moscow, 1965). It is more than likely that Mabbett's view of the *varṇa* also held in Campā, where the terms *vaiśya* and *śudra* occur in only one inscription: *brāhmaṇa* and *kṣatriya* are, of course, mentioned frequently.

269. These terms are explained in Chapter 1, Note 64. Specific information on such commodity flows is almost always only inferential, but the *Chin Shu* (chüan 97, f. 16 v) does note that in one of the *Bnaṃ* kingdoms tribute (or perhaps imposts generally: 貢賦) was paid in gold, silver, pearls, and aromatics.

270. Li Tao-yüan 酈道元 *Shui-Ching Chu* 水經注 (early 6th century A.D.), chüan 36, f. 23r, citing the *Lin-I Chi* 林邑記 ; and *Shu-i Chi* in *Han-Wei Ts'ung-shu*, f. 6r.

271. *Hsin T'ang-Shu*, chüan 222C; *Man Shu* 蠻書 chüan 10.

272. *Hsin T'ang-Shu*, chüan 222C, f.5v and p. 237 above. Abū Zayd described Kalāh in closely similar terms in the 10th century: Ferrand, *Relations de voyages*, vol. 1, p. 96; G. R. Tibbetts, "The Malay Peninsula as known to the Arab geographers," *MJTG*, vol. 8 (1956), pp. 24-25.

273. *Hsin T'ang-Shu*, chüan 222C; *Man Shu*, chüan 10: this latter text mentions only a silver coinage; E. H. Johnston, "Some Sanskrit inscriptions of Arakan," *BSOAS*, vol. 11 (1943-46), pp. 357-385, especially 383-385.

274. George Coedès, "Etudes cambodgiennes, XXV: Deux inscriptions sanskrites du Fou-nan," *BEFEO*, vol. 31 (1931), pp. 6, v. XI and 7, v. XI. The inscription in question was retrieved from the Pràsàt Pràṃ Loveñ at Tháp-muơi in the Plaine des Joncs.

275. *Liang Shu*, chüan 54, f. 7v.

276. *Liang Shu*, chüan 54, ff. 5v-6r; repeated almost verbatim in *T'ai-p'ing Yü-lan*, chüan 788, f. 15v where the primary source is given as Chu Chih's *Fu-nan Chi* (Cp. Note 3 to Chapter 3). For speculations as to the location of this kingdom see Pelliot, "Le Fou-nan," *BEFEO*, vol. 3 (1903), p. 264, note 1 and "Deux itinéraires," *BEFEO*, vol. 4 (1904), p. 280 [in the Irawadi valley or bordering the coast of the Indian Ocean]; Dato Sir Roland Braddell, "Malayadvipa: a study in early Indianization," *MJTG*, vol. 9 (1956), pp. 1-20; Robert Heine-Geldern, "Le pays de P'i-k'ien, le Roi au Grand Cou et le Singa Mangaradja," *BEFEO*, vol. 49 (1959), pp. 361-404 [both favoring a location in Sumatra]; Wolters, *Early Indonesian Commerce*, Appendix B, pp. 259-260 [on the mainland]. According to the Chinese sources cited above, the ruler of the kingdom had access to an Indian text (天竺書) of about 3,000 words which supposedly bore some similarity to a Buddhist *sūtra* (佛經). The fact that the ruler sent tribute to one of the Kings of the Mountain would seem to afford some qualified support for a location on the mainland.

277. *Hsin T'ang-Shu*, chüan 222C; *Man Shu*, chüan 10.

278. Sahai, *Les institutions politiques*, p. 87.

279. Coedès, *Inscriptions du Cambodge*, vol. 5 (1953), pp. 12-13.

280. Sahai, *Les institutions*, pp. 90-91. For *sāhasa* in later Javanese texts see J. Gonda, *Sanskrit in Indonesia* (Nāgapura, 1952), p. 180. Later Cam kings also administered justice in accordance with the *vyavahāra*: Majumdar, *Champa*, Book I, p. 150.

281. Inscription from Pràsàt Nǎk Buos: Coedès, *Inscriptions*, vol. 6 (1954), p. 155.

282. Majumdar, *Champa*, Book III, pp. 4-8.

283. Cp. Robert Lingat: "Le droit hindou a apporté, moins des prescriptions que des normes, moins des institutions toutes faites que des cadres pour ordonner des institutions existantes ou en formation" [*Les régimes matrimoniaux du sud-est de l'Asie*. Publication de *l'Ecole Française d'Extrême-Orient*, No. 34 (1952), p. 112]; Coedès, *Les états hindouisés*, p. 455.

284. R. K. Chaudhary, "Some aspects of feudalism in Cambodia," *Journal of the Bihar Research Society*, vol. 47 (1961), pp. 246-268. Cf. also the pertinent discussion in Sahai, *Les institutions politiques*, chap. 8.

285. Reinhard Bendix, *Max Weber. An intellectual portrait* (New York, 1962), p. 365.

286. Max Weber, *Staatssoziologie* (Berlin, 1956), p. 103.

287. Literally = "immaculate as a consequence of Tantra," and probably implies the gift of a material object on which the Tantric text was engraved: Casparis, *Prasasti Indonesia*, vol. 2, pp. 31, 36, and 45.

288. Following the interpretation of Casparis, *Prasasti*, vol. 2, pp. 26, 33, 34, and 35.

289. Casparis, *Prasasti*, vol. 2, pp. 28-29. The drinking of an oath was not uncommon in ancient India [Casparis, *ibid*, citing Santosh Kumar Das's reconstruction from information in the *Dharmaśāstra* of Nārada and Yājñavalkya, both dating to about the 4th century A.D.], and has been documented for Kampuchea in comparatively recent times [George Coedès, "Les inscriptions malaises de Çrīvijaya," *BEFEO*, vol. 30 (1930), p. 55, citing Moura (1883) and Leclère (1904)] and for the Batak of Sumatra as recently as the 19th century [Hall, "State and statecraft in early Srivijaya," pp. 89-91, citing G. A. Wilken (1893)].

290. Lawrence Palmer Briggs [*The ancient Khmer empire*. Transactions of the American Philosophical Society, New Series, vol. 41, pt. 1 (1951), p. 17] interprets this event as "apparently introducing a sort of feudalism into Fu-nan." Even if the event did take place (and it is by no means certain that it was anything more than an archetyped element in Fu-nan mythology), neither text nor context affords any hint of an impersonal contractual relationship; the implication, if any, is of personal benefices held at the royal pleasure.

291. Coedès, "Deux inscriptions," pp. 6, v.7 and 7, v.7. Kauṇḍinya Jayavarman was reigning at the turn of the 6th century.

292. George Coedès, "Etudes cambodgiennes, XXXVI: Quelques précisions sur la fin du Fou-nan," *BEFEO*, vol. 43 (1943-46), pp. 6-7.

293. Auguste Barth, *Inscriptions sanscrites du Cambodge* (Paris, 1885), no. VI, pp. 38-44.

294. Coedès, *Inscriptions du Cambodge*, vol. 5, pp. 49-52. Maleṅ was almost certainly the Malyaṅ that by the 13th century had become one of the main territorial divisions of Kampuchea.

295. Sahai, *Les institutions politiques*, p. 140.

296. Bennet Bronson and George F. Dales, "Excavations at Chansen, Thailand, 1968 and 1969: a preliminary report," *Asian Perspectives*, vol. 15 (1973), pp. 28-30; Bronson, "The late prehistory and early history of Central Thailand with special reference to Chansen," in Smith and Watson, *Early South East Asia*, pp. 330-331.

360 Nāgara and Commandery

297. Bronson, "The late prehistory and early history of Central Thailand," p. 330. For previous discussions of this sherd see P. D. R. Williams-Hunt, "Archaeological discoveries in Malaya 1951," *JMBRAS*, vol. 25, pt. 1 (1952), pp. 186-188; G. de G. Sieveking, "The prehistoric cemetery at Bukit Tengku Lembu, Perlis," *Federation Museums Journal*, New Series, vol. 7 (1962), pp. 25-54; B. A. V. Peacock, "The Kodiang pottery cones: tripod pottery in Malaya and Thailand, with a note on the Bukit Tengku Lembu Blackware," *Federation Museums Journal*, New Series, vol. 8 (1964), pp. 4-20.

298. Michael J. Walker and S. Santoso, "Romano-Indian rouletted pottery in Indonesia," *Mankind*, vol. 11 (1977), pp. 39-45.

299. Bronson and Dales, "Excavations at Chansen," p. 28. See also Bronson, "The late prehistory and early history of Central Thailand," p. 330.

300. Louis Malleret, *L'archéologie du delta du Mékong*: vol. 2, *La civilisation matérielle d'Oc-èo* (Paris, 1960), pp. 201-2 and plate LXXXIV (2).

301 Malleret, *La civilisation matérielle d'Oc-èo*, pp. 216-7 and plate XC.

302. Cp. Note 64 above. It is not without interest in this connection that, if the late Victor A. Velgus's reading of *Chʽien-Han Shu*, chüan 28, pt. 2, f. 32 recto et verso be accepted, a ruler of Kāñcī sent a mission as far as China as early as A.D. 2: "Some problems of the history of navigation in the Indian and Pacific Oceans" in Yu V. Maretin and B. A. Valskaya (eds.), *The countries and peoples of the East* (Moscow, 1974), pp. 50-63; also in Russian in *Africana* (1969), pp. 135-152.

303. Mentioned but not described by Bronson, "The late prehistory and early history of Central Thailand," p. 333 and Smith and Watson, *Early South East Asia*, p. 258.

304. The kingdom of Campā is discussed on pp. 394-397 below.

305. It will be evident from these comments that I am in agreement with Anthony Christie that the form *ɣuən źiĕn 混慎 by which Chinese annalists referred to the mythical progenitor of the Funanese royal line was not, as has been conventionally assumed, a transcription of Kauṇḍinya, the name of a brāhmaṇa *gotra* prominent in Mysore in the 2nd century A.D., and also the style of the ruling family of the kingdom of *Po/Pʽo-li* (variously 波婆 利/黎/里): see Note 47 to Chap. 6. [See Christie, "The provenance and chronology of early Indian cultural influences in Southeast Asia," p. 8]. The tale of this adventurer, which was apparently current in the Lower Mekong valley in the 3rd century A.D., found its way into three Chinese dynastic histories: *Chin Shu*, chüan 97, f. 16v; *Nan-Chʽi Shu*, chüan 58, f. 4r; and *Liang Shu*, chüan 54, ff 2v-5v. The much later encyclopedia *Tʽai-pʽing Yü-lan* (A.D. 983), chüan 347, f. 14v draws on an independent tradition and, alone of the four texts, quotes its source (probably at second-hand to judge from the majority of quotations in this compilation) as the *Wu-shih Wai-kuo Chuan* 吳時外國傳, a work long since lost but in Sung times believed to contain material from the 3rd century A.D. In some texts the name of the hero is transcribed as *ɣuən dʽien 塡, *—— tien 滇 (both of which versions would improve the accuracy of the alleged transcription), or *—— ɣuậi 潰 (which is clearly a graphic error). In any case, there is nothing in either the transcription or the myth in which it occurs to warrant an Indian origin, and Christie has suggested a possible connection with Cam *kuno*, meaning "to reverence" ["The provenance," p. 8]. The first author to restore the Chinese name as Kauṇḍinya was Paul Pelliot, "Quelques textes chinois concernant l'Indochine hindouisée," *Etudes Asiatiques publiées à l'occasion du vingt-cinquième anniversaire de l'Ecole Française d'Extrême-Orient*, vol. 2 (Paris, 1925), pp. 248-249. In any case, even if this view should prevail, it would imply only that Kauṇḍinya was a prestigious ascription considered proper for an archetyped culture hero (cp. the charismatic "usurper," the so-called second Kauṇḍinya, mentioned on p. 320 above), not that Indian titularies were in use in the 1st or 2nd centuries A.D. It is not without interest that the *Chin*

Shu (chüan 97, f. 16v) characterizes the vessel in which the founder of the dynasty arrived in Fu-nan as a *po* (cf. p. 271 above), which in the context of the time should be understood as some sort of merchant vessel, a conclusion rendered explicit in *Nan-Chʻi Shu*, *Nan Shih*, and *Tʻai-pʻing Yü-lan* by use of the qualifying graphs 賈人 (= traders). Evidently commercial considerations were not alien to the minds of those who formulated the myth. *Tʻai-pʻing Yü-lan* says that Kauṇḍinya came from the country of *Muo-bʻi̯u 摸趺 ; *Chin Shu* simply that he came from a foreign country (外國); *Nan-Chʻi Shu* that he came from the country of *Kieu/Kiek 激 ; while *Nan Shih* adds that that country lay to the south of Fu-nan; and *Liang Shu* specifies either a marcher territory (徼國) in the south (which is essentially what *Chin Shu* says) or the country of *Kieu in the south. If the former reading holds, 激 above must be a graphic error for 徼; if the latter, 激 and 徼, despite the difference in their MSC vocalizations, in the 5th and 6th centuries were merely alternative graphs for the same sound.

The style *mahārāja* was adopted by a ruler of Campā in about the middle of the 4th century, that is, a century after Fan Shih Man, while the "barbarian script" used in Lin-I at approximately the same time must surely have been of Indian provenance (For both points see p. 396 below).

306. *Chin Shu*, chüan 97, f. 16v. It is usually assumed that the information about Fu-nan contained in this work derived from the reports of Kʻang-Tʻai and Chu Ying, who visited Indochina in A.D. 245. The dynasty lasted from 266-420, so that generalized ethnographic information in the history is unlikely to be significantly later than the 4th century. For the implications of the term *Hu*, see Note 190 above.

307. *Liang Shu*, chüan 54, f. 8r. For the Chinese transcription of Kauṇḍinya see p. 320 above.

308. Christie, "The provenance and chronology," p. 6.

309. *Chin Shu*, chüan 97, f. 16v.

310. Of course, Indian writings relating to other than governmental matters, and all in different styles of *brāhmī* script, were known in Indochina during Fu-nan times, for short inscriptions on seals, intaglios, rings, and other precious objects dating from the 2nd to the 5th century A.D. have been recovered from Oc-èo. However, there is no proof that these objects were inscribed in Southeast Asia; in fact, the implications are that they were imported from the Indian subcontinent. No doubt, though, they familiarized certain Southeast Asian groups with the idea of writing. Cf. Malleret, *L'archéologie du delta du Mékong*, vol. 3: *La culture du Founan*, pp. 275-304; and "Aperçu de la glyptique d'Oc-èo," *BEFEO*, vol. 44 (1963), pp. 189-199.

311. For a conspectus of the scripts used in early Southeast Asia see J. G. de Casparis, "Palaeography as an auxiliary discipline in research on early South East Asia" in Smith and Watson, *Early South East Asia*, pp. 380-394, and *Indonesian palaeography. A history of writing in Indonesia from the beginning to c.A.D. 1500* (Leiden, 1975). See also the stimulating comments of Christie in "The provenance and chronology of early Indian cultural influences," *passim*.

312. A calendrical era which may be said to have begun in the 79th year of the Christian calendar, with which it is to be equated by adding 78-1/4 years. It may have been reckoned from the coronation of the Śaka satrap Nahapāna or, less probably, from the accession of Kaniṣka.

313. The earliest of the Kings of the Mountain in the Mekong valley known to have adopted this style was a ruler, recognized only through a Chinese transcription of his regnal title, namely *Dʻi̯-lji-tʻa-bu̯ât-mu̯â 持梨陀跋摩 (Erroneously *Dʻi̯-liei-bʻu̯ât-mu̯â 持黎跋摩 in *Sung Shu*, chüan 5, f. 6r), who dispatched embassies to the court of the Liu Sung at Chien-kʻang in 434, 435, and 438 (*Liang Shu*, chüan 54, f. 8r). Suggested restorations of the name are Śrī Indravarman or, perhaps more likely, Śreṣṭhavarman. The reconstruction of the suffix is not in doubt. The first recorded ruler of the Cam kingdom to adopt

this style was the Dharmamahārāja Śrī Bhadravarman, who reigned in the second half of the 4th century.

On the Indian subcontinent -*varman* was a component in the styles of several dynasties, including the Pallavas, the kings of Daśapura in Mandasore, the Kadambas of Kuntala in northern Mysore, the Viṣṇukuṇḍins of Āndhra Pradesh, and the rulers of Kāmarūpa in Assam.

314. Although relating to one of the *Bnaṃ* kingdoms, the earliest extant record of the myth occurs in a Sanskrit inscription, dated 657, of King Prakāśadharma-Vikrantavarman of Campā [Text and translation by Louis Finot, "Notes d'épigraphie," *BEFEO*, vol. 4 (1904), pp. 918-925, and R. C. Majumdar, *Ancient Indian colonies in the Far East*, vol. 1: *Champa*, pt. 3 (Lahore, 1927), pp. 16-26. Comments by George Coedès, "Notes sur deux inscriptions du Champa," *BEFEO*, vol. 12 (1912), pp. 15-16]. A Kampuchean version of the legend from later times is discussed by Finot, "Sur quelques traditions indochinoises," *BCAI*, vol. 11 (1911), pp. 20-37. In both these versions the legend is patterned on the validatory myth of the Pallava dynasty of Kāñcī [George Coedès, "La légende de la Nāgī," *BEFEO*, vol. 11 (1911), pp. 391-393], itself only one manifestation of a theme of wide geographical occurrence in which the offspring of a culture hero by a serpent-woman (daughter of the Serpent-King, the snake symbolizing ownership of the soil) establishes his right to rule by demonstrating his ability to handle a weapon (symbolizing authority). Rulership is thus transmitted through the female line although the succession is patronymic [Victor Goloubew, "Les légendes de la nāgī et de l'apsaras," *BEFEO*, vol. 24 (1924), pp. 501-510; Eveline Porée-Maspero, "Nouvelle étude sur le Nāgī Somā," *Journal Asiatique*, vol. 238 (1950), pp. 237-267; Jean Przyluski, "La princesse à' l'odeur de poisson et la Nāgī dans les traditions de l'Asie orientale," *Etudes Asiatiques*, vol. 2, pp. 265-284]. For Western readers the most familiar version of this myth is probably that related by Herodotus (Book IV) of Skythes, son of Herakles by the serpent-woman Echidna and eponymous progenitor of the Scyths.

315. Smith and Watson, *Early South East Asia*, p. 260.

316. Barbara J. Price, "Secondary state formation: an explanatory model," in Ronald Cohen and Elman R. Service (eds.), *Origins of the state: the anthropology of political evolution* (Philadelphia, 1978), pp. 161-186.

317. David L. Webster, "On theocracies," *American Anthropologist*, vol. 78, no. 4 (1976), p. 819.

318. This feature was cited as characteristic of theocracies in general by both Elman R. Service [*The origins of the state and civilization* (New York, 1975), p. 301] and Webster ["On theocracies," p. 818].

319. Professor Wolters notes, with documentation, that four kinds of royal gifts are mentioned in Pre-Aṅkor epigraphy, namely (i) a wide range of offices involving honorable responsibilities (Cp. p. 311 above); (ii) presents from rulers; (iii) titles of honor; and (iv) the confirmation of secular and religious privileges ("Khmer 'Hinduism' in the seventh century," pp. 433-434).

320. The term "culturological attraction" was coined by Leon E. Stover, *The cultural ecology of Chinese civilization* (New York, 1974), *passim*, and applied to the integrative processes of theocracies by Webster, "On theocracies," p. 818.

321. L. de la Vallée Poussin, *Dynasties et Histoire de l'Inde depuis Kanishka jusqu'aux invasions musulmanes* (Paris, 1935), pp. 360-361; Coedès, *Les états hindouisés*, p. 360. This continuation of Hinduization beyond the seas is in fact implicit in the cycle of myths relating to the legendary culture hero Agastya, who is credited with having worshiped in Malayadvīpa and other parts of Southeast Asia. See R. Ng. Poerbatjaraka, *Agastya in den Archipel* (Leyden, 1926); Ordhendra C. Gangoly, "The cult of Agastya," *Rupam*, no. 1 (1926), pp. 1-16; K. A. Nilakanta Sastri, "Agastya," *TBG*, vol. 76 (1936), pp. 471-545.

322. Chie Nakane, "Tripura . . .", *Minzokugaku Kenkyu*, vol. 19, pt. 2 (1955),

pp. 58-99 [In Japanese; English summary on pp. 58-59].

323. E. R. Leach, "The frontiers of Burma," *Comparative Studies in Society and History*, vol. 3 (1960), pp. 49-68.

324. David E. Sopher, "The swidden/wet rice transition zone in the Chittagong hills," *Annals of the Association of American Geographers*, vol. 54, no. 1 (1964), pp. 107-126.

CHAPTER 8

Beyond the Gate of Ghosts
Urban Imposition in the Sinicized Territories

> The customs barrier at Ghost Gate —
> Ten men go out,
> Nine men return.[1]

The cities that arose in the manner described in the preceding chapters were not the earliest manifestations of urbanism in the realm that is today conveniently subsumed under the term Southeast Asia. Several centuries before a conflux of cultural forces transformed the settlement patterns of the so called Indianized territories, the southward extension of Chinese political authority had led to the imposition of an urban system in the northern territories of what is now the Democratic Republic of Việtnam. For analogues of these Chinese cities we can look to the Roman cities and towns that were being laid out in Britain during the early centuries of the Christian era. Like the Roman colonial cities, the Chinese foundations were established primarily for political, legal and social purposes, specifically to permit metropolitan officials and indigenous folk who had adopted Chinese culture as far as possible to live the good life, which meant a life among such decencies and elegancies of civilization as could be preserved on an imperial frontier. Neither in Britain nor in Việtnam did the colonial creations emerge as a response to the needs of indigenous society, with the result that both were in their early years exceedingly insecure. But whereas in Britain an imperial policy initiated during the reign of Septimus Severus (A.D. 193-211) undermined the social basis of urban life so that cities were shrunken and civic spirit decayed for some two centuries before the Imperial Rescript finally dealt them the *coup de grâce*, in Việtnam a colonial hegemony that fostered urban life for a thousand years ensured that a proportion of the cities established by the Chinese administration would develop roots in the local society and regional economy. As a result many of these foundations sustained their existence long subsequent to the elimination of Chinese authority in A.D. 968.

The Commanderies of Chiao-chih and Chiu-chen

Việtnamese histories — all written subsequent to the 13th century A.D. — devote lengthy sections to the glories of Việt kingdoms alleged to have flourished in Tong-King and neighboring territories from early in the 3rd millennium B.C. The earliest putative dynasty comprised a line of kings (王) styled Hùng 雄, who traced their descent ultimately from Thân Nông, the Divine Farmer (神農), in Chinese mythology the inventor of both agriculture and pottery. The period of more than two and a half millennia during which this dynasty supposedly ruled over the Kingdom of Văn-Lang (文郎國) witnessed the establishment of the Việtnamese cultural inventory item by item in etiological myth. From a date corresponding to 258 B.C., the annals assume a quasi-historical, as opposed to an archetyped mythological, character, with the conquest of Văn-Lang by Thục vương, either a ruler of Thục 蜀 or a ruler styled Thục, who then founded the kingdom of Âu-Lạc 甌駱 . If the former translation be preferred, there is no reason to suppose that the systematizing compilers of the Việtnamese annals intended to denote by Thục anything other than the old kingdom of Shu — or at least a territory once incorporated in Shu — which was represented in Chinese chronicles by the same character and located on the appropriate border of Văn-Lang, and which had played a not negligible role in the upper Yangtzŭ valley during the era of the Contending States. The fact that Shu had been incorporated in the kingdom of Ch'in in 316 B.C. would not, I think, have deterred the Việtnamese annalists from invoking its armies more than half a century later at a date appropriate to the unfolding of their theme. In any case, the new kingdom survived barely five decades before being constituted as a tributary of a South Chinese border state.

The earlier European scholars who attempted to reconstruct the ancient history of Việtnam were virtually all members of the prestigious Ecole Française d'Extrême-Orient in Hànội, with interests and competencies that were primarily documentary and/or art-historical. Impressed by the evident archetyping of events and the heroizing of characters in the Việtnamese annals, and aware of the patent patterning of the dynastic succession on the Chinese model, they not unnaturally rejected out of hand the traditional account of pre-Chinese times. Since 1954, however, archeologists of the Democratic Republic of Viêtnam have attempted to establish a connection between the kingdom of Văn-Lang and the later phases of the recently discovered archeological culture of Phùng-nguyên, which seems to have flourished throughout the 2nd millennium B.C. The central tracts of this culture area, they note, included the sites traditionally ascribed to both Mêlinh (Phong Châu 峯州), the capital of Văn-Lang, and Loa Thành, the capital of Âu-Lạc.[2] By implication, if not always explicitly, these authors imply that the level of socio-cultural integration achieved in Văn-Lang and Âu-Lạc was approximately equivalent to that connoted by the ancient annals, in other words that these two polities were urbanized societies integrated into maturely evolved state structures. I have already given my reasons for rejecting this view on the evidence at present available, for regarding the pre-Chinese kingdoms as chiefdoms rather than true states, and for categorizing their so-called capitals as the seats of paramount chiefs rather than as maturely developed metropoleis (Note 199 to Chapter 2); and I shall return to the matter at the end of this section.

On my interpretation of the admittedly inadequate evidence, three phases are discernible in the early urbanization process in the territory at present known as Tong-King. Each phase was associated with a particular mode of political organization, in chronological order that of a *de facto* tributary relationship with a Chinese-*style* kingdom, of protectorate status in the Chinese state, and finally of full incorporation in the Chinese empire.

As early as 208 B.C.[3] the Lạc[4] peoples of Tong-King had been incorporated in the kingdom of Nan Yüeh (南越 **Nəm Giwăt, *Nâm Jiwɒt), a quasi-autonomous territory ruled from P'an-yü (番禺 *P'iwɒn-ngi̯u)[5] by a Chinese warlord, a former official in the imperial government, who was in all probability himself an immigrant of the second generation.[6] It would appear that the Chinese régime rested lightly on the local Lạc chieftains and, in fact, constituted probably hardly more than a tributary relationship. Confirmation of the indirect nature of this rule is afforded by the fact that only two commandery seats were established, one at Chiao-chih (交趾 *Kau-tśi)[7] for the collection of tribute from the delta of the Sông Cai, and the other at Chiu-chen (九真 *Ki̯əu-tśi̯ĕn) to supervise similar activities in the lower parts of the present-day provinces of Thành-hóa, Nghê-ân, and Hà-tinh. There is no reason to suppose that either of these settlements was anything other than a fortified frontier post where a *sú-gia* received the tribute of Lạc chieftains.

Conditions in the Tong-King basin appear not to have changed significantly when in 111 B.C. the armies of Han Wu-ti overran Nan Yüeh and integrated Chiao-chih[9] and Chiu-chen into a protectorate of the Empire administered under indirect rule.[10] The countryside was apportioned in three commanderies, each under the supervision of a *t'ai shou* 太守, by adding to the two administrative units already established another, Jih-nan (日南 *Ńźi̯ět-nậm),[11] comprising the coastal plains as far south as the Col des Nuages, where lay the frontier settlements of the Lin-I.[12] In addition, a governor (*tzʻŭ shih* 刺史) with authority over the whole of the former kingdom of Nan Yüeh was based for the first five years of the occupation at Luy-lâu,[13] in the heart of the Tong-King delta. Subsequently the seat of government was transferred to the capital of Ts'ang-wu (*Tsʻang-nguo* 蒼梧) commandery[14] within the boundaries of the empire proper. In any case local customs seem not to have been interfered with and Lạc chieftains and paramounts, in whose persons were institutionalized the ultimate rights to land, were confirmed in their traditional authority, some of the more prominent being appointed to the office of subprefect.

Although Chinese colonial policy did little to disturb the traditional political framework in northern Indochina, it is possible to glimpse the outlines of incipient social change. In the first place, the Chinese hegemony extended into the Sông Cai delta the channels of trade that had been developed between North China and the Hsi valley as early as the time of the Chʻin dynasty (221-207 B.C.),[15] and in so doing probably helped to consolidate the political power of those chieftains (*quận lang* 官郎)[16] whose settlements were favorably situated with regard to this trade. At the same time Chiao-chih became the destination of a stream of immigrants, both voluntary and involuntary, from regions farther north. *Bona fide* Han Chinese farmers and traders established themselves more or less permanently in the delta[17] side by side with renegades, fugitives and those banished from the soil of Han. When in the year A.D. 9 the Governor-General of Chiao-chih declined to acknowledge the legitimacy of Wang Mang's rule, a new stream joined the flow of immigrants, on this occasion made up of Confucian officials and literati who for one reason or another found the new regime in China Proper uncongenial. As a group these new arrivals were possessed of a deeper awareness of their cultural heritage than were most of the earlier immigrants, and their arrival may not have been unrelated to the emergence of a conscious policy of sinicization that had become apparent at the beginning of the first century A.D.[18] The official history of the Han records blandly that the governor who was in charge of the commandery from A.D. 1-25 "transformed the populace by rites and justice."[19] In addition to effecting agricultural improvements, founding schools, and attempting to replace certain of what were, to officialdom, opprobrious local customs with Chinese proprieties, the governors of the three commanderies recruited a militia on the Chinese pattern and instituted a cadre of native officials to staff administrative posts at the lower levels.[20]

Chinese political influence was exercised most strongly in the lowlands, where Lạc tribal society was exposed to — and absorbed a constellation of traits from — a fairly well integrated but hybrid culture subsuming both Han and Yüeh characteristics, with the result that a marked dichotomy was initiated in the evolutionary pattern of the indigenous culture. On the alluvial plains an increasing degree of sinicization moulded the mores and customs of the people now known as Viêtnamese, whereas in the valleys of the surrounding uplands folk such as the Mường preserved to a high degree their ancient ways of life.[21] These latter have no part in a study of urbanism for obvious reasons, but in the lowlands the Han-Yüeh cultural innovations, while leaving many local customs intact, tended to compete with and undermine the authority of those chieftains who, in response to political and commercial opportunities afforded by the Chinese presence, were in process of extending their control over available reservoirs of labor, that is were assuming leadership over confederations of villages and seeking to escape from the constraints on their personal aggrandizement inherent in chiefdom society. When in A.D. 39 the resentment of this class manifested itself in open revolt, Chiao-chih was incorporated in the Chinese polity as the southernmost province of the empire, and a hierarchy of commanderies and prefectures established on the pattern current in Han China.[22] Once the Tong-King basin constituted an integral part of the Chinese empire, the combination of a bureaucratic centralism that effectively prevented the functioning of a provincial administration in isolation, the presence of a cadre of officials with a deeply ingrained consciousness of their own ethnic superiority, and the introduction of a traditionally sanctioned ethos that subordinated the individual to society to an extreme degree, ensured an acceleration in the sinicization of the indigenous folk that had already been initiated by the policies of

Chinese officials such as Hsi Kuang 錫光 (A.D. 1-25), Jen Yen 任延 (A.D. 29-33), and Su Ting 蘇定 (A.D. 34-40.)[23]

An integral part of this process of sinicization was the establishment of *hsien* cities (Sino-Việt. *huyện* 縣), one of the principal instruments of Chinese political and cultural expansion from the days of Ch'in Shih Huang-ti onwards. These cities were wholly Chinese creations, established primarily for the administrative and social convenience of officials. If they sent down economic roots into alien soil, that was fortuitous and contingent upon forces beyond the consideration of their founders. It has traditionally been believed that the *hsien,* as an administrative district under a centrally appointed official, was an innovation of the state of Ch'in 秦, which existed in the Wei valley from 897-221 B.C.[24] Certainly it was constituted as the basis of centralized control in that state as early as 350 B.C.,[25] a development, it has been suggested, of the frontier foundations established by semi-independent vassals of the Chou emperor.[26] Recently Professor Creel has proposed that the *hsien* may have been first devised as an administrative instrument in the Yangtzŭ valley state of Ch'u 楚, instituted on a state-wide scale in Chin 晉, and finally adopted in Ch'in.[27] However that may be, it was a Ch'in ruler who in 221 B.C. brought the last of the former Contending States under his control and imposed the *hsien* as the standard administrative unit throughout the unified territories. Under the succeeding Han dynasty, *hsien* administration was extended through the passes of the southern mountains into the Hsi delta;[28] and when, in A.D. 39, the Sông Cai basin was incorporated within the Empire, this was the tradition of urban life that was imposed there too.[29]

Information about the twenty-two *huyện* cities (henceforward referred to by this Việtnamese form of the word) and the unknown number of subdistrict-level settlements established in Tong-King during this period is scanty, as the material preserved in both Chinese and Việtnamese annals, apart from a few bare references, relates only to the provincial capital. Yet this restricted information is not without interest as it illustrates well the vicissitudes of fortune and the impermanent nature of even the most important settlements of the time. Under the new regime of direct rule the seat of government was maintained at Luy-lâu,[30] which had already been the headquarters of the Inspectorate-General for a few years after the Han conquest of Nan Yüeh. The site of this settlement was located by Claude Madrolle in the present-day village of Lũng-khê in the *phu* of Thuận Thành in Bắc-ninh

Province,[31] but Dr. Jeremy Davidson has recently shown that it was more likely on, or close to, the site of Cổ-lõa.[32]

The degree of urban development represented by Luy-lâu remains uncertain. It is unlikely that the foundation of 111 B.C. was more than an administrative focus and residential site for an alien elite residing temporarily and reluctantly among "barbarians," but there is some evidence that, by the end of the 2nd century A.D., the settlement was beginning to acquire two other functions characteristic of the mature *hsien* city in China, namely cultural and commercial activities. In the troublous times that marked the dissolution of the Han dynasty, numerous members of the Chinese scholar class sought refuge in the relatively peaceful political backwater of Chiao, bringing with them both the official Confucian ethic and sometimes a personal Taoist morality and mysticism.[33] In the 2nd and 3rd centuries Indian and Indo-Scythian Buddhists introduced Mahāyāna doctrines to Chiao-chih.[34] Among the more prominent of these proselytizing Buddhists were the Indian Khâu-đà-la 丘陀羅, the *upāsaka* Tu-định 修定 from *Bʻi̯u-nậm,[35] Khang Tăng-hội 康僧會,[36] son of a Sogdian merchant resident in Chiao-chih, the Indo-Scythian Kalyāṇarūci, who in 255-6 made a Chinese translation of the *Fa-hua San-mei Ching* 法華三昧經,[37] and the Indian Mārajīvaka who arrived in Chiao-chih from *Bʻi̯u-nậm in about 294.[38] One of the earlier converts to Buddhism in Chiao-chih was the Chinese Mou Po 牟博, a former Taoist adept from Tsʻang-wu, who elected to study the Mahāyānist classics in Tong-King as early as 194 or 195, and who, with Khang Tăng-hội, is jointly credited with the establishment of the Āgama 教宗 school of the Tʻien-tʻai 天台 sect of Buddhism in Tong-King.[39] As a result of this religious activity, numerous wats were established in the neighborhood of *Luy-lâu*,[40] and within a few decades the city had become one of the main staging posts for Buddhist monks journeying between India and China, a role that it continued to play well into the 8th century. Most of our information about these voyages relates to the 7th century, when it was customary for Chinese monks journeying to India, the Holy Land of their faith, to start their voyage in earnest from Tong-King. At the same time Indian Buddhists en route to China would probably make their first acquaintance with the Chinese language at this point. In fact the wats of Tong-King may well have been the most likely places in which to find fellow monks competent in both Chinese and some other tongue of the South Seas such as Cam or Javanese, or perhaps Sanskrit, so that the region would have been a convenient halting point where a Javanese or Indian monk could have the intricacies of Chinese grammar explained in his own language. In I Ching's 義淨 compendium of biographies[41] we read of Ming Yüan[42] 明遠, Hui Ming[43] 慧命, and Wu Hsing[44] 無行 passing through Tong-King on their way to India, while Tan Jan[45] 曇閏, Chih Hung[46] 智弘, and the Sogdian Saṃghavarma[47] all spent fairly extended periods in the area. At the same time monks from Chiao-chih were also undertaking pilgrimages to India, among them Vận-kʻi 運期 (who was fluent in the *Kʻuən-luən 崑崙 language, presumably Malay, the *lingua franca* of the Archipelago), Mộc-xoa-đê-ba[48] 木叉提婆, Khuy-sung[49] 窺沖, and Huê-diệm 慧琰, as well as at least two from Ai 愛 prefecture,[50] namely Trí-hành[51] 智行 and Đại-thặng-đang[52] 大乘燈. Meanwhile Tongkinese Buddhism had been steadily becoming more diversified. In the 6th century an Indian monk Vinītarūci,[53] practicing the *pi-kuan* 壁觀 method of Bodhidharma 菩薩達摩 at the Kiến-sơ Wat 建初寺,[54] had founded the first school of Dhyāna Buddhism, a sect that was strengthened when a Kuang-Chou Chinese, Wu Yen-tʻung[55] 無言通, established a second school in the 9th century.[56] Under these circumstances it is not surprising that a number of Buddhist texts were translated into Chinese for the first time in Tong-King, one of them — the last two chapters of the *Nirvāṇa Sūtra* 涅槃後二卷 — being officially presented to the Chinese court in 676 by the administration of Chiao-chih.[57]

Concurrently Chiao-chih was forging trade relations with other parts of the *Nan-Hai* and even with realms beyond it. In fact, from the 2nd to the 6th century, when it yielded precedence to Kuang-tung, Chiao-chih was the eastern terminus of the South Asian sea-route that linked the Middle East to China.[58] To this locality came in the 9th year of the Yen-Hsi reign-period of Emperor Huan [A.D. 166] the famous embassy allegedly, though dubiously, from the Roman emperor Marcus Aurelius,[59] to be followed in the fifth year of the Huang-Wu reign-period [A.D. 226] by an apparently genuine Syrian merchant.[60] In this connexion we may also recall that as early as the middle of the 3rd century A.D. the trade relations of a Mōn emporium probably situated in the extreme north of the Siamo-Malay Peninsula extended as far as Parthia in the west and Chiao Chou in the east.[61] A sizeable proportion of Tong-King commerce appears to have been of an entrepôt character, in which commodities were transshipped in both directions between the South Seas and China proper, though the region itself was well known as a contributor of bananas, areca nuts, shark skins, python bile, and kingfisher feathers.[62] That its emporia were by no means totally eclipsed by Kuang-tung even in later times is evident from a memorial in which Lu chih 陸贄 (754-805), one of the most eminent of all T'ang ministers of state, advocated the establishment of an agency specifically to promote the development of Kuang-tung commerce in competition with ports on the Tong-King Gulf.[63]

Activities such as these must inevitably have done a good deal to diversify the social structure and economic institutions of the chief Chiao settlements, but these are matters that can now be reconstructed only in generalized form from the implications of developments in subsequent centuries. What is certain is that Chiao-chih as a whole, and its seat of government in particular, had become part of a system of religious order that reached from China to India, and of a trade network that extended from the China Sea to the Mediterranean.

The relative impermanence of administrative cities in the early centuries of Southeast Asian history is well demonstrated in Tong-King. To a large extent this instability was the result of tensions inherent in the colonial situation, where the legitimate aspirations of the subject populace were as a matter of policy subordinated to the broader aims of one of the world's two most powerful empires. But to the series of transformations induced by government fiat and popular revolt, manifested primarily in structural modifications to the administrative hierarchy, in the case of Tong-King must be added an additional suite of geomantically inspired changes that affected mainly the locations and morphologies of individual settlements. Like their counterparts throughout much of the traditional world, Chinese bureaucrats were aware that the fortunes of a city could be assured only if its site and form were adapted to the currents of the cosmic breath (ch'i 氣). These dynamic forces of the *genius loci* (hsing shih 形勢) were modified from place to place by the form of the terrain and from hour to hour by the dispositions of heavenly bodies, and it was analysis of these fluctuations that constituted the basis of the pseudo-science of *feng shui* 風水, the art of adjusting the features of the cultural landscape so as to minimize adverse influences and derive maximum advantage from auspicious conjunctions of forms.[64] Something of the way in which these two forces, the socio-political and the pseudo-scientific, interracted to mould the evolution of the urban hierarchy in Tong-King during the period of Chinese political domination is evident from the following sequence of events.

As early as A.D. 142-3, for unspecified reasons probably not unconnected with an abortive rebellion, the seat of government was transferred from Luy-lâu a short distance northwards to

Long-uyên 龍淵,⁶⁵ hitherto merely a huyện headquarters; but during an administrative reorganization at the end of the 2nd century that replaced the quận 郡 of Giao-chỉ by the châu 州 of Giao 交, the capital was reinstated on its former site, the ruins of which were restored and embellished and accorded the new honorific of Dinh-lâu 赢樓 (Anc. Chinese *Ḭäng-lə̯u), perhaps with the sense of Restored Capital.⁶⁶ The capital remained on this site until 229, when the Wu government had occasion to put down a revolt. As the "virtue" of the old capital had thereby been irreparably impaired, and the feng-shui of the site irremediably distorted by treason, the newly appointed Governor established his administration once again at Long-uyên, where it remained until the last years of the century, when Governor Tʻao Heng 陶橫 relocated the city, presumably again for geomantic reasons, on a new site some 14 li to the westward.⁶⁷ In about 306 it was moved a further 10 li westward, probably for similar reasons. During the 4th and 5th centuries Chinese rule, although afflicted by surges of disaffection and irredentism, consistently and successfully fostered Long-uyên as a node in the web of Southeast Asian commerce and as a focus of Buddhist scholarship. Meanwhile the character uyên, having been appropriated to the style of a member of the ruling house of Liu Sung (A.D. 420-479), had become taboo, with the result that Long-uyên became known (in writing at least) as Long-biên 龍編.⁶⁸ A century or so later a spate of turbulence that plagued the provincial administration of the Sui 隋 dynasty from the time of its founding in 581 was clearly not consonant with a propitious chʻi, and in 607 the Emperor sanctioned yet another migration of the capital, this time to a site on the right bank of the Sông Cai in the vicinity of present-day Hà-nội, where was built the new city of Tông-bình 宋平,⁶⁹ seat of the reconstituted commandery of Giao-chỉ.⁷⁰

With the advent of the Tʻang 唐 dynasty, the administrative divisions of the Chinese empire were again reorganized, and in 622 Tông-bình became the capital of the Protectorate-General of Giao 交州大總管府,⁷¹ later to be reconstituted as the Grand Government-General 大都督府, and finally, half a century later, as the Protectorate-General (Second Class) of the Pacified South [An-nam] 安南中都護府,⁷³ comprising a dozen prefectures [州] and fifty-nine sub-prefectures [縣].⁷⁴ In 757 the name only was changed to Protectorate-General of Tiĕn-nam (Ch. Chen-nan) 鎮南中都護府, but reverted to Protectorate-General of An-nam in 768.⁷⁵ The Protectorate-General was an instrument of

Beyond the Gate of Ghosts 375

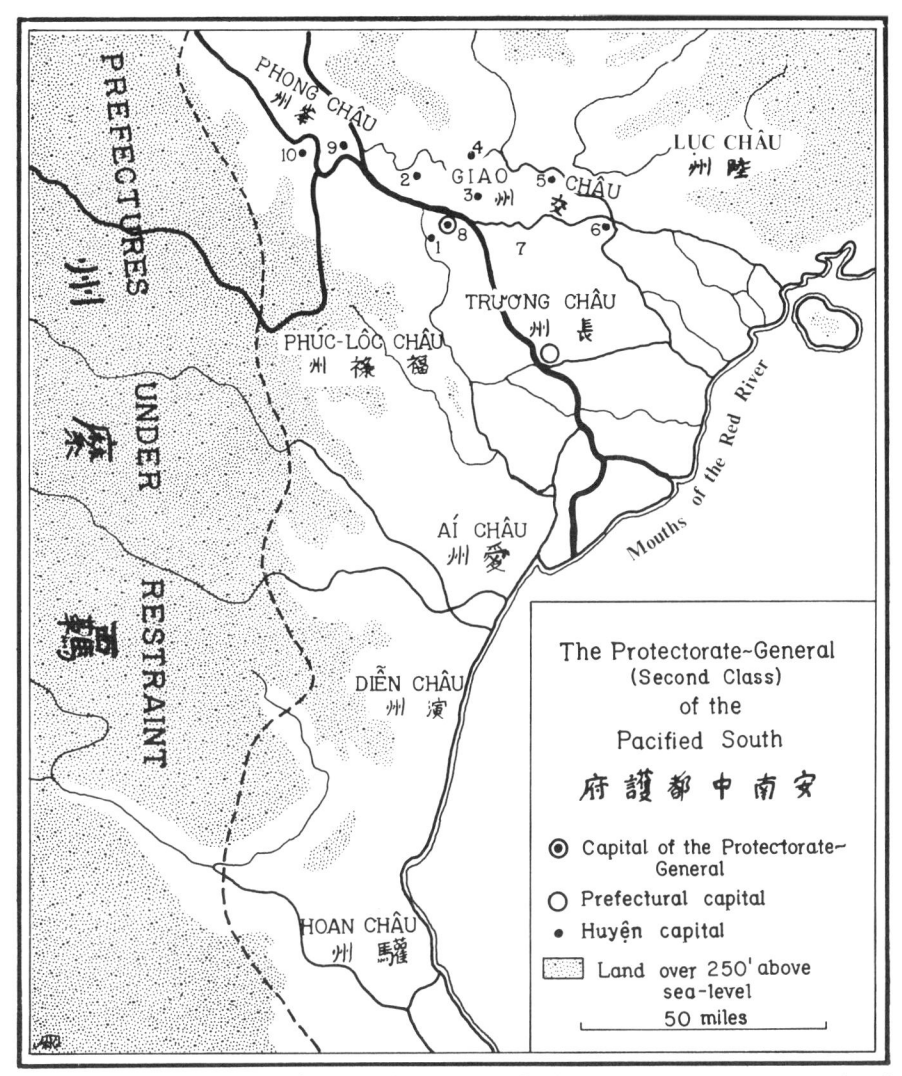

Fig. 20. Identifable features of the Protectorate-General of the Pacified South in ca. A.D. 800. The site of the capital of the Protectorate-General is well established (see pp. 376-377 of text), and the names of the seven Regular Prefectures (正 州) located in the Tong-King delta indicate the approximate locations of these units, although it is impossible to assign them boundaries. The siting of the prefectural seat of Trường, at Văn-dương, is little more than an informed guess. Of the score or so huyện cities in these seven prefectures, only a handful can be located with precision, and these are mostly in Giao Prefecture: (1) Tống bình, (2) Thái-bình, (3) Bình-đạo, (4) Vũ-bình, (5) Long-biên, (6) Chu-diên; (7) the general location of Nam-định huyện has been established but the precise site of the capital is unknown; (8) the seat of Giao-chỉ huyện was apparently also the capital of the Protectorate-General. In Phong Prefecture the two huyện cities marked are (9) Gia-ninh and (10) Thừa-hóa. It is certain that, in addition to the huyện seats that cannot be identified, there were other towns that endured for varying period of time (see pp. 378-379 of text).

The pecked line marks the approximate spatial limit of urbanization under the Protectorate-General.

government that had been developed by the T'ang to cope with the exigencies of border administration. Altogether there were seven of these units spaced in an arc round the land frontiers of the Empire, An-nam being the only one on the southern flank of the Chinese homeland.[76]

The seven prefectures that were located in the Tong-King delta and on the coastal plains as far south as Hoành-sơn shared in a system of administration common to the Empire as a whole,[77] but Chinese control over the neighboring uplands was often only nominal. From time to time attempts were made to bring them within the prefectural hierarchy, but more often than not the more remote tracts, at least, were constituted as "Prefectures (or Subprefectures) under Restraint" 羈縻州 (縣) ruled by indigenous chieftains, what would today probably be called Scheduled Territories.[78] Their numbers, designations, and boundaries were subject to almost continual change,[79] and there is no evidence that the Chinese administration ever succeeded in establishing, even temporarily, any mode of urban life in these regions. Even in the lowlands the three centuries of the T'ang hegemony were a period of political and social instability, during which the capital was moved repeatedly in response to internal uprisings and foreign invasions. Twice between 622 and 663 the seat of government was displaced.[80] In 687, the capital, together with its citadel known as Tử Thành 子城, were sacked during a local uprising,[81] and in 722 an indigenous chief, aided by Khmer and Cam forces, was equally successful.[82] Finally, in 767, after "Malaysian" (Côn-lôn 崑崙 and Chà-bà 爪哇) raiders had again exposed the inadequacy of the fortifications surrounding Tống-bình, the government was transferred to a fortified enceinte (la-thành 羅城) on the site of present-day Hà-nội;[83] but between 785 and 805 it was again located at Luy-lâu.[84]

At some time between 808 and 819 this citadel was entirely reconstructed on a larger scale, and given the name An-nam La-Thành (Citadel of the Pacified South 安南羅城).[85] The settlement is described only in summary fashion, but the meager information at our disposal places it squarely within the Chinese tradition of urban design. The citadel turned its back on the north, the realm of *yin*, of cold and dank darkness (appropriately depicted as a snake coiled about the Black Tortoise), for in the rampart on this side there was no gateway. However, the axial plan was evidenced by gateways breaking the lines of the walls on the other three sides. Both eastern and western gates consisted of three portals, that on the south — as befitted the main entrance to the city — of five.

Yet once again cosmic forces proved more powerful than human planning, and in 825 geomantic considerations encouraged the re-establishment of the capital at Tống-bình.[86] Hitherto such considerations have not been elaborated on in the records, but in this instance the reasons are stated. The texts are not entirely unambiguous, but it seems that the government geomancers had come to recognize that the Bắc river 北江, flowing to the northward of the city, was an unpropitious stream [逆水], an instrument through which evil influences from the north were being channelled into the district, where they bred revolt in the minds of the populace. The *feng-shui* experts then chose a new site on the right bank of the Sông Tô-lịch 蘇歷江, not far from the foundations of a citadel that had been laid on the site of present-day Hànội during the occupation of 767, but which was still unfinished nearly sixty years later. However, some months after construction had recommenced, the geomancers demanded that the location should be changed to the opposite bank of the river, where the new capital was eventually erected on the foundations of the former citadel. But the guardian spirits of abandoned Luy-lâu were still considered powerful enough to induce the governor of the province to erect a funerary temple, where placatory sacrifices might be offered. Despite these precautions, the improved *ch'i* of the site did not prevent the capital being occupied by troops from Nan Chao in 863. The T'ang administration transferred its government temporarily to Hải-môn 海門 [87] but, after a decade of warfare, the Chinese general Kao P'ien recovered the city and rebuilt an enlarged enceinte (đại la-thành) on or very close to the former site. The only sector of the new foundation of which a description has survived is the fortified core. This was surrounded by double defense works, consisting of an inner rampart with a perimeter distance of something less than six kilometers, flanked on all sides by a secondary outerwork that afforded protection against the arrows of besiegers. Within the walls were government offices, the treasury of the Protectorate, granaries, residences of officials and quarters for 5,000 troops,[88] together with an ambitious house-building project initiated by the Chinese general Kao P'ien.[89] That such accretions developed fairly commonly around T'ang forts in Tong-King, both generating and being generated by, true urban functions, is apparent from the role assigned to such foundations in the surviving literature.

The only cities to be accorded even the minimal descriptions noted above were the successive seats of government of the Protectorate-General. That there were other foundations is evident from the nature of the political regime, in which a score of more huyện were organized in seven prefectures, with each huyện focusing on a huyện seat[90] (Fig. 20). The prefecture about which we are best informed was that of Giao 交 . Occupying the eastern sector of the delta that comprises the present-day provinces of Vĩnh-yên and Sơn-tây, it comprised the following eight huyện:

Nam-định 南定	Unidentifiable.[91]
Long-biên 籠編	In the neighborhood of Bắc-ninh.[92]
Bình-đạo 平道	Between the Red river and the Sông Cà-lồ, and bordering the present Canal des Rapides.[93]
Vũ-bình 武平	Occupying the northwestern corner of the prefecture, coincident with the modern huyện of Yên-thế in Bắc-giang province and part of Thai-nguyên province.[94]
Thái-bình 太平	Between the Red river and the Sông Cà-lồ.[95]
Chu-diên 朱鳶戴	Occupying the whole of the eastern tracts of the delta.[96]
Tống-bình 宋平	In the neighborhood of present-day Hà-nội.[97]
Giao-chỉ 交趾	To the west of present-day Hà-nội, and extending from the Red River to the foothills of the mountains, that is, occupying the western tracts of modern Hà-đông and the eastern fringe of Sơn-tây.[98]

To the northwest of Giao, at the apex of the delta, was the prefecture of Phong 峯, consisting of the huyện of Gia-ninh 嘉寧, Thừa-hóa 承化, Tân-xương 新昌, Châu-lục 珠綠 and Tung-sơn 嵩山, of which only the first two can now be located. Gia-ninh followed the course of the Red river into the upper part of the delta,[99] and Thừa-hóa extended still farther up the valley in a northwesterly direction.[100] In the prefecture of Trường 長, which occupied the broad plains of the east-central delta, only the prefectural seat at Văn-dương 交陽 can be identified[101]— and that only in regional terms — although the names of three other huyện survive in Chinese records, namely Đồng-thái 銅蔡, Trường-sơn 長山, and Ki-thường 其常. Finally, the prefecture of Ái 愛 was established on the coastal plains of present-day Thánh-hóa (but nothing further is known of this political unit, not even the location of the prefectural capital), together with three more prefectures still farther southwards on the coastal plains of North Annam: Hoan 驩, Diễn 演 and Phúc-lộc 福祿. Judging from the dimensions of the citadels of Luy-lâu and An-nam La-Thành, even the larger *huyện* capitals must have been small affairs. But such inferences may be misleading, for written and archeological records alike refer only to the fortified core of the city, and we have no means at all of discovering to what extent this was, in any specific case, an isolated military and administrative post or the focus of an agglomeration of population. Certainly Luy-lâu (with its government offices, its numerous wats and its residential housing), and Tống-bình and the An-nam La-Thành in their heyday, were sizable centers of population which surely qualified as true urban foci.

In addition to these *huyện* seats, there were also other foundations known today only by name. For example, when the troops of Nan Chao invaded the Protectorate-General in 863, there were at least two citadels besides the one known as Đại-La. One of these was the enceinte of Tử Thành mentioned above, the other was an earlier fortified site beside the Sông Tô-lịch. Moreover, at different times during the T'ang hegemony, other *huyện* seats were established and endured for longer or shorter periods. Only rarely can these be located with certainty, but in the case of Từ-liêm 慈廉, Ô-duyện 烏延, and Vũ-lập 武立, three *huyện* united in 621 to form the prefecture of Nam-từ 南慈, it is possible to make broad territorial identifications[102] — although, of course, the sites of the *huyện* seats themselves are at present unascertainable.

I have already had occasion to refer to Dr. Davidson's argument for the urbanization of society in Tong-King prior to the incorporation of the Red River delta into the kingdom of Nan Yüeh at the end of the 3rd century B.C. Of the process of urbanization in general in Việtnam he writes:

> From observation of the urban-rural interdependent relationship in the late historical period, certain factors concerning the development and structuring of towns in Viet-Nam . . . become apparent. The settlement that would develop into an important centre was strategically sited for offence and defence, for accessibility to the surrounding countryside by river and land routes which afforded ease of military manoeuvre, whence military supremacy, and for control over the flow of produce. Because of its commanding position this dominant settlement achieved an administrative function, and since it was central to the trade cycle of the region, it became the market town, the focus for the exchange of produce which in Vietnamese terms included products that were specialties of certain villages. These craft and produce specializations coming together at the central market-place probably aided the development of street guilds and wards. Since not all settlements were self-supporting, mining communities for example, the market-place as a redistribution point was essential

to the continued existence of such dependent communities. The
administration of the exchange of goods and the machinery for the
maintenance of order necessary to the continuedly smooth operation
of different sectors of society were naturally located at such
favourable sites. The town as a political, social, and economic
space was thus engendered, enabling city-dweller and peasant to
achieve a symbiotic relationship.[103]

After which Dr. Davidson adds, ". . . it now appears that most of these aspects of urbanism are observable in the period prior to Nam-Viet."

Even if this last statement were to hold true, it could be rejoined that it is not so much the presence of individual institutions that constitutes a settlement as urban as the specific character of those institutions and the manner in which they articulate with the functional subsystems of society. As far as I have been able to ascertain from summaries of recent archeological reports in European languages, including a compendious statement by Dr. Davidson himself and others by Mr. Nguyễn Phuc Long and Mr. Hà Văn Tấn,[104] even the later Phùng-nguyên/Văn Lang cultural inventory implies a level of sociocultural differentiation at which a primarily tribal society was only beginning to be integrated into low-level chiefdoms. In fact, Linh Nguyên and Hoàng Hưng have already proposed an interpretation very close to this. As summarized by Dr. Davidson, they have suggested that Phong Châu "was the ruling centre of a loosely knit confederation of tribes of different ethnic composition."[105] The founding of Âu-Lạc could then have signaled either a conquest of Văn-Lang by a ruler from the northward (as one reading of the so-called chronicles might be held to imply) or a transfer of power between lineages within the old chiefdom of Văn-Lang (as most traditional historians have thought). In any case, the paramountcy was probably strengthened by the change, however it may have come about.

Dr. Davidson summarizes the implications of archeological research in Việtnam during the past quarter of a century as follows:[106]

> One sees from the distribution of Bronze Age sites three centres:
> (1) the area around the confluence of the Hồng River (Phùng-nguyên = Việt);
> (2) a shift to the more southerly Thanh-hoá region (Đông-sơn = Việt); and
> (2a) a series of Bronze Age sites, sparse and dwindling as they move inland — very few drums have been found in this inland and border region — mounting up the Hồng to:

(3) the Yúnnán area (Diān)...

Given this distribution, the conservative dates advocated for Phùng-nguyên and the Hông-bàng dynasty, the dates and finds of old bronzes, especially Heger I drums, in Yúnnán, one may propose that the Diān [Tien] area was a part of, and secondary to, the Văn-lang hegemony in the early period, a recipient of Phùng-nguyên - Dông-so'n (I-II) culture. Then in the third century B.C. this outpost of the confederation increased in importance, rose up against the Hùng leadership of the confederation, overthrew it and replaced it with the short-lived Thục kingdom of Âu-lạc, centred on the territory of the capital of the now vanquished Hùng-vu'o'ng. Archaeological evidence from North Vietnamese sites of this period shows that certain axes and "ploughshares," etc., quite unlike those usually found in the Vietnamese culture settlements, are common to Shízhaìshān [Shih-chai Shan]. Vietnamese traditions native to the area (Phú-thọ, Vĩnh-phú, Hà-tây) and relating to the struggle between the Hùng-vu'o'ng and Thục regard the Thục as the adversary. In 208 B.C., Triêu Đà overthrew the Thục. The vacuum that the Ailao-Thục had left in their Yúnnán homeland during their brief supremacy in the Vietnamese delta (258-208) permitted some other group of the confederation (their vassals?) to gain control and to develop what we now know as the rich Bronze Age civilization of Diān (second-first century B.C.)

With this set of inferences I am in provisional agreement. If the term "confederation" were changed to "chiefdom," the preceding paragraph would be unexceptionable as an account of power shifts of the type that are an all but inevitable accompaniment to the latter mode of political organization. The point at which I must part company with Dr. Davidson is when he claims that, "The discoveries of the Phùng-nguyên culture complex on what is traditionally Phong-châu territory argue strongly for the acceptance of Văn-lang and the Hung-vu'o'ng (?-258 B.C.) as historically valid."[107] Perhaps the discoveries in question do support the inference of a polity of some kind in what is now Tong-King prior to the 3rd century B.C. but, in my judgment, they imply a level of social, political, and economic integration far below that of the historical kingdoms presupposed by the Việt

annals, even during the half-century of Âu-Lạc dominance. For that
time, I think it not unreasonable to postulate a two- or three-tier
settlement hierarchy, encompassing the seat of a paramount set amid
tributary villages, possibly with district chiefs mediating between
the two from larger-than-average villages. The caches of bronze
arrowheads, bronze hoes, and bronze and stone axes that have come
to light within the enceintes of Cô̋-loa are entirely in keeping
with the redistributive mode of economic integration that
characterizes most chiefdoms. Furthermore, I doubt if the craft
specializations implicit in archeological assemblages from
Đồng-khôi (stone), Dậu-dương (stone), Gò Bông (pottery), Gò Mun
(pottery), Thiêu-dương (pottery), and Đồng-dậu (possibly bronze)
would have necessitated, as Dr. Davidson suggests, "some centrally
located market as a redistribution centre for specialized craft
goods produced at various 'factories'."[108] The requisite exchanges
would more likely have been effected within the framework of a
redistributive system focused on the seat of the paramount.[109]

The Commandery of Jih-nan

We have seen that under the Former Han the narrow strip of
coastal plain between the Porte d'Annam and the Col des Nuages, the
southernmost territory of the Chinese empire, was constituted as the
commandery of Jih-nan 日南. In the 2nd century A.D. the capital
of this commandery was located at Hsi-chüan (西捲 *Siəi-g‘i̯wän)[110]
in the neighborhood of present-day Ba-đôn, and hsien headquarters
were established at Chu-wu (朱吾 *Tśi̯u-nguo),[111] Pi-ching (比景
*Pji-ki̯ɒng),[112] Lu-yung (盧容 *Luo-i̯wong),[113] and Hsiang-lin (象
林 *Zi̯ang-li̯əm).[114]

It appears that Chinese control over this commandery was
somewhat tenuous, with the prefectural cities standing as islands
of governmental authority amid a sea of so-called "barbarians."[115]
These colonial foundations had been established primarily to serve
the political purposes of the Chinese government and had no
nourishing roots in the cultural, social, or economic life of the
countryside. Indeed, there is a good deal of evidence to show that
Chinese rule, together with the exactions and regularized
bureaucratic administration that it promoted, were not invariably
welcomed by the indigenous folk. In such circumstances the role of
the hsien foundations was restricted to that of fortresses
maintained for the restraint of a dissident populace. The
inhabitants of Hsiang-lin prefecture were particularly turbulent.
A revolt in A.D. 100 within the prefecture made it necessary for

the government to appoint a Commissioner of Military Affairs 象
林將吳長史.[116] This did not prevent another uprising in 137,
this time by tribes "from beyond the frontiers of Jih-nan,"
including a group known to the Chinese as Ch'ü-lien (區憐
*K'iu-lien).[117] This and another outbreak in 144[118] were both quelled
by diplomatic means, by persuasion as the Chinese were wont to
phrase it, but this traditional instrument of frontier government
as practiced by the Middle Kingdom proved inadequate to its task
some half-century or so later when a member of the Ch'ü lineage 姓
區 established an autonomous territory in Hsiang-lin.[119] The
Chinese administration was apparently content to accept this *fait
accompli* as reflecting actual conditions in the former
prefecture, and between 220 and 230 the governor of Chiao-chih
received an embassy[120] from the new principality, which was
rubricated in Chinese annals as Lin-I (林邑 *$Li̯əm$-·$i̯əp$).[121] This
was the name by which the Chinese henceforward referred to the
ethnic group, closely associated with the Ch'ü lineage, which, from
a hearth in Hsiang-lin prefecture[122] in the neighborhood of
present-day Hué, extended its control northwards, occasionally to
the Hoành mountains, and finally southwards to include present-day
Quảng-nam.

By 248 the Lin-I had established their northern frontier on
the Giang river,[123] and it is at this time that we first hear of a
Lin-I urban center. Among the territories prised from the Chinese
grasp was the city of Ch'ü-su (區粟 *$K'iu$-$si̯wok$),[124] in the
immediate vicinity, perhaps even on the site of, the former
commandery seat of Hsi-chüan.[125] Whether the old Chinese colonial
fort had been renamed by the Lin-I or whether Ch'ü-su was a separate
foundation is unknown. In 268 the Lin-I sent their first embassy
to the court of Wu in the company of a representative of Fu-nan,[126]
and in 284 we hear of another similar mission to the court of Chin.[127]
It is probably from this time that there dates the conscious
adoption by the Lin-I of certain elements of Chinese culture.[128]
Doubtless the administrative demands of emergent statehood rendered
their rulers especially receptive to the appeal of the material
aspects of Chinese civilization, and it is certainly not fortuitous
that techniques of city planning were, allegedly, among these
earliest borrowings.[129] At the same time the Lin-I, from their
agriculturally meager base of marsh, sand dunes and mountain
spurs, were casting covetous eyes toward the extensive
agricultural lands of Chiu-te (九德 *$Ki̯əu$-$tək$) commandery.[130]
The attempts of Chinese prefects to impose inflated duties on
merchandise entering the tribal areas did nothing to
ameliorate the frustrations of the Lin-I.[131] Various

frontier incidents during the later years of the 3rd century and
early decades of the 4th culminated in 347 in the occupation by the
Lin-I of the greater part of the commandery of Jih-nan.[132] Raids
farther north into Chiu-te in succeeding years brought Chinese
retribution and the abandonment of Jih-nan,[133] but not the
pacification of the frontier, which was the scene of skirmishing,
interspersed with diplomacy when a strong Chinese administration
rendered raiding unprofitable, for another century. That the Lin-I,
or at least their rulers, did not regard themselves as wholly alien
to Chinese culture is clear from the fact that in 433 a ruler of
the tribal confederacy petitioned the Emperor of Liu Sung that he
be appointed to the governorship of Chiao-chih. However, his
territory was considered to be too distant from the seat of the
commandery, and a Chinese was appointed to the post.[134] Finally, in
446 some three centuries of frontier friction were brought to a
temporary close by a determined governor of Tong-King. Both the
fortress city of Chʻü-su and the capital of the Lin-I, at Văn-xá in
the neighborhood of Hué, were put to the sack.[135]

The fortress of Chʻü-su

There can be no doubt that by this time there were
substantial urban foci in the territories of the Lin-I. When they
first appeared it is impossible to say, but descriptions of both
Chʻü-su and the capital city were incorporated in *Shui-Ching Chu* 水
經注, an extended commentary on the *Classic of the Waterways*,
compiled by Li Tao-yüan 酈道元 [136] at the beginning of the 6th
century A.D. For neither city is the text free of ambiguity, but
the urban character of the settlements described is readily
apparent.

Let us examine first the account of the fortress of Chʻü-su
in the *Shui-Ching Chu*, as this may incorporate a stratum of evidence
of earlier date than anything in the description of the capital.
This material found its way into a work of Taoist inspiration, the
Lin-I Chi 林邑記, which now survives only in quotation in later
compilations. This collection of *mirabilia* has traditionally been
attributed to the Taoist sage Tung-fang Shuo 東方朔,[137] but
internal evidence in the text makes it unlikely that it was
compiled much before the end of the 5th century.[138] In any case,
quotations from this work, including a description of Chʻü-su, were
incorporated in chüan 36 of the *Shui-Ching Chu*.

It would appear that strategic considerations had played
some part in the siting of this city, for it guarded both the

southern approaches to the Porte d'Annam and the entrance to the route that led up the Sông Giang[139] to the Mu-Gia pass and so to the plains of the middle Mekong. Viewed from the point of view of the Chinese officials who founded the original fortress of Hsi-chüan in this position, it controlled the northern entrance to Jih-nan and constituted a bastion from which Chinese administration could be deployed among the tribal populations of that prefecture and beyond, and to which Chinese forces could withdraw when threatened by the uprisings that were endemic to the frontier. It was doubly fortunate that a fortress on a site possessing these regional strategic recommendations should also have controlled the valley of the lower Sông Giang, where were the most productive padi lands of Jih-nan. Morover, probably as a result of the establishment of the commandery seat at this point, the estuary of the Giang had become the focus for maritime commerce along this stretch of coast. As the *Shui-Ching Chu* put it, "It is from this estuary that one sets sail for Fu-nan and the other kingdoms [of the south]."[140] Or, in the words of the *Chin Shu*: "At first the *kuo* [territories; in the majority of cases sc. chieftainships and chiefdoms] beyond the frontier used to offer precious objects in barter for other merchandise brought over the sea-lanes" 初徼外諸國嘗齎寶物自海路來貿貨賄.[141]

In order that the fortress might function the more effectively, the tactical aspects of the site had been selected with care, the skills of the engineer being reinforced by a judicious exploitation of natural features. The city was, in the words of the *Shui-Ching Chu*, "situated between two rivers (to north and south respectively)... with streams and rivulets flowing at the foot of the walls to east and west ... and with hills on three sides" 其城治二水之間三方際山南北瞰水東西澗浦流湊城下.[142] This situation would have offered few advantages to a city generated by the imperatives of commerce; rather it was the sort of situation attractive to the founders of a Chinese colonial city established to serve the purposes of frontier administration, and which only subsequently attracted to itself secondary exchange functions. The importance of that role in the turbulent situation prevailing in Jih-nan is evident in the frequency with which Chʻü-su featured as a focus of military activity in the five centuries or so of its existence: seized by the Lin-I in 248,[143] the scene of their defeat by a Chinese punitive expedition in 350,[144] besieged by Hsiang Tao-sheng 相道生 in 431,[145] sacked by Tʻan Ho-chih 檀和之 in 446,[146] and captured by

386 *Nāgara and Commandery*

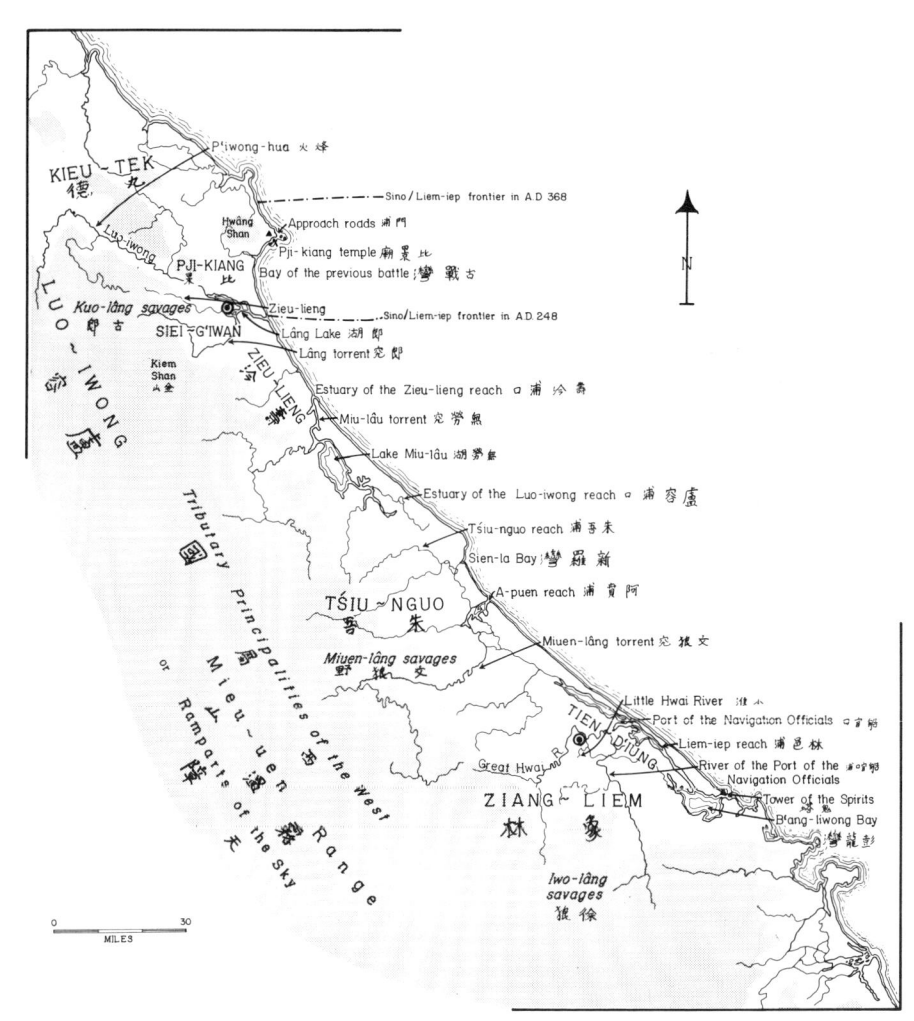

Fig. 21. The toponymy of Jih-nan commandery in the 4th century in so far as it can be reconstructed from the *Shui-Ching Chu* and other early Chinese sources. Based on the work of Rolf Stein in "Le Lin-yi," *Han Hiue*, vol. 2, pts. 1-3 (Pékin, 1947). The circled dots represent respectively (i) in the north the fortress of *Chü-su* and (ii) in the south the capital of the Lin-I, c. A.D. 450.

Transcriptions of the names of topographical features have been simplified in the interests of cartographic expediency: for more accurate renderings consult the text.

Liu Fang 劉方 in 605,[147] to mention only the more significant engagements. That the city played the same strategic role in the view of the Lin-I during the periods when they controlled it is explicit in a remark of the *Shui-Ching Chu* that the weapons of the Lin-I were collected in Ch'ü-su "because of the difficulties presented by a dissected terrain" 阻崄地險故林邑 兵器戰具悉在區粟 .[148] The astrological aspects of the site of Ch'ü-su, which were by no means unimportant, especially during the reign of an emperor with Taoist proclivities, have been touched on by Stein in his monograph on the Lin-I, pp. 45-46.

Amid these natural defences rose those of the city itself, which were popularly, and perhaps correctly, believed to have been patterned on technical innovations introduced from China between 313 and 317 by a certain Wen 文 , who later became "king" of the Lin-I with the regnal name of Fan Wen 范文 .[149] However, it is not easy to discern specifically Chinese features in the form of the city. The enceinte, more than 6 *li* in perimeter,[150] consisted of a plinth of brick courses some 20 feet in height surmounted by a brick wall of 10 feet. Above this rose five-tiered, lighter structures of wood, which in turn supported towers up to eight *chang* in height.[151] The walls were broken by no less than thirteen gates,[152] and the upper brick courses were pierced by square loopholes. The *Shui-Ching Chu* also adds a curious phrase to the effect that on its western flank the wall of the city formed ten angles 城西折十角 . The import of this remark is not clear and might at first glance be referred to a defense system involving something like Cairati's bastioned trace of later times, complete with re-entrants and oreillons. However, the capital of the Lin-I was also alleged to exhibit convolutions of one sort or another in its northwestern corner, and it may be that we are here dealing with a symbolic attribute. If so, I am at a loss to explain its significance. Another possibility is that separate accounts of one and the same city may have been distributed confusedly between Ch'ü-su and the capital.[153] The only feature of the city that manifestly betokened Chinese influence was the orientation of all the main buildings or, perhaps, all the buildings in the palace complex 宮殿 , towards the south.[154] It was estimated — on what authority is not stated, but possibly deriving from reports of the campaigns of 350, 431 or 446 — that there were about 2,100 dwelling houses 屋宇 in the city. Finally, a typically elliptical, but nevertheless significant, phrase may be construed as meaning either that markets were established round the outskirts of the city or

that markets and habitations surrounded the city 市居周繞.
I am inclined to prefer the former interpretation, and to regard
the markets as accretions analogous to those that grew up under the
walls of the ecclesiastical fortresses of Merovingian Europe: the
points, that is, where the dwellers within the walls transacted
business with the peasants of the surrounding countryside, rather
than foci of local exchange for an extramural agricultural
population. The first situation is that characteristic of the
imposed city, the colonial city, whereas the latter circumstance is
more consonant with the spontaneously generated city that arises in
realms of primary urban generation. I admit that this rendering
interprets the graphs in the light of preconceived notions, but at
least it does no violence to the text.

Of the population of Ch'ü-su the *Shui-Ching Chu* says nothing
apart from one obscure reference to some alleged descendants of
Ch'in exiles 秦餘徙民 having become completely assimilated to
frontier life 染同夷化 .[155] "The old customs of Jih-nan,"
says the author, rather sadly, "have been completely transformed."
Rolf Stein was almost certainly correct in interpreting these
remarks as a Han, or perhaps later, rationalization of the
continued presence of "barbarians" in a commandery that the Chinese
were accustomed to believe had been under Chinese occupation since
Ch'in times (221-207 B.C.). There is no reason to postulate a
population significantly mesticized at the time of compilation of
either the *Lin-I Chi* or the *Shui-Ching Chu*, the more especially as the
presence of Ch'in emigrés among the Lin-I belongs to a cycle of
legends prominent in Indochinese folklore.[156] This legendary aspect
of the matter is not inconsistent with the remark, with which the
Shui-Ching Chu concluded its account of this topic, that the
assimilated exiles used nests for dwellings and took their night's
lodging in trees. Perhaps this phrasing reflects the common
Austronesoid preference for stilted houses, but it also has
overtones of both Indochinese and South-Chinese folklore.[157]

The capital of the Lin-I

The lengthy statement in the *Shui-Ching Chu* relating to the
capital of the Lin-I[158] appears to have been compounded of reports
deriving from two punitive campaigns. Generally speaking, Li
Tao-yüan's information relating to the environs of the capital
dates from the expedition of T'an Ho-chih in 446, whereas that
relating to the city itself seemingly derives from 344. The city
was situated some 40 *li*[159] from the coast and at the foot of a low

spur of the Chaîne Annamitique. It was thus on the inner edge of the narrow coastal plain and in a position to draw on the resources of both mountain and lowland. Ready access to the uplands was certainly an asset in view of the role of forest products in the trade of this coast.[160] Equally important was the fact that the city was situated at the hub of a system of natural waterways that afforded easy communication in all directions. The Bô river[161] provided both access to the coastal lagoons and a route to the interior. Northwards the Lagune de l'Ouest offered a sheltered waterway that linked up with the Han river and the neighboring prefecture of Chu-wu; southwards the Lagune de l'Est[162] led to the Lagune de Câu-Hai[163] and ultimately, through an ample breach in the cordon of sand dunes, to the sea at the Tower of Spirits (鬼塔 Fig. 21).[164] The tactical features of the site of the city reproduced in essence those enumerated for Ch'ü-su: a mountain spur to the rear, padi fields before, and streams directed into a system of double moats on all sides.[165]

When we come to discuss the plan and architecture of the capital it is difficult to sift fact from symbol and folklore. The enceinte of the city was somewhat larger than that at Ch'ü-su, just over 8 *li*, and like Ch'ü-su, was elongated from east to west.[166] There were four gates, the most important of which pierced the eastern wall, so that we may say that the city faced in that direction. The northern gate, which fronted on to the Bô river, was apparently kept permanently closed 路斷不通 . In this we may see possibly a reflection of the Chinese innovations at the beginning of the 4th century or perhaps a cultural symbolism shared by both the Chinese and the Lin-I, or even simply a prudent desire on the part of the latter to run no risk of surprise attack by exasperated Chinese officials from the north. We have already seen that *An-nam La-Thành*, seat of the Protectorate-General of the Pacified South, was constructed in 819 with no gate in its northern wall. Internally the capital comprised about fifty quarters, each crammed with houses: "where purlins and ridgepoles touch and eaves of [adjoining] dwellings render mutual support" 連甍接棟檐宇 相承 as the *Shui-Ching Chu* put it. Only one of these quarters is mentioned specifically, the one called Enceinte of the Western Quarter 日西區城,[167] which enclosed a rocky eminence 石山[168] adjoining the Bô river. Judging from its restricted area, a mere 320 *pu*, or about 400 square meters, in relation to the extent of the city it was one of the smaller quarters. The use of the character *ch'eng* 城 in the above quotation, however, clearly indicates that its seperateness was emphasized by its own wall on at least two sides. There is no hint as to the role of this quarter in the functioning of the city as a whole.

On turning to the architectural features of the city, seeds of suspicion are sown as soon as we realize that the character and dimensions (though not the extent) of the walls are precisely the same as in the case of Chʻü-su, with the sole exception that the towers apparently did not rise above seven *chang* in height. This gives added significance to what might otherwise have been accepted as coincidence, namely the fact that the descriptions of the respective courses of the Nguôn Nậy river to the north of Chʻü-su[169] and of the Bô river to the north of the capital are identical except for one graph.[170] The suspicions aroused by these coincidences are strengthened by the discovery, remarked on above, that equivocal phrases concerning meanders and sinuosities that occur in descriptions of the northwestern sector of, or approaches to, the capital are parallelled in the case of Chʻü-su by a reference to ten angles.[171] One other detail may not be entirely devoid of symbolic overtones. The *Shui-Ching Chu*[172] remarks, apropos of the towers mentioned above, "flying turrets and owls' tails welcome the winds and support the clouds" 飛觀鴟尾迎風拂雲. The flying turrets may be nothing more than literary hyperbole, but the so-called "owls' tails" are a distinctive feature of Chinese architecture, probably from the time of the Former Han onwards.[173] They are in fact the fish that are often to be seen at either end of the ridgepoles of important buildings, and which are associated with a cycle of legends, widespread through South China and Southeast Asia, which are concerned with hybrid creatures that are both fish and fowl. Moreover, in China these legends are closely associated with the Fan lineage, and especially with Fan Li 范蠡, a *merchant* who is credited with the introduction of *fish* culture into the Yüeh country, and, among other feats, *the building of a city* after the pattern of the Kʻun-lun 崑崙. Now it will be recalled that the introduction of *city planning techniques* into the territories of the Lin-I was attributed to Fan Wen, a *merchant*, whose rise to prominence was contingent upon the miraculous transformation of some *fish*. Is it still possible to accept the "owls' tails" as fact, or were they literary embellishments whose symbolism was readily apparent to Li Tao-yüan's readers? Clearly a city built by a member of the Fan lineage ought to exhibit such features. All that we can be certain of is that, if they did appear on the towers of the capital of the Lin-I, they were indicative either of Chinese influence or of a substratum of symbolism common to both cultures. In any case, Li Tao-yüan was not complimentary about the architecture of the capital. In a sentence typically charged with irony and implication, he described it as "soaring upwards like a mountain wall [that is robust] but of inept construction" 騫薵崟崟但制造壯拙.[174]

The *Shui-Ching Chu* also adds that there was a total of eight sacred buildings 廟 within the enceinte, both temples 神祠 and pagodas 鬼塔, and appends a note to the effect that their overall appearance was reminiscent of Buddhist architecture 佛刹. There are also references to a brick (or tiled) palace, oriented to the east, ornamented with "owls' tails," with carved gates painted blue and with passages glazed with red lacquer. Cow dung 牛屎[175] was smeared on the walls, allegedly imparting to them a green sheen 青光. This information would assume significance as a token of Indian influence but for the fact that the whole of this passage relating to the palace has the aspect of an interpolation, interdigitated as it is with an account of the Enceinte of the Western Quarter. It also introduces a topic that fascinated the Chinese throughout these early centuries of the Christian era, namely the fact that, to the south of the tropic of Cancer, at certain times of the year a gnomon cast a shadow to the south. The significance of such a phenomenon for the Chinese, whose culture was permeated with the symbolism of an ominous, threatening north opposed to a benign, auspicious south, is readily apparent. On f. 19 verso of chüan 36, Li Tao-yüan reports an interrogation by Emperor Ming of the Han (A.D. 58-75) of a visitor from Jih-nan in which the notion that in that territory one turned north to see the sun 日南郡北向視日耶 was refuted.[176] The Sung encyclopedia *T'ai-p'ing Yü-lan*[177] also contains a passage relating that among the Lin-I "doors always opened to the north to face the sun" 皆開北戶以向日, but then immediately contradicts itself by remarking that "[they also face] east or west without any fixed rule" 或東西無定. In this context we are surprised to find Li Tao-yüan also writing that in the walls of the buildings making up the palace complex no apertures faced south 合堂瓦殿南壁不開.[178] Apparently this was achieved by turning a gable end in that direction 南頭長屋脊出南北.[179] And Li Tao-yüan adds, "The south, apparently, turns its back on the sun" 南擬背日,[180] echoing a phrase used in his earlier account of Emperor Ming's interrogation.[181]

There were doubtless other Lin-I settlements in the former commandery of Jih-nan and farther southwards, but none is mentioned in the surviving literature, with the possible exception of the Port of the Navigation Officals,[182] situated in all probability at the point where the Hương Giang[183] entered the Lagune de l'Est.

The evidence discussed above is unsatisfactory for our present purposes, particularly as it is virtually impossible to sift fact from folklore. It cannot be doubted that incipient urban life existed in the territories of the Lin-I, but it is still a matter for speculation whether the towns were originally Chinese colonial foundations or were generated within the cultural context of tribal groups in transition from folk to peasant society. In the case of Chʻü-su, the Chinese administration of Jih-nan seems to have been responsible for the founding of a commandery seat in the neighborhood, but there is still an element of doubt as to whether the Lin-I renamed this settlement or established their own city near by. Such evidence as we have demonstrates some degree of affinity between the morphology of the Lin-I city and that of the representative Chinese urban form of the time, but whether this was the expression of cultural borrowing or of a factor common to the cultures of South China and North Annam is difficult to say; and the problem is not made any simpler by the fact that it has to be viewed through Chinese eyes. Even the Viêtnamese annals, late in any case, are based on the earlier Chinese accounts of the Lin-I, and are valuable only for the specifically Viêtnamese folklore that they incorporate. We should remember, too, that remnants of the partially sinicized Li peoples of Tong-King seem to have withdrawn southwards after the failure of the rebellion of A.D. 39, and may have been instrumental in introducing Chinese customs among the Lin-I.[184] In any case, Chinese government seats such as Hsi-chüan must have been centers of cultural diffusion among — to judge from later analogies — not unresponsive tribesmen.

*　*　*　*　*　*　*　*　*　*

It must be admitted that the preceding discussion has done no more than demonstrate that the origins of urbanism in Tong-King and North Annam are still obscure, and that only the broadest of outlines are at present discernible. Yet it is surely safe to say that by the end of the 1st century A.D. urban nuclei in Chinese style had come to constitute prominent features of the delta landscape. In succeeding centuries they were extended, with varying degrees of permanence, along the coastal plains of North Annam as far south as the vicinity of the Hoành mountains. By Tʻang times these powerful instruments of sinicization had already gone far towards inducing that dichotomy between urban or peasant lowlander on the one hand and tribal hillman on the other that has ever since been a distinctive feature of Indochinese ethnology.

At the same time these Chinese colonial foundations served as instruments for the promotion of a class stratification which, long before T'ang times, had lost a good deal of its original ethnic basis. At the apex of the social pyramid were the Chinese Protector and other Chinese high officials and military personnel. Below them were ranged in appropriate order lesser Chinese bureaucrats, together with exiles from the society of Hua, mainly disgraced politicians. Although banished to the farthest bounds of the empire, a sentence which was itself a badge of infamy, these political exiles were still Chinese mandarins and therefore, among barbarians, not realistically able to sink too low in the social scale. In fact, in the Protectorate their status was likely to have have been relatively higher than their disgraced condition would have permitted in the Chinese metropolitan territories, Central Hua as they were called. However, although the boundary between colonial master and indigenous subject was virtually impermeable in a downward direction, it was permeable enough upwards given the right circumstances. In the first place, there was a class of persons of Chinese ancestry who, although born among the sights and sounds of the tropical south, had yet preserved, sometimes for many generations, their Chinese speech and culture and what in later times and in other regions was called a creole life-style.[185] In many respects this class bridged the great divide between Chinese and indigenous folk, between Hua 華 and Man 蠻 peoples. Some even achieved high office in the administration, notably Teng Yu 登祐, who rose to be Protector of Annam.[186] The key to social advancement in such cases was a familiarity with the Chinese classics, an accomplishment that was open not only to Chinese but also to indigenes blessed with the requisite leisure and endowed with the necessary energy. The Buddhist faith also afforded a likely avenue of advancement (note the Giao monks who undertook pilgrimages to India, p. 372 above), as also may have military proficiency.

Below these elite strata of society labored the artisans, shopkeepers, and government and private servants in the cities, and the great mass of the peasantry who were reclaiming the deltaic lowlands of the Red River valley for *padi* cultivation but whose achievements are, not unexpectedly, ignored in the literary records of the time. In fact, these farmers, on whose labors ultimately depended the prosperity of the Protectorate, made less impression on the literati, whose records are the only ones we possess, than did the swidden cultivators of the uplands, whom their betters in the cities regarded as barely human, and whose stilted houses were often compared unflatteringly to birds' nests.[187] Another group who are largely ignored in the writings of the time are the merchants, their involvement in a complex network of exchanges reaching from the Mediterranean to North China being documented only in a poorly articulated archeological record. The manner in which commercial transactions were organized is presumably irrecoverable.

To judge from the meager evidence available, the colonial cities of Tong-King were of only moderate size, and certainly less impressive than their analogues, whether at the provincial or *hsien* level, within the boundaries of China proper.[188] Indeed, the built forms of the majority of these foundations, even as late as T'ang times, were considerably less impressive than that of Cổ-loa in an earlier period. What distinguished them from the fortified settlements of the Lạc chieftains was not the quantity of labor invested in monumentality and defensive works, but rather their functions as theaters for the acting out of more diversified life-styles, as nodes in more highly differentiated social networks, and as functional centers of societal control at a greatly increased scale. In this last role the cities of Tong-King radiated ties of interdependence, both commercial and religious, that linked them not only to the urban hierarchy of the Chinese empire but also to cities and societies at the other end of Asia.

The Lin-I and the Kingdom of Campā

At the beginning of the 7th century A.D. inscriptions from present-day Quảng-nam attest the existence in that province of a polity bearing the name Campā.[189] When this honorific was first used in that area is unknown, but rulers proclaiming Sanskrit styles had been recorded epigraphically from the middle of the 4th century. The earliest of these was a certain Bhadravarman, who dedicated a shrine to Śiva Bhadreśvara at Mĩ-sơn and established the dominance of the cult of Śiva-Uma at his court.[190] This is usually located on the site of present-day Trà-kiệu on the strength of stone inscriptions in a script identical with that used at Mĩ-sơn that have come to light there. Two of these inscriptions are in Sanskrit and delimit the territory dedicated to Bhadreśvara at Mĩ-sơn; the third, which enjoins respect for "the nāga of the king," is the oldest text in the Cam language, and therefore in any Indonesian dialect.[191] The significance of this last is that it testifies to the presence of a Cam-speaking population to the south of the Bay of Tourane in the 4th century and the use of that language side by side with Sanskrit for epigraphic purposes. Other inscriptions associated with Bhadravarman have been found as far south as Phú-yên Province, but it is Quảng-nam, encompassing the archeological sites of Mĩ-sơn, Trà-kiệu, and Đồng-dương, that seems to have constituted the sacred hearth of Cam culture.

Now, although the Chinese sources provide no overt indications of Lin-I ethnic affiliations, the names, or more probably the styles, of most of the rulers preserved in those texts seem to have been cast in Cam, or at least Indonesian, forms. The *$b^c_{\underset{\sim}{i}}$wɒm 范 (MSC fan, Việt phạm) component that occurs in no less than eleven Chinese transcriptions of royal styles between the 3rd and 6th centuries,[192] for example, was almost certainly an attempt to render an ethnonym of the type beiam, as in Cam beiam, a name by which the Cams are still known to certain tribes of upland Indochina.[193] Moreover, the variant readings *ɣuo-d'ât (MSC Hu-ta 胡/湖達) and *s$\underset{\sim}{i}$u-d'ât (MSC Hsü-ta 須達) employed by the Chinese for the style of a ruler at the turn of the 5th century[194] have been plausibly restored as, respectively, Cam hadah, hudah and Bahnar sodah, both signifying "brilliant;"[195] while there can be no doubt that *ɪang mwai (MSC Yang Mai 陽邁) in the styles of two 5th-century rulers transcribes Cam Yaṅ Maḥ, meaning Golden Prince.[196] It is to be inferred, therefore, that at least some elements of the Lin-I population, and particularly the ruling strata, were Cam-speaking, perhaps altogether Cam in culture. This being so, it is natural to conclude that the Hinduized Cams whom we encounter in Quảng-nam from the second half of the 4th century onward were essentially the same people as those whom the Chinese had already been describing under the rubric of Lin-I for a century and a half, and who had established a capital in the southern part of Hsiang-lin Prefecture, probably in the neighborhood of Hué. On this view, the capital was transferred from Van-xá to Trà-kiệu in 605. This has, in fact, been the preferred interpretation of traditional Chinese and Viêtnamese annalists, as well as of most Western scholars.

The main impediment to a too ready acceptance of this point of view is the circumstance that the Lin-I, as they appear in Chinese sources, exhibit few characteristically Indian cultural traits (The "barbarian script" mentioned below and the smearing of cow dung on the palace walls might be exceptions) whereas the Cams of Quảng-nam were already strongly Hindu by the second half of the 4th century. Moreover, the Lin-I and Cam dynastic lines appear to overlap, with Chinese texts sometimes providing both styles (or names) and dates at variance with those elicited from Hindu epigraphic sources. From time to time attempts have been made to resolve these incompatibilities by equating the styles of certain Lin-I rulers with Hindu honorifics occurring in epigraphic documents. The results of these attempts have been rather less than successful. A favorite strategy has been to identify the Lin-I ruler known to the Chinese as *B⁽i̯wɒm ɣuo-dˤât (MSC = Fan Hu-ta) with the [Dharmamahārāja Śrī] Bhadravarman, partly on the grounds of the supposed contemporaneity of these two rulers and partly because the Chinese record that the former — in the manner of a Hindu ruler — had himself eulogized in "barbarian script" on a stela outside the east gate of his capital.[197] Others, suspecting that Bhadravarman's inscriptions might be several decades older than A.D.400, have suggested that *B⁽i̯wɒm B⁽i̯u̯ət (MSC = Fan Fo), the style ascribed to a ruler who came to the throne of Lin-I in 349, was a Chinese transcription of Bhadravarman.[198] This is a phonetically unacceptable suggestion, but there is an outside chance that the *b⁽i̯u̯ət component in the Lin-I ruler's style transcribed Buddha, and that the name of his capital, which the Chinese rendered as *B⁽i̯u̯ət-pâu (MSC = Fo-pao) City 佛保城,[199] could have been a Chinese rendering of Buddhaguptapura; in which case it would be in order to postulate a ruler styled *Buddhagupta.[200] However, no such name or style occurs in extant Cam epigraphy. As a way of resolving this impasse, Rolf Stein has suggested that the rulers of Lin-I with their capital at Van-xá were quite different from those with Sanskrit styles who left their epigraphs in Quảng-nam and Phú-yên, and who appear — at this distance in time, at any rate — to have been much more thoroughly Hinduized than their neighbors to the north.[201] Nevertheless, Stein proposes that they were subsequently conquered by the Lin-I. On the evidence currently available, this is an attractive, but by no means conclusive, hypothesis. In any case, the Chinese histories are in fundamental agreement with Hindu epigraphy from the 5th century onwards.

Whatever may have been the truth of the matter, it is certain that by the beginning of the 5th century A.D. Quảng-nam had become the base for a polity of considerable importance. From this sacred territory, which was known by the honorific Amarāvatī, a succession of rulers extended their power to include the restricted lowland embayments of the southern Annamite coast, namely — as they figure in Cam epigraphy — Vijaya in present-day Bình-định, Kauṭhāra on the deltaic plain of Nha-trang, and Pāṇḍuraṅga in the lowland of Phan-rang. Although the name Campā had been attested since the beginning of the 7th century A.D., Chinese annalists continued to use the ethnic ascription of Lin-I until 758, when they adopted the so-far unexplained term *γwan jiwang (MSC Huan Wang 環王). The search for the original of this transcription is in no way helped by the fact that the Cams themselves continued to refer to their kingdom as Campā. Pṛthivīndravarman and Indravarman I (reigning respectively in the middle and at the end of the 8th century) both claimed — accurately enough by all accounts — to reign over the entire kingdom of Campā, and Harivarman I, early in the 9th century, assumed the title of Supreme Lord of Śrī Campāpura (Śrī Campāpuraparameśvara).[202] Probably the adoption of the new name was in some way associated with a concurrent migration of the center of gravity of the kingdom that is known to have occurred southward from Mĩ-sơn to Kauṭhāra and Pāṇḍuraṅga. Finally, in the Hsin T'ang-Shu, *Tśi̯äm b'uâ (MSC = Chan-p'o 占婆) is used as a synonym for Huan Wang, and after the arrival of a Cam embassy in China in 877, all texts used the form *Tśi̯äm City (MSC = Chan Ch'eng 占城) to denote both capital and kingdom.[203]

Information about the settlement hierarchy in the Cam polity from the 5th century onwards is even more exiguous than that relating to the Lin-I. A succession of capitals are mentioned only in the most general of terms, and other urban forms virtually not at all until Chao Ju-kua in the 13th century described a three-tier hierarchy in terms of the capital, district cities (hsien 縣), and market centers (chen 鎮), with an implied fourth, and lowest, tier of agricultural villages.[204] The most that can be said about the early centuries is that the general configuration of events implies a political organization not greatly dissimilar to that in the Mekong valley at the same time. The recurrent rise and fall of "dynasties" (sc. descent groups) and the transference of power between families is not at all inconsistent with the notion of "a matrix of chieftainships integrated into a continually changing pattern of chiefdoms" (p. 143 above), while the manner in which Śaivite doctrine was used to support the integrity of the kingdom, together with the prominence of brāhmaṇas in the life of the court, bespeak a generally similar pattern of political development. In about eighty per cent of those published inscriptions from Campā which mention particular religious sects, Śiva is recognized as the principal member of the Trimūrti, while Bhadravarman's dedication of a liṅga with the personalized honorific -iśvara was the first instance of what was to become standard practice in both Campā and Kambujadeśa. Indeed, the Mĩ-sơn inscriptions furnish the oldest extant reference to a liṅga in the whole of Southeast Asia.[205]

Notes and References

1. The Gate of Ghosts was the name of a narrow gorge only thirty paces wide through which the traveller had to pass on his way from what is now Kuang-tung to Tong-King: Liang Tsai-yen 梁載言, *Shih-tao chih* 十道志, apud *T'ai-p'ing Yü-lan* 太平御覽 chüan 172, f. 9v. I owe the reference to the folk saying to Edward H. Schafer, *The vermilion bird: T'ang images of the South* (Berkeley and Los Angeles, 1967), p. 31.

2. For representative views of the scholars of the Ecole Française d'Extrême-Orient, see especially Henri Maspéro, "Etudes d'histoire d'Annam: IV, Le royaume de Văn-Lang 文郎國," *BEFEO*, vol. 18, fasc. 3 (1918), pp. 1-10, and "Etudes d'histoire du Viet-Nam: le royaume de Văn-Lang," *Dân Việt Nam*, no. 1 (1948), pp. 1-12; Léonard Aurousseau, "La première conquête chinoise des pays annamites (III siècle avant notre ère)," *BEFEO*, vol. 23 (1923), pp. 137-262; Cl. Madrolle, "Le Tonkin ancien," *BEFEO*, vol. 37, fasc. 1 (1937), pp. 263-332. Maspéro went so far as to deny the authenticity both of the name Văn-Lang 文郎 (which can be read as Tattooed, or Painted, Men), which he regarded as a mislection of the old Chinese name Yeh-Lang 夜郎 (*loc. cit.*, p. 2) and of the royal style Hùng 雄, which he interpreted as a scribal error for Lạc 雒 (*loc. cit.*, p. 7). Văn-Lang is now known to have been a transcription in Chinese characters of *vlang* (or *blang*: Mod. Việt. *dang*), denoting a (presumably totemic) bird of the heron family.

According to Việtnamese tradition, the site of Mêlinh, the capital of Văn-Lang, is marked even at the present day by the celebrated temple dedicated to the Hùng Vương in the village of Hi-cương, near Việt-trì, in the prefecture of Lâm-thao, Phú-thọ province.

3. This is the traditional date when Chao T'o 趙佗 (Sino-Việt. Triệu-Đà) is alleged to have extended his control over the chiefdoms of Âu-Lạc, but more than half a century ago Henri Maspéro ["La commanderie de Siang," *BEFEO*, vol. 16, fasc. 1 (1916), pp. 49-55, and "Bulletin critique," *TP*, ser. 2, vol. 23 (1924), pp. 373-393] made a case for changing this date to 181 B.C.

4. In Chinese texts this ethnonym is rendered by a variety of graphs: 雒駱 駱洛 and 鵅, all, except the last which is apparently *hapax legomenon* and does not figure among Karlgren's reconstructions, being restored to an Archaic form ** *glâk*. Lạc is the Sino-Việtnamese form. The classic account of the Lạc tribes is to be found in Ssŭ-ma Ch'ien, *Shih Chi* 史記 chüan 43, f. 9 verso, with supplementary information in Li Tao-yüan, *Shui-Ching Chu* 水經注 chüan 37, f. 6 verso; *Shih Chi*, chüan 113, f. 1 verso; *T'ai-p'ing Kuang Chi* 太平廣記 chüan 482; and *T'ai-p'ing Huan-yü Chi* 太平寰宇記 chüan 170.

5. Close to present-day Kuang-tung. On this city in ancient times see Nakamura Kushirō 中村久四郎 "Tō-jidai no Kanton," *Shigaku Zasshi* 唐時代の廣東史學雜誌 vol. 28 (1917), pp. 242-258, 348-368, 487-495, and 552-576.

6. Chao T'o, whose biography is to be found in *Shih Chi*, chüan 113 and *Ch'ien-Han Shu* 前漢書 chüan 95. In 179 B.C. he claimed that he had resided among the Yüeh for forty-nine years. As he was to live for another forty-two years, thus reaching the age of at least ninety-one, it is rather unlikely that he had been born in China proper. See *Ch'ien-Han Shu*, chüan 95, f. 9b.

7. Present-day Bắc-bô. The semantic significance of this toponym has been a subject of extended debate. Cl. Madrolle ["Le Thanh-hóa," *TP*, ser. 2, vol. 7 (1906) pp. 382-5, *Le Thanh-hoá* (N.D.) pp. 4-7 and "Le Tonkin ancien," *BEFEO*, vol. 37, fasc. 1 (1937), p. 309] derived it from a postulated sobriquet of a tribal group (the Crossed Toes) that had subsequently been transferred to the

land itself. More probable is the suggestion of Edouard Chavannes [*Les mémoires historiques de Se-ma Ts'ien*, vol. 1 (1895), p. 38] that, as Chiao-chih appeared in the *Shu Ching* as Nan Chiao 南 趾, meaning the Chiao of the South, only the *chiao* component could be considered a transcription of an indigenous name. Thus Tong-King would have been known both as "the Chiao at the mountain foot" (Chiao-chih) and as "the Chiao of the south." A conspectus of the whole problem is to be found in Ch'en Ching-ho, "Kiao-tche ming tch'eng k'ao," *Bulletin of the Faculty of Letters, National University of T'ai-wan* (T'ai-pei, 1952) and Paul Pelliot, *Notes on Marco Polo*, vol. 1 (Paris, 1959), pp. 233-234. See also Nguyễn Phuc Long ["Les nouvelles recherches archéologiques au Việtnam," *Arts Asiatiques*, vol. 31 (1975), p. 14] who suggests that Chiao-chih signified "territories occupied by the peoples who worshipped the *Kiao long* (the crocodile-dragon totem)." The name was applied to a commandery of Tong-King from Han to T'ang times, and was also the name of a *hsien* under the Sui and the T'ang.

8. Sino-Việt. Cửu-chân.

9. Sino-Việt. Giao-chỉ.

10. *Shih Chi*, chüan 113, ff. 4a-6b; *Ch'ien-Han Shu*, chüan 95, ff. 10v-13r.

11. Jih-nan = South of the Sun, a name bestowed by Chinese officials in recognition of the fact that, for a greater or lesser number of days between the spring and autumn equinoxes, the gnomon cast its shadow toward the south, a phenomenon which they encountered only when the Han extended its control to the south of the tropic of Cancer. For the significance of the toponym Jih-nan in the symbolic imagery of South China in early times see Wheatley, *The pivot of the four quarters* (Edinburgh and Chicago, 1971), pp. 460-461, Note 41. The urbanization of this southern commandery is discussed in the second part of this chapter.

12. See pp. 382-392 below.

13. See below. For possible reasons why Luy-lâu should have been chosen as the seat of the Inspector-General in preference to P'an-yü, the capital of the former kingdom of Nan Yüeh, see Wang Gungwu, "The Nanhai trade," *JMBRAS*, vol. 31, pt. 2 (1958), pp. 17-18.

14. Present-day Wu Chou 梧州 at the confluence of the Kuei and Hsi rivers in Kuang-hsi Autonomous Region.

15. Cp., for example: (i) *Huai-nan tzŭ* 淮南子, compiled at the court of Liu An 劉安, Prince of Huai-Nan in c. 120 B.C. (chüan 18, f. 27): ". . . gains from the lands of the Yüeh in the form of rhinoceros horn, elephant tusks, kingfisher feathers, and pearls, both regular and irregular" 又利越之犀角象齒翠珠璣. (ii) Ssŭ-ma Ch'ien's description of the Nan Yüeh capital of P'an-yü (*Shih Chi*, chüan 129, ff. 8v-9v) as "an emporium for the collection of rhinoceros horn, elephant tusks, tortoise-shell, pearls, fruit and cloth;" and Pan Ku's 班固 remark (in *Ch'ien-Han Shu*, chüan 28B, f. 31b) that "most of the Chinese merchants trading [in the same city] had become exceedingly rich."

16. Until well into the 20th century this term was still used in official Việtnamese documents, though with the components reversed to accord with the structure of that language, to denote the *thô lang* of the Mường (cp. Thai *thô ti*) who, in Thành-hóa, themselves also use this title [Jeanne Cuisinier, *Les Mường. Géographie humaine et sociologie* (Paris, 1948), p. 315].

17. These remarks would have applied in all likelihood to numerous officials as well, for only the least distinguished among candidates for office would have been assigned to Chiao-chih, and once there, remote from influential friends, it would have been difficult to arrange for a transfer to a more attractive post.

18. It is, of course, from this period that date most of the numerous tombs of Chinese officials and sinicized local notables that have featured so largely in the archaeological record of Tong-King. See Henri Parmentier, "Anciens tombeaux au Tonkin," *BEFEO*, vol. 17, fasc. 1 (1917), pp. 1-32 and "Le tombeau de Nghi-vê;" *BEFEO*, vol. 18, fasc. 10 (1918), pp. 1-7; O. Jansé, *Archaeological research in Indochina*; 3 vols: Harvard-Yenching Institute Monograph Series, vol. 7 (Cambridge, Mass., 1947), vol. 10 (1951), and Institut Belge des Hautes-Etudes Chinoises (Bruges, 1958); and "Rapport préliminaire d'une mission archéologique en Indochine," *Revue des Arts Asiatiques*, vol. 9, pts. 3 and 4 (1935), pp. 144-153 and vol. 10, pt. 1 (1936), pp. 42-52; L. Bezacier, *Le Viêt-Nam: I, De la préhistoire à la fin de l'occupation chinoise* (Vol. 2 of *Asie du Sud-Est* in the series entitled *Manuel d'Archéologie d'Extrême-Orient*: Paris, 1972), pp. 255-261; Nguyễn Phuc Long, "Les nouvelles recherches," pp. 97-101.

19. *Ch'ien-Han Shu*, chap. 28C. The governor referred to was Hsi Kuang 錫光 (S.-Viêt. Tích Quang).

20. Lê Tắc 黎崱 *An-nam chí-lược* 安南志畧 (13th century), quyển 11, f. 1 recto et verso.

21. Though seemingly absorbing in their turn a distinctive assemblage of traits from neighboring folk societies, notably those of Thai stock. It is interesting — if the parallelism between developments in the Chinese province of Chiao-chih and those in the Roman province of Britannia may be pursued briefly — to recall R. G. Collingwood's words [*Roman Britain and the English settlements* (Oxford, 2nd. edition 1937), p. 194]: "The Flavian movement for the development of towns, therefore, would inevitably divide the population of Britain into two classes, distinct not in social standing or in legal status or in blood, but in habits and education and culture: one somewhat intensely romanized, the other romanized in a much lower degree or hardly at all. And there is good evidence that this is what actually happened. The townsfolk, even the poorest and lowest in the social scale, learnt Latin; learnt in many cases to read and write; learnt to live in a Roman way. The country-folk, in particular the villagers, acquired hardly anything of all this."

22. According to the *Ch'ien-Han Shu*, chüan 28 C, f. 6, the commandery [*chün* 郡] of Chiao-chih comprised the following *hsien* 縣, here listed under their present-day Viêtnamese vocalizations : *Luy-lâu* 羸陵, *An-dịnh* 安定, *Câu-lậu* 苟屚, *Mi-linh* 麊泠, *Khúc-dương* 曲昜陽, *Bắc-đái* 北帶, *Kê-từ* 稽徐, *Tây-vu* 西於竽, *Long-biên* 龍編, and *Chu-diên* 朱鳶㢤. In A.D. 44 Ma Yüan 馬援, the Chinese conqueror of Tong-King, subdivided *Tây-vu* into two *hsien*, *Phong-khê* 封谿/溪 and *Vọng-hải* 望海 [Ssŭ-ma Kuang 司馬光, *Tzŭ-chih t'ung-chien* 資治通鑑 (1084), chüan 43, p. 5]. In a much quoted table of *hsien* at different periods in Chinese history, Li Chi [*Formation of the Chinese people* (Cambridge, 1958), p. 235] recorded no *hsien* in the southern Chinese provinces of Kuang-hsi, Kuang-tung and Kuei-chou, and omitted Tong-King from consideration altogether, even though it constituted an integral part of the Chinese empire from A.D. 43 to 968. In fact, as early as 111 B.C. when Nan Yüeh was incorporated in the Empire as the *ch'en-shih-pu* of Chiao Chou 交州 (S.-Viêt. Giao Châu), which included large tracts of present-day Kuang-tung, Kuang-hsi and Tong-King, its territory was divided into seven commanderies comprising 56 *hsien*.

23. Sino-Viêt., respectively, Tích Quang, Nhâm Diên, and Tô Đinh.

24. E.g., Chao I 趙翼 *Kai-yü Ts'ung-k'ao* 陔餘叢考 in *Ou-pei Ch'üan-chi* 甌北全集 (1877), chüan 16, ff. 8v-10r; Yao Nai 姚鼐 *Hsi-pao Hsüan Wen-chi* 惜抱軒文集 [*Ssŭ-pu Pei-yao* ed.], chüan 2, f. 1r; Ch'i Ssŭ-ho 齊思和 "Chan-Kuo chih-tu k'ao," *Yen-ching Hsüeh Pao* 戰國制度攷 燕京學報 vol. 24 (1938), p. 214; Derk Bodde, *China's first unifier. A study of the the Ch'in dynasty as seen in the life of Li Ssŭ (280? - 208 B.C.)* (Leiden, 1938), pp. 135-139 and Appendix, pp. 238-243.

25. *Shih Chi*, chüan 5, ff. 16-17.

26. Wolfram Eberhard, *Conquerors and rulers* (Leiden, 1952), pp. 11-12.

27. H. G. Creel, "The beginnings of bureaucracy in China: the origin of the hsien," *The Journal of Asian Studies*, vol. 23, no. 2 (1964), pp. 155-184.

28. According to the *Kuang-tung T'ung-chih* 廣東通志, vol. 1, chüan 3, as early as A.D. 222 twenty-two *hsien* cities had already been established in Kuang-tung province.

29. For a brief outline of the extension of *hsien* administration throughout the Chinese empire, see Sen-dou Chang, "Some aspects of the urban geography of the Chinese hsien capital, "*AAAG*, vol. 51, no. 1 (1961), pp. 23-45, and the same author's "The historical trend of Chinese urbanization," *loc. cit.*, vol. 53, no. 2 (1963), pp. 109-143.

30. *Luy-lâu* is the Việtnamese vocalization of the name of the capital of Giao-chỉ province. In Chinese records it occurs under various orthographies: *ljwię̆ 贏屚 ; *liạn 贏 ; *iäng 贏屚 (though in this series the modern corrupted form has come to coincide with the *ljwię̆ group): *lᵊu 屚樓慺. Although *ljwię̆ lᵊu 贏陸 appears to be the sole form sanctioned by the official histories, the general instability of the graphs has induced some confusion in the writings of modern authors. Henri Maspéro ["Etudes d'histoire d'Annam, V," *BEFEO*, vol. 18, fasc. 3 (1918), p. 11] transcribed the official form into French as *Lien-cheou* (= MSC *Lien-shou*); Paul Pelliot ["Meou-tseu ou les doutes levés," *TP*, vol. 19 (1918), p. 328] and Emile Gaspardone ["Matériaux pour servir à l'histoire d'Annam," *BEFEO*, vol. 29 (1929), p. 82] as *Ying-leou* (= MSC *Ying-lou*); while Trần Văn Giáp ["Le Bouddhisme en Annam des origines au XIIIe siècle," *BEFEO*, vol. 32 (1932), p. 209] rendered 贏樓 as *Lei-leou* (= MSC *Lui-lou*). So far as Việtnamese historiography is concerned, it has been customary to read the first graph as *luy*, though E. Nordemann opted for *Doanh-lâu* in his *Chrestomathie Annamite*, p. 46, as did Cl. Madrolle in some of his early works, e.g., *Indochine du Nord* (Hanoi, 1923). In 1937 Henri Maspéro wrote: "Les prononciations des caractères, qui servent à écrire les noms au Tonkin sous les Han sont très souvent incompréhensibles, mais comme elles sont données par les contemporains, il faut bien les accepter. Mon impression personelle est que les Han ont conservé, sans les changer, les graphies qu'ils ont trouvées adoptées par l'administration des rois de Nan-yue . . ." [reported in Cl. Madrolle, "Le Tonkin ancien," *BEFEO*, vol. 37 (1937), p. 200]. In this instance the local pronunciation of 贏 would appear to have resided somewhere between *ljwię̆ and *iäng. Presumably it was an attempt to reproduce such a vocalization that led Meng K'ang 孟康 (whose *Han-shu Yin-i* 漢書音義 is preserved in part in *Ch'ien-Han Shu*, chüan 28C, f. 12r) to insist that the graph 贏 should be read as *liạn (孟康曰贏音連), and which induced the author of the 3rd-century *Ti-tao Chi* 地道記 to devise the graph 贏. Madrolle ("Le Tonkin ancien," p. 281) claimed that this orthography was still used by local Việtnamese scholars in the earlier years of the present century to designate the ruins of the ancient city. However, it must be remembered that his informant was *tri-phủ* of Thuận Thành, and thus a member of the class most likely to cherish an ancient text, such as *Ti-tao Chi*, containing references to neighborhood landmarks. In other words, it may have been the *tri-phủ's* own knowledge of ancient texts rather than local custom that dictated his remarks to Madrolle.

Madrolle's attempt (1937: 281-2) to attach eponymous and chronological significance to the several forms of this name (e.g. 贏屚 = ruined citadel; 贏陸 = beneficent citadel), even if sustained, need not invalidate the preceding remarks, for Chinese authors customarily tried to interpret a foreign toponym at the same time as they transcribed it.

The second element in the official form of this name is rare but Yen Shih-ku 顏師古 (581-645: *Ch'ien-Han Shu*, chüan 28C, f. 12r) provided a *fan ch'ieh* 反切 Chinese pronunciation of *lᵊu (*lâi 來 + k'ᵊn 口), which Meng K'ang (*loc. cit.*) confirmed with an *yin-yün hsüeh* 音韻學 vocalization. For further comments on the vocalization of this name and its descriptive imagery, consult Jeremy H. C. S. Davidson, "Urban genesis in Viet-Nam: a comment," in R. B. Smith and W. Watson (eds.), *Early South East Asia* (New York and Kuala Lumpur, 1979), pp. 311-312.

31. Madrolle ["Le Tonkin ancien," pp. 279-288] selected this particular site from among a considerable number of possible locations, all exhibiting remains of fairly substantial settlements, mainly on the basis of (i) the meager locational information provided by the *Ch'ien-Han Shu*, chüan 28C, f. 12r; (ii) rather superficial archeological investigations previously undertaken on the site by Henry Wintrebert, for several years Resident of Bắc-ninh Province; and the existence of certain shrines dedicated to Sĩ Nhiếp, who has been traditionally associated with Luy-lâu. However, the *Yüan-ho chün-hsien t'u-chih* 元和郡縣圖志, compiled by Li Chi-fu 李吉甫 in 814, placed Luy-lâu 75 *li* to the *west* of Hà-nội. Madrolle rejected this, the earliest specific directional information extant, on the grounds that it would have located the provincial capital in the foothills of the Mường country, and suggested that "west" was here a mislection for "east." Madrolle's arguments are cumulatively impressive, but they by no means constitute proof of the identification, and I have chosen to adopt Dr. Davidson's interpretation (see below). It must be remembered that the shrines honoring Sĩ Nhiếp may well be late foundations, and that the local traditions associating him with Luy-lâu may be nothing more than instances of the well attested tendency of popular memory to associate folk heroes with sites hallowed on quite other grounds. And, as mentioned above, Madrolle's ruins are not the only ones that might accord with the little that we can glean from literary texts concerning the physical form of Luy-lâu: they happen to be one of the very few sites that have been even partially excavated. Nor should the generally reliable testimony of Li Chi-fu be rejected out of hand.

32. Davidson, "Urban genesis," pp. 311-312, note 25. It is noteworthy, though, that Nguyễn Phúc Long still adheres to Madrolle's identification: "Les nouvelles recherches," p. 23.

33. Cp. the preface to *Mou-tzŭ li-kan* 牟子理惑 in *Hung ming chi* 弘明集, a collection of Buddhist texts compiled by Shih Seng-yu 釋僧祐 toward the end of the Southern Ch'i 南齊 dynasty, A.D. 479-501 [Jap. Trip., Tōkyō ed., 霜 4]: ". . . after the death of Emperor Ling 靈帝 [A.D. 189] the Empire was disturbed. Chiao-Chou alone was relatively peaceful, and men of non-conformist temperament 異人 came from the north to reside there. Many devoted themselves to cultivating gods and demons, abjured cereals 辟穀 and [sought for] immortality 長生."

34. Trần-Văn Giáp, "Le Bouddhisme en Annam des origines au XIIIe siècle," *BEFEO*, vol. 32 (1932), pp. 191-268; Samy, "Histoire du bouddhisme en Indochine," *Revue Indochinoise*, vol. 24, no. 7-8, pp. 77-81. Cp. the reply of the monk T'an Ch'ien 曇遷 (S.-Việt. Đàm-thiên) when asked by the Emperor Kao 高帝 (A.D. 479-482) of the Southern Ch'i dynasty to undertake a missionary enterprise in Tong-King: "Lian-lęu [i.e. Luy-lâu] is much closer to India by sea than we are, so that before the doctrine of the Buddha had reached Chiang-tung 江東 (= China of the Ch'i dynasty) there were already more than a score of *caitya* in the territory of Lian-lęu and over 500 monks were reciting from fifteen rolls of texts" [Trần Văn Giáp, "Le Bouddhisme en Annam," pp. 208-9, 235, quoting from *Thiền-uyển tập anh ngữ-lục* 禪苑集英語錄, a collection of biographies of monks of the Dhyāna school compiled in 1337. I have not seen this work, the several editions of which are apparently all in Hànội. In the original text of the *Thiền-uyển* the Chinese Emperor is referred to as Cao-tổ 高祖 of the Tùy (Sui 隋) dynasty (581-618), but we know from *Kao-Seng Chuan* 高僧傳 (chüan 13, f. 75 recto) that T'an Ch'ien died between 478 and 483. Trần Văn Giáp has, therefore, emended Tùy to read 齊 (Ch. = Ch'i: p. 210), which, incidentally, is in accord with the reference to China as Chiang-tung, denoting the relatively limited territory under the control of this particular dynasty].

35. Cô-châu Pháp-vân-Phật bản-hành ngữ-lục (see Note 38 below), here quoting *Báo cực truyện* 報極傳 (for which see Trần Văn Giáp, "Le Bouddhisme en Annam," p. 218, note 1); *Cô-châu tứ-pháp phả-lục* 古珠四法譜錄, also quoting earlier sources. In some texts the name of the monk is written Cà-la-chà-lê 伽羅闍梨, which may be restored as Kālācārya or the Swarthy Sage, presumably a soubriquet applied by the Việtnamese to an Indian, or possibly Southeast Asian, Buddhist.

36. Chinese = Kʻang Seng-hui. It was common practice among Chinese annalists to employ the first or second syllable of a particular ethnonym as the *hsing* of a person of that ethnic origin. In this case Kʻang was derived from Kʻang-chü 唐居, that part of Kirghizistān around the Talas and Chu valleys. Khang's biography is included in *Kao-Seng Chuan* 高僧傳 (Tōkyō Tripit. vol. 35, chap. 2, f. 3 r et v).

37. Sino-Việt = Chi Cương Lương 支疆良. Trần Văn Giáp ("Le Bouddhisme," pp. 213-4) equates Chi Cương Lương with the *śramana* Chiang Liang Lou-chih 疆梁婁至 mentioned by Fei Chʻang-fang 費長房 in *Li-tai san-pao chi* 歷代三寶記 [see also Paul Pelliot, *TP*, vol. 22 (1923), p. 100] and with a certain Chih Chiang Liang-lou 支疆梁楼/樓 mentioned in Nanjio's catalogue [Appendix 2, no. 22], and restores both forms as Kalyāṇarūci.

38. Sino-Việt. = Ma-la-ki-vực 支疆梁接樓. Biography in *Kao-Seng Chuan* (*Tōkyō Trip.*, vol. 35, chap. 2, f. 53 recto). In *Thiền-uyển* this name occurs as Ma-la-kì-thành 摩羅耆城 : emendation by Trần Văn Giáp, "Le Bouddhisme" pp. 211-212. A Jīvaka is also mentioned in *Cổ-châu Pháp-vân-Phật bản-hành ngữ-lục* 古珠法雲佛本行語錄, a late (1752) compilation recounting the history of Việtnamese Buddhism from the period of the Three Kingdoms until about 1750. I have not seen this work and my information is from Trần Văn Giáp, pp. 216-218, who also resolves discrepancies between this text and certain Chinese sources [*Kao-Seng Chuan*; *Fo-tsu li-tai tʻung-tsai* 佛祖歷代通載 (Tōkyō Trip, vol. 35, ch. 10, folio 41 verso)].

39. Sino-Việt. = Mâu Bác. See *Mou-tzǔ li-kan*, Note 33 above. Translation and annotation by Paul Pelliot, "Meou-tzǔ ou les doutes levés, *TP*, vol. 19 (1918-19), pp. 255-433. See also Trần Văn Giáp, "Le Bouddhisme," p. 214. The period from the beginning of the 3rd to the end of the 6th century witnessed the dominance of Indian Buddhism in Tong-King. Note that Mou Po journeyed first to South China and then to Tong-King in pursuance of his studies, a response to the manner in which the Indian doctrines had diffused along the sea route towards the east.

40. These included the Thành-đạo 成道 Wat housing the Pháp-vũ 法雨 Buddha at Đông-cốc; the Nam-Giao Học Tổ 南郊學祖 Wat, commemorating Sĩ Nhiếp (Shih Hsieh), at Lũng-khê; the Phi-tương Wat, consecrated to the Pháp-lôi 法雷 Buddha, at Thành-tương; the Pháp-điện 法電 Wat at Phương-quan; the Phúc-nghiêm 福嚴 Wat at Mãn-xá; the Pháp-vân 法雲 Wat at Khương tự. For details see Madrolle, "Le Tonkin ancien," pp. 292-296.

41. *Ta-Tʻang Hsi-yü Chʻiu-fa Kao-seng Chuan* 大唐西域求法高僧傳 (c. A.D. 705).

42. Sino-Việt. = Minh Viễn. This monk's Sanskrit name was Cintādeva, rendered in Ancient Chinese as *Ṭi̯ən-tâ-dʻiei-bʻuâ 振多提婆.

43. Sino-Việt. = Huệ Mạnh.

44. Sino-Việt. = Vô Hành. This monk's Sanskrit name was Prajñadeva, rendered in Ancient Chinese as *Bʻuân-ńi̯ak-dʻiei-bʻuâ 般若提婆.

45. Sino-Việt. = Đàm Nhuận.

46. Sino-Việt. = Trí Hoằng.

47. Rendered in Anc. Ch. as *Tsʻəng-ka-pʻuâ-muâ 僧伽跋摩 ; Sino-Việt. = Tăng-cà-bạt-ma.

48. A Sino-Việt. rendering of Sanskrit Mokṣadeva.

49. This monk's Sanskrit name was rendered in Sino-Việtnamese as 質呾囉提婆 = ? Citradeva.

50. Present-day Thành-hóa.

51. This monk's Sanskrit name was Prajñadeva. For the Sino-Việt characters see Note 44 above.

52. This monk's Sanskrit name was Mahāyāna-pradīpa, rendered in Sino-Việt. characters as 莫訶夜那鉢地巴波. The preceding information has been culled from I Ching's *Memoir*, Tōkyō Tripit. vol. 35.

53. Rendered in Sino-Việt. characters as Tì-ni-đa-lưu-chi 毘尼多法支.

54. In the present-day village of Phù-đổng, Tiên-du huyện, in Bắc-ninh Province.

55. Sino-Việt.= Vô Ngôn Thông.

56. For information on both these monks see *Thiền-uyển tập anh ngữ-lục* and *Cổ-châu Pháp-vân-Phật bản-hành ngữ-lục*, f. 14. Summarized by Trần Văn Giáp, "Le Bouddhisme," pp. 235-236.

57. This particular translation was the work of Tie Hien 智賢 (Skt. name = Jñānabhadra) and Huāi Nieng 會寧 [Tōk. Trip., vol. 35, chap. 7, f. 95 recto, and *Sung Kao-Seng Chuan* 宋高僧傳 chüan 2].

58. *Chiu T'ang-Shu* 舊唐書 chüan 41, f. 33 verso: "the kingdoms of the South Seas that, since Han times, have come to present tribute, have necessarily come by way of Chiao-chih."

59. *Hou-Han Shu*, chüan 118, folio 10v. The complete passage has been translated by F. Hirth, *China and the Roman Orient* (Shanghai, 1885), p. 42. Cp. E. Chavannes, "Les pays d'Occident d'après le *Heou Han Chou*," TP, vol. 8 (1907), p. 185. I have here adhered to the traditional dating of this alleged embassy, but it has been suggested on fairly strong grounds that the event actually took place during the reign of Elagabalus (A.D. 218-222). See B. Broeler and F. Bömer, *Fontes historiae religionum indicarum* (Bonn, 1939), p. 131, and E. R. Hayes, *L'école d'Edesse* (Paris, 1930), p. 77.

60. *Liang Shu* 梁書 chüan 54. The complete passage has also been translated by Hirth, *China and the Roman Orient*, p. 48.

61. See p. 214 above.

62. *Hsin T'ang-Shu*, chüan 43A, f. 9v.

63. *Ch'üan T'ang Wen* 全唐文 chüan 473, ff. 14 r - v.

64. For summary discussions of the conceptual bases of *feng shui*, and for bibliographic references, see E. J. Eitel, *Feng-shui, principles of the natural science of the Chinese* (Hong Kong, 1873); J. J. M. de Groot, *The religious system of China*, vols. 2 and 3 (Leiden, 1892); Joseph Needham, *Science and civilisation in China*, vol. 2 (London, 1956), pp. 359-363; and vol. 4 (1962), pp. 239-245; Stephan D. R. Feuchtwang, *An anthropological analysis of Chinese geomancy* (Vientiane, 1974). For the application of this pseudo-science to urban design see Wheatley, *The pivot of the four quarters* (Edinburgh and Chicago, 1971), pp. 419-423.

65. Also written 龍周. The precise site of this settlement is disputed, one group of researchers preferring the village of Quê-dương in Võ-giàng subprefecture, another affirming the claims of Đông-yên village in Yên-phong subprefecture. Both villages are in Bắc-ninh province. See Viện Sử học, *Lịch sử thủ đô Hànôi* (Hànôi, 1960), p. 13.

66. This account is based on material in *Ta-Ch'ing i-t'ung chih* 大清一統志 [ed. by Hsü Ch'ien-hsüeh 徐乾學 c. 1730], article on *Ku Chiao-Chou* 古交州, which is itself a collation of earlier sources.

67. *Yüan-ho chün-hsien t'u-chih* 元和郡縣圖志. chüan 38, f. 5 verso.

There is every reason to suppose that Tʻao Heng would have wished to channel a more propitious chʻi into his capital, for he had been sent by the Wu 吳 emperor specifically to reclaim the allegiance that Giao-châu had just accorded to the Chin 晉 dynasty.

68. This is the explanation offered by the Ta-Chʻing i-tʻung chih in its notice on the administrative divisions of the state of Chʻi (under the rubric Kuang-tung), but Tongkingese folklore, reported by Madrolle ["Le Tonkin ancien," p. 297], prefers a validatory myth in which the name (which can be translated as Dragon Twist) commemorates the appearance of two entwined [編] dragons in the shallows of a near-by river. Cp. also the Tʻang poet Lu Kuei-meng 陸龜蒙 who turned a couplet on this very point: Chʻüan Tʻang shih 全唐詩 han 9, tsʻe 10, chüan 9, f. 7v.

Việtnamese antiquarians and topographers have almost invariably located Long-biên on the site of present-day Hà-nội. Representative of traditional opinion are the remarks of Nguyễn Trại 阮廌 in 1435 in his Dưdia chí 輿地志 [a topography of Việtnam that forms the sixth and final quyển of the collected works of that author under the title Úc-trại tập 抑齋集 (Úc-trại being the hiệu of Nguyễn Trại)]: "Long-biên is the present-day city of Thăn-Long 昇龍城 where King Cao 高王 founded the Great Citadel 大羅城 ." In the light of our present knowledge such a location is inadmissible, as indeed was pointed out over half a century ago by Henri Maspéro. ["Le protectorat général d'Annam sous les Tʻang," BEFEO, vol. 10 (1910) p. 575]. It is still impossible to specify the precise location of the ancient capital, but Cl. Madrolle has demonstrated beyond doubt that during the four and a half centuries or so of its existence the city occupied a series of sites all in the vicinity of the north bank of the Sông Thiap in Bắc-ninh: ["Le Tonkin ancien," pp. 299-302].

69. Chinese = Sung-pʻing. Originally this name had been applied to a commandery created during the 5th century A.D., probably during the rule of the Liu Sung [Nan-Chʻi Shu, chüan 14, f. 14 recto; Tʻai-pʻing Huan-yü Chi, chüan 170, f. 6 recto]. For the approximate site of Tông-binh see Maspéro, "Le protectorat général," pp. 552-555.

70. Sui Shu, chüan 31, f. 6 recto.

71. Tʻung Tien 通典 chüan 32, folio 4 verso; Tzŭ-chʻih Tʻung-chien, chüan 190, f. 8 recto; Chiu Tʻang-Shu, chüan 41, f. 33 verso; Hsin Tʻang-Shu, chüan 43A, f. 7 verso. Yüan-ho chün-hsien tʻu-chih, chüan 38, f. 9 verso alone places — presumably erroneously — the formation of the Grand Government-General in the fourth year of Wu-te, i.e. 621.

72. Tzŭ-chʻih Tʻung-chien, chüan 190, f. 22 recto; Tʻung Tien, chüan 32, f. 4 verso.

73. The Tʻang hui-yao 唐會要 chüan 73, f. 17 recto dates the imperial decree establishing the Protectorate-General to the 7th day of the 3rd month of the first year of Tʻiao-lu, that is 22 April 679, but the Hung-chien lu 弘簡錄 chüan 2, f. 17 verso refers this event to the 8th month of the 1st year of Kʻai-yao, or 18 September-16 October 681; the Chiu Tʻang-Shu, chüan 5, folio 7 verso agrees with this latter version in recording a date equivalent to 12 October 681.

74. For general remarks on the Protectorate-General see Henri Maspéro, "Le protectorat général d'Annam sous les Tʻang: Essai de géographie historique," BEFEO, vol. 10 (Hanoi, 1910), pp. 539-584 and 665-682. Maspéro's reconstruction relies heavily on five Chinese works: Tʻung Tien by Tu Yu 杜祐 (c. A.D. 812), chüan 184, ff. 23 et seq; Yüan-ho Chün-Hsien Tʻu-chih by Li Chi-fu 李吉甫 (A.D. 814), chüan 38; Chiu Tʻang-Shu by Liu Hsü 劉昫 chüan 41, ff. 33 recto et seq; Tʻai-pʻing Huan-yü Chi by Yüeh Shih 樂史 (A.D. 976-983), chüan 170 and 171; and Hsin Tʻang-Shu by Ou-yang Hsiu 歐陽修 (A.D. 1061), chüan 43A, ff. 7 verso et seq. There are, of course, no Việtnamese works contemporary with the events described, and such later Việtnamese histories, topographies, and encyclopedias

as do deal, usually in an extremely perfunctory manner, with this period are of little practical significance.

75. *Chiu T'ang-Shu*, chüan 41, f. 33 verso; *Yüan-ho chün-hsien t'u-chih*, chüan 38, f. 9 verso; *Hsin T'ang-Shu*, chüan 43A, f. 8 recto; *T'ai-p'ing Huan-yü Chi*, chüan 170, ff. 2v - 3r; Bui Quang Tung, "Tables synoptiques de chronologie vietnamienne," *BEFEO*, vol. 51 (1963), p. 32.

76. Robert des Rotours, "Les grands fonctionnaires des provinces en Chine sous la dynastie T'ang," *TP*, vol. 25 (1927), p. 246. For a general discussion of provincial government under the T'ang (which unfortunately has little to say about the South), see Denis C. Twitchett, "Varied patterns of provincial autonomy in the T'ang dynasty," in John Curtis Perry and Bardwell L. Smith (eds.), *Essays on T'ang society* (Leiden, 1976), pp. 90-109.

77. Territories such as these were designated "regular prefectures" 正州 .

78. Edward Schafer, mindful of China's classical past, renders *chi-mi chou* literally as "bridle and halter counties," thereby appropriately continuing into T'ang times the old euphemism that the Chinese emperor harnessed subjected barbarians to the imperial polity by the power of his "virtue." Schafer continues, "Thus the bestial aliens were bound by the leash of Chinese moral superiority, which they duly recognized in accepting the novel but hybrid administration [*The vermilion bird*, p. 71]. Twelve hundred years later the French still found it necessary to administer Phongsaly, the northernmost province of the former Protectorate of Laos, as a military territory under the direct control of the French army. An obvious earlier analogue of this situation that springs to mind is the distinction between the civil (lowland) and military (upland) zones of Roman Britain.

79. There is an incomplete enumeration of these territories in *Hsin T'ang-Shu*, chüan 43C, f. 12 verso that includes 41 Prefectures-under-Restraint.

80. Maspéro, "Le protectorat général," p. 556, note 3.

81. *Hsin T'ang-Shu*, chüan 4, f. 2 verso; *Tzŭ-ch'ih t'ung-chien*, chüan 215, f. 3 recto; *Yüeh-shih Lüeh* 越史畧 chüan 1, f. 9 verso [in *Shou-shan Ko Tsung-shu* 守山閣叢書]; *Đại-Việt sử-kí toàn-thơ* 大越史記全書 ngoại kỉ, q. 5, f. 4 recto. Tử Thành was a small edifice, with a perimeter of only 900 paces, that had been built in 621 by Ch'iu Ho 丘和 [*Đại-Việt*, ngoại kỉ, q. 5, f. 3 recto].

82. *Hsin T'ang-Shu*, chüan 207, f. 1 verso; *Chiu T'ang-Shu*, chüan 8, f. 8 recto and chüan 184, f. 2 recto; *Tzŭ-ch'ih T'ung-chien*, chüan 212, f. 6 verso; *Hung-chien lu*, chüan 64, f. 21 verso; *Đại-Việt sử-kí toàn-thơ*, ngoại ki, quyển 5, f. 4 verso.

83. *Yüan-ho chün-hsien t'u-chih*, chüan 38, f. 3 verso. 羅城 was a term widely used in East Asia from Sui times onward: cp. Chinese *lo-cheng*, Japanese *rajō*.

84. *Hsin T'ang-Shu*, chüan 43A, f. 7 verso. For comments on this topic see Paul Pelliot, "Deux itinéraires de Chine en Inde à la fin du VIIIe siècle," *BEFEO*, vol. 4 (1904), p. 135.

85. *T'ang Hui-yao*, chüan 73, f. 17 verso; *An-nam chỉ lược* 安南志畧 chüan 9, f. 3 verso - 4 recto. It is not unlikely that the name of *An-nam La-Thành* had been bestowed on the city originally founded on this site by the Imperial Commissioner Chang Po-i 經畧使張伯儀 in 767 [*ibid*.].

86. Phạm-công-Trứ 范公著 *Đại-Việt sử-kí toàn-thơ* 大越史記全書 (1665): *Ngoại-kỉ toàn-thơ* 外紀全書 (from the beginnings to A.D. 967), q. 5, folio 7 verso, and Li Tế Xuyên 李濟川 *Việt-điện u-linh tập* 越甸幽靈集 (1329), folio 10 recto [here quoting *Giao-châu kỉ* 交州記 of Master Triệu 趙公, late-ninth century]. The role of geomancy in the siting of this citadel is not mentioned in any of the Chinese sources, a circumstance that led

Maspéro ["Le protectorat général," p. 553] to stigmatize the Viêtnamese accounts as echoes of local legends. To me they have the ring of truth. Closer to legend, however, is the continuation of the story in the Ðại-Việt sử-kí toàn-thơ: "When Li Yüan-chia 李元嘉 transferred his capital to the bank of the Sông Tô-lịch, he built a small town. A geomancer advised him: 'Your forces are inadequate for the construction of a large town [but] within fifty years a person by the name of Kao will establish on this spot the seat of the Protectorate-General'" — clearly a validatory myth devised subsequent to the enlargement of the citadel by the Chinese general Kao P'ien 高駢 (Sino-Việt. = Cao Biền) in the winter of 866/7.

87. *Tzŭ-ch'ih T'ung-chien*, chüan 250, f. 8 verso.

88. *Việt-sử lược* [quyển 1, f. 12 verso] and *Ðại-Việt sử-kí toàn-thơ* [ngoại kỉ, q. 5, ff. 14 recto - 15 verso] record a perimeter distance of 19,805 paces. These distances may or may not be in approximate agreement, depending on the length assigned to the pace, but Ssŭ-ma Kuang 司馬光 *Tzŭ-ch'ih T'ung-chien* 資治通鑑 chüan 250, f. 19v in any case records a perimeter distance of only 3,000 paces. The massive fortifications still visible in Hà-nội bear no relation to this T'ang foundation, but are the remains of Lí and Trần capitals subsequently constructed on the same site. Tongkingese folklore, however, archetyping rather than discriminating, has for long designated these remains as La Thành. Indeed, this identification is made explicitly in both *Bắc-Thành địa-dư chỉ* 北城地輿志 quyển 1, f. 3 recto [I have not seen this work, and am relying on information contained in Maspéro's "Protectorat Général," p. 558] and *Ðại-Nam nhất-thống-chi* 大南一通志. f. 14 verso. The editors of the *Khâm-định Việt-sử thông-giám Cương mục* 欽定越史通鑑綱目 [compiled in 1859; revised from 1871 to 1878, and printed in 1884] alone seem to have escaped this error. The number of troops in the garrison is from *Việt-sử lược*, quyển 1, f. 12 verso. *Tzŭ-ch'ih T'ung-chien* [chüan 250, f. 11 verso] reads "more than 400,000" 四十餘萬聞], an impossible figure for such a garrison, yet one that has been copied with an alarming lack of critical acumen into the *Ðại-Việt sử-kí toàn-thơ, ngoại kỉ*, quyển 5, f. 15 recto.

89. *Tzŭ-chih T'ung-chien*, chüan 250, f. 19v.

90. *Hsin T'ang-Shu*, chüan 43. The account of Tong-King included in this chapter apparently relates to the closing years of the T'ang dynasty. It was this list of administrative divisions that, being eventually incorporated in abridged form in the *Cương mục*, acquired canonical authority in Việtnamese historiography. The remarks which follow owe much to the synthesis of Henri Maspéro, "Le Protectorat Général d'Annam sous les T'ang," *BEFEO*, vol. 10 (1910), pp. 539-584, 665-682.

91. Maspéro, "Le Protectorat Général," pp. 567-569.

92. *Loc. cit.*, pp. 569-575.

93. *Loc. cit.*, pp. 575-578.

94. *Loc. cit.*, pp. 578-579.

95. *Loc. cit.*, pp. 579-580.

96. *Loc. cit.*, pp. 580-584.

97. *Loc. cit.*, pp. 551-563.

98. *Loc. cit.*, pp. 563-567.

99. *Loc. cit.*, pp. 666-667.

100. *Loc. cit.*, p. 667.

101. *Loc. cit.*, pp. 668-680.

102. *Loc. cit.*, p. 563.

103. Jeremy H. C. S. Davidson, "Urban genesis in Viet-Nam: a comment," in R. B. Smith and W. Watson (eds.), *Early South East Asia* (New York and Kuala Lumpur, 1979), p. 305.

104. Jeremy H. C. S. Davidson, "Archaeology in northern Viet-Nam since 1954," in Smith and Watson, *Early South East Asia*, pp. 98-124; Nguyễn Phuc Long, "Les nouvelles recherches archéologiques au Việtnam," *Arts Asiatiques*, vol. 31 (1975), pp. 3-154; Hà Văn Tấn, "Nouvelles recherches préhistoriques et protohistoriques au Việtnam," *BEFEO*, vol. 68 (1980), pp. 113-154. For a recent Chinese view see Lü Shih-p'eng 呂士朋 *Pei-shu shih-ch'i ti Yüeh-Nan* 北屬時期的越南 Monograph No. 3, Southeast Asia Studies Section, New Asia Research Institute, Chinese University of Hong Kong (Hong Kong, 1964), p. 14.

105. Linh Nguyên and Hoàng Hưng, "Vấn đề Hùng-vương và khảo cổ học," cited in Davidson, "Archaeology in northern Viet-Nam since 1954," p. 114. Nguyễn Phuc Long is equally explicit: "Le processus de la formation du Vănlang s'est déroulé lentement sur la base d'une fédération des tribus, des régions, aboutissant à une union territoriale dans le cadre d'une communauté culturelle" ("Les nouvelles recherches," p. 6).

106. Davidson, "Archaeology in northern Viet-Nam," pp. 114-115.

107. Davidson, "Urban genesis," p. 305. Davidson here cites Châu Trương hoàng, "Nền văn hóa khảo cổ học duy nhất trong thời đại đồng thau Việt-nam và vấn đề nước Văn-lang của Hùng- vương."

108. Davidson, "Urban genesis," p. 306.

109. Cp. the constellations of specialized manufacturing settlements that surrounded the ceremonial and administrative centers at Cheng Chou and Hsiao T'un on the North China plain in Shang times: Wheatley, *The pivot of the four quarters* (Edinburgh and Chicago, 1971), chap. 1, especially Figs. 1 and 2.

110. Sino-Việt. = Tây-quyển.

111. Sino-Việt. = Châu-ngô.

112. Sino-Việt. = Tī-cảnh.

113. Sino-Việt. = Lo-dung.

114. Sino-Việt. = Tương-lâm.

115. *Ch'ien-Han Shu*, chüan 28B, f. 6 recto; *Hou-Han Shu*, chüan 33, f. 8 recto; *Chin Shu*, chüan 15, f. 9 recto; *Shui-Ching Chu*, chüan 36, f. 18 verso. The same information was later also incorporated in Viêtnamese annals, e.g., Lê Tắc's 鰲 寅 *An-nam chỉ-lược* (first half of the 14th century), quyển 1, f. 3 verso [Japanese edition of 1884 translated into French by Camille Sainson, *Mémoires sur l'Annam* (Pékin, 1896)], and *Khâm-định Việt-sử thông-giám cương-mục* 欽定越 史通鑑綱目 tiền biên (1859), quyển 2, ff. 5 recto and 27 verso [translated into French by A. des Michels, *Les annales impériales de l'Annam* (Paris, 1889)]. The conclusions of Henri Maspéro as to the location of Hsiang-lin are no longer acceptable ["La commanderie de Siang," *BEFEO*, vol. 16, fasc. 1 (1916), pp. 49-55]. There is a perceptive study of this topic by Lao Kan 勞榦 "Hsiang-Chün Tsang-k'e ho Yeh-Lang-ti kuan-hsi," *Liu-t'ung pieh-lu* 象郡牂柯和夜郎的關係 六同別錄 chüan 3 (hsia), *Academia Sinica, Bull. Nat. Res. Inst. of History and Philology, wai-pien*, 3rd. series (Li-chuang, 1946). Today this is a rare journal, which I have not been able to consult, but the substance of the article is summarized by R. A. Stein in Appendix V of "Le

Lin-yi, sa localisation, sa contribution à la formation du Champa et ses liens avec la Chine," *Han Hiue* 漢學 vol. 2, fasc. 1-3 (Pékin, 1947). The present exposition relies heavily on Stein's interpretation.

116. *Hou-Han Shu*, chüan 4, f. 22 recto and chüan 116, f. 32v. For the office of Commissioner of Military Affairs see *Hou-Han Shu*, chüan 38, f. 3 verso. Maurice Durand ["*Cương-mục*, quyển 2," *BEFEO*, vol. 47, fasc. 1 (1955), p. 414, note 4] translates *chang shih* 長史 as "Délégué en Chef." Some texts use the form 長吏.

117. Sino-Việt Khu-liên. *Shui-Ching Chu*, chüan 36, f. 24 recto; *Hou-Han Shu*, chüan 116, f. 3 verso: *Cương-mục*, q. 2, f. 19 recto.

118. *Hou Han Shu*, chüan 116, f. 3 verso; *Cương-mục*, q. 2, ff. 19 verso-22 recto.

119. *Shui-Ching Chu*, chüan 36, f. 24 recto; *Liang Shu*, chüan 54, f. 2 recto, *Chin Shu*, chüan 97, f. 14 verso. The personal name of this chieftain is written *Lien* (連 *liän*: Sino-Việt. = Liên) in *Chin Shu* and *T'ai-p'ing Yü-lan*, chüan 52, f. 6 recto; *Ta* (達 *d'ăt*: Sino-Việt. = Đạt) in *Liang Shu*; and *K'uei* (逵 *g'jwi*: Sino-Việt. = Quí) in *Shui-Ching Chu*. If *Lien* is indeed the authentic reading, and European scholars have tended to accept it as such, then there is little reason to doubt a connexion, so far not elucidated in specific terms, between this chieftain and the tribal group that rebelled in 137 (despite the slight discrepancy in the sound of the names). The fact that all three of the graphs representing the alleged personal names share the same radical and are somewhat similar in general appearance tends to support the conjecture that we are dealing with graphic errors. But in that case it would be logical, in the absence of compelling reasons to the contrary, to adopt the reading of the earliest of the three texts, namely *G'jwi* as recorded in the *Shui-Ching Chu* (early 6th century) rather than the *Liän* of *Chin Shu* (A.D. 646). However, as Stein has already pointed out ("Le Lin-yi," p. 209), Chinese authors not infrequently cast their transcriptions of foreign ethnonyms in the form of Chinese family and personal names. *K'iu* would then be read as an ethnonym of wide application, with *Liän*, *G'jwi* or *D'ăt*, together with *Siwok* [*K'iu-siwok* 區眾], *Siei* [*Siei-k'iu* 西區 : vide Note 167], et al., as tribal names. *K'iu* employed in this sense invites comparison with a modern ethnonym used in the same manner, namely *Kha* (Khùa in the dialect of Quảng-bình, according to R. P. Cadière, "Les hautes vallées du Song-Gianh," *BEFEO*, vol. 5 [1905], p. 349; to the Việtnamese the Kha are known as Moï). It may be significant that in the hinterland of Quảng-tri the Moï are to this day known as Ca-lo, the latter element in the name representing a specific tribal appellation [*Vide* R. P. Cadière, "Note sur les Moi du Quang-tri," *BIIEH*, vol. 3 (1941), p. 101].

Chin Shu, loc. cit., refers these events vaguely to the end of the Han dynasty, but *Shui-Ching Chu* is a little more specific in relating them to the period Ch'u-p'ing 初平 of Emperor Hsien 獻 i.e. 190-193. Other accounts of these happenings are to be found in *Nan-Ch'i Shu*, chüan 58, f. 66 recto; *Sui Shu*, chüan 82, f. 1 recto -3 recto; *Nan Shih*, chüan 78, f. 1 verso et seq.; *Wen-hsien T'ung-k'ao*, chüan 331, f. 2600, as well as in Việtnamese annals: *Việt-sử-lược* 越史畧 q. 1, f. 5 recto; *An-nam Chí-lược* 安南志畧 q. 7, ff. 1 verso recto; *Đại-Việt sử-kí* 大越史記 ngoại-kỉ; *Đại-Việt sử-kí toàn-thư* 大越史記全書 ngoại-kỉ; *Cương mục*, tiền biên, q. 3, f. 20 verso.

120. This embassy was dated by Pelliot, "Le Fou-nan," p. 151.

121. Sino-Việt. = Lâm-âp. The polity of the Lin-I (the precise form it took is unknown) crystallized in Hsiang-lin, the southernmost prefecture in the commandery of Jih-nan. The name Hsiang-lin was made up of a Chinese trope (*hsiang* = elephant) which had long been in use to denote in vague fashion the partly explored, vaguely forbidding regions of South China and its borderlands, together with a Chinese transcription, *lin*, of an indigenous element, presumably an ethnonym . It is, of course, possible that *hsiang* was also an indigenous word rationalized into a familiar form: the predilection of Chinese scholars for the transcription that was at the same time an interpretation is well known. In that

case, the name would have comprised transcriptions of two indigenous elements. Traditional scholarship, both oriental and occidental, has predicated the elimination of the Chinese element by aphaeresis when the territory passed out, de facto, of Chinese hands, upon which — so it is presumed — the Chinese added the graph i (in Han times customarily used to denote the seat of a subprefecture) to describe the emerging polity of the [Hsiang] Lin. This is, indeed, a venerable theory that has been espoused by virtually all scholars from Li Tao-yüan [Shui-Ching Chu, chüan 36, f. 24 recto] at the beginning of the 6th century A.D. to Georges Maspéro and Léonard Aurousseau in the 20th. However, Rolf Stein has suggested that i (* ·i̯əp), too, may represent an ancient indigenous word. By means of a series of linguistic analogies, and by arguments based on I Ching's use in the 7th century A.D. of a variant transcription 臨邑 (*Li̯əm-·i̯əp, but significantly **Bli̯əm-·i̯əp in Archaic Chinese), he has sought to relate the term Lin-I to the PRM-KRM consonantal complex that manifests itself in toponyms and ethnonyms throughout peninsular Southeast Asia. It is impossible here to do justice to the intricacies of Stein's thesis, for which the reader is referred to "Le Lin-yi," Appendix VI and, for contrary arguments, to J. J. L. Duyvendak's review of this work in TP, vol. 40 (1951), pp. 336-351.

Note that the form 臨邑 also occurs in Tuan Kung-lu's 段公路 Pei-hu lu 北戶錄, probably from the end of the 9th century [Quoting Wan-Sui li 萬歲曆], but Stein is of the opinion that Tuan may have been influenced by I Ching's work instead of transcribing independently. See Stein, loc. cit., p. 221, note 207.

122. Cf. Shui-Ching Chu, chüan 36, f. 24 recto: "This kingdom constituted the prefecture of Hsiang-lin in the time of the Ch'in and the Han;" and Hou-Han Shu, chüan 33, f. 17 recto: ". . . Hsiang-lin, the present-day kingdom of the Lin-I."

123. Shui-Ching Chu, chüan 36, f. 18 recto (Gloss by Li Tao-yüan), and f. 22 verso. In the ancient toponymy of Jih-nan Commandery this river was the Shou-ling (壽泠 *Zi̯əu-lieng: Sino-Việt = Thọ-lạnh). Though the text statement is doubtless true in substance, Li Tao-yüan is guilty of an anachronism, for the prefecture of Shou-ling was not established until 289 (Sung Shu 宋書 chüan 38, f. 10 verso).

124. Sino-Việt. Khu-túc.

125. Shui-Ching Chu, chüan 36, f. 22 verso; San-Kuo Chih (Wu) 三國志 (吳), chüan 16, f. 53 recto. Stein has confirmed that Li Tao-yüan's equation of Hsi-chüan with Ch'ü-su, though based on dubious reasoning, was in fact justified ("Lin-yi," p. 12).

126. Chin Shu, chüan 3, f. 9 verso. An earlier embassy that is dated between A.D. 220 and 230 was accredited to the governor of Chiao-chih, not to a reigning Chinese dynasty.

127. Chin Shu, chüan 97, f. 15 recto. The latter paragraph states that during the T'ai-k'ang period of Emperor Wu [the Lin-I] for the first time came to offer tribute 武帝太康中始來貢獻. Apparently the annalists of Chin chose to ignore not only the embassy to Chiao-chih (Notes 120 and 126) but also the joint mission to the Wu court in 268. See also Nan-Ch'i Shu, chüan 58, f. 7 recto, and Ma Tuan-lin, Wen-hsien T'ung-k'ao, chüan 331, f. 2600.

128. According to Shui-Ching Chu, chüan 36, f. 25 recto, an important stimulus to this diffusion of technology was provided by the activities of a certain Wen (文 *Mi̯uən), allegedly a Chinese from Yang Chou (f. 25 verso, quoting Chiang-tung chiu-shih 江東舊事, though some recent authors (e.g. Stein, "Lin-yi," p. 243; Coedès, Etats, p. 89) have regarded him as possibly a sinicized Lin-I. Some texts accord him commercial affiliations (Shui-Ching Chu, loc. cit., Chin Shu, chüan 97, ff. 15 recto et verso), either in South China or in the Lin-I territories. In the version of his life that was incorporated in Chinese annals and encyclopedias, between 313 and 317 he introduced to the Lin-I new concepts of military strategy. When he later succeeded to the throne he took as his

regnal style the expression that later Chinese authors rendered as Fan Wen (范
文 *Bʻiwăm miwən), the former element doubtless representing a Chinese
transcription of an indigenous name, perhaps — as Stein has suggested ["Le
Lin-yi," Appendix VII] — Brahm or Prohm, but more probably an honorific cognate
with the word beiam which some upland tribes of Viêtnam still apply to the Cams
[Anthony Christie, "The provenance and chronology of early Indian cultural
influences in South East Asia," in Himansu Bhusan Sarkar (ed.), R. C. Majumdar
Felicitation Volume (Calcutta, 1970), p. 9.

129. Shui-Ching Chu, chüan 36, f. 25 recto: "instructed King Fan-I in the
building of walls and moats" 教王范逸制造城池 ; Chin Shu, chüan 97,
f. 15 verso: ". . . in the construction of palaces, dwellings, cities walled and
unwalled" (or ". . . the construction . . . of walls and [the layout of]
cities"). . . 作宫室城邑 . Other items in the complex of innovations
allegedly adopted by the Lin-I at this time included weapons of offense and
defense, as well as the planning of strategy on a large scale. Shui-Ching Chu,
(loc. cit.), Liang Shu (loc. cit.) and Wen-hsien Tʻung-kʻao (chüan 331, f. 2600)
add the adoption of war chariots.

130. This, at any rate, is one of the reasons adduced by the authors of Chin
Shu, chüan 97, f. 16 recto: 林邑少田食日南之地; Liang Shu, chüan 54,
f. 2 verso: 林邑先無田土食日南地肥沃. Identical phrasing in
Nan shih, chüan 78, f. 2 verso (except that 素 is substituted for 先), and
Đại-Việt sử-kí, ngoại-kí, q. 4, f. 14 recto. And the statement has the support
of physiography. The narrow strip of lowland between the Porte d'Annam and Col
des Nuages, hemmed in between lagoons and sand-dunes on its shoreward side and
mountain spurs on its landward flank, is even today one of the least productive
parts of the whole east coast. The only extensive tracts of good agricultural
soil in this region lie along the lower reaches of the Sông Giang. See, for
example, Henri Brenier, Essai d'atlas statistique de l'Indochine française
(Hanoi, 1914), map. XXI; Henri Russier, Indochine française (Hanoi, 1931), p. 53;
"La riziculture de l'Indochine," Exposition coloniale internationale (Paris,
1931); Pierre Gourou, L'utilisation du sol en Indochine française (Paris, 1940),
chap. 7, pt. 4.

131. According to the Chin Shu, chüan 97, f. 16 recto, Liang Shu, chüan 54,
f. 2 verso, and Nan Shih, chüan 78, f. 2 verso, Chinese officials in the several
prefectures of Jih-nan were levying tolls of from 20 to 30 per cent (presumably
ad valorem) on merchandise imported by sea into the tribal areas 太守多食利
侵侮十折二三. An important outcome of the introduction of taxation into
these tribal territories was the migration of a group of Wen-lang (文狼
*Miuən-lâng) to a site rendered by the Chinese as Chʻü-tu-chʻien (屈都乾
*Kiuət-tuo-kân), which some authors have equated with the Ptolemaic Καττιγαρα
Cp. pp. 447-448 below. See Chin Shu Ti-tao Chi as quoted in Shui-Ching Chu,
chüan 36, f. 23 recto.

132. There is a résumé of the troubled relations between the Chinese provincial
administration and the tribal groups of the frontier in Hou-Han Shu, chüan 116,
f. 3 verso et seq. Events leading up to the invasion of the Lin-I and their
occupation of the commandery are detailed in Chin Shu, chüan 97, f. 16 recto.
Đại-Việt sử-kí, ngoại-kí, quyển 4, dates the final events to 348.

133. Chin Shu, chüan 97, ff. 16 recto et verso; Shui-Ching Chu, chüan 36, ff. 21
verso and 22 verso; An-nam Chí-lược, q. 8, f. 4 recto; et al.

134. Sung Shu, chüan 5, f. 12 verso and chüan 97, f. 48 verso; Đại-Việt sử-kí,
ngoại kí, q. 4, f. 17 verso; Đại-Việt sử-kí toàn-thơ, q. 4, f. 16 verso;
Cương-mục, Tiền biên, q. 3, ff. 26 verso - 27 recto.

135. Sung Shu, chüan 5, f. 14 verso and chüan 97, ff. 1 recto et verso; Liang Shu,
chüan 54, ff. 4 recto et verso; Nan Shih, chüan 78, ff. 4 recto et verso;
Nan-Chʻi Shu, chüan 58, ff. 7 recto et seq. [These last three texts record the
date as 445: 22nd year of Yüan-chia]; Việt-sử lược, chap. 1, f. 9 verso;

Đại-Việt sử-kí, ngoại-kỉ, q. 4, f. 18 recto; Cương-mục, Tiền-biên, q. 3, f. 27 recto. Đại-Việt sử-kí toàn-thơ, ngoại-kỉ, q. 4, f. 11 recto erroneously places these events in 436 (13th year of Yüan-chia). See also Shui-Ching Chu, chüan 36, f. 29 recto. I am here adopting Stein's identification of the site of the capital: "Le Lin-yi," chap. 2.

136. There is a biography of Li Tao-yüan in Wei Shu 魏書 chüan 89, ff. 9 verso-10 verso. But note a parallel passage in Pei Shih 北史 chüan 27, f. 10 recto, in which the period of his prefectship among the tribal groups of Hu-nan is reported as 512 to 516, instead of 477 to 499 as in the earlier account. Subsequently he held the post of Marshal of the Pacified South 安南將軍, though there is no evidence that he ever travelled in those regions.

137. In Nan-fang ts'ao-mu chuang 南方草木狀, allegedly compiled by Chi Han 嵇含 (sometimes Hsi Han 稽含) in the second half of the 3rd century A.D. [Cf. Chin Shu, chüan 72, f. 6 recto; Wen-hsien T'ung-k'ao, chüan 205, f. 1704], but in fact a 12th-century forgery: see Ma Tai-loi 馬泰來 "The authenticity of the Nan-fang ts'ao-mu chuang," T'oung Pao, vol. 74 (1978), pp. 218-252.

138. Léonard Aurousseau [Review of Georges Maspéro's Le royaume de Champa in BEFEO, vol. 14 (1914), p. 10, note 1] noted the presence in the existing text of records of events that took place after the death of Tung-fang Shuo.

139. Anciently the Lu-yung (盧容 *Luo-i̯wong) river.

140. This is a quotation from K'ang-T'ai's Fu-nan Chi, concerning which see p. 149 above. Cf. Wen-hsien T'ung-k'ao, chüan 331, f. 2600.

141. Chin Shu, chüan 97, ff. 15 verso - 16 recto.

142. Shui-Ching Chu, chüan 36, f. 18 verso. This and subsequent references in this chapter are to the Ssŭ-pu ts'ung-k'an edition of the Shui-Ching Chu.

143. P. 383 above.

144. Shui-Ching Chu, chüan 36; Chiu T'ang-Shu, chüan 41.

145. Sung Shu, chüan 97, f. 48 verso; An-nam Chí-lược, q. 8, f. 5 recto; Đại-Việt sử-kí, q. 4, f. 17 recto; Cương-mục, Tiền-biên, q. 3, f. 26 recto.

146. Sung Shu, chüan 97, f. 48 recto; Nan-Ch'i Shu, chüan 58, f. 7 recto et verso; Liang Shu, chüan 54, f. 4 verso; Nan Shih, chüan 78, f. 4 verso; Wen-hsien T'ung-k'ao, chüan 331, f. 26; Đại-Việt sử-kí, ngoại-kí, q. 4, ff. 18 recto - 19 recto; Đại-Việt sử-kí toàn-thơ, ngoại-ki, q. 4, f. 11 recto et verso; Cương-mục, Tiền biên, q. 3, ff. 27 recto - 28 verso; Việt-sử lược, q. 1, ff. 9 verso - 10 recto; An-nam Chí-lược, q. 4, f. 7 recto and q. 8, f. 5 verso.

147. Sui Shu, chüan 53, f. 42 recto; Đại-Việt sử-kí, ngoại-kí q. 6, f. 1 verso; Đại-Việt sử-kí toàn-thơ, ngoại-kí, q. 5, f. 1 verso.

148. Shui-Ching Chu, chüan 36, f. 19 recto.

149. Cf. Note 128 above. Popular belief in the innovatory role of Fan Wen is attested by a sentence on f. 19 recto of chüan 36 of Shui-Ching Chu which is apparently intended as a quotation from Lin-i Chi: "Numerous walls and ramparts date only from [the reign of] the king of the Lin-I [called] Fan Hu-ta (*Bʻi̯wəm ɣuo-dāt)" 多城壘自林邑王范胡達始. This king was ruling in c. A.D. 400, so that the remark must have been an interpolation in Tung-fang Shuo's text or, possibly, Li Tao-yüan was using an already expanded version of the Lin-I Chi, or — and this is perhaps the most likely interpretation — Li Tao-yüan himself appended an annotation which was later incorporated in the text.

150. 6 li 170 pu. If we accept a li of 400 meters (see Note 5 to Chapter 3),

the perimeter was about 2 kms. As the *Shui-Ching Chu* adds that the city was 650 *pu* from east to west, and assuming a rectangular shape, the meridional distance was 515 *pu*, i.e. the extreme dimensions were only about 720 meters x 570 meters. This and the following architectural details are taken from ff. 18 verso - 19 recto of *Shui-Ching Chu*, chüan 36.

151. The *chang* 丈 or 10 *Chinese* feet, like the *li*, has varied considerably during Chinese history. *Vide* John C. Ferguson, "Chinese foot measure," *Monumenta Serica*, vol. 6, (1941), pp. 357-382. Assuming a foot of Om. 23, which is Ferguson's estimate for the time of the Western Chin (A.D. 265-316), the towers would have been about 60 feet in height.

152. This is an unusual number of gates, but could possibly have been the result of a layout such as was prescribed by the *Kʻao-kung Chi* 考工記 or, for that matter, the *Arthaśāstra*, that is twelve gates (three on each of four sides) together with another adventitious or, perhaps, main gate: see Wheatley, *The pivot*, pp. 411-414.

153. Stein ["Le Lin-yi," pp. 52-53] has suggested, with the necessary caution, that the "ten angles" of Chʻü-su may have been connected with the Stream of the Nine Coils of the Dragon 九曲龍溪, a name applied by the *Ðại-Nam nhất-thông chí* (1882), paragraph on Quảng-bình, f. 29 recto et verso, to a series of meandering reaches of the Sông Giang in the neighborhood of the village of Cao Lao, that is, close to the site proposed for the ancient city. The geomantic associations of this district are clearly evident in the paragraph devoted to it in the *Ðại-Nam*: "The head [of the dragon] looks towards the unsettled abyss 生淵, its tail constitutes the Stream of Gems 球溪. This stretch of water is famous. In the places of the Dragon's Tongue and Nostril it winds through *nine* meanders . . . Water flows from the Head and from the Tongue of the Dragon, so that there is always a trickle in the bed of the stream and it never dries up."

154. Cf. Wheatley, *The pivot*, chap. 5.

155. *Shui-Ching Chu*, chüan 36, f. 19 recto.

156. *Vide* Stein, "Le Lin-yi," Appendix VII. Descendants of Han Chinese were also allegedly to be found in the 4th century among the Western Tributaries (Hsi Shu 西屬, possibly for Hsi-Lʻu 西虜: *Siei-dʻuo*, a tribal group located to the south of the Lin-I): *Chʻu-Hsüeh Chi* 初學記, compiled by Hsü Chien 徐堅 in c. A.D. 700, chüan 6, f. 9 recto, *sub verbo* 漢柱. Both those at Chʻü-su and these latter are doubtless related to the so-called Ma Liu (馬留 *ma liəu/ liəu) whom Indochinese folklore describes as descendants of Chinese troops who remained in the south after the campaign of Ma Yüan (馬援 : Sino-Việt = Mã Viện) in A.D. 41-43, and who, in consequence, were closely associated with the pillars, boats and horses, all of bronze, attributed to that culture hero [*int. al.*, *Wu-lu* 吳錄 ; *apud* Chʻu-Hsüeh Chi, loc. cit., chüan 6, f. 9 recto; *Shui-Ching Chu*, chüan 36, f. 30 recto et verso; *Tʻai-pʻing Yü-lan*, chüan 187, f. 7 recto; *Chiao-Kuang Chih* 交廣志. *apud Yün-lu Man-chʻao* 雲麓漫鈔, chüan 5, f. 2 recto (*She-wen Tzǔ-chiu* 涉聞梓舊 edition); *Chin Shu*, chüan 15, f. 9 recto; *Liang Shu*, chüan 54, f. 1 recto; *Nan Shih*, chüan 78, f. 1 recto; *Ta-yeh shih-i lu* 大業拾遺錄 by Tu Pao 杜寶, *apud TPYL*, chüan 959, f. 3 verso; *Tʻung Tien*, chüan 188, ff. 1007-8; Tuan Chʻeng-shih 段成式 *Yu-yang Tsa-tsu* 酉陽雜俎 chüan 4, f. 4 verso (*Ssǔ-pu Tsʻung-kʻan* edition); Liu Hsün 劉恂, *Ling-piao Lu-i* 嶺表錄異 chüan A, f. 4 verso (*Wu-ying Tien* edition); *Man Shu*, chüan 1; *Tʻai-pʻing Huan-yü Chi*, chüan 171, f. 8 recto; *Hsin Tʻang-Shu*, chüan 222B, f. 1 recto; Chou Chʻü-fei 周去非 *Ling-wai Tai-ta* 嶺外代答 chüan 10, f. 7 recto (*Chih-pu-tsu-chai Tsʻung-shu* edition)].

157. *Shui-Ching Chu*, chüan 36, f. 19 recto. This passage should be considered in the light of its continuation, the whole being composed in *fu*-style. As Rolf Stein has pointed out ("Le Lin-yi," p. 15), "Si le passage précédent se présente comme un essai d'historiographe d'expliquer la présence de barbares dans un pays *administrativement* sinisé, celui-ci confirme cette présence par une évocation

lyrique reflétant la crainte sacrée de la forêt et de la montagne et l'assimilation des barbares à des démons." The passage in question runs: "The suburbs [of Ch'ü-su] adjoin the mountains which, covered with thorn scrub and dense foliage, raise their forest [mantle] through gloomy vapors and lowering distances to touch the clouds. It is not the sort of place in which a human being would be at peace" 員郭接山榛棘蒲薄騰林拂雲幽煙冥縕非生人所安.

158. *Shui-Ching Chu*, chüan 36, ff. 25 verso - 27 verso.

159. *Shui-Ching Chu*, chüan 36, f. 24 recto. We are indebted to Rolf Stein for the detective work that resulted in the identification of the site of this capital: "Le Lin-yi," chap. 2.

160. Chief among these forest products from the hills backing the coastal plain in later times was *gaharu* (Cham = *gahlā*). Even in the time of the Lin-I it was an important export (*Wen-hsien T'ung-k'ao*, chüan 331, f. 2600; *Kuang Chih*, apud *T'ai-p'ing Yü-lan*, chüan 982; *Nan-chou I-wu Chih*, ibid; *Ta-yeh Shih-i Lu*, ibid; *Teng Lo-fou shan shu* by Chou Fa-chen, ibid.). From *Shu-i Chi* (in *Han-Wei Ts'ung-shu*, f. 6 recto) we learn that "In Jih-nan there are forests of 1,000 *mou*, whence come celebrated aromatics" 日南有千畝林名香出其中. Cp. *T'ai-p'ing Kuang-chi*, chüan 414, ff. 1 verso - 2 recto. When Liu Fang sacked the capital of the Lin-I (a later capital situated probably at Trà-Kiệu, not the one discussed here) he carried away 2,000 *chin* of *gaharu* [*T'ai-p'ing Yü-lan*, chüan 982, f. 6 recto]. The collection of aromatics is an especially important theme in the folklore of this stretch of coast: cf. Rolf Stein, "Jardins en miniature d'Extrême-Orient," *BEFEO*, vol. 42 (1942), pp. 64-76, and *Shui-Ching Chu*, chüan 36, f. 23 recto: "[The Wen-Lang (*Mi̯uən-lâng* 文狼), a tribal people of Quảng-trị] make it their business to collect aromatics, which they trade with other people at the markets." Also *Shu-i Chi*, loc. cit.: "In Jih-nan there is a market for aromatics; it is the place where traders barter all [kinds of] fragrant substances."

161. Anciently the Great Huai 大淮 river.

162. Anciently the Lin-I Reach 林邑浦.

163. Anciently P'eng-lung Bay 彭龍灣.

164. The affinity of the Lin-I for the sea is clearly evident in the texts relating to them, and is affirmed by an admittedly poetic passage in the *Shui-Ching Chu*, chüan 36, f. 21 recto: "[The territory of the Lin-I] was bounded by seas that carried the traffic of all countries."

165. Perhaps we should not read objective reality into the rhythmically parallel Chinese phrases (*Shui-Ching Chu*, chüan 36, f. 26 recto), which may betoken nothing more than lyrical evocation: 西南際山東北瞰水, but the general statement is true even of the site of the capital as reconstructed by Stein. The presence of *padi* fields close to the walls of the city is not certain, but is implied by Stein's judicious emendation of *yin* 因 in a meaningless jumble of characters to *t'ien* 田 ["Le Lin-yi," p. 93].

166. 8 *li* 100 *pu* = about 4 kilometers, depending on our interpretation of the length of the *li* (Cf. Note 5 to Chap. 3).

167. Or, perhaps, the "city"(sc. quarter) of Hsi Ch'ü (*K'i̯u). For *k'iu* as an ethnonym see Note 119 above. Hsi (*siei 西) is also a fairly common element in Indochinese place-names, e.g. the commandery seat Hsi-chüan; Hsi-t'u 西屠, a territory bordering the Lin-I to the south (*T'ai-p'ing Yü-lan*, chüan 790, f. 9 verso, quoting *Chiao-Chou I-nan Chuan*, probably of Chin date. See Stein, *Lin-yi*, pp. 110-111); Hsi Ku-lang torrent 西古郎究, present-day R. de Trốc [*Shui-Ching Chu*, chüan 36, f. 18 recto]; et al. It is often difficult to decide whether this element should be transcribed or translated.

168. Stein ["Le Lin-yi," p. 105, note 81] observes that such an eminence is lacking at Văn-xá, where he proposes to locate this city. However, in the South Chinese provinces, *shih-shan* (*shek shaan* 石山) denotes the artificial mountain that plays an important role in the art of the miniature garden. It is conceivable, therefore, that it may have been used in this technical sense in Li Tao-yüan's account of the capital of the Lin-I.

169. Cp. p. 387 above.

170. *Shui-Ching Chu*, chüan 36, ff. 25 verso - 26 recto: 三重長洲 [a difficult phrase: Aurousseau, *BEFEO*, vol. 14, fasc. 9 p. 21, translates as ". . . (dessine) 3 longues îles accolées; Stein, "Le Lin-yi," p. 93, as "En triples îles allongées"] 隐山遶西衛北迴東 . The passage relating to Ch'ü-su on f. 18 recto merely substitutes 而 for 迴.

171. *Shui-Ching Chu*, chüan 36, f. 26 recto: 北邊西端迴折曲入 . Cf. chüan 36, f. 18 verso.

172. Chüan 36, f. 26 recto.

173. This and the following remarks are taken from Rolf Stein's lengthy excursus "L'ethnique du Lin-yi," Appendix VI to "Le Lin-yi." See also Matsumoto Bunsaburo 松本文三郎, "Shi-bi-kō," *Tōhōgakuhō* 鴟尾考 東方學報 vol. 13, pt. 1 (1942), pp. 1-29, and Marcel Granet, *Danses et légendes de la Chine ancienne*, vol. 2 (Paris, 1926), p. 531.

174. *Shui-Ching Chu*, chüan 36, f. 26 recto.

175. The *Wu-ying Tien* edition of the *Shui-Ching Chu* reads *nien* 年 (= year) for *niu* in this phrase, an obvious mislection which is corrected in all other editions that I have been able to consult.

176. *An-nam Chỉ-lược*, quyển 15, f. 2 recto attributes this interrogation to Emperor Ming of the Chin (322-325), but the passage contains so many corruptions that there is every reason to prefer the testimony of *Shui-Ching Chu* to that of the 14th-century Viêtnamese text. Li Tao-yüan was here citing the *Ku-chin Shan-yen* 古今善言 of Fan T'ai 范泰 , who lived at the time of the Liu Sung dynasty (420-479). The visitor was Chang Chung 張重 (tzŭ Chung Tu仲 馬) who, although a dwarf, was *chi-li* 計吏 in Jih-nan (Cf. *Chiao-Chou ming-shih chuan* 交州名士傳 apud *T'ai-p'ing Yü-lan*, chuan 375, f. 1 verso).

177. *T'ai-p'ing Yü-lan*, chüan 786, f. 5 recto; mutilated in *Pei Shih*, chüan 95, f. 10 verso and *Chin Shu*, chüan 97, f. 15 recto.

178. *Shui-Ching Chu*, chüan 36, f. 26 verso.

179. Lit. "the two extremities of the elongated roof project to north and south."

180. This phrase as constituted in all editions of the text reads 南擬背日, which makes no sense (Cp. Aurousseau's translation, *BEFEO*, vol. 14, fasc. 9, p. 23). The emendation adopted here was proposed by Stein, "Le Lin-yi," p. 100.

181. "The houses of officials and of the people are oriented, according to preference, towards the east, west, south or north; they turn their backs without any fixed rule" 官民居止隨情面向東西南北迴背無定.
There are two final sentences relating to the capital which appear to refer to conditions after the sack of the city in 446 rather than in more normal times: "In the suburbs there are neither markets nor villages. The towns have few inhabitants and along the desolate shore of the sea there lives no human being" [*Shui-Ching Chu*, chüan 36, f. 27 recto. Note that the sentences immediately following tell of the grief of the King of the Lin-I on returning to his ruined capital].

182. *Shui-Ching Chu*, chüan 36, f. 29 recto.

183. Anciently the Reach of the Port of the Navigation Officials 船官口浦.

184. The *Hou-Han Shu* [chüan 116, f. 3 verso] mentions Li savages "beyond the frontiers" of Chiu-chen, that is, in Jih-nan.

185. In the West Indies, Mauritius, and Spanish America, the word creole is used in two distinct senses, signifying respectively a person of native birth but of European descent, *or* a person of mixed European and Negro birth. The meaning I have in mind here is the first of these — the Chinese who had been born in Nan Yüeh — but the other type of creole was also to be found in Tong-King. The earliest *recorded* example of a Chinese who married a woman of Việt is possibly the great Chao Tʻo, though doubtless the practice had been fairly common even before his time. By the Tʻang period, persons of mixed descent probably constituted a significant proportion of the population.

186. Chang Cho 張鷟 *Chʻao-yeh chʻien-tsai* 朝野僉載 (8th century, with Sung additions), chüan 1, f. 5v.

187. Cf., for example, p. 388; *Chiu Tʻang-Shu*, chüan 176, f. 8v; *Hsin Tʻang-Shu*, chüan 184, f. 1 r.

188. Bases for estimating population sizes among the colonial foundations in Tong-King are entirely lacking, but *Hsin Tʻang-Shu* gives a figure of nearly 100,000 taxable persons for the Protectorate (chüan 43A, f. 9v), implying perhaps a total population of 200,000-250,000.

189. Campā was the name of a city of considerable commercial significance on the Ganges river in the neighborhood of present-day Bhāgalpur. As early as the 7th century B.C., it was the capital of the kingdom of Anga, but subsequently declined in importance and, by Mauryan times, had lost its pre-eminence to Tāmraliptī.

For general works on the kingdom of Campā and Cam culture see J. Leuba, *Un royaume disparu: les Chams et leur art* (Paris, 1923); R. C. Majumdar, *Ancient Indian colonies in the Far East. Vol. I: Champa* (Lahore, 1927); Georges Maspéro, *Le royaume de Champa* (Paris, 1928: first published in *Tʻoung Pao*, vols. 11-14, 1910-1913); Jean Y. Claeys, "Introduction à l'étude de l'Annam et du Champa," *Bulletin des Amis du Vieux Hué*, vol. 21. (Hanoi, 1934); Philippe Stern, *L'art du Champā et son évolution* (Toulouse, 1942); Jean Boisselier, *La statuaire de Champa — Recherches sur les cultes et l'iconographie* (Paris, 1963).

190. Auguste Barth and Abel Bergaigne, *Inscriptions sanscrites de Campā et du Cambodge*. Notices et Extraits des Manuscrits de la Bibliothèque Nationale XXVII (Paris, 1885-1893), p. 199; Louis Finot, "Notes d'épigraphie, I: Deux nouvelles inscriptions de Bhadravarman Ier, roi de Champa," *Bulletin de l'Ecole Française d'Extrême-Orient*, vol. 2 (1902), pp. 185-187 and "L'inscription de Chiêm-sơn," *loc. cit.*, vol. 18 (1918), pp. 13-14; Majumdar, *Champa*, Book III, pp. 4-9; B. C. Chhabra, "Expansion of Indo-Aryan culture during Pallava rule," *Journal of the Asiatic Society of Bengal*, vol. 1 (1935), pp. 47 ff. For a description of the ritual center at Mĩ-sơn see Henri Parmentier, "Les monuments du cirque de Mĩ-sơn," *BEFEO*, vol. 4 (1904), pp. 805-896.

191. Inscriptions of Hon Cuc, Chiêm-sơn [Finot, "Deux nouvelles inscriptions," p. 186; and "Deux nouvelles inscriptions indochinoises," *BEFEO*, vol. 18, no. 10 (1918), p. 13; Majumdar, *Champa*, pp. 8-9], and Đông-yên-châu [George Coedès, "La plus ancienne inscription en langue chame," *New Indian Antiquary*, Extra Ser. I (1939), pp. 46-49].

192. *Bʻiwɒm ji̯ung (MSC Fan Hsiung 范熊), reigning in 270; *Bʻiwɒm i̯ĕt (MSC Fan I 范逸), reign ended in 336; *Bʻiwɒm mi̯uən (MSC Fan Wen 范文), succeeded to the throne in 336; *Bʻiwɒm bʻi̯uət (MSC Fan Fo 范佛), ascended the throne in 349; and seven rulers between about 400 and 510, including *Bʻiwɒm

γuo-dʻāt (MSC Fan Hu-ta 范胡達), who was reigning at the turn of the 5th century.

193. Anthony Christie, "The provenance and chronology of early Indian cultural influences in South East Asia," in Himansu Bhusan Sarkar (ed.), *R. C. Majumdar Felicitation Volume* (Calcutta, 1970), p. 9. For a possible relation of words of the *beiam* type to the consonantal groups BRM/PRM and, by extension KRM, that is widespread in Indochina, see Stein, "Le Lin-yi," Chap. 6.

194. *Nan-Chʻi Shu*, chüan 58, f. 4v; *Chin Shu*, chüan 10, folio 35r and chüan 97, f. 14v; *Liang Shu*, chüan 54, f. 54r.

195. Christie, "The provenance and chronology of early Indian cultural influences," pp. 9-10.

196. Maspéro, *Le royaume de Champa*, p. 67. *Nan Shih*, chüan 88, f. 41v; *Wen-hsien Tʻung-kʻao*, chüan 331, p. 2600; *Shui-Ching Chu*, chüan 36, f. 27v; and *Ðại-Việt Sử-ký, ngoại-kỷ*, q. 4, f. 17r all associate this name with the Cam term for a particular type of gold.

197. *Shui-Ching Chu*, chüan 36, f. 26v. This identification was widely disseminated, if not first proposed, by Maspéro, *Le royaume de Champa*, p. 63.

198. E.g., George Coedès, *Les états hindouisés d'Indochine et d'Indonésie* (Paris, 1964), p. 95.

199. *Shui-Ching Chu*, chüan 36, f. 27r.

200. Christie, "The provenance and chronology," p. 9.

201. Stein, "Le Lin-yi," pp. 71 and 111.

202. References in Maspero, *Le royaume de Champa*, p. 96.

203. Summarized in Paul Pelliot, "Deux itinéraires de Chine en Inde à la fin du VIIIe siècle," *BEFEO*, vol. 4 (1904), pp. 196-197. Late texts such as *Tung-hsi-yang Kʻao* 東西洋考, compiled by Chang Hsieh 張燮 (prefaces composed by friends of the author dated 1617 and 1618), *Hsi-yin-hsüan tsʻung-shu* 惜陰軒叢書 edition, chüan 2, f. 2r., assert that the capital was transferred to Chan Chʻeng after the Cam armies had been defeated by the governor of Annam in 809 — a statement which, although unconfirmed by contemporary sources, is a reasonable enough proposition.

204. Chao Ju-kua 趙汝适 *Chu-fan Chih* 諸蕃志 : Feng Chʻeng-chün's 馮承鈞 edition, Shanghai, 1938), p. 3.

205. A problem that, despite its importance for a study of state origins in Southeast Asia, cannot be discussed here is the possible relationship of the ruling families of Campā to those of Fu-nan, in both of which the ethnonym *bʻiwɒm is prominent. A suite of variable but persistent traditions locates Cams originally in various parts of the middle and lower reaches of the Mekong valley, whence they were allegedly driven out and founded the kingdom of Campābassac in what is now southern Laos. Mme. Eveline Porée-Maspero, while drawing attention to an apparent alternation of ruling families (or at least styles) and power in Lin-I and Fu-nan, has suggested that history does not contradict tradition and that the Fu-nan known to the Chinese was one with the most ancient Campā [*Etude sur les rites agraires des Cambodgiens*, vol. 1 (Paris and La Haye, 1962), pp. 144-149]. This is an idea with far reaching implications for Southeast Asian historiography, and deserves a great deal of further study.

CHAPTER 9

Envoi

About two thousand years ago the highest level of political centralization and the highest degree of societal differentiation attained anywhere in Southeast Asia (in the restricted sense in which the term has been employed in this work) did not exceed that order of development which is associated with the chiefdom, a type of proto-state comprising a system of chieftainships. Some of these polities, mainly those in the highlands but including certain lowland groups such as the Cams, were apparently integrated by segmentary sets of lineages and lineage heads, others seemingly by cross-cutting associations of various types. Strictly speaking, these latter groups — like the Plains Indians of North America — produced only the morphology and much of the cohesion of the true chiefdom, while lacking its kinship structure. In either case, as far as can be determined from the inadequate evidence available, levels within the settlement hierarchy were poorly differentiated. Shortly after this time, however, in the western territories of the region hitherto incipient status differences were elaborated and more clearly defined and the power of centralized leadership enhanced when paramounts, probably with quite other ends in view, began to assimilate themselves to certain aspects of Indian deities whose prestige transcended that of the old territorial spirits. In territory after territory in western Southeast Asia particularly favored chiefs managed to "promote" (in the technical sense specified on p. 24) their own interests so as, temporarily at least, to monopolize the paramountcy. Henceforth sanctity would be incidental to sovereignty instead of a prerequisite for it, and attainment of the royal office would *ipso facto* substantiate the charismatic nature of an individual in socially recognized terms.[1] And to disseminate the cognized values of the center through the lower-order systems of the provinces, these early paramounts progressively extended and diversified the linkages that bound lesser chieftains to their courts, principally through marriage alliances, gifts of office, rank, and territory, and what has been termed "culturological attraction."[2] At the same time, the settlement of Indians directly from the subcontinent probably served to confirm and consolidate the emergent notion of western Southeast Asia as an integral part (not merely an extension) of the South Asian, principally Hindu, cultural milieu. The outcome of these religio-political transformations and the socio-economic changes associated with them was the crystallization of a relatively well defined urban hierarchy that in morphology, function, internal structure, external relationships, and quality of life can properly be regarded as representing a new level of sociocultural integration. What cannot be determined with any degree of exactitude on the evidence at present available is for how long indigenous paramounts and chiefs had been influenced by, and possibly experimenting with, Indian governmental practices before they finally adopted the Sanskrit chancellery terminology, together with the use of the *praśasti* and the foundation stele, that from the 4th century A.D. onward render them visible in the historical record. The first appearance of Indian artifacts has been dated with some degree of certainty at Chansen and rather less precisely at Oc-èo, Beikthano, and a few other sites, but the gestation periods for ideological borrowings (the type of development that is hinted at by the foreign scripts employed in the early Bnaṃ and Lin-I kingdoms) are still matters for speculation. Yet it is evident that, although the new "Indianized" polities retained and elaborated the old pyramidal authority structures attributed to prehistoric chiefdoms, and although at least some of the earliest centers of Indianized culture were raised on the sites of previously existing Metal Age settlements, the urban hierarchy that developed *pari passu* with the adoption and adaptation of Indian conceptions of government and social organization signified a transition from culture to civilization. It is in this new patterning of authority relationships, which was neither Indian nor indigenous, that the roots of the traditional urban hierarchy in western Southeast Asia must be sought.

In the northern tracts of what is now the Democratic Republic of Việtnam the prehistoric settlement pattern was transformed in quite another manner. In the deltaic plains of Tong-King and on the coastal lowlands of North Annam, a hierarchy of Chinese-style administrative centers was imposed on the populace with increasing firmness as the status of those territories changed from tributary to protectorate to full incorporation in the Empire

of Han. The primary purposes of these colonial foundations were to
provide bases for the military control of the subject population,
to simulate the cultural milieu of a metropolitan Chinese city as
closely as was possible on this far southern frontier of empire,
and to diffuse the values of Chinese civilization among the Man
peoples so that they might one day enter into full participation in
the comity of Hua. This last task was a particular responsibility
of all Chinese officialdom in the provinces, but most notably of
hsien magistrates, whose duties were idealized as follows by the
Hsü Han Chih:

> They exhibit virtue and encourage righteousness; they restrain
> licentiousness and punish wickedness; they mediate in litigation
> and suppress banditry; they assist the people in their seasonal
> activities. In autumn or winter they collect revenue and render up
> their accounts to the *chün* or state to which they are subordinate.[3]

That these magistrates were often other than models of rectitude
and, no less than the commandery governor Hsi Kuang cited on
p. 369, failed in the long run to "transform the populace by rites
and justice"[4] is amply attested by the vicissitudes of a millennium
of Chinese colonial rule. Nevertheless, the impress of the Chinese
presence was profoundly apparent on both urban and bureaucratic
forms long after the passing of the Chinese hegemony. For the last
two thousand years, the morphology of the traditional Việtnamese
city at all times has been much closer to that typical of the Sinic
culture realm than to that of any indigenous or Indianized
settlements so far known from Southeast Asia. The Pre-Chinese
settlement pattern in Tong-King and Annan can only be a topic for
speculation but even if, as Dr. Davidson contends,[5] some Han-period
settlements were built on Bronze Age sites, there can be no doubt
that the traditional Việtnamese urban hierarchy (as distinct from a
scatter of individual settlements), owed its origin and principal
distinguishing characteristics to the imposition of Chinese
authority patterns in Han times.

    The consequences of the contrasting origins of the urban
hierarchies in the so-called Indianized and Sinicized culture
realms of Southeast Asia were apparent long subsequent to the
formative phases with which we have been concerned in this volume.
In fact, they have not been totally expunged even today. Despite
not inconsiderable discrepancies in their morphologies, structures,
functioning, and life styles, Burmese cities, say, have
traditionally had more in common with their Khmer or Javanese
analogues than with the urban forms of the Việt state. In the
Indianized realms, the pyramidal structure of the early kingdoms
whose origins we have been discussing was progressively elaborated

into what Professor Tambiah has aptly categorzied as a "galactic polity," on the analogy of "a central planet surrounded by differentiated satellites, which are more or less 'autonomous' entities held in orbit and within the sphere of influence of the center."[6] Whereas a chiefdom had consisted of a number of chieftainships arranged around a central paramountcy, the representative kingdom of the Indianized realms similarly came to comprise an array of satellite territories disposed about a central domain controlled directly by a supreme ruler. Typically these satellites fell into two classes. Nearest the centrally situated royal domain was an encircling zone of territories authority over which had been delegated to royal kinsmen and court favorites, while beyond these formally constituted benefices was another zone of quasi-independent polities whose principal concession to the authority of the high king was the presentation of tribute at expedientially determined intervals.

As each component of a major kingdom was constituted as a smaller-scale version of that kingdom, the dissolution of an integrated polity was always likely to result in the formation of a series of independent but minor kingdoms. The cyclical repetition of this process does much to explain why the political surface of Southeast Asia during the first fifteen hundred years of the Christian era exhibited continual, and often violent, shifts in the arrangement of its power foci, patterns which had no sooner crystallized than they began to dissolve, only to be replaced in the course of time by others no less mutable than their predecessors. Yet, in spite of these fluctuations in political fortunes, persistent centroids of political power, usually (though not invariably) situated in the lower and middle tracts of major river valleys, are clearly discernible beneath the flux of surficial transformations. Eleventh-century Pagan, 12th-century Kaḍiri, and 13th-century Kambujadeśa immediately come to mind as among the more impressive manifestations of these centroids of political power. The combined testimony of archeology, epigraphy, and literary chronicles implies that several of these cores of political power were first consolidated during the 7th and 8th centuries, a period which appears to have witnessed a general expansion in the scale of Southeast Asian polities, with a relatively small number of major kingdoms asserting their dominance over, and often absorbing, the rest.[7]

The ultimate source of all authority in these galactic polities continued to be a thearchic kingship which mediated between the planes of existence, between macrocosmos and microcosmos, between gods and men. And outwards in all directions from this quintessentially sacred axis of the world there radiated a finely calibrated declension of power and virtue in which sanctity and socio-political rank were precisely matched, descending ineluctably, as a 14th-century Javanese manual of rules of worship has it, from god-king to priest to prince to lord to headman to master to retainer.[8] This disposition of power and authority flowed logically enough from two implicit principles of statecraft which Clifford Geertz has generalized as the Doctrine of the Exemplary Center and the Doctrine of the Theater State.[9] The former of these principles signified that the royal court, and indeed the whole ritual precinct of the capital city, by being constituted as an image of celestial order, served as an idealized structural model for society at large. The rituals and ceremonies celebrated there, the style of life and the forms of social organization that obtained there functioned as mirrors to the larger community, as inculcators of appropriate attitudes and values, and as symbolic statements about the nature of society.[10]

By the Doctrine of the Theater State, the second of his principles of statecraft, Professor Geertz means simply the material realization of the Exemplary Center. As he writes, "The ritual life of the court . . . formed not just the trappings of rule but the substance of it. Spectacle was what the state was for; the central task was less to govern — a job the villagers largely accomplished for and among themselves — than to display in liturgical form the dominant themes" of their high cultures.[11] To this role of ceremony as reflecting and expounding the splendor and greatness of the court should be added the equally important function of generating power and its material manifestation, wealth, at the axis of the kingdom. And as each territorial component of the kingdom, whether appanage, benefice, province, circuit, or district, replicated at its own appropriate scale the realm of the supreme ruler, the primal fount of authority and power, so the capital of the high king both represented and embodied the integrity of the whole state.

Implicit in this conceptualization is the idea that the state was defined not by its perimeter but by its center, from which it follows that the fundamental obligation of the center was to itself. By ensuring its own power and prestige among the kingdoms of the world, the capital worked in the best interests of the populace at large. One way in which the power of the capital was affirmed was by modeling its plastic form, either actually or notionally, on principles of celestial order, and it was these sacrally sanctioned arrangements which served to relate political practice to political theory. For the initiated, the plastic symbolism of many of these capitals afforded a commentary on the place of man in his family, his city, the kingdom, the world, and the universe, so that a journey through such a city transcended both art and function to assume the character of a religio-philosophical experience.[12]

Underpinning the political superstructures of these kingdoms were two developed modes of economic integration, known technically as redistribution and mobilization, which were jointly responsible for a generalized movement of commodities and services step by step up the urban hierarchy from the provinces toward the capital.[13] However, Professor Tambiah has cautioned against the belief that all the surplus resources of the provinces actually reached the capital of an early Southeast Asian kingdom.[14] He points out that, at each collection level, officials appropriated that portion of the revenue proper to their political and social stations and transmitted the rest upward to the next higher ranking collection center. As a result of this creaming off of commodities at successive levels — so Tambiah contends — only a miniscule proportion of the taxes, fees, and fines imposed at the lower levels eventually trickled into the royal treasury. However that may be, the system did provide powerful monarchs such as Jayavarman VII of Kambujadeśa, Hayam Wuruk of Majapahit, or Aniruddha of Pagan with control of strategic economic resources extending far beyond the simple exploitation of labor pools. Moreover, Professor Tambiah is certainly correct in emphasizing the importance of state (which in practice meant royal) monopolies of foreign trade and the taxation of domestic commerce as supplements to the redistributive and mobilizative processes; in particular as providing fluid resources which, through their disbursement to officials, retainers, and servants, could be used as a means of governmental control. In Professor Tambiah's view, it was primarily the ability of a ruler to manipulate this commercial sector of the economy that permitted some kingdoms to become more powerful than their neighbors.

In the northern regions of Việtnam, the urban hierarchy evolved under conditions very different from those we have been discussing. For nearly a millennium Tong-King and northern Annam formed part of a succession of centralized bureaucratic empires even the smallest of which was very much larger than the combined areas of the Việt territories. Although the structure of local government established during the earlier years of the T'ang dynasty represented a deliberate attempt to achieve a balance of power between local and metropolitan interests, the destiny of the Protectorate was still inextricably linked with that of the Chinese polity. The decisions of the Metropolitan Protector — the title of the ranking official in the Protectorate for much of the Tʻang period — were inevitably dictated by policies formulated in Chʻang-an for the benefit of the empire as a whole rather than directed to the narrow advantage of Tong-King, and the economy of the region was as closely tied to that of the central power as the peripheral position of the territories permitted (Not even a system of government-supervised roads and waterways furnished with post-stations at regular intervals could offset the isolating effect of 1,500 miles of difficult travel). When, in the 10th century, the Việts established the independent state of Ðai Cô Việt, they found themselves encumbered with a set of long-established administrative and economic relationships that practically guaranteed the continuation of the urban hierarchy more or less as it had developed under Chinese tutelage. In subsequent centuries, although the Việts pushed their southern frontier deep into Cam territory (and ultimately beyond even that), so strong was the inertia inherited from the colonial period that the apex of the urban hierarchy remained anchored in the Tong-King delta — except for a brief interval at the end of the 14th century — until late in the 18th century, when it was moved first to Qui-nhon and subsequently to Hué.

Figure 22 depicts in broadest outline the principal urban hierarchies that had evolved in Southeast Asia by the second half of the 14th century in so far as they can be reconstructed from available sources.[15] The first point to notice is that each hierarchy is functionally composite. Theoretically each could be analysed in terms of its functional components — administrative, political, economic, religious, ceremonial, and so forth — but the limitations of extant data make such an attempt unrealistic in practice and the hierarchies will here be treated as unified and comprehensive systems.

The nature of the sources precludes the discrimination of anything more complex than a three-level hierarchy, with the implication, of course, of a fourth and lowest level composed of the villages and hamlets that provided the subsistence basis of all Southeast Asian kingdoms, but which are not represented at all on Fig. 22. At the apex of each hierarchy was the capital of a kingdom. On the mainland and in Java these were the seats of government of territorial states of considerable spatial extent.

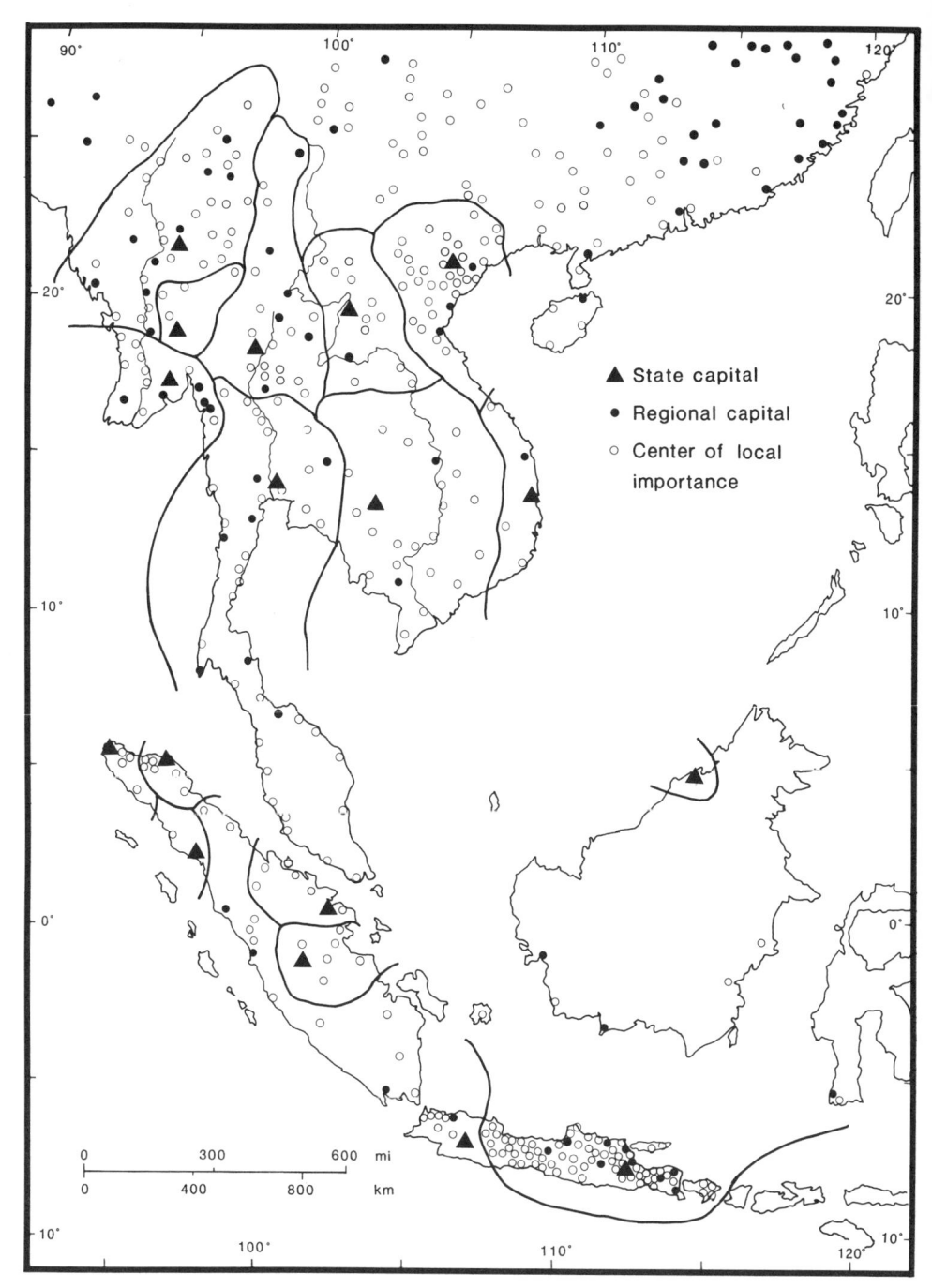

Fig. 22. The principal urban hierarchies in Southeast Asia in the second half of the 14th century [Adapted from Kernial Singh Sandhu and Paul Wheatley (eds.), *Melaka: the transformation of a Malay capital c. 1400-1980*, vol. 1 (Kuala Lumpur, 1982), p. 24].

In what is present-day Burma, Pegu had become the capital of the
Mōn state in 1369, Ava had been established as the Burmese capital
in 1364, and Taungoo had become the seat of another, though
precariously independent, Burmese dynasty in 1347. In Thailand two
hierarchies focused on, respectively, Ayutthaya and Chiangmai, the
former founded as recently as 1350, the latter in 1296. In the
Mekong valley, the Khmer capital of Yaśodharapura still dominated
the plains of Kampuchea, while farther north the kingdom of Lan
Chang had been founded in 1353 with its capital at Mu'ang Swa. To
the east of the Chaîne Annamitique a northern hierarchy culminated
in the Vietnamese capital at Thăng-long, while a southern system
focused on the Cam city of Vijayapura, then enjoying a resurgence
of its former glory that George Coedès has likened to "le dernier
rayon d'un soleil couchant." In the Archipelago the most amply
developed hierarchy was that controlled from the capital of
Majapahit, which had been founded in the lower Brantas valley in
eastern Java in 1350, although even on that island the system
subsumed within the kingdom of Pajajaran was a substantial competitor.
Sumatra, by contrast, exhibited only incipient hierarchies. Its
interior had hardly experienced even the beginnings of urban
dvelopment, and the ports strung round its coastline were in the
nature of city-states rather than the capitals of territorial
kingdoms. The notable exception was Malāyu, whose capital of
Malāyupura seems at this time to have been far up the Batang Hari
valley, deep in the interior of the island. Berunei's
classification as a state capital is anomalous. Although it had
been known as a trading port as far afield as China since the 9th
century,[17] in the 14th century it cannot have been anything more
than the seat of a coastal chieftain, probably on the scale of the
barangay that the Spaniards encountered on their earliest voyages to
the Philippine Islands in the 16th century. Nevertheless, because
it must have dominated a hinterland producing trade commodities,
Berunei is depicted on the map as a territorial capital. In
reality it was probably not too dissimilar from some Sumatran
trading ports which, because they had fallen under the political
control of aggressive neighbors, are represented on the map as of
only local importance.

  The second-ranking cities in the hierarchy were mainly
provincial capitals or relatively important trading ports, Bassac,
Tenasserim, and Nakhon Sithammarat being examples of the first
type, and Bassein, Martaban, and Tuban of the second. Dagon (on
the site of present-day Rangoon) is included in this class because
the Peguan king Binnya U (1358-85) constituted its great pagoda as

a shrine of more than local prestige. Makasar, although mentioned in the *Nāgara-Kĕrtāgama* (canto 14, stanza 5), in the 14th century was probably little more than the seat of a paramount chief, and figures in this class only because it appears to have been the most important settlement in south Sulawesi.

The third, and lowest, discernible rank in the hierarchies depicted on Fig. 22 comprised a broad band of urban centers ranging in size and importance from, say, Tamiang on the northeast coast of Sumatra and Kelantan on the east coast of the Siamo-Malay Peninsula, both of which were known to Chinese and Javanese alike as profitable ports of call for trading vessels, to local market towns in the interior of Burma or Java, even to the seats of certain minor paramounts which barely qualified as urban. It also included the settlement of several thousand Chinese from Kuang-tung and Fu-kien who had established themselves beside what Wang Ta-yüan called the Old Channel, leading to the Musi river and the former site of Śrī Vijaya.[18] Clearly a category subsuming urban forms as disparate in size and range of functions as those specified here must have been a composite of several ranks, but the quality of the evidence has not permitted their separation. In fact, this level of the hierarchies was the one most affected by the limitations of the data. Because the evidence tended to emphasize politically, administratively, and ceremonially prestigious settlements at the expense of those unconnected with royalty or aristocracy, this was the least thoroughly reconstructed of the three levels. Local market centers were especially poorly recorded. Moreover, the difficulties of locating historical toponyms tended to be exacerbated at this level of the hierarchies, so that possibly as many as twenty per cent of these lower-order centers could be assigned only approximate locations. On the positive side, though, it can be assumed that locational inaccuracies of this type which have survived the reduction in scale inherent in the printing process are unlikely seriously to have subverted the generalized pattern of urban distribution with which we are primarily concerned. Nevertheless, it must be admitted that, strictly speaking, the map depicts not complete urban hierarchies but rather recoverable fragments of hierarchies.

The Capitals

The state capitals of Southeast Asia in precolonial times have been characterized at one time or another as exemplary centers,[19] as eponymous universal axes giving their names to dependent polities,[20] as torches flaring and fading in political space,[21] and as suns to which their kingdoms were but haloes,[22] all of which are only ways of epitomizing these capitals as embodying the concentrated power of their respective states. Underpinning this role of the capital was an annual sequence of ritual and ceremony, a large part of which took the form of illocutionary rites,[23] including the so-called verbal magic that C. C. Berg and O. W. Wolters have discerned in, respectively, Javanese and Malay chronicles,[24] and which surely informed other classical literatures of Southeast Asia. But it was also recognized that these rites would achieve their maximum effectiveness only if they were performed in a terrestrial setting modelled on the world of the gods. To attain that end, the capital was conceived as, and often constructed in the form of, a reduced version of the cosmos, which in western Southeast Asia meant the Indian cosmos. The urban designs developed on this basis assumed dramatically different forms in the different cultural realms of Southeast Asia but almost invariably shared three implicit principles of spatial organization, namely, terrestrial space was structured in the image of celestial space, was developed about an existentially centered point of ontological transition between cosmic planes, and was orientated in relation to the cardinal compass directions.[25] The remarkable manner in which the Khmers combined their agricultural technology and cosmomagical symbolism into a smoothly functioning foundation of statehood has been a subject of frequent comment;[26] but although the plastic expression of this symbolism is better preserved in Kampuchea than in most other parts of Southeast Asia and its interpretation there more fully endorsed by epigraphic documents, analogous uses of symbolism in the interests of political and social integration have been noted in many other parts of Southeast Asia. Even where, as in the capital of Majapahit, there is an almost complete absence of architectural or other plastic evidence, the symbolic basis of urban organization is often to be inferred in existential terms.[27]

The Lower Ranks in the Urban Hierarchies

The *raison d'être* of all the urban hierarchies depicted in Fig. 22 was the sustaining of a highly developed system of redistributive and mobilizative exchanges that had been progressively elaborated within the framework of a set of increasingly powerful polities. The salient characteristic of the hierarchies in the 14th century, as of their predecessors during the best part of a millennium, was the fact that the main centers of redistribution and mobilization were predominantly the main centers of decision-making. It followed that there was an almost perfect locational isomorphism between the administrative and economic components of each composite hierarchy, which consequently, tended to be mutually reinforcing. Moreover, by ensuring that the range of highest-order functions in both hierarchies was coincident with the areal extent of the polity, dynasty after dynasty induced strongly primate arrangements in the settlement patterns; that is, the largest city (in every instance the capital) was several times more populous than any other urban center in the hierarchy and exceptionally expressive of national capacity and sentiment. Ava, Pegu, Ayutthaya, Vijayapura, and Majapahit all exceeded many fold in magnitude of population, area, and diversity of functions any other urban centers in their respective kingdoms; and it was to this variance in scale between the capital and the rest of the urban hierarchy (rather than to absolute size) that the administrative and ceremonial centers owed a major part of the prestige that they enjoyed in the eyes of their populations.

It has been observed in a preceding section that benefices and dependencies typically reproduced on a smaller scale the symbols, institutions, and modes of organization of their major kingdoms. Among the most common replications were the cosmomagical bases of urban design, so that provincial, district, and lesser seats were often constituted as reduced models of their paramount capitals. Not unexpectedly, the symbolic component usually became progressively less prominent as the base of the hierarchy was approached, the level at which district chiefs were able to accumulate only limited surpluses with which to implement the symbolic designs so prominently displayed in the great capitals. Or, as a 14th-century Javanese or Khmer would probably have phrased it, the chiefs lacked wealth because they lacked power, and they lacked power because they had not taken the ritual measures to secure it. In either interpretation the outcome was the same: symbolic designs were most prominent in the upper ranks of the hierarchy, although even at the lowest levels some concessions were usually made to the need to maintain harmony between macrocosmos and microcosmos.

It was during the 14th century that one particular type of city began to assume a new prominence, one in which the adaptive functional subsystem of society was coming to assert its dominance over the integrative, goal-attaining, and pattern-maintaining subsystems,[28] or, as Erik Cohen would put it, the instrumental orientation to environment was coming to prevail over the sentimental, territorial, and symbolic orientations.[29] Although this type of urban form had probably existed in previous periods (possibly Tun-sun and Lo-yüeh were early exemplars), and although in the 14th century it was apparently not completely unrepresented in any of the main cultural realms of Southeast Asia, it achieved its characteristic expression in the Pasisir of the North Javanese coast in the 15th and 16th centuries. Majapahit's involvement in the burgeoning trade with the Middle East and India on the one hand and China on the other, together with its own monopoly over the spices of the eastern islands, had induced the rise of a number of trading cities along its northern coast. Originally constituted as benefices at the disposal of the Majapahit ruler, as early as the 14th century these port cities were developing characteristically commercial orientations, and orthogenetic transformations were beginning to yield to heterogenetic changes[30] as ethnically and socially diverse groups worked out a *modus vivendi* that was fundamentally alien to the brittle socio-political structure of the traditional, territorially based polity.

Heterogeneity of population, in fact, was one of the salient characteristics of these port cities. Van Leur's citation of the experiences of the first Dutch mariners to visit Bantam (admittedly some two centuries after the period with which we are here concerned) can stand repetition as typical of conditions in the Pasisir ports at all times:

> There came such a multitude of Javanese and other nations as Turks, Chinese, Bengali, Arabs, Persians, Gujarati, and others that one could hardly move . . .
>
> They . . . came so abundantly that each nation took a spot on the ships where they displayed their goods, the same as if it were on a market. Of which the Chinese brought of all sorts of silk woven and unwoven, twined and untwined, with beautiful earthenware, with other strange things more. The Javanese brought chickens, ducks, eggs, and many kinds of fruits. Arabs, Moors, Turks, and other nations of people each brought of everything one might imagine.[31]

Tomé Pires, writing early in the 16th century, went so far as to assert that the majority of these Pasisir ports had been founded by traders, some of whom had been foreigners:

> At the time when there were heathens along the sea coast of Java, many merchants used to come, Parsees, Arabs, Gujaratees, Bengalees, Malays and other nationalities, there being many Moors among them. They began to trade in the country and to grow rich. They succeeded in way of making mosques, and mollahs came from outside, so that they came in such growing numbers that the sons of these said Moors were already Javanese and rich, for they had been in these parts for about seventy years. In some places the heathen Javanese lords themselves turned Mohammedan, and these mollahs and

> the merchant Moors took possession of these places. Others had a
> way of fortifying the places where they lived, and they took people
> of their own who sailed in their junks, and they killed the Javanese
> lords and made themselves lords; and in this way they made
> themselves masters of the sea coast and took over trade and power
> in Java.
>
> These lord *pates* are not Javanese of long standing in the
> country, but they are descended from Chinese, from Parsees and
> Kling, and from the nations we have already mentioned . . .[32]

Although in the 14th century the Pasisir lords had probably not yet established their hegemony over Javanese foreign trade, Pires's account of the role of foreigners in these ports was confirmed for the 14th century on at least two occasions by Ma Huan, who noted that Gresik had been founded by Chinese (inferredly between 1350 and 1400) and that in his day (1433) Tuban afforded a haven for numerous emigrants from Kuang-tung and Fu-kien.[33]

It goes without saying that these port cities of heterogenetic transformation were less impressive architecturally than the great capitals, that the rigorously formalized spatial arrangements of the latter were in almost total abeyance, and that ritual experts were much less prominent in the communities residing within their walls. Bubat, the outport of Majapahit on the Brantas estuary, seems to have conformed fairly closely to this stereotype at least as early as the middle of the 14th century. According to the *Nāgara-Kĕrtāgama*, its waterfront was surrounded on three sides by large buildings (*bhawana*, probably warehouses) interspersed with the residential compounds of *mantri*, these last being persons of at least relatively high status.[34] The remark that these structures were clustered in groups (*mapaṇṭa*) has sometimes been taken to imply the existence of ethnic quarters in the port, a feature which seems to have been characteristic of Southeast Asian port cities in all eras.

This then was the stage of urban integration attained in Southeast Asia in the century before the intrusion of the Portuguese initiated a process that would ultimately induce a major restructuring both of political order within the region and of the associated patterns of urbanization. One city in particular was to play a crucial role in this transition. Although it seems to have been founded as a ritual and ceremonial center at the turn of the 15th century, within fifty years Melaka had developed into the premier trading emporium in the whole of Southeast Asia.[35] The basis of Melakan commerce at this time was the exchange of the staple products of the Archipelago for the staple manufactures of India. Melaka was, in effect, a collection center for the spices of Banda and Maluku and a distribution center for the textiles of

Gujarāt, Coromandel, Malabār, and Bengal. It was the very success of the city in dominating the trade of East and Southeast Asia at the point where it flowed in and out of the Indian Ocean, which was also the only point throughout eight thousand miles of seaway at which it was practicable to control the spice trade between the Nusa Tenggara and Renaissance Europe, that brought about its downfall. The power that controlled Melaka Strait during the 15th century was in a position to apply a tourniquet to the world's major artery of trade — as Tomé Pires put it, "Whoever is lord of Melaka [$malaq^a$] has his hand on the throat of Venice"[36]— but when the advantage of a Malay sultan became the arbiter of prices in Lisbon and the Hansa ports, it was bound to invite European intervention. The city was taken by storm by the troops of Afonso d'Albuquerque on August 24, 1511, thereby ushering in a new order of polity and city. Although the old order was never wholly obliterated, it was nearly everywhere so thoroughly transformed that its lineaments now appear only as indistinct traces on a five-hundred-year-old palimpsest.

Notes and References

1. Cp. David L. Webster, advancing the concept of "charismatic office": "Thus, 'charisma', although attached to an individual personality, is not necessarily a product of that personality . . . Socially recognized charisma . . . goes with the job" ["On theocracies," *American Anthropologist*, vol. 78, no. 4 (1976), p. 821].

2. Cf. Note 320 to Chapter 7.

3. *Hsü Han Chih* 續漢志 chüan 28, f. 7r. This work, by Ssŭ-ma Piao 司馬彪 of the Chin dynasty, constitutes the monographic chapters of the *Hou-Han Shu* 後漢書, the rest being from the brush of Fan Yeh 范曄. The *Hsü Han Chih* was not incorporated into the official history until the 11th century.

4. A fact of which Viêtnamese historians have made much. Cf., for instance, Nguyên van Huyên, *La civilisation annamite* (Hanoi, 1941), p. 10.

5. Jeremy H. C. S. Davidson, "Urban genesis in Viet-Nam: a comment," in R. B. Smith and W. Watson (eds.), *Early South East Asia* (New York and Kuala Lumpur, 1979), p. 313. Davidson is here citing a paper by Lê văn Lan (1963).

6. Stanley J. Tambiah, *World conquerer, world renouncer* (Cambridge, 1976), p. 113. Cf. also the same author's "The galactic polity: the structure of traditional kingdoms in Southeast Asia," *Annals of the New York Academy of Sciences*, vol. 293 (1977), pp. 69-97.

7. R. B. Smith, "Mainland South East Asia in the seventh and eighth centuries," in Smith and Watson, *Early South East Asia*, pp. 443-456. Cp. also *ibid.*, p. 261. Dr. Smith further suggests that significant organizational contrasts between the western and eastern sectors of Indianized Southeast Asia may have begun to develop during the 7th and 8th centuries, but it is by no means certain that such a distinction may not reflect the nature and availability of evidence rather than reality. Certainly it would be difficult at this time to prove that 11th-century Kambujadeśa was a more highly differentiated polity than contemporary Pagan.

8. *Rājapatiguṇḍala*, a text (*MS. Or. Leyden 5056*) dealing with the organization of the clergy in 14th-century Majapahit, is included in Theodore G. Th. Pigeaud's *Java in the 14th century: a study in cultural history*, 5 vols. (The Hague, 1960). A transcription of the Javanese passage is to be found in vol. 1, p. 90; an explication in vol. 2, pp. 120-125; and an English translation in vol. 3, p. 90.

9. Clifford Geertz, *Islam Observed: religious development in Morocco and Indonesia* (New Haven, Conn., 1968), p. 36.

10. Some parts of this and the following paragraphs have been published previously in Kernial Singh Sandhu and Paul Wheatley (eds.), *Melaka: the transformation of a Malay capital, c. 1400-1980*, vol. 1 (Kuala Lumpur, 1982), chap. 1.

11. Geertz, *Islam observed*, p. 38. Of course, it is a moot point whether differences between Southeast Asian and Western perceptions of what constitutes theatricality are sufficiently great to require qualification of this concept of the theater state.

12. The cosmomagical basis of urban form in Southeast Asia in early times has been graphically elucidated by, among others, Robert von Heine-Geldern, "Weltbild und Bauform in Südostasien," *Wiener Beiträge zur Kunst- und Kulturgeschichte Asiens*, vol. 4 (1930), pp. 28-78; George Coedès, *Pour mieux comprendre Angkor*

(Paris, 1947), chap. 5; Jean Filliozat, "Le symbolisme du monument du Phnom Bǎkheṅ," *Bulletin de l'Ecole Française d'Extrême-Orient*, vol. 44 (1954), pp. 527-554; Bernard-Philippe Groslier, *Angkor. Hommes et pierres* (Paris, 1956), *passim*; Tambiah, *World conqueror, world renouncer*, chap. 7. For a general discussion of the cosmological ordering of space see Wheatley, "The suspended pelt: reflections on a discarded model of spatial structure," in Donald R. Deskins, Jr., George Kish, John D. Nystuen, and Gunnar Olsson (eds.), *Geographic humanism, analysis and social action*. Michigan Geographical Publications No. 17 (Ann Arbor, Mich., 1977), pp. 47-108.

13. The main modes of economic integration are defined in Talcott Parsons and Neil J. Smelser, *Economy and Society. A study in the integration of economic and social theory* (London, 1956), *passim*; and Smelser, "A comparative view of exchange systems," *Economic Development and Cultural Change*, vol. 7 (1959); pp. 173-182. Both redistribution and mobilization involve a centripetal flow of commodities and services from the periphery of the polity toward the capital but, whereas the former involves the allocation of rewards in conformity with the integrative requirements of society (and consequently operates in the interests of social stratification), mobilization channels resources into the hands of those responsible for the achievement of collective goals. In other words, it subordinates economic arrangements to the pursuit of broadly political purposes. See also Note 64 to Chap. 1. For the application of these concepts to early Southeast Asia see Wheatley, "Satyānṛta in Suvarṇadvīpa: from reciprocity to redistribution in ancient Southeast Asia," in Jeremy A. Sabloff and C. C. Lamberg-Karlowsky (eds.), *Ancient civilization and trade* (Albuquerque, N. Mex., 1975), pp. 227-283. Leonid A. Sedov has discussed the way in which local lineage temples were integrated into the redistributive systems of ten especially large temples in Kambujadeśa during the 10th and 11th centuries in "K voprosu ob ekonomicheskom stroe ankorskoi Kambodzhi IX-XII vv," *Narody Asii i Afriki, Istoriia, Ekonomika, Kul'tura*, vol. 6 (1963), pp. 73-81 [In Russian].

14. Tambiah, "The galactic polity," pp. 85-88.

15. This map has been published previously in Sandhu and Wheatley, *Melaka*, vol. 1, p. 24, where it is accompanied by a discussion of the sources on which it is based and cautions as to its reliability. Yet, despite the expediential judgments that entered into its composition, despite the distortions and stylization inherent in cartographic representation at this scale, and despite the uneven coverage of the several territories resulting from the largely fortuitous survival of evidence, the map is believed to provide a reasonably sound visual impression of the broad pattern of urban development in Southeast Asia toward the end of the 14th century. Generally speaking, the historical record is most adequate for regions bordering the maritime trade route between East and West, and in the neighborhood of the capitals. Minor towns in the interior of the continental territories are almost certainly under-represented, as they probably are in Java, the Tong-King delta, Kampuchea, and the Cam lowlands, despite the relatively dense clusters of symbols assigned to the first two of these regions.

For a conspectus of urban developments in Southeast Asia in centuries immediately following the one to which the map relates see Anthony Reid, "The structure of cities in Southeast Asia, fifteenth to seventeenth centuries," *Journal of Southeast Asian Studies*, vol. 11, no. 2 (1980), pp. 235-250.

16. George Coedès, *Les états hindouisés d'Indochine et d'Indonésie* (Third edition, Paris, 1964), p. 427.

17. Berunei (*Po-ni*: *Bʻuǝt-niei 渤泥 in the Chinese dynastic histories) sent its first mission to the Dragon Throne in 977 (*Sung Shih*, chüan 49, f. 19r). See also Paul Pelliot, "Le Hōja et le Sayyid Ḥusain de l'histoire des Ming," *T'oung Pao*, vol. 38 (1948), p. 267, note 346. Early in the 16th century Pigafetta reported that the settlement housed 25,000 families: Lord Stanley of Alderley, *The first voyage round the world by Magellan*. Hakluyt Society, vol. LII (London, 1874), p. 114.

18. Wang Ta-yüan, *Tao-i chih-lüeh chiao-chu*, vol. 26 of *Wen tien ko-shu chuan, Kuo-hsüeh wen k'u* (Peiping, 1936), p. 84. Cf. O. W. Wolters, "Landfall on the Palembang coast in medieval times," *Indonesia*, vol. 20 (1976), *passim*.

19. P. 423 above.

20. P. 423 above.

21. Cf. Soemarsaid Moertono, *State and statecraft in old Java: a study of the later Mataram period, 16th to 19th century*. Monograph of the Modern Indonesia Project, Southeast Asia Program, Cornell University (Ithaca, N.Y., 1968), p. 61. The simile of the torch flaring in the darkness is from the introductory narrative (*kanda*) to a Javanese *wayang* play.

22. Theodore G. Th. Pigeaud, *Java in the 14th century: a study in cultural history* (The Hague, 1960), vol. 1, p. 10; vol. 2, pp. 29-30; and vol. 3, p. 15.

23. I.e. "performative" rites which were effective simply by virtue of being enacted (J. L. Austin's terminology). Cf. Stanley J. Tambiah, "Form and meaning of magical acts: a point of view," in Robin Horton and Ruth Finnegan (eds.), *Modes of thought. Essays on thinking in Western and Non-Western societies* (London, 1973), pp. 199-229.

24. See, for instance, C. C. Berg, "Gedachtenwisseling over Javaanse geschriedschrijving," *Indonesië*, vol. 9 (1956), pp. 177-216; "Javanische Geschichtsschreibung," *Saeculum*, vol. 7 (1956) and vol. 8 (1957); and "Javanese historiography — a synopsis of its evolution," in D. G. E. Hall (ed.), *Historians of South East Asia* (London, 1961), pp. 13-23; O. W. Wolters, *The fall of Śrīvijaya in Malay history* (Ithaca, N.Y., 1970), *passim*.

25. For an extended discussion of these principles and their implications see Wheatley, "The suspended pelt," pp. 52 ff.

26. Cf. Note 12 above and additionally, for ancient Kampuchea, Bernard-Philippe Groslier, "Agriculture et religion dans l'empire angkorien," *Etudes Rurales*, vol. 53-56 (1974), pp. 95-117. There is an extended evaluation of the Ańkor kingdom from a Marxist viewpoint in Leonid A. Sedov, *Angkorskaia imperia* (Moscow, 1967) and a briefer discussion by the same author, in "Angkor: society and states," in Henri J. M. Claessen and Peter Skalnik (eds.), *The early state* (The Hague, 1978), pp. 111-130.

27. For comments on symbolic elements in the architectural arrangement of Majapahit see Sandhu and Wheatley, *Melaka*, vol. 1, pp. 35-36.

28. These terms are drawn from Parsonian sociology: see, for example, Talcott Parsons, *Societies: evolutionary and comparative perspectives* (Englewood Cliffs, N.J., 1966), and *The system of modern societies* (Englewood Cliffs, N.J., 1971).

29. Erik Cohen, "Environmental orientations: a multidmensional approach to social ecology," *Current Anthropology*, vol. 17, no. 1 (1976), pp. 49-70.

30. This terminology is borrowed from Robert Redfield and Milton B. Singer, "The cultural role of cities," *Economic Development and Cultural Change*, vol. 3 (1954), pp. 53-73.

31. J. C. van Leur, *Indonesian trade and society: essays in Asian social and economic history* (The Hague and Bandung, 1955; originally published in 1934), p. 3, citing in translation G. P. Rouffaer and J. W. IJzerman, *De eerste schipvaart der Nederlanders naar Oost-Indië onder Cornelis de Houtman, 1595-1597: Journalen, documenten en ander beschieden* (The Hague, Linschoten Vereeniging, 1915-1929), vol. 1, p. 74 and vol. 2, p. 293.

32. Armando Cortesão, *The Suma Oriental of Tomé Pires*, 2. vols. Hakluyt

Society, Second Series, nos. LXXXIX and XC (London, 1944): English transl. in vol. 1, pp. 105-106, Portuguese text in vol. 2, p. 386. The term *mollah* which occurs in this passage is a Persian form from the Arabic *mawlā*, signifying a member of the Muslim religious classes in general.

33. J. V. Mills, *Ma Huan. Ying-yai Sheng-lan* (Cambridge, England, 1970), pp. 89-90.

34. Pigeaud, *Java in the 14th century*, vol. 1, p. 66; vol. 3, p. 102; vol. 4; pp. 290-292.

35. The rise of Melaka to commercial pre-eminence in the flux of competing polities that characterized Southeast Asia at the turn of the 15th century is described in Kernial Singh Sandhu and Paul Wheatley (eds.), *Melaka: the transformation of a Malay capital* (Kuala Lumpur, 1982), vol. 1, chap. 1 and vol. 2, chap. 46.

36. Cortesão, *The Suma Oriental*, vol. 2, pp. 287 and 510.

APPENDIX

Urban Centers in the Ptolemaic Corpus

Although the Γεωγραφικὴ Ὑφήγησις (*Instruction in Practical Cartography*) has long been attributed to the astronomer Klaudios Ptolemaios, who lived in Alexandria during the 2nd century A.D., it is not at all certain precisely what this author contributed to the corpus that bears his name. Aware that the import of an astronomical observation was contingent on the precision with which the observer could define his position on the surface of the earth, Ptolemy set out to construct, or at least to compile a manual for the construction of, a more accurate map of the world than had hitherto existed. His method is specified as follows (Bk I, chap. 4): -

> If visitors to different countries had made similar observations, it would be possible to construct a definitive map of the inhabited world; but only Hipparchus [2nd century B.C.] has recorded altitudes of the Pole Star and noted which places are situated in similar latitudes (and then for only a few of the immense number of positions needed to construct a map of the world): while a few later writers have noted that certain places are situated on the same meridian . . . but distances between points, especially from east to west, have been calculated only approximately . . . so that the proper method of constructing a world map would be first to plot those positions determined by accurate observations, and then to manipulate the data for positions obtained from other sources so as to fit them into this framework with the least possible distortion.[1]

Ptolemy's attempts to attain the accuracy he desired were subverted by four circumstances, three of a theoretical nature and one arising from practical considerations. In the first place, he followed Posidonius (c. 135-50 B.C.) in assuming a terrestrial circumference of 180,000 *stadia*,[2] which implied that a degree of latitude or longitude at the equator was equivalent to 500 *stadia*, and this error accumulated progressively eastward from the prime meridian until it reached a maximum in eastern Asia. But even the Mediterranean was accorded a longitudinal extent of 62° instead of 42°. Second, owing to the fact that Ptolemy had no real knowledge of the so-called Fortunate Isles (vaguely identified with Madeira and the Canary Islands), which defined his prime meridian, all his longitudes, reckoned eastward, were about seven degrees less than true. Third, Ptolemy had no astronomical observations from the region of the equator, so that he was forced to calculate its position relative to the northern tropic. As the Posidonian degree was only five-sixths of a true degree, he misplaced the equator some 230 nautical miles too far to the north. The constancy of these errors over the whole map has led some scholars to devise arithmetical formulae to convert Ptolemaic co-ordinates to true latitudes and longitudes,[3] but these exercises have inevitably been thwarted by the manner in which Ptolemy constructed his graticule. Outside the Mediterranean world, and over extensive territories even within it, his co-ordinates could not have been derived from astronomical observation. In the ancient world latitudes were obtained by measuring either the altitude of Polaris or the duration of the longest day. Within the frontiers of the Roman Empire such observations were perhaps not too infrequent, but beyond the *limes* they hardly existed at all. Even in the Mediterranean the instruments available for such observations were of limited accuracy, yet Ptolemaic latitudes are recorded to within five minutes. A Ptolemaic longitude was even less reliable. In theory it represented the difference in time between the place in question and the prime meridian passing through the Fortunate Isles, but until accurate marine chronometers were invented in the 18th century such a calculation was never more than, at best, an informed estimate.

In the absence of astronomical (or, as they were called at the time, *meteoroscopic*) data, when fixing positions Ptolemy had to rely on a primitive form of dead reckoning.[4] Within the confines of the Roman Empire, overland distances were known fairly accurately, but the vagaries of wind and weather and the lack of compass and log rendered marine itineraries, particularly those outside the trade-wind zone, prodigious sources of error. However, Ptolemy reduced all the sailing times available to him to an average of 516 *stadia* a day. He then made strenuous efforts to reconcile the positions obtained in this way with "authority," that is with the conclusions of earlier writers of repute.

The Γεωγραφικὴ Ὑφήγησις, as Ptolemy called his manual on map-making (the *Geographia* or *Cosmographia* as it became known to later centuries) in its present form comprises eight books. The first and the beginning of the second present a discussion of the principles

and methods of map construction, including a critique of the work
of Ptolemy's near-contemporary Marinos of Tyre. The next five
books and part of the seventh consist of tables of the latitudes
and longitudes, expressed in degrees and minutes, of more than
eight thousand places set out in a crude regional arrangement. In
the concluding sections of Book VII this information is summarized,
and a general description of the dimensions of the known world
provided. Book VIII explains how to divide the world-map into
twenty-six regional maps and appends a short list of co-ordinates
of principal cities in which, contrary to the practice throughout
the rest of the work, latitude is denoted by the length of the
longest day and longitude as the difference in time of a
particular place from Alexandria. The earliest surviving copies of
the *Geographia* are in the form of Byzantine manuscripts from the
13th and early-14th centuries. Some of the manuscripts incorporate
maps, others do not. Among those which do, two traditions can be
discriminated: an A version which contains twenty-six maps. all
inserted in Book VIII, and a B version, furnished with 64 maps
distributed throughout the text. Both traditions often include, or
were intended to include, a world map, either on one sheet or
spread over four sheets. In some manuscripts the single-sheet map
carries the name of Agathodaimon, an artificer of Alexandria, whose
dates are unknown.

The traditional view of the *Geographia* as transmitted in the
Byzantine manuscripts was that it was compiled in its entirety, both
text and maps, by Ptolemy. This was not so very different from the
conclusion of Father Joseph Fischer in 1932 that the text is
Ptolemy's composition and that the surviving maps are derived from
versions prepared by Ptolemy — with the exception, of course, of
the world map drawn up by Agathodaimon.[5] However, the lateness of
the manuscript tradition, inconsistencies and contradictions
between the eight books, the inclusion of material that could not
have been known to Ptolemy, and discrepancies between text and maps
have forced some recent scholars to the conclusion that the
Geographia as we now know it is a cumulative text. Certainly the
case for this assumption is strengthened by the absence of any
mention of a *Geographia* in eight books by any contemporary of Ptolemy
or by any extant writer during the immediately succeeding centuries.
Nor is the *Geographia* mentioned in any of the numerous surviving
lists of Ptolemy's works, not even in the dictionary of ancient
authors compiled by Suidas of Byzantium in the 10 th century. When
the *Geographia* is mentioned by other authors, it is nearly always in
connection with the theoretical discussion in Book I. The

principal proponent of this view of the Ptolemaic compendium as a composite text was the late Leo Bagrow, who held that the *Geographia* in its present form is a 10th-11th century Byzantine compilation of Ptolemaic writings, while the maps (except for the world map by Agathodaimon) were constructed in the 13th and 14th centuries on principles specified by Ptolemy but using information that was continually being augmented over the best part of a millennium.[6] On this interpretation Ptolemy himself would have been responsible only for Book I of the *Geographia* and some general instructions at the beginning of Book II, together with information in Book VIII about the limitations of the regional maps and the schedule of principal cities.[7] In short, in Bagrow's view, the compendium of co-ordinates was assembled during the course of twelve centuries, provided late in its evolution with maps by three or four different hands, and furnished with authority by ascribing its authorship to Ptolemy. Whether or not this particular interpretation is valid in all its ramifications, there can be no doubt that the *Geographia* as it is now constituted is, to a degree still to be determined, a cumulative text, the reliability and significance of which must be evaluated book by book, section by section, paragraph by paragraph, and sometimes word by word. And we are not likely to make much progress in that task until all the main manuscript traditions have been subjected to the most rigorous textual scrutiny and collation.

The difficulties inherent in the explication of any part of the *Geographia* are all exacerbated in those sections of Book VII which, under the rubrics "Location of Trans-Gangetic India" (Τῆς ἐκτὸς Γάγγου Ἰνδικῆς θέσις) and "Location of the Sinai" (Σίνων θέσις), list co-ordinates for nearly 140 settlements and physiographic features in Southeast Asia, interspersed with sundry descriptive comments. The latitudes and longitudes, as we have seen must have been read off a map constructed on other principles, and afford only minimal guides to location, while the great majority of the toponyms have so far defied identification. In fact, many of them appear so strange that a casual reader might be forgiven for regarding the relevant sections of Book VII as a farrago of nonsense. That they are not simply that, despite their distortions of land shapes and their garbling of names, is attested by occasional correspondences with other bodies of evidence, but a proper understanding of Book VII still eludes us. And it will continue to do so until linguists with the requisite competencies mount a sustained and concerted investigation of the toponyms sprinkled so tantalizingly over the map. The master key to the rationale of the Ptolemaic geography of Southeast Asia lies in toponymic identification rather than supposed sailing times and distances, and certainly not in the manipulation of latitudes and longitudes.

As long ago as 1925 Louis Renou prepared a redaction of Book VII based on the combined testimony of what he believed were the most reliable representatives in each of seven manuscript families established by Otto Cuntz two years previously.[8] The map of Trans-Gangetic India that accompanies some manuscripts is constructed on a rectangular projection with straight parallels and meridians intersecting at right angles, a cartographic expedient which Ptolemy was prepared to tolerate for small areas only (II, 1, 10 and VIII, 2, 6).

Among the places listed in what is today Southeast Asia are about thirty settlements each designated as a *polis* (πολις),[9] a term which in Ptolemy's time signified an urban center where one would have expected to find at least some basic institutions of government in addition to retailing and various types of services;[10] six trading ports each specified as an *emporion* (ἐμπόριον), which denoted "an authorized sea-coast (not inland) mart in the Orient where *non*-Roman dues were levied by *non*-Roman authorities;"[11] five *metropoleis* (μητρόπολεις) or chief cities of their respective territories; and one *basileion* (βασίλειον) or royal city. Of course, these classifications were determined by hearsay, whether by Ptolemy or by one of those who added to his list of co-ordinates, and, especially in the case of the *poleis*, the supposed Southeast Asian exemplars may not have possessed all the attributes implied by their class in the Graeco-Roman world.

Attempts to restore the original names of these settlements, or indeed of the other features listed in the *Geographia*, have thus far met with little success. The late George Coedès thought that Trans-Gangetic India was "remplie de toponymes à consonance sanskrite."[12] But a *consonance* is all it was. Recognizable Sanskrit words, explicit or inferred, are relatively infrequent. *Takola* (Τάκωλα), a mart on the coast of the Golden Chersonese (Χρυση Χερσονήσος: VII, ii, 5), was assuredly the *Takkola* mentioned as a likely destination for seafaring merchants in a gloss in the *Mahāniddesa* and again in the *Milinda-Pañha* (both probably dating from the 2nd or 3rd century A.D.), and also the place listed as *Talaittakkolam*, an alleged conquest of Rājendra Cola I, in a Tanjāvūr inscription of 1030/1.[13] *Maiandros* (Μαίανδρος), the name of a mountain range in the western part of Trans-Gangetic India (VII, ii, 8), was probably a rendering of *Mahendra*. *Tamara* (Ταμάρα), a *polis* or small town (the text is not specific on this point: VII, ii, 24) is almost certainly to be restored as Sanskrit *Tāmra*, meaning "copper," as the *Geographia* locates it squarely in the Copper Country (Χαλκίτις Χώρα: VII, ii, 20), "where there are very many mines of that metal." *Têmala* (Τημάλα : VII, ii, 3), a *polis* in the Silver Country, may have been a Hellenized version of the Sanskrit tree-name *tamāla*, but there is no firm basis for this assumption. There can be no doubt, though, that the ethnikon *Nangalogai*, "signifying 'realm of naked men'" (Ναγγαλόγαι ὅ σημαίνει γυμνῶν κόσμος) and applied to a group inhabiting the territory beyond the *Maiandros* range (VII, ii, 18), was a direct borrowing of the sense and sound of the Sanskrit *nagnaloka*.[14] It is tempting to speculate that this may be a reference not to a society at a primitive stage of development but to the prominence of naked ascetics and mendicants in an Indianized social context, perhaps to the Pāśupatas mentioned on p. 292. It will be recalled that I Ching noted that before his time one of the *Bnaṃ* polities had been known as the Kingdom of Naked Men (Note 2 to Chapter 3).[15] The *Aginnatai* (Ἀγιννάται) of *Salinê* (Σαλίνη) island (VII, ii, 26), by contrast, who "constantly go naked" and whose name probably derived from the Sanskrit *nagnata*, denoting a wandering mendicant, may have owed their appellation to their low level of cultural attainment. Their island may have been one of the Andaman or Nicobar groups. A few other names on the Ptolemaic map of Southeast Asia may or may not be of Sanskrit origin, and two apparently incorporate the Sanskrit component *nāgara*: *Konkonagara* (Κογκοναγάρα) in the Golden Chersonese (VII, ii, 25) and *Kokkosanagora* (Κοκκοσαναγόρα) in the territory of the *Sinai* (VII, iii, 5). It has been suggested that the former of these names was a Greek transcription of Sanskrit *Kanakanāgara*, meaning Golden Capital,[16] an appropriate enough designation for a city on the Golden Peninsula, but it could equally, and with a closer phonetic correspondence, have been a rendering of *Gaṅganāgara*, denoting River Capital. Such a name has in fact been preserved in Malay legend.[17] Some other names, notably *Kattigara* (Καττίγαρα), "the anchorage of the *Sinai*" (ὅρμος Σίνων: VII, iii, 3), sound vaguely Sanskritic, although they have no meaning in that language. At least one name, *Iabadiou* (Ἰαβαδίου: VII, ii, 29) appears to be a transcription of a Prākrit form *Yāvadiu* (rather than of the Sanskrit *Yāvadvīpa*) = Java Island. In any case the equivalence of the two names is confirmed by the Ptolemaic annotation that *Iabadiou* signified "Barley Isle." Cape *Maleoukolon* (Μαλεουκόλον ἄκρον, in some MSS Μελεουκόλον: VII, ii. 5) in the Golden Chersonese has been shown to be a Greek transcription of Tamil *malaikkāl*, signifying "foot of the mountain." Moreover, Jean Filliozat has suggested that the mountain rising behind this promontory was very likely the Mount *Maleus* (Latin < Tamil *malai* = mountain) mentioned by Pliny in his *Natural History* as a place where shadows fell to the north during the winter half of the year, to the south during the summer half.[18] In other words, Mount *Maleus*, and by implication Cape *Maleoukolon*, even allowing for Pliny's statement being in round figures, were situated close to the equator. Professor Filliozat goes on to point out that in all Southeast Asia, indeed in the whole of the Indian culture realm, only one locality can meet the physical requirements of a prominent cape backed by a sizeable mountain on or close to the equator, namely Ujung Inderapura below Gunung Kerinci (also known as G. Inderapura) on the west coast of Sumatra.[19]

For the rest, apart from a few purely Greek descriptive names such as the Golden Peninsula, the Copper Country, or the Islands of Satyrs (which may or may not have been translations of either indigenous or Indian names), the sources of the Ptolemaic toponymy are seldom better than conjectural, and usually not even that.

The prevailing view of the disposition of land and sea as it is displayed in the maps accompanying some manuscripts of the *Geographia*, or as it can be reconstructed anew from the Ptolemaic co-ordinates, has been that the coastline traces out the shape of peninsular Southeast Asia to produce an outline that, although grossly distorted, is still readily recognizable. This belief is at least as old as the 16th century, when contemporary Western discoveries were added to Ptolemaic maps — the so-called "modern Ptolemies" — on the assumption that their coastlines were in general agreement with the reality that is depicted on a present-day map. In this century Gerini,[20] Berthelot,[21] and Wheatley,[22] among others, have each in principle accepted the validity of this style of interpretation. On this view, the territories lying immediately to the east of the Ganges delta represent modern Burma, an identification not without supporting evidence. *Kirradia* (Κιρραδία: VII, ii, 16), for instance, is presumably the country of the Kirāta, a forest people diffused widely to the east and northeast of Bengal.[23] *Argyra* (Ἄργυρα: VII, ii, 3), the Silver Country, is likely to be the Ptolemaic expression of the nexus of ideas, involving the Pyū who dominated the Irawadi valley for much of the first millennium A.D., which was discussed in Note 11 to Chapter 4. The name of the *Katabêda* (Καταβηδα: VII, ii, 2) river survives even today in Kutabdia/Cheduba Island,[24] while the *emporion* of *Barakoura* (Βαρακοῦρα: VII, ii, 2), slightly farther south on the Ptolemaic map, was probably a transcription of the name which appears in Burmese MSS of the *Niddesa* as *Parapura*, in Thai versions as *Parammukha* and *Parapura*, and in a late-7th or early-8th century inscription from Mrohaung as *Pureppura*.[25] *Bêsynga* (Βησύγγα: VII, ii, 4) *emporion*, near the estuary of the *Bêsyngas* river (Βησύγγα ποταμοῦ ἐκβολαί: VII, ii, 4), was probably the same place as the **B'ji̯e̯-tsuong* 皮宗 that envoys from a ruler of Kāñcī to the Han court recorded as a port of call on the voyage from India to Jih-nan,[26] as the **Pji-si̯ung* 比嵩 that lay "across the Great Bay of Chin-lin from Fu-nan,"[27] and as the *Vesuṅga* mentioned in the *Mahāniddesa*, but its precise location is unknown. Possibly the initial syllable may represent Mon *bi* = river.[28]

It also follows from this interpretation that the *Chrysê Chersonêsos* (VII, ii, 5) was the Ptolemaic depiction of the Siamo-Malaysian peninsula, with the promontory (ἀκρωτήριον: VII, ii, 7) between *Zabaipolis* (Ζάβαιπόλις) and *Thagora* (θαγόρα) ending in present-day Pointe de Cà Mau. The main impediments to acceptance of this view are the river system of the Golden Chersonese, which is not easily accommodatable to the drainage pattern of the Siamo-Malaysian peninsula, and the absence of archeological evidence for substantial settlements in the southern half of that peninsula in early times — although this latter argument may not carry much weight in the light of the comments in Chapter 6 on the prevailingly insubstantial character of traditional settlements in the Malaysian world. However, the similarity of the river system to the distributaries of a delta, coupled with co-ordinate manipulations that at the time could be deemed to point to the Irawadi valley, have led a number of investigators, among them C. Lassen, Sir Henry Yule, J.W. McCrindle, St. A. St. John, and V. Kanakasabhai, to locate the Golden Chersonese in Lower Burma.[29] *Takola*, the *emporion* of the Chersonese, is then often identified with the Tuikkulā (Burmese, but Mōn *Tuikgala* would be chronologically more apposite) near Ayitthima in the Sittōng subdivision of Shwegyin district. But this expedient raises as many problems as it solves, not the least being the abandonment of some of the toponymic identifications proposed above.

Thus far no one has made much sense of the toponyms and ethnonyms scattered through the territories surrounding the Great

Gulf. *Thinai* (Θῖναι: VII, iii, 6), *metropolis* of the *Sinai* (Σῖναι: VII, iii, 1), was presumably the "very great inland city called *Thin* (Θίν) [or *Thina* (Θίνα)]" which the *Periplus of the Erythraean Sea* relegated to the far north, "below Ursa Minor."[30] There is no doubt in my mind that the names *Thinai* and *Thin/Thina* derived ultimately from *Dzʽi̯ĕn 秦, the style of the dynasty which unified most of China in 221 B.C., by way of an intermediary Middle Persian *čīn*,[31] but establishing the origin of the name still leaves open the location of the people it designates. For the realms beyond the Golden Chersonese, Ptolemy himself, on his own admission (I, xiv, 1), seems to have had no information other than a summary by Marinos of Tyre of a voyage by an otherwise unknown Alexander, supplemented in part from the interrogation of mariners who traded with India (I, xvii, 5). Alexander had reported that, from the Golden Chersonese, "the coast faced south" for a distance of 20 days' sailing, whence the course lay southeast "for some days" to *Kattigara*. On the present interpretation, for reasons that have never been satisfactorily explained, Ptolemy or his Byzantine successors committed the egregious error of extending the lands of East Asia southward beyond even the equator and then westward to join up with an eastward projection of the East African coast.

The most reasonable, although surely not definitive, interpretation of the eastern sectors of the Ptolemaic map of Southeast Asia is that worked out during the past forty years by scholars of the Ecole Française d'Extrême-Orient. While holding to the belief that the map constructed from Ptolemaic co-ordinates does indeed reflect in a general way the run of actual coastlines, these scholars have changed the prevailing ideas as to which coastlines are involved. In the first place, the Chrysê Chersonêsos is identified with the southern half (instead of the whole) of the Siamo-Malayan peninsula,[32] so that the *Perimoulikos* Gulf (Περιμουλικὸς κόλπος): VII, ii, 5) becomes no more than a bay on the east coast of that peninsula, the Great Gulf the Ptolemaic designation for the present-day Gulf of Thailand, and the most easterly lands more or less coincident with the territories of the *Bna̭m* kingdoms of the lower Mekong valley.[33] This thesis is entirely in accord with R. A. Stein's recognition of *Kattigara* in the Chinese transcription *K'i̯u̯ət-tuo-ku̯ən/kân* 屈都昆乾 (MSC = *Chʽü-tu-kʽun/chʽien*), the name of a territory that was incorporated in the Fu-nan polity early in the 3rd century, conquered by a king of Campā between 336 and 340, and settled by some two thousand refugees from Chu-wu prefecture in the Chinese commandery of Jih-nan (p. 382 above) at an undetermined time, perhaps as early as the 1st century A.D., but certainly by the end of the 3rd.³⁴ *Kattigara* is rubricated in the *Geographia* (VII, iii, 3) not as a *polis*, a *metropolis*, or an *emporion* but simply as "the anchorage of the *Sinai*." This could mean that it was the main roadstead in Indochina where *Sinai* vessels dropped anchor to trade with the indigenous population, but most investigators have regarded it as situated within *Sinai* territory, and usually as an important, if not the principal, port of the *Sinai*.

The precise site of this port has occasioned a good deal of discussion without providing a definitive conclusion. The *Geographia* is explicit that it was situated to the southwest of the capital of the *Sinai* (I, xvii, 4). If the *Sinai* were Chinese from the land — as the *Periplus* puts it — "under Ursa Minor," then this statement could have been true only in the most general sense; but if the *Sinai* were the previously mentioned refugees from the Chinese commandery of Jih-nan (not necessarily ethnic Chinese but possibly former dwellers in Chinese-controlled territory), then both they and their capital could have been located in southern Indochina. To the east of the *Sinai*, according to the *Geographia* (I, xvii, 4), was "an unknown land of muddy lakes and tall reeds so thick in the stem that the local folk use them to cross the marsh" [presumably by the making of articulated paths or rafts], a description nicely in accord with conditions in the Mekong delta, especially in that part known as the Plaine des Joncs.³⁵ Stein's proposal, based on an early Chinese itinerary, of a site for Ch'ü-tu-k'un (that is *Kattigara*) in the neighborhood of Cap Saint-Jacques has the merit of locating the Ptolemaic settlement in southern Indochina but does not allow for its position to the southwest of the *Sinai* capital.³⁶ In what is thus far the most thorough review of the matter, Louis Malleret concluded that the most likely site for *Kattigara* was Thnal Mray (known to the French as Cent Rues), with the *Sinai* capital in the vicinity of Prei Nokor.³⁷ In connection with this line of argument, the Ptolemaic gloss (VII, iii, 6) that *Thinai* "had neither walls of copper nor anything else worthy of mention" is not without interest. I suspect that Ptolemy, probably through the intermediacy of Marinos and the voyager Alexander, was here referring to a stratum of mythological notions that were manifested in the several Southeast Asian toponyms incorporating the element *tamra* (Sanskrit = copper), as well as in the themes of bronze (or copper) works (columns, boats, horses, etc.) associated with the name of Ma Yüan.³⁸ Moreover, Stein has pointed out that the possible founders of *Kattigara* had come from Chu-wu prefecture, whose inhabitants were reputed to live solely on fish — which in

this context almost certainly meant raw fish.³⁹ If the Great Gulf
was indeed the Gulf of Siam, it seems likely that both the
Fish-eating *Sinai* themselves (Ἰχθυοφάγοι Σίναι: VII, iii, 4) and the
Fish-eating Aethiopians (Ἰχθυοφάγοι Ἀιθίοπες: VII, iii, 1 and 3)
in *Sinai* territory which the Ptolemaic corpus places along the
eastern shore of the Great Gulf may have been in some way connected
with the fish eaters from Chu-wu.

Other restorations of Ptolemaic toponyms in East Asia are no
less conjectural than those already discussed. *Brammapolis*
(Βραμμαπολις: VII, iii, 15), in *Sinai* territory, might have been
connected with the *b⁽ⁱwɒm 邑 (*beiam*: see p. 395) component in the
styles of early Cam and Fu-nan rulers.⁴⁰ If *Tamara*, as suggested
above, is to be read as Sanskrit *Tāmra*, then the likelihood of a
Tāmrapura having existed in the vicinity of Bà Phnom (Note 59 to
Chap. 3) should not be overlooked. The designation Copper Country
may have reflected an awareness of the Phetchabun or Lopburi ores
but more probably, I think, was another expression of the
mythological complex mentioned in the previous paragraph.
Finally — so far as this style of interpretation is concerned — it
is possible that the *Dorias* river (Δορίας: VII, ii, 7 and 11) may
have incorporated the Sanskrit element *dvāra*, which figured on the
shores of the Gulf of Siam in early times in the name of the polity
of Dvāravatī, an honorific adopted after that of Kṛṣṇa's capital in
Gujarāt (Cf. Chap. 5).

An alternative way of interpreting the outline of the Golden
Chersonese has been to subsume within the Ptolemaic peninsula both
the Siamo-Malayan peninsula and the island of Sumatra.⁴¹ This
expedient has become considerably more attractive since Professor
Filliozat's identification of Cape *Maleoukolon* with Ujung Inderapura
(p. 445 above). Apart from *Iabadiou* (p. 444 above), the islands in
the Indian and Prasodic Seas have not been identified with any
degree of certainty. The skeptical may speculate with Pijnappel
and Yule that the name *Sabadibai* (Σαβαδίβαι: VII, ii, 28) is nothing
more than a doublet of *Iabadiou*, perhaps through the agency of Arabic-
speaking informants.⁴² Duplication is not uncommon in the Ptolemaic
text. Even in the Mediterranean, the island of Elba is recorded
twice, once under a Latin, and once under a Greek name. In India,
Ujjayinī appears first as *Ozêne* (Ὀζήνη) but later as *Ozoamis*
(Ὀζοαμίς). In Trans-Gangetic India, I think it is not unlikely
that *Mareoura Metropolis* (Μαρεούρα μητρόπολις: VII, ii, 24) was the
same place as *Bareuaora* (Βαρευάορα: VII, ii, 24), even though the
two names came to be assigned to different river valleys — and

although there are variant readings of the latter name that do not sustain the phonetic similarity. Into the three Satyr Islands (Σατύρων νῆσοι τρεῖs: VII, ii, 30) that are placed to the northeast of Java the imaginative may read a sailor's tale inspired by reports of the orang-utan (*Pongo pygmaeus*, Linn.), a species restricted, during historical time at any rate, to Kalimantan and Sumatra. The five *Barousai* (Βαροῦσαι: VII, ii, 28) islands, supposedly to the west of Java and southwest of the Golden Chersonese, sound very much as if they may have owed their name to Barus, a polity on the west coast of Sumatra which by the 7th century had become famous throughout East Asia for its camphor. But these exercises in toponymic identification, and others like them, amount to little more than idle speculation, entertaining enough but yielding little secure understanding.

Recently W. J. van der Meulen has proposed entirely new principles of interpretation of the Ptolemaic data relating to Trans-Gangetic India.[43] This author rejects the idea that even a distorted map can be, or ever has been, constructed from the Ptolemaic co-ordinates. What appear to be coastlines on the map, he contends, are really sailing routes "which could (and fairly often would) run parallel to a coast." He then asks,

> But since the sailors of those days were not bound to coastal shipping, what guarantee do we have that these places were always located along the same coast, that the sailing route did not cross from mainland to island, from island to island or from one mainland to another? What assures us that those who told about their voyages mentioned every crossing and that those who noted down the sequence of places and their distances paid due attention to taxonomic consistency? Thus, in particular, they could have mentioned an island and then places (on that island). Ptolemy, however, or more probably his source, would have lifted this island out of context and placed it with the others in a special "list of islands." Thus no trace of crossings would remain.

On this assumption, Van der Meulen reconstitutes the so-called Ptolemaic coastline as what he calls "the sailors' route" (or, on another occasion, "the Ptolemaean odyssey").[45] Starting from the Ganges delta, this route leads across the Bay of Bengal to a landfall on the coast of peninsular Thailand, and thence round the northwestern tip of Sumatra and along the whole length of the west coast to Sunda Strait. Thence the voyager supposedly worked his way "through a combination of channels through the marshland which runs from the mouth of the Masuji at the southern end to the mouth of the Komering at the northern."[46] Embarking on the sea again in the neighborhood of Jambi, he set sail for southern Indochina, before again crossing the South China Sea (according to Van der Meulen depicted as a river in the Ptolemaic text) to

Sarawak and Kalimantan, in the southwestern corner of which was
Kattigara. Van der Meulen points out that the geometrical figure
developed by the voyage as far as Indochina approximates to the
shape of the Golden Chersonese on the Ptolemaic map,[47] as indeed it
must if the supposed coastlines are really sailing routes.

The toponymic pattern that emerges from this reconstruction
negates virtually all the locational identifications of previous
investigators, even such seemingly secure ones as *Iabadiou, Katabêda*,
and *Maleoukolon* (although it does leave intact a few phonetic
correspondences, e.g., *Kirradía* < Kirāta; *Nangalogai* < Nagnaloka). But
the main objection to this reading of the text is its denial of the
existence of coastlines on the Ptolemaic map. That over much,
perhaps most, of his map Ptolemy relied primarily on sailing times
and itineraries converted to standard distances is not in dispute.
In fact, he admitted as much, while warning against the excesses
and hyperbole of some previous travelers (Note 4 above). But his
actual sources are all but unknown and there is no means of
discovering precisely what information was available to him,
exactly what form it took, or what cross-checking was possible.
That Ptolemy ignored the peninsular shape of India while listing
more than 400 of its toponyms surely argues against an exclusive
reliance on maritime logs in that part of Asia. Moreover, he seems
to have had access to more information than he recorded, as witness
his casual dismissal of a myth concerning the walls of *Thinai*
without a clear statement as to what the myth was about in the
first place (p. 448 above). There is simply no way of knowing what
sort of elaborative and explanatory information was combined with
the sailing directions that were relayed to Ptolemy (or to those
who may have augmented or amended his co-ordinates in subsequent
centuries) by Graeco-Roman or Indian travellers. Eggermont has
given reasons for believing that, for India at any rate, both Pliny
or Ptolemy availed themselves of "excerpts from an extensive Greek
text that showed Sanskrit words accompanied by their Greek
translations."[48] Whether or not such explicatory texts existed for
Trans-Gangetic India (where the purely Sanskrit component was
almost certainly less conspicuous), it is far from proven that
Ptolemy (and his redactors) consistently mistook sailing directions
for coastlines.

In support of his thesis, Van der Meulen relies on a second,
empirically derived principle, namely the prevalence of Sanskrit
original forms for the Ptolemaic toponymy, both as actual names and
as translations of, or calques on, indigenous terms.[49] But a very

high proportion of his restorations are, in my view, suspect. I can see no justification, for instance, for deriving Rhabana ('Ράβανα) from a postulated but unattested (and unlikely) *Rāj Bnaṃ, or even from the often postulated Kuruṅ Bnaṃ (p. 147 above); Bêsynga (p. 446) from Bahih Siṃhala (in the sense of Outer Ceylon); Sindai (Σίνδαι) from siddha ("the blessed spirits who have 'arrived' and have been admitted amongst the semi-deities"); Perimoula (Περιμουλα) from prī/priya (= delighting in, beloved) + mula (= root); Lêistai (Λησταί) from leśtas (which "portrays exactly the furtive ways of these people and the fleeting glimpses the voyagers sometimes had of these silent barterers"); Kortata/Kordathra etc. (Κορτατα/Κορδάθρα) from Kra (place-name) + Sanskrit tata (= spread out, extended) = Malay bambang → P'an-p'an = Chinese transcription (cf. p. 234 above); Pagrasa (Παγράσα) < bhāga (= country) + rasa (plant essence) = Malay Tanah Sari = Tenasserim; Korandakaloi (Κορανδάκαλοι) < karaṇḍa (= basket), perhaps "'basket rogues' who . . . cheated (karaṇḍakhala), or simply . . . basket makers (karaṇḍakara);" Tougma (Τούγμα) < tūru-gmā (= rich earth, "an acceptable substitute for Śrīkshetra"); Attabas (Αττάβας) < āttāmbhas (= without water) = Malay kering or, with infix -um-, Kumering: hence the Kumering river which "has indeed 'periodic' spells of dryness;" or Thêriôdês (Θηριώδης) = abounding in game < tiryagja = Malay binatang (= animal): hence Binatang, near the Rajang estuary. Fanciful, and sometimes fantastic, as these alleged correspondences are, only occasionally is it possible to suggest a convincing alternative. One such instance, though, is Maleoukolon, which is almost certainly a transcription of a Tamil phrase (p. 445 above) rather than, as Van der Meulen suggests, a compound of Malayu + kulya = channel, signifying "the channel that conveyed the voyagers directly to Malayu." With the style of argument illustrated above goes the assumption that the Ptolemaic sources "remained true to certain literary standards and conventions, such as the use of synonyms (including Sanskrit synonyms for Malay names), artificial word explanations, allusions and maybe even the omitted syllable game . . ."[50] However, in Trans-Gangetic India and the Sinai territories, on only three occasions is a Greek translation explicitly offered in explanation of a Sanskrit name: Nangalogai is defined as "realm of naked men" and Aginnatai as "those who constantly go naked" (p. 444 above), while Iabadiou is translated specifically as "Barley Isle" (p. 444). These annotations are valuable clues to the recognition of two Sanskrit phrases and a Prākrit, but I do not find the extension of this principle in, for example, the following derivation of Mareoura

(Μαρεοΰρα) at all convincing.
> The most likely derivation of the name seems to be maryâvara.
> Since maryâ means landmark, boundary, but also moral law and vara
> means best, very, this name could well be a synonymous substitute
> (fairly common in Indian literary usage) for the surname of the old
> Mon capital Thatön, that is, Sudhammavatī.[51]

And Van der Meulen's two papers comprise a tissue of such arguments on a scale not seen since the publication of Colonel Gerini's massive *Researches on Ptolemy's Geography of Eastern Asia* more than seventy years ago. George Coedès's characterization of that earlier work when it first appeared would seem equally applicable to Van der Meulen's reconstruction: "trop ingénieux pour être toujours convaincant."

The aim of this excursus has not been to attempt yet another reconstruction of the Ptolemaic geography of Southeast Asia but rather to evaluate its potential contribution to an understanding of the settlement pattern in the proto- and early-historic periods. An exigent problem is, of course, the reliable identification of place-names, and we have seen that that desideratum is still far from achieved. Yet the record of some thirty urban-style settlements, together with trading marts and capital cities, must carry important implications even if most of the names cannot be restored nor their locations identified. At their face value, the several classes of cities listed in the *Geographia* would seem to imply a particular level of sociocultural integration stated in terms of the Graeco-Roman experience. But it must be remembered that the specific urban categories employed in the *Geographia* to order settlement data were essentially Western classical constructs imposed on the evidence by Ptolemy or his successors, or by the original informants themselves (whoever they may have been). There is no guarantee that these Mediterranean urban types were precisely replicated in Southeast Asia, so that somewhere in the transmission process Asian categories were almost certainly transposed into those familiar to Western cartographers. The success and consistency with which this was achieved cannot be estimated until the Ptolemaic urban hierarchy has been much more fully elucidated than is at present possible and its components subjected to rigorous comparison with those of the Mediterranean world. For the present, all that can be stated with certainty is that, in the *Geographia* as it has been transmitted to us, *poleis* are distributed fairly evenly throughout the main landmass of Trans-Gangetic India (which may have included Sumatra); that they are relatively more common in Trans-Gangetic India than in the territories of the *Sinai*, and are completely unrepresented in the southern islands; that only one *metropolis* is situated to the west of the Golden Chersonese (wherever that may have been), three to the east, and one in the southern archipelago; and that five of the six *emporia* are to the west of or in the Golden Chersonese, with only one to the east. Curiously, only one *basileion* is listed for the whole region, and that is situated in what is almost certainly present-day Burma. But it cannot be emphasized too strongly that this is a summary of the Ptolemaic information, not of an actual situation at a particular time in the past.

The Ptolemaic toponymy is also pregnant with implications for the nature and chronology of the so-called Indianization process, and therefore bears indirectly on the progress of urbanization and state formation in Southeast Asia. Some names (although far fewer than Van der Meulen postulates) can at present be ascribed Indian (Sanskrit, Prākrit, Tamil) origins, and others will doubtless be elicited in the future. But this leaves unanswered the question as to who coined or transmitted the names. Were they adopted by indigenous folk under Indian influence, or imposed by Indians resident in or passing through Southeast Asia (*Maleoukolon* might have been such a one), or were they modeled on local toponyms and ethnonyms by Sanskrit scholars or Prākrit-speaking informants (*Nangalogai* could have been an example)? And, of all three types (if, in fact, all three are represented in the Ptolemaic toponymy), what proportions were, respectively, descriptive appellations, translations, and calques?

Underlying all these lines of inquiry is the even more fundamental question of the extent to which the *Geographia* is a cumulative text. It would be of fundamental importance to establish that, say, a Sanskrit or Tamil name was currently in use by one or another ethnic group, whether transient or resident, when Ptolemy compiled the core of the *Geographia* in the 2nd century A.D. *Kattigara* comes close to that desideratum if we accept the mention of the name in a Chinese source relating to the 3rd century. And so do names such as *Takola* and *Bêsynga*, which seem to be mentioned in the *Mahāniddesa*. If the name Malaikkāl (*Maleoukolon*) was indeed connected with the Mount *Maleus* mentioned by Pliny, then it was probably in use a century or so before Ptolemy lived, while Professor Wolters has declared his confidence that, "the Chinese evidence of the early third century [relating to present-day Indonesia] is consistent with Ptolemaic evidence."[52] But the antiquity of only a handful of names has so far been adequately demonstrated by cross-references to other early sources. Other books of the *Geographia* which are better elucidated than Book VII have been shown to include material that could not have been known in Ptolemy's time, and it would surely be imprudent to reject the likelihood that some later data may also have been incorporated in those sections dealing with one of the least known parts of the Ptolemaic world. At the present time there is no reason to disregard Leo Bagrow's warning of nearly forty years ago: "If 'Ptolemy's' data are the only source for us, we cannot merely on their basis determine the time or the questions of migrations of peoples, the existence of cities, et cetera."[53]

456 Nāgara and Commandery

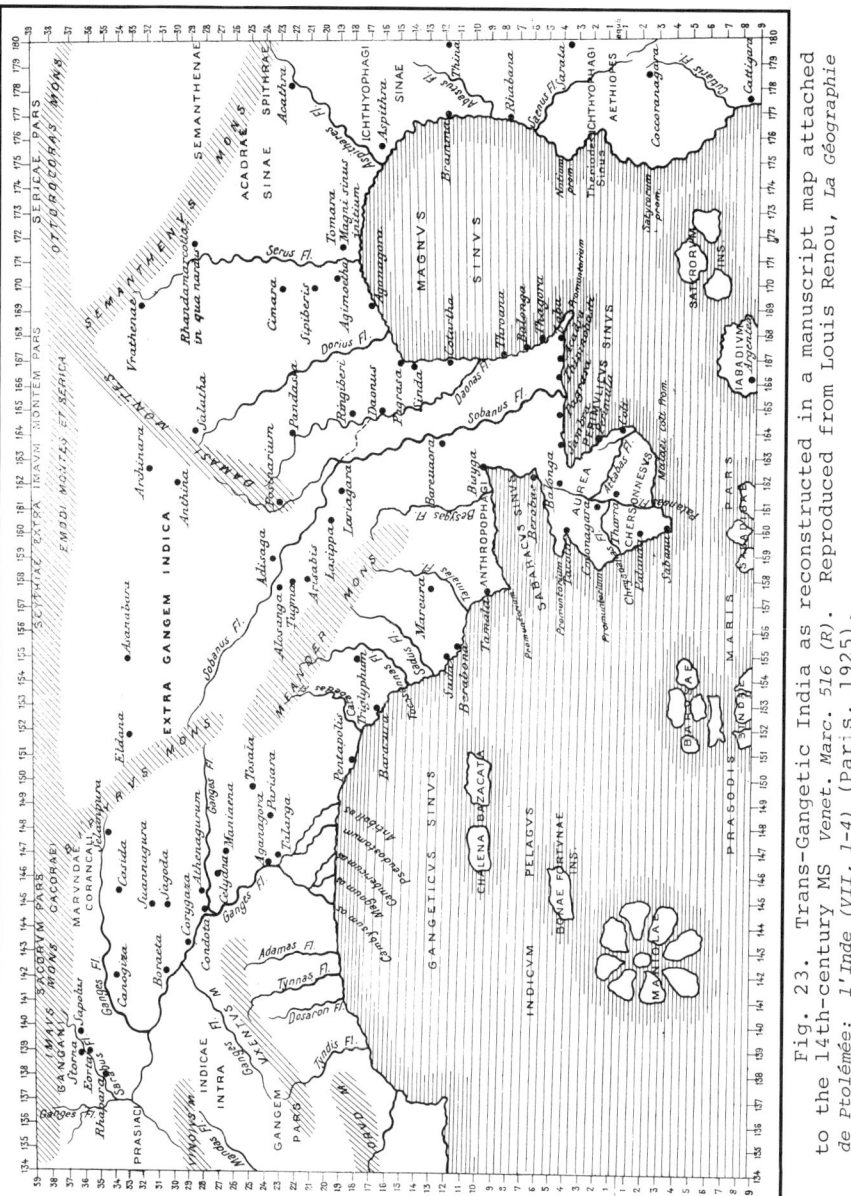

Fig. 23. Trans-Gangetic India as reconstructed in a manuscript map attached to the 14th-century MS Venet. Marc. 516 (R). Reproduced from Louis Renou, *La Géographie de Ptolémée: l'Inde (VII, 1-4)* (Paris, 1925).

Notes and References

1. I have tried to render this turgid and involved passage into easily intelligible English. A more literal translation may be consulted in E. H. Bunbury, *A history of ancient geography*, vol. 2 (London, 1879), pp. 554-555.

2. The Olympic *stadium* was equivalent to 600 Greek, or 606-3/4 English, feet. Thus 10 *stadia* would have been approximately equivalent to one nautical mile.

3. E.g., G. E. Gerini, *Researches on Ptolemy's geography of Eastern Asia* (London, 1909); T. G. Rylands, *The Geography of Ptolemy elucidated* (Dublin, 1893), pp. 36-80; André Berthelot, *L'Asie ancienne centrale et sud-orientale d'après Ptolémée* (Paris, 1930).

4. Ptolemy admitted as much in Book I, iii, 5 when he noted that, although his map ought to have been based on astronomically fixed positions, there were so few of these that it inevitably became necessary to estimate locations from travel reports. He cautioned, though, that the cartographer should make more allowances than had his predecessor, Marinos of Tyre, for the exaggerations and general unreliability of travelers' estimates.

5. Joseph Fischer, *Claudii Ptolemaei Geographiae Codex Urbinas Graecus 82* (Leiden, 1932). Father Fischer believed that the maps prepared by Ptolemy had subsequently become separated from the text and had undergone a degree of modification before being reunited with the text.

6. Altogether there are more than forty MSS. of the *Geographia* surviving in whole or part. A Latin translation, accompanied by maps, was printed for the first time in 1475: *Claudii Ptolem. Cosmographiae* [sic] *Libri primi capita* (f. 60 recto, col. ii) (Bononia). Misdated as 1462. This was followed by numerous other editions during the latter part of the fifteenth and early sixteenth centuries. In 1533 the Greek text was edited by Erasmus: Κλαυδιος Πτολεμαῖον Ἀλεξανδρεως φιλοσοφον . . . (Basileae) and in 1618 P. Bertius published both the Greek and Latin texts: *Theatrum Geographiae Veteris* (Leiden). All these early editions abound in textual errors, and the first attempt at a critical edition was that by F. G. Wilberg and C. H. F. Grashof: *Claudii Ptolemaei geographiae libri octo* (Essen, 1838-45), who completed only the first six books. C. F. A. Nobbe's edition (*Claudii Ptolemaei Geographia*, Leipzig, 1843-45) was complete but his readings were not annotated and often selected promiscuously from aberrant texts. C. Müller's great edition ended with Book V (*Claudii Ptolemaei Geographia*, 1883) in A. F. Didot's *Bibliothecum Graecorum Scriptorum*, but was continued to Book VIII by J. Fischer, S. J. (1901). The year 1932 saw the publication of Fischer's *Claudii Ptolemaei Geographiae Codex Urbinas Graecus 82* (Leiden), a sumptuous reproduction of an indifferent MS., and also of a poor English translation by E. L. Stevenson: *The Geography of Claudius Ptolemy* (New York); and in 1938 H. von Mžik translated Book II into German: "Des Klaudios Ptolemaios Einführung in die darstellende Erdkunde," *Klotho*, Band 5, Teil 1.

During the early years of this century, in the English-speaking world the writings of E. H. Bunbury were still authoritative on matters Ptolemaic, and even today the lucidity of this author's style is unsurpassed. A summary of his views appears in *A history of ancient geography*, vol. 2 (London, 1879), pp. 546-644. On the European continent Father Joseph Fischer held undisputed sway as the doyen of Ptolemaic scholars; the following are typical of his numerous papers: "Die Handschriftliche Überlieferung der Ptolemäus-Karten," *Verhandlungen des achtzehnten Deutschen Geographentages zu Innsbruck* (Berlin, 1912), pp. 224-30; "An important Ptolemy manuscript in the New York Public Library," *United States Catholic Historical Society; Historical Records and Studies*, vol. 6, pt. 2 (New York, 1913), pp. 216-34; and "Ptolemäus und Agathodämon', *Kaiserliche Akademie der Wissenschaften in Wien, Denkschriften,* philosophisch-historische Klasse, Bd. 59, Abhandl. 4 (1916), pp. 71-93. During the same period Albert Herrmann, Professor of Historical Geography at Berlin, was producing a spate of papers, such as "Marinus, Ptolemäus und ihre Karten," Zeitschrift der Gesellschaft für Erdkunde zu Berlin (1914), pp. 780-7; "Die Seidenstrassen von China nach dem Römischen Reich," Mitteilungen der Geographischen Gesellschaft in Wien, Bd. 63 (1915), pp. 472-500; "Marinus von Tyrus," Petermanns geographische Mitteilungen, Ergänzungsheft 209 (1930), pp. 45-54.

From the second decade of this century there appeared occasionally papers which, although they attracted little attention at the time, are now seen to have been pioneers of the modern approach to Ptolemaic studies. Such, for example, are those of L. O. Th. Tudeer, "On the origin of the maps attached to Ptolemy's Geography," Journal of Hellenic Studies, vol. 37 (London, 1917), pp. 62-76; and "Studies in the Geography of Ptolemy: I, the Scholia of Nicephorus Gregoras," Annales Academiae Scientiarum Fennicae, Ser. B. T. 21, No. 4 (1927); and of B. Dinse, "Die handschriftlichen Ptolemäus-Karten und die Agathodämonfrage," Zeitschrift der Gesellschaft für Erdkunde zu Berlin (1913), pp. 745-70. Later came two papers by W. Kubitschek, "Die sogenannte B-Redaktion der ptolemäischen Geographie," Klio, Bd. 28 (Göttingen, 1935), pp. 108-32, and "Studien zur Geographie des Ptolemäus: I, Die Ländergrenzen," Akademie der Wissenschaften in Wien, philosophisch-historische Klasse: Sitzungsberichte, Bd. 215, Abt. 5 (1935). In 1930 P. Schnabel published his "Die Entstehungsgeschichte des kartographischen Erdbildes des Klaudios Ptolemaios, Sitzungsberichte der Preussischen Akademie der Wissenschaften, philosophisch-historische Klasse, Bd. 14 (1930), and eight years later his Text und Karten des Ptolemäus (Leipzig, 1938), in both of which he sought, by a comparison of the different manuscripts, to establish the connexion between the Ptolemaic maps and the history of the text of the Geographia. In the same period H. von Mžik was also investigating this topic: "Neue Gesichtspunkte zur Würdigung der 'Geographie' des Klaudios Ptolemaios für die Orientalistik mit den einleitenden Abschnitten der 'Weltschau' des (Pseudo-) Moses Xorenaçi in deutscher Übersetzung," Litterae Orientales, Heft 54 (Leipzig, 1933), pp. 1-16.

Finally, this important period in the development of Ptolemaic scholarship was brought to a virtual close in 1945 with Leo Bagrow's "The origin of Ptolemy's Geographia," Geografiska Annaler, Årg. 27, Häft 3-4 (1945), pp. 318-87, though the ideas which found their final expression in that paper had been adumbrated in two short articles in the 1930's: a review of J. Fischer, De Cl. Ptolemaei vita operibus Geographia praesentim eiusque fatis in Imago Mundi, vol. 1 (1935), pp. 76-7, and "Entstehung der 'Geographie' der C. Ptolemaeus," Comptes Rendus du Congrès International de Géographie, Amsterdam, 1938, vol. 1 (1938), pp. 380-7. There is a summary of Bagrow's conclusions in his History of cartography. Revised and enlarged by R. A. Skelton (London, 1964), pp. 34-37.

7. Bagrow suggests that this list may have been drawn up for the benefit of students of astronomy who were using Ptolemy's manual called the Syntaxis (History of cartography, p. 35).

8. Louis Renou, La Géographie de Ptolémée: l'Inde (VII, 1-4) (Paris, 1925); Otto Cuntz, Die Geographie des Ptolemaeus, Galliae, Germania, Raetia, Noricum, Pannoniae, Illyricum, Italia (Berlin, 1923). In what follows, I have not always adopted Renou's readings.

9. This figure must remain inexact because some poleis listed, correctly enough, in Trans-Gangetic India appear to have been situated in the Ganges or Brahmaputra valleys [e.g., Sapolos (Σάπολος), Storna (Στόρνα), Kōrygaza (Κωρυγάζα), Aganagara (᾽Αγαναγάρα), etc.] and others farther east may also have been outside the bounds of present-day Southeast Asia.

10. It goes without saying that the classical conception of the polis as an autonomous city-state on the pattern of 5th-century Athens had long been superseded by that of the city as an instrument of local government within an all-encompassing empire. The most comprehensive discussion of this transformation is still that by A. H. M. Jones, The Greek city from Alexander to

Justinian (Oxford, 1940), but a shorter account is incorporated in Mason Hammond, *The city in the ancient world* (Cambridge, Mass., 1972), chaps. XIX and XX.

11. E. H. Warmington, *The commerce between the Roman Empire and India* (Cambridge, 1928), p. 50.

12. George Coedès, *Les états hindouisés d'Indochine et d'Indonésie* (Third edition, Paris, 1964), p. 43.

13. Sylvain Lévi, "Ptolémée, le Niddesa et la Bṛhatkathā," in G. Van Oest (ed.), *Etudes Asiatiques publiées à l'occasion du vingt-cinquième anniversaire de l'Ecole Française d'Extrême-Orient* (Paris, 1925), vol. 2, pp. 1-55 and 431-432; Wheatley, "Takola emporion," *The Malayan Journal of Tropical Geography*, vol. 2 (1954), pp. 35-47; Dhanit Yupho, "Takola," *Silpākọn*, vol. 11, no. 4 (1967), pp. 36-43.

14. George Coedès, *Textes d'auteurs grecs et latins relatifs à l'Extrême-Orient depuis le IVe siècle av. J.-C. jusqu'au XIVe siècle* (Paris, 1910), p. 177 sub Nangalogai.

15. Cf. O. W. Wolters on Śaivite ascetics in the lower Mekong valley in Pre-Aṅkor times in "Khmer 'Hinduism' in the seventh century," in R. B. Smith and W. Watson (eds.), *Early South East Asia* (New York and Kuala Lumpur), pp. 431-433.

16. W. J. van der Meulen, "Suvarnadvīpa and the Chrysē Chersonēsos," *Indonesia*, no. 18 (1974), pp. 17 and 29. A city named *Kanakapurī* is assigned to Dvīpāntara (p. 257 above) in the *Kathāsaritsāgara*: Sylvain Lévi, "K'ouen Louen et Dvīpāntara," *Bijdragen tot de Taal-, Land-, en Volkenkunde van Nederlandsch-Indië*, vol. 88 (1931), p. 623.

17. Sir R.[ichard] O. Winstedt (ed.), "The Malay Annals or Sejarah Melayu," *Journal of the Malaysian Branch of the Royal Asiatic Society*, vol. 16, pt. 3 (1938), p. 48 [Rumi transcription]; C. C. Brown, "Sĕjarah Mĕlayu or 'Malay Annals'," *loc. cit.*, vol. 25, pts. 2 and 3 (1952), p. 18 [English translation].

18. *Naturalis Historia*, VI, xxii, 6.

19. Jean Filliozat, "Pline et le Malaya," *Journal Asiatique*, vol. 262 (1974), pp. 119-130.

20. Gerini, *Researches on Ptolemy's geography of eastern Asia*, *passim*.

21. Berthelot, *L'Asie ancienne centrale et sud-orientale*, pp. 372-417.

22. Wheatley, *The Golden Khersonese. Studies in the historical geography of the Malay Peninsula before A.D. 1500* (Kuala Lumpur, 1961), *passim*.

23. Cp. the *Kirradai* (Κιρράδαι) mentioned in the *Periplus of the Erythraean Sea*, transl. by G. W. B. Huntingford, Hakluyt Society, Second Series, no. 151 (London, 1980), p. 55. The first scholars to make this identification were probably Sir Henry Yule and A. C. Burnell, *Hobson-Jobson. A glossary of colloquial Anglo-Indian words and phrases. . .* , new edition by William Crooke (London, 1903), p. 203. It is not without implications for the sources on which the *Geographia* was based that the people known as *Kirāta* (as opposed to their territory) are listed in VII, ii, 15 under a corrupted version of the Pāli form of their ethnonym: *Piladai* (Πιλάδαι) *et var.*, *Tiladai* (Τιλάδαι) *et var.*, both for *Kiladai* (Κιλάδαι) < *Kilāta* [See J. Ph. Vogel, "Ptolemy's topography of India: his sources," *Archaeologica Orientalia in memoriam Ernst Herzfeld* (New York, 1952), p. 234, note 14; P. H. L. Eggermont, "The Murundas and the ancient trade-route from Taxila to Ujjain," *Journal of the Economic and Social History of the Orient*, vol. 9 (1966), pp. 280-281]. For the Kirāta in Indian literature see Beni Madhab Barua, *Aśoka and his inscriptions*, second edition (Calcutta, 1955), p. 100, and Bimala Churn Law, *Historical geography of ancient India* (Paris, 1954), p. 98.

24. Lévi, "Ptolémée, le Niddesa et la Bṛhatkathā," p. 22

25. E. H. Johnson, "Some Sanskrit inscriptions of Arakan," *Bulletin of the School of Oriental and African Studies*, vol. 11 (1943-46), pp. 369-370.

26. *Ch'ien-Han Shu*, chüan 28, pt. 2, f. 32 recto et verso. For this interpretation of the text see Victor A. Velgus, "Some problems of the history of navigation in the Indian and Pacific Oceans," in Yu V. Maretin and B. A. Valskaya (eds.), *The countries and peoples of the East* (Moscow, 1974), pp. 50-63.

27. *T'ai-p'ing Yü-lan*, chüan 788, f. 6 r et v, citing *Sui Shu*.

28. Gerini [*Researches*, pp. 77, 729 and 750] went so far as to derive the name from [Old] Mōn *Bī-ching/sing* = Elephant river, i.e., the Irawadi.
It is also tempting to speculate on a possible relationship between Ptolemaic *Pentapolis* (Πεντάπολις: VII, ii, 5), presumably some sort of league or federation of five cities, and the Mōn "Kingdom of the Five Cities" (Proto-Mōn = *Puṅ Sun*) that was absorbed into the Fu-nan polity during the 3rd century A.D., although the Ptolemaic context does not imply a location at all close to that suggested on p. 213 above.

29. C. Lassen, *Indische Alterthumskunde*, vol. 3 (Leipzig, 1858); Sir Henry Yule, "Map of ancient India from classical sources," in W. Smith, *An atlas of ancient geography, Biblical and classical* (London, 1874); J. W. McCrindle, *Ancient India as described by Ptolemy* (London, 1885); St. A. St. John, "Takkola," *Actes du Onzième Congrès International des Orientalistes* (Paris, 1897), pp. 217-233; V. Kanakasabhai, "The conquest of Bengal and Burma by the Tamils," *Madras Review* (1902).

30. J. I. H. Frisk, "Le Périple de la Mer Erythrée," *Göteborgs Högskolas Årsskrift*, vol. 33 (1927), p. 126. For comments on the declension of *Thina* or *Thin*, which in the *Periplus* occurs only in the accusative and genitive cases, see note 65 to chap. 7.

31. I am here following Paul Pelliot in deriving the Greek forms from Irānian *Čīn* rather than from the customarily postulated Sanskrit *Cīna*: *Notes on Marco Polo*, vol. 1 (Paris, 1959), p. 267.

32. George Coedès, Review of *The Golden Khersonese* in *T'oung Pao*, vol. 49 (1962), pp. 433-439.

33. For the minutiae of this interpretation and its toponymic identifications see Louis Malleret, *L'archéologie du delta du Mékong*, vol. 3: *La culture du Fou-nan* (Paris, 1962), chap. 25.

34. R. A. Stein, "Le Lin-yi," *Han-Hiue*, vol. 2 (1947), pp. 108-123; also Wheatley, *Golden Khersonese*, pp. 21-22, and note 131 to chap. 8. The name *Kattigara* is still something of a mystery. *K'įuət-tuo* may have transcribed Sanskrit *kūṭa* = mountain, although *k'įuət* alone sufficed in *G'ji-tuo-k'įuət* 耆 闍 崛, a Chinese rendering of *Gṛdhrakūṭa* cited by Stein ("Le Lin-yi," p. 123); *-gara* may represent simply Sanskrit *gara* = locality, or perhaps *gṛha* = house; *-n* was a regular Chinese transcription of *-r* in foreign names, e.g., An-hsi < Arsak, Ta-tan < Tatar, Huan-ch'ien < Khwārizm, etc. Other examples are cited by Stein, p. 112, note 90. For reasons why this interpretation of the name is preferable to that of Otto Franke [*Geschichte des Chinesischen Reiches*, vol. 3 (Berlin-Leipzig, 1937), pp. 212-214], who proposed an original *kastināgara* = tin city, see Malleret, *La culture du Fou-nan*, p. 440.

35. A location for the *Sinai* in Indochina does not fit well with the statement in the *Geographia* (I, xvii, 4) that, from the capital of the *Sinai*, one route led into Bactria by way of the Stone Tower and another down into the Ganges valley at Pāṭaliputra. However, the text allows that this information may relate not to the capital of the *Sinai* but to that of the *Sēres*, in which case the description of the uncharted terrain presumably does likewise. It is a case of swings and roundabouts. Ptolemy committed a series of gross errors in his depiction of East Asia and it is unlikely that any single consistent system of explanation will account for all his aberrations.

36. Stein, "Le Lin-yi," p. 120.

37. Malleret, *La culture du Fou-nan*, chap. 25. My own feeling is that Malleret attributed too high a degree of precision to the Ptolemaic evidence, but this is not to deny the persuasiveness of a location for *Kattigara* in southern Indochina.
   The earlier scholars in this field tended to assign *Kattigara* to some part of China: e.g., Pijnappel, "Ptolemaeus en de Indische Archipel," *Bijdragen tot de Taal-, Land- en Volkenkunde van Nederlandsch-Indië*, vol. 3 (1870), pp. 36-68; H. Kiepert, *Lehrbuch der alten Geographie* (Berlin, 1878), p. 44; Gerini, *Researches*, p. 302; Berthelot, *L'Asie ancienne*, p. 414. Bunbury, somewhat surprisingly, was prepared to locate the *Sinai*, and by implication *Kattigara*, in present-day Kampuchea or Cochin China [*A history of ancient geography*, vol. 2, pp. 606-607], while Paul Pelliot ["Note sur les anciens itinéraires chinois dans l'Orient romain," *Journal Asiatique*, 11th series, vol. 17 (1921), p. 141; *Notes on Marco Polo*, vol. 1 (Paris, 1959), p. 234, and other papers] was inclined to derive *Kattigara* from *$K\breve{o}g\text{-}\hat{t}\underset{\sim}{i}\partial g$ (cf. note 7 to chap. 8) and consequently to place the port in Tong-King. The first author to propose a location in southern Indochina was Albert Herrmann [*Das Land der Seide und Tibet im Lichte der Antike*. Quellen und Forschungen zur Geschichte der Geographie und Völkerkunde, vol. 1 (Leipzig, 1939), p. 80; "Der Magnus Sinus und Cattigara nach Ptolemaeus," *Comptes Rendus du Congrès International de Géographie, Amsterdam, 1938*, vol. 2 (1938), pp. 123-128. In his previously published *Historical and commercial atlas of China* (Cambridge, Mass., 1935), pp. 20, 22, and 27, Herrmann had followed Pelliot in locating *Kattigara* in Tong-King]. Subsequently Paul Levy, in a mostly unpublished study ["Le Kattigara de Ptolémée et les étapes d'Agastya, le héros de l'expansion hindoue en Extrême-Orient," *The Twenty-first Congress of Orientalists* (Paris, 1948), p. 223: cf. also Stein, "Le Lin-yi," pp. 1, 122, and 318], Stein, and Malleret arrived at similar conclusions.

38. Stein, "Le Lin-yi," appendix IV.

39. Fish as a dietary staple was, and is, so common among coastal peoples of Southeast Asia that it would hardly have merited special comment. The information about the fish-eaters of Chu-wu is derived from *Hsüan-chung Chi* 玄中記, by an otherwise unknown member of the Kuo 郭 family (probably Chin dynasty), as preserved in *T'ai-p'ing Yü-lan*. See Stein, "Le Lin-yi," pp. 63-64 and 123.

40. Stein, "Le Lin-yi," pp. 223ff. According to the *Shuo Wen* 說文, in the 1st century A.D. *Brāhm* or *Brāhma* was transcribed by the graph 梵 (*$b^{\zeta}\underset{\sim}{i}wpm$).

41. E.g., W. Volz, "Südost-Asien bei Ptolemäus," *Geographische Zeitschrift*, vol. 17 (1911), pp. 31-44. An interesting variation on this reading,which was quite common in earlier times was presented by Manuel Godinho de Eredia at the turn of the 17th century. Although he spent most of his life in Melaka, Eredia was introduced to the Classical writings of the West during a Jesuit education in Goa. The chief interest of his reconstruction lies in his interpretation of the Ptolemaic isthmus as a land-bridge linking Cape Rachado on the Malaysian side of Melaka Strait with Pulau Rupat on the Sumatran side. See his *Declaraçam de Malaca e India Meridional com o Cathay* (1613), chap. 22 and *Informação da Aurea Chersoneso* (1597-1600), both translated and annotated by J. V. Mills, "Eredia's Description of Malacca, Meridional India, and Cathay," *Journal of the Malayan Branch of the Royal Asiatic Society*, vol. 8, pt. 1 (1930), pp. 1-288.
   Another possibility, raised by Filliozat's identification of Cape *Maleoukolon*, is that the so-called Golden Peninsula was in fact the island of Sumatra, while the Sabarac and Perimulic Gulfs (Κόλπος Σάβαρακὸς: VII, ii, 4; Περιμουλικὸς Κόλπος: VII, ii, 5) were respectively the northwestern and southeastern entrances to the Strait of Melaka. The Siamo-Malayan peninsula would then be the tract of land projecting southeastwards on the Ptolemaic map toward the promontory between *Zaba* and *Thagora* (VII, ii, 7). This interpretation obviously implies that for some reason or other some voyagers — at least those known to Ptolemy's informants — were not using Melaka Strait. That Tamil mariners were, in fact, sailing along the west coast of Sumatra is evident from Filliozat's researches.

42. Pijnappel, "Ptolemaeus en Indische Archipel," p. 48; Sir Henry Yule, "Notes on the oldest records of the sea route to China from western Asia," *Proceedings of the Royal Geographical Society* (1882), p. 649.

For Arabic *dīb* < Sanskrit *dvīpa* or Pāli *dīpa*, cp. *Sūwarndīb* سُورن د يب *Suvarṇadvīpa*: e.g., al-Bīrūnī, *Kitāb Abī al-Rīḥān Muḥammad bin Aḥmad al-Bīrūnī* (c. 1030). Edited with English transl. by Eduard Sachau, *Alberuni's India* (London, 1887), p. 201.

43. W. J. van der Meulen, "Suvarṇadvīpa and the Chrysê Chersonêsos," *Indonesia*, no. 18 (1974), pp. 1-40, and "Ptolemy's geography of mainland Southeast Asia and Borneo," *idem, no. 19 (1975), pp. 1-32*.

44. Van der Meulen, "Suvarṇadvīpa," p. 5.

45. Van der Meulen, "Suvarṇadvīpa," pp. 27 and 19.

46. Van der Meulen, "Suvarṇadvīpa," p. 31.

47. Van der Meulen, "Suvarṇadvīpa," pp. 26-27.

48. Eggermont, "The Murundas," p. 277.

49. Van der Meulen, "Suvarṇadvīpa," pp. 16-22.

50. Van der Meulen, "Ptolemy's geography," p. 31.

51. Van der Meulen, "Ptolemy's geography," p. 29.

52. O. W. Wolters, *Early Indonesian commerce: a study of the origins of Śrīvijaya* (Ithaca, N.Y., 1967), p. 57. Cf. also Van der Meulen, "Suvarṇadvīpa," p. 18.

53. Leo Bagrow, "The origin of Ptolemy's *Geographia*," *Geografiska Annaler*, vol. 27, pts. 3-4 (1945), pp. 318-87.

ADDENDA

Pages 50 and 52. —— During the last fifteen years or so, published discussion of the data from Northeast Thailand by scholars not directly involved in the excavations has been sporadic, most presumably awaiting the publication of final site reports before venturing an opinion. However, the voice of the skeptic has been heard from time to time, notably in W. Marschall, "On the Stone Age of Indonesia," *Tribus,* vol. 23 (1974), pp. 71-90 and H. H. E. Loofs-Wissowa, "Thermoluminescence dates from Thailand: comments," *Antiquity,* vol. 48 (1974), pp. 58-62. While this monograph has been in press the validity of what have been called the "long dates" as opposed to the "short dates" has been debated at some length in the pages of the *Journal of Southeast Asian Studies,* vol. 14, no. 1 (1983): Loofs-Wissowa, "The development and spread of metallurgy in Southeast Asia: a review of the present evidence," pp. 1-11; with rejoinders by Donn Bayard and Pisit Charoenwongsa and by Wilhelm G. Solheim II, pp. 12-25; and a surrejoinder by Loofs-Wissowa, pp. 26-31. Moreover, Charles [F.W.] Higham and Amphan Kijngam have recently interpreted radiocarbon evidence from the Khorat site of Ban Nadi as implying that the dates hitherto proposed for bronze-working at Ban Chiang (and probably also at Non Nok Tha) should be revised to 2000-1750 B.C. and for the appearance of iron to c.400-200 B.C. ["Irregular earthworks in N.E. Thailand: new insight," *Antiquity,* vol. 56 (1982), p. 103, note]. When expert opinion is so divided, the layman can only wait for time to settle the dispute.

Page 117, Note 196. —— Add: H. H. E. Loofs-Wissowa, "Report on an archaeological jouney to the Socialist Republic of Vietnam," *Bulletin of the Indo-Pacific Prehistory Association,* vol. 2 (1980), pp. 31-39.

Pages 141-145. —— A third view of the nature of the Fu-nan polity is implicit in a recent study by Kenneth R. Hall, "The 'Indianization' of Funan: an economic history of Southeast Asia's first state," *Journal of Southeast Asian Studies,* vol. 13, no. 1 (1982), pp. 81-106.

Page 252, Note 24. —— Since this note was written, Dr. Janice Stargardt has published a detailed account of certain aspects of her archeological researches in South Thailand: *Satingpra I: The environmental and economic archaeology of South Thailand.* Institue of Southeast Asian Studies, Studies in Southeast Asian Archaeology No. 1 (Singapore, 1983).

Page 259, Note 70. —— To the references listed in this note, add: J. G. de Casparis, "Some notes on the epigraphic heritage of Srivijaya," *SPAFA [SEAMEO Project in Archaeology and Fine Arts] Digest,* vol. 3, no. 2 (1982), pp. 29-34 and Boechari, "On the date of the inscription of Ligor B," *loc. cit.,* pp. 35-36.

Page 265. —— In a recent paper Professor H. B. Sarkar has sought to demonstrate that the *Niddesa* was in existence as early as the middle of the 3rd century B.C. If this claim is substantiated and if the Southeast Asian toponyms incorporated in the text were indeed familiar to certain Indian communities at that time, these conclusions would have important implications for the beginnings of cultural exchange between India and Southeast Asia. See "A geographical introduction to South-East Asia: the Indian perspective," *Bijdragen tot de Taal-, Land- en Volkenkunde,* vol. 137, nos. 2-3 (1981), pp. 297-302.

Page 293. —— In a book published while the present work was in press, Professor Wolters has confirmed my inference by explicitly categorizing his "men of prowess" as the "big men" of anthropological literature: *History, culture, and region in Southeast Asian perspectives* (Singapore, 1982), pp. 5-6.

Page 341, Note 89. —— To the studies of coastal morphology listed in this note, add: Pierre-Yves Manguin, "Sumatran coastline in the Straits of Bangka: new evidence for its permanence in historical times," *SPAFA Digest,* vol. 3, no. 2 (1982), pp. 24-28.

Pages 349-350, Note 165. —— A somewhat different view of the implications of Khmer kinship is propounded by Professor O. W. Wolters in *History, culture, and region in Southeast Asian perspectives* (Singapore, 1982), chap. 1.

General Index

Matter in the *Notes and References* is indexed only when it adds substantially to information in the main text.

Agriculture: origins of 50, 52; in the northern highlands 67; in Tong-King 67-71; in Annam 73-77; swidden cultivation 53, 67, 81, 89, 100, 113; in the lower Mekong valley 77-81; sugar-cane 79; terracing 64-65, 105; plow 66; spade 64, 105; and population pressure 277, 342; innovation 277. *See also* Animal husbandry
Aí Prefecture 378
Amarāvati 396
Amoghapura 125, 144, 320
Animal husbandry 50-51, 53, 64, 89, 101
Aninditapura 125, 144
Aṅkor Bórěi 132, 134, 136, 137, 145, 155, 294
An-nam 375-376
Arakan 184-185, 290, 309
Archeology: in Southeast Asia 43-45, 58, 95; furnishing primary evidence 58; megaliths 58-62, 74-75, 103, 110, 212; Older Megalithic 59; Younger Megalithic 59, 60; in Mekong delta 111; in Burma 184; of the Môn 204-211; in the Malaysian world 240; in peninsular Thailand 254
Architecture: in Fu-nan 123, 145; at Oc-èo 127-133; at Beikthano 169-172; at Hmawza 175; of Pyū capital 176-177; of Sudhammapura 202; of Haṃsavatī 202; at Nakhon Pathom 206; at Ku Bua 207; at Mu'ang Bon 209; in Dvāravatī 212; at Ū Thòng 226; in Langkasuka 233; in Kaḷāh 234; in Walaiñ 237; on the Diëng upland 238; in Śrī Vijaya 243; at Luy-lâu 376; in Ch'ü-su 387-388; of the Lin-I capital 391-392; "owls' tails" in the Lin-I capital 390
Argyra 233, 445-446
Arimaddanapura 181-182, 197
Artisans and craftsmen: in Oc-èo 133; in Pre-Aṅkor Kampuchea 314-315; in Tong-King 393
Âu-Lạc 91, 117, 366, 367, 380

Ava 427
Ayutthaya 427

Bagrow, Leo 442, 455
Bali 181, 237, 256-257
Ban Chiang 83
Bantam 431-432
Barakoura 446
Barousai Islands 450
Barus 237, 256, 450
Bassac 427
Bassein 427
Bayard, Donn T. 82
Beikthano 167-173, 183, 190-191, 294, 420
Benedict, Paul K. 57-58, 83, 99
Benjamin, Geoffrey 49, 275
Berunei 238, 246, 427, 436
Bhadravarman, Dharmamahārāja Śrī 289, 308, 362, 394, 396, 397
Bhadreśvara 144, 317, 394
bhakti 291-292
Bharukaccha (Barygaza, Broach) 273, 287
Bhattacharya, Kamaleswar 290
Bhavapura 125, 144
Bhīmapura 125, 144, 320
Boserup, Ester 276, 342
Brāhmaṇism, Brāhmaṇas: in Tārumā 87, 299; consecratory roles of 286; *vrātyastoma* 295; functions of 298; in Tun-sun 298-299; in P'an-p'an 299; in the Red-Earth Kingdom 299; in Kalimantan 299; status and provenance of 300-302; miscegenation in Tun-sun 301; differences between roles in India and Southeast Asia 302-303, 315; as government officers 309-310; and sacrifice 352; in Bangkok 353-354; in Campā 397
Brammapolis 449
Bronson, Bennet 50, 242, 243, 244, 245, 259, 321
Buddhism, Buddhists, Buddhist remains: at Beikthano 172; at Hmawza 173; among the Pyū 180; in Arakan 184; among the Môn 200; at Ku Bua 207-208;

465

at Mu'ang Bon 209; at Sī Thep 210;
in Khorat 211; at Mu'ang Fa Daed 212;
in Kedah 232; at Śrī Vijaya 239; in
early Southeast Asia 272, 321; Buddha
Dīpaṁkara 272, 273, 321, 340; at
Chansen 272, 321; in Chiao-chih 371-
372, 403-405; Āgama school of the
T'ien-t'ai sect 371; wats in the
neighborhood of Luy-lâu 371; Dhyāna
school in Chiao-chih 372; texts
translated in Chiao-chih 372

Cakrāṅkapura 125, 320
Campā, Cam 76, 181, 182, 307, 308, 322, 358, 394-397, 417
Chansen 85, 208, 316, 321, 420
Chen-la 290, 307, 312, 313, 320
Chiangmai 427
Chiao-chih (*Kau-tśi, Giao-chỉ)
  Commandery 67-72, 367-368, 399-400, 405
Chiefdom: definition of 11, 34-35;
  settlement patterns in 11-13, 422;
  variability of 12-13; patrimonial
  character of 13-14; law in 14-15, 37;
  economic integration of 15-16;
  religious organization in 17-18; in
  prehistoric Southeast Asia 90-91,
  419; in Fu-nan 121, 142-144, 305;
  authority of the paramount 289, 294;
  nāgara as 304; among the Pyū 306;
  Canāśa as 306; in Việtnam 367
Chin-lin 165, 446
Chiu Chen (*Kiə̯u-tśiə̯n) Commandery 367-368
Chiu-te (*Kiə̯u-tək) Commandery 383-384
Chopper-chopping tools 46, 51
Christie, Anthony H. 61, 323, 337, 360, 418
Chrysê Chersonêsos 272, 443, 445, 446, 461
Ch'ü-su (*K'i̯u-si̯wok) Fortress 77, 383-388, 410
Chu-wu City, Prefecture 382, 389, 448-449
Coedès, George 48, 88, 124, 132, 155, 158, 202, 211, 224, 226, 229, 286, 300, 302, 311, 328, 427, 443
Coinage 316
Colani, Madeleine 66, 74-77
Cổ-loa 91-93, 371
Confucianism 371
Conical clan 11, 35
Copper Country 445
Couto, Diogo do 80, 112
Culturological attraction 326, 362, 420

Dagon 427-428
Damais, Louis-Charles 250, 253, 256, 257
Davidson, Jeremy H. C. S. 117, 371, 379-382, 403, 409, 421

Dhanvipura 125, 312
Diëng upland 238
Dong Lakhon 211
Dong Si Mahā Phót 210
Dorias River 449
Dhruvapura 125
Đông-sơn Culture 48, 56
Dupont, Pierre 200, 202
Du'wop City 202
Dvāravatī 203-206, 215, 224-225, 449
Dvīpāntara 267, 268

Ecotypes, Ecosystems 89-90, 100, 111, 116, 274-275, 277, 340-341, 343
Entitation, problem of 3-4
Ethnic groups: Lạc 67-72, 91, 367, 369, 399; Man 65, 223, 270, 421; Lji (Li, Lai, Loi) 73, 108; Yeh-lang 73, 108; Lu-yü 73, 108; Ku-lang 73, 108; Shih-p'u 73, 108; P'o-liao 73, 108; Chiu-pu-shih 73, 108; Wen-lang 73, 108, 316, 412; Hsü-lang 74; Ai-lao 165; K'un-lun 270; Kachin 279-284, 344; Mường 369; Chü-lien (*K'i̯u-lien) 383; Bahnar 395; Nangalogai 444, 454; Aginnatai 444; Sinai 444, 448-449, 460
Ethnographic parallels 116
Exchange: modes of 15-16;
  redistribution and mobilization in
  chiefdoms 15-16, 315, 358, 424, 436;
  administered trade 19, 38; silent
  barter 74, 109; traders at Ku Bua
  207; markets 315; in Tong-King 382.
  See also Trade and commerce

Fan Ch'o 65-67, 179
Fan [Shih] Man 121, 142-143, 144, 322
Fan Wen 387, 411-412, 413
Feng-shui 373-374, 377, 405
Ferrand, Gabriel 251, 254, 257, 286, 346
Filliozat, Jean 297, 353, 445, 449, 461
Flannery, Kent V., model formulated
  by 23-27; involving: processes 23,
  mechanisms 23-26, socio-environmental
  stresses 23; systemic pathologies 26;
  limitations of model 27; exemplified
  275, 325-326, 419
Friedman, Jonathan 279-284, 343, 344
Fu-nan: location and extent of 119,
  145, 150-151; dynastic myth of 120,
  121, 148, 320; urban hierarchy in
  120-127, 145; missions to the Chinese
  court from 120, 153, 313; emergence
  of chiefdom 121-123; capitals of 124,
  145, 155; pura in 125-127, 144;
  Indo-Scythian cultural influence in
  128; style of ruler of 147, 159, 308;
  ruler taming elephants 348

Geertz, Clifford 423
Gio-Linh 74-77, 110

Gorman, Chester F. 98-99, 100
Groslier, Bernard Philippe 62, 78, 162
Gunung Jerai 236, 255
Gurun 237, 257

Halin (Hanlan) 179, 183, 191, 194-195
Haṃsavatī (Pegu) 202, 222-223
Hà-nội 376-377
Hall, Kenneth R. 355-356
Haripuñjaya (Lamphun) 210, 215, 227-228
Harivikrama 175
Harris, David R. 53, 55
Heine-Geldern, Robert von 45, 48, 59, 95
Higham, C. F. W. 216, 218
Hindu, Hinduization: of Southeast Asia 287-303, 327-328, 362; of institutions 304, 322, 359; *Smṛti* canon 307; varna in Kampuchea 315; law code 316; titularies 322; cultural milieu 420; chancellery terminology 420; implications of the Ptolemaic corpus for 454
Hmawza (Old Prome) 173-180, 183, 192
Hoabinhian Culture 46, 51, 66
Ho-lo-tan Kingdom 233, 251
Hsiang-lin City, Prefecture 382, 383, 410
Hsi-chüan City 382, 385
Hsi-li-i Town 181, 195
Huan Wang Kingdom 397
Hun Pʻan Huang 121, 320
Hutterer, Karl L. 97
Hydraulic systems: allegedly in Tong-King 68; in Gio-Linh 74-75; in Tārumā 87-88; in Fu-nan 88, 134, 136-141, 162; irrigation works 278-279, 343

Iabadiou (Yāvadiu) 233, 444, 449
Indrapura 125
Insignia of office 312, 356
Integrative Levels, Theory of 24, 40
Īśānapura 125, 156

Jacques, Claude 141
Java 181, 237-239, 241, 268, 273, 334, 335, 355, 444
Java City 237, 242
Jayacandravarman 175
Jayavarman I 144, 290, 307, 311, 312
Jih-nan 368, 382-392, 400
Johor Lama 247

Kalāh, Kolo Kingdom 234-235, 254, 309
Kampheng Sèn 206-207
Kan-tʻo-li Kingdom 233, 251, 313
Karpūradvīpa 268
Katabēda River 446
Katāha 135, 236, 268, 288, 335, 336
Kattigara 74, 154, 412, 444, 447-448, 454, 460, 461

Kauṇḍinya Jayavarman 144
Kauthāra 396, 397
Khorat 85, 90, 211-212, 215, 216-218
Kings, Kingship: in early Southeast Asia 307-308; duties of 308; styles of 308-309; thearchic 307, 326; the Hùng dynasty 366, 381, 422
Kinship: Local lineages 276; generalized exchange among the Kachin 279, 343, 345; in genealogical structure of the Kachin 280; in ancient Kampuchea 349-350; kindred 350; Chʻü *(*Kʻiu)* 383; Fan lineage 390
Kirradia 445
Kirsch, A. Thomas 343, 344, 350
Konkonagara 444
Kota Cina 242, 260
Kota Tampan 46
Ko-ying 259
Krom, Nicholaas J. 48, 286
Kṣatriya, Kṣatra 296-297, 327
Ku Bua 207, 213, 215
Kuñjarakuñja 238, 258
Kʻun-lun 130, 267, 270, 271, 339

Lamb, Alastair 236, 254
Langkasuka 231-232, 233, 241, 249, 252, 309, 319
Law: in chiefdoms 14-15, 37; Hindu code of 316; in Fu-nan 316; among the Pyū 316-317; in Kampuchea 317; in Campā 358
Leach, Edmund 284, 343
Leur, Jacob Cornelis van 286, 351, 431
Lévi-Strauss, Claude 283-284, 343-344
Liṅga 144, 204, 238, 290-291, 322, 324, 387
Liṅgapura 125, 144
Lin-I *(*Liəm-·iəp)*: frontier settlements of 268, 383; controlling Chʻü-su 383; missions to Chinese courts 383; capital of 388-392, 416; and Campā 394-397; ethnic affiliations 395; styles of rulers 395; origin of name 410-411; invasion of Jih-nan Commandery 384, 412; affinity for sea 415
Long-uyên (Long-biên) City 373-374, 378, 405, 406
Lopburi (Lavapura) 85, 115, 208, 214, 224, 227
Luce, Gordon H. 178, 179, 187, 224
Luy-lâu City 368, 370, 376, 377, 379, 400, 402-403
Lu-yung City 382

Mabbett, I. W. 315
Maiandros 443-444
Majapahit 427, 429, 431
Malāyu 237, 256, 427
Maleñ 320
Maleoukolon Cape 444-445, 449, 454

Malleret, Louis 81, 110, 127-136, 140, 148, 159, 162, 461
Mareoura Metropolis 449
Martaban 427
Melaka 432-433, 438
Mêlinh (Phong Châu) 367
Metals and Metallurgy: beginnings of 53, 98; iron in Borneo 101; bronze drums 102; scenting gold 74, 109; gold in Southeast Asia 271; in Tong-King 382
Meulen, W. J. van der 450-453
Mi-chen 203, 223-224
Mi-no-tao-li Town 181, 196, 224
Mĩ-sơn 290, 394-395
Mōn (Rman): location and extent of 199-202; culture hearth of 200, 222; western tradition 202-203, 214; eastern tradition 203-211, 214; polity 203-211; capitals 204-206, 215, 219; settlement hierarchy 215-216; royal styles among 309
Mu'ang Bon 209
Mu'ang Fa Daed 212, 229
Mu'ang Swa 427
*Muo[k]-Xâ-siĕn 237, 256

Naerssen, F. H. van 297, 306
Nāgara: formation of 273-287; nature of 303-321; government of 307; settlement hierarchy in 327; functions of 327
Nakhon Pathom 206, 213, 224, 226
Nakhon Si Thammarat 427
Nan Chao 193
Nan-Yüeh 67, 104, 367, 368
Naravaranāgara 124, 155
Non Nok Tha 83, 98

Oc-èo 78, 127-136, 158, 159, 294, 312, 316, 324, 361, 420
Ô-duyên City 379
Orang Laut 244, 261

Padi (Rice): domestication of 53, 55, 82, 83; in Yün-nan 65; in Tong-King 72; in the lower Mekong valley 79-81; floating rices 80-81, 112, 113; at Oc-èo 81; use of, in trial by ordeal 81; diffusion through Southeast Asia 82-89; at Non Nok Tha 82-83; at Ban Kao 83-84; on the Plaine des Joncs 88; in early ecosystems 89, 325; saline-soil races of 106. See also Agriculture
Pagan: See Arimaddanapura
Pajajaran 427
Palembang 239, 246
Pānduranga 396, 397
P'an-p'an (*B'uân-b'uân) Kingdom 234, 237, 243, 246, 252-253, 299, 309, 313, 320
P'an-yü City 267, 399

Pegu 427
Pelliot, Paul 148
Phanat 210
Phong Prefecture 378
Phong Tük 208, 213
Phùng-nguyên Culture 91, 116, 117, 367, 380
P'i-ch'ien Kingdom 316
Pīlakkavanaka 184
Pires, Tomé 431-432
Port of the Navigation Officials 392
Prefectures (Subprefectures) under Restraint 376, 407
Prehistory of Southeast Asia 43-94
Ptolemaic geography: deficiencies in 439-440; compilation of 440, 454; structure of 440-441; transmission of 441-442; Southeast Asia in 442-443; reconstructions of 445-453, 457-458
Purandarapura 125, 156
Pureppura 184, 446. See also Barakoura
Pūrnavarman 87-88, 294, 309
Pyū (P'iao); location of 167, 188-190; burial urns 172; coinage 172, 316; dynasties 173-174; capitals 179-180; embassies to the Chinese court 177, 195, 313; urban hierarchy 180-181, 182-183; garrison towns 180-181, 195, 196; dependencies of 183; tribes of 183, 197; royal styles among 309; trade among 316; law 316-317

Raktamrttika 144
Red-Earth Kingdom 144, 234, 243, 251-252, 309
Rice: See Padi

Sabadibai 449
Sahai, Sachchidanand 311-312, 317, 320
Śambhupura 125, 144, 156
Samrôn Sen 78, 81
Samudrapura 125
Sanctity 27-28, 282
Śailendra 239
San-fo-ch'i Kingdom 243, 245, 246
Sañjaya 238
Satingphra 241
Satyrs, Islands of 445, 450
Scripts 322, 324, 358, 361, 420
Seluyut 181, 237, 255, 316
Settlement, pattern of: in chiefdoms 11-13; in vicinity of Tien Lake 64; in the Mōn territories 214; in Khorat 216-218, 228; in the Malaysian world 242-248, 261; of the nāgara 327; in Tong-King and Annam 392
She-p'o: See Java
Shih-chai Shan 64, 96, 278
Simhapura (Lion City) 234, 241, 247, 252
Sinicization process 369-370, 421
Sī Thep 209-210

Śiva, Śaivism: of Vyādhapura 124; in
  Fu-nan 143, 144, 147, 155, 290, 348;
  Pyū ruler assimilated to 180; at Ū
  Thòng 204, 290; at Muʿang Sima 211;
  on Wukir Hill 238; on the Diëng
  upland 238; in Campā 289, 290, 394,
  397; in Arakan 290; in Java 291; in
  Kalimantan 291; devotionalism in the
  lower Mekong valley 291-295;
  devotionalism in Indonesia 349;
  Pāśupatas at Khmer courts 292, 302,
  444; Śrī Piṅgaleśa 307; offenses
  against 317; cult of the liṅga 324
Solheim, Wilhelm G., II 51-56, 95, 99,
  114
Śreṣṭhapura 125, 134, 144, 311
Śrī Canāśa 211, 306, 309
Śrī Harṣavarman 204
Śrī Kṣetra 173-180, 192, 223
Śrī Tāmrapaṭṭana 184, 203
Śrī Vijaya 239-240, 242, 247, 255, 258-259, 306, 310-311, 319
Stargardt, Janice 250, 252
State: origin of 10; definition of 34;
  nāgara 303-306; galactic polity 422-423; doctrine of the theater state
  423, 435
Stein, Rolf A. 130, 396, 409, 414, 447
Styles and Titularies: Great King of
  Fu-nan 123, 322; Śailarāja of Fu-nan
  147, 296; Parvatabhūpāla of Fu-nan
  147, 296; Dharmamahārāja of Campā
  294; Rājādhirāja of Tārŭmā 294, 309;
  royal usages 308-309; in Śrī Vijaya
  310-311; in Fu-nan and Chen-la
  311-312, 357, 449; mahāsena in Pyū
  kingdom 312; in the Red-Earth Kingdom
  312-313; in Pʿan-pʿan 313; adoption
  of -varman suffix 324, 361; in Java
  355; of Lin-I rulers 395; Śrī
  Campāpuraparameśvara 397
Sudhammapura (Thatōn) 202, 222
Suvarnadvīpa, Suvarṇabhūmi
  (Suvaṇṇabhūmi) 222, 223, 264, 265-266, 268, 287, 331, 333, 334
Suvarṇapura 268, 336
Svargadvārapura 125, 156, 225
Symbolism of urban form 423-424, 429,
  430, 435-436

Takkola, Takola 268, 443, 446
Talain: See Pyū
Tamandarapura 125, 320
Tamara 444, 449
Tambiah, Stanley J. 422, 424
Tāmraliṅga, Tāmbraliṅga Kingdom 236-237, 268
Tāmrapura 125, 145, 320
*Tʿan-liəng Island 225
Tan-tan Kingdom 234, 237, 253, 314
Tārŭmā 87, 232-233, 250, 253, 294
Taungoo 427
*Tʿâ-γuân 225

Tenasserim 427
Teng-liu-mei Kingdom 247
Thăng-Long City 427
Thagora 446
Thap Chumphon 209
Thin, Thina Metropolis 270, 338, 447
Thừa-hóa Prefecture 378
Tien, Lake, Kingdom, King of 64, 91, 97,
  104, 116, 285
Tirčul: See Pyū
Tŏng-bình City 374, 376, 377, 378, 379
Trương Prefecture 378
Trade and Commerce: at Oc-èo 134, 316;
  at Tun-sun 213-214, 316; at Ku Bua
  214, 316; at Kalāh 236; at Seluyut
  237, 316; focused on Śrī Vijaya 240,
  260; between India and Suvaṇṇabhūmi
  265-266; to and through Southeast
  Asia 269-273, 321, 325; Po-ssŭ
  commodities 270, 337; Indian traders
  in Southeast Asia 286, 287, 296, 327,
  352; in aromatics 315, 415; among the
  Pyū 316; Persian merchants 337; in
  Chiao-chih 368, 372-373; Syrian
  merchant in Chiao-chih 372; in
  Jih-nan 383; markets at Chʿü-su 387;
  at Melaka 432-433
Tsʿang-wu Commandery 368
Tuban 427, 432
Tuk Mas 238
Tù-liêm City 379
Tʿu-min Town 181, 196
Tun-sun Kingdom 212-214, 231, 301, 309,
  316
Tư Thành 376, 379

Ugrapura 125, 144
Urban genesis: urban imposition 5-6;
  primary and secondary urban
  generation 6-7, 32, 388; approaches
  to the study of 21-23, 39
Urbanism, Urbanization: concept of 1-10; models of 2; definition of 2-5;
  urban process 4-5; as level of
  sociocultural integration 1, 7, 20;
  as creator of effective space 8; in
  Roman Britain 365; hsien (huyện)
  cities in Tong-King 370, 371, 377-379, 401; migration of Tong-King
  capitals 373-377; hsien (huyện)
  cities in Jih-nan 382; Chinese
  colonial cities in Tong-King 394,
  420-421; crystallization of an urban
  hierarchy in western Southeast Asia
  420; urban hierarchy in Tong-King
  424-425; principal urban hierarchies
  in Southeast Asia in the 14th century
  425-432; 14th-century capitals 428-429; in the Ptolemaic corpus 439-462
Ū Thòng 204-206, 213, 215, 226, 333

Vaiśālī 184
Văn-Lang 91, 117, 366, 367, 380, 399

Vijayapura 396, 427
Vraḥ Vnaṃ 124, 134
Vũ-lâp City 379
Vyādhapura 124, 132, 290

Walaiń Kingdom 237, 238, 242, 256
Wales, H. G. Quaritch 110, 200, 209, 212, 214-215, 218, 226, 228, 236
Williams-Hunt, Peter D. R. 211, 216, 218, 228
Wolters, O. W. 125, 141, 239, 242, 243, 253, 256, 257, 259, 260, 291-294, 302, 362, 429
Wu Chin-ting 64

Yaśodharapura 427

Zabaipolis 446
Zābaj (Jāvaka) 245, 267

Index of Principal Texts and Inscriptions

An-nam Chí-Lược 68, 401, 409
ʿAjāʾib al-Hind 109
ʾAkhbār al-Ṣīn waʾl-Hind 256
Aranyaparvan 307
Arthaśāstra 264, 307, 331-332, 414

Batang Hari Inscription 239
Baudhāyana Dharmasūtra 272, 300
Bṛhatkathā 264
Bṛhatsaṁhitā 264

Caddanta Jātaka 209
Cāmadevīvaṃsa 210
Capitulo 6 da Grande e Admiravel Cidade que se Discobrio nos Matos do Reino Camboja
Chiao-Chou Wai-yü Chi 67
Chiêm-sơn Inscription 417
Chʿien-Han Shu 71, 194, 360
Chin Shu 78, 111, 120, 322, 323, 360-361, 385
Chiu Tʿang-Shu 177, 178, 183, 194, 195, 197, 224
Cô-châu Pháp-vân-Phật Bản-hành Ngữ-lục 403

Đại-Việt Sử-ký Toàn-thơ 407-410, 413
Dīpavaṃsa 200, 266

Fa-hua San-mei Ching 371
Fī Taḥqīq mā liʾl-Hind 109
Fu-nan Chi/Chuan 149, 213, 229

Geographike Huphegesis 272, 439-442, 457
Glass Palace Chronicle 178, 193, 195

Hàn Čei Inscriptions 144, 163
Hikayat Marong Mahawangsa 297, 351
Hìn Khôn Inscription 211
Hìn Tăng Inscription 211
Hon Cuc Inscription 417
Hou-Han Shu 187, 188, 405, 421
Hsin Tʿang-Shu 105, 111, 124, 177, 180, 190, 194, 195, 223, 224, 225, 257, 397
Hsüan-chung Chi 108
Hua-yang-Kuo Chih 173, 188
Huai-nan Tzŭ 400
Ḥudūd al-ʿĀlam 109, 188

Jātakamālā 265
Jātakaṭṭhavaṇṇanā 265
Jinakālamālī 214, 227

Kalyāṇī Inscriptions 200
Kan-wet-khaung-kon Inscription 192
Kao-Seng Chuan 251, 403
Karang Berahi Inscription 319
Kathākośa 264
Kathāsaritsāgara 264, 266, 267, 288, 331
Kedukan Bukit Inscription 244
Khâm-định Việt-sử Thông-giám Cương Mục 68, 407-410, 413
Kitāb al-Masālik waʾl-Mamālik 256
Kota Kapur Inscription 239, 319
Kuang-Chou Chi 67-68
Kuan-tzŭ 71, 107
Kutai Yūpa Inscriptions 232, 241

Liang Shu 121, 124, 127, 142, 143, 213, 214, 229, 232, 241, 308, 316, 323
Ligor Stele Inscription 240
Lin-I Chi 384

Mahābhārata 291, 307
Mahākarmavibhaṅga 263, 265, 267, 336
Mahāniddesa 237, 265, 443, 446
Mahāvaṃsa 200, 266
Mānava Dharmaśāstra 300, 301, 307, 317
Man Shu 65, 105, 106, 178, 179, 181, 194, 197, 223, 224
Maunggun Gold Plates 192
Milinda-pañha 264-265, 443
Mĩ-sơn Stele Inscription 317, 394
Mou-tzŭ Li-kan 403
Muʾang Sima Inscriptions 211
Muʿjam al-Buldān 254
Murūj al-Dhahab wa-Maʿādin al-Jawhar 255, 256
Myazedi Inscriptions 189

Nāgara-Kĕrtāgama 428, 432
Nan-Chao Yeh-shih 193
Nan-Chʿi Shu 120, 123
Nan-chou I-wu Chih 121, 229
Nan-fang Tsʿao-mu Chuang 413
Nan-Hai Chi-kuei Nei-fa Chuan 147, 187
Nan Shih 229
Nan-Yüeh Chih 69

471

Palas Pasemah Inscription 239
Paramatta-Dīpanī 265
Periplus Maris Erythraei 269, 270, 271, 272, 337
Phnom Bàyaṅ Inscription 290
Ph'u Khiau Kău Inscription 211
Pràsàt Ampĭl Rolǔ'm Inscription 156
Pràsàt Trapāṅ Run Inscription 157
Purāṇas 268, 291, 334

Raghuvaṁśa 267
Rājapatiguṇḍala 423, 435
Rāmāyaṇa 264, 268, 307
Rasavāhinī 266
Rās Mālā 269, 335

Sabokingking Inscription 245
Sambór-Prei Kŭk Inscription 156
Sāsanavaṃsappadīpikā 266
Sejarah Melayu 243, 249
Shih Chi 63, 68, 91
Shih-chi Cheng-i 149
Shui-Ching Chu 67, 108, 149, 338, 384-392
Shwezayan Pagoda Inscriptions 202-203
Sīhaḷavatthuppakaraṇa 251, 266, 333
Sui Shu 127, 241, 252, 308, 314, 356
Suma Oriental 431-432, 437-438
Sung Shih 227

Tabā'i' al-Hayawān 109, 188
Ta-Ch'ing I-t'ung Chih 405, 406
T'ai-p'ing Huan-yü Chi 69, 149, 188, 193, 195

T'ai-p'ing Kuang Chi 68-69
T'ai-p'ing Yü-lan 121, 128, 149, 194, 195, 223, 225, 229, 391
T'ang Hui-yao 223
Tăn Kraṅ Inscription 307
Tao-i Chih-lüeh 428, 437
Tà Prohm Inscription 156
Ta-T'ang Hsi-yü Ch'iu-fa Kao-seng Chuan 147, 156, 187, 255
Taungdwingyi Thamaing 179, 180, 183, 195
Telaga Batu Inscription 260, 310-311, 317, 319, 356
Thăm Lekh Inscription 317
Thiên-uyển tập anh ngữ-lục 403
Tiruvācakam 347
Ts'e-fu Yüan-kuei 194, 195, 223, 225
Tugu Inscription 87, 232-233, 253
T'ung Tien 149, 225, 229, 234, 250
Tzŭ-ch'ih T'ung-chien 406-410

Vắt Căkret Inscription 157
Vetālapañcaviṁśatikā 300
Việt-điện U-linh Tập 407
Võ-canh Inscription 125, 297, 309

Wai-Kuo Chuan 81, 113, 121, 153
Wen-hsien T'ung-k'ao 109, 194, 195, 227, 357
Wukir Inscription 348

Yüan-ho Chün-hsien t'u-chih 403, 405

তোমায় আমায় মিল হয়েছে কোন্‌ যুগে এইখানে।
ভাষায় ভাষায় গাঁঠ পড়েছে, প্রাণের সঙ্গে প্রাণে।
ডাক পাঠালে আকাশপথে কোন্‌ সে পুবন বায়ে
দূর সাগরের উপকূলে নারিকেলের ছায়ে।
গঙ্গাতীরের মন্দিরেতে সেদিন শঙ্খ বাজে,
তোমার বাণী এপার হতে মিলল তারি মাঝে।
বিষ্ণু আমায় কইল কানে, বললে দশভুজা,
'অজানা ওই সিন্ধুতীরে নেব আমার পূজা।'
মন্দাকিনীর কলধারা সেদিন ছলোছলো
পুব সাগরে হাত বাড়িয়ে বললে, 'চলো, চলো।'
রামায়ণের কবি আমায় কইল আকাশ হতে,
'আমার বাণী পার করে দাও দূর সাগরের স্রোতে।'
তোমার ডাকে উতল হল বেদব্যাসের ভাষা—
বললে, 'আমি ওই পারেতে বাঁধব নতুন বাসা।'
আমার দেশের হৃদয় সেদিন কইল আমার কানে,
'আমায় বয়ে যাও গো লয়ে সুদূর দেশের পানে।'

THE UNIVERSITY OF CHICAGO
DEPARTMENT OF GEOGRAPHY
RESEARCH PAPERS (Lithographed, 6×9 inches)

LIST OF TITLES IN PRINT

48. BOXER, BARUCH. *Israeli Shipping and Foreign Trade.* 1957. 162 p.
56. MURPHY, FRANCIS C. *Regulating Flood-Plain Development.* 1958. 216 pp.
62. GINSBURG, NORTON, editor. *Essays on Geography and Economic Development.* 1960. 173 p.
71. GILBERT, EDMUND WILLIAM. *The University Town in England and West Germany.* 1961. 79 p.
72. BOXER, BARUCH. *Ocean Shipping in the Evolution of Hong Kong.* 1961. 108 p.
91. HILL, A. DAVID. *The Changing Landscape of a Mexican Municipio, Villa Las Rosas, Chiapas.* 1964. 121 p.
97. BOWDEN, LEONARD W. *Diffusion of the Decision To Irrigate: Simulation of the Spread of a New Resource Management Practice in the Colorado Northern High Plans.* 1965. 146 pp.
98. KATES, ROBERT W. *Industrial Flood Losses: Damage Estimation in the Lehigh Valley.* 1965. 76 pp.
101. RAY, D. MICHAEL. *Market Potential and Economic Shadow: A Quantitative Analysis of Industrial Location in Southern Ontario.* 1965. 164 p.
102. AHMAD, QAZI. *Indian Cities: Characteristics and Correlates.* 1965. 184 p.
103. BARNUM, H. GARDINER. *Market Centers and Hinterlands in Baden-Württemberg.* 1966. 172 p.
105. SEWELL, W. R. DERRICK, et al. *Human Dimensions of Weather Modification.* 1966. 423 p.
106. SAARINEN, THOMAS FREDERICK. *Perception of the Drought Hazard on the Great Plains.* 1966. 183 p.
107. SOLZMAN, DAVID M. *Waterway Industrial Sites: A Chicago Case Study.* 1967. 138 p.
108. KASPERSON, ROGER E. *The Dodecanese: Diversity and Unity in Island Politics.* 1967. 184 p.
109. LOWENTHAL, DAVID, editor, *Environmental Perception and Behavior.* 1967. 88 p.
112. BOURNE, LARRY S. *Private Redevelopment of the Central City, Spatial Processes of Structural Change in the City of Toronto.* 1967. 199 p.
113. BRUSH, JOHN E., and GAUTHIER, HOWARD L., JR., *Service Centers and Consumer Trips: Studies on the Philadelphia Metropolitan Fringe.* 1968. 182 p.
114. CLARKSON, JAMES D., *The Cultural Ecology of a Chinese Village: Cameron Highlands, Malaysia.* 1968. 174 p.
115. BURTON, IAN, KATES, ROBERT W., and SNEAD, RODMAN E. *The Human Ecology of Coastal Flood Hazard in Megalopolis.* 1968. 196 p.
117. WONG, SHUE TUCK, *Perception of Choice and Factors Affecting Industrial Water Supply Decisions in Northeastern Illinois.* 1968. 93 p.
118. JOHNSON, DOUGLAS L. *The Nature of Nomadism: A Comparative Study of Pastoral Migrations in Southwestern Asia and Northern Africa.* 1969. 200 p.
119. DIENES, LESLIE. Locational Factors and Locational Developments in the Soviet Chemical Industry. 1969. 262 p.
120. MIHELIČ, DUŠAN. *The Political Element in the Port Geography of Trieste.* 1969. 104 p.
121. BAUMANN, DUANE D. *The Recreational Use of Domestic Water Supply Reservoirs: Perception and Choice.* 1969. 125 p.
122. LIND, AULIS O. *Coastal Landforms of Cat Island, Bahamas: A Study of Holocene Accretionary Topography and Sea-Level Change.* 1969. 156 p.
123. WHITNEY, JOSEPH B. R. *China: Area, Administration and Nation Building.* 1970. 198 p.
124. EARICKSON, ROBERT. *The Spatial Behavior of Hospital Patients: A Behavioral Approach to Spatial Interaction in Metropolitan Chicago.* 1970. 138 p.
125. DAY, JOHN CHADWICK. *Managing the Lower Rio Grande: An Experience in International River Development.* 1970. 274 p.
126. MACIVER, IAN. *Urban Water Supply Alternatives: Perception and Choice in the Grand Basin Ontario.* 1970. 178 p.
127. GOHEEN, PETER G. *Victorian Toronto, 1850 to 1900: Pattern and Process of Growth.* 1970. 278 p.
128. GOOD, CHARLES M. *Rural Markets and Trade in East Africa.* 1970. 252 p.
129. MEYER, DAVID R. *Spatial Variation of Black Urban Households.* 1970. 127 p.
130. GLADFELTER, BRUCE G. *Meseta and Campiña Landforms in Central Spain: A Geomorphology of the Alto Henares Basin.* 1971. 204 p.

131. NEILS, ELAINE M. *Reservation to City: Indian Migration and Federal Relocation.* 1971. 198 p.
132. MOLINE, NORMAN T. *Mobility and the Small Town, 1900–1930.* 1971. 169 p.
133. SCHWIND, PAUL J. *Migration and Regional Development in the United States.* 1971. 170 p.
134. PYLE, GERALD F. *Heart Disease, Cancer and Stroke in Chicago: A Geographical Analysis with Facilities, Plans for 1980.* 1971. 292 p.
135. JOHNSON, JAMES F. *Renovated Waste Water: An Alternative Source of Municipal Water Supply in the United States.* 1971. 155 p.
136. BUTZER, KARL W. *Recent History of an Ethiopian Delta: The Omo River and the Level of Lake Rudolf.* 1971. 184 p.
139. MCMANIS, DOUGLAS R. *European Impressions of the New England Coast, 1497–1620.* 1972. 147 p.
140. COHEN, YEHOSHUA S. *Diffusion of an Innovation in an Urban System: The Spread of Planned Regional Shopping Centers in the United States, 1949–1968,* 1972. 136 p.
141. MITCHELL, NORA. *The Indian Hill-Station: Kodaikanal.* 1972. 199 p.
142. PLATT, RUTHERFORD H. *The Open Space Decision Process: Spatial Allocation of Costs and Benefits.* 1972. 189 p.
143. GOLANT, STEPHEN M. *The Residential Location and Spatial Behavior of the Elderly: A Canadian Example.* 1972. 226 p.
144. PANNELL, CLIFTON W. *T'ai-chung, T'ai-wan: Structure and Function.* 1973. 200 p.
145. LANKFORD, PHILIP M. *Regional Incomes in the United States, 1929–1967: Level, Distribution, Stability, and Growth.* 1972. 137 p.
146. FREEMAN, DONALD B. *International Trade, Migration, and Capital Flows: A Quantitative Analysis of Spatial Economic Interaction.* 1973. 201 p.
147. MYERS, SARAH K. *Language Shift Among Migrants to Lima, Peru.* 1973. 203 p.
148. JOHNSON, DOUGLAS L. *Jabal al-Akhdar, Cyrenaica: An Historical Geography of Settlement and Livelihood.* 1973. 240 p.
149. YEUNG, YUE-MAN. *National Development Policy and Urban Transformation in Singapore: A Study of Public Housing and the Marketing System.* 1973. 204 p.
150. HALL, FRED L. *Location Criteria for High Schools: Student Transportation and Racial Integration.* 1973. 156 p.
151. ROSENBERG, TERRY J. *Residence, Employment, and Mobility of Puerto Ricans in New York City.* 1974. 230 p.
152. MIKESELL, MARVIN W., editor. *Geographers Abroad: Essays on the Problems and Prospects of Research in Foreign Areas.* 1973. 296 p.
153. OSBORN, JAMES F. *Area, Development Policy, and the Middle City in Malaysia.* 1974. 291 p.
154. WACHT, WALTER F. *The Domestic Air Transportation Network of the United States.* 1974. 98 p.
155. BERRY, BRIAN J. L., et al. *Land Use, Urban Form and Environmental Quality.* 1974. 440 p.
156. MITCHELL, JAMES K. *Community Response to Coastal Erosion: Individual and Collective Adjustments to Hazard on the Atlantic Shore.* 1974. 209 p.
157. COOK, GILLIAN P. *Spatial Dynamics of Business Growth in the Witwatersrand.* 1975. 144 p.
159. PYLE, GERALD F. et al. *The Spatial Dynamics of Crime.* 1974. 221 p.
160. MEYER, JUDITH W. *Diffusion of an American Montessori Education.* 1975. 97 p.
161. SCHMID, JAMES A. *Urban Vegetation: A Review and Chicago Case Study.* 1975. 266 p.
162. LAMB, RICHARD F. *Metropolitan Impacts on Rural America.* 1975. 196 p.
163. FEDOR, THOMAS STANLEY. *Patterns of Urban Growth in the Russian Empire during the Nineteenth Century.* 1975. 245 p.
164. HARRIS, CHAUNCY D. *Guide to Geographical Bibliographies and Reference Works in Russian or on the Soviet Union.* 1975. 478 p.
165. JONES, DONALD W. *Migration and Urban Unemployment in Dualistic Economic Development.* 1975. 174 p.
166. BEDNARZ, ROBERT S. *The Effect of Air Pollution on Property Value in Chicago.* 1975. 111 p.
167. HANNEMANN, MANFRED. *The Diffusion of the Reformation in Southwestern Germany, 1518–1534.* 1975. 248 p.
168. SUBLETT, MICHAEL D. *Farmers on the Road. Interfarm Migration and the Farming of Noncontiguous Lands in Three Midwestern Townships. 1939–1969.* 1975. 228 pp.
169. STETZER, DONALD FOSTER. *Special Districts in Cook County: Toward a Geography of Local Government.* 1975. 189 pp.
170. EARLE, CARVILLE V. *The Evolution of a Tidewater Settlement System: All Hallow's Parish, Maryland, 1650–1783.* 1975. 249 pp.
171. SPODEK, HOWARD. *Urban-Rural Integration in Regional Development: A Case Study of Saurashtra, India—1800–1960.* 1976. 156 pp.

172. COHEN, YEHOSHUA S. and BERRY, BRIAN J. L. *Spatial Components of Manufacturing Change.* 1975. 272 pp.
173. HAYES, CHARLES R. *The Dispersed City: The Case of Piedmont, North Carolina.* 1976. 169 pp.
174. CARGO, DOUGLAS B. *Solid Wastes: Factors Influencing Generation Rates.* 1977. 112 pp.
175. GILLARD, QUENTIN. *Incomes and Accessibility. Metropolitan Labor Force Participation, Commuting, and Income Differentials in the United States, 1960–1970.* 1977. 140 pp.
176. MORGAN, DAVID J. *Patterns of Population Distribution: A Residential Preference Model and Its Dynamic.* 1978. 216 pp.
177. STOKES, HOUSTON H.; JONES, DONALD W. and NEUBURGER, HUGH M. *Unemployment and Adjustment in the Labor Market: A Comparison between the Regional and National Responses.* 1975. 135 pp.
179. HARRIS, CHAUNCY D. *Bibliography of Geography. Part I. Introduction to General Aids.* 1976. 288 pp.
180. CARR, CLAUDIA J. *Pastoralism in Crisis. The Dasanetch and their Ethiopian Lands.* 1977. 339 pp.
181. GOODWIN, GARY C. *Cherokees in Transition: A Study of Changing Culture and Environment Prior to 1775.* 1977. 221 pp.
182. KNIGHT, DAVID B. *A Capital for Canada: Conflict and Compromise in the Nineteenth Century.* 1977. 359 pp.
183. HAIGH, MARTIN J. *The Evolution of Slopes on Artificial Landforms: Blaenavon, Gwent.* 1978. 311 pp.
184. FINK, L. DEE. *Listening to the Learner. An Exploratory Study of Personal Meaning in College Geography Courses.* 1977. 200 pp.
185. HELGREN, DAVID M. *Rivers of Diamonds: An Alluvial History of the Lower Vaal Basin.* 1979. 399 pp.
186. BUTZER, KARL W., editor. *Dimensions of Human Geography: Essays on Some Familiar and Neglected Themes.* 1978. 201 pp.
187. MITSUHASHI, SETSUKO. *Japanese Commodity Flows.* 1978. 185 pp.
188. CARIS, SUSAN L. *Community Attitudes toward Pollution.* 1978. 226 pp.
189. REES, PHILIP M. *Residential Patterns in American Cities, 1960.* 1979. 424 pp.
190. KANNE, EDWARD A. *Fresh Food for Nicosia.* 1979. 116 pp.
191. WIXMAN, RONALD. *Language Aspects of Ethnic Patterns and Processes in the North Caucasus.* 1980. 224 pp.
192. KIRCHNER, JOHN A. *Sugar and Seasonal Labor Migration: The Case of Tucumán, Argentina.* 1980. 158 pp.
193. HARRIS, CHAUNCY D. and FELLMANN, JEROME D. *International List of Geographical Serials, Third Edition, 1980.* 1980. 457 p.
194. HARRIS, CHAUNCY D. *Annotated World List of Selected Current Geographical Serials, Fourth, Edition. 1980.* 1980. 165 p.
195. LEUNG, CHI-KEUNG. *China: Railway Patterns and National Goals.* 1980. 235 p.
196. LEUNG, CHI-KEUNG and NORTON S. GINSBURG, eds. *China: Urbanization and National Development.* 1980. 280 p.
197. DAICHES, SOL. *People in Distress: A Geographical Perspective on Psychological Well-being.* 1981, 199 p.
198. JOHNSON, JOSEPH T. *Location and Trade Theory: Industrial Location, Comparative Advantage, and the Geographic Pattern of Production in the United States.* 1981. 107 p.
199-200. STEVENSON, ARTHUR J. *The New York-Newark Air Freight System.* 1982. 440 p.
(Double number, price: $16.00)
201. LICATE, JACK A. *Creation of a Mexican Landscape: Territorial Organization and Settlement in the Eastern Puebla Basin, 1520–1605.* 1981. 143 p.
202. RUDZITIS, GUNDARS. *Residential Location Determinants of the Older Population.* 1982. 117 p.
203. LIANG, ERNEST P. *China: Railways and Agricultural Development, 1875–1935.* 1982. 186 p.
204. DAHMANN, DONALD C. *Locals and Cosmopolitans: Patterns of Spatial Mobility during the Transition from Youth to Early Adulthood.* 1982. 146 p.
205. FOOTE, KENNETH E. *Color in Public Spaces: Toward a Communication-Based Theory of the Urban Built Environment.* 1983. 153 p.
207-208. WHEATLEY, PAUL. *Nāgara and Commandery: Origins of the Southeast Asian Urban Traditions.* 1983. 473 p.
(Double number, price: $16.00)

175423